THE MICROECONOMICS OF COMPLEX ECONOMIES

THE MICROECONOMICS OF COMPLEX ECONOMIES

Evolutionary, Institutional, Neoclassical, and Complexity Perspectives

WOLFRAM ELSNER

TORSTEN HEINRICH

HENNING SCHWARDT
University of Bremen, Bremen, Germany

AMSTERDAM • BOSTON • HEIDELBERG • LONDON
NEW YORK • OXFORD • PARIS • SAN DIEGO
SAN FRANCISCO • SINGAPORE • SYDNEY • TOKYO

Academic Press is an imprint of Elsevier

Academic Press is an imprint of Elsevier
The Boulevard, Langford Lane, Kidlington, Oxford OX5 1GB, UK
Radarweg 29, PO Box 211, 1000 AE Amsterdam, The Netherlands
225 Wyman Street, Waltham, MA 02451, USA
525 B Street, Suite 1800, San Diego, CA 92101-4495, USA

Notice
No responsibility is assumed by the publisher for any injury and/or damage to persons or
property as a matter of products liability, negligence or otherwise, or from any use or
operation of any methods, products, instructions or ideas contained in the material herein.
Because of rapid advances in the medical sciences, in particular, independent verification
of diagnoses and drug dosages should be made

British Library Cataloguing-in-Publication Data
A catalogue record for this book is available from the British Library

Library of Congress Cataloging-in-Publication Data
A catalog record for this book is available from the Library of Congress

ISBN: 978-0-12-411585-9

For information on all Academic Press publications
visit our website at http://store.elsevier.com/

Typeset by MPS Limited, Chennai, India
www.adi-mps.com

Printed and bound in the United States of America

15 16 17 18 19   10 9 8 7 6 5 4 3 2 1

Working together
to grow libraries in
developing countries

www.elsevier.com • www.bookaid.org

Dedication

Wolfram Elsner dedicates this book to his wife Angelika, who gave so much for it, his children Katja, Daniel, and Nina, and grandchildren Lia, Leonel, and Ida Malin.

Torsten Heinrich dedicates this book to his parents, Sigrid Heinrich and Günter Heinrich.

To Rebekah—Henning Schwardt.

Contents

IV

HISTORY OF THOUGHT
AND CONTEMPORARY
MODELS IN COMPLEXITY
ECONOMICS

V

FURTHER APPLICATIONS:
INFORMATION, INNOVATION,
POLICY, AND METHODOLOGY

For Solution Keys, Further Reading, and more, see Companion Website and Instructors'
Manual for this book http://booksite.elsevier.com/9780124115859
and
http://textbooks.elsevier.com/web/product_details.aspx?isbn=9780124115859

Preface: A Complexity Microeconomics, "Post-Crisis"

"A surgeon, an engineer and an economist are discussing which of the three disciplines would be the oldest: The surgeon spoke first and said, 'Remember at the beginning when God took a rib out of Adam and made Eve? Who do you think did that? Obviously, a surgeon.' The engineer was undaunted by this and said, 'You remember that God made the world before that. He separated the land from the sea. Who do you think did that except an engineer?' 'Just a moment,' protested the economist, 'before God made the world, what was there? Chaos. Who do you think was responsible for that?'" **Told by Franco Modigliani[1]**

"[...] the paradigm shift from a geocentric to a heliocentric worldview facilitated modern physics, including the ability to launch satellites. In the same way should a paradigm shift from a component-oriented to an interaction-oriented, systemic perspective (as promoted by complexity science) enable us to find new solutions to urgent societal problems." **Dirk Helbing and Alan Kirman[2]**

ECONOMICS AFTER 2008

Lingering Crises, Increased Socioeconomic Volatility, and the Struggle for Answers

Economists being responsible for "chaos," as mentioned in the little metaphor above. Admittedly, economics has not been really successful so far in contributing to the solution of the most basic problems of mankind. Contributing to the solution of the problems of the world nowadays would mean to give useful advice for a more sustainable, and socially and regionally inclusive, more stable, and reliable economic development, where all agents may become capable of learning, investing in their human and social capital, and innovating in a broad sense. And many professional practitioners, entrepreneurs, and politicians, supported by an increasing number of critics from the ranks of academic economics itself, nowadays think that economists have increasingly failed to inform such actions. Among these problems figure those of a sustainable use of resources, climate protection, of food safety, health, and education provision for all, an income distribution considered fair, efficient, and just by most, social inclusion, power control, or more participation.

The *neoliberal* recipes, however, have largely been "De-regularisez! Privatisez! Le marché va de lui-même." And their singular trust in market forces for achieving social and economic improvements does no longer appear sufficient to an increasing number of discontents from both outside and within economics. Rather,

---

[1]Economics Nobel Laureate, in his lecture "My Evolution as an Economist" at Trinity University, San Antonio, TX, USA, March 24, 1987; repr. in: *Lives of the Laureates. Eighteen Nobel Economists*, edited by W. Breit and B.T. Hirsch, Cambridge, MA, London, UK: MIT Press, 4th ed., 2004, p. 115.

[2]"Rethinking Economics Using Complexity Theory," *Real-World Economics Review*, **64**, 2013, p. 23.

we have experienced the most severe financial meltdown and economic crisis since 80 years, if not in history, aggravated by food and resource, climate, health, social, political, and even moral crises. Markets and industrial and financial corporations often appeared helpless, and the latter at times desperately called in the most massive support of the state (budget and central banks) and, thus, taxpayers.

This crisis, still lingering, appears to be a case, a prominent one indeed, of a most basic complexity-economics issue, a case of collective negative unintended consequences of what appeared rational individualism. This outcome of a fallacy of aggregation reflects increased, but insufficiently recognized systemic complexity, including ubiquitous social dilemmas, reinforced by an overly individualistic cultural framework.

Since the beginning of the financial crisis 2007–2008, the big established printed media have become particularly critical against economics and its "mainstream". In the *New York Times*, for instance, famous physicist and economist Mark Buchanan argued in 2008 that economics were the only nonmodern discipline left, as its mainstream had no developed complexity approach, also arguing that "this economy does not compute" the way the economics mainstream's pure market model and its "rational" individuals allegedly do (Buchanan, 2008). In the *Times*, economists were declared "the guilty men" of the financial crisis (Kaletsky, 2009a). And the same newspaper called for a "revolution" in economic thought (Kaletsky, 2009b). And while the *Financial Times* diagnosed the "unfortunate uselessness of most state-of the-art economics" in the monetary field (Buiter, 2009), the *New York Times* again, right at the beginning of the crisis in 2007, had hope that "in economics departments, a growing will to debate fundamental assumptions" would emerge (Cohen, 2007), just in order to express its disappointment on that 2 years later: "ivory tower unswayed by crashing economy" (Cohen, 2009).

The *Scientific American* just stated: "The economist has no clothes" (Nadeau, 2008).

Against that background, many of these and other established newspapers and journals, printed or "blogosphere," non- or semi-academic, discovered existing paradigmatic alternatives as "hip heterodoxy" (Hayes, 2007) or "a brave army of heretics" (Warsh, 2009 on economicprincipals.com).

Noncomplex Advice for Complex Problems?

Answers of the "mainstream" of economics to complex structures and processes, to increasing power differences and conflict, uneven development, ecological deterioration, food and energy crises, etc. have indeed remained insufficient. They have been derived from a less complex core model, a model of a market economy, partial-market equilibrium, or general equilibrium across partial markets, with presupposed perfect information, rationality of agents, selfish individual behaviors that yield a beneficial collective result, i.e., the invisible hand metaphor and paradigm, with the behavior of all agents corresponding to an average or representative agent, efficient prices that reflect all relevant information, and an inherent tendency toward the (ideally unique and stable) general equilibrium.

Consequently, the advice of the "mainstream" of economics has increasingly been criticized as being simplistic, and thus often inappropriate. The approach appears designed to apply a certain mathematical approach in order to yield a predetermined equilibrium for an economic system, at the cost of assuming identical agents and no direct interaction among them, in a pure prices–quantities world (see, e.g., Foster, 2005, 2006, pp. 1072–1075). A number of well-known complexity economists, such as A. Kirman, H. Föllmer, or D. Colander, in their famous "Dahlem Report" (2009b), straightforwardly stated that "mainstream" economics were predominantly responsible for the financial crisis. Others have argued that the economics "mainstream" were less about providing instrumental knowledge but rather just an easy unifying value-base for society (see, e.g., Nelson, 2001). This reminds of an older critique, according to which the "hidden methodology" of the "mainstream" would consist of a particular rhetoric (see, e.g., McCloskey, 1983).

It also seems that the policy advice of shaping the world according to such an ideal "market" model has made the world even more complex and overly turbulent by removing stabilizing institutional coordination forms and thus disembedding markets from social institutions. Markets then often tend to increasingly fail. It has been argued that the crises of the market economy then are unintended "collapses of complexity" (see, e.g., Mirowski, 2010). At any rate, appropriate complexity reduction will be as necessary for problem solving in the real world as a proper acknowledgment and treatment of its complexity.

While the neoclassical "mainstream" assigned the properties of perfect information and rationality to the individual, with resulting systemic optimality, equilibration, and alleged stability and "proper" complexity, others who have contributed to the neoliberal revolution, such as *Hayek* and the Hayekians, have adopted the other extreme, i.e., while they acknowledge that the individual may not be perfectly informed, they allot perfect knowledge to the market system as a whole, yielding the same systemic results of market optimality.

However, appropriately complex answers to the real-world complexity, with its many, and heterogeneous, agents directly involved and interacting, and even more potential relations of different kinds among them, may indeed imply a mix of different and diverse "allocation mechanisms" and coordination forms—including institutional forms, hierarchies, private and public, and networks—rather than a monism derived from an ideal, "pure" model of a "market". In a real-world economics, we will have to drop the idea of a simplistic, noncomplex structure or process, and a predetermined, optimal, and stable equilibrium. A whole and rich world of rigid economic analysis has been opened up through this.

What Is Neoclassical "Mainstream" Economics—And Does It Still Exist?

Many economists, therefore, have tried again, in recent years and in particular in the post-2008 or post-crisis years, to scrutinize, reconsider, and (re-)define the "hard core" of such an economics "mainstream," or neoclassical paradigm, such as methodological individualism, instrumentalism, or equilibration, and to find out, whether it really still exists, as a coherent, and dominating, research program. Does it really still exist in face of an obvious and considerable diversification of economics in research and methodology, its partitioning in many new fields, such as experimental and behavioral economics, complex modeling, game-theoretic applications, network analyses, or systems simulations in computers?

Many have stressed its surprising ability to change in its alleged hard core of axioms and assumptions, its resilience, persistence, and continuing discursive power together with its continuing dominance (see, e.g., Arnsperger and Varoufakis, 2006; Kapeller, 2013). In fact, a big "advantage" of neoclassical economics is that it provides an integrated theory of everything, with a consistent, if wrong, answer to anything.

Others argue that in its strict sense, considering the historical origins of neoclassical economics, it has not only diversified, having even become fragmented, but also dissolved, and thus does, in fact, no longer exist. Therefore, the very term should be discarded, and the focus of a critique laid on the methodological aberrations still existing everywhere in the discipline, i.e., deductivism and the obsession with (specific) mathematical modeling—rather than being occupied, as it should, with uncovering the "nature of social reality" and developing appropriate research methods (see, e.g., Lawson, 2013; for a discussion of mathematics for a future economics, see, e.g., Keen, 2012; Giannakouros and Chen, 2012). D. Colander straightforwardly concluded "the death of neoclassical economics" (Colander, 2008).

A "Cognitive Dissonance"?

Others have argued that the economics "mainstream" has become subject to a cognitive dissonance between its inner values, or political-economic commitments, and socioeconomic reality, particularly after the financial crisis 2008ff. (see, e.g., Kessler, 2010). Such dissonance would have to do with clinging to a hard-core model of the "perfect market" and related normative "superior insights," which then were to be protected against empirical counterinstances (see, e.g., Kapeller, 2013).

On the other hand, most "mainstream" economists are mostly doing research with assumptions deviating from, and often results inconsistent with, the basic general equilibrium model. But the core model usually would remain unswayed by such research, and research results then forced to fit into those superior insights and a priori truth. This would particularly be the case in public and political statements, policy advice, funded private expertise, and—last not least—in textbooks and teaching (see also, e.g., Elsner, 2008).

The standard (micro-)textbook, against this background, has assumed a particular, and peculiar, structure and format over the last decades: It provides the basic model, unchanged, as it did over decades, in fact since the 1950s (see, e.g., Colander, 2010). Settled results of more relevant research from the last, say, three decades have been added through ever more additional chapters, presented as variants, exemptions, deviations, other results, etc., where each of the latter would fundamentally question the basic model of the first chapters. The very basic structure is left untouched. This results in a strange message given to tens of thousands of graduates worldwide to take with them into their professional lives: Reality out there resembles the perfect-market model of the textbook—plus a number of exemptions, variants, deviations, and other cases, which, however, do not fundamentally question that basic market model.

A "Ruling Mainstream" and a "Pluralist" Approach to Teaching

In this way, economics is, in many respects—textbooks and teaching, policy advice, private expertise, academic personnel recruitment, etc.—, indeed providing unifying socioeconomic norms and rhetoric, even in contrast to many of its own better research insights.

And its mainstream is livelier than ever, in terms of science politics. Namely with the new evaluation business exerted by a new ranking industry, it would further profit from a trend of cumulative self-reference inherent in the citation-impact factors, which eventually work against pluralism in academic recruiting, publishing, and teaching (see, e.g., Lee and Elsner, 2008, 2010), with the danger of increasing paradigmatic monism in the economics discipline.

Nevertheless, the pure-market belief system has been widely questioned in the face of the crises of the economy, society, environment, and politics, and the call for a more pluralistic approach in the discipline, and particularly in academic teaching, and here not the least in microeconomics, has become louder in recent years (see, e.g., Keen, 2009; Raveaud, 2009).

Complexity Economics for Complex Problems? The Secular Quest for New Microfoundations

A long-lasting argument, put forward and extensively dealt with already by *Adam Smith*, and made most famous perhaps by Karl Marx, is that markets inherently tend to undermine themselves and may generate cyclical and/or structural crises—and even more so the more disembedded from social institutions they were.

In recent economics debates, particularly post-crisis, this has specifically led to a widespread quest for new microfoundations among both critical mainstream economists and the heterodox economic branches (see, e.g., Ayres and Martinás, 2005; Mirowski, 2010; King, 2012; Duarte and Lima, 2012; Heinrich, 2013). Among them, the president of the American Economic Association in 2006–2007, George Akerlof, has called for new microfoundations in his presidential address (Akerlof, 2007). And this is in a longer tradition of pleas and declarations for reorientations in economics and more pluralist perspectives on the discipline (see, e.g., "A Plea for a Pluralistic and Rigorous Economics," 1992, reprinted in the *American Economic Review*).

A future new unifying paradigm, and perhaps new set of general benchmark models, might indeed be provided in the foreseeable future, from both orthodox and heterodox angles, through complexity economics—in fact, considered by some a paradigm shift (see, e.g., Fontana, 2008; an example for an early comprehensive application of complexity microeconomics is, e.g., Tisdell, 2013; see further, e.g., Axelrod, 1997; Beinhocker, 2005; Garnsey and McGlade, 2006; Chen, 2010; Kirman, 2011). As D. Colander has shown, complexity thinking was always present in the history of economic thought and has provided a rich legacy for a comprehensive modernization of the discipline (Colander, 2008). While A. Kirman and D. Helbing have elaborated on "rethinking economics using complexity theory" (Helbing and Kirman, 2013), R. Holt, B. Rosser, and D. Colander have straightforwardly declared the beginning of a "complexity era in economics" (Holt et al., 2011).

Complexity (micro-)economics results from a number of sources, from the analysis of dynamic and complex systems, the resurgence of biological analogies, modern statistical nonequilibrium physics, population thinking, and evolutionary economics, networks analysis, applications of (evolutionary) game theory, experimental behavioral economics, the new analytical opportunities of complex modeling and related computer simulations, and from evolutionary-institutional economics (see, e.g., Foster, 2005, 2006).

Also note that such efforts came and today come from different organizational sources, some of which are beyond just disciplinary research. The Mecca of complexity economics has been the *Santa Fe Institute*, with its books and working paper series. Also, INET, the *Institute for New Economic Thinking*, was founded by famous George Soros in 2009, in an effort to reconsider economic theorizing from scratch.

The Ideal "Market," the Real-World Market, Embedded in Its Counter-Principles, and a Mixture of Allocation Mechanisms

Complexity (micro-)economics implies that a real-world market economy will have to be conceptualized as a complex phenomenon, embedded in a set of mechanisms and entities that basically are its counter-principles, such as bureaucracies (hierarchy), networks, jointly learned (informal) social rules and institutions, and the state. Only all of these together give life, sense, meaning, and workability to a spontaneous, decentralized mechanism that we are used to calling a "market," while both limiting and enabling the market to work at all, when otherwise it might not even come into being.

It is not that a decentralized economic system would not be adequate per se. On the contrary, decentralization may be one of the requirements for an economic system to deal with complexity, which, however, in turn, may itself stem from fragmentation and individualization. But assuming isolated selfishly maximizing individual agents, all being of one kind, is certainly not the answer to real-world direct interdependence and related complexity. Coordinating real-world agents and simplifying their often intricate decision problems, so that they become capable and inclined of long-run learning, investing, innovating, or sometimes acting at all, might require a trinity of

- coordination through jointly learned institutionalized cooperative interaction to solve ubiquitous social-dilemma and collective-good problems (informal institutions);
- discursive deliberation and agreed upon collective action through formal organization, namely, properly legitimized and formed public action (organization, planning, or the state);
- decentralization with some spontaneous individualist reaction of agents to price changes (markets).

Therefore, a new understanding of the economy as a (what we will call) directly interdependent and complex system, where agents have different strategic options and mixed, and often intricate incentives to act, has been developed. Where agents are directly interdependent, they have to recurrently directly interact and learn from this experience, if they like it or not—uncertain as they are. In complex systems, effective coordination, thus, is all but obvious, trivial, simple to achieve, or self-stabilizing. Only real time, history, process, and recurrent interaction with learning and behavioral innovation will provide the frame for

generating solutions to the complex coordination problem, involving perhaps, but not necessarily, reduced systemic complexity. This will also give room for search, innovation, joint learning, the creation of collective and shared information, cumulative process, and long-run development. Note that behavioral consequences of rationality may be completely different under such different settings, namely, learned and recognized interdependence and long-run perspectives (futurity) (for a classical treatment, see, e.g., A. Sen's "rational fools," Sen, 1977). But there is no guarantee at all in complex structures and resulting evolutionary processes that an effective or instrumental coordination, i.e., coordination that serves problem solving, will actually emerge—or be stable.

Nobel Prizes for Such a Microperspective

With a complexity perspective coming up in economics and gaining dominance in cutting-edge economic research, complexity economists have also become eligible for the Nobel Prize. The Nobel Prize 2009, for instance, was awarded to one of the leading representatives of evolutionary-institutional economics, Elinor Ostrom (1933–2012; who shared it with Oliver Williamson), who has focused on collective-good and social-dilemma problems in a broad array of real-world applications, theoretically, by formal modeling, computer simulation, and laboratory experiment, applying game theory, doing empirical research, and developing highly relevant policy advice. We consider this and the earlier and later Nobel Prizes for G. Myrdal, H. Simon, D. North, J. Harsanyi, J. Nash, R. Selten, A. Sen, G. Akerlof, D. Kahnemann, V. Smith, R. Aumann, T. Schelling, J. Stiglitz, E. Maskin, R. Myerson, or R. Shiller indications of the paradigmatic diversification of economics and of the advancement of complexity microeconomics, which this textbook represents.

Revising Basic Assumptions, Closing the Gap Between "Doing" and Teaching

As said, much of applied research undertaken in the frame of mainstream economics deviates more or less in its assumptions or results from the perfect, general-equilibrium market economy model, and increasingly so. But also, many economists still do hesitate to draw the general consequence of thoroughly revising basic presumptions, perspectives, theories, models, and methods of received conventional economics. While they would agree that there is little evidence for self-equilibrating, stabilizing, and efficient market economies to be found in any concrete investigation, they would rarely state this in a general way and with all implied consequences, and particularly so in teaching.

As D. Colander stated in a review of the development of U.S. economics textbooks, the Samuelsonian textbook template that had emerged after 1948 (when Samuelson's famous textbook appeared for the first time) and still dominates today, with its supply/demand/partial-market equilibrium core, was no longer consistent with the cutting-edge research of the profession since the 1980s:

> The economics texts [...] did not change with the profession, and as of 2010 most texts had not incorporated that new [behavioral, game-theoretic, complexity, ... – W.E.] approach in their core structure. This has created a gap between what economists do and what they teach. *(Colander, 2010, p. 1)*

Toward a Broader Problem Solving . . .

A growing portion of economists is reconsidering complexity, real-world phenomena, and relevance. They no longer want to lay the idea of some efficient, equilibrating, and stable ideal market economy into the hands of millions of academically trained young professionals around the world as *the* common thread for their future professional and societal lives. As said, long-run large-scale problem-solving capacities of economies, societies, global corporations, financial markets, or governments have not increased over the last decades but rather seem to have deteriorated. The rigid and theoretically strong alternatives for increased problem-solving capacities of economic agents in the future have been far developed in economics. On the status quo, shortcomings, and potential reforms of economic education in the USA and Europe, see the reviews of Colander (2007, 2009a).

A New Teaching: Redrafting and Recrafting Microeconomics. . .

Thus, many economists have advocated the introduction of new teaching and related new types of textbooks (for an early assessment of complexity economics for teaching economics, see, e.g., *The Complexity Vision and the Teaching of Economics*, Colander, 2000b). Colander also stated:

> As more and more of the stock of teaching economists become trained in these new approaches and methods [of complexity economics – W.E.], we can expect to see a major change in the texts. *(Colander, 2010, p. 1)*

Similarly, S. Reddy, in an extensive review of the widely used textbook Mas-Colell et al. (1995ff.), concludes:

> [...] there is not very much by way of a developed alternative body of theory expressly concerned with strategic interaction. Who will create it? *(Reddy, 2013, p. 4.)*

It took meteorology more than 30 years, more than 100,000 person-years and at least $30 billion to make the step from simple methods (analog meteorology) to the modern simulative/computative meteorology (Farmer, 2011, p. 30). That is what will be needed in economics as well. And it is the feeling of many economists nowadays that the discipline is indeed already approaching this threshold of collective investment.

This textbook redrafts basic microeconomic modeling and teaching from scratch, on the basis of the wealth and breadth of complexity economics that have evolved in the last three decades. The perfect-market model has mostly become a very special case in the newly recognized and analyzed universe of complex structures, their potential processes, and system behaviors. And microeconomics is no longer exclusively markets but a broader set of interrelated coordination problems and potential coordination forms. This reflects the fact that the real world, too, is much broader and much more diverse in its forms, critical factors, mechanisms, and processes than reflected by the conventional core of microeconomics. The latter does not even sufficiently resemble the real world.

And again, to be sure, microeconomics does not lose its accessibility for rigor, formal modeling, and empirical testing, nor for good "teachability" in this way, but it will gain in relevance, professional usefulness, and problem-solving capacity.

ABOUT THIS TEXTBOOK

Guidelines of the Textbook

Among this textbook's distinguishing guidelines figure the following:

- *Rigid and cutting-edge*: It is rigid and cutting-edge with regard to settled economic research methods and results. And it has a large methodological part that provides the methods required for this textbook, and, above that, a deeper theoretical understanding of the complexity of economic systems.

- *New structure from scratch*: It refers to that cutting-edge research and settled research methods and results in a new and more appropriate structure.
- *Real world*: Besides its abstract and rigid approach, it has a strong real-world perspective.
- *Pluralistic*: It is plural(istic) in its perspective on different theoretical paradigms, and assumes a comparative, integrative, and synergetic approach—including a set of core models, representing diverse perspectives on economic complexity.
- *HET perspective*: It has a strong history-of-economic-theory approach, e.g., by embedding neoclassical economics in its own history and the history of its critique, and by developing a history of economic complexity thinking, starting with no one less than Adam Smith and his theory of emerging social rules, and ending with recent core models in economics.
- *Multilevel*: It is a multilevel textbook. It is accessible for the introductory teaching level, in a particular selection and combination of informal chapters, although it mainly is at intermediate level, and in other particular parts, it is advanced.
- *Multipurpose*: It is a multipurpose textbook, usable not only for microeconomics at the different levels and in one- or two-semester settings, but also usable for courses in industrial economics/industrial organization, game theory, mathematical/complexity economics, behavioral economics, or history of economic thought, and also as a second textbook for courses with prescribed standard curriculum in microeconomics. Thus, also instructors who prefer the standard teaching canon may find themselves profiting from adding chapters from this textbook.
- *Modularity*: It is built in a modular approach, where certain strings of chapters can be used for the different courses

mentioned, as required or supplementary reading, but also individual chapters can be used as stand-alone readings (in spite of dense cross-references among the chapters, which are not crucial to understanding a particular chapter). The practical value for some instructors from this will be that virtually any individual chapter can be selected or skipped.

In particular, this textbook develops complexity in economics methodologically from game theory, via simulation and evolutionary game theory, guided by an institutional perspective on the economy, leading to a variety of models and applications, such as the analysis of dynamic systems or network analysis.

Its Overall Structure and Content

The book has five parts. For the detailed structure of parts and chapters see Figure 1. More details are given below and in the Didactics section.

- PART I—Basics of the Interdependent Economy and Its Processes
- PART II—Markets: General-Equilibrium Theory and Real-World Market Structures
- PART III—Further Tools and the Analysis of Complex Economies
- PART IV—History of Thought and Contemporary Models in Complexity Economics
- PART V—Further Applications: Information, Innovation, Policy, and Methodology

Some Points in Particular

- *Introductory part*: The introductory part (Part I, Chapters 1–4), being largely informal, may be used at introductory-level teaching in a variety of economics and social-science courses (see Didactics section), but may also be perceived and

used, in higher-level courses, as some kind of a review section. The latter may also be applied to the neoclassical economics chapter (Chapter 5).

- *Prerequisites clarified and provided*: The prerequisites required for using any chapter of this textbook are clarified (see Didactics section) and provided in this textbook, considering that some undergraduates may be ill-prepared to work with the core chapters of this textbook at the intermediate level (with the possible exception of method-intensive mathematical/complexity economics or game theory courses taken before).

- *History of thought and the set of contemporary core models*: Only few textbooks in economics include the history of thought (often ending already with Keynes). And many economists find the idea of presenting recent theoretical and methodological developments in a history-of-thought perspective, as opposed to a uniform accepted-practice perspective convincing; they may find it difficult to give up the idea of a unique single-core model for a whole set of diverse core models. But exactly this (in Chapters 6, 12, and 13) was appreciated by external commentators in preparation of the textbook

- *The simulation chapter*: Discussants in preparation of this book also considered the simulation chapter (Chapter 9) as one of the central points of the methodological part (Part III) of the book. But instructors should exactly know what they can expect here. We do recount models from the literature. Also, we do enable students to recreate simulations, but in a very concise and short way. So students and instructors will need to employ additional resources, many of which are, however, freely available on the internet, as we can, of course, not cover programming in detail in an economics textbook. We do have code, in the *Python*

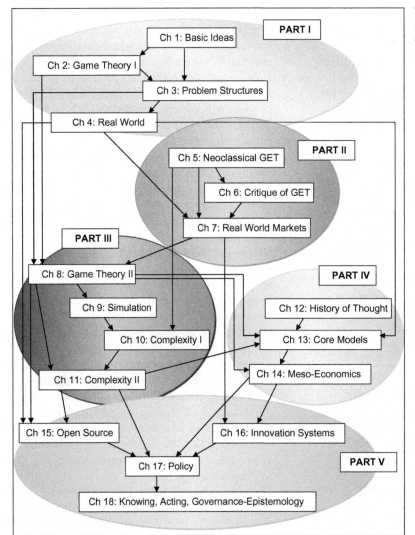

FIGURE 1   The structure of the textbook and the interdependence of the parts and chapters.

language, which also is freely available and widely used.

- ***The overall profile with regard to teaching level and to required versus companion reading***: The book's profile has been identified, as mentioned, as either a main reference for a pluralist intermediary/ advanced microeconomics course, or a companion book to a more conventional textbook in a standard-but-open course, or an additional reading text in a variety of specialized courses—with its issues that are not usually covered in an economics textbook (complexity, history of thought, simulation, contemporary core models, information and innovation economics, policy, critique of neoclassical economics, epistemology, etc.).

For more details on the usage of this textbook, see *Didactics* section.

Its Competition

Closest to our textbook is Samuel Bowles' book *Microeconomics* (Bowles, 2004). It resembles ours in terms of the complexity perspective in general, the stories from the real world, the breadth of the perspectives adopted, in particular evolutionary and institutional perspectives, and the more embedded use of game theory (embedded in proper evolutionary-institutional story telling and substantive interpretation). Bowles is famous for having written important and often path-breaking papers for more than 40 years. His book is also rebuilding real-world micro from scratch. It is in parts above the level of ours, i.e., it is mostly advanced. So it requires more from the potential student. Also, it is not really a full-fledged textbook but something in between a textbook and a research monograph. Nevertheless, with its new perspective, it has already been a big-seller—which confirms that there indeed is a need for a genuine complexity textbook like ours "out there."

A new microeconomics textbook-like book based on Bowles' book has been announced by the *Santa Fe Institute* in 2012: Samuel Bowles and Duncan Foley, *Coordination, Conflict and Competition: A Text in Intermediate Microeconomics* (no publisher given). The table of content can be accessed at: http://tuvalu.santafe.edu/~bowles/books.htm. It is more textbook-like.

For a detailed and updated overview and comparison of recent microeconomic textbooks, mainstream and heterodox ones, see the *Instructors' Manual* and the *Companion website* of our textbook at http://booksite.elsevier.com/9780124115859 and http://textbooks.elsevier.com/web/product_details.aspx?isbn=9780124115859.

This review shows that a number of economists, including some most established and prominent ones, and again, both from the mainstream or heterodoxy, are elaborating on new microfoundations of emergent system properties and evolving behavioral structures, which is also our common thread. Thus, some modern textbooks also are approaching complexity economics. Those economists have been developing and teaching such perspectives, theories, and models during the last 20 years or more. But, still, our reviews also show that there is an unmet demand for appropriate and comprehensive textbooks "out there" with the profile and particular accessibility of this textbook as described earlier. This is where we come in.

Enjoy working with the textbook!

An annotated *list of selected micro-textbooks*, selected monographs on evolutionary, institutional, and applied game-theoretic economics of interactive economies, and other further readings can be found at the *Instructors' Manual* website and the students' *Companion Website*, http://booksite.elsevier.com/9780124115859 and http://textbooks.elsevier.com/web/product_details.aspx?isbn=9780124115859.

References

A plea for a pluralistic and rigorous economics. Am. Econ. Rev. 82, 1992, xxv.

Akerlof, G.A., 2007. The missing motivation in macroeconomics. Am. Econ. Rev. 97 (1), 5–36.

Arnsperger, C., Varoufakis, Y., 2005. A most peculiar failure: how neoclassical economics turns theoretical failure into academic and political power. Erkenntnis. 59, 157–188.

Arnsperger, C., Varoufakis, Y., 2006. What is neoclassical economics? The three axioms responsible for its theoretical oevre, practical irrelevance and, thus, discursive power. Real-world Econ. Rev. 38, 2–12.

Axelrod, R., 1997. The Complexity of Cooperation. Agent-based Models of Competition and Collaboration. Princeton University Press, Princeton, NJ.

Ayres, R.U., Martinás, K. (Eds.), 2005. On the Reappraisal of Microeconomics. Edward Elgar, Cheltenham, Northampton.

Beinhocker, E.D., 2005. The Origin of Wealth: Evolution, Complexity, and the Radical Remaking of Economics. Harvard Business School Press, Boston, MA.

Bowles, S., 2004. Microeconomics. Behavior, Institutions, and Evolution. Sage and Princeton University Press, New York, Princeton.

Buchanan, M., 2008. This economy does not compute. N.Y. Times. October (1), OP-ED.

Buiter, W., 2009. The unfortunate uselessness of most "state of the art" academic monetary economics. Financ. Times. March (3).

Chen, P., 2010. Economic Complexity and Equilibrium Illusion. Essays on Market Instability and Macro Vitality. Routledge, London, New York.

Cohen, P., 2007. In economics departments, a growing will to debate fundamental assumptions. N.Y. Times. July (11), 6, Section B.

Cohen, P., 2009. Ivory tower unswayed by crashing economy. N.Y. Times. March (4).

Colander, D., 2000a. The death of neoclassical economics. J. Hist. Econ. Thought. 22 (2), 127–143.

Colander, D. (Ed.), 2000b. The Complexity Vision and the Teaching of Economics. Edward Elgar, Cheltenham, Northampton.

Colander, D., 2007. The Making of an Economist, Redux. Princeton University Press, Princeton, NJ.

Colander, D., 2008. Complexity and the history of economic thought. Middlebury College Economics Discussion Paper 08-04, Middlebury, VT. <http://sandcat.middlebury.edu/econ/repec/mdl/ancoec/0804.pdf> (accessed 27.12.13.).

Colander, D., 2009a. The Making of a European Economist. Edward Elgar, Cheltenham, Northampton.

Colander, D., Föllmer, H., Kirman, A., et al., 2009b. Dahlem Report. The financial crises and the systemic failure of academic economics. <http://www.debtdeflation.com/blogs/wp-content/uploads/papers/Dahlem_Report_EconCrisis021809.pdf> (accessed 27.12.13.).

Colander, D., 2010. The evolution of U.S. economics textbooks. Middlebury College Economics Discussion Paper No. 10-37, Middlebury College, Middlebury, VT.

Cullis, J., Jones, P., 2009. Microeconomics. A Journey Through Life's Decisions. Pearson/Prentice Hall, Harlow, UK.

Duarte, P.G., Lima, G.T. (Eds.), 2012. Microfoundations Reconsidered. The Relationship of Micro and Macroeconomics in Historical Perspective. Edward Elgar, Cheltenham, Northampton.

Elsner, W., 2008. Art. Market and State. International Encyclopedia of Public Policy. O'Hara, P.A. (Ed.), vol. III, Public Policy. <http://pohara.homestead.com/Encyclopedia/Volume-3.pdf>.

Farmer, J.D., 2011. The challenge of building agent-based models of the economy. Presentation at the European Central Bank, Frankfurt, June 10. <http://www.ecb.europa.eu/events/conferences/shared/pdf/conf_ecb_ny_fed/Farmer_pres.pdf?b2e9fbef4de78d132289f880fc83b0b8> (accessed 23.12.13.).

Fontana, M., 2008. The complexity approach to economics: a paradigm shift. Working Paper 01-2008, University of Torino, Italy. <http://www.cesmep.unito.it/WP/2008/1_WP_Cesmep.pdf> (accessed 27.12.13.).

Foster, J., 2005. From simplistic to complex systems in economics. Cambridge J. Econ. 29 (6), 873–892.

Foster, J., 2006. Why is economics not a complex systems science? J. Econ. Issues. XL (4), 1069–1091.

Garnsey, E., McGlade, J., 2006. Complexity and Co-Evolution. Continuity and Change in Socio-Economic Systems. Edward Elgar, Cheltenham, Northampton.

Giannakouros, P., Chen, L., 2012. Reclaiming math for economists: a pedagogical approach to overcoming a persistent barrier to pluralism in economics. Int. J. Pluralism Econ. Educ. 3 (2), 118–143.

Hayes, C., 2007. Hip heterodoxy. Nation. June (11).

Heinrich, T., 2013. Technological Change and Network Effects in Growth Regimes: Exploring the Microfoundations of Economic Growth. Routledge, Oxford, New York.

Helbing, D., Kirman, A., 2013. Rethinking economics using complexity theory. Real-world Econ. Rev. 64, 23–51.

Holt, R., Rosser, J.B., Colander, D., 2011. The complexity era in economics. Rev. Polit. Econ. 23 (3), 357–369.

Kaletsky, A., 2009a. Economists are the forgotten guilty men. The Times, TIMESONLINE. February (5).

Kaletsky, A., 2009b. Now is the time for a revolution in economic thought. The Times, TIMESONLINE. February (9).

Kapeller, J., 2013. Model-Platonism in economics: on a classical epistemological critique. J. Inst. Econ. 9 (2), 199–221.

Keen, S., 2009. A pluralist approach to microeconomics. The Handbook of Pluralist Economics Education. Routledge, London, New York, pp. 120–149.

Keen, S., 2012. Maths for pluralist economics. World Econ. Assoc. Newsl. 2 (1), 10.

Kessler, A., 2010. Cognitive dissonance, the global financial crisis and the discipline of economics. Real-world Econ. Rev. 54, 2–18.

King, J.E., 2012. The Microfoundations Delusion. Metaphor and Dogma in the History of Macroeconomics. Edward Elgar, Cheltenham, Northampton.

Kirman, A., 2011. (The Graz Schumpeter Lectures). Complex Economics: Individual and Collective Rationality Routledge, London, New York.

Lawson, T., 2013. What is this "school" called neoclassical economics? Cambridge J. Econ. 37, 947–983.

Lee, F., Elsner, W. (Eds.), 2008. Publishing, refereeing, rankings, and the future of heterodox economics. On the Horizon. 16 (4), (special issue).

Lee, F., Elsner, W. (Eds.), 2010. Evaluating economic research in a contested discipline. Rankings, pluralism, and the future of heterodox economics. Studies in Economic Reform and Social Justice, Wiley-Blackwell, Special Issue of the American Journal of Economics and Sociology, 695.

Marglin, S.A., 2008. The Dismal Science: How Thinking Like an Economist Undermines Community. Harvard University Press, Cambridge, MA.

Mas-Colell, A., Whinston, M.D., Green, J.R., 1995ff. Microeconomic Theory. Oxford University Press, Oxford.

McCloskey, D.N., 1983. The rhetoric of economics. J. Econ. Lit. 22 (2), 481–517.

Mirowski, P., 2010. Inherent Vice: Minsky, Markomata, and the tendency of markets to undermine themselves. J. Inst. Econ. 6 (4), 415–443.

Nadeau, R., 2008. The economist has no clothes. Sci. Am. March (25).

Nelson, R.H., 2001. Economics as Religion. From Samuelson to Chicago and Beyond. Pennsylvania State University Press, University Park, PA.

Raveaud, G., 2009. Pluralism in economics teaching: why and how. What Next. Dag Hammarskjöld Foundation, <http://www.dhf.uu.se/whatnext/papers_public/Raveaud%20-%20Pluralism%20in%20economics%20teaching.pdf> (accessed 27.12.13.).

Reddy, S., 2013. Reading Mas-Colell. Game theory: too much and too little? <http://ineteconomics.org/reading-mas-colell/game-theory-too-much-and-too-little> (accessed 23.12.13.).

Sen, A.K., 1977. Rational fools: a critique of the behavioral foundations of economic theory. Philos. Public Aff. 6 (4), 317–344.

Tisdell, C.A., 2013. Competition, Diversity and Economic Performance. Processes, Complexities and Ecological Similarities. Edward Elgar, Cheltenham, Northampton.

Warsh, D., 2008. A brave army of heretics. May 25. <www.economicprincipals.com> (accessed 27.12.13.).

Acknowledgments

Chapter 4 makes some reference to: Wolfram Elsner, "The 'New' Economy: Complexity, Coordination and a Hybrid Governance Approach," *International Journal of Social Economics*, **31.11-12** (2004), pp. 1029–1049, and to: id., "Real-World Economics Today: The New Complexity, Co-ordination, and Policy," *Review of Social Economy*, **LXIII.1** (2005), pp. 19–53.

Chapter 12 is in minor parts based on: Wolfram Elsner, "Adam Smith's Model of the Origins and Emergence of Institutions: The Modern Findings of the Classical Approach," *Journal of Economic Issues*, **XXIII.1** (1989), pp. 189–213, and on: Wolfram Elsner, Sebastian Berger, "European Contributions to Evolutionary Institutional Economics: The Cases of 'Cumulative Circular Causation' (CCC) and 'Open Systems Approach' (OSA)," *Journal of Economic Issues*, **XLI.2** (2007), pp. 529–537.

Section 13.12 is based on: Wolfram Elsner, "The Theory of Institutional Change Revisited. The Institutional Dichotomy, Its Dynamic, and Its Policy Implications in a More Formal Analysis," *Journal of Economic Issues*, **XLVI.1** (2012), pp. 1–43.

Chapter 14 is based on: Wolfram Elsner, "Why Meso? On 'Aggregation' and 'Emergence' and Why and How the Meso Level Is Essential in Social Economics," *Forum for Social Economics*, **36.1** (2007), pp. 1–16, on: Wolfram Elsner, Torsten Heinrich, "A Simple Theory of 'Meso.' On the Co-Evolution of Institutions and Platform Size—With an Application to Varieties of Capitalism and 'Medium-Sized' Countries," *Journal of Socio-Economics*, **38** (2009), pp. 843–858, Wolfram Elsner, "The Process and a Simple Logic of 'Meso.' On the Co-Evolution of Institutional Emergence and Group Size," *Journal of Evolutionary Economics*, **20.3**, 2010, pp. 445–477; and on: Wolfram Elsner, Torsten Heinrich, "Coordination on 'Meso'-Levels: On the Co-Evolution of Institutions, Networks and Platform Size," in: Stefan Mann (Ed.), *Sectors Matter! Exploring Mesoeconomics*, Berlin, Heidelberg, New York: Springer, 2011, pp. 115–163.

Chapter 16 is partly based on: Wolfram Elsner, Gero Hocker, Henning Schwardt, "Simplistic vs. Complex Organization: Markets, Hierarchies, and Networks in an Organizational Triangle—A Simple Heuristic to Analyze Real-World Organizational Forms," *Journal of Economic Issues*, **XLIV.1** (2010), pp. 1–30.

Chapter 17 is in parts based on: Wolfram Elsner, "Interactive Economic Policy: Toward a Cooperative Policy Approach for a Negotiated Economy," *Journal of Economic Issues*, **XXXV.1** (2001), pp. 61–83.

Chapters 1–3, 5–7, and 8–10, and parts of Chapter 13 are partly based on the book: Wolfram Elsner (in collaboration with Torsten Heinrich, Henning Schwardt, and Matthias Greiff), *Microeconomics of Interactive Economies. Evolutionary, Institutional, and Complexity Perspectives. A "Non-Toxic" Intermediate Textbook*, Cheltenham, UK, Northampton, MA, USA: Edward Elgar, 2012. We gratefully acknowledge the permission given by Edward Elgar Publishing to draw on previously published material.

Claudius Gräbner, worked with the authors through the revisions of all chapters of the book and even authored some sections. The authors are much indebted to Claudius.

The authors are grateful to *Professor Shuanping Dai*, PhD, and to *Yanlong Zhang*, MA, who have contributed to Chapters 10 and 13, to *Dr. Miriam de Blasi*, who has contributed to Chapter 15, to *Yasar Damar*, MA, who has contributed to Chapters 7 and 13, and to *Dr. Matthias Greiff*, who has contributed to Chapters 5 and 6.

Many have commented on earlier versions of this text. We are grateful to *Professors Ping Chen*, Shanghai and Beijing, *Philip A. O'Hara*, Perth, AUS, *Paul D. Bush*, Fresno, CA, *Peter Dorman*, Olympia, WA, and *Alexander Lascaux*, Moscow/Hertford, UK, for comments, encouragement, and support. Finally, we would like to thank generations of students who have worked with and commented on parts and earlier versions of this text.

Last not least, we thank the *publisher* and its responsible Senior Acquisition Editor, *Dr. Scott Bentley*, who in a committed, elegant, and enjoyable way, organized a 10-month two-staged review process with 11 anonymous *reviewers*. These, in turn, got involved with this book in a way that was far beyond their usual responsibility. We learned a lot from them, not least about the informal "deep structures" of teaching and learning in the USA. This book profited enormously from, in sum, 22 detailed reviews.

About the Authors

Wolfram Elsner (*1950) studied economics at the University of Cologne, Germany, received the PhD at the University of Bielefeld in 1977 and the venia legendi ("Habilitation" as used in German-speaking academia, also called "venia docendi") in 1985. He then left academia to work in the "real world" for 10 years. He has worked as head of a municipal economic development agency for 4 years. Later, he worked as head of the planning division of the Ministry for Economic Affairs in a German state ("Land") and as director of that state government's economic research institute for 6 years (until 1995). He also served as that state's official for industrial defense conversion policy through the nineties (1992–2001), managing a state conversion program and EU funds allocated to this purpose. During this time, he returned to academia as a full professor of economics at the University of Bremen in 1995 and has served in many academic functions, local, national, and international, since then. He is an adjunct professor at the doctoral faculty, economics department of the University of Missouri at Kansas City and co-director of the iino—*Institute for Institutional and Innovation Economics*, University of Bremen. He is Managing Editor of the *Forum for Social Economics*, co-editor of the book series *Advances in Heterodox Economics* (Routledge), and President of the *European Association for Evolutionary Political Economy*—EAEPE. He has authored many articles in more than a dozen different journals and has edited or co-edited many books.

Torsten Heinrich (*1982) teaches economics at the University of Bremen placing a focus on evolutionary economics and simulation. He studied economics at the Dresden University of Technology (TU Dresden), Germany, and the Universidad Autónoma de Madrid, Spain, and received a master's degree in economics from the Dresden University of Technology in 2007. He took up a position as teaching and research assistant at the University of Bremen and continued to do research on economic growth, chaos and complexity in economics, network externalities, the economic aspects of the information and communication technology, and simulation in economics. He received a PhD at the University of Bremen in 2011 for a dissertation on the role of network effects in technological change and economic growth. He currently holds a Post-Doc position at the University of Bremen.

Henning Schwardt (*1977) studied economics and political science at Christian-Albrechts-University, Kiel, Germany, and at Stockholm University, Sweden. After graduating with a master's degree in economics, he went to Madrid, Spain, for doctoral classes in economics and international relations at the Universidad Autónoma de Madrid. Following the "suficiencia investigadora," he took up a position as teaching and research assistant at the Institute for Institutional and Innovation Economics at the University of Bremen, Germany, where he received the PhD promotion in 2012. Currently, he holds a Post-Doc position in Bremen.

Didactics: How to Work with This Textbook at Introductory, Intermediate, and Advanced Levels, and in Different Kinds of Courses

"The purpose of studying economics is so as not to avoid being deceived by economists." **Joan Robinson**[1]

BEYOND THE "ECONOMICS OF THE X": A DIFFERENT TASK, A DIFFERENT STYLE

Famous economist Axel Leijonhufvud, in a legendary story about the "nation of the Econs," characterized the usual syllabus of microeconomics as the economics of the "x", demand and supply, the totem of the tribe of the micros (Leijonhufvud, 1981, Chapter 12). This indeed is the standard textbook structure: "demand—supply—partial-market equilibrium (equilibrium prices)—general equilibrium—welfare," nowadays supplemented by add-ons about "nonperfect markets," market failures of all kinds, game theory, some nonequilibrium dynamics, some complex recent phenomena such as information and innovation economics, and public policies.

Since its perspectives, questions, approach, contents, material, examples, references, etc. deviate from standard textbooks, this textbook needs to also be somewhat different in style compared to a textbook that conveys a completely settled, standardized, codified, and "obvious" body of knowledge. The body of knowledge of this textbook is comparatively new, less standardized, and less codified yet, and thus often more unfamiliar or even surprising vis-á-vis the settled patterns of thought, that often refer to the everyday consciousness and language, often also the language of the media—and of students. Therefore, we often look at issues, statements, propositions, and examples from different angles.

This is also why we strive to inform students about the variety of newly available critical literature in order to demonstrate that there is a whole new world to learn. Often, our chapters have comparatively many references and even more *further readings*. While standardized textbooks tend not to "disturb" and "confound" students with "too much" literature, we have found that it is most important for students to learn how numerous, how diverse, and how rich the critical literature "out there" really is. An important didactical issue and an issue for attitudes toward professional life and life in general.

We would, of course, not expect students to read and learn more than they are required by standard textbooks and in standard courses.

[1]Robinson, J., (1955) 'Marx, Marshall And Keynes', Occasional Paper No. 9, The Delhi School of Economics, University of Delhi, Delhi.

But we think we have to explain more, in order to establish the new perspectives and the so far more uncommon and unfamiliar ways of thinking.

Complexity economics is about often intricate structures, with lasting tensions or contradictions, with resulting continuing, often open-ended process, with multiple equilibria, thus often open indeterminate results. However, we will see that, nevertheless, a lot of specific, "hard," and "rigid" knowledge can be learned.

SAMPLE SYLLABI: ROADMAPS FOR TEACHING IN DIFFERENT FORMATS

The "stand-alone" use of this textbook as a required prime source, as said, can be applied to undergraduate, graduate, and post-graduate, introductory, intermediate, and advanced micro, each as a one- or a two-semester course, depending on the local givens of a department's or school's programs.

Furthermore, it can be used, as a required main textbook or as a supplementary reading for elective courses in Game Theory, Industrial Economics or Organization, Mathematical or Complexity Economics, Behavioral Economics, or History of Thought. For all these options, see the sample syllabi in Table 1.

Finally, it can be assigned as a companion volume, with certain individual chapters or chapter strings selected, in certain specialized economics courses with some complexity perspective aimed at.

For an overview of potential uses of the textbook, see Table 1. Note: Chapter numbers in brackets indicate noncore chapters that may be skipped or used in parts only. Also note that

TABLE 1 Overview of Sample Syllabi/Roadmaps for Teaching with This Textbook in Different Settings

Course Level / Course Type	Introductory/Undergraduate (First Year)	Intermediate/Undergraduate (Second and Third Year)	Advanced/Graduate/ Post-Graduate (Fourth Year and Above)
One-Semester Course or Two-Semester Course, First Semester	1, 2, 3, 4, (5), (12)	(Focus on theory and methods) (4), 5, 7, 8, 9	6, (8), (9), 10, 11, 13, (14)
Second Semester	./.	(Focus on history of economic thought, core models and applications, policy and methodology) (12), 13, (14), 15, 16, 17, 18	./.
Courses in Game Theory and/or Industrial Economics/Organization (Intermediate)	./.	(2), 7, 8, (9), (11), 13, 15, 16	./.
Course in Behavioral Economics (Intermediate)	./.	3, 8, (13), (14), (15)	./.
Course in History of Economic Thought (Intermediate)	./.	12, (5), 6, 13, (14)	./.
Courses in Mathematical and/or Complexity Economics (Advanced)	./.	./.	6, (8), 9, 10, 11, 13, (14), (15), (18)

TABLE 2   Formal Prerequisites of the Parts of the Textbook

Part	Prerequisites
Part I: Basics of the Interdependent Economy and Its Processes	None
Part II: Markets: General-Equilibrium Theory and Real-World Market Structures	Introductory Microeconomics; Basic Analysis; Basic Algebra
Part III: Further Tools and the Analysis of Complex Economics	On top of the above: Dynamic Systems/Basic Differential Calculus (Intermediate Analysis)
Part IV: History of Thought and Contemporary Models in Complexity Economics	On top of the above: Basic Game Theory, Evolutionary Game Theory; Complexity Theory/Dynamic Systems; Simulations (Parts II and III of the textbook provide this)
Part V: Further Applications and Interactive Economic Policy	On top of the above: Basic Understanding of the Methods and Models Used in Heterodox Economics (Parts II through IV of the textbook provide this)

NOTE

For supplementary teaching material (lecture slides), exercises and solution keys, sample exams, and further readings, teachers may visit the *Instructors' Manual website*, and students may visit the textbook's *Companion Website*, http://booksite.elsevier.com/9780124115859 and http://textbooks.elsevier.com/web/product_details.aspx?isbn=9780124115859.

---

there are some few chapter doublings in the first line and the columns of the matrix. The curriculum for a particular course in the microeconomic training across the different levels, or for different courses at a particular level of a program is, of course, subject to the local conditions and, thus, to the discretion of the academic lecturer.

PREREQUISITES FOR PARTICULAR PARTS

Parts II through V take into account that the great majority of the readers are familiar with—mostly neoclassical—introductory microeconomics. The more formal Parts III and IV are slightly more demanding in the mathematical prerequisites they require. An overview is given in Table 2.

Reference

Leijonhufvud, A., 1981. *Information and Coordination. Essays in Macroeconomic Theory*. Oxford University Press, New York, Oxford, incl. in Chapter 12 a reprint of the paper: Life among the Econ. West. Econ. J. 11 (3), 1973, 327–337.

List of Abbreviations

All-D	always defect (strategy)
CCC	circular cumulative causation
CG	collective good
CKR	common knowledge of rationality
CPR(-G)	common pool resource (-game)
FOC	first-order conditions
GT	game theory, game-theoretic
GET	general equilibrium theory
HET	history of economic thought
H&S	Hub and Spoke (hierarchical network structure)
IPR	intellectual property rights
MC	marginal costs
MR	marginal returns
NE	Nash equilibrium
NSI	national systems of innovation
OS	open source
PO	Pareto optimum
PD	Prisoners' Dilemma
R&D	research and development
RSI	regional systems of Innovation
SESDS	successive elimination of strictly dominated strategies
SG	supergame
SME	small and medium-sized enterprises
TFT	tit-for-tat (strategy)
TIC(T)	tele-information and -communication (technologies)
TMS	Theory of Moral Sentiments
VAC	value-added chain
VoC	varieties of capitalism
WN	Wealth of Nations

BASICS OF THE INTERDEPENDENT ECONOMY AND ITS PROCESSES

1

Introduction to the Microeconomics of Complex Economies

"The degree to which economics is isolated from the ordinary business of life is extraordinary and unfortunate." **Ronald Coase**[1]

"Why is Economics Not An Evolutionary Science?" **Thorstein Veblen**[2]

"Why is Economics Not a Complex Systems Science?" **John Foster**[3]

[1]Nobel Laureate in Economics, "Saving Economics from the Economists," *Harvard Business Review*, December 2012.
[2]*The Quarterly Journal of Economics*, **12.4** (1898), pp. 373–397.
[3]*Journal of Economic Issues*, **40.4** (2006), pp. 1069–1091.

1.1 INTRODUCTION: A MICROECONOMICS OF DIRECT INTERDEPENDENCE

Many economic situations are characterized by a direct interdependence among the agents involved. The behavior of one, or some, or all of them influences the options that are open to the others and the results they can achieve. Given different options for behaviors in a certain situation, then, which one do agents choose? And will their choices result in an outcome that they can be satisfied with, for themselves, or as a group? Or are situations conceivable, in which individuals, who make individually optimal decisions, generate outcomes that *unintentionally* leave them all, or at least some, worse off in an interdependent setting?

As you may infer from these questions, it is important to be aware that economic situations cover a much *broader and more fundamental range of circumstances* than the mere exchange of goods and services for money. Rather, they include companies having to decide on how to handle joint research and development (R&D) projects, or firms choosing price and quality of product varieties in competitive setups, but also such situations as taking up studies and attending lectures in an effort to acquire knowledge and skills that may amongst other things serve to increase future earnings potential, and many more. All such situations involve *several behavioral options* that are open to the agents as well as results for agents that depend also on *decisions made by other agents*. Such directly interdependent, and thus *interactive*, situations and their consequences in truly *multipersonal* (or "social") decision situations (and thus "socio-"economy) are at the center of this textbook.

1.2 DIFFERENT PROBLEM STRUCTURES IN DIRECTLY INTERDEPENDENT DECISION SITUATIONS

1.2.1 Degree of Conflict

Social decision situations, where interdependent agents exercise a mutual influence on their respective results, can be differentiated by the degree of conflict that is inherent to them. When referring to degree of conflict here, we mean the *tension that can arise between an individually optimal decision and the eventual result on an aggregate level*, i.e., the outcome that individually optimal decisions may produce when exercised together that in turn feeds back to individual results.

The simplest and fully "optimal" case is one where individually optimal (i.e., "rational," maximizing) behavior by each agent leads to a result that is also the optimal social, collective outcome. On the other side of the spectrum are situations, in which individually rational, maximizing behavior results in a socially suboptimal outcome and which is reflected in comparatively worse individual results as well. The latter would mean that decision criteria *beyond a sole focus on immediate individual maximization* might allow the agents to realize superior results. How to solve such situations so that even narrowly conceived rational individuals can attain improved results is a question that we will discuss repeatedly throughout the book.

1.2.2 Rationality and Optimality

Note that the *concept of rationality* as utilized in most economics textbooks and teaching material differs somewhat from the general use of the term and from the use of the term in other disciplines. Beyond the coherence of behavior and assumptions, and the mere "purposefulness" of behavior with regard to a specific objective, in "mainstream" economics the rationality concept includes the assumption that individually *maximizing* behavior, which we also may call *individualistic* behavior, is optimal for reaching an objective (i.e., an economic outcome captured in terms of costs and benefits of an action). Such "optimality" of behavior is governed by certain mathematical conditions that we will explain in detail in Chapters 2 and 5. A "rational" decision in these circumstances is thus by definition also an "optimal" decision, which in fact results in a significant difference between *different concepts of rationality*. As a baseline and reference point, we follow this understanding of rationality. However, eventually it will be necessary to *adapt a rationality concept* that is more closely oriented on its use in other disciplines and more appropriate for a *more realistic microeconomics* or *"real-world* microeconomics."

1.2.3 Pareto Criterion

In economics, a commonly used criterion for evaluating and comparing situations is the Pareto Criterion. A situation is defined a *Pareto Optimum* (PO) if from there no agent's situation can be improved without reducing the payoff of someone else at the same time. Note that this criterion does not include a broader judgment regarding the desirability of an outcome including some redistribution. A situation where one agent controls all available resources or receives the entire payoff in a given setup, while the rest of the group have or receive nothing, nevertheless is Pareto-optimal according to that definition, just as is a situation where all agents control or receive equal shares. If a situation is not Pareto-optimal, if it is *Pareto-inferior* compared to another *Pareto-superior* one, then, according to the definition, at least one agent's payoff can be improved without a concurrent reduction

in anyone else's payoff. If the individually optimal decisions lead to an outcome that is a PO, we assume the degree of conflict to be relatively low. If individually optimal decisions lead to a Pareto-inferior outcome, in turn, the degree of conflict is assumed to be relatively high, as agents' interests in others' decisions and their preferred choices do not concur.

1.2.4 Social Optima and Social Dilemmas

You may imagine these situations along the following lines. As we consider agents and their behaviors, and the overall result to be expected from their decisions, every agent needs to have at least two behavioral options, A and B. If individually optimal decisions result in a PO, we can say that every agent rationally wants to choose, say, option A and that this choice leads to an optimum on the group level as a side effect. In the second case, every agent's individually optimal choice is B, but the outcome is not optimal. In fact, they would all prefer everyone to choose A. But no one has an individualistic incentive for this choice. Even if all other agents choose A, an individual can attain her best payoff by opting for B. However, if all agents choose B, the result will be suboptimal, on a group level as well as for each of them. But as they all individualistically prefer B, rational and individualistic agents deciding freely will not be able to solve the situation and reach the Pareto-superior result. Such situations are thus called social dilemmas.

1.2.5 Coordination Problems

In between these two types of outcomes is a variety of situations, in which individually optimal behavior cannot be defined without knowing about the choices of the other agents in a situation. That is to say, within the setup as described above, if all other agents choose their option B, the last agent would also choose B, but if the others opt for A, so would the last one choosing. There is no clearly optimal behavior for an individual, but different options become more or less attractive, depending on what the other agents in a group opt for. Such problem situation is therefore called a coordination problem. Once the agents in a group have coordinated on a type of behavior, they have no reason to change their behaviors, at least not individually. Note, however, that there is no guarantee that the coordinated situation would be the best among the possible outcomes. It is, by definition of the problem structure, superior only to uncoordinated outcomes, though.

Such different types of interdependent situations can be represented with the help of *game-theoretic* tools. Once these have been introduced in Chapter 2, we will discuss these social decision situations for a more detailed analysis.

1.3 COMPETING PARADIGMS IN ECONOMICS: INVISIBLE HAND VERSUS FALLACY OF AGGREGATION

1.3.1 The Invisible-Hand World View

Many economists have been and continue to be very optimistic about such structures of the basic social decision situation. The assumption from which a broad strand of economic theory developed is that individualistically rational behavior would automatically result in a *social optimum* as well. This invisible-hand paradigm certainly served its purpose of developing a narrative, on which newly emerging merchant and trading classes in the *eighteenth century* could emancipate themselves against their feudal overlords. A concept of a *self-organizing* social and economic system, a "market" or *"market economy,"* leading to desirable social outcomes without the need for supervision, served the articulation of their interests perfectly.

Adam Smith (1723–1790), who gave the idea its attractive invisible-hand capture and effectively used it as a topical metaphor against the feudal class of his day, did in fact not completely believe in its general validity, though. For him, pure individual selfishness as the sole motivation would lead to overall undesirable results. Rather, agents were *socially embedded* actors, and needed to become socially embedded in proper ways, if they were to contribute to the general welfare. And they would be willing to be properly socially embedded and to contribute, if only they were allowed sufficient room to choose and would feel sufficiently empowered. Such embeddedness in the social structures of their environment (i.e., social rules and social institutions) was a crucial factor to function both social and economic spheres, and in particular, for "markets" to function for the welfare of all and not just of the most powerful and rich.

This second aspect, however, has been pushed to the background of much of economic theory, and the focus has generally been directed to situations in which individual optimality and social desirability (presumably) perfectly coincide. It has become increasingly clear in the era of modern complexity sciences that the optimality of results in allegedly self-organizing, decentralized, spontaneous "market" systems is by no means certain, though, and that situations, in which the results can considerably be improved by properly structuring the decision problem to enable agents to achieve superior results, are the rules rather than an uncommon exception.

1.3.2 The Fallacy-of-Aggregation World View

Other possible situations, e.g., those related to the social dilemma situations referred to above, can be described in terms of the fallacy-of-aggregation concept (sometimes also called the fallacy of composition). This idea states that the individually "optimal" actions undertaken by the agents may result in socially undesirable (Pareto-inferior) outcomes. In fact, we may relate this to a story that combines the general idea of the fallacy of aggregation with the importance of *expectations* regarding others' behavior in interdependent situations. Imagine a number of firms that have to simultaneously decide on their investment programs. Their investments signify increased demand for others' products (directly or indirectly because of increased purchasing power of the workers employed). In that case, a decision where all invest may be profitable for all. If, on the other hand, only some invest, their spending may not be profitable because the lack of investment by others can signify an overall demand that is not high enough to lead to an amortization of the investment spending undertaken. In short, if enough companies invest, everyone's investment will be worthwhile. If not enough firms invest, those who did will lose money, they produce a positive *"external" effect* for all firms who profit from the additional demand that is created by the investment spending. As individualistically rational agents, no one will invest and the collective situation may remain in economic stagnancy for a long time.

1.3.3 A Continuum of Complex Decision Structures

Depending on the relative strength of the effects involved, we may imagine the situation as a coordination or a dilemma problem. Either, it will become worthwhile to invest if enough other companies invest (their increased demand may necessitate additional production capacities to satisfy it), or a company may be unequivocally better off not investing, while still preferring all others would engage in investment programs and profiting from the additional demand this would create. If additional demand can be met by increasing the degree of utilization of existing production structures (as would be the case in a recession), the second case becomes more likely. However, if the scenario is true for all companies, none will invest, and the overall result is worse than it would have been if every firm had invested.

The degree of conflict thus differs depending on the overall problem structure that agents face. It has become clear that there is a continuum of problem structures beyond the individually easily solvable case of rational decisions resulting in a PO. In the case of coordination problems, expectations regarding others' behavior are crucial, whereas dilemma problems cannot be optimally solved by rational individualistic agents. In the case described, a fiscal program to stimulate demand and possibly transform the dilemma problem into a coordination problem may be a way out. More generally, an easy way out may be to call for *enforcing socially optimal behavior*, which, however, is not an easy task for a number of reasons. An endogenous solution that is attained and can be maintained by the agents themselves would of course be preferable. How such solutions may be developed (by the public agent) will be discussed in Chapters 2, 3, and 17.

1.4 UNCERTAINTY, STRATEGIC UNCERTAINTY, AND BOUNDED RATIONALITY

1.4.1 Uncertainty and Expectations

Uncertainty (sometimes also called strong or true or radical uncertainty[4]) describes a situation in which agents do not know about future

---

[4]In many textbooks, uncertainty is simply used in the sense of risk, which always is still calculable as just some probability attached to a variable or parameter. To be sure, complexity economists acknowledge the fundamental existence and pervasiveness of uncertainty, which is no longer calculable and, therefore, often is termed "strong," "true," or "radical" uncertainty. Thus, our use of uncertainty throughout this textbook is always in the above sense of this "strong uncertainty." We just use the word uncertainty, though.

states of a system. This can manifest itself in different ways, as (i) they may not know in which different states the system may be in the future or (ii) they may know about the different states, without, however, being able to put probabilities on them and on that basis calculate risk (or it may be a mixture of both). Economic situations are generally characterized by such uncertainty, and increasingly so, the longer the time horizon that we have to consider.

In situations characterized by direct interdependence, we can also introduce the concept of *strategic uncertainty* (or *initial strong strategic uncertainty*). This term specifically captures the notion of not knowing how other agents will behave (at least in the beginning of a longer interaction relationship, when agents do not know each other sufficiently well). As the results that agents can achieve depend on the behavior of others, they will form *expectations* about these others and make their own choice based on these expectations. But being able to form expectations about the behavior of others presumes that agents have some knowledge, or at least can formulate some assumptions, about the others' motivations. The less they know, or the less sure they can be about the assumptions they have made, the higher is the *degree of uncertainty* under which agents take their own decisions.

1.4.2 Behavioral Patterns

If agents were not able to change that situation of uncertainty, it would mean the end of our analysis. There would be no regularities in behavior we could observe, at least no systematic ones, and hence there would be no foundation from which an analysis could be developed. But obviously there are behavioral patterns that are regularly repeated, that are observed, and that thereby allow agents to form expectations regarding future choices of behavior by others. These regularities are the reflections of *social rules* and *social institutions* that guide agents' behaviors, concepts to which we will soon return.

1.4.3 Bounded Rationality

Another aspect that presents problems for agents when taking decisions is that they cannot handle the amount of data available in any given moment. When we assume rationality of the agents, but concede their *limited cognitive capacities*, we speak of boundedly rational agents. They would have to be able to handle all available data in any given moment in order to optimally inform their decisions.

For instance, if there were only 10 commodities available and each commodity available only in 5 different quantities, the rational individualistic agent would have to be able to calculate her perfect preference order among around 5^{10} or 9.8 million different commodity bundles within a logical second. Consider the several thousand items available in any regular supermarket and the number of different quantities available for each. A "rational" individualistic consumer would need to have a brain of the size of the universe to store his "preference function."

Hence, there is no reason to suspect that the decisions eventually taken by real-world agents would in any structured way lead to "optimal" results for them. This is independent of any interdependence among agents so far. We merely concede that agents' capacities are limited.

Even if they were to make purely rational decisions on the basis of a strict cost–benefit analysis based on the information they have, they might end up with *any* kind of result. They may have taken the best possible decision given the information they had, but some crucial piece may still have been missing. Of course they can *learn* and *adapt their behavior*, but, again, they have limited capacities and therefore cannot continuously analyze and possibly upgrade all of their decisions frequently, an aspect that becomes all the more important once we recognize that the *environment* they are moving in may be *continuously changing* over time.

Furthermore, they do not face all relevant situations on a frequent basis, but some decisions have to be taken only occasionally. An upgrading of decision rules based on earlier experiences is obviously difficult in this case. Such *decision rules* are embodied in the *social rules* and *social institutions* that structure interactions in groups in order to reduce the environmental complexity. We discuss these rules in Sections 1.6 and 1.7 and Chapter 3.

1.5 PATH DEPENDENCE, NONERGODICITY, AND CUMULATIVITY IN PROCESSES OF CHANGE

1.5.1 Path-Dependent and Nonergodic Process

Change is a constitutive element of economic systems. Environmental changes, technological development, *adaptations* of rules to allow for better results to be achieved, and other influences combine to create an economic sphere that is constantly in flux. We can employ the concept of *path dependence* for capturing some of the principal dynamics in these processes (see also Chapter 13 for a particular core model of such dynamics). Another characteristic that economic systems show is the *nonergodicity* of processes of change they undergo.

Ergodicity in systems (of agents, particles, or other elements) means that the properties and the constitution of the system usually do not change over space and time. So you can relatively easily tell future states of the system. Those systems may even return to earlier statuses, much like a mechanical system. Often, the property of ergodicity is also related to

the idea of a *representative agent* or element, so that you can conclude from the properties and behavior of one to those of all others. Nonergodic systems on the other hand do consequently exhibit a nontrivial development on the local and global scale; they are path dependent and usually their development is not reversible but *irreversible*. They cannot assume the same status again that they had assumed before on their development path.

The state of a nonergodic, path-dependent system depends on the path the system followed to that moment. The shape of this path is not predetermined, however. As can be appreciated from what has been said until here, influences from a number of sources can have an impact on the path taken and the shape of a situation that results from it in a given moment. In socioeconomic systems, *learning* capacities of agents and the solutions to collective problems employed in a group can differ, for instance, and are likely to have an influence on future developments in their specific group and circumstances. At the same time, *random shocks, stochastic events*, or *accidents of history* influence the development that an economic system is undergoing.

1.5.2 Complexity and Cumulative Process

As said, such influences and the resulting reactions and developments are typically irreversible in complex economic systems. We use complexity to describe situations that involve a number of heterogeneous agents having different behavioral options to choose from, possibly pursuing different objectives.[5]

Even a number of individually minor incidents may combine to have a significant influence on the overall dynamic of such a system

[5]For the moment it is sufficient to describe the conditions leading to complexity in socioeconomic systems. Numerous heterogeneous agents with various behavioral options in strategic interdependence face situations that can be characterized as complex. As usual, there exist a large number of definitions of complexity, depending on the particular perspective of a subdiscipline, the research question or field of application at hand. We will provide and shortly discuss a number of conceptions and explain a more specific definition for proper use in complexity microeconomics in Chapter 10.

as behavioral decisions reinforce one another in a *cumulative process*. Accordingly, there will be no predetermined endpoint for the development either, *no predetermined unique equilibrium* at which it comes to rest. Rather, economic structures are reflections of ongoing processes, of which change is a constitutive characteristic. Such systems do not return to prior states in a sufficiently long time interval. In this way, approaches based on *multiple equilibria* can therefore serve as first approximations to an enhanced understanding of problems in that sphere (for such models, see Chapters 6, 10, 11, and 13).

1.6 SOCIAL RULES AS INFORMATIONAL AND "EXPECTATIONAL" DEVICES

1.6.1 Social Rules

If we know some agents from a group, we will increasingly be able to formulate assumptions about other members of this group. This is because behavior in groups follows *social rules*. Such rules serve a dual function. On the one hand, they make decisions *less complex*, i.e., easier for individual agents because there exist rules that agents can orient their decision on. In fact such rules are necessary for individuals because of the vast amounts of data available to them in every moment, from which they have to filter information that has to be analyzed in order to take a decision. If you have a rule to guide you, that process is much easier to go through. In fact, as the sheer amounts of data available are substantially beyond individuals' capacity to process, we need to have constructs that support us and facilitate the taking of decisions for us.

1.6.2 Satisficing

Here, social rules help by providing guidelines that agents can automatically follow and apply in their decisions. As long as the outcome is satisfactory (meets the *aspiration level* of an agent), such *satisficing* behavior is not in need of further changes. The formation of the aspiration level in turn depends on the environment in which agents are moving, as this shapes the reference frame on which agents draw. Here, we can already identify a first *feedback* cycle among behavior and outcomes that is mediated through the social rules followed and will have an impact on changes of these rules in the future. However, given this complex, uncertain, and ever-changing environment, the individual agent can no longer know, whether she improves "globally" or only "locally," i.e., whether she is climbing the Mount Everest or just a little hill in her neighborhood. Satisficing behavior usually refers to, intends, and is "satisfied" with only local improvement.

1.6.3 Common Knowledge

Social rules also help to form expectations about other agents' behaviors. Therefore, such social rules have to be common knowledge in the groups in which they apply. They help to *reduce complexity and uncertainty* surrounding the possible choices of other agents. This is a crucial function in situations that are characterized by a direct interdependence of agents, in which one's results immediately depend not only on one's own but also on the others' behaviors. Our expectations regarding others' behavior thus matter for our own choice of behavior in such situations, and the formation of expectations must eventually be facilitated by a common knowledge of rules governing social situations.

1.6.4 Enabling Action

The existence of social rules and common knowledge regarding such rules allows agents to interact in a purposeful manner. As you will have realized, the existence of such rules does not imply their optimality for given situations. They facilitate agents' decision making by reducing uncertainty in situations characterized by their direct interdependence. There is no reason to suspect that the outcome for the agents that results should be in any way optimal for them, alone or as a group, especially if we assume satisficing behavior under bounded capacities to be a more appropriate approximation to real-world agents' decision making. But the rules allow reaching some outcomes, instead of letting agents face situations that they cannot solve at all. By reducing the options available to the agents in the first place, and thereby reducing complexity, social rules thus make situations accessible to the agents and only thereby permit them to reach a result. For many situations, thus, what may appear as a constraint on behavioral options in the form of social rules is in fact a necessary first step enabling agents to reach a decision at all, or help them attain a superior outcome relative to the situation without.

1.6.5 Stable Systems of Interconnected Rules

Additionally, we can point to the fact that there is no reason to suspect that different groups would have developed the same rules for solving their collective problems. On the contrary, different groups most likely have developed *different sets of rules* (or *cultures*) for addressing the relevant problems that they have been facing in their possibly specific environment and over time. Finally, as groups apply numerous rules for a broad range of problem sets, and these *rules are linked to one another* (aligned with the broader "world view" emerging in a group), the transfer of selected ones from one group to another can prove difficult, and lead to

results that were not anticipated nor desired, if they do not integrate with the prevailing set there.

As rules are *learned* and over time *habituated*, and therefore applied without every time undergoing a rigorous process of consideration and evaluation, it is on the other hand likewise difficult to simply mandate the change of broader sets of rules. This does not mean change would not happen, though. It does mean that there is no single direction into which systems move and that could be identified based on universally valid axioms. Rather, they develop path dependently, as mentioned.

1.7 SOCIAL RULES AND SOCIAL INSTITUTIONS AS SOLUTIONS TO COORDINATION AND DILEMMA PROBLEMS

1.7.1 Recognizing Different Problem Structures

In "social" (i.e., multiagent) decision situations individual agents have to decide, as said, under *recognized interdependence*. Observing such social situations in general more closely has shown us that the degrees of conflict of interests between the agents involved differ depending on the problem structure they face, with considerable implications for their different individual and aggregate (or common or collective) outcomes. For a group to be able to sustain situations and some degree of social cohesion, we have recognized that different situations require different kinds of rules, depending on the *underlying problem structure they strive to solve*. As different groups can be expected to have developed different sets of rules over time, their ability to commonly or collectively confront economic situations and problems can be expected to differ.

1.7.2 Coordination Problems and Dilemma Problems, Coordination and Cooperation, Rules and Institutions

For different problem structures, different social rules are needed for the agents if they are to reach a Pareto-optimal result. For just *coordinating* on a Pareto-optimal outcome, a *social rule* suffices. Achieving a Pareto-optimal result in a *social dilemma* situation is more complicated.

The complication results from the problem structure and individually optimal behavior therein. In a social dilemma, even in the socially optimal situation therein, agents have a persisting dominant incentive to change their behavior to further increase their payoffs (in the example above, choose *B* instead of *A*). How to incentivize the individuals not to do so (in favor of a collective long-run increase of their payoffs, the PO in that structure) is thus a relevant and necessary consideration when attempting to *structure policies* in order to improve the economic situation for a population. Within a population or group, *social institutions* fulfill the role of *stabilizing* socially preferable behavior patterns and mutual behavioral expectations, and thus of *sustaining the socially preferable situation* that agents can profit from in the longer term. Agents thus have to be *socially embedded* such that the individualist temptation to opt for a short-term advantage (the absolute maximum) does not overturn the longer term perspective, and the social institution is reaffirmed by the behavioral choices of the agents and kept alive.

If agents opt for the individually optimal behavior in a social dilemma structure, the others can follow suit and the overall result will be a Pareto-inferior outcome. This also leads to a reduction of the payoff attainable by the individual agent who first opted for the short-term gain. We call the achieving of the Pareto-optimal result in a dilemma situation the result of common *cooperation*. Cooperation is defined as *coordination plus sacrifice*. The sacrifice here

would be the *forgoing of the individualistic short-run maximum*. The social institution that contains the behavior leading to this outcome accordingly needs to be endowed with a sanction mechanism in order to *make agents abstain from the short-run maximum*, which, in turn, would not be attained anyway but lead to the Pareto-inferior dilemma situation if applied by all. A social institution, therefore, is considered a *social rule plus sanction mechanism*. How this can be represented formally, what the sanction mechanism will be, and how and why the threat of a sanction is credible will be discussed, once some game-theoretic concepts have been introduced (see Chapter 3).

There are a huge number of definitions of the term "institution" in the literature, most of which are just more or less colloquial. Our use throughout this textbook is strictly distinct from the general social rule. While the former is strictly related to the solution of a social dilemma in the long run (with an always dominant incentive *not* to be coordinated), the latter is related to the solution of a less problematic coordination problem (where coordination is in everyone's immediate short-run interest). Therefore, the social institution needs to be learned in a process and applied in the long run. As a habituated and semi-conscious rule, it has to lead to behavior including the sacrifice of a possible short-term maximum. This has to be supported by mutual sanction capacity for unilateral deviation. Otherwise short-run rational maximizers would never learn to cooperate and to attain the Pareto-superior social situation.

1.7.3 Sacrifice and Sanction, Repeated Interaction and Time Horizon

The sacrifice that is involved in adhering to the social institution is based, as said, on the resistance to the temptation of applying the individually rational behavior under a short-run perspective to the detriment of the individual and the group's longer term results. With that, however, agents put themselves in the position of potentially suffering from such behavior by others who, for their part, might not act based on the social institution. But if the situation can be structured to include an endogenous sanction, there may be a way to stabilize the Pareto-optimal result. As we will see in the game-theoretic analyses that follow, such mechanisms can be built relatively easily into games that are played *repeatedly*. A *longer time horizon* of interactions is thus a very basic mechanism that can help to bring about improvements in the results agents in groups can achieve.

Arguing for the adoption of a longer time horizon is easiest based on *learning* by the agents. This is important insofar as the ability to learn differentiates these agents from the ones in a number of economic models, where it is posited that all agents have all necessary information at the outset. We will discuss this aspect again in Chapter 3.

1.7.4 "Common" and "Collective"

Note that we use the idea of a *common* problem and its solution to describe a simple *coordination problem* and its solution (the social rule), where each agent has an *immediate interest to be coordinated* with the others (see 1.2.5). We use the term of a *collective* problem and its solution to describe a *social dilemma problem* and its solution, in which it is always in the short-run individualist interest *not* to contribute to the *collective good* or to exploit the contributions of others, where, in other words, the solution depends on the *short-run sacrifice* and, therefore, as this sacrifice is not individualistically "rational" on an *endogenous sanction* for non-contribution, i.e., a reciprocating punishment through the others by not contributing next time as well, as we have described above. As the institution thus is not individualistically "rational" it can come into existence only in a

process of habituation and semiconscious application, a "rationally adopted irrationality," so to speak. We will discuss this and explain the issue more specific, exact, and with more illustration in Chapter 3.

1.7.5 Costs as Opportunity Costs

The sacrifice of a short-term advantage that may be individually realizable, if the others generally obey the rule embodied in the institution, may be seen as the *opportunity cost* of the long-term improved result. An opportunity cost, the most general form of economic costs, describes the gains that another (the next best) alternative would provide although this other option is not pursued. If you buy good *I*, and then do not have enough money for good *II*, the unit of good *II* you do not buy is the opportunity cost of acquiring the last unit of good *I*. The outcome that an agent does not realize because she opts for another kind of behavior is the opportunity cost of the outcome realized. The opportunity cost is a relevant decision variable in fact—if it is higher than the gain promised from the option realized, another decision should be taken by the agent. In directly interdependent decision situations such calculation is more complicated, because *expectations about the reaction of other agents* have to play a part in the considerations of the agents, as these shape the true opportunity costs of, as well as benefits from, decisions.

1.7.6 Incomplete Contracts, Reciprocity, and Trust

Behaviors and institutions are especially important when exchanges are concerned that are not executed simultaneously, but where some agents have to get active first, and have to rely on others to follow suit and honor commitments they may have entered into in order for long-term projects to become viable (think of *R&D* activities that run for long periods and rely on *sequential* contributions by the involved firms). *Reciprocity* and *trust* become necessary ingredients in order to bridge over time. The necessity to put trust into the interaction partners is most relevant as written *contracts* are necessarily *incomplete*. They cannot contain provisions for every contingency. Therefore, they can support *long-term* exchanges (that do not coincide in time and/or place) but may not provide sufficient certainty and hence may not restructure a situation so that all potential problems for agents are provided for with a solution mechanism. To strengthen the foundation for a relation, an alteration of the nature of the underlying problem structure is going to be helpful or even required. And, again, some degree of trust is going to have to be invested (i.e., learned), especially at the beginning of a new partnership.

1.7.7 Transforming and Solving a Social Dilemma

If we develop the analyses of social problem structures based on narrowly rational agents, we have to be aware that we have to involve some kind of *transformation of the original social dilemma* situation, as a dilemma is a problem that an individualistic and rational agent will not be able to solve. As long as we build our analyses on agents that we assume to be rational in the individualistic economics understanding, we have to alter the situation they face, for a superior outcome to be systematically realizable. As you will see, the solution concepts employed in game-theoretic analyses and the tools developed for other methodological approaches to economic questions require some defined rationality of the agents to work. We can later introduce behavioral motivations that are broader and more real-world related, but a first baseline and reference point can be the "rational" individualistic agent. Finding mechanisms that allow even these types of agents to solve specific problem structures, such as social dilemmas, without having to fall back on an external enforcer, suggests that a strong solution mechanism may have been found. We will introduce you to related solution conceptions in Chapter 3.

1.8 THE PUBLIC GOOD CHARACTER AND POSITIVE EXTERNAL EFFECTS OF SOCIAL RULES AND SOCIAL INSTITUTIONS

1.8.1 Types of Goods: Private and Collective

We can understand social rules and social institutions as the collective solutions to a common problem. We have seen that they *increase the problem-solving capacities* of agents by offering behavioral guidelines and reducing uncertainty in the formulation of expectations about other agents' behavior. When social rules and institutions exist, they thereby have the character of what is called a *public good*. That means, they are *nonrival* and *nonexclusive* in consumption. Nonrivalry signifies that one agent's use of a good does not prevent or reduce its use or usefulness by and to others. Nonexcludability signifies that once others have made their contributions or the good is already in existence, agents cannot be excluded from the generated benefits or prevented from using the good.

Goods that are rival and exclusive are so-called *private goods*, in contrast. *Rivalry* means that one agent's consuming of a good means that others cannot consume it. *Excludability* in turn means that agents can be excluded from utilizing the good (through technical conditions and through provisions defining the transfer of rights of ownership and assorted other rights).

Given these dimensions for categorizing goods, we can additionally distinguish two other types of goods, namely, *club goods* that are characterized by excludability and nonrivalry, and *commons* that are already existing and received by the agents, characterized by nonexcludability and rivalry (the latter comes into existence at a certain level of use, thereafter it is overused and thus rivaling).

Different groups of agents have found different arrangements, as said, structuring their treatment of goods that are characterized by their nonexcludability, so-called *collective goods*. As will be taken up below, a number of problems result here, regarding production in the case of public goods and exploitation and consumption in the case of the commons. Depending on how a group's approach to the collective sphere is defined and formed, the consequences and the relative success in the economic sphere may considerably differ between groups, as the relation to and treatment of nonexcludable goods bears significantly on the overall economic structures and success that populations or groups can realize. Table 1.1 gives a short overview of basic types of goods.

1.8.2 Decision Situations and Rules and Institutions as Systems of Externalities

When agents follow social rules and social institutions to inform their behavioral decisions, they create a positive effect on other agents, as these can take better-informed behavioral decisions themselves. There are,

therefore, so-called *positive external effects* in the application of social rules and social institutions (or simply put: rules, in the following). And benefiting agents *cannot be excluded from profiting* from these external effects.

These positive external effects in the case under consideration here may coincide with *positive network externalities*, because one agent's application of a rule does not only provide positive effects on the other agents, but because additionally the usefulness of rules may *increase with the number of agents applying* them in their decision-making processes. Or, the other way around: if a rule is not followed by a sufficient number of agents, so that there is not a sufficient coherence in behavior, any given rule fails to reduce uncertainty sufficiently, leading to a reduction or relapse of problem-solving capacities of the agents in a group. What constitutes a sufficient number of agents may depend on the problem in question.

Agents always have the choice of contributing to the collective good of a social institution, or of not contributing, which would result in its weakening, and potentially even its deterioration and eventual breakdown, if it already existed, or in its not coming into existence at all. Agents have to contribute to the institution's *emergence*, *maintenance*, and *reproduction*; they affirm it through their behavior. The breakdown of the institution would signify a worsening of the results achievable by the agents in a group. We thus find *negative external effects* of not

TABLE 1.1   Basic Types and Properties of Goods

	Rivalry	Nonrivalry
Exclusion/excludability	Private goods	Club goods
	← Overuse	
Nonexclusion/nonexcludability	Commons (preexisting, usually natural or infrastructural goods, rivaling at overuse)	Public goods, including commons at proper use

contributing, and positive external effects of contributing to the maintenance of the social institution by adhering to its prescriptions on this level of social relations as well. The positive external effects of the rules and institutions are derived from the positive external effects of the concurrent behavior patterns on the results achievable by other agents.

1.8.3 Network Externalities and Increasing Returns to Scale of Institutions

Related concepts are *economies of scale* or *increasing returns to scale*. Economies of scale is the term used for describing falling average costs as a result of increasing production volumes or numbers. The more a firm produces of a good, the cheaper every single unit becomes. To expand production is thus a generally advantageous strategy to pursue in this case because it purports a potential cost advantage over other producers in a similar market segment. Returns to scale are derived from production technologies and refer to the proportionality of output changes following changes in all input factors (the latter changed in a fixed relation with each other). If output increases over-proportionally following an equal increase in all inputs, we refer to this as increasing returns (with constant and decreasing returns as the equivalent categories for proportional and under-proportional increases; we will explain this in more detail in Chapter 5). Economies of scale is a consequence of increasing returns to scale.

The application of a rule shows a similar characteristic to that of economies of scale in the *number of both agents that use it and times it has been used by agents*. The more often agents apply a rule, the less they have to invest in the taking of decisions in similar situations any longer, as they can simply apply a rule in a

certain situation without further consideration. Thereby they also reduce the necessary effort level for other agents, because they increasingly know what to expect from their peers. The more agents apply a rule and the more often a rule has been applied, the less costly its application becomes.

1.8.4 Degeneration of Institutions and Institutional Lock-In

However, that may mean that the rule itself is in use long after its problem-solving capacity has started to diminish. A change in the environment may lead to results that are increasingly far from what would be attainable if different behavioral options were chosen. The diminishing cost of applying the rule may simply make the cost of switching to a new rule (or even set of rules) seem prohibitive to the agents. They might profit if the new rule was established and used by a sufficient number of agents for a sufficient number of times (though they do not necessarily know that, especially as they act under uncertainty). But the initial cost of switching may prevent them from doing so, even as that reduces their long-term economic results. The network effects related to the characteristics of social rules may prevent their adaptation to newly arising challenges or the adaptation of newly emerging opportunities. The institution then may degenerate from a problem-solving device into an abstract behavioral prescription or *abstract norm*, and agents would be considered to be "rationally" trapped in an *institutional lock-in*.

1.8.5 A Variety of Institutional Systems Including "Markets" as Sets of Institutions

Still, social rules and social institutions are not like natural laws. They are subject to change, deviation, surprise, individual adaptation, being not followed or even broken. And at times some drastic changes in the overall framework of rules structuring groups' interactions may occur. Consider, for instance, that it has been a mere 200 years since the organization of economic exchanges in spontaneous decentralized systems called *"markets,"* concurrent to the radical reinterpretation of the role of the individual in society. We consider "markets," like any other system of allocation of resources and of decision making, particular sets of social rules and social institutions, and they may exhibit extremely different sets of rules and institutions, including very short-run individualistic behaviors. So they are required to be regulated and embedded in *proper sets of rules and institutions*, if they are to generate the positive results, in face of coordination problems and social dilemmas, usually expected from them. And since their coming into existence, the institutional structures of markets have undergone substantial differentiation and changes over time as well.

1.9 "INSTRUMENTAL" AND "CEREMONIAL" DIMENSIONS OF SOCIAL INSTITUTIONS

1.9.1 Life Cycle and Degeneration of Institutions

Originally, social rules and social institutions are assumed here to emerge as *problem-solving* devices enabling agents to solve the common and collective problems as described above. This function is described by their so-called *instrumental* dimension. Rules and institutions may, however, eventually appear, as said, to the individual agent as *norms*, prescriptive behavioral requests. This may introduce a change in the *motivation* for maintaining the rule as well. The normative aspect can be considered as an additional dimension

of the rule, a dimension in which the original problem-solving character is no longer consciously present. If even the original problem has ceased to exist and changed, and the *motivation to solve problems* has been substituted by another motivation, a so-called *ceremonial* dimension may become a dominant part of the overall character of the rule. Over time, all rules and institutions may acquire an increasingly pronounced ceremonial dimension.

In more detail, the typical *life cycle* of a rule contains a number of stages. Being established as an instrumental rule, it eventually acquires a normative dimension, becoming a, still instrumental, norm. It will be handed on from generation to generation with a fading consciousness about which problem it was meant to solve originally. But still it may be a proper problem-solving device. Once the normative character is thus established, however, and the original problem may even have disappeared, it turns into an abstract norm over time. As that stage is reached, and as it still will be maintained and defended by its proponents, the *motivation* for keeping it as an abstract norm will have changed and its ceremonial dimension is established. The ceremonial motivation will usually be to *maintain differential power and status* rather than solving objective common problems. Some may profit more from the outmoded, "petrified" rules than others and lose their power and status if a new instrumental institution would be emerging from a new interactive learning process.

1.9.2 Ceremonial Value and Motivation: Power and Status

Thus, an increasing dominance of the ceremonial aspect of rules derives from status and distinction, power and hierarchy considerations of agents. The ceremonial is thus a *value dimension* in which differential power and status are the dominating influence factors, instead of the *value of a primary problem solving*. They have their roots in a desire for leadership and superiority of some and feelings of *identity* and *belonging* of their followers, which together may reduce individuals' fears under conditions of uncertainty. The social stratification that emerges in groups is reinforced by accordingly defined "acceptable" behavioral patterns of individuals, depending on their rank in the population. The resulting structure is strengthened by *narratives* (beliefs, folkways, fairy tales, or *"enabling myths"*) that combine to form an ideological framework that justifies the hierarchical structures in place. In turn, individuals are further emotionally conditioned to accepting prevailing hierarchical structures by sets of *ritualized* behaviors that reinforce their attachment to the ceremonial system in place.

Changes in the environment reduce a rule's usefulness in a new situation. So, over time a reduction in a rule's problem solving, instrumental capacity may come about. However, related to the emergence of rules' ceremonial dimension, the original problem-solving motivation for maintaining rules is driven to the background, and increasingly replaced by ceremonial considerations regarding their preservation. The stronger these considerations are, the more petrified a group's social structure has become, the more difficult it gets to change rules according to instrumental needs and considerations. The situation, as mentioned, is considered *locked-in* (the conceptions of *ceremonial dominance* and of a *lock-in* are very relevant and prominent in economics and will be explained in more detail with their original reference theories and models in Chapters 12 and 13).

We can additionally point again to the cost factor mentioned above, contributing to the conservation of rules beyond their instrumental usefulness and justification. The cost-reduction per application reduces the attractiveness of establishing a new rule that is more costly to follow at first. Establishing a new way of coordinating agents' behaviors may be difficult to formulate and may also be difficult to organize if larger numbers of agents are involved: A collective coordination or cooperation problem again, or, more generally, a problem of *common and collective action capacity*.

1.9.3 Coordination and Change

We have to note, though, that even a strongly ceremonially dominated rule is not without any problem-solving capacity. This capacity is merely reduced, possibly substantially reduced, relative to that of other possible behavioral patterns in certain circumstances. But it still allows some coordination of agents, even if hierarchical, and hence the achieving of some coordinated outcome, where without any rule no such outcome might be feasible. But the result is not as good as it could be under different rules given the circumstances. We can thereby appreciate that different sets of rules will result in *different levels of problem-solving capacities* by groups and whole populations. There will also be a dynamical component to this, as, at least periodically, some general sets of rules or some environments may be more conducive to change than others.

1.10 REAL-WORLD MICROECONOMICS

1.10.1 Assessing Different Complex Decision Situations

Placing direct interdependence of agents at the heart of microeconomic theory permits the addressing of complex situations in which a number of strategic issues emerge. Imperfect knowledge is inherent to such situations and no uniquely optimal behavior can generally be identified. Rules and institutions are required for supporting agents in their ability to actually take decisions by reducing complexity through some rule-based behavior.

Actions may further be *context dependent*. The same agent may act differently in seemingly similar situations (going out at night, but either with friends or with family, for instance). Two agents facing the same situation may likewise behave differently, for instance, depending on the institutional context that they were brought up and socialized in.

Understanding decisions and forecasting likely behavior—crucial in interdependent settings were expectations regarding others' choices matter greatly for own behavior—become core aspects here, and *tools for assessing situations* and structuring one's surroundings in a way that make it accessible and interpretable in a commonly shared way are necessary for agents to act consistently. Such consistency in behavior is usually the outcome of shared social rules and institutions. Neglecting the importance of direct interdependence among agents and of uncertainty may thus remove crucial factors from an analysis of an economic problem. Finally, these aspects are already identifiable when we pretend that situations can be described with the help of well-defined objectives (payoffs) of the agents. Conflicting goals that cannot be represented in a single dimension and are not translatable into a single unit of measurement to calculate optimal trade-offs further complicate matters.

1.10.2 Integrating Direct Interdependence

Hence, we have chosen to start our introduction to microeconomics by focusing on ways to make directly interdependent decision situations more accessible. The usual introduction focuses on situations where individually and socially optimal results are simultaneously achieved by individual agents without a problem. Those agents then are focused solely on themselves, receiving all required information

without effort, cost, or uncertainty, usually in the form of equilibrium prices against which "optimal" behavior is calculated without any influence of agents on each other. Such a setup is, in fact, applicable only in a very limited number of circumstances and most economically highly relevant issues cannot be adequately addressed in such a way. As stated above, the optimality of results in spontaneous decentralized systems under individualistic motivation is by no means certain. Therefore, we consider it appropriate to establish your awareness for these issues from the very beginning.

1.10.3 Integrating Uncertainty

Uncertainty likewise plays an important role when addressing modern economies. General circumstances have become more difficult to foresee and calculate. Increasing numbers of involved agents, and direct interdependence, between them, have made it increasingly difficult for economic agents to adopt longer term perspectives. At the same time, of course, agents have an incentive to try and reduce these effects in order to stabilize their environment.

For instance, a constitutive characteristic of economies over the last couple of centuries has been changes in technology and structures. This has resulted in unforeseeable changes in social, political, economic, and ecological matters. A view on the *economic subsystem* as isolated from the rest of the whole system, i.e., the *societal and natural subsystems*, and operating under a set of predetermined and unalterable "laws" can then not necessarily adequately address related issues.

1.10.4 Reducing Uncertainty in the Corporate World Through Power and Control

As an additional crucial point, an uncertain environment coupled with the requirements that modern production technologies impose forces companies to *strive to increase controlling their environment* and reducing potential sources of disruptions. A number of instruments are available (managing demand, securing supplies, reducing potential competition, exerting all kinds of power, amongst others) for putting longer term activity on a more secure footing and a number of effects resulting from characteristics of technologies may contribute there (network economies, lock-ins, etc.). The importance of and interest of agents in control bridges to traditionally neglected issues of *power*, as these lie beyond the ability to tweak results in one's favor by influencing outcomes in a given price–quantity space. Should companies fail to stabilize their environment and in fact end up in a situation where they actually have to compete for resources, customers and technological advances, a noticeable waste of resources may result, not their *a priori* determined socially optimal allocation.

1.10.5 Integrating Social Rules and Social Institutions

Behavioral rules serve a dual instrumental purpose. They facilitate the reaching of decisions by agents, by limiting the effort necessary for them to orient themselves in certain situations through reductions of complexity. Relatedly, they reduce the strategic uncertainty of agents in directly interdependent situations, again facilitating the taking of decisions and realization of improved results for the agents.

Depending on the problem structure faced, different rules or institutions are needed for the solution of common and collective problems. As sets of rules develop over time, different groups show different problem-solving capacities. At the same time, the transfer of selected rules from one group to another is unlikely to be successful, as rules have developed in complex path-dependent processes

and are structured in complementary sets. Solutions may be reached that can typically be differentiated by their overall economic effectiveness. *The better suited a set of rules is for solving collective problems, the more successful the population or group in question is likely going to be.*

1.10.6 Integrating Institutional Change and Petrifaction

Rules and institutions undergo changes over time in not only in reaction to but also contributing to changing environments. Their problem-solving, instrumental component is reduced as a function of two related phenomena. The first is the fact that the repeated application of a rule leads to its habituation and "semiconscious" application. An effect of such habituation is a reduction in the cost of applying it. New, potentially better suited rules may then be difficult to establish, as they signify elevated costs or effort during the process of their establishment. This refers to the individual agents who have to unlearn something and adopt something new, at the same time that the relevant population environment has to do the same in order to make use of the potential for improvement that a new rule may offer (if applied by sufficient numbers of agents).

The second conserving force is related to the fact that the motivation for maintaining rules changes over time. The original problem-solving objective behind them may be pushed to the background by ceremonial considerations that have developed for a given set of rules. Some agents profit within given structures and gain due to the social position they have reached. Keeping this social position may be a strong motivation for maintaining given rules, even if their change might promise economic improvements. Others may simply be unwilling to give up their established patterns of thought and "world view," even if they could gain thereby. Over time, therefore, a system of rules and institutions may well lose its problem-solving capacity and degenerate into a power-based justification for a sclerotic hierarchy. Continued impulses for change will be required to prevent this dynamic to dominate the system and to regain appropriate common coordinated and collective cooperative action capacity.

1.10.7 "Markets" as Widely Differing Sets of Institutions

In fact, the principal focus of much of microeconomic theory, the "market," is a social construction, a set of institutions, serving to moderate some societal conflicts, namely the allocation and distribution of available resources. This construct has developed over time and has been shaped by earlier conditions that find their reflections in current structures. Depending on how earlier conditions and power distributions have been shaped in detail, current *"market" arrangements differ*, thus offering different solutions to the same general problem structures in different populations and groups. An understanding of the rules surrounding the interactions in markets and any other form of coordination, cooperation, allocation or organization can then significantly enhance our understanding of the problems involved and the solutions reached, stressing the different problem-solving abilities of different populations and groups. The widely varying forms and understandings of "markets" will be explained in detail in the more theoretical Chapters 5–7 as well as in the more applied Chapters 4, 15, and 16.

1.10.8 Looking Behind the Veil of Everyday Solutions

When observing economically relevant behavior, we see the solutions that are implemented by populations and subpopulations (groups) of agents. The *surface of the real world* is full of *"solutions,"* instrumental and appropriate ones, or ceremonial, locked-in, and petrified ones, as we have explained. Whether these are appropriate or highly inappropriate, we can assess only by analyzing the problem structure behind that surface or veil. The objective of analyzing such situations and solutions is to *identify and understand the underlying, often hidden or tacit problem structures*, be they different "markets," hierarchies, networks, governments, or other formal or informal systems. Only thereby can we understand basic problems and processes in economic matters and eventually arrive at statements regarding the *desirability of change*, the *potential for improvement*, and the *scope of potential policy intervention* to shape conditions of the interaction processes among the individual agents.

1.10.9 What is Microeconomics? ... and the Next Step

Microeconomics thus becomes *"the" science of complex coordination, cooperation, and organization* among individual agents in processes under conditions of direct interdependence and uncertainty.

The next step towards an analysis of different socioeconomic situations is the acquisition of *tools* and *methods* for understanding different problem structures so as to be able to identify and recognize them and then be able to devise adequate proposals for how to deal with them in later steps.

Further Reading

Alverson, H., 1986. Culture and economy: games that "play people". J. Econ. Issues. 20 (3), 661–679.

Beinhocker, E.D., 2007. The Origin of Wealth. Evolution, Complexity, and the Radical Remaking of Economics. Harvard Business School Press, Boston, MA.

Fontana, M., 2008. The complexity approach to economics: a paradigm shift. Working Paper No. 01, Universitá di Torino. <http://www.cesmep.unito.it/WP/2008/1_WP_Cesmep.pdf> (accessed 14.05.13.).

Foster, J., 2005. From simplistic to complex systems in economics. Cambridge J. Econ. 29 (6), 873–892.

Friedman, J.W., 1994. Problems of Coordination in Economic Activity. Economics as Science of Coordination. Kluwer Academic Publishers, Boston, Dordrecht, London.

Henrich, J., Boyd, R. (Eds.), 2004. *Foundations of Human Sociality. Economic Experiments and Ethnographic Evidence from Fifteen Small-Scale Societies*. Oxford University Press, New York, NY.

Hodgson, G.M., Samuels, W.J., Tool, M.R., 1994. The Elgar Companion to Institutional and Evolutionary Economics, vol. 2. Edward Elgar, Aldershot, Brookfield.

Further Reading—Online

For further reading, see the textbook website at http://booksite.elsevier.com/9780124115859

Tools I: An Introduction to Game Theory

"In football, everything is complicated by the presence of the opposite team." (French original: "Au football, tout est compliqué par la présence de l'équipe adverse.") [1]

2.1 INTRODUCTION

We all know the following situation: Person A is about to enter a building through a narrow doorway when person B attempts to leave through the same exit. Trying to show good manners, person A will politely step aside in order to let person B pass—however, so will person B, in her case to let person A pass. It only takes a moment for the both of them to realize that the other person is trying to let them pass, A realizes that B stepped aside; B realizes that A is waiting for her to pass. So they will again enter the doorway at the same time only to find that this attempt to coordinate has also failed.

[1] Attributed to Jean-Paul Sartre.

The Microeconomics of Complex Economies.
DOI: http://dx.doi.org/10.1016/B978-0-12-411585-9.00002-6

We are faced with a situation that seems to be both simple, almost trivial, and difficult to resolve, thus complex. There are only two individuals involved (A and B), they can choose between only two options (to wait or to enter the doorway), their objective is the same: to resolve the situation and pass the doorway either A first or B first—it does not even matter who passes first.

When faced with the situation it may seem like a game: choose a strategy and hope for some luck. Depending on what the other person does you win (i.e., you are able to pass) or you lose. And this idea is not at all wrong. Many interactive situations, in fact, most of the social sphere may be conceptualized as one in a family of strategic games, each with its own rules. There are games in which the players share a common objective like in the present example and games where they try to exploit each other. There are games that offer an obvious best choice option to all those involved and games where the resolution is tricky and full of uncertainty (like in the present case). There are games with only two agents and only two options per agent and those with millions and millions of participants and an infinite continuum of possible strategies. There are games which may be played repeatedly and games that only offer one single try.

It is obvious that in an interactive world, it is always a simplification to reduce a social situation to one game. The game can merely be a model; it is a way to analyze the structure that lies beneath the social interaction, its possibilities and opportunities, the development paths of the interaction, less likely and more likely outcomes. A word of warning should not be foregone: Oversimplification results in inaccurate models; assuming a strategic game as a model (or as part of a model) implies a number of other assumptions (such as rational decision making) that are not always justified. The skilled and careful use of strategic games in models of social interactions, however, reveals a whole new layer in the social system that is investigated—the layer of strategies and their consequences. This chapter will give a basic introduction to the modeling with strategic games, an introduction to game theory. More formal concepts and advanced methods will be discussed in Chapter 8.

2.2 UNDERSTANDING A STRATEGIC GAME

To distinguish our model games from the common sense term for recreational games, we may specify our models as *strategic games*. A strategic game is characterized by a set of participants, a set of behavior options for each of the participants, and a set of rules as well as the information available to each of the participants. The participants in a strategic game are commonly called *agents*; the options among which an agent chooses are referred to as her *strategies*.

There are many possible forms of games; some of the more prominent ones, including repeated games and sequential games, will be explained in Chapter 8. One form, however, is as universally applicable and powerful as a model as it is simple and easy to use as a theoretical concept: simultaneous 2-person 2-strategy normal-form games. Common to this group of strategic games is that the game involves two agents each of which chooses between only two strategies and the choices are to be made simultaneously without any possibility for collusion between the two agents.

		Player B	
		Pass	Wait
Player A	Pass	0 **0**	1 **1**
	Wait	1 **1**	0 **0**

FIGURE 2.1 Anti-coordination game; payoffs of the row player (A) highlighted in bold face.

BOX 2.1
_____

ORDINAL AND CARDINAL UTILITY

In game theory, utility is commonly given as a cardinal measure, i.e., specific (quantified) payoffs are stated and payoff and utility variables are treated as standing for exact quantities. This, however, is not required for normal-form games in pure strategies. It would be sufficient to be decidable if one option A is (given the choices of the other players) preferred to another option B, if instead B is preferred to A or if the agent is indifferent between the two as long as this preference order is consistent. This is known as ordinal utility measure. For details on theoretical requirements for game-theoretic preference functions see Chapter 8.

The game introduced in Figure 2.1 is a member of this group. We can write it as shown in Figure 2.1. The strategies of player A are given in the rows, those of player B in the columns; for 2×2 strategies there are four possible outcomes for which the payoffs of both players are given (see Box 2.1 for details on the concepts utility and payoff in game theory). Payoffs of the row player (A) are given in the lower left (bold), those of the column player (B) are given in the upper right of the respective field. This _matrix notation_ is commonly used to write strategic games.

The view obtained from writing the game in matrix notation (Figure 2.1) is the following: As said, both agents try to pass through the door, one first, then the other. There are two solutions that allow to accomplish this end: A waits and B passes or B waits and A passes. There are also two less fortunate outcomes namely one where both agents attempt to pass and another one with both agents waiting for the other one to pass and neither of them actually attempting to move through the doorway.

Game theory offers a number of approaches to solve strategic games and make predictions regarding outcomes. Before these methods are discussed, however, the following section will illustrate that strategic games may be used to model a broad range of concepts and phenomena in interactive economics.

2.3 THE INVISIBLE HAND AND THE FALLACY OF AGGREGATION AGAIN
_____

In Chapter 1, we introduced two general concepts of economic modeling, the invisible hand and the fallacy of aggregation. Both tell illustrative stories of the direct interaction of rational agents. The invisible hand describes a situation where every agent chooses the socially optimal option out of her incentive to maximize individually. Say, every agent has an option to contribute (costs: 1) or not to contribute (zero cost) to a public good and receives three times her own contribution (benefit: 2 or 0 respectively) and twice the contribution of the other player(s) (2 or 0 respectively); see Figure 2.2.

The concept of optimality in interactive situations, specifically the _Pareto optimum_, has been introduced in Chapter 1. It is easy to see that the game will arrive at the socially optimal (and single Pareto-optimal) point (4,4). Consequently, this model justifies ignoring the micro-level of direct interactions (since everyone chooses equivalently and optimally). A different story is told by the _fallacy of aggregation_.

Say, as before, the agents choose whether to contribute or not; but this time, they only receive twice the payoff of their opponents.

		Player B	
		Strategy 1	Strategy 2
Player A	Strategy 1	4 4	2 2
	Strategy 2	2 2	0 0

FIGURE 2.2   Social optimum game.

		Player B	
		Strategy 1	Strategy 2
Player A	Strategy 1	1 1	2 −1
	Strategy 2	−1 2	0 0

FIGURE 2.3   Prisoners' dilemma game.

We can see that the second strategy seems to be strictly better (strictly dominant) against the first one, the most likely outcome would therefore be (0,0) which of course is *Pareto inferior* compared to (1,1); see Figure 2.3. The message conveyed by this metaphor is that it is possible that agents choose a socially suboptimal situation and do so rationally. Social interactions may take any form out of an extensive continuum of game structures with different properties. Though it should be carefully chosen which game structure applies, game theory as a method is extremely powerful when considering socioeconomic systems. To quote from one of the most important recent game theory textbooks, Hargreaves Heap and Varoufakis: "One is hard put to find a social phenomenon that cannot be so described [as a strategic game.]" (2004, p. 3).

The game given as an example for the metaphor of the invisible hand is called a social optimum game; it is symmetric and for both players the first strategy is preferable to the second no matter what the opponent does (a *strictly dominant strategy*). Both players choosing this strategy leads to a situation where neither of the players has an incentive to unilaterally deviate from this outcome which brings stability to

this result and justifies it being called an equilibrium—specifically a *Nash equilibrium*. This property (no incentive for unilateral deviation) does not hold for any of the alternative three possible outcomes; the Nash equilibrium is thus unique and it is furthermore the only Pareto-optimal outcome. The game discussed for the fallacy of aggregation is a *prisoners' dilemma*; it is a *symmetric* game as well, it too contains a *strictly dominant* strategy for both players, leading to the single Nash equilibrium. However, this time the Nash equilibrium is the only outcome that is not Pareto optimal.

Thus far, both games are 2-person, 2-strategy normal-form games; however, the same two games may be defined as n-person games with the same results. All n agents choose one of the two strategies. In order to make this choice, every agent will take into consideration the possible choices of all the other agents. Say among the other agents, there are n_1 who choose the first and n_2 that opt for the second strategy such that $n_1 + n_2 = n - 1$. In the social optimum game, the payoffs resulting from the two strategies, Π_1 and Π_2, are as follows:

$$\Pi_1 = -1 + 3 + 2n_1 = 2 + 2n_1$$
$$\Pi_2 = 0 + 0 + 2n_1 = 2n_1$$

That is, by choosing n_1 the agent awards herself and every other agent an additional payoff of 2. She will—as long as she is rational—find that this option is always preferable no matter how many other agents made the same choice (i.e., no matter which value n_1 assumes). For the prisoners' dilemma on the other hand, the payoffs resulting from the two strategies are as follows:

$$\Pi_1 = -1 + 0 + 2n_1 = -1 + 2n_1$$
$$\Pi_2 = 0 + 0 + 2n_1 = 2n_1$$

It is easily seen that the second term, the one resulting from the contributions of other agents, is equal in both games. However, the first, individual, term becomes negative in the prisoners' dilemma. This does again not depend on what the other agents do. No rational agent would therefore be willing to contribute by playing strategy 1 in this game.

Hence, provided that all agents are sufficiently informed and act rationally, we can predict that a social optimum game will result in all agents contributing as much as possible, while a game of the prisoners' dilemma type will prevent rational agents from contributing at all. As mentioned, the two games reflect two different if not oppositional economic principles, the invisible hand, which for more than two centuries has guided classical and neoclassical thought, and the fallacy of aggregation, which describes a more complex, conflictive, and interdependent setting.

Having discussed the game theory models of two radically different stories, of two opposite ways of conceptualizing economic reality, it has become clear that game theory is a method. It is a powerful tool, perhaps the most appropriate one to investigate socioeconomic systems, but it is nothing more than that. One concept may be modeled using game theory just as well as an entirely different one.

2.4 HOW NOT TO PLAY A GAME

2.4.1 Pareto Dominance

After detailing a number of illustrative examples in the previous sections, it is now time to proceed to the core concepts of game theory. The above examples have shown that there are more preferable outcomes and less preferable outcomes. Some outcomes should definitely be avoided.

For instance, considering the anti-coordination game again, the agents will want to avoid to be coordinated (i.e., being stuck in the doorway or waiting for nothing). However, things are not always as easy: In the prisoners' dilemma game (Figure 2.2), player B

wants to avoid the lower left field; player A does not agree—she is very much in favor of getting to exactly this field. Hence, it is imperative to obtain a neutral, general, and robust notion which outcomes are bad for all of the involved and definitely to be avoided.

The concept is called Pareto dominance, named in honor of the Italian economist Vilfredo Pareto. The concept recognizes that payoffs of different agents are fundamentally uncomparable. Utility of agent A cannot be transformed into utility of agent B and vice versa. Still an outcome is still doubtlessly preferable if both agents improve or if one agent improves while the other retains the same payoff. Such an outcome is called *Pareto superior*; the other one is called *Pareto dominated* or *Pareto inferior*.

Pareto Optimality and Suboptimality

A desirable outcome is one that is not Pareto dominated by any other possible outcome. This may be illustrated as in Figure 2.4: in a figure with the payoffs of both agents on the two axes, an outcome is Pareto dominated if there is another outcome to the upper right of this outcome. Outcome X is Pareto dominated by outcome Y. Outcomes Y, V, and W, however, are not Pareto dominated. Such an outcome is called *Pareto optimal* or a *Pareto optimum of the game*.

A simple way of finding Pareto optima in a strategic game is to go through the possible outcomes one by one and cross every outcome out that is Pareto dominated by another (any other) one; see Figure 2.5.

2.5 HOW TO PLAY A GAME

2.5.1 Dominance

It has been discussed which outcomes are desirable. The question now is: How do we manage to achieve one of them?

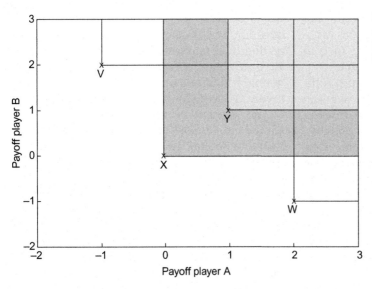

FIGURE 2.4 Outcomes in prisoners' dilemma game (Figures 2.2 and 2.5) and Pareto dominance: X is Pareto dominated by Y; Y, V, and W are Pareto optimal.

FIGURE 2.4 Outcomes in prisoners' dilemma game (Figures 2.2 and 2.5) and Pareto dominance: X is Pareto dominated by Y; Y, V, and W are Pareto optimal.

		Player B	
		Strategy 1	Strategy 2
Player A	Strategy 1	1 1	2 −1
	Strategy 2	−1 2	−0 −0−

FIGURE 2.5 Pareto optima in a prisoners' dilemma game. (Crossed payoffs indicate Pareto dominated outcomes; all other outcomes are Pareto optima.)

		Player B	
		Strategy 1	Strategy 2
Player A	Strategy 1	0 0	1 1
	Strategy 2	1 1	0 0

FIGURE 2.6 Best answer strategies (payoffs underlined) in an anti-coordination game.

Obviously in the prisoners' dilemma game above, neither player would be inclined to play their second strategy. Any possible payoff they could obtain with this strategy is less than the alternative given the other player's choice. Such a strategy is called a *strictly dominated strategy.* No rational agent will ever make this choice. A strategy for which every payoff (given the choice of the opponent) is better than all alternatives is called a *strictly dominant strategy.*

2.5.2 Best Answers

Returning to the anti-coordination game (Figure 2.1), we find that there are no dominant or dominated strategies in this game.

Hence, the concept of dominance is not helpful in predicting outcomes.

Still, it is clear which outcomes are preferable and thus to decide which strategy the agents choose given the choice of the other player. This concept is termed the best answer strategies. If a strategy 1 of player A leads player B to choose her strategy 2 then strategy 2 of B is called the best answer (or a best answer since there may be several strategies with equal payoffs) to strategy 1 of A. Every player has at least one best answer strategy corresponding to every choice of the other player(s). It is helpful to identify all best answer strategies to all the strategies of all the players in a game: Underline the payoff the player hopes to achieve as a best response to the choice(s) of the opponent(s) (Figure 2.6).

2.5.3 Nash Equilibria

An outcome that is achieved as a result of every player playing her best answer strategy is called a Nash equilibrium named in honor of game theorist and Nobel memorial laureate John Nash. Every involved strategy is the best answer to the strategies of the other player(s), thus no player has an incentive to unilaterally deviate from the Nash equilibrium. It follows that a Nash equilibrium is—for rational players—an absorbing state, an outcome that is dynamically stable (if there were the option that one or more players revise their choices), an outcome that is more probable than others.

To obtain the set of Nash equilibria in a strategic game, underline the best answer payoffs and identify the outcomes for which all payoffs for all players are underlined. Figure 2.6 does this for the anti-coordination game discussed earlier in this chapter: the Nash equilibria are the lower left and upper right fields, the outcomes in which the players choose different strategies.

2.6 HOW MANY GAMES CAN WE PLAY?

So far we restricted the considerations in this chapter to a specific type of games: Games that are limited to exactly one time period in which all agents act simultaneously. These games are referred to as normal-form games (because they are conveniently represented in the matrix form, also called normal-form, as shown above). However, many different types of games are conceivable. The agents may choose strategies sequentially—in this case, the second player knows the decision of the first one when she chooses her strategy (sequential games). Normal-form games may be played repeatedly, which means that the agents remember choices and outcomes from previous periods (repeated games). This allows more complex strategies since they may contain instructions for more than one period and since they may also take the opponents' actions and reactions into consideration. Repeated games may be repeated for a certain time or indefinitely; they are also called supergames, particularly in case of indefinite repetition. These different types of games also require refinements of some of the game-theoretic concepts; these will be detailed in Chapter 8.

2.7 SUMMARY

This chapter offered a basic understanding of what a strategic game is, how it is used in modeling interactive situations, and how the central concepts of basic game theory—best answers, dominance, Nash equilibria, and Pareto optimality—are applied. Game theory is only one in a number of methods that may be used to analyze and understand economic interactions and their consequences. Until very recently, a large part of the profession of economics chose to forego using game theory—though this is now slowly but steadily changing. This was because direct interactions are very difficult to fit into general equilibrium models which in turn made it possible for the first time to analyze the economy as a whole and the nontrivial interdependence between different sectors, still one of the most important accomplishments in the history of economics. However, this came at the cost of sacrificing heterogeneity and direct interaction and reducing the social sphere to an agglomeration of homogeneous agents. The elaborate models of perfect markets in effect shifted the attention away from strategic interactions to another part of economic reality. The market perspective will be explained in Chapters 5 through 7 while Chapter 8 and the following chapters explain more advanced methods for the analysis of interactive economies.

A broad perspective on interactive economics using and applying the methods explained in this chapter will be detailed in Chapters 3 and 4.

Chapter References

Hargreaves Heap, S.P., Varoufakis, Y., 2004. Game Theory: A Critical Introduction. Routledge, London, New York.

Further Reading

Binmore, K., 2007. Game Theory: A Very Short Introduction. Oxford University Press, Oxford.
Bowles, S., 2006. Social interactions and institutional design. In: Bowles, S. (Ed.), Microeconomics: Behavior, Institutions, and Evolution. Princeton University Press, Princeton, NJ, pp. 23–55. , Chapter I.

Further Reading—Online

For further reading, see the textbook website at http://booksite.elsevier.com/9780124115859

EXERCISES

1. Identify:
   a. the Pareto optima in the anti-coordination game (Figure 2.1) and in the social optimum game (Figure 2.2)
   b. the best answer strategies and Nash equilibria in the prisoners' dilemma (Figure 2.3) and the social optimum game (Figure 2.2)
   c. whether there are strictly dominant strategies in the social optimum game (Figure 2.2)?

2. Consider the following game and identify Pareto optima, best answer strategies, and Nash equilibria. Are there strictly dominant strategies?

		Player B	
		Strategy 1	Strategy 2
Player A	Strategy 1	2 4	3 3
	Strategy 2	1 1	4 2

3. How many Nash equilibria, how many best answer strategies, and how many Pareto optima does a 2-person 2-strategy normal-form game have at least? How many (of any of those concepts) does it have at most? Consider as an example the following game.

		Player B	
		Strategy 1	Strategy 2
Player A	Strategy 1	0 0	0 0
	Strategy 2	0 0	0 0

CHAPTER

3

Problem Structures and Processes in Complex Economies

"We may speak of households, firms, and government as the primary economic agents which carry on their activities with-in the framework of a set of evolving economic institutions. But these agents and economic institutions also interact with an external environment which can be classified in a variety of ways. One simple classification might be: (1) the framework of legal and political institutions [...]; (2) the complex of social institutions that make up what may loosely be referred to as the social environment; (3) the evolving body of scientific and technical knowledge (and the institutions through which such knowledge is developed and transmitted); (4) the physical environment; [...]." **Robert A. Gordon**[1]

OUTLINE

[1]Then President of the American Economic Association, Presidential Address: "Rigor and Relevance in a Changing Institutional Setting," *The American Economic Review*, **66.1** (1976), pp. 1–14, p. 11.

The first and second chapters have introduced you to the basic conditions that agents face in real-world economic decision situations and basic tools for representing and analyzing these. In this chapter, we will in more detail introduce you to the variety of problem structures agents have to deal with and to solution mechanisms for these problems that we can derive with the help of the game-theoretic methods you have learned about.

3.1 A CONTINUUM OF SOCIAL PROBLEM STRUCTURES

As explained in Chapter 1, agents interacting directly and facing situations characterized by their direct interdependence opens the possibility for the emergence of various types of problem structures. Depending on the type, these are solved more easily or with more difficulty, if at all. A solution here means the achieving of a Pareto-optimal outcome. The difficulty of achieving such an outcome depends on the basic problem structure. These problem structures can be represented by games.

If individually optimal strategy choices lead to a Pareto-optimal outcome, the problem is minor (nonexistent, in fact, in the game-theoretic setups we consider here). The *coordination problems* we have mentioned in Chapter 1, however, do already not involve an ex-ante optimal strategy, as the optimal choice for an agent depends on the choices of the other agents in the game. We will see that different types of coordination problems exist with differing degrees of *asymmetric interests* of the agents regarding which outcome exactly to coordinate on, as a consequence of asymmetric payoffs in the coordinated outcomes. Finally, there are *dilemma problems*. As we will see, the basic problem there is such that it cannot be solved by "rational" agents. All relevant aspects of the situation are integrated in the payoffs for them and the only aspect that matters for them is to

try and realize a payoff that is as high as possible. Still, there are ways for dealing with a dilemma situation, as we will also see, as the situation can at times be transformed, thus at least potentially allowing agents to improve their results.

We will use *normal-form games*, introduced to you in Chapter 2, to describe these basic problem structures. As the basic outline of the problems can be captured in 2×2 games, we use these for purposes of presentation. It must not be forgotten, however, that usually more agents and more behavioral options, i.e., strategies, are involved, making problems potentially much more difficult to solve than may appear from a 2×2 normal-form game.

3.1.1 An Invisible Hand at Work: A Social Optimum Structure

Figure 3.1 shows a *social optimum game*. As you see, each agent's first strategy is strictly dominant and therefore their only sensible choice. When facing such situations, the agents achieve a socially optimal outcome simply by following their individually optimal behavioral pattern. There is no conflict of interests between the agents; the Pareto-optimal outcome is reached. If agents would primarily face these kind of problem structures, we could limit ourselves to abstracting from the interdependence of their decisions and use individual optimization problems as the basis for analyzing problems, effects of constraints, etc. However, such

		Player B	
		Strategy 1	Strategy 2
Player A	Strategy 1	3 3	2 2
	Strategy 2	2 2	1 1

FIGURE 3.1   Social optimum game.

situations are only one of a number of different ones that agents face. And for all others, we cannot neglect the influence that the interaction of agents has on the overall outcome.

Many of these additional problems take the form of coordination problems. These involve possibly numerous combinations of mutual best answers in pure strategies in which at least one of the resulting pure-strategy Nash equilibria is Pareto-optimal. In contrast to the social optimum games, and also the dilemma games that we will explain below, there are no strictly dominant strategies in coordination games. As a result, expectations regarding other agents' behavior start to matter greatly here, because an individual's best strategy choice now depends on what the other players (are expected to) do.

We can distinguish between a number of gradually distinct types of coordination problems. The distinction that is interesting for us at this point, in terms of the resulting differentiation of problem structures agents face, is based on two different aspects. The first is whether all Nash equilibria are Pareto-optimal or only some, or even only one, of them. The other is whether the payoffs in the Nash equilibria are the same for all agents, or whether some profit more than others in certain Nash outcomes.

3.1.2 A Simple Coordination Problem

Figure 3.2 shows a *basic coordination problem*. There are two Nash equilibria, in the upper left and lower right cell of the matrix. If both agents choose their first strategy, or both choose their second strategy, they end up in a Pareto-optimal situation. As both agents get the same payoff within a Nash equilibrium, and the same payoff in either Nash equilibrium, they have no preference regarding which one they reach, as long as they can coordinate on one of them (drive on the right- or

FIGURE 3.2   Basic coordination game.

FIGURE 3.3   Assurance game.

left-hand side of a street; choose one communication technology from a number of equivalent possible options; etc.).

3.1.3 Another Coordination Problem: Assurance

A variant of this problem is one in which only one of the two Nash equilibria is Pareto-optimal. Such a problem is depicted in Figure 3.3. It is often called *assurance game*. For making the problem structure plausible, imagine, for instance, that the strategy leading to the Pareto-superior Nash equilibrium may have become available later than the other one. In that case, agents would have to believe that everyone else is aware of the new option (which our game-theoretic actors of course are, but which real-world agents may not be) and to trust that everybody else is equally aware and that everybody is willing to switch strategies. As there still are two Nash equilibria in the game, both are equally rational choices for agents, provided they believe that everyone else will be playing that particular Nash strategy. If an agent can be assured that everyone will choose the strategies leading to the Pareto-superior outcome, it is rational for her to do so as well. If that assurance is not given, there may be situations in which it is rational to opt for the other strategy.

3.1.4 Assurance Extended: Stag Hunt and the Problems of Trust and Signaling

Yet another variation of this type of situations is called a *stag hunt game* (Figure 3.4),

Player B

		Strategy 1	Strategy 2
Player A	Strategy 1	3 3	2 1
	Strategy 2	1 2	2 2

FIGURE 3.4 Stag hunt game.

adapted from a story told by *Jean-Jacques Rousseau* (1759). Two agents go hunting. If they both focus their efforts on a stag (strategy 1) they will catch it. They have to coordinate their efforts though. If one deviates and tries to catch a hare (strategy 2), she can do that alone, but the result attainable is smaller than her share of the stag would be. Should the other player, however, make that decision, she could not catch the stag on her own. If the players cannot communicate during the hunt, the temptation to change strategies and switch to unilaterally hunting a hare may increase over time. A switch of strategies may then appear increasingly favorable, be it only to insure against a change of mind of the other player(s) (for a general example see Box 3.1).

In addition to the general problem of a coordination of strategies, there is a *second problem involved* here therefore. As you can see, the payoff for strategy 2 is the same independently of the other player's choice of strategy. It can be seen as the safe option. As long as you are sure that the other agent will choose strategy 1,

---

BOX 3.1

IMMIGRATION AS AN EXAMPLE OF COORDINATION PROBLEMS

Obviously, a number of factors matter for decisions regarding migration and the destination sought. Some aspects, at least, can be captured in a coordination game setting, though. These relate to positive external effects (see Chapter 1) that living close to people with a shared cultural background may result in. Such effects may in this case result, for instance, from existing networks offering support to new arrivals, helping finding work, finding a place to stay, with administrative issues to offering an easier arrival in the new environment, reducing the negative emotions

that a complete loss of familiarity and cultural embeddedness might conceivably lead to.

You may also think of a stag hunt-type situation, where the decision is whether to move, or to stay. Staying is the safe options, moving only offers an improvement of the situation where someone does not have to go it alone. Obviously, as you can appreciate, numerous scenarios are conceivable, where the overall situation agents face then determines whether coordination problems may be adequate for capturing a problem faced, or whether other problems structures appear more appropriate.

---

there is no reason for you not to do so either. As soon as you have doubts, though, the *safe strategy* may be the better option for you. Choosing it, you can be sure to avoid the loss that you would face in case of a strategy switch by the other player. Such games allow a Pareto-optimal outcome to be reached, and there is no reason why players would not want to try and do that. But if they cannot communicate (which by assumption they cannot), or maybe fear a mistake may be made by the other player in deciding on her strategy, or simply assume the other is so distrustful or simply fearful as to rather choose the safe option for herself, they may have no choice but to do the same. Their expectations regarding the motivations of the other player(s) in the game matter greatly now (for an example see Box 3.2). Depending on how they assess

the other(s), one or the other strategy is their best choice. That includes how they assume they are perceived by the other(s), as their choice depends on what they expect, etc. *Rules supporting agents* in their choice of the strategy make it easier for agents to take the risk of losing out through their strategy choice, by *signaling* that everyone is expected to make a certain choice and thus reducing the risk of other choices (a failure to coordinate) within a given group.

3.1.5 Coordination with Asymmetric Interests: Battle of the Sexes

Another coordination problem is one in which the agents profit from coordinating, but to different degrees. In such a case, we speak

---

BOX 3.2

EFFORT AT THE WORKPLACE AS AN EXAMPLE OF A STAG HUNT GAME

You have seen the basic stag hunt problem in Figure 3.4. As an example, imagine that workers can choose the effort level they are willing to put into their work. Say there is a minimum effort they will in any case show leading to a safe overall result as given by the payoffs of strategy 2. However, all workers involved have the choice of increasing their effort (choose strategy 1). When all do, the overall result they can achieve signifies an improvement over the regular effort outcome. When not everyone of those involved chooses a higher effort level, however, that improvement in overall results is unattainable, meaning we need a concerted effort by all those involved for an improvement. If the higher outcome is not attained, those workers that

have opted for a higher effort level see a reduction of their overall payoff (due to the extra energy spent that is not leading to the satisfaction of better results, frustration with such an outcome, etc.).

Now, if they have to fear that some coworkers may not be willing to put extra effort into their work, they would thus face a reduction of their payoffs. If there are additional issues of possibilities for monitoring each individual effort, this is exacerbated, in fact. This also requires that every worker perceives the basic situation in the same way, namely, that extra effort is worthwhile if everyone contributes. Again, expectations about other agents play a crucial role in the behavior eventually adopted, by the workers in this case.

---

of asymmetric interests among the players. See Figure 3.5 for an example of such games. These are called *battle of the sexes games*. As an example for a situation that may be captured by a simple coordination game, we had referred to coordinating on the application of a given communication technology. Here, we may assume that companies have invested in developing such technologies, and have thus incurred costs (technology 1 being developed by player A, and technology 2 by player B). For effectively communicating, they both need to use the same technology, however, meaning one has to switch to the other's technology, incurring additional costs.

As said, the players prefer being coordinated to not being coordinated, but both have different preferences regarding which Nash equilibrium to reach. There is no way to determine at the outset which result may be achieved. For addressing that question, we'd have to analyze the wider situation, so as to understand whether one player might influence the other, or whether the players may be able to negotiate a solution for the situation.

As both prefer being coordinated to being uncoordinated, there is no reason to expect the agents not to follow a rule describing how to achieve coordination. So, once such a rule has come into existence it can be expected to be stable. There are a number of possibilities for such a rule, which ex-ante and without further knowledge cannot be determined, though. Whether it allows agents in turn to reach their best result (for instance, through alternating between the Nash equilibria), or whether it permanently gives an advantage to one (group of) player(s) cannot be answered within this setup. We can say, however, that a rule establishing a coordinated outcome in the game will improve the situation of all players as compared to an uncoordinated outcome (as is true in all coordination games).

3.1.6 An Anti-Coordination Problem: Hawk-Dove

Another interesting variant is the *hawk-dove games* (that are sometimes called *anti-coordination games*, as the Nash equilibria result from players choosing different strategies). As you can see in Figure 3.6, the two Nash equilibria in pure strategies (upper right and lower left) are Pareto-optimal. There is a third Pareto-optimum, though, in the upper left. Even though one player gains with respect to that third Pareto-optimum in a Nash equilibrium, the other one loses.

In a variation of the example for the battle of the sexes game, we might imagine that companies A and B may develop a communication technology, jointly if both choose strategy 1, or abstain from trying to develop it, as strategy 2. The assumption here would be that an adaptation of the developed technology is easy so that companies can profit without having to incur the development costs, and that the

		Player B	
		Strategy 1	Strategy 2
Player A	Strategy 1	3 / 4	2 / 2
	Strategy 2	1 / 1	4 / 3

FIGURE 3.5   Battle of the sexes game.

		Player B	
		Strategy 1	Strategy 2
Player A	Strategy 1	3 / 3	4 / 2
	Strategy 2	2 / 4	1 / 1

FIGURE 3.6   Hawk-dove game.

availability of the new technology promises some gains even for those going alone in development, as compared to the situation where both companies do nothing.

There are relatively strong asymmetric interests in such a setup. But without knowing about broader structures that this particular game may be embedded in, there is, as in the battle of the sexes games, no way of knowing in which equilibrium the players will find themselves. Still, even though one of the players may feel exploited by the other, there is no reason to change her strategy choice, once the coordination on one Nash equilibrium is established. The outcome is stable. A strategy change by the player who is worse off in the Nash equilibrium would lead both to the worst possible result in the game.

3.1.7 A Social Dilemma Problem, and Public Goods and Commons

Lastly, in this continuum of games describing problem structures in directly interdependent decision situations, there are dilemma problems. These are characterized by the fact that the strictly dominant strategies of the players lead them to an outcome that is not Pareto-optimal. Figure 3.7 shows such a game. The Nash equilibrium is located in the lower right cell. The other three results are Pareto-optimal.

FIGURE 3.7 Dilemma game.

You can see that both players would be better off if they both chose their dominated strategy. But in that case, they face the threat of exploitation by the other player. And as rational players, they have to expect that the other tries that exploitation (maximizing her payoff), just as the opponent has to expect that of you. For rational players of the kind assumed in classic game theory, there is no way of solving such a dilemma problem. They are doomed to playing their strictly dominant strategies, even as that takes them to the relatively bad result. Note the difference to the hawk-dove game where the exploiting situation is stable, as a Pareto-optimal Nash equilibrium (that may serve as a reminder that the Pareto-criterion does not include any specific notion of fairness).

In Chapter 1, we had referred to dilemma problems agents may face in relation to *collective goods*, as public goods or as commons. Problems concerning both types of collective goods may be illustrated through a dilemma structure.

Regarding *public goods* the dilemma results from individual incentives for contributing to the provision of these goods, or rather, the lack thereof. We can further distinguish the provision of the public good by a group of agents as well as by private companies. Recall that public goods are characterized by nonexcludability as well as nonrivalry in use. At this point, the relevant fact is that once they exist, no one can be excluded from using them.

Regarding the case of a group provision, imagine that every agent controls some resources. These can be used for private consumption (strategy 2) or split between private consumption and a contribution to producing a public good (strategy 1). As you can see, in that case every agent has an incentive not to contribute. If the other(s) do(es), the agent can utilize the public good and has all her resources available for private consumption. If she contributes, some of her resources will be utilized in the production of the public good, and thus are not available for her exclusive private use. And if the other player chooses not to contribute, the contributing player has to carry the efforts alone, or the overall quality of the public good may suffer, so that in any case the benefit it might bring if fully provided will not materialize. Still, not contributing is the dominant strategy in this case. The public good, from which both would profit, will not be produced by the agents as we assume them to be, then.

If it is a company considering whether to produce a good with public good character, or not, the story is a different one: A private company has no incentive to produce a public good because the nonexcludable character of the good means that the firm cannot charge agents using it once it is in place. It would therefore not have a chance of recovering its investment. Employing its resources where they can generate a product that consumers can be charged for is preferable to the company (you may also assume that private agents might make an ex-ante promise to reimburse the company for production, but as they do not have a reason to make good on that promise once the public good has become available, production/nonproduction and payment/nonpayment are the respective strategy options with nonproduction/nonpayment as the Nash equilibrium).

In both cases, public goods would not be produced by private agents. The provision of public goods is hence a classical economic problem, and often seen as the principal task of government in economic matters. As we will see below, though, there are solutions to dilemma problems which offer ways in which private agents, as a group, can be supported in efforts to contribute to the production of a good with public good properties. That goes even for the rational agents at the heart of the concepts applied here. When considering real-world agents, who are embedded in certain social structures, which additionally they may find difficult to leave, that may change the perception of problems involved from the start (we will take these aspects up in section 3.2).

The second group of collective goods are the *commons*. The problem results from the use of an already existing resource that is nonexcludable but shows rivalry in use (possibly, after a certain threshold has been passed). If nonexcludability is given in the use of resources, then that may mean that agents have an incentive to utilize it beyond its sustainable limits (strategy 2), eventually depleting it. For ensuring its long-term availability, a group needs institutions governing the use of such resources if their depletion is to be avoided (strategy 1) (for a general formulation of the problem structure, see Box 3.3). Historically, different groups have had different degrees of success in the development of such institutions, and therefore different degrees of economic success (see our explanations of Elinor Ostrom's studies in this area in Chapter 13).

In Section 3.2, we will introduce ways that allow even economically rational agents to improve their results in situations that developed from dilemma problems. Once such solution mechanisms have been explained we will adopt a broader perspective, and address the function of institutions as well.

3.2 SOLUTIONS TO SOCIAL DILEMMA PROBLEMS

If agents are to realize a Pareto-superior outcome in a dilemma situation, a transformation of the problem structure or additional capabilities of the agents are necessary because the basic dilemma cannot be solved by the agents as conceived so far. In this section, we will introduce you to some possibilities that allow

BOX 3.3

TRAGEDY OF THE COMMONS

The Tragedy of the Commons is a term used to describe dilemma-type problems in the exploitation of existing (renewable) resources. These kinds of problem arise when individually and socially optimal levels of exploitation do not coincide. We can use the following example:

Let the Commons in this case be a pasture. It is freely accessible and a number of shepherds use it as a grazing ground for their sheep. The pasture has a *maximum carrying capacity* of animals. When the number of animals on the meadow is larger than this maximum carrying capacity, *each* animal loses some weight compared to a maximum weight when the number is at or below the maximum carrying capacity. In this case, the overall weight of the animals on the meadow is given by

$$f(N) = N[\pi^{max} - t(N - N^{max})]$$

N = number of animals on the meadow
π^{max} = maximum weight of an animal
N^{max} = maximum carrying capacity
t = weight loss of each animal for each animal beyond the maximum carrying capacity (with t for "technology," imagine a natural production function).

The maximum of this function, from df/dN (meaning we pretend the number of animals was continuous and not discrete), gives the overall highest weight of all animals combined. The number of animals on the meadow at this point is:

$$N^* = \frac{\pi^{max} + tN^{max}}{2t}$$

Let $\pi^{max} = 100$, $N^{max} = 20$, and $t = 5$. Then $N^* = 20$ ($= N^{max}$ in this case). It is of course conceivable that the weight loss per animal can be compensated by larger numbers of animals for a while so that overall weight increases even as individual weight per animal drops. (Consider the case of $t = 2$ as an example, with all other parameters equal.) If we assume that the meadow is used by two shepherds, a symmetrical distribution of use would imply each one can have 10 sheep grazing. The overall weight of each herd is 1000 then. Now, if one shepherd decides to put an eleventh animal on the meadow, the weight of each animal would drop to 95. The shepherd whose herd continues to number 10 animals now has animals with an overall weight of 950. The one who increased the number of animals to 11, however, sees an increase in overall weight to 1045, whereas the overall weight of all animals on the meadow is reduced, $1995 < 2000$. If both decide to increase the number of animals to 11, the weight of each animal drops to 90, their respective herds bring a weight of 990, respectively. In a normal-form game, this takes the following form:

		Shepherd B	
		10 sheep	11 sheep
Shepherd A	10 sheep	1000 / 1000	1000 / 950
	11 sheep	950 / 1045	950 / 990

For both shepherds, having 11 animals on the meadow is the strictly dominant strategy. Their overall result is, however, worse than it would be if both sent only 10 animals to graze.

We can show this in a more general form as well. Imagine that each shepherd sends the same number of animals onto the meadow. Then for a number S of shepherds, n^*_{social} is the

---

BOX 3.3   *(cont'd)*

---

number that every shepherd sends as his share of the overall socially optimal amount:

$$N^* = \frac{\pi^{max} + tN^{max}}{2t} = \sum_{i=1}^{s} n_i = Sn^*_{social}$$

Now, assume that an individual shepherd takes the decisions of the $S - 1$ other shepherds as given. His rational, maximizing decision problem then derives from:

$$f(n_i) = n_i[\pi^{max} - t(N - N^{max})]$$

or

$$f(n_i) = n_i[\pi^{max} - t(n_i + (S - 1)n^*_{social} - N^{max})]$$

As a result of df/dn_i, this yields

$$n^*_{individual} = \frac{\pi^{max} + tN^{max}}{2t} - \frac{(S - 1)}{2}n^*_{social} >$$

$$\frac{\pi^{max} + tN^{max}}{2t} - (S - 1)n^*_{social} = n^*_{social}$$

When all other shepherds have their share of the socially optimal number of animals on the meadow, every individual shepherd has an incentive to increase his number of animals beyond that number. (Calculate for yourself the number of sheep that an individually maximizing shepherd will put on the pasture, assuming that all others stick to n^*_{social}.)

---

dealing with dilemma problems in a way so that agents can improve the results they can achieve.

3.2.1 Transformation of the Problem Structure: Supergames and Single-Shot Solution

As the players cannot solve the dilemma problem as such, one possibility is to try and change the underlying problem structure. The way to do this is to move *beyond the one-shot game* considered above, and allow agents to meet *repeatedly*. As we will momentarily see, if certain conditions are met, then a *transformation of the game into a stag hunt-type coordination game* is feasible. Such a transformation opens the possibility for agents to improve their results if they can coordinate on the now existing Pareto-optimal Nash equilibrium.

This may, remember, still involve considerable problems in an *N*-person setting, especially if those that attempt to switch to the new Nash equilibrium have to fear losses in case not enough others make the same attempt. In fact, a second aspect that we will explain in section 3.2.2 is what minimum share of agents in a group has to switch strategies, or what minimum share has to generally emerge in a population for the strategy leading to the Pareto-optimal new Nash equilibrium to become the then preferred option in a population of agents.

A *supergame* is a repeated game. Here, the same underlying game is played by the agents in *indefinite or infinite repetition*. As they play the same basic game every time, we can sum up the payoffs of the underlying game over the duration of the interactions. Future payoffs received are discounted in such summation. The logic behind this can be described through the following example: Imagine an interest rate of 10%. If you take 100 units of currency to the bank, you will receive 110 currency units in the following period, or 121 in the period after that if you leave the money at the bank, and so on. These future payoffs are then said to be worth 100 units of currency today. Likewise, for receiving a given amount of money in a future period, the amount of money you have to take to the bank today is lower, the further into the future that money is paid to you. Now, in the case of repeated games you receive nominally constant payoffs every period. These are then discounted to give today's value of the expected stream of income you receive. Imagine you receive a payoff of 121 in the current period, and for two more periods beyond this. At an interest rate of 10%, the current value of this income stream is $121 + 110 + 100 = 331$.

For an infinite series of payoffs, we can make use of the fact that these types of series (infinite geometrical series) converge to a limit value. The discount factor, here δ, is usually a simple expression given by $1/(1 + r)$, where r is the discount rate employed by the agent in the discounting of future payoffs in the formulation of the supergame. To allow for indefinite instead of infinite games, we formulate it as $p/(1 + r)$. For a $p = 1$, the assumption is that the game continues infinitely, for a $p < 1$, there is an endpoint; however, that endpoint cannot be known by the agents, as it is a stochastic event. The game is indefinite, and endgame effects cannot occur. There is always the possibility that there will be further interactions in which behavior can be sanctioned.

Future payoffs are discounted by this factor. For a payoff a, the present value of the payoff received in the following period is δa, the present value of the payoff in two periods time is $\delta^2 a$, and so on. The limit value to which this series converges is $a/(1 - \delta)$. For the numerical example used above that means, if the payoff of 121 is received ad infinitum from today onward, the present value of the overall income stream is $121/(1 - \delta)$, or 1331.

We can use this limit value to represent the value of expected streams of results in supergames. This works for supergames with indefinite repetitions as well, because the endpoint is undetermined there and therefore making use of the infinite geometrical series for expressing the interactions' expected value in the current period makes sense as an approximation for today's value of the income stream. Agents then evaluate the results of the different strategies they have at hand based on the current value of the income stream they can expect from them.

Figure 3.8 shows a dilemma game again, this time in general form. The relations between the payoffs to arrive at a dilemma situation is $b > a > c > d$. The second condition for the payoffs ($(b + d)/2 < a$) assures that in case of a repetition, it is not preferable for the agents to switch back and forth between their strategies. You see that the first strategy of the agents is strictly dominated, the second strategy is strictly dominant, leading them to the nonoptimal Nash equilibrium. As agents could improve the result for both themselves and the others, if they chose their strictly dominated strategy, we call this strategy *cooperation*, and the second strategy *defection* (potentially improving the individual result, however, at the cost of the interaction partner's, or opponent's payoff reduction). The choice in the one-shot game is to defect, no matter what the other player may be expected to do. Now, if agents meet repeatedly, a change is introduced to the strategic situation they find themselves in.

		Player B	
		Strategy 1	Strategy 2
Player A	Strategy 1	a / a	b / d
	Strategy 2	d / b	c / c

FIGURE 3.8 Dilemma game: $b > a > c > d$ and $(b + d)/2 < a$.

The repetition allows them to take *prior strategy choices of other players into account* in their own strategy choice.

This said, when approaching such a problem using game-theoretic analytical methods we have to formulate agents' strategies at the outset of their playing the supergame. When analyzing the situation we do not let agents reconsider their choices after every interaction (every move within the supergame). Rather, they have to formulate a *game plan at the outset*, and then have to follow it until the supergame (the round) is completed. This game plan can include contingencies for the other players' earlier choices, when allowing the agents a memory period over which they remember interaction partners' earlier moves. An easy strategy to build our illustration on is called *tit-for-tat* (TFT) with a memory period of one, thus reflecting a short history of interactions and a one period memory and reaction option. It is nevertheless a good choice for introducing a number of the basic issues involved and, in fact, a simple representative of a generally quite successful type of strategies in repeated dilemma games (as we will see in Chapter 13).

The game plan for a player choosing TFT is, start with cooperation and then mirror your opponent's prior choice in all subsequent interactions. Should two TFT-players meet, they will choose cooperation in every interaction, therefore, as they will both have started cooperating and then choose what the other one did in the preceding interaction.

For a discussion of whether the transformation of the dilemma game into a coordination game can succeed, and under what conditions, we draw on TFT as one component of the strategy set of the agents. The other will be to choose defection in every interaction (All-D). The payoffs that result if two players meet that can choose either TFT or All-D are shown in Figure 3.9.

FIGURE 3.9 Dilemma-based supergame (TFT and All-D).

TFT/TFT in the upper left cell is equivalent to the result achievable if two agents choose the cooperative strategy in the underlying game, thus receiving a, in every move. But, it does so in a way that takes into account the prior choices of the opposing player. As opposed to a strategy that would simply say always cooperate, TFT involves a mechanism to punish an agent who chooses defection. Following the defection of the other player, the TFT player likewise defects in their next interaction. This reduces the payoff in the future round; possibly in all future rounds, depending on the game plan(s) of the other player(s).

Now, whether this threat of punishment can really discipline the players depends on the overall payoffs achievable, because these determine whether the threat is credible or not. In a setup such as this, where agents only decide based on payoffs, a threat's credibility depends on the related payoffs. We will return to this point momentarily.

As $a > c$ continues to be given, the result in the upper left cell continues to be superior to the result in the lower right. But as we can see, the TFT game plan means that the payoffs in the upper right (TFT/All-D) and lower left (All-D/TFT) have not changed proportionally to the underlying dilemma game (and vice versa for the row player). In the first interaction of the supergame, the players receive payoffs b and d, respectively. Afterwards, they get c in each interaction. Therefore, the c is received infinitely often from the second interaction onward, leading to the overall expected payoffs shown in the payoff matrix. The series contains one c that has not been received, namely, the first interaction's payoff, and which therefore has to be subtracted. Now, if

$$b - c + \frac{c}{1 - \delta} > \frac{a}{1 - \delta}$$

holds, then All-D strictly dominates TFT as a strategy, and the Pareto-superior result (as compared to the Nash equilibrium) in the TFT/TFT combination is unattainable for "rational" players. If the relation does not hold, if the inequality is reversed, however, there is no longer a strictly dominant strategy in the supergame. If

$$\frac{a}{1 - \delta} > b - c + \frac{c}{1 - \delta}$$

TFT becomes a best answer to itself, and the outcome in the upper left hence a Nash equilibrium. The strategy combination leading to the result in the lower right continues to be a Nash equilibrium as well. In the resulting game, we would therefore find two Nash equilibria, one of which (upper left) Pareto-dominates the other (lower right). This is a version of a stag hunt-type game. The dilemma problem is transformed into a coordination problem and hence a problem that the agents can solve.

The next step would be the actual solution of the new problem structure, a rule that establishes the changes in behavior patterns that lead to the Pareto-optimal Nash equilibrium TFT/TFT being realized. In the setup considered up to this moment, a rule suffices, because the problem now is one of coordination. We will return to this point in a moment.

The payoffs are given in the game. Jointly, they constitute the problem structure. What we have to ask ourselves then is what *value of* δ is sufficient for the transformation of the problem structure from dilemma to coordination? A quick manipulation of the above condition, that TFT/TFT $>!$ All-D/TFT gives us the *single-shot condition*,

$$\delta >! \frac{b - a}{b - c}$$

The single-shot condition shows us that the less likely a *common future*, meaning the lower the value of p and hence δ, the less likely it is that the transformation into a coordination game succeeds. Conversely, we can say, the longer the time horizon agents adopt for their interaction (reflected in increasing values of p), the more likely it becomes that they can solve a dilemma problem by transforming it into a coordination problem. Also, the transformation is more likely when agents generally value future payoffs relatively higher (as mirrored in a lower discount rate r).

You can see that the threshold value of δ depends on the payoff structure. For a given b, the larger a is relative to c, the more likely it becomes, that the problem can be transformed. Accordingly, the lower the value of b is for given a and c, the more likely it becomes that the transformation succeeds. If you think in terms of *policy*, how to *strengthen relations between agents* and thereby *extend the time horizon* under which they operate can be a valuable guiding question in a number of problematic fields (such as R&D cooperation, for instance, but also in approaching public good contributions or commons exploitation), as can be attempts to reduce the one-time reward from defecting against cooperating interaction partners.

When the single-shot condition is fulfilled, the threat embodied in the TFT strategy becomes a credible one—the strategy says, if you defect on me, I will defect on you in the future. And this is in fact worthwhile for me to do, because in those circumstances, once you have defected, defecting is the least bad option amongst the ones open to me. You, as the first to defect, however, will see your payoff reduced subsequently, and end up worse than in a situation of common cooperation. Expressed with the help of the payoffs that means because

$$d - c + \frac{c}{1 - \delta} > \frac{d}{1 - \delta}$$

that is by definition of the underlying game always fulfilled, as it can be rewritten as

$$\frac{\delta}{1 - \delta} c > \frac{\delta}{1 - \delta} d$$

it pays to defect against a defector. Once you meet someone who defects against you, you are better off defecting yourself. That makes the threat of switching from cooperation to defection in subsequent interactions credible. The defector, on the other hand, faces the payoff relations

$$b - c + \frac{c}{1 - \delta} < \frac{a}{1 - \delta} < \frac{b}{1 - \delta}$$

as soon as the threat of a strategy switch in reaction to her choice, as embodied in the TFT game plan, is made. Defecting, she may hope to continuously exploit the other player(s), always receiving b. The TFT strategy, however, prescribes to choose defection in reaction to such a move in the following interaction in the supergame. This worsens the result that the defector can achieve. And it reduces it below the level of return achievable if she sticks to choosing cooperation in every interaction (as long as the single-shot condition is fulfilled). Therefore, it is effective as a punishment. (See Box 3.4 for an example for another possible way of dealing with this kind of situation.)

When the single-shot solution is fulfilled, that means we have the believable announcement of a strategy change in case of being faced with defective behavior, combined with an effective punishment that results from this strategy change. This leads to a *credible threat* players can make once they have achieved the coordination on the Pareto-superior Nash equilibrium to keep others from deviating from it.

In fact, in more general terms, this result has been known for a long time among game theorists as the *folk theorem*. It tells us that any result from individually rational decisions can be sustained as an equilibrium in a supergame with a finite number of players and a finite number of strategies. A decision is individually rational if the expected resulting payoff is at least as large as the maximin payoff for a player in the game (the minimum payoff that an agent can secure for herself through her own strategy choice; see Chapter 8 for in-depth explanations of folk theorem and solution concepts other than the Nash equilibrium). Which one of the possible Nash equilibria will result in the end cannot be determined on this basis, however.

The construction of the single-shot game relies on the infinite or indefinite repetition of the constitutive game (we may also imagine this as a situation with an endpoint beyond the planning horizon of agents). We stress this to underline that in every interaction, agents still face a dilemma structure. For the rational agent who decides on a game plan today and sticks to it until infinity, this is irrelevant. But if we move beyond the game-theoretic analysis and approach real-world agents, we have to be aware that they do have a choice in every interaction. What the single-shot solution allows us is to show that a dilemma problem may be altered in a way that allows the individual agents to find a solution to it. How this solution is stabilized in real-world situations is not described therein. For real-world agents, we in fact need the institutionalization of behavior, in semiconscious and habitual behavioral decisions. We will take this point up in more detail in Section 3.2.4.

BOX 3.4

UNDERSTANDING AND ALTERING PROBLEM STRUCTURES

We have always assumed complete information for the agents. That means that they understand the problem they are facing, and know that the other agent(s) do so as well. An implicit assumption that was likewise made has been that the individual player is not in a position to alter the problem faced. If they are in a position to exert influence on a situation, however, and given the understanding they have of the situation, they may well attempt to take action for changing the problem faced.

Imagine a company A dominating the market for a specific product and another agent thinking about setting up a company B for entering into that market and share in some of the profits realized therein. As long as A services the market alone (B does no enter), profits of 10 are realized in each period. Should company B enter the market, A's profits drop to six, and B realizes profits of four if A simply accepts that move. If, however, A decides on fighting the entrant through a price struggle, its profits are reduced to two, whereas the entrant, B, realizes a loss. The following situation presents itself:

		Company B		
		Don't enter		Enter
Company A	No price struggle		0 __10__	__4__ 6
	Price struggle		0 __10__	−4 2

Now, note that the best answer to B entering lays in simply accepting the fact—the threat of a price struggle in case of entering is not

credible as it would reduce profits from six to two, something a profit-maximizing agent would abstain from. What company A wants to do in this situation is to change the situation for the entrant—technically, to move the Nash equilibrium that is relevant for the entrant from the upper right to the upper left in order to *deter* her from *entering* the market. Possibilities may include spending on sales promotion and general marketing measures in order to strengthen the own customer base and threaten losses to the entrant (who has to make an initial investment that will have to be recovered) no matter whether or not a price struggle is engaged in, making "not entering" a strictly dominant strategy. Imagine that at a cost of two, the incumbent may influence customers sufficiently strongly for a new entrant to face losses due to a limitation of the customer base she may reach:

		Company B		
		Don't enter		Enter
Company A	No price struggle		0 __8__	−1 4
	Price struggle		0 __8__	−9 0

To abstain from a price struggle is still the best answer to a decision to enter, but not entering has become the strictly dominant strategy for the potential entrant.

Similar effects may be achieved through investments that improve A's cost structure so that even without price struggle an entrant would face losses given the price–cost

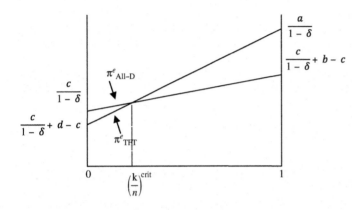

FIGURE 3.10 TFT and All-D payoff schedules in a population.

3.2.2 The Population Perspective

As you have seen, if the single-shot condition is fulfilled, there are two Nash equilibria (TFT/TFT and All-D/All-D) in the supergame we have looked at in the previous section. The best strategy choice for an agent depends on the choice by the player she meets in the game. Broadening the perspective now, we can imagine a population, in which players are randomly matched to play these supergames. The overall size of the group is given by n, the TFT-players in the group are given by k. In this case, the expected payoffs for the players change insofar as they have to include the probabilities that their opponent chooses All-D or TFT. As the best choice for a player depends on the choice of her opponent, both are viable strategy choices. The expected payoff for TFT-players is given by

$$\pi^e_{TFT} = \frac{k}{n}\frac{a}{1-\delta} + \frac{n-k}{n}\left(d - c + \frac{c}{1-\delta}\right)$$

The expected All-D payoff is,

$$\pi^e_{All-D} = \frac{k}{n}\left(b - c + \frac{c}{1-\delta}\right) + \frac{n-k}{n}\frac{c}{1-\delta}$$

As the single-shot condition is assumed to be fulfilled, we know that for some population share, the expected payoff for TFT has to be higher than that for All-D because both are best answers to themselves in the underlying game. A graphical representation of the payoff schedules for this case is shown in Figure 3.10.

The point at which the two payoff schedules intersect gives the population share from which the expected payoff from choosing TFT becomes higher than that of choosing All-D for increasing TFT-shares (an increasing number k in a given population of size n). We call this the *minimum critical mass* of TFT-players that have to be present in a population for the Pareto-superior Nash equilibrium to become viable. The share depends on the payoff structure, including the discount factor. The larger the δ, for a given payoff structure, the further to the left lays the intersection, meaning the smaller the minimum critical mass.

If the agents know about the respective shares in the population, they will decide accordingly and choose the strategy with the higher expected payoff; if they form expectations about the shares, it depends on what these expectations look like. As long as the agents know about the shares of strategies in the population, they have a strictly preferred choice, namely, the strategy with the higher expected payoff. In that case, they will all end up choosing the same strategy, and every agent plays either All-D or TFT in every round she enters. At that point, there is no mechanism within the setup of the game to let them change strategies and lead the agents in the population to choosing the other strategy.

This is of course especially interesting in case of a group in which every agent plays All-D. An All-D population reflects a situation in which each individually optimal decision contributes to an overall, individually as well as collectively, inferior result. A switch of strategies by a sufficient number of agents would promise a Pareto-superior result. But unless for some reason enough players switch strategies to reach the minimum critical mass, that Pareto-superior result is not attainable. As said, within the game there is no mechanism that might lead to such a minimum critical mass forming. For individuals taking their decision autonomously, an All-D environment is a stable, if inefficient, outcome. We may take this as a first hint at the increasing difficulty involved in solving even coordination problems in larger groups. Even though the agents are still matched in pairs of two in the supergames they play, changing their expectations regarding others' choices becomes more difficult as they have to be assured that a sufficiently large number of other players will adopt the globally preferable strategy as well in order to increase expected payoffs to the level where agents are willing to in fact make that choice.

In order to be able to argue for why a group of agents that has been playing All-D might eventually manage to switch to a TFT-outcome, we have to resort to a broader *process story*, for which we have to relax some of the assumptions about the agents. Relaxing those assumptions may allow us to introduce feelings such as frustration from the continued unattractive result obtained (*c* instead of the also possible *a*), learning effects, experimentation due to curiosity, or other motivations that may lead agents to experiment with different behavior patterns and transmit the results they may experience into the larger group.

3.2.3 Agency Mechanisms

The transformation of the problem structure (the single-shot solution) is one way that allows for a potential for agents to improve the results from their interactions. For another possible solution of the dilemma, we have to alter assumptions about the agents. Assume that agents are able to *monitor* other agents and that they have a certain *memory* period over which they can remember others' behavior. Also, they may be able to gain information about other players through third parties, in which case players can build a *reputation*. Additionally, assume that players can *use the information* that is available to them through these different channels and *reject* entering into *interactions* with other agents and so at least to some degree select their interaction partners. In that case, the probability for a TFT-player to interact with another TFT-player is presumably larger than their share in the population, the probability of an All-D player interacting with a TFT-player is accordingly lower than the TFT-share of the population. The changes in expected payoffs can be written as:

$$\pi^e_{TFT} = \left(\frac{k}{n}\right)^{\alpha} \frac{a}{1-\delta} + \left(1 - \left(\frac{k}{n}\right)^{\alpha}\right)\left(d - c + \frac{c}{1-\delta}\right)$$

$$\pi^e_{All-D} = \left(\frac{k}{n}\right)^{\frac{1}{\alpha}}\left(b - c + \frac{c}{1-\delta}\right) + \left(1 - \left(\frac{k}{n}\right)^{\frac{1}{\alpha}}\right)\frac{c}{1-\delta}$$

In order to introduce the difference between the share of cooperators in a population and the probability of playing against a cooperator in the following supergame, we have added a parameter representing agency mechanisms in the form of the exponent α. For $0 < \alpha < 1$, the probability of playing with a cooperator is larger than their share in the population for another TFT-player. Accordingly, the probability for an All-D player to interact with a TFT-player is lower than the TFT-share in the population.

Represented graphically, the schedules delineating expected payoffs (payoff schedules in the following text) then change as shown in Figure 3.11 (for the payoff schedules' shape, check the derivatives of the expected payoffs, that will give you $\pi^e(k/n)' > 0$ and $\pi^e(k/n)'' < 0$ for TFT-players and $\pi^e(k/n)' > 0$

and $\pi^e(k/n)'' > 0$ for All-D players). Note that in this approach, the underlying dilemma still exists as in this approach the single-shot condition is assumed not to be fulfilled (if it was, the minimum critical mass would simply be further reduced). As you can see, in this setup there result two intersections of the payoff schedules. The population share of cooperators is presented on the horizontal axis, again. In this case, a population in which both types of strategies continue to be played is one stable outcome, the other is the whole population playing All-D.

To the left of the first intersection, the expected payoff for All-D is higher than that for choosing TFT. No single player has an incentive to choose TFT; hence, the share of these players stays at zero. To the right of the first intersection, the expected payoff for TFT is larger than that for All-D. Hence, agents switch to TFT, and the share of TFT-players in the population increases. To the right of the second intersection, the expected payoff for choosing All-D is higher than that for the TFT-choice. It pays to switch to All-D therefore, and the share of TFT would be reduced. The second intersection, a *mixed population*, is therefore also a *stable outcome* in this setup.

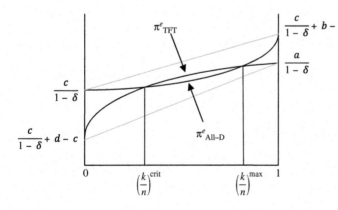

FIGURE 3.11 Payoffs in a population with agency capacities.

The exact intersections of the payoff schedules depend on the payoffs in the underlying game, the time horizon as mirrored in the discount factor, and the strength of the agency mechanisms as represented by the parameter α, where agency mechanisms are stronger the smaller α. The smaller the α is, the steeper the slope of the TFT-payoff schedule for low shares of cooperators in the population. We may interpret it as saying that the stronger the agency mechanisms are, the easier it is for TFT-players to identify and interact with one another. As the share of cooperators can be expected to increase once the first intersection has been crossed, for a given incentive structure, as a consequence, the stronger the agency mechanisms, the smaller the initial share of TFT-players (minimum critical mass) necessary for leading the system to the stable mixed population equilibrium. Note that this is basically a verbal description of what a replicator would show us in quantitative terms, with payoffs as the fitness indicator (for a formal presentation and explanation, see Chapter 8).

These formal approaches to problems individual agents may encounter show that there are a number of factors involved that may lead to changes in the assessment of a situation or that directly may allow agents to make individually preferable choices that lead to overall improved results. The time horizon under which agents make decisions can influence what kind of problem structure they are faced with. This relates to the weight they individually assign to future results (mirrored in the discount rate) and assumptions about the duration of specific interactions with other agents. Expectations about others' likely behavior choices matter once interaction partners are drawn from a larger population. Possibilities for increasing the information about other agents' past behavior and thereby presumably strengthening the base for the formulation of expectations regarding their future choices can also help agents realizing a superior overall result, particularly when coupled with the ability to one way or another have a choice regarding whom to interact with.

3.2.4 Institutionalization and Habituation of Cooperative Behavior: Rationally Rule-Behaving

As we have explained, the representation of problem structures as strictly rational agents would perceive and approach them is a helpful analytical approach, and solutions for specific problem structures, such as dilemma situations, that can be derived in such a setup are very promising for informing policy suggestions. But some questions can only tentatively be answered on this basis.

In the derivation of the single-shot solution, we assume interactions of pairs of agents. These may be able to coordinate on behavior patterns that lead to Pareto-superior results, given that the *time horizon* of their interaction is *sufficiently long* to make this worthwhile. This does, however, only tell us about two agents being able to *transform the problem they face in a long-run relationship*, not about the establishing of a cooperative culture, or the process leading up to such a situation, in a group of agents, where additionally interactions may be short-lived. And formally showing the emergence of a cooperative environment in an N-person game is much more difficult, if possible at all. Nevertheless, we observe such environments in real-world situations. Possible complementary perspectives include ones brought forth by *evolutionary economists* who argue that over time there may have been a selection toward predispositions for cooperative behavior as this translated into advantages for groups against groups in which defective behavior dominated. Still, even given such advantages, human agency and individual perceptions of problem situations and interaction partners mean that cooperation may break down again even if it has emerged. The understanding for the general problems involved and how these may be solved can therefore contribute to stabilizing cooperative environments, help reconstitute cooperation where it has been threatened, and establish cooperation between groups that had previously not been in contact. The results we can derive in 2-player games in the different environments considered above can be helpful starting points for this.

Adopting a population perspective allows us to extend the setup and thereby offers additional insights into a strengthening of cooperative environments, or the conditions for making it easier to advance them. Now, *expectations about others' behavior*, as expressed by the (expected) *probability of meeting cooperative partners*, are introduced into the setup. As we have seen, in the simple framework allowing for two strategies, this will lead to a situation in which either everyone chooses TFT, and hence de facto cooperates in every interaction, or everyone chooses All-D. However, the basic condition for this situation to become possible is still that the single-shot condition is fulfilled, and therefore that agents can expect to play many interactions with one another once they enter into a relation.

Transferring this analytical setup to real-world situations, agents have to *ignore the fact that in every interaction they still face a dilemma problem* and adopt a culture of recognized interdependence and a long-run perspective. Institutions, as social rules plus sanction mechanism (Chapter 1), that establish a rule under which agents *abstain from trying to gain a short-term advantage* over others are the tool-enabling agents in groups to nevertheless show behavior allowing the realization of a cooperative outcome. So, *a rule would suffice under single-shot conditions*, as it enables agents to solve the coordination problem they face there, but, when transferring our results to real-world situations, we have to be more cautious.

The at least latent dilemma structure in the background requires additional mechanisms enabling a stable cooperative environment (for consequences for policies, see Chapter 17).

Allowing for agency mechanisms permits the introduction of another way for establishing a cooperative environment. Agency mechanisms change the expected payoff of agents as a function of the share of cooperators in a population. Expected payoffs for TFT-players increase relative to a situation without agency, whereas those for All-D players are reduced. The problem in this setup may be seen as more pronounced again, as even in the supergames, the dilemma structure may be kept in place. Transferring the analytical setup to real-world problems, we can recognize that further support for the agents, enabling them to maintain cooperative behavior patterns, is going to be a very helpful, even necessary, addition. This support is gained from the institutional structure. Every group interacts under a set of rules and institutions. An institution's rule that is reaffirmed in *semiconscious behaviors*, in a habitual application, can lead agents to show cooperative behavior, even where the basic conditions would lead us to suspect that no such behavior should be observed.

These considerations also allow us to address a further question: Why extend cooperation to people you do not know about, in a *generalized culture of cooperation*? If agents face an underlying dilemma structure, and their time horizon is short, meaning they do not expect many interactions with the person they are facing at the moment, or if they do not know about that person, why should and do they still opt for a cooperative kind of behavior? Within the different setups utilized so far, there is no answer to this question; in fact, the agents we have utilized for the explanations so far would not make such a choice. What we might argue is that following the behavioral rule of the institution is based on the understanding that the maintenance of the institution (that may have emerged in a setup involving smaller groups) benefits the (larger) group in the long run. However, here some defecting agents may, conceivably relatively quickly, lead to the breakdown of the institution, or at least prevent an extension of it being applied in the larger group as well. Remember that the only thing keeping it alive is agents following it. As long as they do, the *individually rational incentive to defect in a dilemma situation* can be kept in check by generally accepted behavioral rules. If the only reason for them to follow an institution is the long-term benefit of the group this may lead to, we need a very pronounced understanding of this possible long-term development, and a very pronounced check on desires of distinguishing oneself within the group through enhancing one's economic potential in order to limit the temptation of giving in to trying to exploit other players.

An institution provides this. And more *stability* results if cooperation is understood as the result of *habitual behavior* that is enabled by and embodied in social institutions. As also explained, *limited cognitive capacities* (bounded rationality) in complex situations (*n*-player populations) make such behavioral rules necessary, because *agents cannot make conscious decisions in every moment and situation they face*. Furthermore, such institutions likewise *serve to reduce the degree of strategic complexity and uncertainty* that agents face by informing them about socially acceptable behavior patterns and hence about what generally to expect from counterparts in a given situation.

Once *we give up the assumption of strictly (boundedly or not) economically "rational" agents*, decisions no longer have to be purely informed by achievable payoffs. Patterns may emerge that are not strictly "rational" from an individual point of view; the time horizon is short, the single-shot condition therefore not satisfied, and defection the strictly dominant choice, but still cooperation is observed. Other factors shaping behaviors have to play a role here.

A social institution directs agents to play cooperatively even in a dilemma situation. Once it is in place, it may eventually be accepted without the connection to the agents who may have developed it, as a *general norm* in situations where the dilemma structure is in place (the single-shot condition is not fulfilled) and agency mechanisms play no important role (as agents from different peer groups interact, for instance). The institution has in that case become detached from any specific relations, and constitutes a generally accepted code of behavior. Agents accept these behavioral rules independently of the exchange relation they are about to enter as a generally applicable norm. This effect is called *reconstitutive downward causation* as it involves an institution that has emerged and is now established on the aggregate ("macro" or "meso," see Chapter 14) level affecting individual agents' choices, their behavior on the micro-level.

But, you still have to believe in another person adhering to the institution, even if for her that means *sacrificing* the potential gain from another possible behavioral option. For a cooperative outcome to become possible, you have to believe the other person to be willing to forego the short-term gain that defection promises, even if you do not expect to have a long-term relation with the person; what is more, the other person has to come to the same assessment, as otherwise she may defect in order to protect herself from being exploited, and not even from the desire to try and exploit you. The reputation of agents matters here.

But once a generally cooperative environment has emerged, it may be more easily sustained as agents do not consciously decide on whether they think other players follow the institutional rule or not, but simply habitually take a certain decision in a given moment. Once the behaviors and results have repeatedly been reaffirmed, there is no reason for further continued questioning of behavioral decisions. Individual agents simply habitually apply certain behavior patterns in this case. Likewise, expectations may not be consciously formed any longer, but simply be the result of habitual thought patterns that the agents are unaware of. Only once agents are caught by surprise when others start not to act in accordance with the institution might they be forced to reconsider their behaviors.

This connects to another aspect of relations between agents that can be included in our considerations, namely, *trust*. When referring to trust, we usually imply that agents have faith in others to make choices that do not harm them, even though the others have the possibility to do so (for their own gain). A functioning institutional frame supporting cooperative behavior can then lead to the constitution of a more trustful environment as agents who are willing to engage in cooperative behavior can be perceived as trustworthy by others. This in turn may allow for the emergence of habitually trusting behavior, in selected interaction arenas or groups at first, and in turn, potentially, transferred to the general environment, detached from personal relations and transferred to less familiar acquaintances or even strangers (also see Chapter 14).

Further Reading

Foster, J., 2005. From simplistic to complex systems in economics. Cambridge J. Econ. 29 (6), 873–892.
Friedman, J.W., 1994. Problems of Coordination in Economic Activity. Economics as Sciences of Coordination. Kluwer Academic Publishers, Boston, Dordrecht, London.
Kosfeld, M., Okada, A., Riedl, A., 2009. Institution formation in public goods games. Am. Econ. Rev. 99 (4), 1335–1355.

Ostrom, E., 2000. Collective action and the evolution of social norms. J. Econ. Perspect. 14 (3), 137–158.
Pelligra, V., 2011. Intentions, trust and frames: a note on sociality and the theory of games. Rev. Soc. Econ. 79 (2), 163–188.

Further Reading—Online

For further reading, see the textbook website at http://booksite.elsevier.com/9780124115859

EXERCISES

1. Briefly describe the range of problem structures that agents can face in interdependent decision situations.
2. What distinguishes social optimum and social dilemma situations from coordination problems?
3. What problem that agents may face beyond a necessity for assurance does a stag hunt game illustrate?
4. What game can you use for describing a coordination problem with asymmetric interests between the agents? Also, think of an example of a situation where this may be helpful for understanding a real-world problem.
5. Which are considered typical examples of social dilemma situations? Where do the specific problems arise from in these?
6. How can agents who take their decisions exclusively based on their payoffs realize a Pareto-optimal result in a social dilemma problem?
7. What condition has to be fulfilled when a social dilemma problem is changed in a repeated game? Derive this condition from the payoffs of the agents.
8. What can you learn about the possibilities for Pareto-improvements in dilemma situations from the single-shot condition?
9. In a dilemma game as shown in Figure 3.8, let $a = 4$ and $c = 2$. For calculating payoffs in the related supergame, let $\delta = 0,9$ ($\delta = 0,5$). What is the maximum value of b

for which the single-shot condition still holds?

10. In a dilemma game as shown in Figure 3.8, let $b = 10$ and $c = 2$. For calculating payoffs in the related supergame, let $\delta = 0{,}8$ ($\delta = 0{,}5$). What is the minimum value of a for which the single-shot condition holds?

11. Assume a population perspective on a dilemma-based supergame. Calculate the value for $(k/n)^{crit}$ (the intersection of the payoff schedules as shown in Figure 3.10).

12. How can institutions support agents when it comes to realizing improved results in dilemma situations? Why does a simple rule not suffice in such a situation?

Approaching Real-World Interdependence and Complexity: Empirical Phenomena in the Global Economy*

"[...] aggregate transaction costs as a whole had a clear increasing trend in the history of the industrial revolution and division of labor, which was driven by increasing network complexity and innovation uncertainty. [...] Reducing transaction costs is the main argument for financial deregulation, which is the root of the current financial crisis." **Ping Chen**[1]

"There tends to be a lack of communication and co-operation in the supply chain, and the process is not marked by a great deal of trust." **Oliver Loebel**[2]

*This chapter was coauthored by Claudius Gräbner.

[1]Author of the book *Economic Complexity and Equilibrium Illusion*, London, New York: Routledge, 2010; interview in *World Economics Association Newsletter*, **3.4** (2013), p. 10.

[2]Secretary General of the European Technical Contractors Committee for the Construction Industry, in: *European Innovation* (published by the European Commission, Enterprise and Industry DG, ISSN 1830-4338), November 2006, p. 9.

The Microeconomics of Complex Economies.
DOI: http://dx.doi.org/10.1016/B978-0-12-411585-9.00004-X

4.1 INTRODUCTION

Today's economies are inherently *complex*, in terms of *numbers of agents* involved in economic processes and *agents' heterogeneity* (for a detailed and more formal explanation of complexity, see Chapter 11). And this may easily be more the case than ever before. In order to properly understand complex economies, we are required to apply adequate tools. In Chapters 1–3, we have acquired some basic theories and tools, which already enable us to shed some light on important basic aspects of the real-world economy. In this chapter, we will explain real-world issues, and you may practice the application of your theoretical knowledge acquired so far and of those tools.

The central aspects of today's economies to be scrutinized are:

1. *Value-added chains* (VACs) are functionally and spatially *decentralized* and largely *fragmented*, not only on a national, but on a *global* level, and, thus *many*, and many *heterogeneous agents* are involved in any production and innovation process of ever more complex products (see, e.g., Ruigrok and van Tulder, 1995; Amin, 1999; Kingston, 2000; Rupert, 2000; Perraton, 2001; Biswas, 2002; Bair, 2008; Baldwin and Venables, 2010; Li et al., 2010).
2. Digitized microelectronic and *network-based tele-information and communication technologies* (TICs) have become ubiquitous, and with this, *external effects* of individual decisions on others, namely, the increasing value (utility, benefit) of a growing technology network for those already in it through the adoption of this technology by a new user (*network externality*) (see, e.g., Orlikowski and Iacono, 2000; Hutter, 2001; Gottinger, 2003; Shy, 2001, 2010). Note that we deviate from the usual abbreviation for TICs as ICTs—*information and communication technologies*. We consider it more important to stress the fact that this communication is not just a technology but a long-distance interaction (tele = remote).
3. *Local clusters* and *networks*, each involving *many and different agents*, have become important *organizational forms* in the economy, shaping the behavior of the agents involved by providing *new forms of coordination and cooperation* among firms and people under conditions of increasing uncertainty. Famous cases of spatial agglomerations that have developed effective coordination and cooperation and, have been, superior systemic performance, are the *Silicon Valley* or the so-called *Third Italy* (see, e.g., Lazonick, 1993; Baker, 1996; Cox, 1997; Rallet and Torre, 1998; Steiner, 1998; Tichy, 1998; Maillat and Grosjean, 1999; Gertler et al., 2000; Malmberg et al., 2004; Feldman and Braunerhjelm, 2006; Orsenigo, 2006; Bair, 2008; Coe et al., 2008; Sturgeon et al., 2008; Lane and Probert, 2009; Diez-Vial and Alvarez-Suescun, 2010; Garon, 2012; Kamath et al., 2012).

It becomes immediately clear that *direct interdependencies* and *direct interactions* among economic agents, with related *strategic uncertainty* and requirements of rule-based *coordination* or institutionalized *cooperation* do matter in these contexts—as pointed out in Chapters 1–3. If direct interactions among agents occur recurrently and sequentially, this will generate path-dependent, cumulative, open evolutionary processes where coordination and cooperation may emerge.

Direct interdependencies have always been present in real economies and have been anticipated by socioeconomists from all perspectives from the very beginning of modern economics in the eighteenth century (for a history of complex economic thought, see Chapter 12).

We will introduce some basic issues of complex economies of our times. The problems have already been investigated by economists employing methods of complex microeconomic analysis, and we will refer to their empirical work frequently in the following. If you are interested in cases presented in this chapter, this will enable you to conduct some additional investigation by starting with the contributions referenced here.

The remainder of this chapter is structured as follows: We first consider the era of so-called *neoliberal deregulation* of markets and states, which was launched in the mid-1970s. We will explain why this cannot be a cure under conditions of complexity, as it was postulated, but aggravates problems of uncertainty, market failure, and noncoordination/noncooperation rather (Sections 4.2.1 and 4.2.2). We then take a more detailed look on the implications of global deregulation for VACs (Section 4.2.3) and explain the new *ambiguous role of TICs* with respect to *coordination*, i.e., technological and behavioral *standardization* (Section 4.2.4) and their *network effects*. We also consider cumulative and path-dependent evolutionary processes, looking at *practical examples* (Section 4.2.5). Thereafter, we show how individual economic agents commonly *react* to economic complexity under conditions of *individualistic and uncertain decision-making*, i.e., how they use *larger hierarchies and power* in an effort to *maintain control* over their increasingly volatile environment, but also how they engage in *cluster coordination* and *network cooperation*, and, finally, how they combine hierarchy/power and the new coordination/cooperation forms into hub&spoke network forms (Section 4.3). We conclude the chapter by considering what the real-world experience tells us for further microeconomic theory and modeling (Section 4.4).

4.2 THE SPECIFIC INHERENT COMPLEXITY, VOLATILITY, AND UNCERTAINTY OF TODAY'S REAL-WORLD ECONOMY

4.2.1 The "Organized Capitalism Plus Welfare State and Proactive Policies," 1930s Through 1970s: A Shaping Role for Social Institutions

After the *Great Depression*, which began in 1929, after the experience of the proactive and interventionist so-called *New Deal* 1933−1938 in the USA during the era of President Roosevelt, after John Maynard Keynes' theoretical revolution in favor of proactive state agency (details in Chapter 12), and after the experience of war- and defense-industries-led growth during *World War II*, a socio-politico-economic paradigm of some "organized capitalism" cum welfare state and proactive policies had come to prevail (see Box 4.1), up to the late 1970s (which, of course, also had to do with the then existing competition between the two large political world systems, "western" capitalism and "eastern" state socialism, which ended by the end of the 1980s). This, however, through its very economic and social success (stabilization and growth), while leaving the system unchanged in its basic microeconomic structures, entailed *ever-growing integrated corporate hierarchies* (the so-called "Fordist," highly formalized and bureaucratic production system), thus ever more narrow *oligopolistic market structures* with ever higher concentration and centralization of capital, also some social codetermination by *trade unions* and corporate *labor representatives*, and some proactive and interventionist macro-regulating policies cum some welfare state.[3] "Organized capitalism" meant that whole areas of

---

[3]This was also called bastard-Keynesian economic-policy paradigm; bastard-Keynesian, as, different to Keynes' analysis and reform program, governments left the microeconomic structures untouched; again, for more detail on Keynes and Keynesianism, see Chapter 12.

BOX 4.1

"ORGANIZED CAPITALISM PLUS WELFARE STATE" AND "DEREGULATED NEOLIBERAL MARKET ECONOMY" COMPARED (NONEXHAUSTIVE)

Key properties of the "organized capitalism plus welfare state"-economy (post-WWII—end of 1970s):

- strong hierarchies in large corporate organizations;
- production in companies mostly organized at the national level;
- reinvestment of profits for future production capacity and product lines;
- open support (directly and indirectly) for domestic producers by the country's political leadership;
- strengthened workers' rights and increasing wage share of GDP as a result of stronger trade unions power in tandem with the socioeconomic competition with the soviet-communist world, and of better education;
- more inclusive and extended social systems (for the same reasons as mentioned before);
- increasing social upward mobility;
- from the 1970s onward, transition from industry to services, or, from an industrial to a postindustrial society (including social trends such as a decline of traditional family structures, an improved social standing of women, and of minorities);
- slowly noticeable broader impact of the rise of information technology.

Key properties of the "deregulated neoliberal market economy" (since end of 1970s):

- emergence of increasingly transnational corporations and the spatial fragmentation of VACs;
- outsourcing and functional fragmentation of the VACs: dominant hub&spoke network structures;

- supported by increasing capacities and capabilities in IT;
- erosion of workers' rights, and falling wage share in GDP, stagnating real wages, "flexibilization" and precarization of labor;
- reduction of depth and extension of social systems;
- privatization of public sector services;
- political focus on austerity policies, usually at the expense of labor and weaker social groups;
- deregulation of the financial sector, with cascades of derivatives and increased leveraging; much higher incidence of financial crashes and financial sector-induced crises since the early 1980s;
- company orientation on short-term financial indicators, reduction of funds for reinvestment in the operations of the company.

Under a systemic perspective, the recognition of the interaction of these distinct aspects is an important feature of analysis.

There are some shifts within the system as described. The increased utilization of IT (TIC) in production processes, organization, and service provision, may exacerbate some of the mentioned aspects and may strengthen specific transmission channels between them. Industrial and postindustrial economies' general tendencies toward monopolization, or at least oligopolization (see Chapter 7 for details) may be further strengthened as there are network effects on the customer side of markets in IT products. If related information and knowledge in production is proprietary, these tendencies can be expected to gain yet more traction. In sum, there are noticeable dynamics potentially pushing technological systems and subsystems toward lock-ins on specific standards

---

BOX 4.1 *(cont'd)*

(for more detail see Chapter 15). At the same time, the fragmentation of value-added chains raises issues of compatibility of operations between autonomous agents. Positions of dominance in production networks, and possible power to dictate standards, may increase power imbalances between agents, or, can be a valuable instrument of control for already influential agents. Again, tendencies toward lock-ins are fostered. While standardization is necessary for easing, or even enabling, interactions, the resulting limitation of available alternatives also puts bounds on the innovative potential. Tensions

regarding innovative capacity and interoperability on large scales can be expected to persist, if not increase. The economic changes described in this box are also influenced by and do interact with other—political and social—processes. For instance, much of the developing world has succeeded in leaving behind some brutal forms of dictatorship and oppression over the last decades. Some developing countries also commenced a catchup process with the developed world in economic and technological.terms. Modern information and communication technology may have played a part in this.

---

socioeconomic life were—after the disastrous experience with classical liberalism, i.e., with *economic-policy abstinence* and defeatism, and subsequent crisis and depression in the 1930s—increasingly *embedded into systems of social rules and institutions*, such as *labor-protection law* and rules of *wage determination*, for *setting up and doing business*, for *production* and products, for *international trade* and foreign direct investment, some *currency regulation*, for dealings with *money and finance, unemployment* compensation and protection, public further education for unemployed, health care systems, retirement and pension legislation, and so on.

However, this socioeconomic and political micro- and macro-constellation had, for instance, through endowing the laboring classes with some basic rights, inherently caused some organized *income distribution struggle* between large corporate capital and organized labor from the 1960s onwards, with increasing *price-push inflation* by "big corporation" and sometimes some *wage-push* through organized labor, further, a tendency toward *output restriction* and *price increase* by big oligopolistic corporations, including their negative output reaction rather than price reduction in

downswings, and, in all, a combined tendency toward *stagflation* with, in the end, increasing *unemployment* again. In a phase of increased income distribution struggle and social conflict (end of 1960s and beginning of 1970s)—a phase that was alleged to be characterized by "overcomplexity," particularly for public agency, and, thus, by "state failure"—the time seemed ripe for a return to a "liberal" politico-economic paradigm, this time, once and for all, dismantling the welfare state and labor rights, reducing state activity, and restoring the power of "the markets."

4.2.2 "Market Deregulation" as the "Neoliberal" Response to the Complexity Challenge

Politico-Economic Paradigm Change, the Era of "Neoliberal" Deregulation, and its Outcomes

As a response to those economic and social problems of that earlier economic paradigm—prepared and supported by some theoretical *economic-paradigm change* (the so-called "monetarism," "supply-side economics," and "new market and competition economics" revolution, in political terms the so-called "neo-liberalism" revolution) and enforced by the leading corporations, the finance sector, corporate think tanks, mass media, publishers, etc.—most governments switched over from proactive welfare-state policies to the *deregulation of markets* and their *disembedding from many social rules and institutions*, which had cared for organizing stability, interest balancing, and the common good for all. This entailed the organization by the governments of an *exclusive global layer for productive and capital traffic*, tightened corporate and property rights, *reduction of state* activity and of public wealth (*privatization*), *reducing labor rights* and the welfare state, etc., in order to deregulate economic behavior in general and to allow for the emergence of new markets and for *less binding social rules and institutions*.

Markets and capitalist market economies have been deregulated on a comprehensive, large-scale, and long-run basis since then. This includes:

1. *labor law*, with a subsequent reduction of average labor costs and a long-run redistribution into profits worldwide;
2. the *law of setting up business*, which has fostered *outsourcing* and *functional VAC fragmentation*;
3. *foreign-trade law*, which supported the international expansion of the largest companies, the *global spatial VAC fragmentation*, and global hub&spoke-type sourcing networks;
4. the *law of banking and of the financial speculation sector*, which increased overall systemic volatility up to the *Great Recession* and crises of 2007ff. (see, e.g., Chen, 2010).

Further, this included

5. the dispensing of former public property and wealth (*privatization*), with a subsequent *regulation of oligopolistic competition* in postal, traffic, IT sectors and energy;
6. the reduction of the welfare state and social security.

This was declared to provide the best answer to the macroeconomic problems mentioned, to *reduce the complexity of the decision problems of the state* (politicians and bureaucracies), to generate global competition, to make "markets" provide more "efficiency," and thus to enhance economic growth to the benefit of all.

The historically emerged arrangements of *social rules and institutions* was *abandoned* on a large scale, which opened up new space for action and profit-making for corporations, particularly for the large and internationally active ones that had all opportunities to expand into a newly deregulated "free" global space and *control fragmented and cheap labor worldwide*, and for the money and finance industries. But at the same time, it *increased the volatility* of the system as a whole, and *turbulence* (i.e., the relative rate of change of external conditions) and *uncertainty* for individual agents, even for the largest and most powerful corporate benefiters.

In addition, *new large public−private deregulation bureaucracies* entered the action space, which—in contrast to the official "neoliberal" rhetoric—further *increased the complexity of the individual decision situation*, even for the largest players. While the "neoliberal" rhetoric *intended a reduction of systemic complexity* through "more market," this indeed was perhaps achieved for the public agents and for politicians, but the individual decision situations for most private agents included increasing complexity.

And whether the system complexity as a whole was in fact increased or reduced must remain an open question for the time being (for more detail on the alternative measures of *complexity* see Chapter 11).

What corporate leaders, think-tank spokesmen, and "neoliberal" and "neoconservative" policy makers and economists had in mind, declared, and predicted was a revival of the "invisible hand" metaphor. In theoretical terms, this implied that maximally unregulated "markets" were some sort of *social optimum games* (see Chapter 3), with an inherent tendency toward *predetermined and stable equilibrium* (see Chapters 5 and 6). Therefore, all that had to be done was to enable every agent to follow her *short-run individualistic selfish interest in the "markets."* If everybody would be doing so, the social optimum for society would be achieved automatically.

Deregulated Markets Are Not a General Cure—on Relevant Real-World Modeling

Unfortunately, this has never been the case and was not the case here. *Adam Smith*'s metaphor of the "invisible hand" was embedded in his theory of strong informal social and formal legal *institutions* (for more details, see Chapter 12). After a long story of 40 years of "neoliberal" deregulation, institutions-, rules-, and state-dismantling, privatization, redistribution of rights, income, wealth, and power to the upper ranks, the global economy has, in fact, experienced a phase of *increasing volatility, turbulence, complexity of individual decision problems,* and *macroeconomic and financial crises*— with its preliminary climax of the *Great Recession* of 2007ff.

And as we already know from the preceding chapters, most real-world microeconomic decision problems are represented by *coordination and dilemma games.* In spontaneous decentralized systems, such as deregulated markets, with more or less intricate direct interdependencies, a simple deregulation, disregarding direct interdependencies and a long-run perspective, but enforcing short-run individualism rather, may easily be a counterproductive measure to achieve a high performance of the system. It might only be superior in the sense of *individualistic redistribution* of the powerful, as a prisoners' dilemma, *chicken*, or *hawk-dove game* compared to a social optimum game. This might be the case the more powerful agents are enabled by the governments to increase the *asymmetry of payoffs* in their favor.

We will describe the "ideal" market in Chapter 5. What underlies this model of an ideal market is an agent with perfect information on present givens and the future, where all information is a collective good but provided without any problems. Uncertainty, asymmetric information, or bounded rationality is assumed away. Similarly, direct interdependence, externalities, or power relations do not play a role. And if agents could be assumed to have equal preferences, a pure coordination through the price mechanism would be unproblematic (see Chapters 5 and 6).

In this chapter, we will show that external effects, incomplete information, bounded rationality, etc. indeed play a central role in reality and this leads to particular behaviors, actions, reactions, and economic forms in the real world.

To be sure, any *model* and any *modeling* have to make *assumptions* and in the previous chapters we have used a number of them. Many of the assumptions are not realistic, e.g., the initial characterization of the agents in our games. The art of economic modeling is to choose the most effective assumptions in order to get a tractable, but equally adequate and thus illuminating, model of reality. Assuming central problems away is not a good start.

We will confine us below, for didactical reasons, on *coordination and dilemma games*, being aware of three *methodological issues*: First, in some cases, *other game structures*, be it variants of a coordination game, or be it anti-coordination games rather than a social dilemma, may be more adequate to map some real-world problems; second, we will abstract in this chapter, for the time being, from dynamic aspects in modeling, such as those represented in, e.g., the Schumpeterian idea of an *innovative individual entrepreneur* or in other issues of *break outs from static coordination and cooperation forms* (for Schumpeter, see Chapter 12); third, we will always have to take care for the trade-off between model simplicity and empirical relevance (or explanatory power).

You have already learned from the notion of *bounded rationality* (see Chapter 1) that for economic agents to make reasonable decisions and to perform well in the real world, some *reduction of the complexity and uncertainty*, which inevitably exists in real-world situations of strategic interdependence, is required. This is usually carried out through emerging social rules and institutions that individual agents, in myriads of social interactions, tend to adopt and follow for reasons of their long-run interest (for the basic idea, see the *single-shot logic* in Chapter 3).

So it is highly questionable whether the deregulation of markets was a good measure, and the concept of the *fallacy of aggregation* (see Chapter 1) gives you a first hint about why it usually is not. This is why critical liberals in the tradition of A. Smith's theory of social institutions (see Chapter 12) always have considered de-regulated markets moral "suckers". Certainly, the link between the striving of individual agents to reduce complexity and the overall economic performance is not a trivial one and will have to be further specified throughout this textbook (see in particular Chapters 6, 7, 10, 11, and 13 on *levels of system complexity and effective individual decision-making*).

The Global Deregulated Economy in an "Institutional Disequilibrium"?

The globalization process has been analyzed by many as a long-run political and public-administrative project, (de)regulated, on the one hand, by liberalization, and global empowerment of capital, and corporate concerns and, on the other hand, by still national regulation and control of the more general interests and social concerns (labor regulation, employment, health, social security, etc.; see, e.g., Jones, 2000; Kingston, 2000; Rupert, 2000; Perraton, 2001, 678ff.). The global layer of exclusive corporate activities has been characterized as being largely *disembedded* from the historically developed arrangements of social institutions that used to

exist in the nation-states and in national and regional—local cultures. The "neoliberal" construction of the global space, in that critical perspective, also *reduced collective action capacities, coordination, cooperation*, and *social control* for societies and governments (see, e.g., Amin, 1999; Jones, 2000; Standing, 2001; Biswas, 2002).[4] The global system, therefore, has been called a system in institutional disequilibrium, characterized by an *increasing excess demand of international collective goods*, while their supply decreases (Padoan, 2001). In this way, the global economy would not provide enough institutional structure to reduce complexity sufficiently to make agents (companies, governments, and societal agents of all kinds) capable to behave in coordinated, cooperative, and thus problem-solving ways, but it would even add to *increasing complexity* and *turbulence* for individual decision makers, and to *systemic volatility* (see the cumulation of crises worldwide since the 1990s).

In this context, even the most powerful corporate global players face an increased level of complexity, uncertainty, and turbulence, a degree of complexity that has been considered even *overcomplexity* (see, e.g., Armstrong, 2001, 533ff., 541ff.), as it has been *made* through institutional disembedding and could be easily reduced through institutional reembedding (on overturbulence for firms, see also, e.g., Cordes, 2008). As a result, also *transaction costs* often tend to increase, particularly as uncertainty often increases *information costs* considerably.

Note that we are talking about *basic information* here, which is to be *shared* in order to *remediate strategic uncertainty*, a *collective good*, the provision of which is all but trivial—and, in fact, to be carried out through the very process of learned institutionalized cooperation, and then available in abundance. As long as this has not collectively succeeded yet, an

---

[4]On the other hand, *social media*, such as Twitter and Facebook, generally are expected to increase collective action capacity through providing opportunities of organizing collective events or of building new networks (for details on this, see Chapter 15).

individualistic strategy to acquire information needed may indeed have to incur *infinite transaction (information) costs*. (This, in turn, is not to deny that other kinds of information may be private goods, good for individual competitive use, which, thus, may have private utility, be scarce, and, therefore, have an individual price and can be acquired through a "market".)

This also generates an incentive structure such that *even the most powerful corporate hierarchies* find it necessary to *increase their power even more* and faster in order just to *maintain the earlier level of control* over their socioeconomic environment. As a consequence of this, social and economic inequality becomes an ever more striking problem, both on a national and global scale (Stiglitz, 2012; Galbraith, 2012).

4.2.3 Fragmentation of the VACs and Technological Standardization

Spatial and Functional Fragmentation

Through the combined processes of *outsourcing* and *global distribution* of the corporations' production and labor force, VACs were fragmented (in terms of greater numbers of smaller agents involved) both in a spatial and in a functional (i.e., vertical supply) dimension. In an effort to *reduce labor costs* and to make use of an enhanced, and on average cheaper, labor force worldwide, products were no longer produced in one single firm. Rather, different components of a certain end product are produced by different specialized subcompanies (functional disintegration of VACs), which are often operating in different places all over the world (spatial disintegration of VACs) (see, e.g., Lane and Probert, 2009). By doing so, firms allocate production steps according to the required type of labor into the countries, in which the respective type of labor is cheapest and/or abundant and the social and juridical framework allows production with maximum margin. The most profitable steps in the VAC are kept within the own company of the

assembler and brand holder of the final product, while less profitable steps are outsourced into subcontractors.

The *clothing industry* provides numerous recent examples, but also the *Apple Corporation* was in the news because of its subcontractors in Asia, where expenditures for employee security and wages were lowest. This process also comes with the *redefinition of the boundaries of the corporate organization* (see Chapter 16 for more on this).

A System of Externalities, Entailing "Inappropriability"

Due to the fragmentation of the VACs and the corresponding division of labor, the individual firm's production, and in particular R&D and innovation efforts, will face a constant *information and knowledge outflow* across the firm's boundaries into other firms (customers, users) of the VAC that can make good use of it, based on the exchange of products (parts) among firms. This outflow of new knowledge to many others is unavoidable. It may entail a situation, in which *R&D costs cannot be fully recovered by the sales price*, as the customers would know that the new knowledge embodied in the new product cannot easily be protected or kept secret, but will *tend to become open information very quickly* (on (in)appropriability conditions and strategies, see, e.g., Cohen et al., 2000). Consequently, some positive externalities are inevitably generated and potential profits cannot be properly appropriated through revenues (see, e.g., Andersen and Frenz, 2008; Waterman and Ji, 2012). This is known as inappropriability in the industrial and innovation systems literature.

However, in a functioning, cooperatively coordinated production and innovation system (VAC)—disregarding, for the time being, a hierarchical order- and control-based coordination in hub&spoke supplier networks—such inappropriability will be healed through a *related smooth and continuous inflow of positive externalities* (new knowledge) from other firms (suppliers).

A working system, *effective governance*, or even deliberate management, of such *externalities exchange*, in fact, requires an established learned *system of coordination, cooperation*, and *related trust* (see, e.g., Bresnahan et al., 2001; Moore and Davis, 2004; Dobusch and Schuessler, 2012, 625ff.; for the *Silicon Valley* case, see, e.g., as the classical study Saxenian, 1994; for the *Third Italy* case, see, e.g., as the classical study Brusco, 1982).

If, however, such a coordination and cooperation system has not stably emerged yet, a rational firm, under certain conditions, might be incited or even forced to adopt a *free-rider position*, i.e., to reduce its own R&D efforts and to exploit the positive externalities generated by the other firms in the same VAC, i.e., a knowledge that inevitably comes across them.

A Social Dilemma Involved

Let us describe the situation in more abstract terms. In order to do so, we try to simplify the problem as much as possible, making use of your game-theoretic skills acquired so far. While producing *integrated and increasingly complex products* involves an obvious problem among many different and formally independent firms of *coordination on the same technological standards*, also a social dilemma problem is involved.

Assume we investigate a VAC consisting of two firms, *A* and *B*. As knowledge-intense and continuously innovated product parts and, with this, new knowledge (that cannot easily be protected, e.g., through formal patenting and licensing, for different reasons; see again, e.g., Cohen et al., 2000) are permanently exchanged between the two, innovations and new production techniques invented by one firm are revealed to the other firm almost immediately.

Therefore, individualistic, short-run rational firms have an individualistic incentive not to invest into the R&D of new products and technologies at all and to *avoid own major R&D expenses*, hoping that the other will bear the

R&D costs for his part, and will innovate and send technologically updated parts along the chain. The free-rider firm then might hope to *do reverse engineering* with the products it gets delivered and in this way learn from the innovation of the other without much own effort. But if no firm invested into R&D, there would be no innovations at all. To formulate this problem as a normal-form dilemma game should be easy (see Exercise 2 at the end of this chapter).

By applying game-theoretic reasoning, we can clarify a severe problem faced by many VACs in the global economy. In reality, VACs normally consist of many more than two firms, intensifying the problem into an *n*-agents public-good game with greater anonymity. The dilemma situation, particularly the incentive to defect, may be expected to be more severe if there are more than two firms involved with less transparency.

The Necessity of Technological Compatibility and Behavioral Coordination and Cooperation

Functional fragmentation obviously requires ensuring *technological* (and, with this, also *behavioral*) *compatibility* or (as used with IT systems) *interoperability* in the VAC, in an effort to coordinate and generate some minimum *reintegration* of the VAC, and with this a more effective production and innovation, even on a fragmented basis (see, e.g., Langlois, 2003; Nagler, 2008; Hyndman et al., 2010). (We might also talk of a *quasi-reintegration*, as the integration will remain based on a fragmented structure and will not be led back into on large hierarchy.) In the previous example, we assumed some successful coordination between the two firms, because if they had been unable to coordinate on compatible technologies, product parts would not have been interchangeable effectively between the two firms.

Thus, international restructuring, it has been argued, is as much a *struggle over the problems of uncertainty and transaction costs* through *new forms of coordination and cooperation* as it has been an effort for the provision of cheap labor, resources, and new sales opportunities (see, e.g., Ruigrok and van Tulder, 1995; Raikes et al., 2000). We will see in the next sections that the problem of technological interoperability is not an exemption or fringe phenomenon but the rule and at the core of modern manufacturing processes.

An Example: Interaction with Service Providers and Customers

The production process in general has not only been separated into many different production steps. In particular, manufacturing processes and *service* provision have become divided from each other and "outsourced" into autonomous units. Thus, these new units also are directly interdependent with each other and with the other components of the VAC, and, again, collective learning processes that ensure proper coordination and cooperation between them are required (see, e.g., Rabach and Kim, 1994). This will be facilitated through the emergence of *dense interaction in close spatial relations* (see, e.g., Bennett et al., 2000; Goldenberg, 2010).

On top of that, and independent of the first argument, manufacturing firms, with their generally limited knowledge and uncertainty about the different dimensions, future potentials, and further path-dependent developments of their complex technologies and products, increasingly need to interact and coordinate nowadays not only with their prime suppliers and service firms but also with their lead customers (users), in order to gain more information on use profiles and future directions of innovating the product or technology (see, e.g., Prandelli et al., 2008; Yang and Liang, 2010). To put it simpler, a company has to secure dense contacts with its most important customers in order to respond adequately to their future needs and to sustain the business relation.

With all this, it has been argued in the empirical industrial-economics literature, information and technological knowledge have become increasingly *user- and context-specific* and often even *tacit*. Note that tacit knowledge is not easily accessible to codification and formal transfer. So, it must be *jointly developed* and *collectively learned* in a dense multilateral interaction process, often with mutual plain *imitation*, *learning from doing* of the others, based on *trust* and institutionalized cooperation. Again, effective action is not feasible unless governed by coordination and cooperation (see, e.g., Casciaro, 2003; Gereffi et al., 2005; Ruys, 2005; Gibbon, 2008).

Note that our argument for learned rule-based coordination and institutionalized cooperation particularly applies to the ideal situation of *many independent firms*, usually *small- and medium-sized enterprises* (SMEs), acting on an *equal footing*.

They have, as argued above, as a "net" of firms, in the first instance a *technological and behavioral standardization problem* in any regular production (P) process, i.e., a common *coordination* problem, playing a coordination game. In the second instance, in particular in *innovation processes* (some ΔP), there also exist social dilemma problems, and they are involved in prisoners' dilemma games, having a collective cooperation problem (the terminology you have learned in the previous chapters).

Note that we have argued and will further explain later that alternatively, large *hierarchies* exert more *power-based forms of coordination* over many SMEs in global sourcing *hub&spoke networks*, which combine hierarchy/power and the basic fragmented net structure. This may have some advantage of effectivity over ideal voluntary and learned SME networks. However, we will consider below the obvious disadvantages for the SMEs or the regions involved that their dependence on large powerful corporate hierarchies has.

4.2.4 Digital Information, Competing Network Technologies, and Network Externalities

Digital Microelectronic Technologies of Tele-Communication and -Information, and Resulting Network Effects

Today's economies are characterized by digital, microelectronic, and network-based telecommunication technologies. We will explain "network-based" technologies further later in this chapter; for now it is sufficient to know that the benefit or utility of such technologies increases for each user the more users they have.

Under such circumstances, no individual economic decision can be made that does not have a related technical information and communication dimension, and no such technically related decision can be made that does not require at least a (technical) *coordination*. Economic decisions need to be based on technical compatibility and, as used in TIC contexts, *interoperability*. Existing technologies in practical use in production and/or innovation systems, thus, must fit to each other, i.e., agents need to use technologies which work out together.

For instance, if agent *A* wants to send an encrypted email to agent *B*, both agents need to use compatible encryption software; and two firms working together in the same VAC need to match their manufacturing decisions. Or think of two software firms forced to use compatible computer languages, if they do not want to block (or lock-in) any further development or a consulting agency forced to use the same computer operating system as its client. As a student, you may also have already experienced a discussion with your fellow students about which kind of presentation software you are going to use for your project presentation. If you failed to coordinate on a unique software (e.g., PowerPoint, Keynote, or LaTex), your group performance would decline significantly.

In this way, no decision seems to be makeable and no information or innovation can be generated that does not involve *externalities*, positive, if coordination has been attained, and negative if not. This entails a strong *direct mutual interdependence* of the decisions of agents and provides numerous possibilities for the application of our game-theoretic concepts from the preceding chapters.

Also, it appears obvious that the benefit of a technology for any individual user in general increases with the *size of the network* (or *installed base*), i.e., the *number of users*, of that technology—thus, any additional member joining that network of users will generate another marginal *network externality* on all others (see, e.g., Koellinger and Schade, 2010; see more on that below in this Section 4.2.4).

Close-to-Zero Marginal Costs of Information Reproduction

Digital microelectronic technologies have added to the *collective-good* characteristic of basic information not only through that system of externalities (for the system of good types, see Chapter 1, Table 1.1) but also through the fact that the reproduction of digital information nowadays usually takes place at near-to-zero marginal costs (i.e., additional costs per copy) and *only the first copy does incur high costs* (including risk-taking, learning costs, time and effort, and trial and error—also considered high *initial fixed and sunk costs*, which need to be incurred in the beginning and cannot always easily be liquidated later).

The economy, in this sense, has entered a stage of some *potential informational abundance*, which then would bear little resemblance to the conventional mainstream economic assumption of ubiquitous scarcity.

Also, the technical facilities for *reproducing information* have become so widespread that the information is no longer under full control of the original producer (if there is only one identifiable producer at all).

This may add to the fact that digital micro-electronic information often has become subject to *nonexcludability*, contributing to the requirement of basic coordination and cooperation to deal with such information as a *collective good*.

Network Technologies and Network Externalities

As said, the total benefit of *basic (technological) information*, or *knowledge*, required to coordinate agents on one standard in production and innovation (as is the case with collective goods in general), *increases with the number of its users*. Basic information, in this sense, is a "systemic" factor. Note that this is the case because of its properties of a collective good, i.e., *nonrivalry* and *nonexcludability*.

The technological basis of the economy has become *network-based* with TICs (see Box 4.2 for information about network technologies and network effects). Since network-based technologies are more useful for the individual user the more users share the same network, each agent, with her technological decision in favor of one out of several competing technology networks, generates, willingly or not, positive or negative external effects on third parties. This depends on her decision to join a specific network or another competing network. Network technologies with their network externalities in use have thus come to govern largely the dynamics of the economy,

---

BOX 4.2

DEFINITION: NETWORK TECHNOLOGIES AND NETWORK EFFECTS

A network technology is a technology, the use of which by different agents in an interconnected system (a fragmented VAC, a digital microelectronic TIC system, combined hard- and software systems) requires compatibility and interoperability (among hard- and software, different supplier parts, interconnected and communicating automata) to be defined through technical standards, interoperation protocols, communication interfaces, etc. The different hardware and software elements, components, modules, etc., with their designed and engineered interoperability, then form a network wherein users can easily exchange hard- and software elements, signals, and information, can easily communicate, etc. In systems with a division of labor, namely fragmented VACs, and with dense exchange (many interactions per time period), transactions, and communication, it will be the case that the more elements (users and their interoperable equipment) enter that network, the higher the value of the network to the individual user will be (network effect, network externality). Also for incumbent users, the value of the network will increase with an increase in the total number of users in that network. Any additional user entering a particular network, thus, generates a positive external effect for the incumbent users and a negative external effect on the users in a competing network. There will also be a positive externality of that decision on those, who will still have to make a decision on entering one of the competing networks in the future (by improving the general knowledge base for their future decisions, then better knowing, how many people are in which network, and the relative benefits of these networks) (see, e.g., Katz and Shapiro, 1994; Shy, 2001; Gottinger, 2003; Varian et al., 2004).

---

and an efficient individualistic (i.e., autonomous) maximization is becoming a near-to-irrelevant exemption, as it would fail to take the decisions of others and the external effects of one's own and the others' choices into account (see, e.g., Hutter, 2001; Nagler, 2008).

A Game-Theoretic Example: A Three-Agent-Two-Technology Coordination Problem

Consider an example in order to clarify the importance of network effects and the collective-good character of basic information. Again, we turn to the problem of *technology choice* from competing, noninteroperable network technologies (for the related full-fledged model, which is a core model of modern complexity economics, see Chapter 13).

Consider three agents, A, B, C, who have to make a decision on one of the two noninteroperable technologies, T_1, T_2. You may think of T_2 as a DVD of the HD type and T_1 as the Blu-ray type (see Figure 4.1).

We assume T_1 to be superior over T_2 ex ante, while, however, agents initially do not know about this and do not prefer one technology over the other and thus will randomly choose. Which technology will be chosen is path dependent, and how often a technology will be chosen will explain ex post its relative superiority or inferiority.

Obviously, every agent who takes a decision will generate positive or negative externalities on the others, whether she intends to do so or not. Assume B decides first (perhaps she had to because her new investment was most due). Whichever technology she chooses, say T_2, she will generate positive externalities on the other two, since these will know better what to do whenever they will have to decide.

In particular, they know that if they would choose the same technology as B did, they will be capable of communicating, producing, and innovating at least together with B, i.e., one-third of the relevant population of the example.

Assume C chooses next (perhaps she had to reinvest equipment next). She may choose T_1 (perhaps because her engineers have convinced her that T_1 is superior and that these benefits would even exceed the benefit from being able to communicate with B). In choosing T_1, she will generate another positive externality on agent A, making A's future choice even better informed and easier. But she also generates a negative externality on B since B's opportunities to communicate and produce with the rest of the population will be limited.

Finally, agent A chooses. Whichever technology she chooses, she will generate a positive externality on one of the other two and a negative externality on the other one, as you (see Figure 4.1) will be able to explain yourself.

In more formal terms, this can be captured as: $\Pi_{T1} = n_{T1} + 1$ and $\Pi_{T2} = n_{T2}$. This may yield the following payoff structure (see Figure 4.2 as a numerical example). It is a *coordination problem* as we know it from Chapters 1–3, a three-agent coordination game though (in Exercises 3 and 4 at the end of this chapter, you are asked to provide a normal-form representation of the game and to calculate the Nash equilibrium (NE)).

Note from Figure 4.2 that

1. the payoffs for fully coordinated situations (all three agents make the same choice, see lines 1 and 8) are preferable over payoffs of weakly coordinated situations (i.e., two out

Technology	T_1		T_2
Agent	A	B	C

FIGURE 4.1 Choice between competing network technologies—an illustration.

A	B	C	Π_A, Π_B, Π_C	$\sum_{i=A}^{c} \Pi_i$	NE	PO
T_1^*	T_1^*	T_1^*	$4^*, 4^*, 4^*$	12	Yes	Yes
T_1^*	T_2	T_1^*	$3^*, 1, 3^*$	7	No	No
T_1^*	T_1^*	T_2	$3^*, 3^*, 1$	7	No	No
T_1	T_2^*	T_2^*	$2, 2^*, 2^*$	6	No	No
T_2	T_1^*	T_1^*	$1, 3^*, 3^*$	7	No	No
T_2^*	T_2^*	T_1	$2^*, 2^*, 2$	6	No	No
T_2^*	T_1	T_2^*	$2^*, 2, 2^*$	6	No	No
T_2^*	T_2^*	T_2^*	$3^*, 3^*, 3^*$	9	Yes	Yes

FIGURE 4.2 A coordination problem of technology choice with three agents (A, B, C) and two competing network-TICs (T_1, T_2, with $T_1 > T_2$)—a numerical example (with payoffs Π for $1T_1 = 2$; $1T_2 = 1$; $2T_2 = 2$; $2T_1 = 3$; $3T_2 = 3$; $3T_1 = 4$; the coordinated agents are marked with a star in each case).

of three agents make the same choice, see lines 2–7);

2. a full coordination on the inferior technology is a NE of the coordination game implied;

3. a fully coordinated situation at the inferior technology (T_2) (see line 8) is superior to all noncoordinated (isolated) adoptions of the superior technology (see line 4 for the isolated agent A, 6 for isolated agent C, and 7 for isolated agent B) and equal to weak coordinations (two agents coordinated) on the superior technology (lines 2, 3, 5).

Note also that this structure reflects networks effects, as explained, with increasing payoffs for each user, with an increasing number of choices (users) for any technology.

Also note that no strategy (technology choice) is strictly dominant. While full coordination on T_1 is a Nash equilibrium, full coordination on T_2 is as well. And a choice of T_1 by the first agent does not necessarily trigger the others to fully coordinate with the first on T_1,

as they may yield the same payoffs with a coordination of the two of them on T_2.

Finally note that path dependence would play a major role if the situation would be considered as a process in a larger population, as we will see (as a complex model and computer simulation in Chapter 13).

You may have noticed that our example involved three firms. It is straightforward to verify that the problem would not come up like this, if we only considered two firms. However, there might be the case of an oligopoly with two large corporations (a *duopoly*), where each has produced one of the competing technologies and each wanted to *set the general standard* (in a broader market with many small buyers), e.g., by being *first mover*, gaining some advantage for their technology (see further below in this section; for such battle in a duopoly model, see Chapter 7). While the central mechanism does not change fundamentally, if more than three agents are taken into account, a few other issues arise in that case. Therefore, the problem of technological choice is scrutinized in more detail in Chapters 15 and 16.

Competing Network Technologies, Uncertainty, and Potential Blockage of Action

With competing and *nonstandardized (noninteroperable) technologies*, users may get particularly uncertain, reluctant, and passive, and often completely blocked in their decisions to adopt a new technology, in order not to experience *later regret*, when another technology than the one they have chosen may turn out to become the larger and more useful net or standard for the whole economy. This has indeed become a latent feature of a decentralized economy based on network technologies (see, e.g., Tirole, 1995, section 10.6; Wettengl, 1999). The introduction of color TV, videotape systems, HDTV, computer operating systems, or second-generation DVDs have been instances from the more recent industrial history that demonstrate the ubiquity of *latent collective blockages of action* and, with this, impeded dissemination of new technologies (e.g., Weitzel and Westarp, 2002; Gauch, 2008). If competing technology suppliers keep struggling for first-mover advantages and for their product or technology to become the standard, a *blockage of information and innovation flow* may result, and interoperability and standardization may also be blocked, resulting in further customer caution. There are pervasive tendencies in the real-world TIC sectors, it has been argued, to generate *innovation at suboptimal levels* (see, e.g., Miller, 2001).

Incentives to Wait Versus Incentives to be the "First Mover"

If a firm is the first mover and is successful in setting the standard for the corresponding industry, it will be able to secure *monopoly profits* in that industry and (by controlling the standards of the industry) to exercise control over the industry. This strategy is, however, often very risky as to be the standard setter, a firm needs a certain minimum critical mass of customers and if it fails to get them, losses will be generally very high.

On the other hand as said, it sometimes also pays to wait until other players make their moves and to exploit the information revealed by them through their choices. Which effects dominate depends on the specific situation.

In these cases, we may easily see that besides coordination problems, there may also be *dilemma problems* involved.

"Basic Information" as a Collective Good: Sharing Knowledge in Fragmented VACs and on Network-Based Technologies

As such basic information often cannot, and generally should not, be kept secret and fully appropriated individually, production and innovation systems, in turn, need to be properly *collectively governed* or *managed* in the VAC or an innovation system, as said. This requires a proper *institutional setting* for the fragmented, decentralized production and innovation process in general. If such an adequate institutional setting is missing, this may reinforce individualistic reactions of the economic agents.

This is due, as said, to the fact that much information, and, in fact, the most basic information display the features of a collective good. Technological and behavioral information or knowledge that are required to be shared for coordination in a fragmented VAC is characterized by nonrivalry of use and nonexcludability, sometimes assuming the form of inappropriability of profit from R&D expenses, as mentioned (see Chapter 1, Table 1.1, again for the basic *classification of goods*). Information, therefore, must be shared, the technology be coordinated as a standard, in order to guarantee interoperability (compatibility) and coordination, and thus an effective production and innovation of complex products (for such *"knowledge" commons*, see also, e.g., Hess and Ostrom, 2007).

Note that generally we may make a distinction between just static *data* (just informational bits, where it is open, whether the agent can make use of it or not), further *information*, which displays some *contextual use* for the agent, and *knowledge*, which is considered an *active asset* for the agent, which he can fully make use of. Thus, data, information, and knowledge may be distinguished according to the degree of *active absorption* and application by the agent.

"Inappropriability" and "Open Source" as a Potential New General Economic Principle and as a Business Model

Shared basic technological (and related behavioral) *knowledge*, required for coordination, has the objective property of an *open-source element* in the VACs and innovation chains, i.e., a collective good provided. It is, in that sense, also inappropriable, i.e., no exclusive individual profit can be drawn from it. The open-source dimension of the economy appears so important that we will devote a complete chapter to its detailed scrutiny (see Chapter 15). For now, we just take the open-source property of basic information as a reflection of a collective, basically inappropriable good.

As mentioned, in the fragmented VAC, any *delivery*, *sale*, and *supply* implies a distribution of (technical) information, which very quickly may become *general knowledge* depending on the so-called absorption capacity of the others. The others cannot easily be technically excluded from receiving the new information contained, as the information contained in delivered goods and services may quickly diffuse. The R&D investment of a firm then may not be paying in terms of yielding a usual return rate because *parts of the benefit and profit just drain out* onto others. This is because the information produced and contained in goods and services, and used for technological standardization and related behavioral coordination, basically is not a private good.

On the other hand, firms not only have to externalize benefits from their own research, but also receive benefits from the research efforts of other firms. This *exchange of information benefits* is an important factor for the profit rate of each firm to become "usual" again. R&D expenses then must lead to *mutual positive externalities*, if the VAC or innovation system shall be effectively working, producing, and innovating.

In all, while inappropriability—as a technical condition and implication of the given property of a collective good, or *openness*, of basic information—generates a system of externalities and with this a coordination problem, this very coordination problem can be *solved* only in a *learned system of trusting* that externalities, while given away, will be received as well in the system of deliveries in a VAC or innovation chain, and of resulting coordination, a commonly "well-governed," or perhaps even deliberately "well-managed," system.

As basic information in the context described is not a private good, the rules of the economy have to be adjusted respectively in order to guarantee an effective information circulation between economic agents. Joint use of basic information is welfare-enhancing under those conditions and increasingly becomes a necessity for coordination (see, e.g., Reinstaller and Hoelzl, 2004).

However, in an established production or innovation system, also *exploiting basic information* generated by others may be a *dominant rational opportunistic strategy* in an individualistic cultural environment. Under certain conditions, it may be an option to *wait*, or to postpone, or completely *avoid own effort and expenses*, and to try to receive relevant basic information just from others. Thus, also a *dilemma structure* is involved. Therefore, it is necessary for an economy to find an adequate *setting of social institutions* securing an effective circulation of information and to sustain a Pareto-superior equilibrium.

Again, we will explain the collective-good character of information and the new economic principle and business model of OS in greater detail in Chapter 15.

4.2.5 Network-Technology Choice as Path-Dependent Process

Technology Choice as a Path-Dependent Process: An Example of the Choice of a Computer Operation System

Consider a consulting firm C facing the decision problem of choosing the kind of smartphone, which its employees are requested to use. As the operating systems are mutually incompatible and need to be adjusted to the rest of the IT infrastructure of the firm, all employees must use the same type of smartphone. The choice is to be made between BlackBerry smartphones, smartphones based on the Android operating system, and iPhones.

The choice is particularly of interest as the data transfer and communication between the firm and possible clients would be highly facilitated if the client used the same operating system.

Consider the firm chooses to give iPhones to their employees. This might be the case, because two of the most important clients use an OS X operating system and the firm wants to preserve the current business relation. It might also be a completely arbitrary choice, e.g., because the CEO personally likes Apple products.

Consider the following possible events:

1. The two clients choose to change their business focus and leave the market. Other firms use mostly GNU-Linux-based operating systems because of their decreasing costs and their greater flexibility. The exit of the two clients and the choices of the other firms pose negative external effects on C and represent a severe risk. Another change of the operating system might be too costly for C, which now has a severe disadvantage against its competitors using GNU-Linux systems.
2. Apple further restricts the compatibility of its products, and transfer costs from OS X

systems to other systems increase significantly. Although C preserved the relation to two important customers, it now has severe disadvantages in communicating with others. If, maybe because of the decreased compatibility of the iPhones, many new firms decide to choose Android phones, the business situation of C would further decrease.

3. Because of a security problem with Android smartphones, many firms decide to switch to iPhones and BlackBerries. C might attract clients from other competitors and increase its market share and thus its profits.

In any case, the further development of the firm will be highly dependent on the earlier (and at the time of the choice potentially arbitrary and poorly informed) selection of the operating system. For C it was completely impossible to foresee these and other developments, but the earlier choice of the operating systems nevertheless shapes its further development path.

The Importance of Path Dependence and Cumulative Process in the Real World: The Case of Microsoft and the Market for PC Operation Systems

The key conception of path dependence, as already introduced in Chapter 1, states that the development path of an economic system depends on past events and is *time-dependent*. In other words, the trajectory of a path-dependent system depends on the path the system has followed to that moment. The shape of this path, however, is never predetermined, as *exogenous random shocks*, *stochastic events*, or *accidents of history* as well as potential unpredictable and not determinable *endogenous* bifurcations and systemic structural changes and transitions influence the development that a complex economic system is undergoing (for the formal details of complex-system dynamics, see Chapters 10, 11, and 13).

One of the most famous business tales is well-suited to illustrate the importance of the concept of path dependence and of its relevance in real-world economies and business.

The well-known story is about Bill Gates and the beginning of the software company Microsoft. Gates founded the company together with Paul Allen in 1975. In 1980, IBM, at that time the leading producer for firm computer systems, planned to enter the market for personal computers. The company was focused on hardware development and thus had no own suitable operation system. Therefore, it contacted Microsoft, which, however, had no operating system to offer and redirected IBM to Digital Research. Their CEO, David Kildall, however, escaped the representatives of IBM, who again contacted Microsoft. Gates and Allen then agreed to develop an adequate operation system, but as they had never written such a program, they bought the license of an already existing system called Quick and Dirty Operation System (Q-DOS), made some minor changes, and after relicensing it sold it to IBM, which in turn relabeled it PC-DOS. In their contract with IBM, Allen and Gates, however, secured the rights on the "new" operation system so that they could sell it independently from IBM computers, then under the label "MS-DOS".

Although the performance of MS-DOS was poor, it became quite successful, mainly because of its low price and the fact that programs designed for other operation systems could easily be executed under MS-DOS but not vice versa.

In 1987, Gates (Allen left Microsoft in 1982 because of health problems) faced another important choice: Because MS-DOS was still a comparably slow system and was unable to make use of some major innovations in the hardware sector, it was only a question of time until it was to be outcompeted by other systems.

There were several possibilities for Microsoft and the success of the different strategies depended heavily on how the market would evolve in the future. Reliable foresights were, however, impossible, i.e., the companies in the sector truly faced strong uncertainty.

Gates could have invested a lot of money in the development of a new operation system and try to convince his current MS-DOS customers to switch to the new system. This was a promising option indeed, because there was no technological standard set for the new generation of computer systems, and by being a "first mover" one could—provided that one gets a critical mass of initial customers—secure long-term monopoly revenues. On the other hand, this option was also very risky as the resources of Microsoft were tiny compared to major competitors such as Apple and IBM and a "false bet" would probably have meant the end of the company.

Therefore, Microsoft could also exit the operation systems market without harm and focus on developing applied solutions for the new operation system. In this case, Microsoft would "wait" until a standard had developed and then fit its products to the dominating system. This option was clearly less risky than the first one.

Another option for Gates was to sell Microsoft to one of their major competitors. By doing so, he would have had a good opportunity of becoming part of the new mother company, setting the new standard without bearing much risk.

In fact, which strategy would turn out to be the best was impossible to forecast. Minor, even random events could determine the further development of the market for operation systems and once a certain standard had been established, and a certain development path had been taken, it was highly improbable that the situation was going to change again. Gates therefore decided not to bet on one single path, but tried to be prepared for whichever development the sector was going to take. He invested into the development of MS-DOS in order to sustain its customer base some time further, he also started a joint venture with IBM, in which they tried to push forward the development of IBM's operation system, he also started negotiations with companies working with the UNIX standard and even bought stocks of one of the most important UNIX developers in order to sustain his chances in the UNIX market if it became the new standard. He also developed some applications for the Apple operation system and, finally, invested into the development of Windows. Note that his engagement for Apple also entailed access to Apple's technological knowledge, which then helped tremendously in the development of Windows.

The rest of the story is well known. Although in the first years Windows sold very poorly and suffered some serious technical flaws, it turned out to be the winner of the operation systems market and indeed defined the new standard.

We do not know whether Gates knew something about path-dependent processes, but the story shows that *path dependence* is a critical property of economic systems. Developments often are strongly dependent on early, smaller, or even accidental events, then triggering a certain development path of a whole sector.

The above did not aim to glorify the story of Microsoft. Especially after becoming a big corporation itself, the firm implemented mostly "individualistic" and proprietary business strategies. We will return to the case of operation systems in the chapter on the economic openness principle (Chapter 15).

In sum, if we want to describe economic systems properly, we need to be aware of their path-dependent nature and bear in mind that the *reality we observe* often represents *only one possible realization* and that other realizations, which were equally or even more probable in the past, could have been completely different of what then became the standard.

4.2.6 Interoperability—Standardization of Technologies and Behaviors, and the Roles of Collective Rationality and Public Policy—The Example of the Internet Standard

The existence of competing network technologies implies that the necessity of technical *standards*, *interfaces*, and *protocols* has become ubiquitous. This is represented by a coordination problem, and in fact a recurrent one, with a cumulative process with *multiple and often Pareto-different NEs*, as indicated in the numerical example (Figure 4.2) above. So, there are different potential standards where the system may settle at (see also, e.g., Ponte and Gibbon, 2005; again for the formal model and simulation, see Chapter 13).

In the real world, the *public (policy) agent* (be it political parties, government, public administration, different specialized state or semi-state agencies or different kinds of intermediaries), with its (ideally) somewhat broader and more long-run perspective and rationality, through its principle of *hierarchy*, usually requires, supports, or organizes processes of standardization among competing corporations, thus avoiding or shortening long-lasting standard wars, customer blockages, or lock-ins on inferior technologies. For instance, international private–public bureaucracies, such as ICANN, the famous *Internet Corporation for Assigned Names and Numbers*, have been established to assist the development of technological standard setting, interface definitions, and transfer protocols, moderating the conflicts of interests among different major national-champion corporate players with their technological standards (see, e.g., Weitzel and van Westarp, 2002).

For a more precise definition of the *role of policy* of *neutral agents* vis-á-vis the interaction system of the private agents, see Chapter 17.

As an example for a *standard war*, consider the two different internet protocols IPv4 and

IPv6. The current standard which is used by almost every internet user is IPv4. Every time you want to access the internet with your computer, it requires an IP address which is assigned to your computer via an internet protocol.

The problem of the current standard IPv4 is that the amount of possible addresses is limited to about 4.3 billion due to the method the addresses are created. As more and more people want to access the internet, there are no "free" addresses available and in the near future, computers won't be able to receive an IP.

Two reactions to this problem are possible: (i) switch the standard to IPv6 which allows the creation of over 3.4×10^{38} addresses (which are more than 7.9×10^{28} times as many as with IPv4). There are no drawbacks from a functional point of view or (ii) prevent users from getting an own IP but use virtual LAN networks: Then, many users "share" an IP provided by their provider. Then, the possibilities to act in the internet will be reduced for these users. The "advantage" is that the provider does not need to change its protocol standard to IPv6.

This is an example for a situation in which a truly superior technology, IPv6, does not replace the inferior one, IPv4, because the latter has much more users than the first and the actual users want to avoid the costs of changing the standard although this change would be highly desirable from a societal point of view.

4.2.7 In All: A "Complexity Challenge"

In this section, you may have learned about the ubiquitous presence of external effects, "informational" collective-good problems, coordination and cooperation problems, and the fact that a simple deregulation of markets does not help in reducing the *complexity of the individual decision problem* or of the economy as a whole. We further explained which role TIC and disintegrated VACs play in a modern decentralized and individualized economy. They give rise to coordination and dilemma problems, for instance as related to technological choice, which are ubiquitous for most economic agents. Strong mutual dependence and uncertainty about the action of others characterize the economic environment for most agents.

For the economic agents, and for economists as well, this represents a considerable "complexity challenge" (Rycroft and Kash, 1999). Any microeconomic analysis must take these fundamental givens—complex structures and mechanisms—into account and must avoid assuming them away.

We also encountered the methodological challenge the economist is facing while doing her analysis: the choice of the proper game structure, and the choice of the proper degree of model simplification.

According to our (preliminary) definition of *complexity*, we can finish this section stating that the economy is complex, i.e., involves a large number of heterogeneous and interdependent agents, each having different behavioral options to choose from. Complexity microeconomics is on the track to develop tools to fruitfully deal with this problem (see more on this in Section 4.4).

4.3 INDIVIDUALISTIC VS. COMMON AND COLLECTIVE, STRATEGIES TO COPE WITH COMPLEXITY

4.3.1 Power and Hierarchy, Hub&Spoke Clusters and Networks

"Power-Ization": Hierarchy, Power, Collusion—Increasing Control to Compensate for Increased Turbulence

As indicated, the presence of *network effects* alone already tends to *favor cumulative corporate growth* and in this way bigger corporations.

As an example, consider *Microsoft* again, which as a single economic agent commands considerable portions of a relevant core technology and thus has cumulatively attracted the great bulk of the relevant global demand for operation systems and applied software, the largest global market share one individual firm could ever channel to itself.

We will further explain reasons in favor of cumulative differential firm-size growth in Chapter 7.

Furthermore, under the regime of "neoliberal" deregulation of industries and sectors, as described—which also included the loosening and reduction of competition and antitrust policies, under a new mainstream conception of "markets" and "competition"—corporations have had no longer any regulative limits to *increase their size and power* and to exploit their power advantages at the cost of the rest of the economy, as were set under the earlier competition, antitrust, and anticollusion policies.

We have already explained that deregulated markets do not resolve ubiquitous and intricate coordination and cooperation problems, especially not in face of increased complexity, interdependence, and uncertainty. Rather, it seems to increase uncertainty, volatility, and turbulence, and the complexity of the individual decision problems, leading to *less problem-solving capacity* rather than to more.

The individual economic agent, of course, cannot change the systemic properties and system dynamics, and the most powerful corporations in total are profiting individualistically from this anyway, as it provides them differential advantages over the rest of the economy and society. But even the most powerful have to take complexity, uncertainty, and turbulence as given and have to *develop individualistic countermeasures* in order to sustain their position and former level of control in the markets. Especially with bigger economic players, we frequently observe:

- the reinforcement of *hierarchy*, *power*, and *oligopolistic/monopolistic positions*;
- oligopolistic *collusion* and *cartelization*;
- raising *barriers to entry*, against new firms, usually SMEs;
- *mergers and acquisitions* with competitors and SMEs, mostly in a lasting liaison with large financial entities;
- *standard-setting* in their own interest, as first movers, exploiting network effects, and related lobbying for their "intellectual property rights";
- general political *lobbying* and *rent-seeking* for effortless profit-making, and increasing protection of *property rights* (see, e.g., Block, 2000, 55ff.; Ponte and Gibbon, 2005; again, for more details, see Chapter 7).

Note that *hierarchy* in fact is another potential *organizational solution to the problem of coordination and cooperation under complexity*, and the *dominating* one in a global corporate economy—as distinct from learned coordination and institutionalized cooperation among independent and equal agents. It is a solution that dominates economic reality, but has considerable *drawbacks* in terms of *dependence* of large economic, societal, and ecological areas, whole regions and nations, on *volatile decisions* of small groups and committees of people (see, e.g., the large global corporate network centralization study: Vitali et al., 2011)—compared to ideal jointly learned decentral solutions among independent SMEs.

Note, however, that hierarchy is, or is based on, a system of institutionalized behaviors as well, such as organizational routines, and a culture of learned rules in positions of superiority and inferiority. We will deal with the evolutionary theory of intrafirm institutions ("routines") in Section 13.8.

Hub&Spoke Networks

When large power differences and large hierarchies interfere with direct interdependence, fragmented VACs, and basic network structures, then hierarchical network structures, such as hub&spoke networks will probably result, as superior differential powers will be able to organize many smaller agents in sourcing and supplier relations. This is why the global corporate economy nowadays is characterized by global hub&spoke supplier networks, where the big "hub" corporations, usually (still national) "champions," command layered global sourcing systems, with the main suppliers of subsystems functioning as their "spokes" (see, e.g., Bair, 2008; Sturgeon et al., 2008; Coe et al., 2008; Lane and Probert, 2009).

Hub&Spoke Clusters

And as far as global corporate agents in this way can control fragmented VACs and innovation systems (on both global and local levels), it has been argued, they also *control information flows*, entry, and access to resources and play their roles as *key agents*, following the postulates of large-scale production under the conditions of global spatial and functional fragmentation (see, e.g., Swyngedouw, 1997; Raikes et al., 2000, 392ff.). Against this backdrop, also spatial clusters may adopt structures of hub&spoke, as just dependent *satellite platforms* consisting of local firms around, and in favor of, local branches of global corporations (for a number of related case studies, see, e.g., Markusen, 1996).

Hub&spoke clusters may indeed be highly innovative as long and as far as a powerful hub enforces innovations in its very own interest. However, the more power-based, hierarchical, and hub-centered a cluster becomes, it has been argued in the empirical literature, the more risky and precarious the cluster may become as well, i.e., it may be prone to some inappropriate downward swings, premature aging, or abrupt abandonment (see, e.g., Tichy, 1998; Saxenian, 1994; Markusen, 1996).

It is therefore highly probable that this kind of individualistic organizational structures are not optimal in order to guarantee

comprehensive and sustainable innovations and to make full use of the potentials of regional coordination forms such as clusters (e.g., Gallaway and Kinnear, 2002, p. 446; Baker, 1996; Pratt, 1997; Armstrong, 1998).

4.3.2 Industrial Clusters and Networks in General

A Two-Stage Conception of Emergence

Another possible reaction, less individualistic in terms of a *longer run and more interactive engagement* of firms in a regional multiagent setting is entering and actively participating in relatively new *spatial forms of coordination and cooperation* such as local and regional clustering.

Local clustering has indeed become a kind of *spatial organization of firms and production/ innovation* in the last few decades, in particular for the most advanced, high-tech, globalized, and outsourced parts of the corporate economy, and as a kind of *countermeasure against too much fragmentation* and related volatility and turbulence (from the exploding literature on spatial firm clusters, see, e.g., Krugman, 1991; Feser, 1998; Mizrahi, 1998; Maillat and Grosjean, 1999; Breschi and Malerba, 2001; Peoples, 2003; Malmberg et al., 2004; Orsenigo, 2006; Bair, 2008). It is characterized by *recurrent, long-termed*, and *frequent interactions* (*high interaction density*) with *nearby located* suppliers, service providers, customers, competitors, and different societal, semipublic, and public agents and intermediaries (proximity).

At first sight, the emergence of such *quasi-integrated forms of* (*parts of*) *the VAC* or innovation system, such as spatial industrial clusters of many corporations, seems to be opposed to globalization and fragmentation. However, striving for *spatial and cultural proximity* through some form of *spatial institutional reembedding* appears to be exactly a *measure against the volatility and turbulence* of the economic environment and related *complexity of the individual decision situation* (see also, e.g., Gertler et al., 2000; Torre and Gilly, 2000; McCann, 2007; Nousala, 2010).

Which of the two basic actions, individualistic hierarchical versus interactive/cooperative, corporations choose, and in which particular combination, depends on their learned orientations—short-termism, individualism, and hierarchy, or *recognized interdependence* and *long-term perspectives and interaction*—and also, of course, on the *degree of uncertainty* and their *particular incentive structure*. Many high-tech firms, for instance, clustered around *Silicon Valley*, in an attempt to optimize their relatively uncertain R&D processes and thus to profit from the *regional open information flows* there. For their most standardized production processes, however, the same firms may distribute manufacturing all over the world, in order just to exploit different institutional frameworks, different labor conditions, raw material conditions, or different prices in different countries.

Clusters Tend to Outgrow the Market

Clusters thus are "functional" systems of relations and as such *emerge from spontaneous arm's length "market" actions*, under conditions of complexity, as soon as agents start settling in spatial proximity (see, e.g., Elsner, 2000, 413ff.).

Their actions then may outgrow that market in that they establish ever more stable, long-run, and dense interactions. These interactions yield more and more stable relations, which get increasingly resistant against conventional "market signals" (i.e., prices). This is because their recurrent, stable, and long-termed interactions lead them to develop parallel and similar ways of thinking, speaking, behaving, planning, and expecting their mutual actions. They get better knowledge of each other and in this way may develop more stable expectations about the other's future

behaviors, i.e., some form of *trust*, leading, after a period of trial and error, effort, experimentation, and investment of time, to some coordination/cooperation (e.g., Farrell, 2009; Haekli, 2009).

Imagine two companies, A and B, doing business in the same regional agglomeration or local *business district*. They start a buyer—supplier relation with A the buyer and B the supplier, at this time considered a pure arm's length market action. This means that the motivation for A to choose B as her supplier might simply be that B offered the lowest price and was closest. With time passing by, their interactions repeat and get denser, stable expectations and mutual trust emerges. If now another firm offers A a lower price for the same product, it might well be that A rejects this offer because it wants to sustain its relation to B—after having invested so much time and effort, risk-taking, and trial and error, and having gained a reliable and *stable relation in an uncertain environment* (high "relational" fixed sunk costs). In this way, the interactions outgrow the market in the sense that the new interaction relation is resistant against simple competitive low-price offers, i.e., a pure "market-based" signal from outside the relation. The relation is characterized by *long-term reciprocity* of behaviors, rather than short-run price-value equivalence.

The reasons for that may be considered from manifold perspectives: Consider for example the necessarily *incomplete character of formal contracts*, i.e., the impossibility of stipulating any eventualities of a business relation in a formal contract. Therefore, a business relation always involves *uncertainty*, which can significantly be reduced if one has learned to know one's business partner sufficiently well (e.g., Vlaar, 2008). This is just one reason why stable and settled expectations, mutual trust, and coordination/cooperation attained may outweigh low-price offers from outside the relation.

The process described is not necessarily all clear and conscious to the agents. It nevertheless represents an evolutionary process of *collective learning* of correlated behavior that *coordinates* firms and makes them *cooperate*, deliberately or not, in largely *out-of-market*, institutionalized ways, and helps them solve some the basic collective coordination and dilemma problems of production and innovation in the VACs and in technology choice (see also, e.g., Lazonick, 1993; Steiner, 1998; Dupuy and Torre, 1998; Saxenian, 1994).

More Deliberate Agreements: "Strategic Networks"

Inside a given cluster, "but also, of course, across clusters," there may arise *"strategic" networks of subsets of the cluster firms*, which develop even more intense relations by some form of a *conscious, deliberate agreement*, informal or formal. Often, these "strategic networks" are project-based and temporary. They are multilateral, i.e., encompass more than two agents.

Imagine firms *A*, *B*, and *C* in a cluster that involves three more firms, *D*, *E*, and *F*. But *A*, *B*, and *C* have *deliberately* developed a somewhat *"denser" relationship*, as they got involved in a common *future-oriented* and *consciously planned* project and have collectively solved, through cooperation, the dilemma problems involved. Their relation will become qualitatively different than the other, thus, more than just *functional*, relations in the cluster. While all firms are forming a cluster, only *A*, *B*, and *C* are forming a "strategic network."

For more detail, see Box 4.3.

Open-Source Networks in Particular

A special case of a network is an open-source (OS) network, which has succeeded to *govern, or manage, information as a collective good*. Insofar they are based on a learned, stable, institutionalized cooperative behavior, this kind of "strategic network" may be largely self-organizing and self-sustaining (in the sense of an endogenously emerged structure), and thus capable of a more comprehensive *collective action* to overcome dilemma structures when dealing with information exchange and knowledge sharing. In this way, they are often reported to be able to *speed up innovation* (e.g., Nagler, 2008; Chertow and Ehrenfeld, 2012). Insofar as *commercial* firms are involved, their profit-making with an *OS-based business model* may be based on competitive *services* rather than exclusive technological knowledge or formal *patents* on *source codes*—as a considerable number of firms in the software industry have been practicing, such as, e.g., *Red Hat, IBM*, or *Oracle* (formerly also *Sun Microsystems*). Many different forms of OS-based business models have emerged and are practiced nowadays. There obviously are many reasons even for commercial firms to adopt principles of OS and run variants of OS strategies as their business models. Because OS-networks, and open-access and information-*openness* principles, are central examples of complex, evolutionary, and institutional microeconomics, we will explain them in greater detail in Chapter 15.

4.3.3 Taking Stock

We may *conclude* this section with two particularly interesting, even though preliminary, results:

First, while economic agents in general face direct interdependencies in different possible *network structures*, large economic players in particular may *accumulate differential power*, in particular through so-called *network effects*, and therefore may be able to *shape network structures* according to their hierarchical interest, particularly hierarchical hub&spoke structures. From a broader societal, more long-term, and sustainability point of view, however, structures with low power differentials and little hierarchy, and with corresponding governance rules based on equal footing of agents, aiming at *open information flows* and *nonexclusion* of agents, appear to

BOX 4.3

DEFINITION: SPATIAL INDUSTRIAL CLUSTERS AND FIRM NETWORKS

A spatial (regional, local) industrial cluster is a regional group or *agglomeration* of firms or firm branches or plants in a region, which belong to different (statistically defined) industries or branches related to a VAC and that are interconnected—both in *vertical* (supplier) and *horizontal* (competitor) relations—through *recurrent* and *"dense"* (frequent per time unit) interactions. They form *long-termed* and relatively *stable* functional, i.e., *supplier* (vertical and complementary), relations and also *competitor* (horizontal and substitutive) relations. They include manufacturing and service industries. While there are direct vertical supplier relations along *goods and services flows*, the horizontal relations may exist just through *information exchange* among employees and through *workers' mobility* among cluster firms. Also customers may switch among competitive firms in the cluster. And in most effective clusters, competitors often exchange production capacities between those with a current bottleneck and those with current overcapacities (e.g., Saxenian, 1994).

Through dense interaction, the cluster generates and provides, in an *evolutionary interaction history*, the "raw material," i.e., *stable mutual expectations and trust*, for more advanced forms of coordination and cooperation, namely, deliberately agreed-on multilateral arrangements: "strategic" networks. In this way, clusters and networks together may be explained by a *two-stage model*, with a more spontaneous historical emergence of behavioral rules and institutions within a cluster and a more *deliberate*, often only *temporary* and *project-based*, multilateral arrangement through creation of a network on that basis.

More comprehensive clusters may include intermediaries, consultants/advisors/scientists, experts, and public, semipublic, and societal agents (organizations, associations, specialized public agencies, etc.), the latter of which are responsible for *specific infrastructures*, "hard" (real-estate sites, streets, buildings) or "soft" (knowledge transfer agencies), which are important for the cluster firms.

Alfred Marshall was the first economist who described and explained the economic advantages of *industrial agglomerations* through *industrial "externalities"* already in 1890, coining the basic mechanisms at work: (i) *supplier pooling*, (ii) *labor pooling*, and (iii) *information pooling*—stating that common information/shared knowledge, against the background of dense interactions, commodities, and service flows, talks among employees, employees' interfirm mobility, etc., typically is *"in the air"* in a cluster (Marshall, 1890/1920; see also, e.g., Quéré and Joel, 1998; Miguélez and Moreno, 2012).

In an evolutionary process, effective coordination and cooperation then may emerge, as we have explained in the previous chapters and will further explain and model throughout this book.

be more favorable to a culture of effective learning and, subsequently, to *fast and sustainable innovation* in a *socially broad* sense (see, e.g., Foray, 1998; Chertow and Ehrenfeld, 2012). This kind of structures seems to recognize the *collective-good character of basic information* and to govern network relations accordingly. More individualistic responses, on the other hand, pursued by large, powerful players, employ effort to artificially change the collective-good characteristics of basic information, focus on *developing exclusion technologies*, and lobby for artificially raised *(intellectual) property rights* (IPR), in order to increase the scope for monopolistic revenues. Although this may be favorable from an individualistic point of view, i.e., in the short-run, it does not appear to be intuitive from a *long-run* and *broader innovation perspective*. The efficacy of the former, common and collective governance mechanisms and resulting *regional innovation systems* (RIS) have been verified by a broad empirical literature, e.g., about the *Silicon Valley*, the *Third Italy*, and, later, upcoming Asian regions (see again the classical sources for the Silicon Valley: Saxenian, 1994, and the Third Italy: Brusco, 1982). We will provide a more in-depth treatment of openness and of RIS in Chapters 15 and 16. For the issue of effective network structures, see models in Chapter 13, Sections 10 and 11. For a final practical example, consider the development of exclusion technologies by large printer corporations such as HP: In order to prevent customers from using cheaper inks or toners of equal quality, HP developed an electronic code which prevents its printers from accepting non-HP inks. This ensures monopolistic gains for HP and comes along with artificial market entry barriers for the market of printer accessories and higher costs for customers.

Second, *policy* seems to matter for *initializing*, *accelerating*, and/or *stabilizing* the governance of information and the emergence of effective network structures. The kind of reactions of agents to increased complexity depends on the incentive structures, the time horizon, and the institutional, often formally legal, framework of the "rules of the game." Thus, also industrial clusters and networks may have to be considered according to the legal and political framework. For network- and cooperation-fostering policies, see Chapter 17. In fact, many economists are dealing a lot with developing *good-governance principles* favorable to effective collective action. These principles serve to prevent cooperation and network structures from restrictive/collusive degeneration, make them

resilient against sharp external changes—and particularly protect clusters and networks against high dependence on hub corporations and related *premature aging*, when a hub gets into trouble or for some reason withdraws— and thus maintain their innovative capacity. These principles usually will include some *openness, parallel and often redundant action* among network participants, *evenness*, and *participation* mechanisms, irrespective of differences of size and power of participants, a learned *long-run perspective*, and learned *reciprocity*. If applied by a critical minimum mass, they might ensure *continuous joint learning* and *institutionalization of collective action* and, subsequently, a high level and continuity of *systemic innovation*, as the theoretical and applied network literature has elaborated (see, e.g., Powell and Smith-Doerr, 1994; Maggioni, 1997, 238ff.; Elsner, 2000, 450ff.; Lazonick, 2001a,b; Lazonick, 2001b Gallaway and Kinnear, 2004; Paoli and Addeo, 2011; Li et al., 2013). Sustainably effective "strategic networks" of this kind, however, might well be ineffective, in the short-run, for the profit of powerful corporate agents. Again, different models of networks, taking into account network structures and their relative performances, will be provided in Chapters 13, 15, and 16.

4.4 IMPLICATIONS OF REAL-WORLD COMPLEXITY FOR MICROECONOMIC THEORY AND MODELING

4.4.1 A More Integrative Picture

This chapter aimed at looking into real-world processes and relating them to the theoretical and analytical tools you have acquired in Chapters 1–3. We tried to identify some important processes and to shed light on some underlying mechanisms. We tried to illustrate the fact that actual economies are complex and all relevant economic decisions are made in situations characterized by strong mutual dependence among economic agents as well as path-dependent processes.

However, there still are some obvious limitations of making more precise statements about the functioning of today's economies. Therefore, this chapter, hopefully, also provided a motivation to investigate more advanced tools and methods to be learned in the remainder of this book. This section will summarize central aspects and give an outlook on the following parts of the book.

In the real economy we have observed:

1. the increasing *complexity and integration of products*, which have themselves become *systems* consisting of many parts, subsystems, and modules, including physical parts, information/software, and services;
2. the increasingly *fragmented character of the VACs*, which have become *functionally* and *spatially* disintegrated into *many individual agents* (firms) involved, being formally independent, on a global scale;
3. the dominant digital/microelectronic *TIC property of the technological base*, which generates (competing) *network technologies* with *network effects* based on increasing utility, or payoff, increasing with the number of applications, installations, or users and with a required and cumulatively emerging, but nevertheless permanently *contested, standardization.*

Obviously, there is a *trade-off* between points 1 and 2, and it is all but certain that point 3 will be supportive in emerging coordination and cooperation in the VACs to generate those complex products. On the contrary, *contested technological standardization* may lead to *ongoing battles for the standard*, e.g., first-mover races, among large oligopolistic suppliers, as explained. These usually are national champions and, thus, are supported by their home governments in the global industrial centers (USA, EU, China, Japan...).

If this is the case, the usual evolutionary cumulative effects toward *one standard* (network effects) may lastingly be *inhibited*—the hazards of path-dependent *lock-in* notwithstanding (see Chapters 13 and 15 for in-depth analyses). Note that the downside of a competitive victory of just one out of a number of competing and noninteroperable technologies may be a *reduced diversity*, and with this a *reduced resilience* of the whole system against external shocks or sudden environmental changes (for more detail on this, see Chapter 11).

If, however, a technological (and behavioral) standard, or a working complex of interoperable technologies, is achieved, technology may indeed be helpful for—and indicative of—an emergent coordination or cooperation along the VACs or in the innovation system.

Then, in general, a (technological and behavioral) standard T_2 may indeed be *superior* over an earlier standard T_1, in terms of its ability to *coordinate* agents on a *higher level of product complexity* and/or, at the same time, coordinating *more agents* in a VAC (i.e., dealing with a more fragmented, longer VAC).

As products are more and more complex, and there are more manufacturing steps outsourced and the VAC thus disintegrated ever more, there is at the same time an increasing necessity of assuring technological compatibility inside a given VAC.

For an illustration, see Figure 4.3. Note that we have chosen arbitrarily linear trade-off lines for the standards. Note also that those lines must, in reality, not necessarily be parallel.

You further encountered the social dilemma involved in technology choice, if it pays (for the investor) to wait and let the others take the risk of early technology adoption, but also the situations, in which it pays for producers to be the first movers with their technologies in order to be able to determine the future standard.

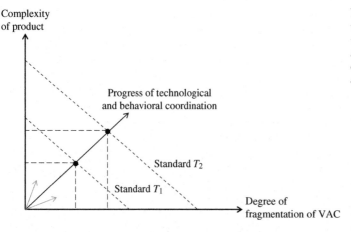

FIGURE 4.3 The trade-off between product complexity and the degree of fragmentation of VACs, as remedied by (technological and behavioral) standardization (coordination or cooperation attained), with a superior and an inferior standard—an illustration.

You also have seen that, although VACs are heavily disintegrated in some cases, they can still be controlled, with some efficacy, by big corporations (the *hierarchical alternative*), because of their ability to set and control technological standards, even at the expense of sustaining technological incompatibilities vis-á-vis competing hierarchical production systems. Big corporations—with their individualistic, hierarchical, and power-oriented behaviors—indeed often even have incentives to *sustain incompatibility* among their own VAC and others', in order to prevent their suppliers and customers from migrating to other systems.

But you also may have learned about the characteristics of more *equal-footed and cooperative industrial clusters and networks*. Here, firms do not strive for a further disintegration of their VAC but have an interest to generate and exploit common and collective positive network effects.

We still are not able to further formalize the mechanisms found. For that purpose, some richer game-theoretic and mathematical tools are required.

4.4.2 What Lies Ahead? The Following Parts of the Book

After this first *applied* chapter, we will take deeper looks at further applied dimensions of microeconomics, such as the complexity and indeterminacy of *real-world markets* (Chapter 7), the *size dimension* of the economy and of its institutionalized coordination (Chapter 14), at technological *openness* issues (Chapter 15), at aspects of the *theory of the firm*, of clusters, networks, and *national and regional systems of innovation* (Chapter 16), or at potential *policy implications* of such complexity microeconomics (Chapter 17).

And after this *introductory part*, we will further and deeper focus on potential *solutions of coordination and cooperation* problems, emerging from microeconomic interactions, entailing coordination and allocation *structures* that become independent of individual agents. Insofar we will be in line with what *classical and postclassical complexity economists* had in mind when considering *decentralized, spontaneous polypolistic systems* and conditions of *emerging, and potentially self-sustaining, solutions* (see, e.g., Chapters 11–13). We will consider such systems under the basic real-world condition of direct interdependencies, intricate structures, fallacies of aggregation, and divergences of collective and individualistic rationalities. Conditions of dynamic and sustained *systemic economic success*, based on continuing both technical and behavioral/organizational innovation, thus will be at the core of what complex microeconomic theorizing, modeling, and complex-systems simulation are about. This will structure the further parts of this book.

In particular, Part II will introduce you to the "mainstream" neoclassical model of an economy, where agents are not directly interdependent (but partial markets are), the *general-equilibrium market economy* (Chapter 5), and to both its critique (Chapter 6) and the theorizing and modeling of real-world markets (Chapter 7).

Part III will introduce you to the *tools* of proper modeling and analysis of complex economies— game theory (Chapter 8), computer simulation (Chapter 9), the formal analysis of different dynamic forms of the economy (Chapter 10), and the comparative formal analysis of dynamics, evolution, and complexity (Chapter 11).

Part IV then will introduce theories and existing core models: historical theories of older and younger founding fathers of complexity (micro)economics (Chapter 12), a core set of current models of complexity microeconomics (Chapter 13), and an exemplary modeling application of the size dimension of emergent coordination (Chapter 14).

Part V will apply what you will have learned so far to real-world topical issues, including technological openness (Chapter 15), a real-world theory of the firm, acting in networks and innovation systems (Chapter 16), and policy implications in a broad perspective, where firms, individuals, business advisors and network coordinators, and semipublic and conventional public agents are envisaged and addressed to act under new perspectives gained and in new ways (Chapter 17).

A final methodologically informed reflection about applying the knowledge learned in the real world and in professional life will conclude (Chapter 18).

At this point, you may already have a clearer understanding of what complexity microeconomics is about, and will be prepared, and endowed, to gain more in-depth knowledge about the economic world of individual agents, their micro-interdependencies and interactions, and their systemic results.

Chapter References

Amin, S., 1999. Capitalism, imperialism, globalization. In: Chilcote, R.M. (Ed.), The Political Economy of Imperialism: Critical Appraisals. Kluwer Academic Publishers, Boston, Dordrecht, London, pp. 157–168.

Andersen, B., Frenz, M., 2008. How technological innovation and emerging organizational forms challenge existing appropriability regimes in music markets: the effects of music downloads and p2p file-sharing. In: First DIME Scientific Conference, April, Department of Management, Birkbeck, University of London. <http://www.dime-eu.org/files/active/0/SC-session2D-Andersen-Frenz.pdf> (accessed 07.06.13.).

Armstrong, M., 1998. Network interconnection in telecommunications. Econ. J. 108 (**448**), 545–564.

Armstrong, P., 2001. Science, enterprise and profit: ideology in the knowledge-driven economy. Econ. Soc. 30 (**4**), 524–552.

Bair, J., 2008. Analysing global economic organization: embedded networks and global chains compared. Econ. Soc. 37 (**3**), 339–364.

Baker, P., 1996. Spatial outcomes of capital restructuring: "new industrial spaces" as a symptom of crisis, not solution. Rev. Polit. Econ. 8, 263–278.

Baldwin, R., Venables, A.J., 2010. Relocating the value chain: offshoring and agglomeration in the global economy. Discussion Paper No. 8163, Centre for Economic Policy Research, London, UK. Available at: <http://www.princeton.edu/~ies/Fall10/VenablesPaper.pdf> (accessed 13.06.13.).

Bennett, R.J., Bratton, W.A., Robson, P.J.A., 2000. Business advice: the influence of distance. Reg. Stud. 34, 813–828.

Biswas, S., 2002. W(h)ither the nation-state? National and state identity in the face of fragmentation and globalization. Glob. Soc. 16 (**2**), 175–198.

Block, F., 2000. Disorderly co-ordination: the limited capacities of states and markets. In: Burlamaqui, L.B., Castro, A.C., Chang, H.-J. (Eds.), Institutions and the Role of the State. Edward Elgar, Cheltenham, Northampton, pp. 53–71.

Breschi, S., Malerba, F., 2001. The geography of innovation and economic clustering: some introductory notes. Ind. Corp. Change. 10, 817–833.

Bresnahan, T., Gambardella, A., Saxenian, A.L., 2001. "Old Economy" inputs for "new economy" outcomes: cluster formation in the New Silicon Valleys. Ind. Corp. Change. 10 (**4**), 835–860.

Brusco, S., 1982. The Emilian model: productive decentralisation and social integration. Cambridge J. Econ. 6, 167–184.

Casciaro, T., 2003. Determinants of governance structures in alliances: the role of strategic, task and partner uncertainties. Ind. Corp. Change. 12 (6), 1223–1251.

Chen, P., 2010. Economic Complexity and Equilibrium Illusion. Essays on market instability and macro vitality. Routledge, London, UK, and New York.

Chertow, M., Ehrenfeld, J., 2012. Organizing self-organizing systems: toward a theory of industrial symbiosis. J. Ind. Ecol. 16 (1), 13–27.

Coe, N.M., Dicken, P., Hess, M., 2008. Global production networks: realizing the potential. J. Econ. Geogr. 8 (3), 271–295.

Cohen, W.M., Nelson, R.R., Walsh, J.P., 2000. Protecting their intellectual assets: appropriability conditions and why U.S. manufacturing firms patent (or not). NBER Working Paper No. 7552. <http://www.nber.org/papers/w7552> (accessed 27.2.14.).

Cordes, C., 2008. A potential limit on competition. J. Bioecon. 10, 127–144.

Cox, K.R. (Ed.), 1997. Spaces of Globalization: Reasserting the Power of the Local. The Guilford Press, London, New York.

Diez-Vial, I., Alvarez-Suescun, E., 2010. Geographical agglomeration as an alternative to vertical integration. Rev. Ind. Organ. 36 (4), 373–389.

Dobusch, L., Schuessler, E., 2012. Theorizing path dependence: a review of positive feedback mechanisms in technology markets, regional clusters and organizations. Ind. Corp. Change. 22 (3), 617–647.

Dupuy, J.-C., Torre, A., 1998. Co-operation and trust in spatially clustered firms. In: Lazaric, N., Lorenz, E. (Eds.), Trust and Economic Learning. Edward Elgar, Cheltenham, Northampton, pp. 141–161.

Elsner, W., 2000. An industrial policy agenda 2000 and beyond—experience, theory and policy. In: Elsner, W., Groenewegen, J. (Eds.), Industrial Policies After 2000. Kluwer Academic Publishers, Boston, Dordrecht, London, pp. 411–486.

Farrell, H., 2009. The Political Economy of Trust. Institutions, Interests, and Inter-Firm Cooperation in Italy and Germany. Cambridge University Press, Cambridge, New York.

Feldman, M., Braunerhjelm, P., 2006. The genesis of industrial clusters. In: Feldman, M., Braunerhjelm, P. (Eds.), Cluster Genesis: Technology-Based Industrial Development. Oxford University Press, Oxford, New York, pp. 1–16.

Feser, E.J., 1998. Old and new theories of industry clusters. In: Steiner, M. (Ed.), Clusters and Regional Specialisation: On Geography, Technology and Networks. Pion, London, pp. 18–40.

Foray, D., 1998. The economics of knowledge openness: emergence, persistence and change of conventions in the knowledge systems. In: Lazaric, N., Lorenz, E. (Eds.), Trust and Economic Learning. Edward Elgar, Cheltenham, Northampton, pp. 162–189.

Galbraith, J.K., 2012. Inequality and Instability. A Study of the World Economy Just Before the Great Crisis. Oxford University Press, Oxford, New York.

Gallaway, T., Kinnear, D., 2002. Free ride: an institutionalist analysis of information in the internet age. J. Econ. Issues. 36 (2), 441–447.

Gallaway, T., Kinnear, D., 2004. OS software, the wrongs of copyright, and the rise of technology. J. Econ. Issues. 38 (2), 467–474.

Garon, J.M., 2012. Localism as a production imperative: an alternative framework for promoting intangible culture heritage. In: Pager, S.A, Candeub, A. (Eds.), Transnational Culture in the Internet Age. Edward Elgar, Cheltenham, Northampton, pp. 346–369.

Gauch, S., 2008. + vs −: dynamics and effects of competing standards of recordable DVD-media. In: Egyedi, T.M., Blind, K. (Eds.), The Dynamics of Standards. Edward Elgar, Cheltenham, Northampton, pp. 47–67.

Gereffi, G., Humphrey, J., Sturgeon, T., 2005. The governance of global value chains. Rev. Int. Polit. Econ. 12 (1), 78–104.

Gertler, M.S., Wolfe, D.A., Garkut, D., 2000. No place like home? The embeddedness of innovation in a regional economy. Rev. Int. Polit. Econ. 7 (4), 688–718.

Gibbon, P., 2008. Governing global value chains: an introduction. Econ. Soc. 37 (3), 315–338.

Goldenberg, J., 2010. Local neighborhoods as early predictors of innovation adoption. MSI reports: working paper series, No. 2. <http://ssrn.com/abstract=1545245> (accessed 30.11.13.).

Gottinger, H.W., 2003. Economies of Network Industries. Routledge, Abingdon, New York.

Haekli, J., 2009. Geographies of trust. In: Haekli, J., Minca, C. (Eds.), Social Capital and Urban Networks of Trust. Ashgate, Farnham, Burlington, pp. 13–35.

Hess, C., Ostrom, E. (Eds.), 2007. Understanding Knowledge as a Commons. From Theory to Practice. The MIT Press, London, Cambridge.

Hutter, M., 2001. Efficiency, viability and the new rules of the internet. Eur. J. Law. Econ. 11 (1), 5–22.

Hyndman, K., Kraiselburd, S., Watson, N., 2010. Aligning capacity decisions in supply chains when demand forecasts are not common knowledge: theory and experiment. Southern Methodist University, Dallas, TX, Mimeo. <http://papers.ssrn.com/sol3/papers.cfm?abstract_id=1545445> (accessed 14.06.13.).

Jones, M.T., 2000. The competitive advantage of the transnational corporation as an institutional form: a reassessment. Int. J. Soc. Econ. 27, 943–958.

Kamath, S., Agrawal, J., Chase, K., 2012. Explaining geographic cluster success—the GEMS model. Am. J. Econ. Sociol. 71 (1), 184–214.

Katz, M.L., Shapiro, C., 1994. Systems competition and network effects. J. Econ. Perspect. 8 (2), 93–115.

Kingston, W., 2000. A spectre is haunting the world—the spectre of global capitalism. J. Evol. Econ. 10 (1), 83–108.

Koellinger, P., Schade, C., 2010. The influence of installed technologies on future adoption decisions: empirical evidence from E-Business. ERIM Report Series Reference No. ERS-2010-012-ORG. Erasmus Research Institute of Management, University of Rotterdam. Available at: <http://repub.eur.nl/res/pub/18463/ERS-2010-012-ORG.pdf> (accessed 13.06.13.).

Krugman, P., 1991. Increasing returns and economic geography. J. Polit. Econ. 99 (3), 483–499.

Lane, C., Probert, J., 2009. National Capitalisms, Global Production Networks: Fashioning the Value Chain in the UK, USA, and Germany. Oxford University Press, Oxford, New York.

Langlois, R.N., 2003. The vanishing hand: the changing dynamics of industrial capitalism. Ind. Corp. Change. 12 (2), 351–385.

Lazonick, W., 1993. Industry clusters versus global webs: organizational capabilities in the American economy. Ind. Corp. Change. 2 (1), 1–24.

Lazonick, W., 2001a. Organizational integration and sustainable prosperity. In: Forrant, F., Pyle, J., Lazonick, W., Levenstein, C. (Eds.), Approaches to Sustainable Development. University of Massachusetts Press, Amherst, MA, pp. 46–89.

Lazonick, W., 2001b. Sustainable Prosperity in the New Economy? Business Organization and High-Tech Employment in the United States. W.E. Upjohn Institute for Employment Research, Kalamazoo, MI.

Li, K., Chu, C., Hung, D., Li, S., 2010. Industrial cluster, network and production value chain: a new framework for industrial development based on specialization and division of labour. Pacific Econ. Rev. 15 (5), 596–619.

Li, W., Veliath, R., Tan, J., 2013. Network characteristics and firm performance: an examination of the relationships in the context of a cluster. J. Small Bus Manage. 51 (1), 1–22.

Maggioni, M.A., 1997. Firms, uncertainty and innovation policy. In: Antonelli, G., De Liso, N. (Eds.), Economics of Structural and Technological Change. Routledge, London, pp. 230–257.

Maillat, D., Grosjean, N., 1999. Globalization and territorial production systems. In: Fischer, M.M., Suarez-Villa, L., Steiner, M. (Eds.), Innovation, Networks and Localities. Springer, Berlin, pp. 50–65.

Malmberg, A., Soelvell, O., Zander, I., 2004. Spatial clustering, local accumulation of knowledge and firm competitiveness. In: Cantwell, J. (Ed.), Globalization and Location of Firms. Edward Elgar, Cheltenham, Northampton, pp. 155–167.

Markusen, A., 1996. Sticky places in slippery space: a typology of industrial districts. Econ. Geogr. 72 (3), 293–313.

Marshall, A., 1890. Principles of Economics. Macmillan, Basingstoke, London (eighth ed.: 1920, Chapter X: "Industrial organization, continued. the concentration of specialized industries in particular localities," pp. 222–242).

McCann, P., 2007. Sketching out a model of innovation, face-to-face interaction and economic geography. Spat. Econ. Anal. 2 (2), 117–134.

Miguélez, E., Moreno, R., 2012. Do labour mobility and networks foster geographical knowledge diffusion? The case of European regions. XREAP Working Paper No. 2012–14. Available at: <http://papers.ssrn.com/sol3/papers.cfm?abstract_id=2120360> (accessed 14.06.13.).

Miller, E.S., 2001. The impact of technological change on market power and market failure in telecommunications. J. Econ. Issues. 35, 385–393.

Mizrahi, S., 1998. Regional co-operation and innovative industries: game-theoretical aspects and policy implications. In: Steiner, M. (Ed.), Clusters and Regional Specialisation: On Geography, Technology and Networks. Pion, London, pp. 81–91.

Moore, G., Davis, K., 2004. Learning the Silicon Valley way. In: Bresnahan, T., Gambardella, A. (Eds.), Building High-Tech Clusters: Silicon Valley and Beyond. Cambridge University Press, Cambridge, MA, pp. 7–39.

Nagler, M.G., 2008. Network externalities, mutuality, and compatibility. Working Paper No. 08–37, NET Institute, Center for Addiction and Recovery Education, Florida. Available at: <http://www.netinst.org/Nagler_08-37.pdf> (accessed 13.06.13.).

Nousala, S., 2010. Emergent structures and geographical scales: what it means for practical policy application. Available at: <http://www.researchgate.net/publication/228268609_Emergent_Structures_and_Geographical_Scales_What_It_Means_for_Practical_Policy_Application> (accessed 14.06.13.).

Orlikowski, W.J., Iacono, C.S., 2000. The truth is not out there: an enacted view of the "digital economy". In: Brynjolfsson, E., Kahin, B. (Eds.), Understanding the Digital Economy: Data, Tools, and Research. MIT Press, Cambridge, MA, pp. 352–380.

Orsenigo, L., 2006. Clusters and clustering: stylized facts, issues, and theories. In: Braunerhjelm, P., Feldman, M. (Eds.), Cluster Genesis. Technology-Based Industrial

Development. Oxford University Press, Oxford, New York, pp. 195–218.

Padoan, P., 2001. Globalization, regionalism and the nation state: top down and bottom up. In: Franzini, M., Pizutti, F.R. (Eds.), Institutions and Social Cohesion. Springer, Berlin, pp. 237–256.

Paoli, A. D., Addeo, F., 2011. Social network research in strategy and organization: a typology. Available at: <http://papers.ssrn.com/sol3/papers.cfm?abstract_id=2060892> (accessed 14.06.13.).

Peoples, J., 2003. Economic gains from regional concentration of business operations. In: Sugden, R., Hartung, C. R., Meadows, G.R. (Eds.), Urban and Regional Prosperity in a Globalized New Economy. Edward Elgar, Cheltenham, Northampton, pp. 159–180.

Perraton, J., 2001. The global economy—myths and realities. Cambridge J. Econ. 25 (5), 669–684.

Ponte, S., Gibbon, P., 2005. Quality standards, conventions and the governance of global value chains. Econ. Soc. 34 (1), 1–31.

Powell, W.W., Smith-Doerr, L., 1994. Networks and economic life. In: Smelser, N.J., Swedberg, R. (Eds.), The Handbook of Economic Sociology. Princeton University Press and Russell Sage, Princeton, New York, pp. 368–402.

Prandelli, E., Sawhney, M., Verona, G., 2008. Collaborating with Customers to Innovate. Conceiving and Marketing Products in the Networking Age. Edward Elgar, Cheltenham, Northampton.

Pratt, A., 1997. The emerging shape and form of innovation networks and institutions. In: Simmie, J.M. (Ed.), Innovation, Networks and Learning Regions. J. Kingsley, London, pp. 124–136.

Quéré, M., Joel, T.R., 1998. Alfred Marshall and territorial organization of industry. In: Oxley, J.E., Yeung, B. (Eds.), Structural Change, Industrial Location and Competitiveness. The Globalization of the World Economy 3. Edward Elgar, Cheltenham, Northampton, pp. 86–103.

Rabach, E., Kim, E.M., 1994. Where is the chain in commodity chains? The service sector nexus. In: Gereffi, G., Korzeniewicz, M. (Eds.), Commodity Chains and Global Capitalism. Greenwood Press, Westport, CT.

Raikes, P., Jensen, M.F., Ponte, S., 2000. Global commodity chain analysis and the French filière approach: comparison and critique. Econ. Soc. 29 (3), 390–417.

Rallet, A., Torre, A., 1998. On geography and technology: proximity relations in localised innovation networks. In: Steiner, M. (Ed.), Clusters and Regional Specialisation: On Geography, Technology and Networks. Pion, London, pp. 41–57.

Reinstaller, A., Hoelzl, W., 2004. Complementarity constraints and induced innovation: some evidence from the first IT regime. In: Foster, J., Hoelzl, W. (Eds.),

Applied Evolutionary Economics and Complex Systems. Edward Elgar, Cheltenham, Northampton, pp. 133–154.

Ruigrok, W., van Tulder, R., 1995. The Logic of International Restructuring. Routledge, London.

Rupert, M., 2000. Ideologies of Globalization: Contending Visions of a New World Order. Routledge, London, New York.

Ruys, P.H.M., 2005. The governance of services. Discussion Paper No. 2005-102, Tilburg University, Center for Economic Research. Available at: <http://ideas.repec.org/p/dgr/kubcen/2005102.html> (accessed 06.06.13.).

Rycroft, R.W., Kash, D.E., 1999. The Complexity Challenge: Technological Innovation for the 21st Century. Pinter, London.

Saxenian, A., 1994. Regional Advantage. Culture and Competition in Silicon Valley and Route 128. Harvard University Press, Cambridge, London.

Shy, O., 2001. The Economics of Network Industries. Cambridge University Press, Cambridge, New York (repr. 2002).

Shy, O., 2010. A short survey of network economics. FRB of Boston Working Paper No. 10-3, Federal Reserve Bank of Boston, Boston, MA. Available at: <http://ssrn.com/abstract=1600783> (accessed 13.06.13.).

Standing, G., 2001. Global flexibility: economic integration, social disintegration? In: Franzini, M., Pizzuti, F.R. (Eds.), Globalization, Institutions and Social Cohesion. Springer, Berlin, pp. 167–181.

Steiner, M., 1998. The discreet charm of clusters: an introduction. In: Steiner, M. (Ed.), Clusters and Regional Specialisation: On Geography, Technology and Networks. Pion, London, pp. 1–17.

Stiglitz, J.E., 2012. The Price of Inequality. How Today's Divided Society Endangers Our Future. W.W. Norton and Company, New York, London.

Sturgeon, T., Van Biesebroeck, J., Gereffi, G., 2008. Value chains, networks and clusters: reframing the global automotive industry. J. Econ. Geogr. 8, 297–321.

Swyngedouw, E., 1997. Neither global nor local: "glocalization" and the politics of scale. In: Cox, K.R. (Ed.), Spaces of Globalization: Reasserting the Power of the Local. Guilford Press, New York, NY, pp. 137–166.

Tichy, G., 1998. Clusters: less dispensable and more risky than ever. In: Steiner, M. (Ed.), Clusters and Regional Specialisation: On Geography, Technology and Networks. Pion, London, pp. 226–237.

Tirole, J., 1995. The Theory of Industrial Organization. MIT Press, Cambridge, MA.

Torre, A., Gilly, J.-P., 2000. On the analytical dimension of proximity dynamics. Reg. Stud. 34 (2), 169–180.

Varian, H.R., Farrell, J., Shapiro, C., 2004. The Economics of Information Technology. An Introduction. Cambridge University Press, Cambridge, New York.

Vitali, S.T., Glattfelder, J.B., Battiston, S.T., 2011. The network of global corporate control, study at the TU Zurich. PLoS ONE. 6 (**10**), Downloaded on January 16, 2013 from: <http://www.plosone.org/article/info%3Adoi%2F10.1371%2Fjournal.pone.0025995>.

Vlaar, P.W.L., 2008. Contracts and Trust in Alliances: Discovering, Creating and Appropriating Value. Edward Elgar, Cheltenham, Northampton.

Waterman, D., Ji, S.W., 2012. Online vs. offline in the U.S.: are the media shrinking? Inf. Soc. 28 (5), 285–303.

Weitzel, T., van Westarp, F., 2002. From QWERTY to nuclear power reactors: historic battles for the standard. In: Geihs, K., et al., (Eds.), Networks: Standardization, Infrastructure, and Applications. Physica, Heidelberg, New York, pp. 33–61.

Wettengl, S., 1999. Initiierung Technologischer Systeminnovationen: Wege zur Vermeidung von Abwarteblockaden in Innovationsnetzwerken (Initiating Technological System Innovations: Ways to Avoid Waiting Blockages in Innovation Networks). Vandenhoeck & Ruprecht, Goettingen.

Yang, K., Liang, H., 2010. Managing service quality: call for a network mechanism. Paper for the 2010 International Conference on Management and Service Science. Available at: <http://ieeexplore.ieee.org/stamp/stamp.jsp?tp=&arnumber=5576662> (accessed 13.06.13.).

Further Reading—Online

For further readings on the issues of this chapter, see the textbook website at http://booksite.elsevier.com/9780124115859

EXERCISES

1. Key Terms
What have you learned so far?
Reconsider the following key conceptions from Chapters 1–3:
- Direct Interdependence
- Complex Decision Structures
- (Initial Strong Strategic) Uncertainty
- (Bounded) Rationality
- Complexity
- Social Optimum Game
- Competing Economic Perspectives: Invisible Hand and Fallacy of Aggregation
- Coordination Problems and Social Dilemmas
- Collective Goods and Externalities
- Opportunity Costs
- Normal-Form Games
- Imperfect/Incomplete Information
- Rationality in the Short-Run and in the Long-Run
- Recurrence and Sequentiality
- Supergames
- One-Shot Result and Single-Shot Solution
- Social Rules and Institutions
- Coordination and Cooperation
- Sacrificing and Sanctioning
- Common and Collective Problem-Solving
- Path-Dependent, Cumulative, and Nonergodic Process
- Increasing Returns
- Learning
- Expectations and Trust
- Instrumental and Ceremonial Dimensions of Social Institutions
- Strategic Games
- Anti-Coordination Games
- Nash Equilibrium
- Pareto Optimum.

Define/explain the following key terms/key conceptions as described in this chapter:
- Lock-in (technological lock-in)
- Global institutional disequilibrium
- VAC fragmentation
- Inappropriability
- TIC
- Interoperability and technological standardization
- Behavioral standardization/institutionalization
- Network technology, network externality/network effect
- Strategic triangle of the economy
- Spatial industrial cluster
- Industrial network
- Functional versus strategic interrelations among firms
- Hub&spoke network structure
- OS.

2. New Properties of the Economy: Complex Products, Fragmented Value Chains, and Network Technologies

  a. Explain the *coordination problems* (i) in the *fragmented VAC* and (ii) in *technology choice* among competing (noninteroperable) network technologies.

  b. Explain the potential *social dilemmas* additionally implied (i) in the innovation process in the fragmented VAC and (ii) in *technology choice* between noninteroperable network technologies. Explain a potential *mutual blockage of (Pareto-superior) action* under conditions of a social dilemma in technology choice. Also explain potential *regret* in technology choice.

  c. Explain potential *inappropriability* in the VAC and the system of both providing and receiving positive *externalities*.

  d. Explain how *interoperable network technologies* may contribute to solving the coordination and dilemma problems for fragmented agents in the VAC, and to producing highly integrated complex products through a fragmented VAC.

3. Technology Choice: Relative Number of Choices and Related Payoffs (1)

  Assume the following numerical *payoff functions* for technologies T_1 and T_2, depending on the number of agents $i = 1,\ldots, n$ having chosen the respective technology:

Number n of Agents I Choosing Respective Technology	Payoff for Each Agent if n-Agents Have Chosen T_1 [$P_{T1}(n)$]	Payoff for Each Agent if n-Agents Have Chosen T_2 [$P_{T2}(n)$]
1	2	1
2	3	2
3	4	3

Determine the *resulting payoffs* for agents A, B, and C, P_A, P_B, P_C, all depending on $T_{1,2}$ and n, in particular depending on the following *choice sequences given* (indicated by X), after all agents have chosen (fill in the bottom right cells in the format: P_A, P_B, P_C):

Agent	T_1	T_2	$P(T_{1,2},n)$
A	X		./.
B	X		./.
C		X	

Agent	T_1	T_2	$P(T_{1,2},n)$
A	X		./.
B		X	./.
C		X	

You may determine the other six possibilities of *choice sequences* on your own.

4. Technology Choice: Relative Numbers of Choices and Related Payoffs (2)

  Further consider an *indefinite series of agents* with *random technology choices*. Determine their changing payoffs, depending on the choices made by each following agent, given the following numerical payoff functions:

Number n of Agents I Choosing Respective Technology	Payoff for Each Agent if n-Agents Have Chosen T_1 [$P_{T1}(n)$]	Payoff of Each Agent if n-Agents Have Chosen T_2, [$P_{T2}(n)$]
1	2	1
2	3	2
3	4	3
4	5	4
5	6	5
6	7	6
7	8	7
...	...	...

See the following example of some sequence:

Agent No.	T_1	T_2	$\Pi(T_{1,2},n)$
1	X		2
2		X	2, 1
3		X	2, 2, 2
4	X		3, 2, 2, 3
5	X		4, 2, 2, 4, 4
6	X		5, 2, 2, 5, 5, 5
7		X	5, 3, 3, 5, 5, 5, 3
...	...	...	...

Build different choice sequences among up to 10 choosing agents in a row, and determine the different results for each.

In particular, give an example for a choice sequence that yields a higher payoff for those who have chosen the inferior technology T_2.

5. New Empirical Phenomena to Cope with Increased Complexity
   a. Explain why and how firms in the global corporate economy tend to organize (or being organized) in
      • spatial industrial clusters,
      • industrial networks,
      • hub&spoke networks.
   b. Explain why *OS-type networks* may be considered superior in collectively governing/managing information and expectations (trust), and to accelerate information and innovation flows. Consider the single-shot solution to explain institutionalized *information exchange* and *knowledge sharing* in OS-type networks.

PART II

MARKETS: GENERAL-EQUILIBRIUM THEORY AND REAL-WORLD MARKET STRUCTURES

5

The Ideal Neoclassical Market and General Equilibrium*

An Economist Abducted by Aliens   © Paul Twomey

Paul Twomey, http://www.feed-charity.org/user/gimage/BeckerCartoon2_350_423.JPG

*Matthias Greiff has contributed to this chapter.

5.1 INTRODUCTION: THE NEOCLASSICAL PARADIGM AND RESEARCH PROGRAM

The neoclassical method and research program are formulated to develop a "pure theory," an abstract model, starting from some abstract axioms and taking as little as possible as given. The objective is to construct an "optimal" equilibrium model of a market economy in a *price—quantity world* and logically deduct *general laws* applicable therein.

However, any model is an imagery, analogy, or metaphor only, relating variables to one another, mostly rather few, and not a theoretical explanation per se. Models can be set up to yield *unique predetermined equilibria*, in "closed" deterministic models, or they can be complex, with many variables, agents and relations, positive feedback loops, etc., no longer apt to yield unique solutions, with open boundaries and being open-ended, as in complexity economics.

Neoclassical economics typically ends up in price—quantity spaces employing the mathematics of *maximization under restrictions* (Lagrange algorithm). *Economism* in that sense is the idea of a "pure" economy, isolated from the rest of society and from the natural environment.

General Equilibrium Theory (GET) as the study of all interdependent ideal partial markets is the comprehensive formulation of neoclassical economics for a simultaneous equilibrium in all partial markets. But the neoclassical paradigm (as any paradigm) cannot straightforwardly be tested and rejected, since "data" are always selected, "stylized facts," evaluated, adapted to the world view of the measurer, and mostly not perfectly selective, but fuzzy and adaptable to different functional forms and formal models.

GET is often named *Walrasian economics*, after its "inventor," Léon Marie-Esprit Walras (1834–1910). Walras considered an exchange economy where agents trade given goods not with each other but with a fictitious auctioneer. There is no direct interdependence of agents but only an indirect interdependence between the collectivities of suppliers and demanders through the aggregates of their supply and demand quantities and prices. Walras was the first to emphasize the interdependence of individual partial markets in his *Elements of Pure Economics* published in 1874, 3 years after the works of William Stanley Jevons and Carl Menger. Walras, Jevons, and Menger thus are considered to be the leaders of the neoclassical or *marginalist revolution*, whose key elements are marginal utility (and marginal productivity in production) and scarcity.

To construct the models, "perfect competition" and "perfect information" are assumed. This means that all agents (firms and households) get all relevant information, past, present, and future, reflected in prices, at no costs. Preferences and production technologies are exogenously given and technology can be accessed and employed by everyone without problems. It is implied that trade may only take place at market-clearing prices, which are computed by the *fictitious auctioneer* (social planner), meaning agents take equilibrium prices as given and maximize utility (households) or profits (firms). This auctioneer announces prices and collects information from all agents regarding how much they would be willing to sell and buy at that price. If the amounts of planned supply and planned demand do not coincide, a new price is called. This process continues until planned demand and supply are equal (*tatônnement*). Only then can exchanges take place. In this setting, a competitive equilibrium is characterized by prices and allocations at which decisions are mutually consistent. Agents can buy and sell exactly the amount they want to at those prices. Supply equals demand (market clearing). At equilibrium, there is no endogenous mechanism that causes a change in prices. However, an exogenous change in preferences or technology will result in a shift of the equilibrium position, hence, a change to new equilibrium prices. Such an equilibrium allocation, as the *"first welfare theorem"* shows, is *Pareto-optimal*.

Early GET models were static models of an economy, abstracted from the time dimension. Soon, however, they were extended to take into account *intertemporal decisions* as well as *risk*.

In our explanation of GET, the starting point is an economic system consisting of households (or consumers) and firms whose behavior will be described in the next two sections (Sections 5.2 and 5.3). Consumers own given resources at the outset which they can consume or sell. Firms buy inputs which they transform into outputs in a production process. The economy, thus, is considered to be an *exchange economy*, i.e., there is no money. However, we can think of one commodity (e.g., gold) as a money commodity, serving as *numéraire* (so that prices express how many units of the numéraire have to be exchanged for acquiring a unit of a specific good).

Having introduced consumer and production theory, we briefly explain *partial equilibrium* analysis, the analysis of one market in isolation (Section 5.4), before we proceed to *general equilibrium* analysis. In a general equilibrium, the partial markets are connected and all agents' decisions are mutually consistent. The general equilibrium, its implications, and the conditions necessary for the model to offer the desired results are considered in Section 5.5. Thereafter, we briefly review the Ramsey intertemporal optimization model and the "New Keynesian" model in Section 5.6. Section 5.7 then presents not only some extensions of the basic framework, mainly focusing on outcomes that result in cases where information is imperfect, but also the effects that constraints preventing the attainment of some conditions for a first-best Pareto-optimal solution may have.

5.2 CONSUMER THEORY

5.2.1 Preferences

With Descartes' division of the world into an inner subjective domain (res cogitans) and an outer objective domain (res extensa), active mind and passive matter became separated. The mind was conceived as having values and being subjective; the individual was defined with reference to reason and consciousness, i.e., with reference to itself. This is known as his famous Cogito ergo sum, "I think, therefore I am" (Descartes, 1637). The outer world, matter, was portrayed as objective and valueless,

working according to universal and unchanging rules.

The Cartesian dualism is at the root of the neoclassical conception of the individual. The subjective mind was relegated to the unscientific domain and it was assumed that individuals do not interact on a subjective level. The individual's autonomy is derived from her "tastes" which remain unchanged. While the unscientific inner world of individuals (tastes) was treated as unobservable and unchanging, choice was observable. The focus shifted from the individual toward choice behavior and individual decision making. Moreover, with this conception the individual was completely detached from her social structure (e.g., class).

The preference-based approach to individual decision making starts from an assumed preference relation (also see Box 5.1). If an individual is offered a choice between apples x and oranges y, she will choose apples if she prefers apples to oranges, formally $x \succsim y$. We assume that the individual has a rational preference relation over the set of all possible choices. Let x, y, z be mutually exclusive alternatives in the set of all possible choices X. A rational preference relation is characterized by:

- completeness: for $x, y \in X$, $x \succsim y$ or $y \succsim x$ or both
- transitivity: for $x, y, z \in X$, $x \succsim y$ and $y \succsim z \rightarrow x \succsim z$
- reflexivity: $x \sim x$ for all $x \in X$.

Moreover, by assuming continuity we exclude lexicographic preferences. Let's illustrate this with a simple two-good example. An agent with lexicographic preferences will choose the bundle that offers the largest amount of the first good x_1 no matter how much of the other good is in the bundle. That is, $(x_1, x_2) \succ (x'_1, x'_2)$ if $x_1 > x'_1$. If both bundles have exactly the same amount of the first

BOX 5.1

REVEALED PREFERENCES

The "revealed preferences" concept was developed by Samuelson. As utility functions themselves cannot be measured, and the concept of utility is applicable only in circular arguments (the assumption is confirmed by behavior that you explain based on the assumption), Samuelson intended to formulate an approximation that permits working with formal models on the basis of observed behavior, as the first attempt at avoiding utility concept problems resulted in fundamentally the same kinds of problem, just one step removed by focusing on the first order conditions for optimality in behavior.

In a first article (Samuelson, 1938), he introduced the basic assumption: preferences are revealed in consumption decisions. If an individual has to make consumption choices between bundles of goods, subject to a budget constraint and without influence on prices or quantities, if the functions describing consumption choices are homogeneous of degree zero, and if behavior is consistent, so that given the choice between any two bundles of goods, an individual always picks the same one (provided they are within her budget), then observation of behavior and data can be used to formulate a preference setting that is noncontradictory.

In a follow-up (Samuelson, 1948), he shows that for the two-good case, revealed preferences, if enough observations are available, result in functions that are equivalent to the

indifference curves of utility theory. These results were generalized by Houthakker (1950), showing the conditions which must hold for integrability of the implied function (integrability implying consistency of behavior) (see also, Samuelson, 1950). A theory of consumer behavior can in this reading be formulated on the basis of revealed preferences.

The condition is called the strong axiom of revealed preferences. If this holds, demand behavior can be reconstructed as satisfying individual utility maximization conditions. It states that if any consumption bundle is revealed to be preferred to another one (having been purchased in a situation where both were affordable) the reverse cannot hold—the second bundle cannot be revealed to be preferred to the first in a situation where both can be afforded. For any comparison of bundles of goods, where this condition holds as "strongly preferred" for at least one pair of bundles, and as at least "weakly preferred" (better or as good as) for all the rest, on inconsistent choices (bundle 1 preferred to bundle n in one situation, but bundle n preferred to bundle 1 in another situation), a consistent (rational) ordering is possible, offering an overall order of bundles that is free of contradictions. The implied function, as said, can be integrated and shown to be equivalent to a preference function.

We will take up the concept and explain criticisms in Chapter 6, together with a number of other critical discussion of neoclassical theory.

good, $x_1 = x'_1$ then the amounts of the second good are compared and the bundle with more of the second good will be preferred. A lexicographic preference relation is rational but

cannot be represented by a continuous function since it is not preserved under limits. With the sequence $\{(1/m)|m \in \mathbb{N}\}$, the bundle $(1/m, 0)$ will always be preferred to $(0, 1)$.

In the limit, however, this preference relation will be reversed:

$$\lim_{m \to \infty} \left(\frac{1}{m}, 0 \right) = (0,0) \prec (0,1)$$

5.2.2 Utility, Maximization, and Demand

Some words on notation: We use subscript $n \in \{1, \ldots, N\}$ to indicate goods and superscript $i \in \{1, \ldots, I\}$ to indicate individuals. Superscript $j \in \{1, \ldots, J\}$ is used for indexing firms. Equilibrium values are denoted by an upper bar. Prices are denoted as row vectors, allocations, endowments, and demand as column vectors, hence their product (e.g., $p\omega$) gives us a scalar (for an overview of the symbols used, see Table 5.1).

An individual's wealth acts as a constraint on her demand since prices are assumed to be positive (goods are desirable). The consumer

cannot spend more than she has. We assume that each consumer has a strictly positive (and finite) endowment of at least one good ($\omega_n^i > 0$ for all i and some n). This results in the attainable set being nonempty and, more importantly, bounded. Our rational consumer is assumed to maximize utility, taking prices as given.

Let there be a finite number of commodities n and assume that utility functions satisfy the following conditions. The utility function u is

- continuous
- strictly increasing in every argument
- at least differentiable twice on the interior of $\mathbb{R}_+^N$
- strictly concave $\partial u / \partial x_n > 0$ and $\partial^2 u / \partial x_n^2 < 0$
- satisfies

$$\lim_{x_j \to 0} \frac{\partial u(x)}{\partial x_n} = +\infty$$

The utility function maps all possible choices of commodity bundles into the real numbers, mathematically $u \colon \mathbb{R}_+^N \to \mathbb{R}$. Commodity bundles that are preferred give a higher utility. The first part of the assumption follows from continuity of preferences and is made primarily for mathematical convenience. The second part means that goods are good, i.e., by consuming more of any good the consumer gets higher utility. Differentiability is assumed for mathematical convenience. Concavity is derived from the assumption of diminishing marginal utility, i.e., the additional amount of utility gained from consuming one extra unit decreases with the amount of the good the individual already consumes. Marginal utility is positive but decreasing. The last condition of this assumption ensures that quantities and prices will be strictly positive in equilibrium. The budget set of consumer i containing all possible bundles that the consumer could buy, given her endowments, is

$$B^i = \left\{ x^i \in \mathbb{R}_+^N \colon px^i \leq p\omega^i \right\}$$

TABLE 5.1 Symbols, Variables, and Parameters for Neoclassical GET

Symbol	Meaning
$p = (p_1, p_2, \ldots, p_N)$	Price vector
$\mathbb{R}^N$	Commodity space
$\mathbb{R}_+^N$	Consumption set
$x^i = (x_1^i, x_2^i, \ldots, x_N^i) \in \mathbb{R}_+^N$	Commodity bundle or demand individual i
$x' = (x^1, x^2, \ldots, x^I) \in \mathbb{R}_+^{IN}$	Allocation
$\omega^i = (\omega_1^i, \omega_2^i, \ldots, \omega_N^i)$	Endowment individual i
$\overline{\omega} = \sum_{i=1}^I \omega^i$	Aggregate endowment
$w = p\omega$	Wealth
λ	Lagrange multiplier
∇	Gradient vector
$\overline{x}, \overline{x}_n^i, \overline{p}$	Equilibrium allocation, equilibrium demand agent i good n, equilibrium price vector

The solution to the consumer's utility maximization problem (UMP) is a bundle of commodities as a function of prices and wealth $x^i = x^i(p, w)$. This is called a Walrasian or Marshallian demand function.[1] For positive prices and wealth let $v(p, w)$ denote the indirect utility function, giving the value of u at $\bar{x}(p)$ (the value of the solved UMP). Since the utility function is strictly increasing (assumption 1), we know that the budget constraint will hold with equality. The consumer spends her wealth completely:

$$v(p, w) = \max_{x} u(x) \text{ subject to } px = w \quad (5.1)$$

Using the Lagrange method (see Box 5.2), we maximize

$$\Lambda = u(x) - \lambda(px - w) \quad (5.2)$$

and get the following first-order conditions (FOCs):

$$\frac{\partial u}{\partial x_n} = \lambda p_n \quad \forall n \in N \quad (5.3)$$

$$px = w \quad (5.4)$$

Assuming that all consumers have positive endowments and thus $w > 0$, we know that in equilibrium they will consume a positive quantity of each good, hence $x_n > 0$ for $n \in \{1, 2, \ldots, N\}$. From Eq. (5.3), we know that in this equilibrium for consumers, marginal utilities (weighted by prices) are equalized, formally

$$\frac{\partial u/\partial x_{n1}}{p_{n1}} = \frac{\partial u/\partial x_{n2}}{p_{n2}} \Leftrightarrow \frac{p_{n1}}{p_{n2}} = \frac{\partial u/\partial x_{n1}}{\partial u/\partial x_{n2}} \quad (5.5)$$

where $n_1, n_2 \in \{1, 2, \ldots, N\}$. Call this the equilibrium condition for consumers.[2] Equation (5.4) tells us that the budget constraint will be binding, i.e., consumers spend their wealth completely. The FOCs of the UMP give us $N + 1$ equations and $N + 1$ variables ($x_1, x_2, \ldots, x_N$ and λ), a system that is solvable in principle.

An Illustration

Using a simple example, we illustrate how we can use the FOCs of the UMP to derive the demand functions. Assume a world with just two goods, x_1 and x_2. (For simplicity, we omit the superscript i indexing individuals.) The utility function is given by

$$u(x_1, x_2) = \alpha \ln x_1 + (1 - \alpha)\ln x_2$$

We set up the Lagrange function and derive the FOCs:

$$\max_{x_1, x_2, \lambda} \alpha \ln x_1 + (1 - \alpha)\ln x_2 - \lambda(p_1 x_1 + p_2 x_2 - w)$$
$$(5.6)$$

$$\frac{\alpha}{x_1} = \lambda p_1 \quad (5.7)$$

$$\frac{1 - \alpha}{x_2} = \lambda p_2 \quad (5.8)$$

$$p_1 x_1 + p_2 x_2 = w \quad (5.9)$$

We combine Eqs. (5.7) and (5.8) to get

$$p_1 x_1 = \frac{\alpha}{1 - \alpha} p_2 x_2$$

---

[1]Since the utility function is concave and we optimize over a compact set B, by the Weierstrass theorem we know that a solution exists. By assuming that u is strictly concave, we get a single-valued solution, i.e., we get a demand function instead of a demand correspondence. Marshallian demand functions are homogeneous of degree zero in (p, w) and they satisfy Walras' Law. A proof can be found in Mas-Colell et al. (1995, p. 52).

[2]This fact was first demonstrated by Hermann Heinrich Gossen in 1854. Gossen's Laws: (i) decreasing marginal utility, $\partial u/\partial x_n > 0$ and $\partial^2 u/\partial x_n^2 < 0$; (ii) utility is maximized if marginal utilities are equalized, $(\partial u/\partial x_n)/p_n = (\partial u/\partial x_{n'})/p_{n'}$; (iii) a commodity has value if there is subjective scarcity, i.e., demand exceeds supply (cf. Niehans, 187−196).

BOX 5.2

THE LAGRANGE MULTIPLIER APPROACH

The utility function $u(x)$ itself has no maximum, utility increases as more of the goods is consumed. The utility maximization problem is a constrained optimization problem, i.e., utility is maximized subject to the constraint that consumers cannot spend more than their available wealth. One way to transform an unconstrained maximization problem into a constrained maximization problem and to solve it is the method of Lagrange multipliers.

For the sake of illustration, assume a consumer in a world with only two goods, x_1 and x_2, and wealth ω. We can write the utility maximization problem as a constrained maximization problem. The constraint $p_1 x_1 + p_2 x_2 = \omega$ is rewritten so that we have zero on the right-hand side, $p_1 x_1 + p_2 x_2 - \omega = 0$. Then, the left-hand side of the rewritten budget constraint is multiplied by the Lagrange multiplier λ and the whole term is subtracted from the utility function:

$$\max_{x_1, x_2, \lambda} \Lambda = u(x, y) - \lambda(p_1 x_1 + p_2 x_2 - \omega)$$

The term λ is called Lagrange multiplier and ensures that the budget constraint is satisfied. The first-order conditions for a maximum are obtained by taking the first partial derivatives of the Lagrange function Λ with respect to x_1,

x_2, and λ and setting them equal to zero. Since we assume that the utility function is concave, the first-order conditions are necessary and sufficient conditions.

$$\frac{\partial \Lambda}{\partial x_1} = \frac{\partial u}{\partial x_1} - \lambda p_1 = 0$$

$$\frac{\partial \Lambda}{\partial x_2} = \frac{\partial u}{\partial x_2} - \lambda p_2 = 0$$

$$\frac{\partial \Lambda}{\partial \lambda} = p_1 x_1 + p_2 x_2 - \omega = 0$$

Now we have a system of three equations which we solve for x_1, x_2, and λ. The specific form of the solution depends on the specific form of the utility function. As can be seen from the last three equations, the budget constraint is satisfied. The consumer spends her wealth completely. By dividing the first and the second equation, we obtain an interesting result:

$$\frac{\partial u / \partial x_1}{\partial u / \partial x_2} = \frac{\lambda p_1}{\lambda p_2} = \frac{p_1}{p_2}$$

At the optimum, the ratio of prices equals the ratio of marginal utilities (=marginal rate of substitution). For our consumer this means that, at the optimum, the utility from the last monetary unit spent on each good must be the same.

---

and rearrange Eq. (5.9) into

$$p_1 x_1 = w - p_2 x_2$$

From the last two equations, we get

$$\frac{\alpha}{1 - \alpha} p_2 x_2 = w - p_2 x_2$$

This equation can be solved for x_2 as a function of prices and wealth:

$$\bar{x}_2(p_1, p_2, w) = (1 - \alpha)\frac{w}{p_2} \qquad (5.10)$$

Inserting Eq. (5.10) in Eq. (5.9) and solving for the demand of x_1, we get

$$\bar{x}_1(p_1, p_2, w) = \alpha\frac{w}{p_1} \qquad (5.11)$$

The last two equations are the individual's Walrasian or Marshallian demand functions, telling us how much of each good the individual will demand as a function of prices and wealth. Note that the demand for each good increases in wealth and decreases in the price of the good. If wealth increases, the consumer buys at least as much of each good as before. And if the price of a good increases, she will buy less of this particular good. The consumer's utility at the optimum is given by the indirect utility function:

$$v(p, w) = u(\overline{x}_1, \overline{x}_2) = \alpha \ln \left[\alpha \frac{w}{p_1} \right] + (1 - \alpha)$$

$$\ln \left[(1 - \alpha) \frac{w}{p_2} \right]$$

An indirect utility function gives utility as a function of prices and income. The direct utility function gives utility as a function of goods consumed.

We can depict optimal consumption in the two-good case (x_1 and x_2) as in Figure 5.1. If the whole budget is used for either good, the amount consumed is given by the intersection at the axes. If both goods are consumed, the maximum possible amounts lay on the budget line between those intersections. This lines slope is given by the relative price ratio, as shown in Eq. (5.5). The optimal consumption bundle is given where the budget line is a tangent to an indifference curve.

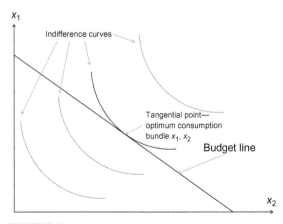

FIGURE 5.1 Marshallian demand—consumption bundles x_1 and x_2.

Indifference curves are sets of points that depict constant levels of utility. Their slope is likewise given by the condition shown in Eq. (5.5). As the budget constraint shows the maximum possible consumption that can be realized, every point to the right of it is out of reach for the consumer. Because more consumption by assumption is better, utility increases on indifference curves that lay further to the right and the optimal consumption bundle is one that is on the budget line. Hence, optimal consumption is given where budget and indifference curves touch in one point. If there was an intersection, there would be an indifference curve in reach signifying utility increases that the buyer could still reach.

5.2.3 Marshallian Demand, Hicksian Demand, and the Slutsky Equation

The dual problem to utility maximization is a minimization of expenditure for reaching a specific utility level u. The general form is thus:

$$\min e(p_i, x_i) \quad \text{subject to } u(x) \geq \overline{u} \qquad (5.12)$$

the result being the Hicksian demand function $h(p, u)$. If u is continuous and locally nonsatiated, the optima of the utility maximization and expenditure minimization will coincide.

A Marshallian demand function shows the quantity of a good demanded depending on its price and overall income and that Hicksian demand shows the quantity of a good demanded depending on its price when all other prices and the level of utility to be attained are kept constant.

Given an expenditure function $e(p, u)$ that shows the minimum expenditure required for reaching a certain utility level, the relation between Hicksian and Marshallian demand is given by:

$$h(p, u) = x(p, e(p, u)) \qquad (5.13)$$

Given the indirect utility function just derived in Section 5.2.2, we can also state

$$x(p, w) = h(p, v(p, w)) \tag{5.14}$$

The two kinds of demand can be related by what is termed the Slutsky equation. More concretely, given changes in prices, this equation relates changes in Marshallian demand, or uncompensated demand, and changes in Hicksian, or compensated, demand (called compensated demand because it shows what changes would be required for maintaining a constant level of utility following changes in prices). What the Slutsky equation does is, it split changes in uncompensated demand into two components, namely, changes that are due to the change in relative prices resulting in substitutions of relatively cheaper goods for relatively more expensive ones (substitution effect, SE) and changes that are due to possible changes in consumers' purchasing power following price changes, the income effect (IE; remember that agents are assumed to possess a certain endowment that they trade the value of which is going to change following price changes):

$$\frac{\partial x_i(p, w)}{\partial p_j} = \underbrace{\frac{\partial h_i(p, u)}{\partial p_j}}_{SE} - \underbrace{\frac{\partial x_i(p, w)}{\partial w} x_j(p, w)}_{IE} \tag{5.15}$$

The derivation is very straightforward. Starting with the total differential of a Hicksian demand function:

$$\frac{\partial h_i(p, u)}{\partial p_j} = \frac{\partial x_i(p, e(p, u))}{\partial p_j} + \frac{\partial x_i(p, e(p, u))}{\partial e(p, u)} \frac{\partial e(p, u)}{\partial p_j}$$

Shephard's lemma tells us that $\partial e(p, u) / \partial p_j = h_j(p, u)$. Using the identities referred earlier, in Eqs. (5.13) and (5.14), namely, $h_j(p, u) = h_j(p, v(p, w)) = x_j(p, w)$, we can substitute and rearrange to arrive at the Slutsky equation. Graphically, we can depict this as follows in Figure 5.2.

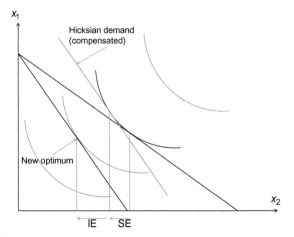

FIGURE 5.2 IE and SE in demand changes following an increase of p_2.

After an increase in the price of x_2, the budget line changes and its slope becomes steeper. The price increase signifies a decrease in consumption potential. The new optimal consumption bundle is given by the tangential of the new budget line and a lower indifference curve. Moving this new budget line in parallel until it touches the indifference curve on which the earlier optimum was located allows a graphic representation of IE and SE of price changes. The SE moves consumption to a point where the relatively cheaper good (x_1) is consumed more. The IE reduces the amount of overall consumption. Note that for x_1, the SE of an increase in p_2 means it is consumed more; the IE then reduces overall consumption.

5.3 PRODUCTION THEORY

5.3.1 The Production Function

We describe firms' production possibilities by a production function F stating the relation between inputs and outputs. For simplicity, assume that there is one output, y, which is produced with two inputs, capital K and labor L (however, also see Section 6.5.3).

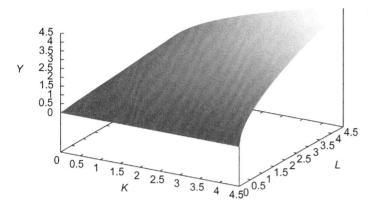

FIGURE 5.3 The Cobb–Douglas production function ($\alpha = 0.5$).

These functions are assumed to be homogeneous of degree one. Often used as an example here is the Cobb–Douglas technology, which is defined by the following production function for $\alpha \in (0, 1)$ and two inputs (K, L):

$$y = F(K, L) = AK^\alpha L^{1-\alpha} \qquad (5.16)$$

In this context, it is also useful to define the marginal product which is the change in total output that occurs in response to a one unit increase in a variable input, keeping all other inputs fixed (the slope of the surface in Figure 5.3). Mathematically, this is the partial differential of the production function with respect to the variable input.

Assume that the production function is differentiable. Then, the marginal rate of technical substitution (MRTS) tells us at which rate one input can be exchanged for another input without altering the quantity of output. To derive the equation for the MRTS, we start with the total differential of the production function (5.16) and set it equal to zero. This is the equation for an isoquant, a contour line through the set of points at which the same quantity of output is produced. We stick to the Cobb–Douglas production function for the derivation, with $A = 1$:

$$\mathrm{d}y = \alpha\left(\frac{L}{K}\right)^{1-\alpha}\mathrm{d}K + (1-\alpha)\left(\frac{K}{L}\right)^{\alpha}\mathrm{d}L = 0$$

If we solve it for the MRTS, it is obvious that the MRTS equals the ratio of the marginal products which is nothing else than the absolute value of the slope of the isoquant:

$$\mathrm{MRTS}_{KL} = \left|-\frac{\mathrm{d}L}{\mathrm{d}K}\right| = \frac{\alpha}{1-\alpha}\frac{L}{K} \qquad (5.17)$$

Figure 5.4 shows isoquants for different levels of output. The shaded areas in the figure are input sets, i.e., combinations of inputs that produce at least some specified amount of output. Formally, isoquant $S(y)$ and input requirement set $I(y)$ are defined as follows:

$$S(y) = \{(L, K):F(K, L) = y\} \qquad (5.18)$$

$$I(y) = \{(L, K):F(K, L) \geq y\} \qquad (5.19)$$

The isoquant is the boundary of the input requirement set. Here, we assume free disposal, i.e., by increasing one input we can produce at least as much output. Moreover, we assume that the law of diminishing returns holds. The law states that if all but one input is fixed, the increase in output from an increase in the variable input declines. For the production function, this implies

$$\frac{\partial F}{\partial K} > 0 \ \text{ and } \ \frac{\partial^2 F}{\partial K^2} < 0 \ \text{ and } \ \frac{\partial F}{\partial L} > 0 \ \text{ and } \ \frac{\partial^2 F}{\partial L^2} < 0$$

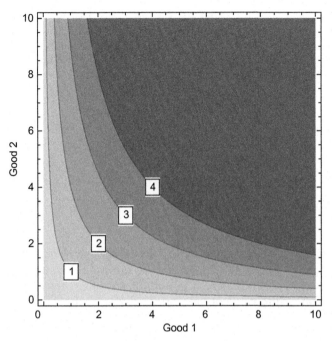

FIGURE 5.4 Isoquants and input sets for a Cobb–Douglas production function ($\alpha = 0.5$).

5.3.2 Cost Minimization and Cost Functions

Let there be a firm with Cobb–Douglas production technology with $\alpha = 0.5$. Input costs are given by the cost of capital r and the wage w. The firm wants to produce output $y = \bar{y}$ taking prices as given. Which amount of capital and labor will the firm choose? To answer this problem, we set up the Lagrangian of the firm's cost-minimization problem:

$$\min_{K,L} rK + wL \quad \text{subject to} \quad F(K, L) \geq \bar{y}$$

$$\Lambda(K, L, \lambda) = rK + wL - \lambda(F(K, L) - \bar{y}) \quad (5.20)$$

Note that we replaced the inequality from the constraint by an equality in the Lagrange function since the firm will not use more of any input than necessary, i.e., production will take place on the isoquant. To figure out which point on the isoquant is cost minimizing, we take FOCs and set them to zero:

$$r = \lambda \frac{\partial F}{\partial K} \quad \text{and} \quad w = \lambda \frac{\partial F}{\partial L}$$

$$F(K, L) = \bar{y}$$

The last FOC states that production will be on an isoquant, i.e., no inputs will be wasted. Combining the first two FOCs, we get the firm's optimality condition for the relative amounts of inputs used:

$$\frac{r}{w} = \frac{\partial F/\partial K}{\partial F/\partial L} = \text{MRTS}_{KL} \quad (5.21)$$

At the optimum, the relative price of inputs has to equal the MRTS.

We now derive the firm's cost function, giving us the minimum cost for producing output $\bar{y}$. For simplicity, we use the Cobb–Douglas production function with $\alpha = 0.5$ (see Figure 5.5):

$$C(r, w; \bar{y}) = \min_{L,K} wL + rK \quad \text{subject to} \quad \bar{y} = K^{0.5} L^{0.5}$$

$$(5.22)$$

Solving the constraint for K yields $K = \bar{y}^2 / L$. By substitution, we rewrite the cost function as:

$$C(r, w; \bar{y}) = \min_L wL + r\frac{\bar{y}^2}{L}$$

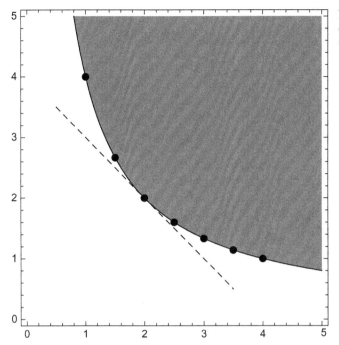

FIGURE 5.5 Input requirement set (gray), isoquant (boundary), and relative prices (dotted line) for a Cobb–Douglas production function.

Taking the FOC and setting zero yields $w = r\bar{y}^2/L^2$. We rearrange the terms to get the conditional factor demand for labor:

$$L(w, r, \bar{y}) = \left(\frac{r}{w}\right)^{0.5} \bar{y} \qquad (5.23)$$

In the same way, we can derive the conditional factor demand for capital:

$$K(w, r, \bar{y}) = \left(\frac{w}{r}\right)^{0.5} \bar{y} \qquad (5.24)$$

We can now write the cost function as:

$$C(r, w; \bar{y}) = wL(w, r, \bar{y}) + rK(w, r, \bar{y}) = 2w^{0.5}r^{0.5}\bar{y} \qquad (5.25)$$

5.3.3 Profit Maximization

Using the cost function, we now turn to the firm's profit maximization problem. A firm's profits are defined as revenue minus cost:

$$\pi(y, L, K; w, r, p_0) = p_0 y - (wL + rK) \qquad (5.26)$$

Since profit maximization implies cost minimization, we can substitute the cost function for $(wL + rK)$. The firm's task is now to choose the level of output y that maximizes profits, taking input prices (w and r) as given. The price of the output p_0 is also taken as given:

$$\max_{y \geq 0} \pi = p_0 y - C(r, w, y) \qquad (5.27)$$

The solution depends on p_0 and the specific form of the cost function. Assume that the firm can sell its complete output at price p_0. The Cobb–Douglas production function exhibits constant returns to scale (see Box 5.3) since

$$F(cK, cL) = A(cK)^{0.5}(cL)^{0.5} = cAK^{0.5}L^{0.5} = cF(K, L)$$

This means that the cost function is linear and average costs (AC $= C(r, w, y)/y$) as well

---

BOX 5.3

RETURNS TO SCALE

Returns to scale is a term that refers to the proportionality of changes in output after the amounts of all inputs in production have been changed by the same factor. Technology exhibits increasing, decreasing, or constant returns to scale. Constant returns to scale prevail, i.e., by doubling all inputs we get twice as much output; formally, a function that is homogeneous of degree one, or, $F(cx) = cF(x)$ for all $c \geq 0$. If we multiply all inputs by two but get more than twice the output, our production function exhibits increasing returns to scale. Formally, we use a function with a degree of homogeneity greater than one to depict this, $F(cx) > cF(x)$ for $c > 1$. Vice versa, decreasing returns to scale are defined by $F(cx) < cF(x)$ for $c > 1$. Increasing returns to scale might prevail if a technology becomes feasible only if a

certain minimum level of output is produced. On the other hand, limited availability of scarce resources (natural resources or managerial talent) might be limiting firm size in which case decreasing returns to scale are more likely. Also, it is possible that a technology exhibits increasing returns at low levels of production and decreasing returns at high levels.

A related term is economies of scale. Economies of scale refer to changes in costs per unit after changes in units of output. When average unit costs fall after increases in output were implemented, we can say that the company realized economies of scale (fixed costs in production are a reason frequently given for their existence, technological factors, increasing returns to scale, may be another cause).

---

as marginal costs $(MC = \partial C(r, w, y) / \partial y)$ are constant.[3]

If the price p_0 is below average costs, the firm will do best if it produces zero output (Figure 5.6B). And if $p_0 > AC$, the firm maximizes profits by producing as much as possible since every additional unit of output increases profits. In this case, the maximum of the profit function is not well-defined (Figure 5.6A). Profit can be visualized as the distance between the revenue function (yp_0) and the cost curve $(C(r, w, y))$.

With decreasing returns to scale, the cost function is convex in y, i.e., the more the

output is produced, the higher the average costs is. If the cost of producing one unit of output is larger than p_0, it is optimal to produce nothing (Figure 5.7A). Otherwise, it is optimal to increase production up to the point where marginal costs (the costs of increasing production by one unit) are equal to p_0. In Figure 5.7B, this is the case where the slope of the cost curve, which gives us marginal costs, is equal to the slope of the revenue function.[4]

In the case of increasing returns to scale, there exists no optimum. The cost function is concave and average as well as marginal costs

---

[3]Mathematically, average costs are the slope of the line going from the origin to a point on the cost curve. Marginal costs are the slope of the cost curve. In the case of constant returns to scale, marginal costs are equal to average costs.

[4]To the right of this point, profits would decrease since the costs of producing one unit more are larger than the revenue from selling the additional unit.

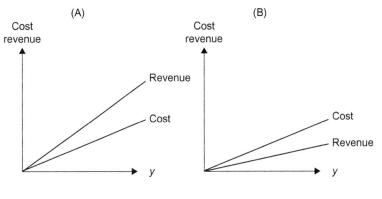

FIGURE 5.6 Revenue and cost for constant returns to scale.

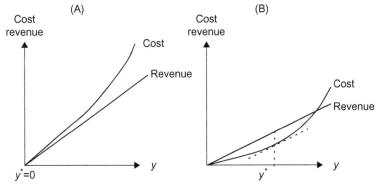

FIGURE 5.7 Revenue and cost for decreasing returns to scale.

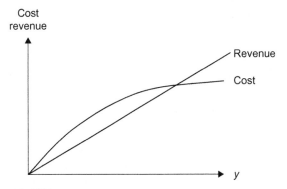

FIGURE 5.8 Revenue and cost for increasing returns to scale.

Note that the discussion of a firm's profit maximization problem relies on two assumptions. First, all output can be sold at the price p_0. Second, all inputs are available in unlimited supply at constant prices. In general, these assumptions will not hold.

5.4 PARTIAL EQUILIBRIUM

We consider a single market in isolation from all other markets. We assume that the consumers and the firms in this market take prices as given, i.e., there is no strategic interaction and they behave as if they were in a perfectly competitive market. We further assume that we can describe consumers and firms by drawing on a representative agent for both of them. The sum of all individuals'

decrease. At some point, marginal costs are below p_0 (and still decreasing), so the firm can increase its profit by expanding production (Figure 5.8).

choices is then mathematically equivalent to the decision of one agent.

Figure 5.9 shows a downward-sloping demand function. We have seen demand

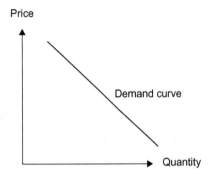

FIGURE 5.9   A stylized demand function.

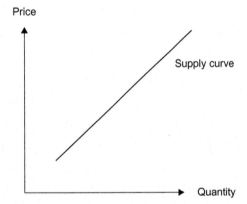

FIGURE 5.10   A stylized supply function.

functions before in Eqs. (5.10) and (5.11). The demand function specifies the quantity the consumer wishes to purchase at various prices.

In a similar way, we can depict the firm's supply schedule connecting all price–quantity pairs which are consistent with the firm's optimum (Figure 5.10). The higher the price of a good, the more a firm is willing to produce and offer, hence, the supply function is upward sloping. In fact, in the perfect competition market, the supply curve is the marginal cost curve. As some inputs to production are assumed to be available only in limited supply, we have a convex cost function and decreasing returns to scale (as in Figure 5.7). Increasing production is only profitable if the good can be sold at a higher price.

Figure 5.11 now brings the demand and supply functions together. The equilibrium price and quantity are given by the intersection of the curves and depict the price–quantity combination at which the consumer and the firm are both satisfied. If the price is above the equilibrium price, there will be excess supply. The firm wants to sell more than it can, hence the firm will cut the price and we move closer to the equilibrium. At a price lower than the equilibrium price, the consumer wants to buy more than is available. There is excess demand, resulting in upward pressure on the price. At the market

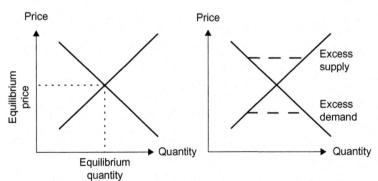

FIGURE 5.11 Supply and demand combined in interaction: equilibrium price and quantity, excess demand and supply.

equilibrium, excess supply and excess demand are both equal to zero. The resulting allocation is Pareto-optimal.

Note that in the analysis of supply and demand, we assumed decreasing returns to scale. For the short run in which some inputs, such as factory buildings, are available in limited supply, this is a reasonable assumption. This is why the upward-sloping supply curve is also known as a short-run supply curve. In the long run, however, we assume that all inputs can be increased (it takes some time to set up a new factory but in principle this is possible). Then the production technology can exhibit constant or increasing returns to scale. In the case of constant returns, the long-run supply curve is horizontal and in the case of increasing returns, it is downward sloping.

5.5 GENERAL EQUILIBRIUM

5.5.1 Welfare Theorems and Walras' Law

Instead of just looking at one market in isolation, as we did in Section 5.4, we look at the complete set of markets now. From the discussion of consumer and firm behavior earlier, in particular Eqs. (5.5) and (5.21), we know that in equilibrium, marginal rates of substitution and technical substitution are equalized:

$$\text{MRS}_{12} = \frac{\partial u / \partial x_1}{\partial u / \partial x_2} = \frac{p_{x1}}{p_{x2}} = \frac{\partial F / \partial x_1}{\partial F / \partial x_2} = \text{MRTS}_{12}$$

(5.28)

General equilibrium analysis allows us to consider all markets simultaneously, instead of just looking at one market in isolation. A general equilibrium is a concurrent equilibrium in all markets, hence the cross effects among markets are taken into account. The combination of equilibrium prices and allocations $(\bar{p}, \bar{x})$ is also known as Arrow–Debreu equilibrium. Wealth is endogenously determined by the

equilibrium price system and the endowments. For the sake of simplicity, we assume that there is no production; we look at an exchange economy. From our discussion of consumer theory, we know that the condition given by Eq. (5.5) has to hold for all consumers, hence we have NI equations. Also, we assume that all markets are in equilibrium, i.e., excess demand z (demand minus supply) is equal to zero:

$$z_n(p) = \sum_{i=1}^{I} \bar{x}_n^i(p) - \sum_{i=1}^{I} \omega_n^i = 0 \quad \forall\, n \in \{1, \ldots, N\}$$

(5.29)

A corollary of Eq. (5.29) is Walras' Law, stating that if $N - 1$ markets are in equilibrium, the Nth market must also be in equilibrium (see Box 5.4).

From Eq. (5.29) we get another N equations, so in total there are $N + \text{IN}$ equations and $N + \text{IN} + 1$ unknowns (N prices, IN unknowns for the allocations, and λ). Since (excess) demand functions are homogeneous of degree zero in prices, we can normalize prices by choosing one good as numéraire and setting its price equal to one. Homogeneity follows from the fact that the budget set does not change if we count in Euros or cents. Now we have a system of $N + \text{IN}$ equations with $N + \text{IN}$ unknowns, and this is as far as Walras got. He just counted the number of equations and unknowns and concluded that an equilibrium existed. However, this need not be true. We will discuss the conditions for existence, together with the questions of uniqueness and stability. For now, we just assume that there exists an equilibrium with positive prices and state some properties of this equilibrium (Debreu, 1959; Arrow and Hahn, 1971; Starr, 1997):

- Theorem 1 (first welfare theorem):
  A competitive equilibrium allocation is an efficient allocation.

BOX 5.4

WALRAS' LAW

If $N-1$ markets are in equilibrium, the Nth market must also be in equilibrium. This follows from simple accounting. If we sum up all individual budget constraints, we see that total expenditure has to equal total receipts, i.e.,

$$\overline{p}\sum_{i=1}^{I}\hat{x}^i(p) = \overline{p}\sum_{i=1}^{I}\omega^i$$

For excess demand functions, Walras' Law implies that they sum up to zero:

$$\sum_{n=1}^{N} z_n(p) = 0$$

For the analysis of general equilibrium, this result proves useful since it implies that if all markets but one are in equilibrium, the last market also has to be in equilibrium:

$$z_n(\overline{p}) = 0 \ \forall \ n \in \{1, \ldots, N-1\} \Rightarrow z_N(\overline{p}) = 0$$

- Theorem 2 (second welfare theorem): Every efficient allocation can be transformed into a competitive equilibrium allocation by appropriate transfers.

The first welfare theorem just states that the equilibrium allocation is efficient in the sense of Pareto: Nobody can be made better off without making someone else worse off. It provides a major argument for market liberals.

The first welfare theorem does not mean that the competitive equilibrium allocation is the social optimum, a claim that would require the comparison of individual utilities. Strictly speaking, there are infinitely many Pareto-efficient allocations. One of them can be achieved by letting individuals trade at market-clearing prices. At the resulting general equilibrium, no individual can increase her utility by trading at the prevailing prices.

In slightly more technical jargon, an allocation $x = (x^1, x^2, \ldots, x^I)$ is Pareto-optimal if there is no other allocation $\hat{x} = (\hat{x}^1, \hat{x}^2, \ldots, \hat{x}^I)$ such that $u(\hat{x}^i) \geq u(x^i) \ \forall i$ and $u(\hat{x}^i) > u(x^i)$ for at least one i. In addition, it has to hold that both allocations are feasible, i.e., the economy cannot consume more than the available endowments, $\sum_{i=1}^{I} x^i \leq \sum_{i=1}^{I} \omega^i$ and $\sum_{i=1}^{I} \hat{x}^i \leq \sum_{i=1}^{I} \omega^i$.

The first welfare theorem now states that the competitive equilibrium, defined by equilibrium prices $\overline{p}$ and allocations $\overline{x}$ that solve the individuals' optimization problems, is Pareto-optimal. What follows is a short sketch of the proof. Suppose that allocation $\hat{x}$ dominates allocation $\overline{x}$ in the sense that $\hat{x}^i = \overline{x}^i$ and $u(\hat{x}^i) = u(\overline{x}^i)$ for $i = 1, 2, \ldots, I-1$, and $u(\hat{x}^I) > u(\overline{x}^I)$. The hat allocation yields the same utility for all agents except agent I whose utility is higher under the hat allocation. Since $\overline{x}^i$ is the solution to agent i's UMP subject to the budget constraint, any allocation that yields higher utility cannot be within the agent's budget set, $\overline{p}\hat{x}^I > \overline{p}\omega^I$. For all agents except agent I, it holds that $\overline{p}\hat{x}^i = \overline{p}\omega^i$. Summing up the budget constraints for all users, we get

$$\overline{p}(\hat{x}^1 + \hat{x}^2 + \cdots + \hat{x}^I) > \overline{p}(\omega^1 + \omega^2 + \cdots + \omega^I)$$

$$\overline{p}\sum_{i=1}^{I}\hat{x}^i > \overline{p}\sum_{i=1}^{I}\omega^i \Leftrightarrow \sum_{i=1}^{I}\hat{x}^i > \sum_{i=1}^{I}\omega^i$$

Put in words, the last equation states that total consumption is higher than aggregate endowment. This contradicts the feasibility of the alternative allocation $\hat{x}$.

BOX 5.5

THREE-AGENTS, TWO-GOODS GENERAL EQUILIBRIUM

This is a simple illustration of an equilibrium in an exchange economy. Agents take prices as given so there is no direct strategic interdependence. No production takes place but three consumers $i = (A, B, C)$ exchange two different goods. Their utility functions are given by

$$u^i(x_1, x_2) = x_1^{a_i} x_2^{1-a_i}$$

with $a_A = 0.4$, $a_B = 0.5$, and $a_C = 0.6$ and endowments $\omega_A = (10, 10)$, $\omega_B = (20, 5)$, and $\omega_C = (5, 10)$. Computing and summing up the individual Walrasian demand functions and equating with aggregate supply, we get the following two equations which have to hold in an equilibrium:

$$17 + 12.5\frac{p_2}{p_1} = 35$$

$$12.5 + 18\frac{p_1}{p_2} = 25$$

Normalizing the price of the first good $p_1^* = 1$, we compute the equilibrium price of the second good as $p_2^* = 1.44$. At these prices, both markets clear simultaneously. Equilibrium allocations are $x^{A*} = (9.76, 10.17)$, $x^{B*} = (13.6, 9.44)$, and $x^{C*} = (11.64, 5.39)$ and utility levels are $u^{A*} = 10.004$, $u^{B*} = 11.3307$, and $u^{C*} = 8.55475$. In comparison, the initial utility levels were $u^A = 10.0$, $u^B = 10.0$, and $u^C = 6.5975$. Hence, exchange resulted in a Pareto-improvement for all agents. Moreover, from the first welfare theorem, we know that the resulting allocation is efficient in the sense of Pareto.

The second welfare theorem states that every efficient allocation is attainable. A way to achieve this is by reallocation of initial endowments. Wealth is transferred and then the market mechanism does its work, so the economy will arrive at the general equilibrium which is efficient. This reveals that the resulting equilibrium allocation is dependent on the initial endowments (see Box 5.5 for an example of an exchange economy).

5.5.2 Existence, Uniqueness, Stability, and the Sonnenschein−Mantel−Debreu Conditions

The two welfare theorems discussed earlier give us some attractive properties of the equilibrium allocations. But with respect to existence, uniqueness and stability of equilibria tell us nothing. In what follows, we will discuss

these three points. Walras counted equations and unknowns and argued that a general equilibrium existed. Formal proofs of the existence of a general equilibrium in competitive markets were developed by Kenneth Arrow and Gerard Debreu as well as Takashi Negishi. The question of uniqueness was analyzed by Hugo Sonnenschein. Finally, we briefly explain the very restrictive conditions that have resulted from these investigations as necessary for allowing for a unique and stable equilibrium, generally known as the Sonnenschein−Mantel−Debreu (SMD) conditions.

Existence

What conditions must be satisfied for an equilibrium to exist? Just counting equations and unknowns is not sufficient. To guarantee existence, we need convexity of preferences (a concave utility function) and a convex production set. The latter implies that we have either constant or decreasing returns to scale, but not increasing returns to scale. Also, it is assumed that each household has strictly positive endowments. Using these assumptions, a general proof of existence was formulated by Arrow and Debreu. Few years later, a different and more compact proof was developed by Negishi. Both proofs rely on the mathematics of set theory, in particular the fixed point theorems developed by Brouwer and Negishi. As these methods are quite sophisticated, we will not discuss them here. For this, the interested reader is referred to Starr (1997, chapter 2) and Mas-Colell et al. (1995, pp. 92–94).

Uniqueness

Knowing the conditions for the existence of an equilibrium, we now turn to the question of uniqueness. Is there a single equilibrium or will there be more than one? As it turns out, there are two stringent conditions under which the existing equilibrium will be unique. In the trivial case, the initial allocation is already Pareto-efficient. No trade will take place and the initial allocation determines the (globally) unique equilibrium.

In the second case, global uniqueness is arrived at by assuming gross substitutability for the demand functions. This means that the demand for each good increases in the price of other goods, $(\partial x_n^i(p))/\partial p_j > 0$ for all $j \neq i$ and all goods $n = 1, \ldots, N$ and individuals $i = 1, \ldots, I$. This requirement translates into a strictly decreasing excess demand function $z_n(p)$ which crosses the x-axis only once. The two conditions for global uniqueness will seldom be fulfilled, so it is likely that there are multiple equilibria. We do not know which equilibrium will be selected. However, if we assume that the economy is at an equilibrium, we know that it will stay there if this equilibrium is locally unique and stable. Local uniqueness is likely (if we exclude perfect substitutes and perfect complements).

Stability

Connected to the question of the uniqueness of an equilibrium is the question of its stability. If the equilibrium is unique, it is also globally stable. After small deviations, the economy will move back to its equilibrium. However, if there are multiple equilibria, some will be locally stable while others will be unstable. Local stability depends on the process which specifies how prices change. If there is more than one locally stable equilibrium, the outcome reached depends on the starting point.

Sonnenschein–Mantel–Debreu

The conditions that have to be fulfilled for arriving at a unique and stable equilibrium are called SMD conditions. The intention was to show that individual demand curves could be aggregated with the resulting market demand curves maintaining their basic characteristics that society could be understood as the sum of its parts and thus represented by a single representative agent. In the end, they had shown that this was not the case.

The problem results as an agent's income is determined by prices and quantities of her endowments, so that, when relative prices change, so does income. For aggregate demand curves, this cannot be ignored, as now a SE and a wealth effect combine in their influence on demand changes. They may be mutually reinforcing or countering one another. The SE refers to relatively cheaper goods being consumed more. The wealth effect is due to changes in the value of the endowments of agents. Wealthier agents consume more, possibly countering effects in markets where demand is negatively affected by SEs. Additionally, more than one price vector may exist that clears markets.

A negatively sloped market demand curve can only be constructed from individual demand curves if these individuals have identical preferences and spend their income on the same goods in the same proportion independently of their income level (basically meaning a world of clones who all consume the same good). In all other cases, the market demand curve can take any form at all. The market demand curve will be continuous, homogeneous of degree zero, and it will satisfy Walras' Law, but market demand is not necessarily monotonically decreasing. In consequence, the SMD conditions mean that equilibrium may be neither unique nor stable unless the very restrictive conditions mentioned are met. (In addition to problems for the model formulation in constructing the benchmark for evaluating market outcomes, this introduces problems relating to equity considerations, for instance, if there are multiple equilibria, which one to try and move the economy to?)

5.6 FURTHER DEVELOPMENTS

5.6.1 Ramsey-Type Intertemporal Optimization

So far, this chapter has only presented equilibria at one single point in time. Neglecting saving and investment, a major component of the economy, however, would constitute a major weakness of the theory. Indeed, their inclusion presents a major challenge because this raises questions such as changes in endowments, information sets, preferences (tastes), changes that could endanger the convexity of the optimization problem, and thus the existence and uniqueness of the equilibrium. If considerations like these are ignored for the moment,[5] the extension of optimization to intertemporal optimization becomes quite straightforward; they were first introduced by Ramsey (1928).

For a simple two-period intertemporal optimization model, consider a single household that lives two periods, 0 and 1. In the first period, it is endowed with capital k_0. It consumes an amount c_0 of k_0 in the first period, the remainder is saved, s_0 (both s_0 and c_0 must be nonnegative):

$$k_0 = c_0 + s_0 \qquad (5.30)$$

The savings of the first period are then available for consumption in the second period, i.e., s_0 equals the endowment in the second period, k_1 which, in turn, equals consumption in the second period, c_1:

$$s_0 = k_1 = c_1 \qquad (5.31)$$

The household maximizes a well-behaved (i.e., concave, continuous, strictly increasing, and twice differentiable in each variable) intertemporal utility function

$$\max U(c_0, c_1) \qquad (5.32)$$

This is mathematically equivalent to the time-static optimization problems; it has a single optimum point, in this case an optimal intertemporal consumption plan. This model can be extended to include more than two (possibly an infinite number of) periods, to include investment, and even to become a full-fledged growth model.

Investment

If the intertemporal savings in the above model are not just savings but yield an interest, we can construct a production theory model. Let the endowment in the second period be a positive (endowment must not be negative) and strictly increasing function F of the first period's savings:

$$k_1 = F(s_0) \qquad (5.33)$$

---

[5]They are partly addressed in DSGE models introduced here and otherwise in game theory approaches in Chapter 8.

The solution is now an intertemporal consumption and investment plan. Note that if we choose a concave, continuous, strictly increasing, and twice differentiable production function, the nonlinearity of the utility function could now theoretically be dropped without affecting the properties of the optimization problem, specifically the existence and uniqueness of a single solution.

Optimization over an Infinite Time Horizon

The model can be applied for an infinite number of timesteps $t = 0, \ldots, \infty$ such that the endowments of the next period k_{t+1} are always produced according to production function F from the savings of the current period, s_0

$$k_{t+1} = F(s_t) \ \forall t \qquad (5.34)$$

The utility function in this type of problems is usually the sum of an infinite sequence of discounted (with factor β) utilities u_t for $t = 0, \ldots, \infty$. Discounting is necessary because otherwise the sum would yield an infinite aggregate utility value. The resulting utility maximization is

$$\max_{\{c(t)\}_{t=0}^{\infty}} \sum_{t=0}^{\infty} \beta^t u_t(c_t) \qquad (5.35)$$

The utility function, however, introduces another difficulty in infinite horizon optimization problems. Note that for the above two-period optimization, we required that the entire endowment has to be consumed in the second period. The rationale of this condition is rather obvious infinite horizon optimizations. In the infinite horizon, however, a final period does not exist. Still, a steady increase of savings toward infinity in order to produce higher quantities while consumption remains around zero is obviously also not a desirable solution. Consequently, the solution of infinite horizon optimization problems must fulfill the condition that the limit of the savings for $t \to \infty$ be finite, the transversality condition.

Usually, this condition is given in the form that the present (discounted) value of the savings or "capital stock" s^0 (for $t \to \infty$) must converge to 0:

$$\lim_{t \to \infty} s_t^0 = 0$$

5.6.2 The Ramsey−Cass−Koopmans Growth Model

Almost three decades later, Ramsey's model of intertemporal optimization was extended into an integrated model of economic growth by Cass (1965), Koopmans (1965), and others. While macroeconomic considerations are not the focus of this book, this section will illustrate the more recent development of neoclassical equilibrium theory with the Ramsey−Cass−Koopmans growth model and give an outlook on real business cycle (RBC) and dynamic stochastic general equilibrium (DSGE) models.

As in the above model, consider one representative household and one representative firm (which may be the same). Household and firm are assumed to live forever. They take prices as given and maximize utility and profits, respectively. There is only one produced good which can either be consumed or invested. Also, we assume that the household has no preference for leisure and supplies one unit of labor each period. In this framework, the only trade-off is the intertemporal trade-off between consumption today and consumption in the future. The solution to the model is an optimal growth path which maximizes social welfare, i.e., the sum of all periods' utility, with β as the discount factor:

$$\max_{\{c(t)\}_{t=0}^{\infty}} \sum_{t=0}^{\infty} \beta^t u[c(t)] \qquad (5.36)$$

This problem of intertemporal optimal allocation is stated and solved as a social planner's problem, i.e., the problem faced by a hypothetical social planner trying to maximize social welfare. It can be shown that a Pareto-optimal allocation that solves the social planner's problem and the allocation arrived at by exchanges in the polypolistic core model are equivalent.

In each time period, we have three goods, labor l_t, capital k_t, and the final output y_t which can either be consumed c_t or invested i_t. Technology is characterized by the production function $y_t = F(k_t, l_t)$ and we assume that capital depreciates at a rate δ so that next period's capital is given by Eq. (5.37), subject to a non-negativity constraint $k_{t+1} \geq 0$:

$$k_{t+1} = (1 - \delta)k_t + i_t \qquad (5.37)$$

The economy is assumed to start with initial capital $k_0 = \bar{k}_0$. The representative household is endowed with one unit of productive time each period and will supply all of it since it does not care about leisure (labor is no argument in the utility function (Eq. (5.36))), hence $l_t = 1 \; \forall t$. For simplicity, it is assumed that there is no uncertainty but perfect foresight:

$$f(k_t) \equiv F(k, 1) + (1 - \delta)k_t \qquad (5.38)$$

The net output $f(k_t)$ can be used for consumption c_t or as capital in next period's production k_{t+1}. We can rewrite consumption as the difference between net output and next period's capital stock, $c_t = f(k_t) - k_{t+1}$, substitute in Eq. (5.36) and rewrite the optimization problem as follows:

$$v(k_0) = \max_{\{k(t+1)\}_{t=0}^{\infty}} \sum_{t=0}^{\infty} \beta^t u[f(k_t) - k_{t+1}] \qquad (5.39)$$

$$0 \leq k_{t+1} \leq f(k_t)$$

$$k_0 = \bar{k}_0 > 0 \;\; \text{given}$$

To derive the mathematical solution would be tedious, hence we will briefly sketch how one would arrive at the solution. First, we would derive the Euler equation, which is a second-order difference equation. Then we use

two boundary conditions, namely, the initial value for k_0 and a transversality condition (stating that the present value of the capital stock converges to zero as time goes to infinity) to solve the Euler equation. The solution is a function which gives us the optimal value for k_{t+1} as a function of k_t, and from the optimal value for k_{t+1}, we can derive the corresponding values for c_t. The complete solution to the social planner problem is an allocation $\{c_t, k_t, l_t\}$. If our economy applies this function each period it is on the optimal growth path.

A hypothetical social planner wanting to maximize welfare should follow this rule, but in reality there is no such social planner. Within the model, however, this can be solved. Negishi (1960) shows that the solution to the social planner's problem is a Pareto-optimal allocation. More precisely, the solution to the social planner's problem yields the set of all Pareto-optimal allocations. From this set, we can select the allocation that is consistent with the firms' and households' FOCs to get the competitive equilibrium allocation, since from the first welfare theorem, we know that the competitive equilibrium allocation is Pareto-optimal. In most cases, the optimization problem is nonlinear and there are no analytic solutions, so numerical methods have to be used.

5.6.3 New Classicals and New Keynesians—Microfoundations of Macroeconomics

Equilibrium, supply and demand determine equilibrium prices which in turn determine output, and thus employment and possibly growth rates. Such a system is stable and follows a smooth and optimal growth path. In reality, however, there are fluctuations in the form of short-run variations in aggregate output and employment. Some economists claim that the fluctuations exhibit no regular pattern but are the consequences of random shocks of various types and sizes. The simplest way New Classical economists model fluctuations is to add shocks to the Ramsey growth model (such a model is fully developed and discussed in Romer, 2006, pp. 180–202). As a consequence, real shocks, i.e., shocks to preferences or technology, which come from outside the model, are propagated through the model and result in fluctuations at the aggregate level. The New Classical Macroeconomics, most prevalent in the work of Robert Lucas and Edward Prescott, was a reaction to Keynesian macroeconomics arguing that involuntary unemployment can arise if aggregate demand is too low. The New Classicals claim that a free price system balances supply and demand in each market, including the labor market, hence there is no place for involuntary unemployment, if we abstract from market imperfections. Fluctuations are explained as responses to real shocks (shocks to real as opposed to nominal variables). Demand shocks result, e.g., from unanticipated changes in fiscal policy. In a supply shock, unanticipated changes in technology cause productivity to change. Since households and firms are assumed to be rational optimizers, fluctuations at the macrolevel are the aggregate effects from households' and firms' efficient responses to shocks. The question now is how to explain persistence. Economies usually show periods of boom and recession which are too long to be just fluctuations. New Classicals in the RBC school claim that shocks are propagated slowly through the whole economy.[6] Also, it is argued that technology shocks do not come in isolation but in waves. Thus, RBC macroeconomists try to explain fluctuations within a Walrasian model of a competitive economy without the need to assume imperfections, missing markets, or externalities.

According to RBC theory, there is no rationale for mitigating fluctuations since they are the consequences of rational adjustments to shocks. Further, there is no place for monetary policy since monetary policy only affects nominal variables, not real variables. Monetary policy has only nominal effects since an increase in the money supply will change the absolute but not the relative price level. Real variables, like preferences and technology, remain unaffected. New Keynesian economics is a response to the New Classicals.[7] Their main disagreement is about how fast prices and wages adjust. New Keynesians have different arguments to explain why adjustment might take time. First, adjusting prices is costly. Second, not all firms adjust prices at the same time, resulting in staggered price adjustment so that overall prices adjust slowly.[8] Third, there can be efficiency wages (Romer, 2006, Section 9.2). Firms pay a wage above the market wage since this increases productivity; a high wage is presumed to increase workers' effort. As a consequence of prices adjusting slowly (sticky prices), households and firms are faced with wrong price signals, leading to misallocations and temporary fluctuations in the real economy. Here, there is a role for monetary policy which can act in order to mitigate fluctuations. Monetary policy has short-run effects as, e.g., an increase in money supply stimulates demand and economic activity. In the long run, however, monetary policy has no effects since prices fully adjust.

---

[6]For a quick review of RBC models, see Romer, 2006, chapter 4.

[7]Two exhaustive references for New Keynesian economics are Walsh (2010) and Woodford (2003).

[8]Sticky prices can be explained by reference to institutional rigidities and bargaining power; here the New Keynesians depart from the assumption of perfectly competitive markets. However, such rigidities can, in principle, be derived from microfoundations.

There are three fundamental assumptions of the New Keynesian model: intertemporal optimization, imperfect competition, and rigidities. The last two components are absent from RBC models, which is the main difference between the two models. In fact, New Keynesian and RBC models employ the same methods. The general equilibrium equations are replaced by equations that give the distance from the equilibrium at a certain point in time and its dynamic development as a difference equation. With additional stochastic components, such models are hence called DSGE models. The method is used in several varieties including the original RBC models, their New Keynesian counterparts, and composite approaches (termed the "new neoclassical synthesis"). The economy is seen as a DSGE system that deviates from the optimal growth path in the short run as a result of exogenous shocks. The models are entirely Walrasian, i.e., they are built up from microeconomic foundations by simple aggregation.

5.7 EXTENSIONS AND TRANSITIONS: THE GENERAL THEORY OF THE SECOND BEST, ASYMMETRIC INFORMATION, AND EFFICIENCY UNDER IMPERFECT INFORMATION

This section offers a look at some interesting results that can be shown in neoclassical models when some of the core assumptions are slightly altered. This will help you to see how sensible the model formulations are to specific assumptions, and how significantly results change at times after what appear to be only slight changes in assumptions. Given that the foundations of policy proposals are often, if only implicitly, rooted in such models, this will help increase your awareness for how an argument for or against certain policy positions may be structured and on which grounds

it is defended. Specifically, this concerns the possibility for an impossibility to attain some optimality condition, in the case of the general theory of the second best, resulting in a situation where the then available best result entails a violation of all other optimality conditions as well. This means that a gradual move toward a first-best solution is usually not possible but that a situation has to be carefully analyzed in order to be able to find how a comparatively good result may be reached given certain constraints that cannot be overcome. The second model to be explained focuses on differences in information availability to different agents, on the demand- and on the supply-side in this case and shows how this may in fact result in the nonconstitution of exchanges that everybody would be willing to enter into, as long as information problems cannot be overcome. Finally, the effects of general imperfect information are shown, which, again, have the effect that the simple policy-kit that the partial and general equilibrium approaches suggest is not adequate as soon as slight changes in the set of assumptions are assumed, as this may lead to optimal tax rates that are in fact positive, and not zero, or markets that are better serviced by few companies instead of many, as is usually presumed.

5.7.1 The General Theory of the Second Best

The general equilibrium model describes a very specific world, in which individual agents' actions produce a result that leaves no room for Pareto-improvements. The model itself seems to suggest a clear cut approach for policies—Let private agents pursue their own business in an undisturbed manner and an optimal result will be the outcome. By extension, we may assume that where this proves difficult or even impossible structures should be put in place that somehow rectify this shortcoming and lead agents to realizing the Pareto-optimum. Specifically, one might intuit that a gradual approach to policies, reducing distortions where possible, can be expected to lead to improvements for the agents, in the Pareto-sense. As we will see, this, however, is wrong.

To this end, we briefly explain the results of the general theory of the second best. Working with the general equilibrium model, a question that may present itself is to which degree it can serve to inform relevant policy decisions in the real world. The general theory of the second best can be drawn on here. In 1956/1957, Lipsey and Lancaster published an article of that title. They discussed a number of specific findings in the literature, predominantly in trade theory and public finance, and provided a general framework for integrating these specific results. The common aspect of the specific models is that some distortion is present in the setup. The question investigated is whether to try and guarantee that the optimality conditions in all other relevant areas are met will lead to an overall second best result (as the global, first-best optimum is not attainable due to the distortion). The answer to this is unequivocally, "no". As soon as optimality conditions are violated somewhere, the best result still attainable usually requires that optimality conditions are violated in some or actually all other related areas as well. For policy proposals, this is interpreted as highly relevant as, given the assumption that the general equilibrium model can basically serve as the foundation for an understanding of real-world economic structures and relations, this means that there is no gradual approach to the first-best optimum. Rather, as soon as some conditions necessary for the first-best optimum are violated, there may be numerous second best results that can be reached and how they can be reached cannot be determined in a general way ex ante. In trade theory, some distortion

may mean that additional tariffs may be required for reaching a second best outcome, in public finance additional taxes may be required. Neither tax rates nor tariff rates have to be proportional to one another but are probably rather distinct from one another and may even come in the form of subsidies. For instance, an example given is that in uniform tax rates, goods that are complements to leisure may be taxed too low, increasing consumption of leisure to a suboptimal level. Overall tax structures for reaching a second best outcome can then become rather complex very quickly. The way to deal with a distortion depends on the overall context faced. And as nobody actually believes that a first-best world was attainable, that means that particular attention has to be paid to policies and policy structures, as well as the overall institutional framework in which activity is embedded.

As Lipsey and Lancaster observe, within the neoclassical framework, the typical economic problem takes the form of an optimization under constraints. We have a function $F(x_1, \ldots, x_n)$ of n variables x_i that is to be maximized (minimized) and a constraint $L(x_1, \ldots, x_n) = 0$ that has to be taken into account in that operation (see the Lagrange Box 5.2). The optimization gives the FOCs (with F_i as dF_i/dx_i, etc.)

$$F_i - \lambda L_i = 0, \quad i = 1, \ldots, n \qquad (5.40)$$

and, from these, the relative conditions for optimality,

$$\frac{F_i}{F_n} = \frac{L_i}{L_n}, \quad i = 1, \ldots, n-1 \qquad (5.41)$$

(where we have picked the nth as numéraire) showing the necessary conditions for attaining the Pareto-optimal allocation sought. Now, Lipsey and Lancaster formulated an additional constraint of the form:

$$\frac{F_1}{F_n} = k\frac{L_1}{L_n}, \quad \text{with } k \neq 1 \qquad (5.42)$$

This additional constraint changes the optimization problem to:

$$F - \mu L - \theta\left(\frac{F_1}{F_n} - k\frac{L_1}{L_n}\right) \quad (5.43)$$

μ and θ will in general be different from λ. The FOCs here are

$$F_i - \mu L_i - \theta\left(\frac{F_n F_{1i} - F_1 F_{ni}}{F_n^2} - k\frac{L_n L_{1i} - L_1 L_{ni}}{L_n^2}\right) = 0 \quad (5.44)$$

For easier representation, we denote

$$\frac{F_n F_{1i} - F_1 F_{ni}}{F_n^2} = Q_i \quad \text{and} \quad \frac{L_n L_{1i} - L_1 L_{ni}}{L_n^2} = R_i$$

As the optimality conditions, we therefore get

$$\frac{F_i}{F_n} = \frac{L_i + (\theta/\mu(Q_i - kR_i))}{L_n + (\theta/\mu(Q_n - kR_n))} \quad (5.45)$$

For these to give the same expressions as the equivalent conditions for the Pareto-optimum (Eq. (5.41)) θ has to be "0", meaning the additional constraint in Eq. (5.42) would be irrelevant. Once some first-best condition cannot be satisfied, for the second best optimum the Pareto-optimality conditions of the rest of the variables likely have to be violated as well. Even if they are in reach, they are no longer desirable. Policy will have to depend on analyses of the circumstances, which will require a lot of information.

5.7.2 Asymmetric Information—The Markets for Lemons

The model of a market for lemons (Akerlof, 1970) considers the outcome of differences in the information available to sellers and potential buyers of a good. The concrete aspect focused on here are differences in information regarding the quality of a certain product between sellers and buyers.

The background would be markets in which buyers use some statistic to form an idea of expected quality of a specific unit of a good because they cannot judge the quality of the specific good they may be about to purchase. Sellers can try to exploit their information advantage and sell low-quality goods. At the same time, owners of good-quality units may be locked in on their product, at least, we can expect them to not receive the true value of their good when selling it.

The general logic is captured relatively easily: Let the sellers know the quality of the good they offer and set their reservation price according to the real value of their particular unit(s). The buyers' reservation price, on the other hand, is oriented on the expected value of an arbitrary unit encountered as she cannot judge the quality and therefore real value of a particular unit. Assume that quality q of goods is distributed uniformly. Further assume that quality is directly mirrored in price, and that for each quality q there is a number of sellers willing to supply the good in question at price p_s, so that $q \leq p_s$ for each seller. The potential buyers, on the other hand, are willing to pay somewhat more than the quality of the product for it, so that for them $p_d \leq kq$, with $1 \leq k \leq 2$. With sufficient information, the price would be somewhere between q and kq, and whoever wanted to trade could.

If, however, the buyers do not know the exact value of a unit, this is not going to work. Assume that they will substitute the expected value of an arbitrary unit to determine their willingness to pay. This is the average value of the units on the market. For any price p, now, every seller with $q \leq p$ will be willing to sell. The average quality for the goods in the market is $q/2$, then (due to the uniform distribution of quality), and the reservation price for buyers is $kq/2$. As long as $k \leq 2$, this is too low to get any seller to sell. In a dynamic situation, we would assume that every seller whose good exceeds the related quality leaves the market, driving down average quality until the point is reached where only the very worst quality products remain and the market has broken down.

In a little more detail, assume the following situation: There are two groups of agents, distinguished by the utility they gain from consumption of a specific good, with M being a bundle of the rest of goods and q_i the indicator of the quality of a particular unit of the good in question:

$$U_1 = M + \sum_{i=1}^{n} q_i \quad \text{and} \quad U_2 = M + \sum_{i=1}^{n} \tfrac{3}{2} q_i \quad (5.46)$$

Note that Akerlof has chosen linear utility functions in order to eliminate all influences that might result from differently shaped utility schedules. A corollary is that individuals spend all their income either on the bundle M or on the second good. Assume the price for a unit of M is unity. That means spending one more unit on bundle M increases utility by one unit ($dU_i/dM = 1$). Regarding spending on the second good, the utility effect for a unit of spending depends on the quality of the good acquired. If $q > p$ then the purchase is worthwhile for agents of type 1, and whenever $3q/2 > p$ it is worthwhile for type 2 agents, because spending of a unit of currency would increase utility more than the same unit spent on bundle M.

Let Y_1 and Y_2 denote the income of all types 1 and 2 agents, respectively. Then, demand D for the good from type 1 agents is of the form:

$$D_1 = \frac{Y_1}{p}, \quad \text{if } q > p \quad (5.47)$$

$$D_1 = 0, \quad \text{if } q < p$$

For type 2 agents, we get the following analogous expressions:

$$D_2 = \frac{Y_2}{p}, \quad \text{if } \tfrac{3}{2} q > p \quad (5.48)$$

$$D_2 = 0, \quad \text{if } \tfrac{3}{2} q < p$$

Accordingly, total demand D is

$$D = \frac{Y_1 + Y_2}{p}, \quad \text{if } q > p$$

$$D = \frac{Y_2}{p}, \quad \text{if } \tfrac{3}{2} q > p > q \quad (5.49)$$

$$D = 0, \quad \text{if } p > \tfrac{3}{2} q$$

Given the assumption of a uniform distribution of quality, average quality at price p is always $p/2 = q/2$. Substituting into the demand conditions shows that in the cases considered here, the reservation price of agents is always $3p/4 = 3q/4$. Trade will never actually take place, even though at any price there would be someone willing to sell and someone willing to pay the asked price if quality could be assured.

Leaving the static environment in which agents simply accept their suboptimal situation, and allowing for search and signaling, for instance, shows the relevance of signals for quality that can therefore become very attractive features for companies to attach to their products. Brand names or guarantees come to mind, but also chains, for instance (as offering an acceptable average quality to those unfamiliar with a specific setting or environment).

The problems highlighted by the model are applicable in a number of markets, actually, and have secured an important place for aspects of asymmetric information in economic analyses. For instance, the impossibility for constituting a working health insurance market (with the characteristics of an insurance market, covering individual risks in a large group) becomes apparent—at every price, a company would attract too many buyers of insurance policies (sellers of individual risk) with problematic risk structures (higher willingness to pay for policies) relative to those with fewer expected problems (lower willingness to pay for policies).

5.7.3 Efficiency and Imperfect Information

This section is based on a review article by Stiglitz (2000) dealing with questions of imperfect information more generally. Assessing the results of numerous research articles, the conclusion drawn is unambiguous—the assumption that markets with somewhat less than perfect information could be approximated in models assuming perfect information is wrong. What he calls information economics shows that even small derivations from the perfect information assumption lead to qualitatively different results in market models. Results that are incompatible with perfect market benchmark predictions can of course be reconstructed in other ways. However, according to Stiglitz, these often rely on reasoning that implicitly relies on imperfect information among the market participants. The constraints that rational agents in such attempts at reconstructing outcomes face can generally be referred back to a lack of relevant information.

The nature of information that distinguishes it from regular goods lies behind this. First, there is a public good component to knowledge or information. But that is not all—a distinctive characteristic is due to the fact that you cannot assess the value of information for determining a market price: If the information is known and its value is clear, a potential purchaser no longer has a reason to pay for it. If it is not known, the price one is willing to pay cannot be based on the content and value it may offer.

Within the world of neoclassical economics, which is asking about efficient allocations of resources among competing ends, the role of prices as signaling scarcity value has long been recognized. The general equilibrium model provides a price vector and resulting allocation that instantaneously produces an efficient outcome (how new information is integrated has always been left out; where that information may come from, as well). In a world of imperfect information, otherwise accepting the neoclassical premise, prices provide other information as well (for instance, regarding quality) and not all scarcity information is included in prices. If information is costly to obtain, this will typically result in a distribution of prices for a given product, or the unique market price may even be the monopoly price as every firm can increase prices in increments that are below presumed costs of search and continue doing so until the monopoly price is reached. In this case, entry will occur at too high numbers and overall results suggest that in this case competitive markets are more wasteful than monopoly markets. Additionally, in that case, a group of firms that can coordinate on lowering prices might induce customers to search one of their outlets so that a reduction in competition may increase efficiency if search costs for agents can be sufficiently lowered (Stiglitz, 1979) (see Chapter 7 for the inefficiencies monopolies introduce when compared to the perfect market benchmark). Then, behavior by consumers as well as by producers can offer information to others and this may affect others' behavior—the independence of the individual agents, the atomistic actor model, breaks down. Likewise, some agents with good or perfect information are not enough to produce an efficient result as soon as there is an, even arbitrarily small, search cost involved for all the rest (which also opens space for distorting information and signals as a strategic objective).

Generally, Stiglitz distinguishes between selection problems (productivity of employees, returns on different assets, private risks of people seeking insurance, etc) as characteristics of items and incentive problems (how hard do employees work, how does someone having bought insurance manage risks, etc) referring to behavior, as general categories agents face once information is imperfect. Market exchanges always include aspects of selecting among hidden characteristics and ways to provide incentives with a view on desirable but unobservable behavior. In sum, the scarcity problem, such as it exists, cannot be solved by prices.

A number of general results emerge that can be compared to assumptions and outcomes in perfect information settings. Integrating information leads to nonconvexities which are reflected in discontinuities. Discontinuities, in turn, mean that there may not be a market equilibrium. Additionally, the first as well as the second welfare theorems do no longer hold; competitive market outcomes are not necessarily efficient. And in an equilibrium, supply and demand need not coincide (unemployment, credit rationing, etc.). Overall, the robustness of the benchmark model with regard to small deviations from the information assumption is very low. Or, as Stiglitz has put it, "(i)nformation economics has made us realize that much of standard economics is based on foundations resting on quicksand" (Stiglitz, 2000, p. 1461). This holds even when we accept the rest of the assumptions made. Critiques regarding those will be presented in Chapter 6.

Externalities and Imperfect Information

As an example, we present a part of a model formulated by Greenwald and Stiglitz (1986). What is shown is that when imperfect information persists, an equilibrium without taxes is not Pareto-optimal and that increased taxes can lead to Pareto-improvements in an economy. For the model formulation, it is important to note that "the distortions that arise from imperfect information or incomplete markets often look analytically like externalities ... and viewing them this way helps identify the welfare consequences of government intervention" (Greenwald and Stiglitz (1986), p. 231). More generally, incomplete markets (meaning markets for some tradables, including for instance risk, are missing) or imperfect information result in competitive market outcomes that are not constrained Pareto-efficient. Action by government typically results in Pareto-improvements compared to the perfect market benchmark (obviously, this is not a case of black and white, but a question of degree).

Start with a market in equilibrium where $x = y$, with x as the demand vector and y the corresponding production vector. Taxes t are the difference between consumer prices q and producer prices p, so that $t = q - p$. A way to approach the problem is to ask whether in this equilibrium, $t = 0$ is part of the solutions for Pareto-optimal allocations. This in turn can be investigated by maximizing government revenue R subject to the condition that household income equals household spending E^h, or

$$\max R = tx - \sum I^h \tag{5.50}$$

subject to

$$E^h(q, z^h; \overline{u^h}) = I^h + \sum \alpha^{hf} \pi^f \tag{5.51}$$

In the expenditure function, u is the household utility level at the competitive equilibrium and α is the share of a household in firm f and thereby its share of profits of that firm. The z^i are a vector of variables other than prices that influence consumption decisions. All z^i, p, q, and π are assumed to be functions of t and I. I^h are lump sum transfers from government to a household h. For determining whether the solution to Eq. (5.50) includes $t = 0$, we proceed as follows.

The total differential of Eq. (5.51) is given by:

$$\frac{dE^h}{dq}\frac{dq}{dt} + \frac{dE^h}{dz^h}\frac{dz^h}{dt} = \frac{dI^h}{dt}$$
$$+ \sum_f \alpha^{hf}\left(\frac{d\pi^f}{dz^f}\frac{dz^f}{dt} + \frac{d\pi^f}{dp}\frac{dp}{dt}\right) \text{or}$$

$$E_q^h\frac{dq}{dt} + E_z^h\frac{dz^h}{dt} = \frac{dI^h}{dt} + \sum_f \alpha^{hf}\left(\pi_z^f\frac{dz^f}{dt} + \pi_p^f\frac{dp}{dt}\right)$$

(5.52)

We know from the definition of taxes that $dq/dt = I + dp/dt$, with I as the identity matrix. This allows rearranging Eq. (5.46) to yield:

$$E_q^h + \left(E_q^h - \sum_f \alpha^{hf}\pi_p^f\right)\frac{dp}{dt} = \frac{dI^h}{dt}$$
$$+ \left(\sum_f \alpha^{hf}\pi_z^f\frac{dz^f}{dt} - E_z^h\frac{dz^h}{dt}\right)$$

(5.53)

Up to this point, we have been following the impact that a small change in taxes t has on household h. For the expenditure function, we know that $E_q^h = x$ (see Hicksian demand) and also that $\pi_p^f = y$. Substituting these expressions and summing over all households yields

$$x + \underbrace{(x - y)}_{0}\frac{dp}{dt} = \sum_h \frac{dI^h}{dt}$$
$$+ \left(\sum_f \pi_z^f\frac{dz^f}{dt} - \sum_h E_z^h\frac{dz^h}{dt}\right)$$

(5.54)

Rearranging again gives us the total compensation payment that government has to make in order to satisfy the constraint formulated in Eq. (5.51):

$$\sum_h \frac{dI^h}{dt} = x - \left(\sum_f \pi_z^f\frac{dz^f}{dt} - \sum_h E_z^h\frac{dz^h}{dt}\right)$$

(5.55)

Differentiating our original maximization problem with respect to t yields

$$\frac{dR}{dt} = x + \frac{dx}{dt}t - \sum\frac{dI^h}{dt}$$

(5.56)

Inserting Eq. (5.55) into Eq. (5.56) yields (where x disappears because the increase in tax revenue of government partly offsets the compensation to households):

$$\frac{dR}{dt} = \frac{dx}{dt}t - (\pi^t - B^t)$$

(5.57)

where

$$\pi^t = \sum_f \pi_z^f\frac{dz^f}{dt} \quad \text{and} \quad B^t = \sum_h E_z^h\frac{dz^h}{dt}$$

This expression gives the derivative of R satisfying the constraint. For the initial equilibrium to be a Pareto-optimum, this must be 0 for $t = 0$, leaving:

$$\frac{dR}{dt} = (\pi^t - B^t) = 0$$

(5.58)

For a Pareto-optimum at $t = 0$, there may thus be no z that is affected by changes in taxes and influences either profits or household utility. Externalities, however, enter utility and profit exactly through these variables z. So in general, the original equilibrium will have been inefficient and taxes will be welfare improving. (For the optimal level of taxation, just rearrange Eq. (5.57) to give an expression of t.)

Chapter References

Akerlof, G.A., 1970. The market for "lemons": quality uncertainty and the market mechanism. Q. J. Econ. 84 (3), 488–500.

Arrow, K., Hahn, F., 1971. General Competitive Analysis. Holden Day, San Francisco, CA.

Cass, D., 1965. Optimum growth growth in an aggregative model of capital accumulation. Rev. Econ. Stud. 32 (3), 233–240.

Debreu, G., 1959. Theory of Value: An Axiomatic Analysis of Economic Equilibrium. Yale University Press, New Haven, London.

Descartes, R., 1637. Discours de la Méthode. Larousse, Paris (1969, ed. André Robinet).

Gossen, H., 1854. Entwicklung der Gesetze des menschlichen Verkehrs, und der daraus fließenden Regeln für menschliches Handeln. Verlag Wirtschaft und Finanzen, Frankfurt a.M. (1987; facsimile reproduction of the first edition).

Greenwald, B.C., Stiglitz, J.E., 1986. Externalities in economies with imperfect information and incomplete markets. Q. J. Econ. 101 (2), 229–264.

Houthakker, H.S., 1950. Revealed preferences and the utility function. Economica. 17 (66), 159–174.

Koopmans, T.C., 1965. On the concept of optimal economic growth. Cowles Foundation Paper 238, December 1965, available online: http://cowles.econ.yale.edu/P/cd/d01b/d0163.pdf, accessed February 2014.

Lipsey, R.G., Lancaster, K., 1956/1957. The general theory of the second best. Rev. Econ. Stud. 24 (1), 11–32.

Mas-Colell, A., Whinston, M.D., Green, J.R., 1995. Microeconomic Theory. Oxford University Press, New York, Oxford.

Negishi, T., 1960. Welfare economics and the existence of an equilibrium for a competitive economy. Metroeconomica. 12 (2–3), 92–97.

Ramsey, F.P., 1928. A mathematical theory of saving. Econ. J. 38, 543–559.

Romer, D., 2006. Advanced Macroeconomics. third ed. McGraw-Hill, Boston, MA.

Samuelson, P.A., 1938. A note on the pure theory of consumer's behaviour. Economica. 5 (17), 61–71.

Samuelson, P.A., 1948. Consumption theory in terms of revealed preferences. Economica. 15 (60), 243–253.

Samuelson, P.A., 1950. The problem of integrability in utility theory. Economica. 17 (68), 355–385.

Starr, R.M., 1997. General Equilibrium Theory—An Introduction. Cambridge University Press, Cambridge, New York.

Stiglitz, J.E., 1979. Equilibrium in product markets with imperfect information. Am. Econ. Rev. 69 (2), 339–345.

Stiglitz, J.E., 2000. The contributions of the economics of information to twentieth century economics. Q. J. Econ. 115 (4), 1441–1478.

Walras, L., 1874. Eléments d'économie politique pure, ou théorie de la richesse sociale. Verlag Wirtschaft und Finanzen, Düsseldorf (1988, fascimile reproduction of the first edition).

Walsh, C.E., 2010. Monetary Theory and Policy. MIT Press, Cambridge, MA.

Woodford, M., 2003. Interest and Prices: Foundations of a Theory of Monetary Policy. Princeton University Press, Princeton, NJ.

Further Reading—Online

For a list of selected intermediate and advanced textbooks, and some more articles, see the textbook website at http://booksite.elsevier.com/9780124115859

EXERCISES

1. Assume that there are three goods, apples, peaches, and pineapples. Construct a *preference relation* that violates the *transitivity axiom*.

2. Draw the *indifference curves* and compute the *marginal rates of substitution* for the following two utility functions:

$$u(x_1, x_2) = x_1 + 2x_2$$

$$u(x_1, x_2) = x_1^{0.3} + x_2^{0.7}$$

3. A consumer spends her entire budget on two goods, bread and beer. How do the quantities consumed change if the price of beer increases (and the price of bread stays constant)? You might use an *indifference curve* to visualize the changes.

4. When is the assumption of firms and households taking prices as given reasonable? Explain!

5. There is a single market with supply given by $X_s = -10 + 3p$ and demand given by $70 - 5p$. Compute the *equilibrium price and quantity*.

6. Explain the *law of diminishing returns* in words and mathematically.

7. Consider an exchange economy consisting of two agents. The agents have the utility function $u_i = \alpha_i \ln x_1^i + (1 - \alpha_i) \ln x_2^i$ with $\alpha_1 = 0.3$, $\alpha_2 = 0.7$ and initial endowments $\omega^1 = (30, 15)$, $\omega^2 = (10, 30)$. Compute *equilibrium allocations and prices*.

6

Critiques of the Neoclassical "Perfect Market" Economy and Alternative Price Theories*

"There is a wealth of important work to be discussed and assimilated into economic theory; however, each of these innovations has been obstructed by the dominant conception of economic value rooted in the imitation of physics." **Philip Mirowski**[1]

*Matthias Greiff has contributed to this chapter.

[1]*More Heat Than Light*, Cambridge: Cambridge University Press, 1989, p. 10.

6.1 INTRODUCTION

The basic model formulation of neoclassical economics as laid out in Chapter 5 has been criticized from various perspectives since its inception. These include focuses on the lack of direct interdependence and the static framework applied, which does not allow us to understand the changing nature of capitalist economies (Veblen, 1898; Schumpeter, 1911; also see Chapters 1, 3, and 12); flawed foundations of, and flawed analogies in, the models derived from the application of tools used in the nineteenth century mechanical physics (Mirowski, 1989; Smith and Foley, 2008); internal inconsistencies in the development of the model (overviews and detailed explanations can be found in Keen, 2009, 2011); the assumption of increasing marginal costs that are necessary to arrive at the stable and efficient equilibrium, but which are empirically unfounded (Lee, 2004; Blinder et al., 1998; for a very early exposition of this observation, see Sraffa, 1926); assumptions formulated regarding the possibility to identify preferences from individual choices alone (e.g., Sen, 1993); and the presumption of exogenously given preferences (Scitovsky, 1976; Galbraith, 2007).

We take up these points in this chapter and revisit some of them in Chapter 7. The starting point will be the very fundamental and comprehensive critique by *Philipp Mirowski* in the late 1980s. Mirowski wrote in a history of thought perspective and traced the historical development of the methods used in neoclassical economics back to classical mechanics, an older branch of physics. It is very informative to have a closer look at the history of neoclassics—something that is widely neglected today. Following this excursus into history and physics, we will detail some of the more important other criticisms of neoclassical economics, including internal inconsistencies of the assumptions and problems to actually measure or observe economic agents' preferences.

The purpose of this chapter is not to slander the widely used methods of neoclassical economics but to show that there are valid criticisms and unresolved issues with this theory. While after more than a hundred years of development general equilibrium theory does have its advantages, there have been attractive alternatives which were not taken up—or at least not developed to the same extent general equilibrium theory was. A prominent example for this is the classical theory of prices, which is based on a very different understanding of value, equilibrium, and competition. A section in this chapter will be devoted to introducing this approach as a possible alternative to neoclassical theory; we will also discuss the main differences between both. Lastly, we will also offer an outlook on Post-Keynesian and Institutional price theories.

6.2 THE MISTAKEN MECHANICAL ANALOGY

In his book *More Heat than Light*, Mirowski (1989) launched a profound critique on neoclassical general equilibrium theory. At the heart of his critique is the metaphor of energy as a mathematical field, and a discussion on how this metaphor, including its mathematical formalism, was adopted in economics. In short, Mirowski claims that the metaphor is inappropriate because neoclassical economics has imitated classical physics but neglected one of the fundamental principles of physics, the conservation of energy, which according to Mirowski has no meaningful equivalent in economics (Box 6.1).

Mirowski describes the marginalist revolution in great detail and shows how the metaphor of utility as a field is imported from physics. The field metaphor is inappropriate because by explicitly taking into account the conservation of energy, several inconsistencies arise in the neoclassical core model. Neoclassical economists did not see the inappropriateness because the use of the field concept in physics was not fully grasped at the time. Consequently, the field metaphor was developed further in economics although upon closer inspection it becomes clear that it has only weak explanatory power and leads to several inconsistencies. In addition to that, the field metaphor is not the all-encompassing

concept that was dominant in the nineteenth century physics any longer, but has been supplanted by newer developments in quantum mechanics and thermodynamics.

In this section, we explain the analogy between classical physics and neoclassical economics. We discuss the analogy between energy and value, before we review Mirowski's critique based on the theory's ontological basis and epistemological interpretation.[2]

6.2.1 Classical Mechanics

According to classical mechanics, we can predict the trajectory of any particle if the particle's position, its mass, and the forces (impulses) acting upon it are known. The philosophical worldview associated with classical mechanics points to a deterministic world in which the behavior of any particle can, in principle, be described accurately. An equilibrium position of the particle is then a point at which the particle comes to rest.

A crucial assumption in classical physics is the conservation of energy, one of the fundamental principles of classical mechanics. It states that in any closed physical system, a system that does not exchange energy with its

---

BOX 6.1

VECTOR FIELDS

A vector field is a mathematical concept, which is used to describe the strength and forces in a subset of the Euclidean space. Maybe the best-known example is a magnetic field. If a magnet is placed in the middle of a table, the magnetic field is not immediately visible. But if shavings of iron are scattered around the table, the shavings will adjust to the forces of the field so that the magnetic field becomes visible. Since the vector field defines direction and strength of its forces, it can be used to represent movements within a space.

---

[2]Epistemology and ontology are two philosophical concepts that are central to Mirowski's reasoning. While "ontological" ("ontology") refers to the *true being* of things, "epistemological" ("epistemology") refers to their *true meaning*.

environment, total energy is conserved over time. More precisely, energy is quantitatively indestructible but can undergo qualitative transformations, e.g., if work is transformed into heat. The conservation of energy is a specific form of a conservation principle, meaning that a "particular aspect of a phenomenon remains invariant or unaltered while the greater phenomenon undergoes certain specific transformations" (Mirowski, 1989, p. 13). The particular aspect which is conserved in classical physics is the amount of energy in a closed system. But what exactly is energy?

6.2.2 From Substance to Field

Early theories described energy as a substance, being embedded in and exchanged between bodies. With the discovery of Leibniz's calculus of variations, the motion of bodies could be described mathematically. An equilibrium corresponds to a stationary value for the function. Later, Hamiltonians were used to describe mechanical systems and mechanical problems were solved for their equilibrium values by integrating the Hamiltonian. The gradient of the Hamiltonian describes a vector field within which each point is associated with a specific amount of energy which depends on the coordinates but is independent of time.

While energy was described before as a substance residing in a body (with the possibility of being transferred to another body), now energy is described as a mathematical field, i.e., a relation between different potentials (see Box 6.1). A potential can be understood as a point in the field characterized by the amount of energy required to bring a particle to this point. The interpretation of energy as a field and the associated mathematical formalism was widely accepted in physics, but on an ontological and epistemological level it was not clear how energy should be perceived. According to Mirowski, "[e]nergy, it seems,

has finally become a purely instrumental and mathematical entity, transformed along its history from a substance to an entity to a relation ..." (Mirowski, 1989, p. 93).

Formally, classical mechanics works with equations of motion which may be written as a Lagrangian (see Chapter 5). This method is analogous to Lagrangian optimization in microeconomics (Box 5.2) though the approach is used for a different purpose and also applied differently in classical mechanics. The Lagrangian L is defined as the difference between kinetic energy T and potential energy V; hence,

$$L = T - V$$

where T, the kinetic energy, generally is defined as:

$$T = \frac{m\dot{q}^2}{2}$$

in mechanics (m denoting the mass of the body in question and $\dot{q}$ the velocity). As m is constant in closed systems in classical mechanics, kinetic energy is a function of position q and velocity $\dot{q} = \partial q / \partial t$ (t being the time); hence $T = T(q, \dot{q})$. q and $\dot{q}$ are vectors containing the position q_i or velocity $\dot{q}$ in each space dimension i, respectively; derivatives are componentwise. Potential energy V is a function of position only $V = V(q)$. Consequently, the Lagrangian reads:

$$L(q, \dot{q}) = T(q, \dot{q}) - V(q)$$

and the Lagrange−Euler equations, derived by differentiating

$$\frac{\mathrm{d}}{\mathrm{d}t}\left(\frac{\partial L(q, \dot{q})}{\partial \dot{q}}\right) - \frac{\partial L(q, \dot{q})}{\partial \dot{q}} = \frac{\mathrm{d}}{\mathrm{d}t}\left(\frac{\partial T(q, \dot{q})}{\partial \dot{q}}\right) - \frac{\partial T(q, \dot{q})}{\partial q}$$
$$+ \frac{\partial V(q)}{\partial q}$$

The Euler−Lagrange equations may be used to derive the path of motion of a mechanical system, specifically with Hamilton's principle of the least action by minimizing physical action (the integral of this Lagrangian over time).

Define $p_i = \partial L / \partial \dot{q}_i$ as the generalized momenta of the system. To obtain the Hamiltonian from the Lagrangian of a constrained (or unconstrained) optimization problem, a Legendre transform has to be applied to the Lagrangian. (Mathematical details of the Legendre transform are comprehensively presented in, for instance, Zia et al., 2009). The Hamiltonian H then is defined as:

$$H = \sum_i \dot{q}_i p_i - L(q, \dot{q})$$

Since

$$\dot{q}_i p_i = \dot{q}_i \frac{\partial L(q, \dot{q})}{\partial \dot{q}_i} = \dot{q}_i \frac{\partial T(q, \dot{q})}{\partial \dot{q}_i}$$

and by definition

$$\frac{\partial T(q, \dot{q})}{\partial \dot{q}_i} = m\dot{q}$$

we get

$$\sum_i \dot{q}_i \frac{\partial T(q, \dot{q})}{\partial \dot{q}_i} = 2T$$

and consequently, the Hamiltonian equals the sum of kinetic and potential energy, which must be conserved in closed systems:

$$H = 2T - L(q, \dot{q}) = 2T - T + V = T + V$$

A more detailed discussion may be found in textbooks on mechanical physics; for a good and extensive explanation, see for instance Calkin (1996).

6.2.3 The Fall of Classical Physics

With the development of modern physics, especially quantum physics, at the beginning of the twentieth century, several ideas of classical mechanics were undermined. Modern physics emphasizes the wave—particle duality,

according to which all matter exhibits both particle and wave properties. With the wave—particle duality, modern physics moved away from the deterministic worldview which was associated with classical physics. According to quantum physics, the dynamics of particles at the atomic or subatomic level cannot be described deterministically because the particle's mass, position, and the forces acting upon it cannot be measured simultaneously with certainty (Heisenberg's uncertainty principle). Moreover, the discovery of Planck's constant revealed that a particle's energy level cannot take all values from a continuum but only certain discrete values, rendering the application of the calculus of variations impossible. Lastly, Henri Poincaré's discoveries in nonlinear dynamics revealed that there are many systems which are not integrable. Integrability, however, was a crucial condition for solving the Hamiltonian function of a dynamic system. The analogies taken from classical mechanics are by themselves not suitable for an open system, such as an economy which is interwoven with the social and ecological system. Notably, much of economic theory did not move beyond these analogies, even as developments in natural sciences pointed away from such concepts to become more refined in their approaches to natural phenomena.

6.2.4 The Mistaken Energy-Value Analogy

In tracing the neoclassical theory of economic value, Mirowski points to the similarity between physical energy and economic value. In classical physics, energy was considered as a substance residing in a body. In classical economics, utility was conceived as a substance residing in a commodity. As the interpretation of energy changed from a substance to a field, a similar development occurred in economics.

While the classical economists held a substance theory of value (e.g., in Marxian theory, labor is the substance which produces value; see Chapter 12), starting with the marginalist revolution, value was interpreted as the result of opposing forces of buyers and sellers. The strength of the forces is independent of any substance but is derived from buyers' and sellers' utility functions. In transferring the model from classical mechanics to a simple exchange economy, the following analogies arose. The three-dimensional Euclidian space corresponds to the *n*-dimensional commodity space, individuals' endowments correspond to the particles' initial positions, and the forces are derived from individuals' preferences. Knowing individuals' endowments and preferences, an equilibrium position, i.e., an allocation of commodities in which no further mutually beneficial trades are possible, can be computed. The analogies are:

- $L = T - V$: utility,
- q: commodity quantities (in physics position in space),
- p: commodity prices (in physics generalized momenta),
- $\dot{q}$: the exchanged volume in commodities (in physics velocity),
- $p\dot{q}$: utility change with the exchange of $\dot{q}$ commodities (in physics twice kinetic energy),
- H and its conservation: a quantity the economic interpretation of which is not usually addressed (in physics energy and its conservation).

In economics, the use of the Lagrangian method is commonplace but the Hamiltonian, though straightforwardly constructed from the Lagrangian, is usually avoided. It was the omission of an important part of the implications of the application of the method of classical mechanics to economic theory that was chiefly deplored by Mirowski's critique.

Mirowski found that this omitted piece would require the constancy of the sum of utility and expenditure. This, however, holds only for special cases.

Specifically, for static optimization problems, the part $\sum_i \dot{q}_i p_i$ of the Hamiltonian (as derived by the Legendre transform of the Lagrangian) is always zero since there is no dynamic change of q, and hence, $H = -L$. Since the value of the Lagrangian is equal to the utility in all optimum points (required by the Kuhn–Tucker conditions), the conservation law requires in this case only that the utility is the same for all optimum points—a rather trivial statement. For dynamic optimization problems like those discussed at the end of Chapter 5 (as well as in Chapter 10), economic conservation laws may be more meaningful and do, in fact, constitute a condition for intertemporal optimization. It does not appear to be possible to give a simple and intuitive economic interpretation for this; other than that it is an optimality condition and/or that it is the sum of utility and intertemporal utility change. It is, however, a central condition implied by the method and the fact that this, its implications, and perhaps its history are not usually discussed in economics may constitute a major problem for the way the discipline of economics operates and for the way it is taught.

The related analogy regarding prices as a conservative vector field (see Section 6.2.2) is usually drawn—even by those who initially developed the neoclassical theory (namely, Fisher, 1892)—directly between forces and prices. As later shown by Hands (1993), the analogy does hold, and there is a conservative vector field involved in this theory; however, its components are not the prices but the quasi-price values obtained from income-compensated demand functions.[3] It should be noted that while general equilibrium theory may appear consistent within itself, there remains a great deal of

---

[3]Income-compensated demand is introduced and presented in more detail in Section 5.2.3.

obscurity around the mathematical consequences of the application of this method in economics. Further, while neoclassical theory does certainly have particular analytical advantages, there were and are a number of promising approaches even in the writings of classical economists that have unfortunately not been pursued.

6.2.5 The Epistemic Break Between Classical and Neoclassical Economics

Mirowski refers to the change from value as a substance in classical economics to value as a field in neoclassical economics as the epistemic break between classical and neoclassical economics. Reasons for the epistemic break are (i) physics envy, i.e., the imitation of physics because physics was considered the most developed and a "serious" science, (ii) the promise of the unification of all sciences, and (iii) a shift in academic standards toward sophisticated mathematical modeling, precision, and internal consistency. The "Achilles heel" in this epistemic break, however, is, as Mirowski argues, the conservation principle, which was ignored by neoclassical economics. In order to apply the mathematical apparatus of classical physics in economics, one has to take the conservation principle into account. But, if this is done, several anomalies arise, leading to Mirowski's claim that the neoclassical theory of value is a bad description of reality, has no ontological significance, and no epistemological interpretation.

The neoclassical theory of value as a mathematical field is derived from agents maximizing their utility subject to a budget constraint. If the mathematical analogy of classical physics is transferred and the conservation principle is taken into account, such a model gives rise to the following results:

1. The model illustrates the interdependencies of markets and the resulting equilibrium prices are such that all markets clear simultaneously (see Section 5.5). Trade is only allowed at equilibrium prices. Unfortunately, equilibrium prices are not necessarily unique.

2. Another weakness of the neoclassical theory of value concerns the system's out-of-equilibrium behavior. For simplicity, let us assume that it is possible to compute unique equilibrium prices for a set of interdependent markets. The question of how markets actually arrive at equilibrium prices cannot be answered, making the model highly stylized and abstract compared to how markets are described by the classical theory of prices. In the neoclassical world, there is perfect competition and the law of one price holds as a consequence. This is radically different from the classical theory, in which natural prices act as center of gravity and market prices fluctuate around them. According to the classical theory, goods are traded at different market prices, but competition forces prices toward natural prices (see also Section 6.5). Such a mechanism, explaining how prices converge toward equilibrium prices, is absent in neoclassical theory. This is closely related to the question of stability, which is concerned with the behavior of the system at positions close to equilibrium. If small deviations from the equilibrium position will be corrected and the system converges back to its equilibrium position, the system is said to be stable. The problem of stability has a fundamentally different structure than the problems of existence and uniqueness because stability is concerned with the adjustment of the system over time, as has been further elaborated by Wellhöner (2002). The neoclassical theory of value, however, remains silent about what happens at positions outside equilibrium and hence cannot answer the question of stability.

3. A consequence of modeling value as a field is that the order of consumption does not matter, meaning that an agent is indifferent about eating soup first and dessert second, and eating dessert first and soup second. This follows from the fact that the vector field is independent of time. Further, the system implies that any type of transaction is as reversible as in mechanical systems—this is a consequence of the conservation laws.

4. Close adherence to the conservation principle yields the result that there is a quantity in equilibrium problems that is to be conserved over time and all transformations. This quantity is for static optimization problems identical to the utility (see Section 6.2.4) but may for dynamic problems become a function of utility, price, and quantity (and functions of these variables, such as expenditure). According to Mirowski, this is the "Achilles heel" of neoclassical economics because it implies that on an ontological level, money and utility are the same thing (Mirowski, 1989, p. 231). If utility and expenditure were not the same thing (see Section 6.2.4), adding them up would be impossible and the neoclassical theory of value would break down.

In Mirowski's critique, the fundamental difference between classical and neoclassical theory of value was stressed. Also, the classical theory of prices represents an alternative which has been adopted by different strands of heterodox economics. Hence, a more detailed discussion of the classical theory of prices will be useful in order to get a deeper understanding between these two competing theories of value. Before we turn to this in Section 6.5, however, we will briefly explain another line of criticism that is concerned with internal inconsistencies of the neoclassical core model and the results that can be found for

firms' behavior in markets and resulting market structures and outcomes in Section 6.3, and discuss the assumptions made about agents' preferences in Section 6.4.

6.3 INTERNAL INCONSISTENCIES

6.3.1 The Impossibility of Horizontal Demand Curves for Individual Firms

Whereas Mirowski focuses his critique on the construction proper of the neoclassical core model, other authors have focused on particular questions regarding the appropriateness of several of the core assumptions used within the model, a point that we will take up later (and have in part already explained in Section 5.5.2, indeed with the Sonnenschein–Mantel–Debreu conditions). Yet others have addressed inconsistencies that arise within this model if we take the assumptions as given and follow their implications. An overview of the latter is given by Keen (2011).

One fundamental assumption of the neoclassical core model, regarding the supply-side, is that companies do not influence each other and that there is no direct interdependence between them. That means there is no functional relation between the decisions of one company and those of others. Additionally, no single company's decisions have an influence on the overall market result; their impact is assumed to be so marginal that it can be ignored in the analysis of the overall market. Therefore, companies act as price-takers who adjust their output so that their marginal costs equal the market price. This assumption is reflected in individual firms facing demand schedules that are horizontal (they can sell whichever quantity they want without influencing the equilibrium market price). The overall demand schedule in the market, on the other hand, is assumed to be negatively sloped, as a reflection of presumed "normal" demand patterns (a price increase reduces demand).

If companies make their decisions independently of one another, that means the decision to increase output q_i that one firm i may take does not lead to reactions by any other producer k in the market, so that $dq_k/dq_i = 0$. As a consequence, overall output changes in the market, dQ, and changes in output by one individual firm are the same, $dQ/dq_i = 1$. This was originally pointed out by the neoclassical economist Stigler (1957, fn. 31).

Now, we have the negatively sloped demand function, or the corresponding inverse demand function $p = p(Q)$. The slope of this market demand function is (dp/dQ). We can multiply this by 1 and use the above relation to arrive at:

$$\frac{dp}{dQ} = \frac{dp}{dQ} \underbrace{\frac{dQ}{dq_i}}_{=1} = \frac{dp}{dq_i}$$

We could also apply the chain rule to derive:

$$\frac{dp}{dq_i} = \frac{dp}{dQ}\frac{dQ}{dq_i} = \frac{dp}{dQ}$$

In any case, we arrive at the result that given the assumptions regarding companies in perfectly competitive markets, the slope of the market demand schedule and the demand schedule that an individual company faces are equal. This introduces a direct contradiction between two of the core assumptions on which the supposed market outcome in a perfectly competitive market rests. If the slope of the market demand curve is negative, $(dp/dQ) < 0$, and the atomistic structure is maintained, the individual demand curve cannot be horizontal. Technically, this means that from the point of view of formalizing companies' decision problems in a price–quantity space, polypolistic market structures are equivalent to oligopolies (for the standard oligopoly models, see

Chapter 7). Keen (2011) explains this in more detail and develops some additional implications, including a negative profit for companies that results from decisions ignoring the above relation and setting price equal to marginal cost. This further entails the consequence that the reference point drawn on for evaluating market outcomes in terms of efficiency, the perfect market model, is logically inconsistent when we take the assumptions made for deriving it seriously and let them be reflected in the model formulations we employ. There will be no socially optimal outcome (understood as maximizing the sum of consumer and producer rents) in the interplay of agents. The foundation for arguments employed to argue for a reduction of government presence in the economic sphere along these lines is thereby void. Note, however, that this does not mean that government was necessarily always needed and would always improve the outcome achievable (see Chapters 7, 12, 14, 16, and 17). What we do find are reasons for more careful arguments and analyses of specific situations before formulating policy proposals. The "black or white" solutions implied by the simplistic model structures discussed above cannot hope to lead to policies and actions that would systematically improve real-world economic results (Box 6.2).

6.3.2 The Impossibility of Simultaneously Independent Supply and Demand and of Upward-Sloping Supply Curves

For the uniqueness of a market outcome (in the price–quantity space of neoclassical analyses) in partial markets, it is required that supply and demand are independent of each other. As Sraffa (1926) has demonstrated, this assumption cannot be sustained. What is more, his analysis shows that in single markets as they are conceived of in the neoclassical

---

BOX 6.2

A SIMULATION OF MARKET OUTCOMES WITH DIFFERENT NUMBERS OF SUPPLIERS

Using simulation as a tool for investigating market outcomes (see Chapter 9 for the method), Keen (2011) finds that the monopoly prediction of a market outcome (see Chapter 7) and simulation results coincide. For a market with many firms, however, there are substantial differences between the prediction in the "perfect market" model and the simulation outcome. The demand curve for both sets of simulations was the same, and so was, in fact, the overall outcome—the competitive market result (with 10,000 firms in the simulation) and the monopoly result showed basically the same total supply, and hence the same market price.

In the simulations, behavior of firms in competitive markets included a provision for changing their individual supplies. The rule was that if a change in individual output resulted in a reduction of individual profits, that change was reversed (so that if an increase in output reduced profits, in the following period output was reduced). Individual firms showed a variety of different output levels, the aggregate result was that of a monopoly market, though. The different output levels may be taken to point to another aspect of real-world markets, namely, the tendency toward larger and smaller companies being present in a market, tending toward oligopolization (see Chapter 7).

---

approach, it is likely that the supply-side determines the price at which a good is sold, whereas the demand-side determines the actual quantity exchanged, and not the interplay of both market sides that simultaneously determines both price and quantity. This result is in fact the one that formed the foundation for classical economists.

Sraffa's starting point is the question of what constitutes a market, in order to address the issue of scarcity of inputs, which is utilized for arguing for upward-sloping supply curves. Put differently, he addresses the assumption of an independence of demand and supply under decreasing returns to scale (see Chapter 5), which are necessarily assumed in neoclassical analyses.

Increasing supply increases costs due to the increased need for a scarce input. As the supply curve is given by the marginal cost curve, this would lead to its upward slope. Sraffa has approached this aspect from two perspectives

on what may constitute a market with a view on factor requirements in production: a narrow definition of a market and a broad definition of a market. (Note that the upward-sloping supply curve can only be conceptualized within the framework of perfect competition, as companies' output will be determined by demand condition as well as cost conditions as soon as they have market power.)

The argument leads to the recognition that the assumption of scarce inputs used for arguing for increasing marginal costs is problematic. If you take a narrow view on what constitutes a market (producers of nails, for instance), the inputs used in production will be used in other markets as well. That means they are more widely available in which case an increase in their price in case of expanding output is not necessarily to justify. This is in fact covered by empirical observations (see Section 6.6) that show companies operating under constant or even increasing returns to scale, and consequently horizontal or even negatively sloped supply curves. As a consequence, demand conditions alone will determine the quantity of output, not the interplay of demand- and supply-sides.

If you take a broad view on markets (such as everyone utilizing iron ore in production), the independence of supply and demand can no longer be assumed. In the broadly conceived markets, changes in factor employment have effects on income and thereby on demand. In this case, every point on the supply curve corresponds to a different demand schedule and the uniqueness of an equilibrium cannot be taken as given. This is a general dilemma for partial market analyses as the desired determination of a factor's or good's unique scarcity value leads to potentially very wrong conclusions then. Think of the labor market, where partial market analyses simply ignore the fact that, in order for there to be a demand, people have to have the means to purchase something—the simplistic formula "higher wages lead to lower employment" cannot be sustained once the labor market is recognized to be embedded in the overall economy.

6.3.3 Summing Up

Taking a number of results shown together, we have seen,

- in Chapter 5, that the Sonnenschein–Mantel–Debreu conditions show that identical preferences with money spent on the available goods in constant shares by all individuals independently of the level of real income are necessarily required for downward-sloping demand curves based on individual preferences to exist;
- in Section 6.3.2, that no difference in the demand curves for single companies and market demand curve even in polypolistic markets can be assumed and that therefore the efficiency condition of "marginal

revenue equals price equals marginal cost" will not hold for individual firms as these would realize a negative profit in this case (note, however, that once interdependence of companies is permitted to be recognized by them, a Cournot oligopoly model with numerous suppliers approaches the perfect market outcome, where, however, constant marginal cost is assumed; see Chapter 7);
- in this section, that independent demand and supply schedules together with upward-sloping supply functions cannot exist in a partial market; and, finally,
- that indeed, upward-sloping supply functions are unlikely unless you take an extremely broad view on what constitutes the market in question in which case the independence of supply and demand cannot reasonably be assumed.

6.4 PREFERENCES AND CHOICE

In this section, we will present arguments brought forth that identify weaknesses in the revealed preferences approach (see Chapter 5). We will also point out consequences for our understanding of the economic sphere and agents' behavior therein, when individual decisions depend on outside influences (by companies or from other individual agents). A simplifying assumption of exogenously given preferences may lead to, sometimes serious, misconceptions of market dynamics and structures. Finally, a more realistic alternative for describing choices, as based on satisficing instead of optimizing behavior, will be introduced.

6.4.1 Problems with the "Revealed Preferences" Concept

The objective of the "revealed preferences" approach was to remove all traces of utility and subjective (unobservable) states, or, unobservable preferences from explanations of consumer behavior (Samuelson, 1938). Choice is to be explained based on observed choice, and the approaches to consumer behavior is thus to be given an empirical foundation. Originally, in fact, the term preferences was not used in the formulation of the basic idea, the focus was on choices, but was only integrated rather late during the process of clarifying the concept. As pointed out in Chapter 5 already, eventually it was shown that based on the assumption of rational behavior by agents, under certain circumstances, observed choices could be translated into constructs that are equivalent to mappings of indifferent schedules. Hence, they can be transferred into utility functions, in fact showing the equivalence of choice sets by rational agents and utility functions constructed for describing and explaining choices by those rational agents under certain conditions. Lately, according to Hausman (2000), the meaning of the term has changed somewhat to include attempts to identify preferences from choices under assumptions about agents' beliefs and expectations. This introduces precisely the subjective notion that was originally tried to do without. We will focus on the original and still broadly used notion here. A number of criticisms were formulated over the years, in sum arguing that the approach has in fact failed to achieve what it set out to.[4] The core of these is that you cannot explain choice based on observation of choice alone but always have to refer to some notion external to choices for interpreting them, such as objectives and expectations (e.g., Sen, 1993).

The assumption that explanations of behavior can be possible on the basis of observed behavior alone hinges on the consistency condition: If a person chooses y when z is also available, this is taken to mean that y is preferred to z. This is translated into the weak axiom of revealed preferences stating that when y is revealed to be preferred to z through agents' choices, z cannot be preferred to y. When this is fulfilled by agents, behavior is consistent and a theory of consumer behavior can be built on its foundation. Now, as Sen (1973) stresses, the choices of y at some times and z at others, even though both are available, are not necessarily inconsistent. They can be seen as inconsistent when we attribute specific motives to the person making these choices. This relies on a step that was precisely the one which Samuelson and those adopting the concept aimed at avoiding.

Sen goes on to stress that maybe the axiom could be seen as a hypothesis to be empirically validated. However, even for small numbers of goods, as soon as they are divisible, the amount of possible combinations becomes extremely large due to their exponential growth—and actually, infinite in the usual calculus-based approach to consumer theory. Even if numerous observations were available, these could not hope to consist of sufficient numbers for confidently not rejecting the hypothesis. That the collection of such data will have to be undertaken in a timeframe in which it may reasonably be assumed that preferences have not changed further underlines the practical impossibility of the notion.

A closely related aspect introduced (see for instance Sen, 1993), which can help exemplifying the impossibility of understanding preferences and beliefs based on choice alone, has been the fact that individual choices can be context-dependent. The overall situation in which people make choices matters for the choices themselves and a decision taken can

---

[4]For a detailed overview, stressing the parallels to the "crisis of hedonism" debate in the early twentieth century, and outlining the broader framework of discussions regarding the relation of economics to other social sciences, see Lewin (1996).

differ depending on those overall circumstances. One core aspect in operationalizing and formalizing individual choice is the independence of a decision from additional available alternatives (see the rationality axioms in Chapter 5). That is to say, if in situation A an individual chooses x over y, she should not choose y over x when a third alternative z becomes available as well in situation B. We can, however, easily construct situations where this is the case. Let x be not taking an apple from a fruit bowl and y be taking an apple. Now, if in situation A there is only one apple in that bowl, people may opt for x. If situation B differs in that there are more apples in the bowl (let z be consuming two apples), an agent may opt for y. The motivation in that case would be not to take the last apple even if you prefer consuming an apple to not consuming one. Such settings can be extended for including additional factors in individual decision-making, such as rules and institutions as norms, more explicitly, which introduce further aspects of motive and preference that are withdrawn from observation but are accessible only through introspection or contextualization, and interpretation. In interdependent situations this is further interesting, because individual behavior depends not only on expectations regarding others' behavior, but also on the interpretations of others' motives: trusting behavior is more likely to be met with a trustworthy response than distrustful behavior. Something that is freely given, say option A, cooperation, when defection, option B, is possible, is more likely to be met with a trustworthy response than the same behavior in the absence of an option that is not chosen and thereby allows to send a signal of trust (e.g., Hausman, 2000). Overall, an interpretation of motivation based on behavior, choice, alone is not possible—we see "chooses," we infer "prefers" and can do so only on the basis of something external to choice, namely, preferences in one guise or another.

6.4.2 Endogenous Preferences and Conspicuous Behavior

Bowles (1998) considers the effect that institutional structures have on individual preferences. These "are reasons for behavior, that is, attributes of individuals that (along with their beliefs and capacities) account for the actions they take in a given situation" (p. 78) and that may therefore be treated "as cultural traits, or learned influences on behavior" (p. 80). A more general discussion of preferences as endogenously formed will be followed by a discussion of more specific influences in this section.

Endogenous Preferences

Providing an overview over a vast literature on individual choices and behaviors, Bowles (1998) stresses the impact that different institutional arrangements have on the value individuals attribute to outcomes of actions and choices, and on their learning and personality development, and hence their perception of situations and changes therein, including overall social relations with other agents. Economic theory ignores those influences, which, in his view leads to restrictions in "explanatory power, policy relevance, and ethical coherence" (p. 75). At the heart of the influence on personality development lies the fact that institutional arrangements influence how and on what terms agents interact. This in turn influences the relative importance of different characteristics and leads agents to draw on different aspects of the general behavioral repertoire in a given situation. In turn, this has an impact on the establishment and solidification of certain types of behavior and habits.

He describes five general channels through which the effects of institutional arrangements, specifically in the economic sphere and therein the structuring of exchange relations, are transmitted. These are, framing and situational construal, intrinsic and extrinsic motivations, effects on the evolution of norms, task performance effects, and effects on the process of cultural transmission.

Each of these transmission channels leads to structures affecting decisions through their influence on values and behavior. The *framing* effect of markets results as the same problem may be perceived differently by individuals in different, e.g., market and nonmarket, environments. An example Bowles refers to is the well-known effect that a service is valued differently by agents when it is provided by government than when it is privately bought. Faced with the same sets of choices, agents may then act differently depending on the specific arrangements structuring their environment. Likewise, results of interactions differ between, rather impersonal, market environments and bargaining environments. In the latter, notions of distributional fairness and other-regarding considerations have a stronger impact on agents' decisions than in the former. Intrinsic or extrinsic *motivations* likewise influence agents' behavior. Again, a number of studies can be drawn on to support this point. When a *quid pro quo* is involved, be it in monetary terms or other, agents' willingness to contribute to a certain task decreases. When they feel they are voluntarily involved in a task, contributions tend to be significantly higher than when obligation and reward are clearly specified. This extends to incomplete contracts, where agents are more willing to advance efforts and reciprocate than in situations where obligations for the involved parties are set out in detail. As far as the evolution of *norms* is concerned, we can observe a reduction of the importance of prosocial behavioral norms the more exchanges are outsourced to market relations. The emergence of prosocial norms and behaviors through repeated interactions, and possibly segmentation and group selection (see Chapters 13 and 14), may in that case be inhibited if relations among agents are predominantly mediated through market

exchanges. The effects of performing *tasks* are traced to learning by doing as a major source of individual learning. What tasks individuals engage in, in turn, is shaped by institutions influencing cost–benefit calculations, narrowly, and acceptable behavior, more broadly, within the set of technologically feasible processes. This may, again, reasonably be assumed to reinforce expectations and thus eventually strengthen certain sets of behavioral norms as agents experience others' decisions and the overall outcome of their actions. Furthermore, the content of tasks, as more passively executing or more actively engaging, shapes agents' behavior outside the work environment as well and thus can have an impact on overall activities that are being pursued. Prosocial behaviors are also likely shaped by the structure and setting of task performance as well. Regarding *cultural transmission* processes, the impact of markets as the main tool for structuring exchanges is less easily shown in studies. Nevertheless, that exchange relations have an impact on the socialization process of individuals has been demonstrated for premarket societies. Observations showing that, for instance, success in schools and in the workplace depends on the same characteristics (perseverance, consistency, punctuality, dependability, etc. with creativity and independence regularly hindering such success) let it appear likely that reinforcement of structures and the behavioral traits most often adopted by agents may reinforce each other. This conjecture is further strengthened by the fact that people showing certain types of behavior are more likely to reach positions of influence and thus positions in which other mechanisms, such as a conformist bias in behavior, can have an impact on final outcomes.

When approaching questions of economic relevance, and problems identified in that realm, therefore, not only which outcome is to be achieved, but also the structuring of processes for doing so has to be in the focus as well. For achieving overall desirable social outcomes, in fact, the recognition of the transmission channels of institutional arrangements on behavior laid out above becomes a crucial aspect as the potential social provisioning offered by the attainable levels of skill and machinery may not be fully exploited if institutional patterns are not given to supporting this. The structures put in place, as seen, are one factor influencing these patterns.

Conspicuous Behavior

The core aspect of T.B. Veblen's approach to economic as part of overall social systems are institutions, "correlated patterns of thoughts" in groups (see Chapters 1, 12, and 13). These do not only enable agents to form expectations about others' behavior, they are also embedded in an overall framework justifying them. This, in turn, provides the ideological framework of the group, the values that are accepted by the members of the group in question. Within this system, it is assumed that individual members of such a group strive for status, recognition that other group members are willing to afford them. How such status is achieved depends on the prevailing value system, as well as on the institutional–technological environment. The value system shapes what is appreciated by group members. The institutional–technological environment in turn defines the space that is open for group members' actions.

Within this framework, we can distinguish between instrumental and ceremonial motivations behind behavior. Functional consideration are considered as instrumental. Ceremonial motivations draw on the desire to send signals conferring abilities for which status is granted within the group. If the desire to send status signals dominates, we speak of conspicuous behavior. In earlier environments, conspicuous leisure was one way for sending signals regarding economic ability. Agents showed that

they commanded enough resources that they did not have to work, which was extended to being able to pay for servants who did not do productive work either. In turn, the signals sent through being able to afford servants were strengthened by letting them show specific behavior patterns, such as standard ways of serving food, for instance, which again required the unproductive use of time and resources (as you had to train people and could not just hire anyone halfway able to balance a plate for when you had guests) (Veblen, 1899).

The general desire for status may be taken as given, and hence behavior to achieve status part of the behavioral repertoire of agents. The outlet individuals choose for doing so, as stated, will depend on a number of factors (and is likely not homogeneous throughout an entire society, as for instance younger individuals may choose signals to distinguish themselves from older members, and groups may adopt specific signals among themselves without, generally, leaving the overall value system of a society, however).

In Western societies, nowadays, a standard way to convey status signals is through conspicuous consumption. With the overcoming of basic economic constraints, space is open to employ economic means for broader signals. Objects are not acquired mainly for their functional properties, but as ways for showing economic means. What the specific objects chosen are is not relevant, as long as other group members are able to identify the signal as such. That basic economic constraints have been overcome does, by the way, not mean that people would no longer be poor—poverty then is a socially defined measure oriented on the minimum consumption ability for being able to fully participate in a society's social sphere and signaling system. This reflects a notion of at least keeping up with a peer group so that agents may not necessarily be leading new waves of consumption articles to prominence, but be part of an eventually following group adopting consumption patterns from earlier buyers.

The ability to successfully send signals in a group depends on a common frame of reference so that they are interpreted by others as has been intended. This, in turn, is not something that would be naturally defined and given. As stated, the general frame will depend on value system and technological possibilities, additionally, within the space opened thereby, fashions and fads can come and go.

Thus, preferences are not exogenous and unchanging. The desire to acquire certain objects and goods can be awakened, so that products can be brought into a, potentially entirely new, market if a demand for them can be created. Companies have numerous tools at hand for doing this, through direct signals (cars, etc.) or indirect ones (products supposedly helping to conform to a society's standards of beauty, for instance).

In this reading, a nontrivial part of economic activity in diversified economies is motivated by the offering of tools for sending signals to the larger social group, embedded in a value system acknowledging consumption as acceptable means for such signals. The introduction of new objects for expanding the range of available specific signals is then a noticeable driver of expanding economic activity (on the advantages of growth for companies which can increase revenue without having to compete too pronouncedly, see Chapter 7). Overall, then, once a certain level of purchasing power has been reached, a continued expansion of the economic sphere is at least partly based on the fulfillment of desires that have first to be created. More

sophisticated ways to send signals on the basis of consumption patterns are a driver of this process. That means a justification of a system as being superior in its ability to satisfy consumer demand falls short of justifying an existing structure because this demand has to be created for keeping the system running in the first place. Continued growth then mainly serves the purpose of limiting the negative impact of competition among producers, as the pie for which they compete continues to increase so that they don't have to take others' share but can enjoy access to increased purchasing power for pushing additional products to consumers (on this also, see Chapter 7 for some more details).

6.4.3 Missing Procedural Aspects of Decision-Making

The economic utility-maximizing agent is usually equipped with enormous computational capacities and complete and transitive preference relations. Therefore, she has no problems in solving difficult optimization problems. Humans do not have unlimited computational capacity and are generally time-constrained in their decision-making process. In reality, people therefore seldom make optimal decisions but employ simplifying decision procedures, which yield acceptable but not necessarily optimal outcomes. These procedures, if they do not exploit all the information available, do not aim at finding optimal (or necessary) behavioral options but satisfactory (or sufficient) options, and require less computational power, are called heuristics (for an example for formalizing such heuristics, see Box 6.3).[5]

---

[5]It is therefore questionable whether modern behavioral economics is on the right track by specifying utility functions with additional variables, which account for decision "defects" (e.g., Berg and Gigerenzer, 2010). In fact, the optimization of these utility functions is even more difficult from a computational point of view. Classical behavioral economists such as Herbert Simon followed a different path by asking the question "what kind of procedures other than optimization humans employ in order to make decisions?"

BOX 6.3

LEXICOGRAPHIC PREFERENCES

One way for formalizing satisficing behavior is lexicographic preferences. Lexicographic preferences describe preference orderings in which one good, characteristic of a good, or bundle of goods, is given absolute preference over one or more others. So, if we have three goods, x, y, and z, with $x_1 = 4$, $y_1 = 5$, $z_1 = 4$ in bundle 1 and $x_2 = 4$, $y_2 = 3$, $z_2 = 7$ in bundle 2, an agent who prefers x to y, and y to z, will choose bundle 1. An agent whose first preference is good z, on the other hand, will choose bundle 2.

This is particularly helpful as it allows integrating one aspect into representations of choices that is crucial to decision behavior but often neglected, namely, what we can represent as the distinction between needs and wants. Needs can be brought into a hierarchical order (a very well-known exemplification of this is Abraham Maslow's "hierarchy of needs"). Within categories of needs, then, a certain degree of substitutability is given, between them this is the case in a very limited fashion at best. Wants, in turn, correspond to preferences within categories of needs. They are shaped and change responding to influences in the social environment but also to earlier decisions taken by an agent.

So agents, for instance as consumers, subdivide needs into many categories that are only loosely tied to one another (changes in prices in one subgroup do not affect expenditure in other subgroups). As a consequence, one can expect that price changes will have an asymmetric impact on changes in consumption choices.

Increases in higher categories of needs will not have an impact on consumption in lower categories, whereas vice versa that may be expected (possibly depending on the magnitude of the changes). Regarding needs, we can assume saturation levels or quantities to play a role; once these have been reached, remaining income can be allocated to different spending categories. Income increases then translate into the possibility to satisfy additional needs. In this case, a representation of utility by one single value will be misleading; a vector in which the components represent the different needs will be more fitting.

Depicting preferences as lexicographic allows accounting for another aspect of human decision-making as well. Often decisions are taken habitually or based in routines, but also, often, only a few selection criteria are drawn on ("procedural rationality"). All of these aspects help reducing problems to manageable sizes (you may limit your search for a new car to a certain brand, or to a certain price range, you may look for a new apartment only in some parts of the city, etc.). Understanding the selection criteria for agents in specific situations is required for understanding their decisions, then (size of an apartment, part of the city in which the apartment is located, upper limits for rent, or any other criteria that may matter for an agent, and the ordering in which they are taken into account as the basis for decisions when moving, for instance).

See, for instance, Chapter 2 in Lavoie (2006).

A common misconception in behavioral economic theory is that heuristics are "bad." Individuals would be "better off" if they made "optimal" decisions in the rational sense. But this reasoning is valid only in a world with perfect knowledge about the world and if time does not play a role for the decision-maker (Simon, 1979, p. 500): If some information is not available or the decision-maker has a limited amount of time in order to make his decision, it might be reasonable to employ decision procedures requiring far less time to be carried out but leading to a satisfactory outcome. Consider for example a chess player: Even the best players do not waste time in searching for the optimal move as it would simply take too much time given their computational power. Even the most modern chess computers would need many years to find the optimal move. Therefore, they employ decision procedures giving them a good move, rather than the unequivocally best one (Simon, 1965, pp. 184–185). Neurobiologists have also shown that the human brain systematically makes intransitive decisions: This intransitivity is deeply rooted in the neural structure of the human brain. One suspects that the reason is that making transitive decisions simply is more time-consuming and in total evolutionary inferior (Kalenscher et al., 2010).

The neoclassical theory circumvents the questions about procedural aspects of choice by assuming an agent with "Olympian" rationality (Simon, 1983) possessing all the relevant information (and if not, the relevant probabilities). But, as in the real-world computational capacities are constrained and information is incomplete, any living organisms rely on heuristics. It also was shown that if there is no perfect information,[6] simple heuristics will give more accurate estimates than the most sophisticated estimation techniques, which are, again, far beyond the computational capacities of any human being (Gigerenzer and Gaissmaier, 2011, p. 455; Wübben and Wangenheim, 2008).

As heuristics are usually oriented on experiences in the past (also compare the definition of institutions in Chapter 1), the choice behavior of individuals exhibits past dependent aspects, which are subject to investigation if one does not act inside the neoclassical framework. Additionally, the aspiration level

(i.e., the threshold beyond which the agent classifies an option as "satisfactory"), might depend on external factors which should be endogenous in an adequate model: The aspiration level might change over time as a result of changes in consumption patterns in the relevant peer group (the social group agents compare themselves to, see also Section 6.4.2), or as a result of habituation, which in turn may be due either to the repeated use of a product with a concurrent loss in satisfaction from its use, or generally to the getting used to certain standards and seeking to expand beyond these (Scitovsky, 1976).

6.5 THE CLASSICAL THEORY OF PRICES AND THE SRAFFIAN CRITIQUE OF THE NEOCLASSICAL THEORY OF VALUE AND PRICE

6.5.1 Foundations of the Classical Theory of Prices

In neoclassical theory, prices are determined by marginal productivities of inputs (see Chapter 5). Prior to the marginalist revolution, which marked the starting point for neoclassical economics, there was no notion of marginal utility, marginal costs, and marginal productivity. Then how are prices determined without any notion of marginal utility, marginal costs, and marginal productivity? According to the classical economists, such as Smith, Ricardo, and Marx, prices must in general be determined by the average costs of production. The average costs of production depend on technology and income distribution.

Classical economists differentiated prices into market prices and natural prices. Market prices are the prices at which goods and services are exchanged. Natural prices are a

---

[6]And as emphasized by Stiglitz (2010, p. 243), a world with almost perfect information is fundamentally different than a world with perfect information.

theoretical construct, and serve as a supposed center of gravity of market prices. Natural prices cannot be observed directly but can be computed based on costs of production. It is assumed that competition will equalize the wage rate and the profit rate. If wage and profit rates are not equalized, natural prices and market prices will differ. Competition, however, will give rise to a process in which capitalists move from sectors with low profit rates to sectors with high profit rates, and workers will move from sectors with low wages to sectors with high wages; thus, there is a tendency toward uniform rates of profit and wages. Due to this tendency, market prices will fluctuate around natural prices which act as a center of gravity. Natural prices are conceived as long-run prices determined by technology and income distribution. To simplify the analysis, we assume that labor is homogeneous. Furthermore, we assume as follows:

1. **Constant returns to scale:** If we double the amount of all inputs, we will receive exactly double the output. If no assumptions are made regarding returns to scale, we cannot make any meaningful statement about what happens when the quantity of outputs produced changes. Hence, in the following, we assume constant returns to scale.
2. **A fixed-proportions technology:** There is only one technology, i.e., one combination of inputs that produces the output. Input factors are used in fixed proportions and there is no substitution of inputs.
3. **Circulating capital:** All produced inputs are completely used up in the production process.
4. **No joint production:** Each production process will produce exactly one output.

In the following sections, we will delineate Sraffa's critique of neoclassical economics theory of value and show a one-commodity model to illustrate the concept of feasibility

and the inverse relation between profits and wages. Then, we will introduce a more general model with n commodities to illustrate how prices depend on distribution. As mentioned above, the concept of natural prices goes back to the classical economists, especially Ricardo (1817). It was formulated mathematically by Neumann (1946) and Sraffa (1960) and an in-depth treatment can be found in Kurz and Salvadori (1997).

6.5.2 Sraffian Critique of Neoclassical Theory of Value and Price

Sraffa's critique of the neoclassical theory of value is based on the problem that arises when defining an aggregate measure of capital. He showed that neoclassical models, which rely on an aggregate measure of capital K, are logically flawed because an aggregate measure of capital cannot exist independently of prices. To define an aggregate measure of capital is impossible because in order to aggregate diverse capital goods (e.g., tractors and computers) into one single quantity of capital requires prices (e.g., the price of tractors and the price of computers).

The overall cost of capital (the asset price) is equal to the present value of profits that can be generated using it. The cost of capital in a period is determined by the interest rate, which is equal to the rate of profit in the perfect market environment that is assumed. The rate of profit, in turn, is equal to the marginal product of capital (its productivity). The price of capital therefore is determined by the profitability with which it can be employed. So, as the measured amount of capital depends on the rate of profit, profit cannot just be its marginal product for the model to escape a circular notion and lose its explanatory power: In order to determine the productivity of capital, it has to be aggregated. This aggregation, however, requires the knowledge of the price of capital, for which its productivity has to be known. Rate of profit and marginal productivity thus are mutually dependent; for determining one, you have to take the other as given. Neoclassical theory, however, sets out to determine both endogenously, and arrive at a unique value for them.

Sraffa's alternative is to use time-dated commodities, i.e., the quantities of commodities and labor which are used as inputs, and the quantities of commodities which are produced. Following Sraffa, we use the term "relations of production" to refer to the processes of production of all commodities by means of commodities and labor per period of time. Since we can (in principle) measure the amounts of inputs and outputs, this implies that Sraffa's theory is based on observables. Of course, this only holds for the actual relations of production since we cannot observe the amounts of inputs and outputs that would be obtained in a hypothetical situation when the scale of production is changed. Using the assumption of constant returns to scale, however, allows us to make inferences about the amount of inputs and outputs that would be observed in any hypothetical situation.

Sraffa shows that, given the relations of production, prices depend on distribution. He goes on and argues that distribution and prices cannot be determined simultaneously and concludes that distribution has to be determined prior to the determination of prices. For a given distribution, Sraffa is then able to determine natural prices (using the assumption of a uniform wage rate and a uniform rate of profit). In contrast to the neoclassical theory of value, Sraffa is able to determine prices without any reference to demand. This implies that his theory of prices is immune to the weaknesses that arise from the Sonnenschein–Mantel–Debreu conditions discussed in Section 5.5.2.

An additional aspect that this approach helps identify is that once time-dated commodities are used in a model (with labor as the only input if you extend the time horizon long enough), the unique relation between cost of capital and the quantity of capital employed breaks down. It is possible that some production processes are preferable (based on the cost they signify) at intermediate levels of capital costs (interest rates) while another is preferable at lower *as well as* at higher rates ("reswitching problem," e.g., Harcourt, 1972; Kregel, 1971; also, Samuelson, 1966). The next two sections show Sraffa's idea in a more analytical way and thus depict an alternative theory of value, which does not require marginal analysis and an aggregate measure of capital.

6.5.3 A Classical One-Commodity Model After Sraffa

In classical economics, production is conceived as a circular flow. At the beginning of the production period, we have a given number of inputs, say x bushels of corn. In the production process, the inputs are transformed into outputs, say y bushels of corn. Production is viable if the surplus or net output y-x is positive, i.e., the system is able to reproduce itself or to expand. If all of the surplus is consumed, then there are exactly x bushels of corn at the beginning of the next period, so the system just reproduces itself. If only part of the surplus is consumed and the rest is invested, our economy starts the next period with more than x bushels of corn and the system grows.

Assume that there is only one commodity, say corn. For the production of one unit of corn, we need a units of input (seed corn) and l units of labor. Let p denote the price of corn, w the wage rate (the price of one unit of labor), and r the profit rate. Assuming that wages are paid at the end of the production period, costs of production are given by

$$p = (1 + r)ap + wl \tag{6.1}$$

Since we assume that production is feasible we assume $a < 1$, meaning that less than one unit of seed corn is needed to produce one unit of corn. We can normalize the price of our single commodity corn by setting $p = 1$, and rewrite Eq. (6.1) to see that the net output $(1 - a)$ is distributed between profits and wages:

$$(1 - a) = ra + wl \qquad (6.2)$$

Another way to see this would be to solve Eq. (6.1) for the wage as a function of the profit rate:

$$w(r) = \frac{1 - (1 + r)a}{l} \qquad (6.3)$$

We see that there is an inverse relation between the wage rate and the profit rate, reflecting and illustrating the class struggle that is inherent in capitalist production. Setting the wage equal to zero we can solve for the maximum rate of profit R. Vice versa, we can set the profit rate equal to zero and solve for the maximum wage rate W. Now we know that the wage rate will be in the interval $[0,W]$ and the profit rate will be in the interval $[0,R]$. Equation (6.3) is an equation with two unknowns, w and r. By setting the wage (the profit rate), we can solve for the profit rate (the wage) and hence arrive at a solution. In order to close the system, we have to fix one of the parameters. We will come back to this issue later.

6.5.4 A Classical N-Commodity Model After Sraffa

Let us now move to an n-commodity world. Assume that there is only one technique for the production of each of the n commodities. This way, we do not have to deal with the choice of techniques. Let $p = (p_1, p_2, \ldots, p_n)$ denote the n-dimensional vector of prices, and let $l = (l_1, l_2, \ldots, l_n)$ denote the n-dimensional vector of labor inputs. Labor is assumed to be homogeneous and profit and wage rates are defined as above. The coefficient a_{ij} denotes the amount of input of commodity j that is needed to produce one unit of commodity i. Cost of production for commodity i is then given by

$$p_i = (1 + r) \times [a_{i1}p_1 + a_{i2}p_2 + \cdots + a_{in}p_n] + wl_i$$

Collecting all coefficients in a matrix

$$A = \begin{pmatrix} a_{11} & a_{12} & \cdots & a_{1n} \\ a_{21} & a_{22} & \cdots & a_{2n} \\ \vdots & \vdots & \ddots & \vdots \\ a_{n1} & a_{n2} & \cdots & a_{nn} \end{pmatrix}$$

allows us to write the prices for all n commodities as

$$p = (1 + r)Ap + wl \qquad (6.4)$$

This economy is viable if the largest real eigenvalue of the matrix A is smaller or equal to one (eigenvalues are explained in Chapter 10). To see how this result is derived, the interested reader is referred to Kurz and Salvadori (1997, pp. 96−97).

Equation (6.4) is a system of n linear equations. The values for A and l are given by the prevailing technology. The unknowns of the system are the n prices, the wage rate, and the profit rate. Fixing one price as a numéraire (e.g., by setting $p_1 = 1$) we are left with n equations and $n + 1$ unknowns. The system is underdetermined; in order to solve it we need to fix one additional parameter. There are various possibilities to solve this: First, we could argue that the wage is determined by class struggle. Second, we could argue that there is a socially determined subsistence wage. And third, we could argue that the profit rate is determined in the financial sector. No matter which way we go, as soon as we fix the wage rate or the profit rate we can compute all the remaining prices. These prices are natural prices which depend on technology (the matrix

A and the vector *l*) and on distribution (*w*,*r*). If the distribution changes, relative prices are affected. If, e.g., the wage rate moves up, prices of labor-intensive commodities increase and prices of capital-intensive commodities fall.

The classical theory of prices is an alternative to the neoclassical theory of prices. Characteristic for the classical theory of prices is the absence of any notion of marginal productivity and the emphasis on distribution, as illustrated by the inverse relation between wages and profits.

6.6 AN OUTLOOK ON POST-KEYNESIAN AND INSTITUTIONAL PRICE THEORIES: SETTING AND ADMINISTERING PRICES

More generally, price theory in the setting of Post-Keynesian economics and institutional economics, particularly the economics of American (or original) institutionalism, provides a further and more far-reaching alternative to the neoclassical modeling of prices. As Lee (2004), amongst others, points out, *Post-Keynesian* as a term for grouping theoretical approaches is not easily defined. In fact, there are a number of broader or narrower definitions of what constitutes Post-Keynesian economic theory. This may partly be the case because a number of theoretical approaches that are not counted as Post-Keynesian in the narrow sense are in fact complementary to these narrow formulations. Therefore, even though more diverse, a broader field can be formulated as well that would then include a number of different, but complementary perspectives, on, for instance, questions of long-term investment and growth dynamics, distribution, the role of the institutional framework in those dynamics, and, especially interesting for us here, prices, approached from a basis that is more rooted in real-world economics.

In this section, we offer a brief overview over Post-Keynesian price theory's principal conceptions, for which we follow Shapiro and Sawyer (2003). Amongst other issues, Post-Keynesian approaches to companies' price setting allow overcoming another conceptual problem in neoclassical theory, namely, the fact that costs cannot be fully determined (but would have to be for strict profit maximization to be possible; see below) and that prices therefore have to be set in a manner that always includes an arbitrary and rule-based element.

At the center stands *pricing power* of the firms. Prices are not cost- or demand-determined but set according to strategic considerations by firms. These prices are operationalized as *markup prices* (for details, see Lee, 2004). The markup is added onto the average variable costs (AVC) in a period. In Chapter 7, we will see that markups are possible in neoclassical monopoly and oligopoly models but that there they are constrained by demand conditions and thus by the exogenously given preferences alone. In contrast, the markup in the Post-Keynesian setting permits an integration of a wider set of possible influences, including the industry structure, influences on demand through, for instance, advertising, and wage setting rules and labor union influence, among others. Prices serve firms to maintain their operability and secure funds for long-term investment projects to be financed internally in order to avoid risk related to external sources of finance. Depending on your needs in a model, you can capture the markup as a percentage *m* of AVC or as a fixed amount *M* added to ACV:

$$p = (1 + m)\text{AVC}$$

or

$$p = \text{AVC} + M$$

Usually, prices are set to cover additional costs and allow for the realization of profits.

However, in practice, there is no fixed relation between average cost and markup.

Changes in average costs may, for instance, lead to a reduction in the markup, if the overall competitive or demand structures are not permissive of (extensive) price increases for a certain product. Vice versa, an increase is conceivable as well. Hence, the markup depends on the conditions a company faces in its market segment and its *discretion* with regard to price setting (note that distributional issues are involved here as well). The *objectives* pursued by a company come into play as well, and different ones may be conflicting here. For instance, aiming at an increase in market share may lead to the acceptance of reduced profits at times. Costs matter in those decisions, but so do, for instance, targeted sales, or the difference between targeted and realized sales, and actions taken by competitors (see also Chapter 7 for presentations of related aspects).

A problem that is very specifically pointed to is connected to the impossibility of the full determination of *real unit costs*. Their final value depends on a number of aspects that can only be known after a few periods, and in fact, can definitely be known only once production has stopped. Examples of such influences are the costs of acquiring equipment, whose contribution to unit cost can only be determined once the machine's use is discontinued and the number of units produced with it known; but also marketing expenditure that influences future sales where the impact on unit costs depends on the number of units sold after they were undertaken, etc. Running costs may also include research expenditure for new products, which have to be covered by revenues from the existing product line.

The covering of costs in a period and realization of a desired profit can of course be attempted based on experience and expectation, but the resulting price to be set will always be somewhat arbitrary under true uncertainty and only local knowledge; and a "profit rate" will likewise be, as true costs cannot properly be determined. Strict profit maximization is hence logically impossible, and not only because of issues of uncertainty and strategic interdependence. True costs and demand (which may depend on a number of factors unknown to or outside the company's scope, such as competitors' strategic decisions, or the overall aggregate demand in an economy) would have to be known, but are not and cannot be. Experience and expectations, and rules of thumb for price setting, in turn, are formulated within the institutional (cultural) framework that companies operate in and the rules they have come to learn and adopt over time that are related to their own learned firm culture and the culture prevailing in their environment, their industry, sector, region, and peer group.

Still, obviously, general requirements are known that have to be fulfilled by companies and guaranteed by the prices they set and can be integrated into economic theory. These provide the foundation for the alternative understanding of the setting of prices introduced here. As said, the operationalization of these concepts is undertaken by means of the markup.

Another aspect to be mentioned here is *administered prices* introduced by the institutionalist economist Gardiner C. Means in the 1930s (Means, 1939; compare Lee, 2004). As Nell (1998) points out, mechanisms for reacting to changes in market demand patterns have undergone significant changes between the period before World War I and the period following World War II. Technical conditions in production up until the beginning of the twentieth century were such that changing demand conditions directly led to changes in prices as production structures were set up for producing a specific amount of a product and changes in that amount were difficult to implement. Prices in this regime fluctuated procyclically to adjust demand to supply (and if nominal wages are assumed to adjust more slowly, real wages moved countercyclically, providing some endogenous counterbalance). In the following decades, through a process that had consolidated itself by the middle of the twentieth century, production structures underwent significant alterations with the result that changes in demand have since then usually been addressed by adjusting the use of production factors, which in the short term is predominantly labor. Prices are kept constant, or slowly increasing, and fluctuations in demand lead to procyclical fluctuations in employment (which is then self-reinforcing as changes in employment will lead to changes in demand in the same direction).

The mentioned administered prices can be seen as a complementary aspect of these broader changes. Companies enter into repeated interactions and contractual relations. Prices are thereby set for a period of time. These are called administered prices; they can be maintained if companies have some degree of market power. The rationale for the company can be understood from a *long-term* perspective, allowing *strategic considerations* regarding growth and market share to become important factors in their considerations and price policies. Prices that can fluctuate in the short term, on the other hand, are called market prices. In this context, we also have to mention Galbraith (2007; also see Chapter 7) who distinguishes market prices, over which companies have no control ("accepted sequence"), and the much larger area where companies have significant power over consumption choices and prices ("revised sequence"). As increased control offers means for reducing the effects of uncertainty, it is generally in companies' interests to try and extend their control over their environment.

The parallel existence of these two types of prices can result in *endogenous macroeconomic cycles*, as demand developments are mutually reinforcing. A reduction in aggregate demand would lead to a reduction in prices in the market sector, and a reduction in employment in the administered sector. Unemployed workers and stable administered prices would further reduce effective macroeconomic demand and thus economic activity. Increasing aggregate demand would be necessary to counter downward adjustments in economies with a mixed price structure, such as the ones that have been emerging since the beginning of the twentieth century. On the other hand, administered prices may also introduce an inflationary dynamic. If companies enjoy market power, they can increase prices even under stable conditions, possibly resulting in dynamics at the end of which stands a generally increasing price level in an economy (which may in turn be leading to *stagflation* as effective demand can subsequently be reduced as well; see also Chapter 4).

6.7 CONCLUSION AND OUTLOOK

We have been dealing with two related aspects of economic theory in this chapter: critiques aimed at the different core aspects and assumptions of the neoclassical general equilibrium approach as well as alternative formulations offered for addressing related issues.

The critiques addressed in this chapter have included:

- the fact that the interpretation of variables from physics models in an economics context does not work as postulated in model formulations in economics; it requires a variety of unwarranted assumptions and may lead to weird implications such as economic conservation laws;
- the fact that taking the assumptions used for formulating neoclassical models seriously, and accepting the modeling strategy employed, leads to the recognition

of inconsistent assumptions in the core model, which includes the assumption of horizontal market demand curves combined with firms' individual demand curves that are negatively sloped (so that a polypolistic market would be distinct from oligopoly markets) as well as the assumption of an upward sloped supply curve in partial markets;

- a number of issues being raised regarding the way that individual preferences are treated; their exogenous nature mirroring presumed customer sovereignty being the determining factor for customers' control over companies (who maximize profit by servicing existing demand as well as they can) in the neoclassical understanding of an economy makes them crucial to the evaluation of market outcomes as socially desirable;
- that the rationality assumption might be a generally useful foundation for understanding and explaining economic outcomes in a general, and generalizable, way can be called into question when considering that more realistic assumptions on individual decision-making, such as satisficing, lead to different outcomes in models, and potentially different evaluations of empirical observations.

These problematic aspects of general equilibrium models in turn may lead one to call into question the normative statement of the overall social desirability of outcomes of market exchanges and related resource allocation patterns, and thus suggest that more careful interpretations of outcomes of economic activities and the outcomes reached are required here. The alternatives presented here have included approaches to matters of production, the formalization of preferences, as well as price theories. These lend themselves to such more careful interpretations, and offer first glimpses at the possibility for gainful

changes in the way the economic sector in a society is treated (on this, see especially Chapter 17). Additional factors, such as issues of power and attempts to integrate other real-world observations into concepts and models, will be further addressed in Chapter 7.

There have been many more alternative promising approaches that have sadly not or only slowly been developed while the general equilibrium theory has been favored by a majority of economists for many decades now. Such alternative methods and models will be introduced in later chapters of this book. This includes alternative methods such as game theory (Chapter 8), simulation (Chapter 9), dynamic systems and complexity (Chapters 10 and 11), and economic models outside the general equilibrium tradition, both historic (Chapter 12) and more recent ones (Chapters 13 and 14).

Chapter References

Berg, N., Gigerenzer, G., 2010. As-if behavioral economics: neoclassical economics in disguise? Hist. Econ. Ideas. 18 (1), 133–166.

Blinder, A.S., Canetti, E.R.D., Lebow, D.E., Rudd, J.B., 1998. Asking About Prices: A New Approach to Price-Stickiness. Russell Sage Foundation, New York, NY.

Bowles, S., 1998. Endogenous preferences: the cultural consequences of markets and other economic institutions. J. Econ. Lit. 36 (1), 75–111.

Calkin, M.G., 1996. Lagrangian and Hamiltonian Mechanics. World Scientific Publishing, Singapore.

Fisher, I., 2007/1892. Mathematical Investigations in the Theory of Value and Prices. Cosimo, New York, NY.

Galbraith, J.K., 2007/1967. The New Industrial State. Princeton University Press, Princeton, NJ.

Gigerenzer, G., Gaissmaier, W., 2011. Heuristic decision making. Annu. Rev. Psychol. 62 (4), 451–482.

Hands, D.W., 1993. More light on integrability, symmetry, and utility as potential energy in Mirowski's critical history. In: De Marchi, N. (Ed.), Non-Natural Social Science: Reflecting on the Enterprise of More Heat than Light. Duke University Press, Durham, NC, pp. 118–130.

Harcourt, G.C., 1972. Some Cambridge Controversies in the Theory of Capital. Cambridge University Press, Cambridge.

Hausman, D.M., 2000. Revealed preference, belief, and game theory. Econ. Philos. 16, 99–115.

Kalenscher, T., Tobler, P.N., Huijbers, W., Daselaar, S.M., Pennartz, C.M.A., 2010. Neural signatures of intransitive preferences. Front. Hum. Neurosci. 4, 1–14.

Keen, S., 2009. A pluralist approach to microeconomics. In: Jack Reardon (Ed.), The Handbook of Pluralist Economics Education. Routledge, London, New York, pp. 120–150.

Keen, S., 2011. *Revised and Expanded Edition: Debunking Economics—The Naked Emperor Dethroned?* Zed Books, London.

Kregel, J., 1971. Rate of Profit, Distribution and Growth: Two Views. Macmillan, London, Basingstoke.

Kurz, H.D., Salvadori, N., 1997. Theory of Production. Cambridge University Press, Cambridge.

Lavoie, M., 2006. Introduction to Post-Keynesian Economics. Palgrave Macmillan, Basingstoke.

Lee, F.S., 2004. Post Keynesian Price Theory. Cambridge University Press, Cambridge.

Lewin, S.B., 1996. Economics and psychology: lessons for our own day from the early twentieth century. J. Econ. Lit. 34 (3), 1293–1323.

Means, G.C., 1939. The Structure of the American Economy. Part I: Basic Characteristics. Government Printing Office, Washington, DC.

Mirowski, P., 1989. *More Heat Than Light—Economics as Social Physics, Physics as Nature's Economics.* Cambridge University Press, Cambridge.

Nell, E., 1998. *The General Theory of Transformational Growth—Keynes After Sraffa.* Cambridge University Press, Cambridge.

Neumann, J.V., 1946. A model of general economic equilibrium. Rev. Econ. Stud. 13 (1), 1–9.

Ricardo, D., 1817. On the Principles of Political Economy. John Murray, London.

Samuelson, P.A., 1938. A note on the pure theory of consumer's behaviour. Economica. 5 (17), 61–71.

Samuelson, P.A., 1966. A summing up. Q. J. Econ. 80 (4), 568–583.

Schumpeter, J.A., 1911/1997. Theorie der wirtschaftlichen Entwicklung—Eine Untersuchung über Unternehmergewinn, Kapital, Kredit, Zins und den Konjunkturzyklus, Duncker und Humblot, Berlin.

Scitovsky, T., 1992/1976. *The Joyless Economy: The Psychology of Human Satisfaction* (revised edition). Oxford University Press, Oxford.

Sen, A.K., 1973. Behavior and the concept of preference. Economica. 40 (159), 241–259.

Sen, A.K., 1993. Internal consistency of choice. Econometrica. 61 (3), 495–521.

Shapiro, N., Sawyer, M., 2003. Post Keynesian price theory. J. Post. Keynes. Econ. 25 (3), 355–365.

Simon, H.A., 1965. The logic of rational decision. Br. J. Philos. Sci. 16 (63), 169–186.

Simon, H.A., 1979. Rational decision making in business organizations. Am. Econ. Rev. 69, 493–513.

Simon, H.A., 1983. Reason in Human Affairs. Harry Camp Lectures. Stanford University Press, Stanford.

Smith, E., Foley, D.K., 2008. Classical thermodynamics and economic general equilibrium theory. J. Econ. Dyn. Control. 32 (1), 7–65.

Sraffa, P., 1926. The laws of returns under competitive conditions. Econ. J. 36 (144), 535–550.

Sraffa, P., 1960. The Production of Commodities by Means of Commodities. Cambridge University Press, Cambridge.

Stigler, G., 1957. Perfect competition, historically contemplated. J. Polit. Econ. 65 (1), 1–17.

Stiglitz, J.E., 2010. Freefall. America, Free Markets and the Sinking of the World Economy. Norton, New York, NY.

Veblen, T.B., 1898. Why is economics not an evolutionary science? Q. J. Econ. 12 (4), 373–397.

Veblen, T.B., 1899. The Theory of the Leisure Class. An Economic Study of the Evolution of Institutions. McMillan, New York.

Wellhöner, V., 2002. Ökonomik–Physik–Mathematik: Die Allgemeine Gleichgewichtstheorie im interdisziplinären Kontext. Verlag Peter Lang, Frankfurt.

Wübben, M., von Wangenheim, F., 2008. Instant customer base analysis: managerial heuristics often "get it right". J. Mark. 72, 82–93.

Zia, R.K.P., Redish, E.F., McKay, S.R., 2009. Making sense of the legendre transform. Am. J. Phys. 77 (7), 614–622.

Further Reading

Philip, A., Sawyer, M.C. (Eds.), 2000. A Biographical Dictionary of Dissenting Economists. second ed. Edward Elgar, Northampton, MA.

Chen, P., 2010. Economic Complexity and Equilibrium Illusion: Essays on Market Instability and Macro Vitality. Routledge, London, New York.

Kirman, A., 2006. Demand theory and general equilibrium: from explanation to introspection, a journey down the wrong road. Hist. Polit. Econ. 38 (5), 246–280.

Reardon, J. (Ed.), 2009. The Handbook of Pluralist Economics Education. Routledge, London.

Van Horn, R., Mirowski, P., 2009. The rise of the Chicago School of economics and the birth of neoliberalism. In: Mirowski, P., Plehwe, D. (Eds.), The Road from Mont Pèlerin. The Making of the Neoliberal Thought Collective. Harvard University Press, Cambridge, pp. 139–178.

Further Reading—Online

For further reading, see the textbook website at http://booksite.elsevier.com/9780124115859

EXERCISES

1. Name five main criticisms of the neoclassical general equilibrium theory and explain briefly.
2. What is an economic conservation law?
3. Why are negative inclined market demand curves and horizontal demand curves for individual companies logically incompatible given the assumptions of the perfect market model? (Show this formally.)
4. Name the principal problems around the assumption of positively sloped supply curves.
5. From what angle and how has the "revealed preferences" approach been criticized?
6. Explain the basic equation of a Sraffian one-commodity model.
7. What are markups and administered prices?

7

Real-World Markets: Hierarchy, Size, Power, and Oligopoly, Direct Interdependence and Instability

"People of the same trade seldom meet together, even for merriment and diversion, but the conversation ends in a conspiracy against the public, or in some contrivance to raise prices." **Adam Smith**[1]

"Technology and the companion commitments of capital and time have forced the firm to emancipate itself from the uncertainties of the market." **John K. Galbraith**[2]

---

[1]*An Inquiry into the Nature and Causes of the Wealth of Nations*, New York: Cosimo Classics, 2007, Volume 1, Book 1, Chapter 10, p. 137, originally published 1776.

[2]*The New Industrial State* (2007/1967), Princeton and Oxford: Princeton University Press, p.139.

7.1 REAL-WORLD PHENOMENA AGAIN, THE CORPORATE ECONOMY, AND OLIGOPOLISTIC MARKET STRUCTURE

7.1.1 Spatial Arenas, Deregulation, Complexity and Uncertainty, Coordination and Dilemma Problems

Real-world markets exist in many specific *geographical spaces*, which often are *overlapping* in manifold ways and also exist *at different levels* (local, regional, interregional, national, international, global). Considering this, there already is nothing like a clear-cut, unique, transparent, and simple ideal "market."

In reality, as explained earlier, markets are also networks of *directly interdependent agents*, facing typical information problems, i.e., (strategic) uncertainty, and *coordination and dilemma problems*. Situations of direct interdependence are genuinely complex and usually have no unique and predetermined outcome, as we have explained in Chapters 1—4 and 6 and will further elaborate in Chapters 8—11.

This chapter, in particular, refers to the earlier *real-world economies* chapter (Chapter 4), with the typical coordination and dilemma problems in the fragmented value-added chains (VACs) and in the *choice of competing network technologies* explained there. A look at those real-world economies showed *tensions* among (i) the required product integration, (ii) the factual VAC fragmentation, and (iii) typically competing network technologies, with the hazards of failing coordination or cooperation. Related information problems (strategic *uncertainty*) and instable expectations and behaviors (*turbulence*) would then persist—particularly occurring in *deregulated markets*, as we have argued. Finally, under conditions of short-run individualistic rationality, uncertainty triggers *reactive tendencies* toward *hierarchization* and *"power-ization,"* as observed, in order for firms to individualistically reduce their uncertainty. But also, the formation of coordinated and cooperative forms such as *spatial clusters* and *networks*, in order to attain some coordination and cooperation, could be observed (see Chapter 4).

As explained in more detail in Chapter 4, markets and capitalist market economies had been *deregulated* on a comprehensive, large-scale, and long-run basis since the mid-1970s, under the political–economic ideology of *"neoliberalism,"* by politicians and state bureaucracies. This included the deregulation of (i) *labor law*, with a subsequent reduction of average labor costs and a long-run redistribution into profits worldwide, (ii) the *law of setting up business*, which fostered outsourcing and functional VAC fragmentation, (iii) *foreign-trade law*, which supported the international expansion of the largest companies, the global spatial VAC fragmentation, and globally fragmented hub&spoke-type sourcing networks, and (iv) the *law of banking and the financial speculation sector*, which increased overall systemic volatility up to the *Great Recession* and crises of 2007ff. (see, e.g., Chen, 2010). Further, this included (v) the dispensing of former public property and wealth (*privatization*), with a subsequent *regulation of oligopolistic competition* in postal, traffic, information, and IT sectors, and (vi) the reduction of the welfare state. The historically emerged arrangements of *social rules and institutions* that had largely stabilized the economy before was *abandoned* on a large scale, which *opened up new space for action and*

profit-making for corporations, particularly for the large and internationally active ones that had all opportunities to expand into a newly deregulated "free" global space. But at the same time this *increased the volatility* of the systems as a whole and the *turbulence* and *uncertainty* for the individual agents, even for the largest and most powerful corporate benefiters.

In addition, the *new large public–private deregulation bureaucracies* entered the action space as new agents, which—in contrast to the intentions and the official "neoliberal" rhetoric—further *increased the complexity of the individual decision situation*, even for the largest players. While the "neoliberal" rhetoric, in fact, *intended a reduction of systemic complexity* through "more market," this indeed was perhaps achieved for the public agents and for politicians (however, note the new deregulation bureaucracies mentioned), but the individual decision situations for private agents included increasing complexity. And whether the system complexity as a whole was in fact increased or reduced must remain an open question for the time being (for more detail on potential measures of *complexity*, see Chapter 11).

Also note that *tele-information and -communication technologies* (TICs or, as typically used, ICTs) do have *size effects* and overall tend to *support* the efficacy of *larger firms* through enlarging opportunities for *economies of scale* (see Chapter 5) and *economies of scope* (as explained in Section 7.2).

As said, real-world activity, against our check of real-world economies, is undertaken in an environment characterized by *uncertainty*, and the more deregulated real markets are the more volatile and turbulent that environment tends to be. For example, changes in aggregate demand often are unforeseeable in complex decentralized networks (among them real-world markets), but have repercussions on more specific sectoral and firm-level demand. Also, other sectors may change in unforeseen ways due to changes in technology, which may result in different demand patterns than expected, technological change may directly affect a firm's position through improved competitiveness by rivals or the availability of new substitutes for its products (for more details on innovation and firm strategy, see Chapter 16).

In this way, a comprehensive tendency *toward proactive (offensive) and reactive (defensive) size and power growth*, as explained earlier, was triggered. In terms of relatively conventional modeling, which also occurs in the mainstream micro textbook, real-world deregulated markets displayed an accelerated and comprehensive development toward an *oligopolistic "market structure,"* in terms of the simple number of (dominant) agents in a market. The related formal models that will be explained in this chapter form an *overlap between a conventional neoclassical micro textbook*, which contains these models at the fringe of their substantial field, and a *complexity economics textbook*, where these models are just one starting point for explaining real-world markets rather. And while these models are dealt with as *exemptions from the neoclassical core model* there, they appear as *prototypes of real-world markets* here. See Sections 7.3–7.6 for this class of models that form an overlapping set.

7.1.2 Hierarchy, Size Growth, "Power-Ization," Oligopolistic Structure, and Persistent Industrial Variety

Hierarchies—i.e., control systems with differential fixed established positions of "superiors" and "inferiors," which in that very way gain power over many natural individuals (be it laborers or consumers)—can be explained as potential solutions to dilemma problems and related initial strategic uncertainty (see Chapter 4; for more details, see Chapter 16). And such large hierarchies, in turn, will be directly interdependent among each other and thus even more *strategically uncertain*. This

chapter thus explains not only a resulting basic tendency toward an *oligopolistic market structure*—at all kinds of spatial levels, even in a local oligopoly of small- and medium-sized suppliers—but also a subsequent *basic indeterminacy* of related *market processes and outcomes*.

Real-world markets empirically are also characterized by a noticeable persistent *variety of firms with different size, organization, internal culture*, and *behavior, coexisting* even in the same industry or region or with production structures that may be servicing similar demand segments. It appears that there exists *no clear-cut, unique first-best solution* for how to organize or which strategy to adopt in complex firm systems. Rather, this is highly contingent in a complex and volatile system. A first explanation for this is discussed under the label of *monopolistic competition*, which is characterized by a *differentiation of products*. The *systemic processes* leading to the *persistent coexistence of variety* will be explained in the theoretical and methodological Chapters 9, 11, 13, and 14 and in the applied Chapter 16. For instance, the interplay of specific internal structures and proprietary (nonopen), or at least hard to communicate (tacit) technological information (see, e.g., Chapter 13 on the *Nelson–Winter* model), leaves space for adopting different ways for firms to act and still maintain a presence in a real-world market, more in some areas (where, for instance, economies of scale matter less) than in others (where these matter more) (again, more on this with some applied innovation theory in Chapter 16).

7.1.3 Proactive Firm Strategy and Planning—Connecting Hierarchy, Size, Power, and Oligopoly to the Theory of the Firm

All the aspects discussed earlier combine to framing an environment, in which companies have an incentive to try and reduce the impact of uncertain future effects through *increasing their control of their environment*, as well as a number of tools at their disposal for actually doing so. Protecting their internal knowledge, securing market positions through *trying to manage demand* and *reducing (the threat of) competition*, or protecting their production structures through guaranteeing their access to inputs, all become components of *companies' strategies*. Growing in *size* through vertical (the buying of producers of input or customers for output) and horizontal integration (buying competitors), with the concurrent tendency toward industrial *concentration*, or growing in *power* through control over large hub&spoke networks, are side-effects of such attempts, but out of their own merits may offer a maintained protection for a firm, reducing the impact of unforeseen events and the dependence on other actors. As *John K. Galbraith*, in the tradition of economists analyzing the large corporate hierarchy (see, e.g., Chandler, 1977), has put it (Galbraith, 2007/1967, p. 139): "Technology and the companion commitments of capital and time have forced the firm to emancipate itself from the uncertainties of the market."

With changes in technology, mirrored in production structures, organizations, and requirements, aspired *control* of markets and *planning* in production and sales have gained in importance over many decades already. Strategic considerations regarding the planning of access to input as well as sales have concurrently become more important as well. This involves an aspect that is generally abstracted from an economic modeling, namely, those preferences and objectives that change over time and are influenced by third actors, either members of a peer group, or companies directly, and are not given and static—so that, at some level, modern economies are good at *satisfying the needs that have been created to maintain given production structures* (for an example, see Box 7.2).

This chapter, in this way, also relates to what in economics and business studies is called the area of the *theory of the firm*. We will approach this area in more detail in Chapter 16.

7.1.4 Overview and Outlook

The development and use of new information and communication technologies contributed to a

- decentralized and fragmented,
- digitized, network-based, and telecommunicating,
- clustered and networking

character of the global economy. Furthermore, the growing importance of financial markets, with their crises and crashes, likewise heralds a turbulent era.

These developments intensified the effects of the direct interdependence of economic agents. Thus, the information required to form expectations and to effectively coordinate agents becomes more difficult to acquire. Hence, markets have become even less effective in solving the complexity challenge.

The global corporate economy has responded to arising challenges

- through *individualist strategies to deal with complexity and turbulence* by gaining more control through size and power, to purchase and merge with other firms, to collude and cartelize, combine with financial agents, and differentiate their products and make them more nontransparent in order to create separate submarkets for their products (*monopolistic competition*—see Section 7.6), and other forms of power strategies like *rent-seeking*, i.e., lobbying and gaining subsidies, government contracts and property-rights protection, privatization of public assets, public—private partnerships, and other advantages from politicians and public bureaucracies,

- through efforts for and battles around setting the (technological and behavioral) *standards* (for these, also see Chapters 4, 13, 15, and 16),
- through using *repeated interaction* in *long-run relationships* and more *stability* based on spatial and cultural *proximity*, thus forming culturally more embedded regional *clusters*,
- through new efforts to establish cooperation through *networks* among firms,
- and finally, through the combination of network structures and power by large corporations forming global-sourcing structures as *hub&spoke* networks, in this way gaining control over global sourcing, labor, and perhaps customers, distributors, and consumers.

In this chapter, we will continue with a short recapitulation of the main reasons why a decentralized spontaneous "market" system inherently tends to degenerate into a system with agents of *size* and *power*—rather than into a(an ideally competitive) system with zero power. Real-world markets tend to be rivaling systems among each *few relevant agents*, thus an *oligopoly* is the typical market structure, rather than polypolistic (close to "perfect") competition among many small entities that are not in a position of influencing each other and each other's results. *Strategic behavior* in real-world conditions is thus a recurrent theme in this chapter.

We then present *oligopoly models* to increase the understanding of particular problem structures that companies may face in real-world markets. Before that, we introduce the usual model of a *"pure" monopoly*, which establishes one of the typical benchmark models of neo-classical microeconomic theory. Even though these models are often formulated with a view on distortions in market outcomes due to economic power (meaning abilities for individual agents to have an influence in the economic sphere, understood just as a price–product

space, as we have seen in Chapter 5), they can still help underlining some particular problems that companies may expect to face in certain situations. Taking up the problems identified for companies in oligopolistic markets, we will then talk about some of the strategies that companies have developed for solving these problems.

7.2 FACTORS LEADING TO SIZE, POWER, AND A SMALL NUMBER OF INTERDEPENDENT SUPPLIERS

Protecting a company in an environment characterized by uncertainty, the increasing outlay of time and capital for establishing structures, and the other aspects mentioned result in companies having an *incentive to try and seek growth*. So there is an inherent tendency of real-world markets toward increasing market concentration. Here is the set of factors that are working in the real world that together endogenously lead to the phenomenon of a highly interdependent and *complex oligopolistic structure* and *indeterminate process outcome*:

- Real-world markets mostly exist in limited geographical firms or commodities *spaces*. They are *networks* of limited sets of *directly interdependent* agents at local, regional, national, interregional, and international spaces.
- Firms tend to grow in size due to *increasing returns to scale* (economies of scale; benefits of large firms, reflected in falling average costs, see Chapter 5) and *economies of scope* (benefits of joint production of two or more products) in the production and cost functions, two supply-side pushes for size.
- Being few, firms tend to avoid competition through informal *collusion* or formal *cartelization*, as competition usually reduces profits and may lead to fierce rivalry and ruinous price competition.

- They then also tend to actively restrict or *deter entry* through *credible threats* (e.g., building overcapacity, increasing marketing budgets, cutting prices, etc., representing *sunk costs* that cannot easily be liquidized or reconverted later.), if entry is not difficult anyway due to the high fixed investment that the given technology may require.
- Given ubiquitous *network technologies*, there is another powerful force supporting the trend toward few large suppliers dominating the markets: *network effects*. These indicate that the benefit of a service or a product becomes more valuable as more people use it, resulting in a cumulative effect that makes *customers/users/consumers* join the largest network (for more detail on network technologies, see some models in Chapter 13 and applied Chapters 15 and 16).
- They tend to *combine with financial corporations* (banks, financial investment dealers, private equity funds, etc.) into global financial entities dominating the global economy (see, e.g., Vitali et al., 2011), not least in order to gain a financial advantage over their industrial competitors, and to *acquire*, or *merge* with, other firms.
- Other well-known cumulative factors in favor of size, power, and small numbers are *first-mover advantages* (with network technologies) in *standard-setting* races, or *learning curves*, both connected to cumulative effects such as economies of scale and network externalities, as well as high initial fixed costs in specialized technology and related hardware. Like increasing returns, they allow for decreasing average costs over time.
- It is additionally advantageous for companies that technological knowledge can often not be copied, or at least not without substantial effort, so that their internal learned knowledge may offer them

an advantage, especially if it has been developing over some time. Complex acquired *tacit knowledge* cannot easily be imitated; particularly by new, young firms that are entering a market and do not yet have a proper *absorption capacity* (again, more on this in Chapter 15).

Thus, a variety of factors, dominating the reality of production and demand sides, tend to make firms gain and exert power over other agents, allowing them to set and possibly fix prices and conditions, thereby redistributing/transferring profit into their own pockets and *commanding global hub&spoke supplier or sales networks* (for more detailed approaches on cooperation for high prices and *"joint dominance,"* see, e.g., Mischel, 1998; Vatiero, 2009; for the highly concentrated multitier global hub&spoke networks dominating the global economy, see again Vitali et al., 2011). With this, they may also generate some *stability and coordination* in the economic sphere.

7.3 PURE MONOPOLY

In this section, we explain the *ideal monopoly* benchmark model describing the effect of the "market structure" of *exactly one large firm* with great power on market outcomes and overall welfare. The firm is selling a good to numerous buyers for which there is no close substitute. Note that for the firms in this as well as the following section, it is assumed that they are homogeneous entities operating under a single objective, namely, profit maximization. Internal structures, with departments possibly pursuing different goals, or conflicts of interest among those who control the company (management and administration) and those who own it (shareholders) are absent, as are potentially conflicting objectives of the whole company (growth might be higher if profit maximization is not attempted), etc.

Note that the formal analysis not only resembles but in fact is narrowly *related to the "market structure" related neoclassical analysis*, in particular of the ideal market as presented in Chapter 5.

The sole seller faces the *downward-sloping demand function* $q = q(p)$ of the *whole market*, which indicates that the quantity q demanded by consumers declines as the price p rises (and *vice versa*) (for some details, see Box 7.1). In the static market under consideration, the threat of entry by potential competitors is not an issue at this stage. Customers buy the quantity of the good that is indicated by the demand function that describes their aggregate decision. There is no direct interdependence in this model.

7.3.1 Price and Output in a Monopoly

This market structure gives the monopolist *market power*. She can change the quantity she offers, and thus determine the price of her product. In what follows, we explain the decision of the monopolist. Profits are given by $\pi(q) = R(q) - C(q)$, where $R(q)$ is the monopolist's revenue function, defined as demanded output times price, and $C(q)$ is the monopolist's cost function, which relates the cost of production to the level of output. The monopolist chooses the quantity q she produces and maximizes profits:

$$\max_q \pi(q) = R(q) - C(q).$$

The first-order condition (FOC) for this problem is given by:

$$\frac{d\pi}{dq} = \frac{dR}{dq} - \frac{dC}{dq} = !0$$

Here, $dR/dq = \text{MR}$ is the *marginal revenue* function of the monopolist and $dC/dq = \text{MC}$ is its *marginal cost* function. MR gives the change in total revenue resulting from the sale of an additional unit of output. MC indicates the change in cost from producing one additional unit of output. The FOC says that a profit-maximizing firm will produce a quantity for which MR equals MC:

$$\text{MR} = \frac{dR}{dq} = \frac{dC}{dq} = \text{MC}$$

This optimality condition holds for all profit-maximizing firms, independently of the market structure assumed. As we will momentarily see, however, marginal revenue develops differently, depending on the market structure assumed.

We had said that the monopoly model serves as one of the benchmark models of neoclassical economic theory. The other is the perfect market model (Chapter 5), which also serves as the point of comparison for the monopoly results with respect to the neoclassical core questions of allocation of resources and efficiency of market outcomes. In the model of a perfect market, a homogeneous good is produced by many firms, none of which can alter market supply through a change in its production in a way that was noticeable on the aggregate level. By assumption, supply changes by any single company have no effect on the market price. Single firms therefore have no option to influence the price of their products directly and have to accept the market price as given. As the price is not subject to change, the only way for the single firm to maximize its profit is to determine the optimal quantity to supply. The revenue function for a firm in a competitive market takes the form: $R^{\text{PC}} = \bar{p}q$. Thus the marginal revenue of a firm is given by the market price: $\text{MR} = p$. Hence the optimality condition for a firm in a competitive market takes the form: $p = \text{MC}$. This means that a firm will produce the quantity at which market price and marginal costs are equal.

<hr>

BOX 7.1

ELASTICITIES AND NORMAL GOODS, SUBSTITUTE AND COMPLEMENTARY GOODS

As you have already seen, in many instances economics assumes that agents' behaviors can be modeled by choosing appropriate mathematical formulations. These typically describe how a change in an independent variable affects the observed outcome in economically relevant situations. An example would be, "an increase in the price of the good increases the quantity demanded of that good."

If we work with a specified function, we can determine the elasticities related to them. Elasticity describes the relative change in a dependent variable in relation to a relative change in an independent variable. Assuming that the quantity demanded q (the dependent variable) can be described as a function of the price p (the independent variable), we get $q = q$ (p). The *price elasticity of demand* would then be given by:

$$\varepsilon_{q,p} = \frac{dq/q}{dp/p}$$

If this price elasticity of demand is larger than 1, we speak of elastic demand; if it is less than 1, we speak of inelastic demand. Only few functions are of a form that leads to constant elasticities over the whole range for which they are defined. Rather, normally, there are elastic and inelastic ranges (see Figure 7.1).

Consequently, there are price ranges for which a change in the price will result in a change in quantity that is relatively larger than the price change (increasing (reducing) overall revenue following a reduction (increase) in the price asked), and areas where the overall change in revenue will be relatively lower than the price change (reducing (increasing) overall

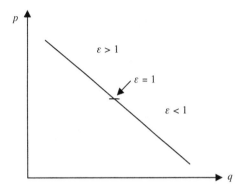

FIGURE 7.1 Elastic and inelastic ranges of a usual demand function (sales function, returns function).

revenue following a reduction (increase) in the price asked).

An idea regarding the expected magnitude of demand changes is important information for companies structuring their price policies; but also, for instance, for governments when deciding tax structure. In taxation we can distinguish between taxes aiming at steering behavior (where the demand change is elastic) and taxes that aim at revenue (where demand is relatively inelastic).

Other elasticities offering information about the economic sphere are the *income elasticity of demand*:

$$\eta_{y,q} = \frac{dq/q}{dy/y}$$

which allows goods to be characterized, depending on the change in demand that can be expected following a change in income. "Normal" goods are those that see an increase in the quantity demanded following increases in income (these are the goods that are usually

---

BOX 7.1   *(cont'd)*

---

used for analyzing markets). Among goods that are increasingly demanded following a price increase one can distinguish between *Giffen goods* (inferior goods—those that cover basic needs and are demanded more frequently when an income constraint gets more pronounced, meaning that price increases have a noticeable impact on real income levels; potatoes having been a typical example) and *Veblen goods* (luxury goods—that are consumed for the purpose of signaling economic potency, as a status symbol, and thereby an example of invidious consumption, as one instance of the more general concept of invidious distinction).

Finally, we want to mention the *cross-price elasticity of demand*, which describes how demand for good 1 may be affected by changes in prices for good 2, as

$$\varepsilon_{q1,p2} = \frac{dq_1/q_1}{dp_2/p_2}$$

If demand for good 1 increases following an increase of the price for good 2, we speak of substitutes (tea and coffee being a typical example). If demand for good 1 falls following an increase in the price of good 2, we speak of complements (coffee and coffee-filters, for instance).

In a monopoly market, the producer faces a downward-sloping market demand curve $q(p)$ that tells her how many units of the commodity can be sold at any given price. Inverting the demand curve to $p(q)$, the inverse demand function shows the price the market is willing to pay for any given quantity of a good. The quantity supplied has an impact on the market price; conversely, if the company decided to set a price, this would determine the quantity it would be able to sell. The revenue that the monopolist can expect to receive if she produces q units of output is $R^M(q) = p(q)q$. Using the product rule of differentiation, the monopolist's marginal revenue can be expressed as:

$$MR(q) = \frac{dR}{dq} = \frac{dp(q)q}{dq} = p + \frac{dp}{dq}q$$

The optimality condition for a monopolist is thus given by:

$$MR = p + \frac{dp}{dq}q = MC$$

This optimality condition states that a monopolist will supply a quantity of a good where the marginal revenue of the last unit sold is equal to its marginal cost. As the monopolist influences the price for all units sold by changing the quantity offered in a market, marginal revenue changes because it includes not only the change in units sold, but also the change in the price of each of these units. In the perfect market benchmark, on the other hand, marginal revenue is constant as firms are assumed to not affect the market price through their decisions. The FOC can be rewritten as follows:

$$p + \frac{dp}{dq}q = p\left(1 + \frac{dp}{dq}\frac{q}{p}\right) = p\left[1 + \frac{1}{(dq/dp)(p/q)}\right]$$
$$= p\left(1 + \frac{1}{\varepsilon}\right) = MC$$

Here, ε is the *price elasticity of demand* (see Box 7.1), which tells us the percentage by which quantity demanded falls as the price increases by 1%. Since we assume a downward-sloping demand function, ε will

---

always be negative. Hence, the equation can be rewritten as:

$$p\left(1 - \frac{1}{|\varepsilon|}\right) = \text{MC} \leftrightarrow p = \frac{\text{MC}}{(1 - (1/|\varepsilon|))} \quad (7.1)$$

The relation between the price elasticity of demand, marginal costs, and price in Eq. (7.1) is called the *Amoroso—Robinson relation*. This relation shows that the monopoly price exceeds the competitive price (=MC) to a degree that is inversely related to the elasticity of demand a company faces. Generally, this degree indicates a firm's market power, and may also be drawn upon for gaining an idea of its position in an oligopolistic market. This market power can be measured through the *Lerner index* that we can deduce by rearranging Eq. (7.1):

$$\frac{p - \text{MC}}{p} = \frac{1}{|\varepsilon|}$$

The index ranges between 0 and 1 (as presumably no company would produce a quantity where $\text{MC} > p$, as here every additional unit would reduce profits). The higher its value, the higher the degree of market power a firm enjoys, or, the higher the *degree of monopoly* in the market.

7.3.2 The Welfare Effect of a Monopoly

After examining the price- and quantity-setting policies of a monopolist, in what follows we will evaluate the welfare effects this market power induces. The question is whether monopoly behavior results in an outcome that can be characterized as optimal from a social point of view. In order to evaluate the outcome we have to introduce a measure of *welfare*. We define welfare as the sum of *consumer surplus* and *producer surplus*.

The consumer surplus is defined as the monetary difference between what consumers are willing to pay and the price they actually pay for the quantity of a good purchased.

Since the market demand curve states the unit price consumers are willing to pay given the quantity on offer we can measure the consumer surplus CS by determining the area under the market inverse demand curve minus the area given by market price times quantity (for an illustration, see Figure 7.2):

$$\text{CS} = \int_0^{q^*} p(q^*)\,\mathrm{d}q - pq^*$$

Given the monopoly price p^M in Figure 7.2, CS depicts the area circumscribed by points E, D, and F.

The producer surplus PS measures the benefit a producer gains by selling a product as the difference between cost of production and sales price. The producer surplus gained for selling an amount q at a price p can be measured by summing up this difference over all units produced:

$$\text{PS} = pq - \int_0^q \frac{\mathrm{d}C}{\mathrm{d}q}\,\mathrm{d}q \quad (7.2)$$

The marginal cost reflects the amount by which a firm's cost changes if the firm produces one more unit of output; since only variable costs change with output, we can define marginal cost as the change in variable cost from a small increase in output. Hence the sum of all marginal costs, which is equal to the area under the marginal cost curve, must equal the sum of the firm's variable costs. Equation (7.2) can be rewritten as:

$$\text{PS} = pq^* - \int_0^{q^*} \frac{\mathrm{d}C_v}{\mathrm{d}q}\,\mathrm{d}q = pq^* - C_v(q^*)$$

Given the monopoly price p^M in Figure 7.2, the producer surplus depicts the area circumscribed by points A, B, D, and E. A socially optimal price—quantity combination is one that maximizes welfare, defined as the sum of producer surplus and consumer surplus:

$$\max_q W = \text{CS} + \text{PS} = \int_0^{q^*} p(q^*)\,\mathrm{d}q - C_v(q^*)$$

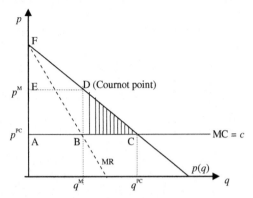

FIGURE 7.2   Price–output combinations in a monopoly and in a market under perfect competition.

The FOC for this problem implies:

$$p(q) = \frac{dC_v}{dq} = MC$$

In a competitive market this condition holds by assumption. In a monopoly market, it does not.

The result of the monopolist's decision is a "deadweight welfare loss," which is formally given by:

$$\int_{q^M}^{q^{PC}} [p(q) - c]dq > 0$$

and is illustrated in Figure 7.2 as the hachured area circumscribed by points B, C, and D. C gives the efficient solution, where price is equal to marginal costs (so that in a market under perfect competition, the consumer surplus is given by the area A-C-F). B is the point where price equals marginal revenue. D, finally, shows the Cournot point, the profit-maximizing price–quantity combination in a monopoly market. Note that among others, this relies on the assumption that a single company will produce a given level of output at the same cost as many small companies.

However, in general, you can also formulate models for situations in which a monopoly leads to fewer welfare losses as a polypolistic supply-side. Also, decades-long economic and policy discussions on the *welfare implications of pure monopoly* have included modeling *opportunities to tax monopolies' profits away* and make more use of these amounts of money through *recycling it through public expenditure.*

7.4 OLIGOPOLY

In oligopoly markets, there are only a small number of firms, serving a particular market. By assumption, they are hence in a position to influence the aggregate quantities (or prices) which means they exercise market power. As a result, as is the case in the monopoly market, the equilibrium price will generally be higher than it would be under perfect competition, and the quantity supplied will generally be lower than it would be under perfect competition. As already mentioned earlier, oligopolistic markets open up some room for strategic interaction.

There are three standard oligopoly models: *Cournot*, *Bertrand*, and *von Stackelberg*. The models are similar in that they are static and considering only one period, excluding repeated interactions. The firms offer one homogeneous good. In the Cournot and Bertrand models, firms make their choices simultaneously while in the Stackelberg model firms make their choices sequentially. In the Cournot model, firms compete by choosing the quantities, and prices then adjust in order to clear the market. In the Stackelberg model, it is also quantities that are chosen. As choices are made sequentially, this allows the first mover to gain a larger market share than that of the competitor firm. Finally, in the Bertrand model, firms compete by choosing prices, and quantities adjust in order to clear the market. The Bertrand model differs in its result since it predicts that two firms competing in prices are sufficient in order to arrive at the outcome that the perfect market model shows as well.

For didactic reasons we present the oligopoly models with only two competing firms, hence we speak of "duopoly." All three duopoly models, however, can be extended to more than two firms without changing the main results.

7.4.1 Cournot (Cournot–Nash) Oligopoly

For a simple illustration of the oligopoly case first considered by Cournot (1838), assume there are two firms (A and B) who simultaneously decide on how much of a *homogeneous good*, q_A and q_B respectively, to produce. The firms face a downward-sloping demand function and it is assumed that the price adjusts in order to clear the market. Thus, the larger the quantity supplied by both firms, $q = q_A + q_B$, the lower the price will be. Formally, this means that the price is a function of output whose first derivative is negative. This function is the inverse demand function $p = p(q)$, with $p'(q) < 0$ for all $q \geq 0$ and, by assumption, $p(0) > c$.

Assume that marginal costs, c, for both firms are identical and constant (both firms utilize the same technology; note that given constant marginal cost, in this interdependent setting, the market price approaches marginal cost with increasing number of firms, see also the Exercises section at the end of this chapter). Firm A's profit maximization problem can then be written as:

$$\max_{q_A \geq 0} \pi_A = p(q_A + \bar{q}_B)q_A - cq_A$$

Here, $\bar{q}_B$ indicates that firm A takes firm B's quantity as given. Deriving the FOC, we get:

$$p'(q_A + \bar{q}_B)q_A + p(q_A + \bar{q}_B) \leq c \quad (7.3a)$$

where the left-hand side corresponds to firm A's marginal revenue and the right-hand side to marginal cost. The FOC holds with equality if firm A supplies a positive amount of the

good, i.e., $q_A > 0$. Firm B engages in the same reasoning so that, given the assumptions made, we can write firm B's FOC as follows:

$$p'(\bar{q}_A + q_B)q_A + p(\bar{q}_A + q_B) \leq c \quad (7.3b)$$

Since Nash equilibrium is equilibrium in choices and beliefs, every firm's belief about the other firm's output is correct, i.e., $q_A = \bar{q}_A = q_A^*$ and $q_B = \bar{q}_B = q_B^*$, where the asterisk denotes a firm's optimal choice of output level. As the goods are homogeneous and both firms utilize the same technology, we further know that $q_A^* = q_B^*$. Adding Eqs. (7.3a) and (7.3b), we arrive at the following condition that has to hold in the Nash equilibrium:

$$p'(q_A^* + q_B^*)\left(\frac{q_A^* + q_B^*}{2}\right) + p(q_A^* + q_B^*) = c \quad (7.4)$$

Equation (7.4) implies that firms are making positive profit since they are charging a price larger than marginal cost (remember that $p' < 0$). Also, the quantity supplied is lower than the socially optimal level. We know this since the demand curve is downward sloping and prices and quantities are therefore negatively related (higher prices meaning lower quantities).

Monopoly, Cournot–Nash Oligopoly, and Polypoly Prices and Quantities Compared

Let us consider an example. For simplicity, we assume that firms are producing with a constant-returns-to-scale technology and face a linear inverse demand function given by:

$$p(q) = a - bq \quad (7.5)$$

In Eq. (7.5), a and b are positive constants. We know that in the perfect competition (PC) market, the price equals marginal cost, $p^{PC} = c$. Output at p^{PC} will therefore be $q = (a - c)/b$. Using the same functions for the monopoly model explained in Section 7.3 we would get $p^M = (a + c)/2$ and $q^M = (a - c)/2b$, respectively, indicating the higher price (as by assumption

$a > c$) and lower quantity (half the perfect market amount in this example) in the monopoly setting.

In the oligopolistic situation, firms interact strategically. Equations (7.6) and (7.7) state firm A's profit maximization problem and the FOC:

$$\max_{q_A \geq 0}(a - b(q_A + \bar{q}_B))q_A - cq_A \qquad (7.6)$$

$$a - 2bq_A - b\bar{q}_B = c \qquad (7.7)$$

We now derive firm A's best-response function q_A^{BR} which is the FOC solved for q_A. We see that firm A's optimal output is inversely related to q_B:

$$q_A^{BR}(q_B) = \frac{1}{2}\left(\frac{a - c}{b} - q_B\right) \qquad (7.8a)$$

Since both firms are identical, firm B's best-response function is given by:

$$q_B^{BR}(q_A) = \frac{1}{2}\left(\frac{a - c}{b} - q_A\right) \qquad (7.8b)$$

Figure 7.3 depicts both best-response functions graphically. The Nash equilibrium is given by the intersection of those functions. It can be derived by substituting Eq. (7.8a) in Eq. (7.8b). Output at equilibrium is:

$$q_A = q_B = \frac{1}{3}\left(\frac{a - c}{b}\right)$$

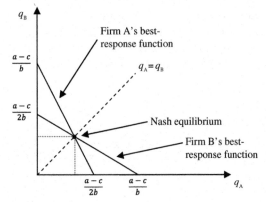

FIGURE 7.3 Best-response functions and Cournot–Nash equilibrium.

Substituting into Eq. (7.5) we get the oligopoly price $p^C = (a + 2c)/3$. In the Cournot oligopoly, total quantity supplied is smaller than at the social optimum, but larger than the quantity in the market if it were a monopoly:

$$\underbrace{\frac{1}{2}\left(\frac{a - c}{b}\right)}_{q^M} < \underbrace{\frac{2}{3}\left(\frac{a - c}{b}\right)}_{q^C} < \underbrace{\left(\frac{a - c}{b}\right)}_{q^{PC}}$$

The Cournot–Nash Oligopoly as a Prisoners' Dilemma—A Numerical Example

If the possibility of collusion is considered, the Cournot model becomes a Prisoners' Dilemma. As described earlier, we assume that both firms are identical. Collusion means that the firms behave as if they were a monopolist and split quantities and profits equally. The Prisoners' Dilemma structure results from the fact that half the monopoly profit is larger than the profit generated in the Nash equilibrium on the one hand, and the fact that with unilateral deviation from the agreed quantities, companies can increase their profits above half the monopoly profits, on the other.

To illustrate this, we resort to a numerical example. Assume that parameters a and b are given by $a = 14$ and $b = 1$. Further assume that constant marginal costs c are given by MC = 2. We know that profit is maximized where marginal revenue is equal to marginal cost. Here, marginal revenue is given as MR = $14 - 2q$. The monopolist's profit-maximizing quantity is consequently $q^M = 6$ which corresponds to a price of $p^M = 8$. Total profits in this case are 36. Two firms colluding would therefore produce three units of output each, generating profits of 18 for every company. Contrast this with the mutual best replies in the Cournot duopoly case. Here, each company would supply four units of the good produced; the corresponding price would be $p^C = 6$. We see that, compared to collusion, Cournot competition results in a lower price and higher quantities. Also, profits would be lower in Cournot competition,

		Firm B	
		Collusion / cartel	Deviation from cartel agreement
Firm A	Collusion / cartel	18 18	20.25 13.5
	Deviation from cartel agreement	13.5 20.25	16 16

FIGURE 7.4 The Cournot–Nash oligopoly as a prisoners' dilemma—numerical example.

namely, 16. Note that the quantities supplied in case of deviating differ depending on what the other company does, therefore strictly speaking not allowing the use of a normal form (simultaneous move) game. For purposes of exposition, the matrix serves, though. It shows that it is in the interest of both firms to achieve collusion. But will collusion be stable?

As can be seen in Figure 7.4, in the one-shot game under consideration at the moment, it will not be. We arrive at this result assuming that one company sticks to the agreement, and then calculate the other firm's best response. The collusion quantity for each company is three units. We plug these into one of the best-response functions and see that the best answer in that case is to produce 4.5 units. The deviating company would see its profits increase to 20.25, whereas the profits of the company sticking to the agreement fall to 13.5. Therefore, the rational choice would be for both to deviate. But if both firms deviate from collusion and play their Nash strategies, they will end up at the Cournot equilibrium. If profits are interpreted as payoffs, this situation corresponds to a prisoners' dilemma.

7.4.2 Bertrand Oligopoly

As in the Cournot duopoly model, for the presentation of the Bertrand duopoly (Bertrand, 1883), we assume a downward-sloping continuous demand function $q(p)$ and

a constant-returns-to-scale technology for both firms. We assume that $q(c)$ is positive and finite, i.e., if price equals marginal cost, a positive and finite quantity of the good is demanded.

In contrast to the Cournot duopoly, competition takes a different form. In the Bertrand duopoly model, firms *simultaneously set prices* and supply adjusts in order to clear the market. The firm that chooses the lowest price captures 100% of the demand. If both firms choose the same price, each firm gets 50% of demand:

$$q_A(p_A, p_B) = \begin{cases} q(p_A) & \text{if} \quad p_A < p_B \\ 0.5q(p_A) & \text{if} \quad p_A = p_B \\ 0 & \text{if} \quad p_A > p_B \end{cases}$$

Firms produce to order, meaning that they produce only what they can sell in the market. For firm A profits are given by:

$$\pi_A = (p_A - c)q_A(p_A, p_B)$$

The Bertrand duopoly model is a simultaneous move game. In the following we will derive the Nash equilibrium. We will show that at the equilibrium prices are equal to marginal cost and each firm captures 50% of the market share.

Consider the situation where both firms set their prices according to $p_A^* = p_B^* = c$. The firms will divide the market equally and each firm makes zero profits. To show that this is a Nash equilibrium we consider what happens when one firm changes its strategy while the other firm keeps its strategy. If a firm rises its price it will sell nothing, so profits will be zero. No firm can gain by raising its price. If a firm lowers its price and charges a price below costs, its market share will rise to 100%, but the firm makes negative profits. Hence $p_A^* = p_B^* = c$ is a Nash equilibrium since no firm can gain by deviating from its strategy (mutual best response).

Next we check if there is another strategy that could be a Nash equilibrium. If the firm which charges the lowest price charges a price below cost, it will incur losses. It will always be rational to charge a price of c or higher because by behaving this way the firm will make no losses. Hence in a Nash equilibrium, firms won't charge a price below c.

What about the following situation in which both firms charge a price above costs? Consider firm A charging a price $p_A > c$ and firm B charging $p_B > p_A$. This is not a Nash equilibrium since firm B can gain by lowering its price and charging a new price p'_B with $p_A > p'_B > c$. Now firm B sells to the entire market earning a positive profit while firm A earns zero profits, but we are not at a Nash equilibrium yet. Firm A can lower its price to p'_A with $p'_B > p'_A > c$. In this new situation, firm A sells to the entire market, but again, this is not a Nash equilibrium. The general point is that at prices above costs, the firm charging the highest price can always increase its profits by undercutting the other firm's price. Competition will drive down prices to the Pareto optimum characterized by $p^*_A = p^*_B = c$.

Lastly, we consider the situation in which one firm charges a price equal to costs ($p_A = c$) and the other firm charges a price above that ($p_B > p_A$). Both firms make zero profit. Such a situation is not a Nash equilibrium since firm A can increase its price slightly to p'_A with $p_B > p'_A > c$, thereby increasing its profits. But then we are back in the case that we discussed in the preceding paragraph. Hence we conclude that $p^*_A = p^*_B = c$ is the unique Nash equilibrium in the Bertrand duopoly model.

In case of constant marginal costs, we get the same result as in perfect competition, completely independent of the number of participating companies. This is known as the "Bertrand paradox."

An Extension: Differences in Cost Structures

As one of the possible extensions of the basic Bertrand model, we briefly consider the case of different cost structures for the producers (other variations include extending the time period to increase the attractiveness of collusion, price-fixing in this case, capacity constraints, or switching costs, which may all be integrated into the other models discussed here as well, of course).

Consider two firms (A and B) with different marginal costs $c_A < c_B$. In this case, the company with higher marginal cost (B) cannot remain in the market, since it would be undercut by the cost leader (A). The cost leader would monopolize the market by charging a price below c_B, i.e., $p_A < c_B$. Whether company A can actually charge the monopoly price p^M_A depends on the marginal costs c_B. If the monopoly price is lower than the marginal costs of the competitor ($c_A < p^M_A < c_B$), the Bertrand–Nash equilibrium is given by: $(p^*_A, p^*_B) = (p^M_A, c_B)$. The cost leader A can set her monopoly price without fearing a market entry by a competitor.

If the monopoly price p^M_A is higher than the marginal cost of company B ($c_A < c_B < p^M_A$), the monopoly price would lead to the market entry of company B. To prevent the market entry, the cost leader will charge a price just below the marginal cost of B. The Bertrand–Nash equilibrium in this case is thus: $(p^*_A, p^*_B) = (c_B - v, c_B)$, with v the smallest monetary unit. The price that provides for entry deterrence is also called the limit price. The potential competition has a disciplining effect on company A. Despite its monopolistic position, the price set and the profits gained are lower than in the pure monopoly model. To sum up, the cost leader will set her price according to the following equation:

$$p_A = \begin{cases} p^M_A & \text{if} \quad c_A < p^M_A < c_B \\ c_B - v & \text{if} \quad c_A < c_B < p^M_A \end{cases}$$

7.4.3 Stackelberg Oligopoly

In the Stackelberg model, firms compete by deciding on their respective *quantity*, as in the Cournot duopoly model (Stackelberg, 1934).

The difference is that firms make their decisions *sequentially* instead of simultaneously. At first, firm A (called the leader) decides about the quantity q_A, taking firm B's reaction into account in that decision. Perfect information is assumed so that firm B can observe firm A's decision. Thereafter, firm B (called the follower) reacts by choosing the quantity q_B.

The Stackelberg model is solved by backward induction. Firm A asks how firm B would react to its quantity decision. The answer is given by firm B's best-response function, which we already know from the Cournot model. We substitute Eq. (7.8b) into the market demand function (Eq. (7.5)) and solve for the price as a function of firm A's output:

$$p(q) = \frac{a + c}{2} - \frac{b}{2} q_A$$

Taking into account this price, firm A now maximizes profits:

$$\max_{q_A} \pi_A = q_A(p - c) = q_A \left(\frac{a + c}{2} - \frac{b}{2} q_A - c \right)$$

The FOC telling us the quantity that firm A will supply is given by $q_A^* = (a - c)/2b$. Substituting in firm B's best-response function gives us the quantity that firm B will supply in equilibrium: $q_B^* = (a - c)/4b$. The price is given by $p^* = (a + 3c)/4$.

The Stackelberg duopoly also results in a situation in which the equilibrium price exceeds the competitive price. In contrast to the Bertrand and Cournot models, firms are in different roles as leader and follower. The leader has the so-called first-mover advantage and generates higher profits than the follower.

7.5 NATURAL MONOPOLY

7.5.1 The Rationale for Natural Monopolies

Real-world markets are characterized by high market concentration. Beside private-sector monopolies, in many societies utilities like electricity, gas, water, and fixed-line telephone services are government-regulated monopolies. Since monopolies are associated with deadweight loss and extra profits which would provoke market entry by competitors, the stability of monopolies and their governmental toleration require an explanation.

One particular set of stable monopolies may be so-called natural monopolies. A natural monopoly is characterized by a *subadditive cost function* which indicates that it is cheaper to produce a given amount of output for a single firm than for many smaller firms. A cost function is subadditive if

$$\sum_{i=1}^{m} C(q_i) < \sum_{j=1}^{n} C(q_j) \quad \forall m < n,$$

$$\text{with } \sum_{i=1}^{m} q_i = \sum_{j=1}^{n} q_j = q$$

Believing that there are natural monopolies, governments frequently grant monopoly rights to public utilities to provide essential goods or services, since, given the conditions for a natural monopoly, it is more efficient to have only one firm serving the market.

Subadditivity may arise due to economies of scale, for instance. Since, in this case average cost falls as output increases (strict subadditivity), the company with the largest production volume in the market could offer the output at the lowest price and displace its competitors. Hence, the market would tend toward a monopoly. To avoid the cost of parallel investments, it may be useful to grant monopoly rights to a company and regulate it.

This is the case in almost every infrastructure sector, where high fixed costs are required to establish the network that delivers a specific good (transport facilities, energy, water) to consumers, but where the marginal cost of supply is constant, so that average costs decline as output rises. If more than one firm takes up production, the average cost is going

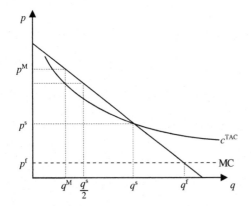

FIGURE 7.5   Strictly subadditive cost curve.

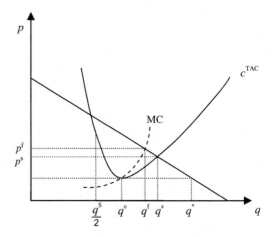

FIGURE 7.6   Weakly subadditive cost curve.

to be higher because each additional firm adds a fixed cost. For a graphical representation, compare quantities and average costs per firm, c^{TAC}, in Figure 7.5. The superscripts f and s designate first- and second-best outcomes. First-best outcome signifies the efficient solution, where price equals marginal cost. The second-best outcome is characterized by the equality of price and average costs.

Decreasing average costs are a sufficient condition for a natural monopoly but not a necessary one. If average costs increase again as output increases beyond a certain point (U-shaped average cost function), there can nevertheless be subadditivity, depending on the level of demand (weak subadditivity). In this case, not every level of output provides the condition for a natural monopoly. Figure 7.6 depicts a U-shaped average cost function.

A natural monopoly is able to supply the total output at lowest costs. However, because of its monopoly position the price it charges can be expected to be higher than its total average cost. The actual price charged depends on how contestable the market is.

A monopoly position is sustainable, if there is no incentive for a competitor to enter the market. That is the case if the natural

monopoly sets a price in a way so that any competing firm that tries to enter the market will incur a loss.

Contestable markets are characterized by free market entry meaning potential competitors (entrants) have free access to the prevailing technology and can enter the market without any penalty if the entry fails. This implies the absence of sunk costs, since the entrant can easily leave the market because the capital equipment that was acquired can be sold or used elsewhere.

In the following we examine the sustainability and efficiency of the natural monopoly in a contestable market and in a market with entry barriers.

7.5.2 Sustainability and Efficiency of the Natural Monopoly in a Contestable Market

In a contestable market, a monopoly price above average cost attracts competitors (entrants) who have free access to the same technology as the established firm (incumbent). The entrants can set a price below the existing monopolist's price and take consumers away. The incumbent firm cannot deter entry if it cannot adjust its prices downward quickly enough. Then, the entrant can engage in a hit and run strategy, entering the market when the price is high, making short-term profits and leaving it without any costs, when the incumbent lowers its price.

The Case of Strict Subadditivity

In case of strict subadditivity (Figure 7.5), the threat of entry of a competitor forces the incumbent to lower the charged price to the level of its average costs to deter entrants. The charged price p^s is the second-best welfare optimal price since it is higher than the marginal cost of the corresponding quantity. The price output combination (p^s, q^s) allows no profitable entry strategy by a competitor; thus the natural monopoly is sustainable, without, however, realizing profits. However, as average costs are higher than marginal costs at this point, the result is not technically speaking efficient.

The Case of Weak Subadditivity

If the incumbent firm has a U-shaped average cost curve (Figure 7.6) and the demand level allows the subadditivity condition to hold, the threat of entry of a competitor would also lead the incumbent to charge the second-best welfare-optimal price p^s. But the resulting price output combination (p^s, q^s) is not sustainable, although the incumbent gains no profits. The firm is not protected from market entry by rival firms, since there is a profitable entry strategy for an entrant. An entrant could challenge the established monopoly by producing a level of output at minimum efficient scale (q^e) and charging a price below p^s. This may cause a price competition that has an end at price p^e. At that point, the demand $q^* - q^e$ is not met. This outcome can be improved by regulating the market through an *entry barrier* or through a *guaranteed minimum price*.

7.5.3 Sustainability and Efficiency of the Natural Monopoly in a Market with Entry Barriers

In real-world markets there are market entry and exit barriers. Thus, the monopoly is not threatened by an entry and has no incentive to set a social-optimum price. On the other hand, subadditivity given, the cheapest way to produce any given level of output is to have one firm producing for the whole market. This raises the question of how to reach a socially optimal price and socially optimal costs simultaneously.

The Case of Strict Subadditivity

Sunk costs are not relevant for the decision to produce for an incumbent since they cannot be recovered. However, they are strategic instruments to deter the entry of a competitor. If an entrant decides to challenge the established monopoly, it has to take into account that the incumbent can trigger a price competition that hinders the entrant from charging a price that would allow for positive profits. Since an entrant has no sunk cost before entering the market, the sunk costs are relevant for its decision to enter the market. Considering the credible threat of the incumbent lowering the prices, a potential entrant may decide against an entry. If the incumbent is protected from market entry by rival firms, it will set the Cournot monopoly price p^M. Society incurs welfare losses. Moreover, the monopoly position is sustainable.

To prevent this loss of welfare the market should be regulated. If the government required the monopoly to set the first-best welfare optimal price p^f, the monopoly would incur losses, since $p^f < c^{TAC}$. Hence, the state would have to subsidize the monopoly or allow the second-best price p^s. This price allows for maximum welfare under the constraint that the company makes no loss.

TABLE 7.1   Effects of Strong and Weak Subadditivity in Contestable and Noncontestable Markets

	Strong Subadditivity	Weak Subadditivity
Contestable market	– p^s (inefficient)	– p^e (inefficient)
	– Sustainable	– Unsustainable
		– Output scaling
Market with entry barriers	– p^M (inefficient)	– p^M (inefficient)
	– Sustainable	– Sustainable

The Case of Weak Subadditivity

In the case of weak subadditivity, the incumbent sets the Cournot monopoly price, since it does not have to fear the market entry of a competitor. Hence, the result is inefficient and the monopoly position is sustainable. But the government has the opportunity to set the first-best price regulating the market, because at p^f the monopoly makes positive profits. For a brief overview, see Table 7.1.

7.6 HETEROGENEOUS OLIGOPOLY AND MONOPOLISTIC COMPETITION

7.6.1 From Homogeneous to Heterogeneous Oligopoly and to Monopolistic Competition

In the oligopoly models presented earlier, we were able to provide a first overview of situations in which companies' decisions have a mutual influence on their respectively resulting profits. In a first extension, to be given in this section, we follow Sweezy (1939), who investigated *how prices* in already existing markets may *change*. His approach integrates the notion that markets have historically grown into oligopolies and that companies in such an oligopolistic setting find themselves in some kind of price equilibrium. In that case, does

any company have an incentive to change its price and if so, how would the others react? Sweezy did not start with formulating assumptions that help define a specific equilibrium that rational companies would find them in if they met in a market without any history of prior relations. Instead he asked how, if companies have over time reached one of the possible equilibria in their market, the situation may change from that point onward, with a specific view on their price policies.

Another basic assumption in the oligopoly models described earlier was that the companies offer a homogeneous product. We will relax that assumption in Section 7.6.2 where we explain the concept of monopolistic competition that has been introduced by Chamberlin (1933) and Robinson (1933) (see also the Appendix to this chapter, introducing the neoclassical formalization of this approach by Dixit and Stiglitz (1977) that has been at the heart of many advances in *neoclassical* modeling over the past decades). In the approach discussed later, a number of companies offer *incomplete substitutes* (*heterogeneous goods*) in a market. The intuition is that in order to *avoid pure (or strict and thus fierce) price competition*, companies can try to *differentiate their products* and thereby gain a certain degree of pricing power—even though the formulation is still wedded to the general notion of companies competing through prices and for profits, resulting in market entry by potential competitors until all profits have fallen to zero.

In fact, companies in real markets have a number of tools at hand to help them stabilize the markets and their market shares or profits and avoid fierce and potentially *ruinous price competition* by aiming at influencing customers' product choice other than price. This point will subsequently be taken, when we turn from the models of oligopolistic markets to addressing further issues that emerge in real-world markets. We will also see there that the tools employed for *stabilizing and securing an individual company's position* can have adverse effects on other companies so that, on the other hand, we find a tendency toward a *destabilization*, *turbulence*, and *indeterminacy* of oligopolistic markets, in the sense that not all companies at the same time can persist and realize a guaranteed and given amount of profits.

7.6.2 Sticky Prices in Oligopoly Markets: A Kinked Demand Curve

Sweezy (1939) addressed the question of sticky prices in markets. Instead of asking what a clearly defined equilibrium in an oligopoly market would look like (given a set of assumptions), he asked how companies might behave in an equilibrium. The point was to find reasons for observed stickiness of prices in markets, especially in markets where you might expect price competition to drive prices down, if you applied a more standard model formulation in the analysis. In order to illustrate the point, he assumed that competitors react in different ways to price changes by other companies, depending on whether these would increase or lower their prices. These different reactions introduce a kink in the demand curve of companies. This means that in situations characterized by *strategic interdependence*, a standard demand function would not be useful.

The basic premise here is that *companies seek the protection of their market shares*. In that case, Sweezy reasoned that it was unlikely that price increases by a company would be met by increases by their competitors. The result is a relatively elastic demand schedule for a firm for prices above the currently charged one. Market share would be lost and total revenue would be reduced if a firm single-handedly raised the price for its product. On the other hand, he assumed that reductions of prices would be met by competitors. Therefore, the demand schedule for the individual firm for

prices below the current one is relatively inelastic. Market shares would not change much, and total revenue would decrease as a consequence. The complete demand schedule a company faces and its marginal revenue are shown in Figure 7.7.

Once firms find themselves in equilibrium in an oligopoly market, the approach can therefore help to understand why market conditions, and particularly the *price, may not change*. Price competition does not make sense for oligopolistic companies. Then, competition could be expected to be exercised through other, nonprice instruments (*nonprice competition*) aiming at strengthening monopoly power and increasing customer loyalty (see Section 7.6.3).

7.6.3 Heterogenization and Monopolistic Competition

The concept of monopolistic competition was introduced by *Chamberlin* in 1933 (Chamberlin, 1933), and in parallel by *Robinson* (Robinson, 1933). Observing market structures, he concluded that the available models of perfect competition and monopoly, respectively, were only incomplete approximations of real markets, where *advertising* and *product differentiation* played a significant role. Commonly

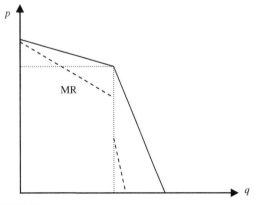

FIGURE 7.7 The Kinked demand curve.

observed market structures, rather, allow firms some *degree of market power*, without enjoying full or "pure" monopoly power, though. At the outset of his concept, thus, stand firms that can *behave like monopolists in their particular market segments*. They do, however, face competition from firms offering *imperfect substitutes* to their products—if price differences get too pronounced, customers will seek a variety that may be less suitable for their needs but that they are willing to except in exchange for the money saved in the purchase in comparison to the preferred option. The reasoning is that in order to *avoid price competition* that may reduce their profits, firms could divide markets and create market segments through product differentiation. As a result, they are assumed to *face downward-sloping demand curves*, albeit more elastic ones than a pure monopolist would. The basic reasoning applied to monopoly markets as explained earlier applies here as well—the degree of pricing power depends on the elasticity of substitution, as seen in the *Amoroso—Robinson relation* in Eq. (7.1).

More specifically, *two separate demand curves* are introduced to illustrate a company's problem structure (see Figure 7.8). One gives a demand schedule for the situation in which all its competitors keep their prices constant, this is relatively elastic (dd). The other refers to a situation in which all firms set the same price. This one is assumed to be relatively inelastic (DD). Note that the reasoning corresponds to that of the kinked demand curve that Sweezy formulated. To the left of the intersection between the dd and DD curves, Sweezy's kinked demand curve corresponds to the dd curve, to the right it corresponds to the DD curve.

As long as *free entry* is assumed, eventually a situation with many companies in the market realizing zero profit would result (see also the formalization of this setting at the end of this chapter). This *connects the idea of a monopolistic component to the competitive market*. If companies realize profits, more competitors enter the market. As companies face downward-sloping demand curves, the *resulting price would in the end correspond to their average costs*, i.e., *zero profits* per unit, while still lying *above their marginal cost*, though. The situation is reversed if the original setup is characterized by losses. In that case, firms leave the market until zero profits are realized.

If *entry barriers* can be erected, the companies in a market may be smaller in number, and we will observe an *oligopoly with heterogeneous products* (heterogeneous oligopoly). We will return to this point in Section 7.7. For a simple illustration of entry deterrence, see Box 7.2. Even though the market structure is described as monopolistically competitive, and continuing entry would eventually drive profits down to zero unless countermeasures were taken, such heterogeneous oligopolies, i.e., including barriers to entry, in fact appears closer to what Chamberlin (and Robinson and Sweezy as well) had in mind. The importance of product differentiation that he noted and the fact that real competition includes a number of nonprice variables (including such aspects as *imperfect information* regarding alternative products and specific product details *on the customer side*), which allow companies to *create market niches* in which they can *exercise market power*, point in this direction.

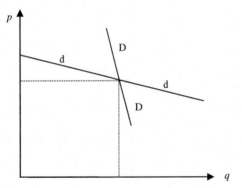

FIGURE 7.8 Demand Schedules in monopolistic competition.

BOX 7.2

A SIMPLE ENTRY DETERRENCE GAME—ILLUSTRATION

1. The game *with entry* (entry deterrence fails) (incredible threat)

    Incumbent I may play *soft* (*S*): He does not expand supply, thus no price deterioration. Thus, *Entrant E* has a chance to make profit after entry.

    I may also play *tough* (*T*): He expands supply, thus price will decline (also at his own expense), with no profit opportunity for *E*.

    The normal-form game resulting in the game matrix is shown in Figure 7.9.

    The announcement of *I* to fight would be an *incredible threat*, given the incentive structure. One *Nash equilibrium* will result: *E* will enter.

    As a three-stage game in extensive form (1.5 interactions, a pre- and a post-entry decision of the incumbent), this is depicted in Figure 7.10.

2. The game when *entry deterrence succeeds* (credible threat)

    I now makes a credible threat through *self-commitment*: He makes a large investment in capacity (production, R&D, advertising) as *sunk costs*. Thus, it pays better for him to expand his production and sales, thus utilizing his extended capacities. Now *T* pays better, $+ \Delta 1$, *S* yields $- \Delta 1$. The new normal form is shown in Figure 7.11.

    Now *T* yields $+1$ (full capacity utilization), while *S* yields -1 for the incumbent. A new *Nash equilibrium* (still two Pareto optimal) results: The newcomer will not enter!

    This is shown as a three-stage game with sunk costs and with entry deterrence in Figure 7.12.

3. An example of *entry deterrence/defending one's monopoly over time*

		Entrant	
		In	Out
	S	2, 1	4, 0
Incumbent	T	1, −1	3, 0

FIGURE 7.9   Entry (deterrence) game—normal form, numerical example.

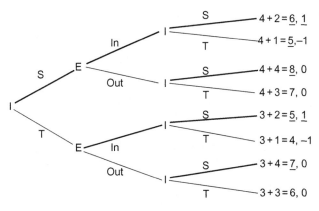

$$4 + 2 = 6, 1$$
$$4 + 1 = 5, -1$$
$$4 + 4 = 8, 0$$
$$4 + 3 = 7, 0$$
$$3 + 2 = 5, 1$$
$$3 + 1 = 4, -1$$
$$3 + 4 = 7, 0$$
$$3 + 3 = 6, 0$$

FIGURE 7.10   Entry (deterrence) game—three-stage extensive form, numerical example.

BOX 7.2   (*cont'd*)

		Entrant	
		In	Out
	S	1, 1	3, 0
Incumbent	T	2, −1	4, 0

FIGURE 7.11   Entry (deterrence) game—normal form with credible threat, numerical example.

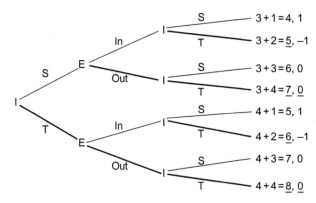

FIGURE 7.12   Entry (deterrence) game—three-stage extensive form with credible threat, numerical example.

		Entrant	
		In	Out
	S	10, 5	b, 0
Incumbent	T	−15, −9	b, 0

FIGURE 7.13   Entry (deterrence) Game—normal form, numerical example, with variable.

Assume that T (a price war) takes place for 1 interaction only, at first (while E is already in). Thereafter, I decides on his *permanent* strategy, and E decides on staying in or exiting as shown in Figure 7.13.

How large must the *monopoly profit b* for I be at the minimum (b_{min}) in order to make him play T forever? (Assume $\delta = 0.9$.) (Note: Apply the single-shot solution as explained in Chapter 3. Use I's T/in-payoff for the first interaction, then b for an infinite geometric series, then deduct b once for the first interaction.)

Solution key:

$$-15 + \frac{b}{1-0.9} - b > ! \frac{10}{1-0.9} \rightarrow \text{Solve for } b!$$

Alternatively, determine the discount factor δ (*future expectation*). How large must δ be at the minimum (δ_{min}) for T to become the superior strategy for I, i.e., to make E exit? In other words, when does it pay for I to defend his monopoly position? (Assume $b = 12$).

Solution key:

$$-15 + \frac{12}{1-\delta} - 12 > ! \rightarrow \text{Solve for } \delta!$$

7.7 HETEROGENEOUS OLIGOPOLISTIC AND MONOPOLISTIC COMPETITION: OPPORTUNITIES FOR STRATEGIC BEHAVIOR OF FIRMS AND THEIR POTENTIAL SOCIAL COSTS

In reality, there are factors that tend to threaten companies' profits in oligopoly markets: reinforced size growth by others through economies of scale in production technology, network effects on the user side, and the other factors mentioned earlier (in Section 7.2). Thus, on the one hand we observe an incentive for companies to try and create a stable environment, in which profits are not threatened, while on the other hand each individual company's measures to try and increase its protection against uncertain events may lead to problems for others. Still, ways have been found for reducing the threats emerging from this situation. For instance, to *avoid price wars* and related turbulence in the oligopoly, oligopolists have chosen early in history to *calm their direct competition down* and *reduce their direct interdependence* through dissolving an important condition of direct dilemma-prone interdependence—which also is an important common condition of all oligopoly models: *product homogeneity.*

Oligopolists may, of course, avoid price competition through *"meet the competition"* clauses (used also as an *entry deterrence*), i.e., a *credible threat* to meet a price-cut by another oligopolist (or potential entrant) through the same price-cut on their sides. What may look like fierce price competition in fact is a device to *enforce price stability as a coordination form.* If a price-cut can be expected to be met by price cuts by competitors, oligopolists have every incentive to maintain high-price strategy coordination. The longer a relatively *stable environment* can be conserved, the better the opportunities to learn about each other and find even

more subtle ways for coordinating their policies (*tacit collusion*). Also remember the *markup pricing* discussed in Chapter 6. Given markup pricing, *decreasing costs* in the environment considered here can be expected to immediately increase profits for companies, since an, at least full, pass-through of cost reductions to prices becomes unlikely.

Product and price differentiation, through *branding, advertising,* or *quality differences,* allowing *market segmentation,* have occurred as a result of the *growing action capabilities of large oligopolistic corporations* vis-à-vis their customers, users, consumers, suppliers, and even politics and public administrations. Large oligopolistic firms divide the market and generate their own market segments (see Box 7.3; for a simple illustration of a company's branding strategy, see Box 7.4), where they can behave similarly to monopolists. Consumers are induced into spending on goods and services because of the name and its image, for instance, rather than because of rational examinations of functional or instrumental quality. In institutional economic terms, we may call this *ceremonial belief,* ceremonial consumption institutions, or ceremonial institutionalized trust. The set of phenomena that emerged this way in real-world markets from the second half of the nineteenth century onward was analyzed as monopolistic competition (see Section 7.6). Monopolistic competition nowadays applies to virtually all important goods and services such as cars, computers, software, telecommunication, and internet services, private water and energy supplies, fuel, etc. Given differentiated products, the *customer/user/consumer has to incur higher costs to collect and process information* on the different brands that, in turn, are deliberately made *nontransparent,* incomparable, or incommensurable to customers by the monopolistic competitors.

Against this background, it becomes obvious that binding consumers/customers/users

---

BOX 7.3

COMPANIES' INFLUENCE ON DEMAND

In the introductory section of this chapter, we referred to a number of avenues open for companies for improving their position in markets and reducing the potential for unforeseeable adverse effects to have a too pronounced impact on a firm's position. One of those was the *management of demand*, including its actual creation. Recognizing that this is in fact a possibility for companies to successfully direct attention and effort is an important point to bear in mind when working with the models presented here.

In these models, companies face external conditions to which they then respond. Technology is given. The *Amoroso–Robinson relation* expresses the profit-maximizing price under given demand conditions. Market power refers to abilities to influence the price–quantity combination in a market to one's advantage. This, in case of monopoly and oligopoly markets, introduces inefficiencies in the static environment considered. The companies still face constraints, though, as they have to take their external environment as given. Not all of their plans and actions will become effective, if taken together. Many actions neutralize each other, and in many cases, as we have seen, the collective outcome is the contrary of what the individual intentions of the oligopolists had been.

Many have contended, however, that demand can largely be managed by powerful oligopolists. Among them is the famous institutionalist economist *John Kenneth Galbraith*. Power then refers not only to realizing advantageous price–quantity combinations, but also to the *ability to change the environment*, within which companies operate, meaning that they can *create conditions*, alone or collectively, that are advantageous to them. Supposed advantages of the setting and system, within which they operate, then often refer to aspects, where companies can do well what they want to do—servicing a demand that they themselves have created. The potential to take influence in the overall socioeconomic system, especially for larger corporations, then becomes much greater than is often acknowledged, and it becomes imperative to realize that influence on agents is not only *exerted through the political sphere*. It extends to numerous other areas as well; for instance, in addition to the points referred to in this chapter already, a shift of research and development costs to the public sector as a consequence of private-sector influence-taking is a pronounced feature of modern economic activity, shifting risk and cost to the public and exploiting the results which emerge (for a more detailed discussion of these issues, see Galbraith, 2007/1967, especially chapters 10,11, and 19; see also, e.g., Rothschild, 1947).

---

to the oligopolist's brand name by advertising, brand management, and reputation building would be a prime strategy for an oligopolist in monopolistic competition. The more she succeeds in *steepening her sales curve* (the demand curve), the more the sales price p that she can realize will tend to be above her marginal revenue (see the *Amoroso–Robinson relation* discussed earlier). Changes in sales can be met through changes in marketing and other measures for securing demand. In contrast to a competition through prices for a given

BOX 7.4

ESTABLISHING A BRAND AS A TOOL FOR REPUTATION

We consider branding as a behavioral signal sent through the repeated production of high-quality goods that serves to convince customers of intentions of future quality production (especially where the quality of a product is not observable before its purchase and use: experience goods).

As a first approach to questions of branding, we may think of one period at some point in time at which the brand was established, i.e., at which earlier production has established a reputation for quality products offered by the producer. Now, if we assume that higher quality production entails higher production costs, the firm may have an incentive to lower the quality of its product in order to increase its short-term profits. One period in this case is defined as the time period needed for information about the product to spread among customers, i.e., for information to be communicated by those who already have purchased the product to those who might still consider doing so. The period ends when every potential customer has made the decision to buy or not to buy. For simplicity, we represent this situation as a game in which the producer and one customer interact, with the firm choosing to maintain a high standard in production, or to lower it, and the customer to purchase the good in question, or not to purchase it (see Figure 7.14).

The firm does not know whether the customer will purchase the product, and the customer cannot observe quality before the purchase. In a given moment, when considerations on a possible future play no role, the firm has a dominant strategy in low quality production. Note that the firm has production costs that cannot be recovered if the customer exits.

Now, obviously, the decision of the firm to produce something or not has to come before a decision of the customer to purchase the product can be executed. If we assume observability of the quality of a product, a representation using the extensive form of the game will be more suitable for representing the decision situation (see Figure 7.15).

If the customer was able to observe the quality of the product before the purchase, high-quality production would pay for the firm, because that would be the only way to actually make a sale and hence to turn a profit (use backward induction for solving the game to arrive at this result).

Assuming again that the overall quality of a product is not observable, we can appreciate the purpose of signaling the intent of certain future behaviors to the customer. In this case, assume additionally that customers will stop purchasing from a firm when their expectations of a high-quality product should be disappointed. For the firm, the question then becomes whether the short-run gain of lowering quality for increasing one period's profits is worthwhile, or not. For this, finally, assume that the decision to plan for future production does not entail a known or planned endpoint,

		C	
		Purchase	Exit
F	High quality	1, 1	−4, 0
	Low quality	5, −1	−2, 0 (Nash equilibrium)

FIGURE 7.14 A firm-reputation game—normal-form illustration, numerical example.

BOX 7.4 *(cont'd)*

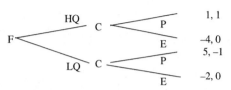

FIGURE 7.15 A firm-reputation game—extensive-form illustration, numerical example.

so that the calculus of an infinite geometrical series can be applied (see Chapter 3). The firm compares the present value of the short-run profit focus to that of the long-run quality (branding) focus:

$$\frac{1}{1-\delta} > 5$$

has to hold for a long-run focus in a high-quality strategy to be worthwhile (when the current value of overall profit is the decisive variable based on which to decide the firm's strategy), i.e., $\delta > 0.8$ has to hold. For a δ as

defined in Chapter 3, containing a probability for the continuation of the interaction and a discount rate for future results ($\delta = p/(1 + r)$), the probability of continued interactions has to lie above 0.8 (the exact value depending on the discount rate r) in order for high-quality production to be worthwhile.

The most recent area of application of *asymmetric information* about the quality of a product and related market failure (as a lack of demand, or, the choice of the exit strategy on part of the customers) is the *internet business*. Asymmetric information is most relevant in the internet, where the customer cannot immediately check the good or service. Thus, the Internet is a *prime area of application* of a "market for lemons" (see Chapter 5). Therefore, among other things, mechanisms of *reputation building* for those producers/suppliers who are interested in selling high-quality products are most important.

---

demand, this changes the focus of competition: instead of competing in markets, companies compete for markets, as the Schumpeterian notion would take it.

7.8 A FINAL CONSIDERATION OF FIRM SIZE AND POWER, STRATEGIC COOPERATION, MONOPOLISTIC COMPETITION, AND REAL-WORLD MARKETS

In the end, the two perspectives of strategic interaction in real-world markets are (i) some collusion/cartelization and price cooperation and (ii) heterogeneous oligopoly, i.e., in total, *monopolistic competition plus strategic cooperation*, would need to be integrated into a more

realistic model of real-world markets. Overall, real-world oligopolistic markets—beyond just either oligopolistic equilibrium with homogeneous goods or monopolistic competition with relative price stability—appear to remain a *complex, unstable,* and *sometimes turbulent form,* due to the factors and mechanisms explained in this chapter and their lasting tensions (for a simplified overview, see Figure 7.16).

Finally, a broader perspective would have to consider and analyze the firm, particularly the large and global firm, and monopolistic rivalry systems, not only in the economy, but also its wider impacts, through the *openness of the economy,* on the exploitation and distribution processes vis-à-vis the social and ecological systems, where all three subsystems form a complete system.

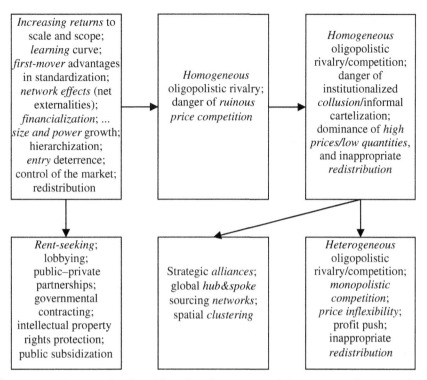

FIGURE 7.16 Factors and issues of real-world markets favoring cumulative size growth, power, oligopolization, and persistent nonoptimality, tension, and instability.

Chapter References

Bertrand, J.L.F., 1883. Théorie Mathématique de la Richesses Sociale. J. des Savants. 67, 499–508.

Brakman, S., Heijdra, B.J., 2004. Introduction. In: Brakman, S., Heijdra, B.J. (Eds.), The Monopolistic Competition Revolution in Retrospect. Cambridge University Press, Cambridge, pp. 1–46.

Chamberlin, E.H., 1933. The Theory of Monopolistic Competition. Harvard University Press, Cambridge, MA.

Chandler, A.D., 1977. The Visible Hand: The Managerial Revolution in American Business. The Belknap Press of Harvard University Press, Cambridge, London.

Chen, P., 2010. Economic Complexity and Equilibrium Illusion: Essays on Market Instability and Macro Vitality. Routledge, London, New York.

Cournot, A.A., 1838. Untersuchungen über die mathematischen Grundlagen der Theorie des Reichtums, Jena 1924 (franz. Original: Recherches sur les principes mathématiques de la théorie des richesses, 1838), Reprint Saarbrücken: VDM Verlag Dr. Müller, 2006.

Dixit, A.K., Stiglitz, J.E., 1977. Monopolistic Competition and Optimum Product Diversity. Am. Econ. Rev. 67 (3), 297–308.

Dixit, A.K., Stiglitz, J.E., 2004. Monopolistic competition and optimum product diversity. In: Brakman, S., Heijdra, B.J. (Eds.), The Monopolistic Competition Revolution in Retrospect. Cambridge University Press, Cambridge, pp. 89–120.

Galbraith, J.K., 2007/1967. The New Industrial State. Princeton University Press, Princeton, NJ.

Mischel, K., 1998. Sticky prices as a coordination success. Atlantic Econ. J. 26 (2), 162–171.

Robinson, J.V., 1933. The Economics of Imperfect Competition. Macmillan, London.

Rothschild, K.W., 1947. Price theory and oligopoly. Econ. J. 57 (227), 299–320.

Sweezy, P.M., 1939. Demand under conditions of oligopoly. J. Polit. Econ. 4, 568–573.

Vatiero, M., 2009. An institutionalist explanation of market dominance. World Competition: Law Econ. Rev. 32 (2), 221–227.

Vitali Stefania, G., James, B., Battiston, S., 2011. The network of global corporate control. PLoS ONE. 6 (10).

von Stackelberg, H., 1934. Marktform und Gleichgewicht. Springer, Wien, Berlin.

Further Reading—Online

For further reading, see the textbook website at http://booksite.elsevier.com/9780124115859

EXERCISES

1. For the inverse demand function $p(y) = a - by$ and the cost function $c(y) = cy$ calculate the profit-maximizing price–quantity combination for a monopolist.
   a. For $a = 200$, $b = 1$, $c = 20$.
   b. For the placeholders a, b, and c for a general result in this setting.
2. Depict the functions from exercise (1) as well as marginal revenue and marginal cost curve and show the Cournot point in the resulting graph.
3. Modify the cost function in exercise (1) to $c(y_i) = cy_i$. For $i = 1, 2$ calculate the best-response functions of two identical companies and determine the quantity that each oligopolist chooses (no storage, all produced units are sold). Which is the resulting market price?
   a. For $a = 200$, $b = 2$, $c = 50$, when companies decide on their output quantity simultaneously.
   b. For $a = 200$, $b = 2$, $c = 50$, when company 1 decides first and company 2, knowing about y_1, deciding later.
   c. For the placeholders a, b, and c for a general result in these two settings.
4. Assume n identical companies in a market described by the functions used in exercise (3). Show that with an increasing number n, the market price converges to the constant marginal cost c.
5. Explain the reasoning behind a kinked demand curve.
6. When might it be considered preferable to have a market serviced by a monopolist? Explain why.
7. Explain the situation when weak subadditivity is a factor in
   a. contestable markets,
   b. markets with entry barriers.
8. What options do companies have for strategic behavior
   a. amongst themselves and
   b. with regard to consumers?
   c. Identify critical assumptions about agents' behavior, options, objectives for arriving at these results.
9. Consider again the game in Figure 7.14. Try and calculate mixed strategies for the agents (in the normal form, i.e., for situations in which agents cannot observe the quality and may consider randomly purchasing the product). How can you interpret the result?

SOLUTION KEYS

For solution keys of the exercises and other material on the subject of this chapter, visit the textbook website www.microeconomics.us.

APPENDIX: A NEOCLASSICAL MODEL OF MONOPOLISTIC COMPETITION

In the late nineteenth century, economists had the perfectly competitive market and the monopoly case as analytical tools at their disposal, as is reflected in Marshall's principles. He was, however, aware that other market forms were not simply hybrids of the two. It was furthermore observed already then that decreasing returns to scale did not stop firms from expanding output or that average costs were decreasing around the realized output level. Both are facts that cannot be reconciled with the perfectly competitive markets of prevailing theory.

Marshall introduced decreasing returns to scale for the individual firm in combination with external economies of scale for the industry as a whole. These external economies of scale create an interdependence of the supply curves, where the combined supply of all firms reduces industry costs and ensures that the combination of lower price and increased supply is in fact an equilibrium outcome. Internal economies of scale (which Marshall thought as important as external ones) could, however, not be represented in this way and, in fact, escaped economists' attempts for the next decades (the verbal discussion that Robinson and Chamberlin offered at the beginning of the 1930s notwithstanding) (Brakman and Heijdra, 2004).

Dixit and Stiglitz (1977) introduced a formulation for modeling a market in which firms produce using a technology that leads to internal economies of scale. Their monopolistic competition model was to lay the foundation for many advances in theoretical mainstream economics in subsequent years.

They open their article referring to the basic issue of welfare economics under a neoclassical perspective, the question whether markets yield the optimum kinds and quantities of commodities. Within that theoretical framework, there are problems with markets' ability to achieve this for three reasons, namely, distributive justice, external effects, scale economies. Their focus is on scale economies—this focus allows the reformulation of the initial question and posing it in terms of quantity versus diversity.

In turn, this reformulation of the question offers the possibility to choose a direct way of including the utility of variety in the formulation—as they put it, "the convexity of indifference surfaces of a conventional utility function defined over the quantities of all potential commodities already embodies the desirability of variety" (p. 297), as the convex shape of the indifference curve includes the assumption that a balanced mix of the available goods is preferred by the agents.

Assume one market in which goods are good substitutes for one another at the same time that they are poor substitutes for the rest of the goods in the economy that is represented as one good.

The usual assumption of an individual actor maximizing utility subject to a budget constraint applies. Let the utility function be of Cobb–Douglas form:

$$U = z^{\alpha} y^{1-\alpha} \qquad \text{(A7.1)}$$

As we have a Cobb–Douglas type function, the corresponding optimum spending in each sector is given by a constant share of income I (as calculated by maximizing utility subject to a budget constraint $p_y y + p_z z = I$):

$$p_z z = \alpha I \qquad \text{(A7.2)}$$

and

$$p_y y = (1 - \alpha) I \qquad \text{(A7.3)}$$

In this, z is the homogeneous good that represents the rest of the economy. The other sector is the monopolistically competitive one. The goods there are assumed to be relatively homogeneous varieties of a general type of good. Hence, y is a composite index of the varieties traded in the second sector. This index is to take a constant elasticity of substitution form:

$$y = \left(\sum_i x_i^{\rho} \right)^{1/\rho} \qquad \text{(A7.4)}$$

For concavity, $\rho < 1$; and $\rho > 0$ to allow for x_i to become zero.

Further assume that all firms in the monopolistically competitive sector produce under equal fixed and marginal costs. In that case, actual labels do not matter, only the total number n being produced. Neglecting problems that result if income distribution plays a role, U can be regarded as representing social indifference curves, or as a multiple of a representative consumer's utility—product diversity can then be interpreted as different consumers using different varieties or as diversification on the part of each consumer.

The price index p_y that is corresponding to the quantity index in Eq. (A7.4), the minimum spending necessary to purchase one unit of the composite good, can be calculated as:

$$\min_{x_i} Q = \sum_i p_i x_i - \lambda \left[\left(\sum_i x_i^\rho \right)^{1/\rho} - 1 \right]$$

leading to

$$p_y = \left(\sum_i p_i^{-1/\beta} \right)^{-\beta} \quad \text{with} \quad \beta = \frac{(1-\rho)}{\rho} \quad \text{(A7.5)}$$

Using a two-stage budgeting process—maximizing utility given the budget constraint in the first step and then maximizing the components in the second step, subject to the constraints given by the respective optimum shares of budget allocated—we can calculate the individual demand schedules for each variant. This gives us

$$x_i = (1-\alpha) \left(\frac{p_i}{p_y} \right)^{1/(\rho-1)} \left(\frac{I}{p_y} \right) \quad \text{(A7.6)}$$

From Eq. (A7.6), it immediately follows that

$$\frac{x_i}{x_j} = \left(\frac{p_j}{p_i} \right)^{1/(1-\rho)} \quad \text{(A7.7)}$$

We see that $1/(1-\rho)$ is the elasticity of substitution between any two variants within the monopolistically competitive sector; we call this elasticity σ—the larger σ gets, the better substitutes the goods in the monopolistically competitive sector are. In fact, as $\sigma \to \infty$ this embodies the perfectly competitive market as a special case.

σ likewise gives the price elasticity of demand for any variant x_i, as can be calculated from the individual demand schedule:

$$-\frac{\partial x_i}{\partial p_i} \frac{p_i}{x_i} = \sigma \quad \text{(A7.8)}$$

To calculate a demand schedule for the sector as a whole, we have to introduce an assumption of symmetry. For symmetric firms, meaning equal quantities and prices respectively for all firms, note that Eqs. (A7.4) and (A7.5) are reduced to

$$y = xn^{1/\rho} \quad \text{(A7.4 ')}$$

$$p_y = pn^{(\rho-1)/\rho} \quad \text{(A7.5 ')}$$

The industry demand curve can then be calculated, using Eqs. (A7.6) and (A7.5'), as:

$$x = (1-\alpha)\frac{I}{np} \quad \text{(A7.9)}$$

This demand function has unit elasticity, meaning that the individual firm's demand schedule is more elastic than the industry's.

Of particular interest under the neoclassical focus in analyses are the welfare implications of this representation of an industry structure. Dixit and Stiglitz distinguish between three results: the equilibrium outcome, a constrained optimum, and unconstrained optimum.

We start with the market equilibrium in order to derive a point of reference for the subsequent comparison. Each commodity is produced by one firm. In the market equilibrium, firms have entered freely until the point at which the marginal firm just breaks even.

There are two conditions to consider. The first is the individual firm's profit maximization; as you know, under neoclassical assumptions, we work with functions that allow formulating marginal revenue equaling marginal cost at the profit-maximizing point. The price elasticity of demand is, as we have seen earlier, given by σ. The companies' profit-maximizing price is calculated in the usual way (see Section 7.3). We hence get (with c as the common marginal cost):

$$p_i \left(1 - \frac{1}{\sigma} \right) = c \quad \text{(A7.10)}$$

As by assumption there is one common equilibrium price, denoted as p_e, we can write

$$p_e = \left(\frac{\sigma}{\sigma - 1}\right)c = \frac{1}{\rho}c \quad \text{(A7.11)}$$

The second condition is that firms enter until the next entrant would suffer a loss. If n is large enough, meaning that the change for all firms that one additional entrant causes is marginal, we can assume that they exactly break even. We can then formulate

$$(p_e - c)x_n = k \quad \text{(A7.12)}$$

where k is the fixed cost incurred by each firm. x_n is given by the demand function we have formulated in Eq. (A7.6).

For the number of firms in the market equilibrium, using Eqs. (A7.6), (A7.11), and (A7.12), we get:

$$n = (1 - \alpha)\frac{I}{p_e}\frac{c}{k}\frac{1 - \rho}{\rho} = (1 - \alpha)\frac{I}{k}\frac{1}{\sigma} \quad \text{(A7.13)}$$

We see the number of firms in equilibrium depends on the cost structure on the one hand (with higher fixed costs leading to a lower number of firms in equilibrium), and on the elasticity of substitution on the other. Note that the number depends negatively on the elasticity of substitution. As we assume internal economies of scale, this result makes sense, as increasing substitutability between any two variants means that the scale in production gets more important which, in turn, should mean fewer big companies will be sharing the market.

However, as has been noted earlier, this does not hold as σ approaches infinity, as in this case a perfectly competitive market outcome is approached, in which the number of firms and the output produced by each is undetermined. Remember that in the perfectly competitive market case, there are no fixed costs of production and hence no scale economies. Now note that the expression given in Eq. (A7.13) depends on the fixed cost incurred

as well—and in fact, if this were to approach zero, as σ approached infinity, we would see the indeterminateness of the number of companies that we find as a result in the perfect competition model.

What is left to find is the equilibrium output of each firm then, which we can calculate from Eqs. (A7.11) and (A7.12) as

$$x_e = \frac{\rho}{\rho - 1}\frac{k}{c} \quad \text{(A7.14)}$$

In this equilibrium solution, we see firms exactly covering their fixed cost. A first-best social optimum would, however, be one where price equals variable cost. Firms would hence incur losses given internal economies of scale because they would have to price below average cost in that case (remember, the scale economies result from the inclusion of fixed costs).

To keep firms from incurring losses, one option is transfers to cover the difference between variable and average cost per unit of output; the other would be regulation to prevent firms from entering the market once average cost is equal to marginal cost. In the latter case, under the conditions set forth here, such a constrained optimum is equal to the market equilibrium outcome, as the loss-preventing prices in both cases are the same from which follows, due to the symmetry assumption used, that number of firms and their respective output levels are equal as well.

We can consequently directly turn to an unconstrained optimum, where the losses incurred due to below-average-cost prices are assumed to be covered by transfers to the companies.

To find the corresponding prices, quantities of output per firm, and number of firms, we maximize an individual agent's utility again. In this case, directly assuming equal prices and quantities for all firms, we get:

$$u = U(I - n(k + cx), xn^{1/\rho}) \quad \text{(A7.15)}$$

in which the overall resource constraint and Eq. (A7.4′) have been used. Differentiating with respect to x and n results in the FOCs

$$-ncU_z + n^{1/\rho}U_y = 0 \qquad (A7.16)$$

and

$$-(k + cx)U_z + \frac{1}{\rho}xn^{(1-\rho)/\rho}U_y = 0 \qquad (A7.17)$$

We know, from the first stage of the budgeting process, that $U_y/U_z = p_y$.[4] From Eq. (A7.16) we thus get, using Eq. (A7.5′), that in the unconstrained optimum, price is equal to marginal cost:

$$p_u = c \qquad (A7.18)$$

Dividing Eq. (A7.17) by Eq. (A7.16) allows us to calculate the output of each firm, as

$$x_u = \frac{k}{c}\frac{\rho}{\rho - 1} \qquad (A7.19)$$

Now, we could derive an expression that defined the number of firms in the unconstrained optimum; however, this would not be easily comparable to the expression giving the number of firms in the market equilibrium case. Hence, an indirect argument is in any case necessary to conclude the comparison between the cases, which is why we skip the exercise.

We see, comparing Eq. (A7.19) with Eq. (A7.14), that the output per firm is equal in all cases under consideration. This means it is not the first-best optimum to push output of firms to the point where economies of scales would be completely exploited when, as in the case considered here, variety is desirable.

Stating this the other way around, we can say that when variety is desirable, it is not socially optimal to fully exploit economies of scale (or, not to leave any "excess capacity" in production unutilized).

Furthermore, as technology does not change in different institutional settings, we see that the market price in the unconstrained optimum is below the price that results in the market equilibrium, as the output produced at the firm level, and hence the variable cost incurred is equal in all cases. Therefore, the number of firms, and thus variety, in the unconstrained optimum has to be above that of the equilibrium case (see also Dixit and Stiglitz, 2004, pp. 102–103).

Note that this model assumption relies on the standard neoclassical set of homogeneity of consumers, with given preferences, perfect information, and so on, and that beyond this, some additional factors are introduced for representing altered cost structures and allow for imperfect substitutes. The agents move in a well-defined space; power is again exerted over a given price-quantity space, enhanced by the introduction of varieties of the good. A result, as in the extensions to the neoclassical core model explained in Chapter 5, is again the *inefficiency of economic activity as soon as small features in the model formulations are altered* with respect to that core model. How far these models carry us in an understanding of real-world economic problems and situations remains open, if you consider the different levels at which very substantial critique can be, and has been, formulated, as explained in Chapter 6.

---

[4]To derive this expression, let p_z serve as numéraire.

PART III

FURTHER TOOLS AND THE ANALYSIS OF COMPLEX ECONOMIES

8

Tools II: More Formal Concepts of Game Theory and Evolutionary Game Theory

Web comic by Randall Munroe, http://xkcd.com/706

The Microeconomics of Complex Economies.
DOI: http://dx.doi.org/10.1016/B978-0-12-411585-9.00008-7

8.1 INTRODUCTION

Game theory is a field of mathematics closely related to economic considerations of preference relations and the effects of direct interdependence on individual "utility" yielding interactive strategic behavior. The field has emerged since the 1940s notably with John von Neumann and Oscar Morgenstern's theory of utility presented in their groundbreaking monograph "Theory of Games and Economic Behavior" (von Neumann and Morgenstern, 1944) and was subsequently complemented by the introduction of concepts of decision making and stable states in interactive situations, in turn allowing the prediction of likely outcomes. Early game theory received notable contributions by John Nash (equilibrium and dominance concepts), John Harsanyi, Robert Aumann (mixed strategy equilibrium concepts), John Maynard Smith, Stephen Jay Gould (evolutionary game theory), Reinhard Selten, Roger Myerson, and Robert Axelrod (strategies in repeated games).

While game theory allows to model far from equilibrium situations, including axioms and analyses entirely different from orthodox neoclassical economic theory, it still requires the assumption of a universal and well-defined rationality of the economic agents. This has been heavily criticized by psychological, experimental, and behavioral economists, who were able to show systematic biases in human decision making (Tversky and Kahneman, 1973). While economic game theory adapted itself to the criticism by considering different kinds of bounded rationality (Simon, 1956) and investigating possible empirically measurable decision heuristics in human decision making (together with the field of experimental economicy, e.g. Fehr et al., 2002), the original approach of game theory may be seen as both inspired and limited by the scientific spirit of the mid-twentieth century, the endeavor to analyze, reproduce, measure, and predict anything with however limited methods (Hargreaves Heap and Varoufakis, 2004, p. 3). Bounded rationality is a usual assumption in multiagent models in game theory. In evolutionary game theory, the focus shifts from individual rational decision making to the dynamic performance of strategies thus relaxing the assumption of universal rationality (Nelson and Winter, 1982; Axelrod, 1984).

Game theory has helped economics and other fields of research to achieve a better understanding of a vast variety of phenomena in socioeconomic systems. It has not only provided a multiplicity of instructive models but also inspired the development of more sophisticated methods both within and beyond the scope of traditional game theory. It might be justified to argue that game theory has been and continues to be for economics what the theory of dynamic systems has been for physics: An area of applied mathematics fitting the needs and developed with the assistance of the academic field it is to be applied to.

8.2 FORMAL CONCEPTS

8.2.1 Games

For a structured approach to game theory, this section will provide definitions, clarify assumptions, and introduce commonly used notations.

A *strategic game* (or just game) is an abstract model of the interaction of directly interdependent subjects (humans, or more generally *agents*). A game is properly described if

1. the set of rules of the game,
2. the set of agents in the game,
3. the set of *strategies* of the agents,
4. the set of *information* available to each agent

are defined.

The set of rules is usually implied in the description of the game as belonging to a particular type of games. For the moment it is sufficient to define the type of normal-form games (further types such as evolutionary games will be introduced later). A *normal-form game* is a game with a defined (finite or infinite) number of agents each of which chooses between (not necessarily identical) strategies with given payoffs for each agent for each

possible *combination of strategies*. Any combination of strategies contains one strategy for each agent participating in the game. The number of strategies per agent may also be finite or infinite. Many concepts, however, do not apply for infinite numbers of agents and strategies; the usual approach that will also be taken in this chapter is that of the number of agents and strategies both being finite. The agents choose their strategies simultaneously, implying that at the time of choosing they are not informed about the choice of their opponents.

Consider a normal-form game with n agents. Let s_i denote abstractly any particular (pure) strategy of the ith agent and S_i the set of all (pure) strategies of the agent i. Further let S be the set of strategies of all agents in the game,

$$S = \{S_i\} \quad i = 1, \ldots, n$$

Let s be any particular feasible configuration of strategies, containing one strategy for each agent, let a particular strategy of agent i be called s_i, and let the strategies of all other agents be written as $s_{-i} = (s_j)_{j \neq i}$, $s = \{s_i, s_{-i}\}$ (read: "s non-i"). The set of all sets of strategies S implies the set of all feasible combinations of strategies s. Therefore, the *set of payoffs* of an agent i resulting from all possible combinations of strategies can be written as

$$\Pi_i(S) = (\Pi_i(s))_{\forall s} = (\Pi_i(s_i, s_{-i}))_{\forall s_i \forall s_{-i}}$$

A normal-form game G with n agents is written as

$$G = \{S_i; \Pi_i(S), I_i\} \quad i = 1, \ldots, n$$

where I_i denotes the set of information of the ith agent. A *2-person normal-form game* is a normal-form game with $n = 2$; thus

$$G = \{S_1, S_2; \Pi_1(S), \Pi_2(S); I_1, I_2\}$$

This special type of normal-form games is the most widely known and used type of strategic games. In addition to this *formal notation*, it may be written in *matrix notation* (Figure 8.1).

		Player B	
		Strategy 1	Strategy 2
Player A	Strategy 1	$\Pi_B(s_{A1}, s_{B1})$ $\Pi_A(s_{A1}, s_{B1})$	$\Pi_B(s_{A1}, s_{B2})$ $\Pi_A(s_{A1}, s_{B2})$
	Strategy 2	$\Pi_B(s_{A2}, s_{B1})$ $\Pi_A(s_{A2}, s_{B1})$	$\Pi_B(s_{A2}, s_{B2})$ $\Pi_A(s_{A2}, s_{B2})$

FIGURE 8.1 Normal-form game in matrix notation (general form).

8.2.2 Agents and Decision Making

With the game, the strategies, the payoffs, and the information set thus defined, what remains to be explained in order to predict strategy choices and payoffs of the game are the properties of the agent. In the above example, we assumed that rational agents would, if possible, always choose strategies to award themselves the highest possible payoff. This is something that must be assumed, since it does not follow from an ex-ante logic nor is it always empirically measurable in human behavior. In fact, it has been firmly criticized by a number of scholars (see the introduction to this chapter). Nevertheless, some kind of regularly predictable decision making has to be assumed in order to derive solutions and predictions. Standard game theory thus requires agents

1. to derive their choices using *well-defined preference orderings*, i.e., their *preferences* for *bundles of goods* must be (see also Chapter 5)
   complete: $a \succ b$ or $a \sim b$ or $a \prec b$
   reflexive: $a \succ b \Leftrightarrow b \prec a$, and
   transitive: $a \succ b$ and $b \succ c \Rightarrow a \succ c$
   If this holds, one may derive an *ordinal payoff measure* Π for any game no matter what kinds of goods the game is originally about;
2. to be aware of common rationality (*CKR—common knowledge of rationality*). That is, agents do not only fulfill condition (1) but are also aware that all other agents fulfill condition (1) as well. Further they are aware that all other agents are aware that all agents are rational, etc.

Note that the agents are neither *envious* nor *benevolent*, i.e., they neither work to decrease nor to increase the payoffs of other agents. They are truly indifferent toward the payoffs of each other. However, CKR (condition (2)) enables agents to anticipate decisions of other agents and react accordingly. In fact, without CKR they were left without any reasonable assumptions about their opponents' behavior and would have to neglect the outcome of other agents completely. In this case, the game is equivalent to an ordinary non-interdependent decision problem—an important point to start with when considering game theory.

8.3 CONCEPTS FROM DECISION THEORY

Thus for now, let us neglect CKR (condition (2)). The strategy choices of the other agents therefore do not appear as willful choices but as random states of the world each applying with a known or unknown but possibly assessable probability. Hence, this is but the first step on the way to modern game theory, the theory of decisions under uncertainty. These concepts are of course applicable when facing initial strategic uncertainty in predicting other agents actions; other agents are however different from mere probabilistic phenomena. If the probabilities are known, it is easy to compute an expected value of the payoff of every strategy and predict that the agent will choose the strategy with the highest expected payoff. Otherwise, there are several general decision concepts that may be applied. Some of them are important benchmark rules for game theory; therefore, we will proceed to review the *minimax* and *maximin* criteria, the *Laplace criterion* or *principle of insufficient reason*, the *Hurwicz criterion*, and the idiosyncratically risk-seeking *maximax* criterion (see Hurwicz, 1953). Note that different authors use two different definitions of the minimax criterion, one of which is equivalent to maximin while the other, introduced by Savage (1951) and sometimes called *Savage's minimax regret* criterion, is not. A detailed overview of decision theory concepts including a demonstrative example of a company choosing an information security system against hacking attacks is given by Finne (1998). It should, however, be added that it is impossible to account for uncertainty in analytical models; the decision mechanisms discussed in this section require assumptions about probabilities for the occurrence of uncertain events, thus defining uncertainty away.

8.3.1 Maximax

For each strategy, consider the highest potential payoff depending on the state of the system (the strategies of other players) and choose the strategy with the highest possible payoff, no matter how unlikely this outcome might be (see Figure 8.2).

8.3.2 Maximin and Minimax

For maximin, consider the lowest potential payoff depending on the state of the system (the strategies of other players) for each strategy and choose the strategy with the highest minimal payoff. Minimax (according to one definition) is the same decision concept: it deals with negative payoffs (costs, years in prison, etc.) and the agent minimizes the maximal possible costs (depending on the state of the system) that may result from one strategy

overall strategies. Any game with positive outcomes can be transformed into a game with costs by subtracting a fixed value higher than or equal to the highest payoff from all payoffs and then transforming the negative payoffs into positive costs by taking the absolute values (see Figure 8.2).

8.3.3 Laplace Criterion

The Laplace criterion states that the agent has no sufficient reason to assume the probabilities of the possible states of the system to be different (therefore also called *principle of insufficient reason*). Equal probabilities are assigned to all possible states to compute and then maximize the expected payoff

$$E(\Pi(s)) = \frac{1}{n} \sum_{i=1}^{n} \Pi_i$$

where $i = 1, \ldots, n$ are the n possible states of the system and Π_i are the payoffs of the strategy s if the system is in state i (see Figure 8.2).

8.3.4 Hurwicz Criterion

The Hurwicz criterion computes a weighted value from the minimum and the maximum payoff of the strategies and is therefore a combination of maximin and maximax.

$$H(s) = \alpha \max_i \Pi_i + (1 - \alpha) \min_i \Pi_i$$

where α is the index of optimism, the level of risk-seeking of the agent. $\alpha = 0$ corresponds to

Player's strategies	States of the system X_1	X_2	Max	Min	Laplace	Hurwicz ($\alpha = 0.25$)
s_1	1	−1	1	−1	0	−0.5
s_2	2	0	2	0	1	0.5
Maximax			2 (s_2)			
Maximin				0 (s_2)		
Laplace criterion					1 (s_2)	
Hurwicz criterion						0 (s_2)

FIGURE 8.2 Comparison of decision theory concepts: maximax, maximin, Laplace criterion, Hurwicz criterion.

the maximin criterion, $\alpha = 1$ corresponds to maximax, and for a two state system $\alpha = 0.5$ corresponds to the Laplace criterion. In the table above, an example of the Hurwicz criterion with $\alpha = 0.25$ is given (see Figure 8.2).

8.3.5 Savage's Minimax Regret

Sometimes this criterion is referred to as just minimax—e.g., by Savage himself (Savage, 1951). The strategy computes the opportunity cost of a strategy for each possible state of the system and selects the strategy with the minimal maximum possible costs. The opportunity costs (or as Savage puts it, losses) are computed as

$$L(s, Z) = \begin{cases} 0 & \text{if } \Pi_{s,Z} = \max_j \Pi_{j,Z} \\ \Pi_{s,Z} - \max_j \Pi_{j,Z} & \text{if } \Pi_{s,Z} \neq \max_j \Pi_{j,Z} \end{cases}$$

where Z denotes the state of the system and $j = 1, \ldots, m$ are the available strategies (see Figure 8.3).

8.4 SOLUTIONS OF NORMAL-FORM GAMES

8.4.1 Dominance of Strategies

As we have seen from the social optimum game and the prisoners' dilemma as discussed in the introduction to game theory in Chapter 2, individually rational decision making on the part of the agents can lead to socially unfavorable outcomes. The structure of the problems as interdependent decision situations, however, defies traditional methods of non-interdependent optimization. Further, using methods of non-interdependent decision theory would also lead to systematic errors as they are unable to take reactions of an "intelligent" opponent into account. A more appropriate course of action is to systematically identify superior and inferior strategies and derive solution concepts from this taking advantage of the (by definition) guaranteed rationality of all players.

The general definition of *dominance* with respect to the set of strategies S_i of an agent i in a normal-form game G is as follows: A strategy $s_i^* \in S_i$ is said to *dominate* another strategy $s_i^\sim \in S_i$ if, and only if,

$$\Pi_i(s_i^*, s_{-i}) \geq \Pi_i(s_i^\sim, s_{-i}) \forall s_{-i}$$

and

$$\exists s_{-i} : \Pi_i(s_i^*, s_{-i}) > \Pi_i(s_i^\sim, s_{-i})$$

$s_i^\sim$ is in this case said to be *dominated* (by s_i^*).

s_{-i} is any possible combination of the strategies of all other agents. That is, the product of the number of strategies per agent (except for agent i) is the number of combinations contained by the set s_{-i}. The inequalities essentially state that for any possible combination of actions of all other agents, the strategy s_i^* must be at least as good (the payoffs for i at least as high) as $s_i^\sim$ and for at least one combination s_i^* must be strictly better (the payoffs for i strictly higher) than the strategy $s_i^\sim$. For 2-person 2-strategy normal-form games (see Figure 8.4), this formula becomes much simpler.

Player's strategies	States of the system X_1	X_2	Opportunity costs X_1	X_2	Min. O.C.
s_1	4	2	0	0	0
s_2	2	0	2	2	2
	Savage's minimax regret				0 (s_1)

FIGURE 8.3   The minimax regret criterion of Savage.

Player B

		s_{B1}	s_{B2}
Player A	s_{A1}	a_B / a_A	b_B / d_A
	s_{A2}	d_B / b_A	c_B / c_A

FIGURE 8.4   Normal-form game in matrix notation (simple general form).

The payoffs of agent A when choosing her dominating strategy s^* for any possible strategy of agent B (s_{B1} or s_{B2}) must be at least as high as the payoffs resulting from her dominated strategy $s^\sim$. More specifically (s_{A1} being the dominating strategy), $a_A \geq b_A, d_A \geq c_A$. Further, for at least one possible strategy of B (s_{B1} or s_{B2}), A's dominating strategy must perform strictly better, i.e., $a_A > b_A$ or $d_A > c_A$.

The stronger form of the dominance criterion is obtained by demanding strictly higher payoffs for any possible combination of the strategies of all other agents. A strategy s_i^* of an agent i in a normal-form game G_0 is said to be *strictly dominating* another strategy $s_i^\sim$ if, and only if,

$$\Pi_i(s_i^*, s_{-i}) > \Pi_i(s_i^\sim, s_{-i}) \forall s_{-i}$$

$s_i^\sim$ is in this case said to be *strictly dominated* (by s_i^*). In terms of the 2-person 2-strategy variant of normal-form games, it is again much easier: s^* is said to dominate $s^\sim$ strictly, if

$$a_A > b_A \quad \text{and} \quad c_A > d_A$$

We can now proceed to predict that strictly dominated strategies will always be abandoned in favor of the respectively dominating strategies. No rational agent will ever choose a dominated strategy, meaning that any dominated strategy is irrelevant for the outcome of the game. This in turn enables us to safely remove any strictly dominated strategy $s_i^\sim$ (of any agent i) from a normal-form game G_0 (obtaining a reduced game G_1) without affecting the outcome of the game. For an illustrative example, see the 2-person 2-strategy in Figure 8.5 and the corresponding reduced game after the elimination of one dominated strategy in Figure 8.6.

With CKR, we can further say that the opponent is informed as well that the first player will never play that strictly dominated strategy. In turn, she also uses game G_1.

FIGURE 8.5 SESDS example: initial game.

FIGURE 8.6 SESDS example: after elimination of s_A^*.

The process may be repeated successively for both players which is a solution concept commonly referred to as *successive elimination of strictly dominated strategies (SESDS)*. This yields a finite sequence $G_0, G_1, G_2, \ldots, G_m$ which ends with a game G_m that does not contain any strictly dominated strategies and thus terminates the process. If G_m contains only (and exactly) one strategy s_i^* for every agent i, the combination of these strategies

$$s^* = \{s_1^*, \ldots s_n^*\}$$

constitutes a unique solution of G_0. In this case, the game G_0 (and all games of the series $G_1, G_2, \ldots$) are called solvable by SESDS. Rational agents will always reach this combination of strategies when playing G_0.

Returning to the two introductory examples, we consider a social optimum game and a prisoners' dilemma starting with the 2-person case. In the social optimum game, the agents choose between either 4 (contributing) and 2 (not contributing) if the opponent contributes or 2 (contributing) and 0 (not contributing) if the other agent does not contribute. According to the above definition, the first strategy (contributing) dominates the second one strictly. For the prisoners' dilemma, the choices are 1 (contributing) or 2 (not contributing) if the other agent contributes and -1 (contributing) or 0 (not contributing) if the opponent does not contribute. This time, the first strategy (contributing) is strictly dominated by the second one. In both cases, the same structure holds for situations with more than two players. We can clearly see that the preference ordering of the two respective strategies does not depend on the choices of their opponents, one is better than the other no matter how other agents act. In other words, this means one of the two strategies is strictly dominant, while the other one—since there are only two strategies in this game—is strictly dominated. The latter can be eliminated for all players reducing the game to one combination of strategies. Since this is obviously true for the 2-person case as well as for the n-person game, we can conclude that both games are solvable by SESDS in both the 2-person case and the general n-person normal-form game.

		Player B	
		s_{B1}	s_{B2}
Player A	s_{A1}	2 2	0 0
	s_{A2}	0 0	2 2

FIGURE 8.7 Coordination game.

		Player B	
		s_{B1}	s_{B2}
Player A	s_{A1}	2 2	3 1
	s_{A2}	1 3	0 0

FIGURE 8.8 Hawk-dove game (also called chicken game).

8.4.2 Nash Equilibrium

While SESDS is a feasible and reliable method to predict a unique rational outcome of games, it does not always yield a solution since not every game has a unique best combination of strategies or more technically not every game contains strictly dominated strategies. Consider as examples the structures known as *coordination game* (Figure 8.7) and *hawk-dove game*[1] or *chicken game* (Figure 8.8) (see also Chapter 3).

In both games, by using SESDS, we cannot predict anything—none of the strategies is strictly dominated. One way to deal with this is simply to accept the fact that rational actors may play both strategies and none of the possibilities can be ruled out—which is a solution of some kind as well. However, it is clear that some of the payoffs are undesirable and even avoidable by simply letting the respective agents choose another strategy. This argument is not per se a valid one since the choices are by definition made at the same time and without knowledge of the action of the other players. Still, we can assume that even rational agents have beliefs about what others will do. Given such beliefs, and thus neglecting any element of uncertainty, the agents have perfect best answer strategies. Any strategy combination that is exclusively composed of best answers offers no incentive to any of the players to reconsider her choice. These mutual best answers or *Nash equilibria* can reasonably be considered more likely outcomes than other combinations of strategies (even more so of course if the game is repeated).

[1]Note that the canonical hawk-dove game awards the agents negative payoffs in the hawk-hawk strategy combination (the lower right field). However, adding the same base payoff to the payoffs of all agents in any possible outcome (strategy combination) does not change the structure and properties of the game. Here, we use this and add a base payoff equivalent in size to the negative payoffs in the hawk-hawk case in order to—for simplicity—avoid negative payoffs since this game will be used and referred to in many examples throughout this chapter.

More formally, a Nash equilibrium is any combination of strategies

$$s^* = \{s_1^*, \ldots, s_n^*\}$$

in a normal-form game G such that

$$\Pi_i(s_i^*, s_{-i}^*) \geq \Pi_i(s_i, s_{-i}^*) \quad \forall s_i \in S_i \ \forall i$$

There may be more than one Nash equilibrium in G (consider the above coordination and hawk-dove games as examples). Even in finite games (requiring the number of strategies s_i for all agents i to be finite), the best answer structure in the game takes a circular form, it is possible that G does not contain a Nash equilibrium in pure strategies at all. For example, in a 2-person game strategy s_{A1} of player 1 is the only best answer to s_{B1} of player 2, s_{B1} is the only best answer to s_{A2} of player 1 which is the only best answer to s_{B2} of agent 2. s_{B2} in turn is the only best answer to s_{A1}. The simplest example of this is the *matching pennies game* (Figure 8.9).

8.4.3 The Relation Between SESDS and Nash Equilibrium

Proposition (1): If a game G is solvable by SESDS and the solution is the combination of strategies

$$s^S = \{s_1^S, s_2^S, \ldots, s_n^S\}$$

s^S is also the only Nash equilibrium in G.

Proof: In order to prove this, we must show that (1) s^S is a Nash equilibrium and (2) no other Nash equilibrium exists in G. For any agent i, s_i^S must be the unique best answer to the rest of the strategy combination s_{-i}^S in G since any other strategy $s_i \in S_i$ must be strictly dominated in G or a subgame G' that contains s_{-i}^S and can therefore not be a best answer to s_i^S. As for any combination of strategies of all players accept i a best answer for i exists, this best answer must be s_i^S. That being true for all agents i, s^S is a combination of mutual best answers and hence a Nash equilibrium. Suppose G contains another Nash equilibrium $s^N = \{s_1^N, s_2^N, \ldots, s_n^N\}$. This means that all strategies s_i^N must be strictly dominated in some subgame G'' of G, the first one (s_i^N) in a subgame containing all other strategies s_{-i}^N. By definition, no best answers to any strategies in a game are strictly dominated in that game, hence if s_i^N is strictly dominated in G_j, it cannot be a best answer to s_{-i}^N and therefore s^N cannot be a combination of mutual best answers and no Nash equilibrium. Thus, any game that can be solved by SESDS has exactly one Nash equilibrium.

It is however possible that a game with exactly one Nash equilibrium is not solvable with SESDS; consider the example in Figure 8.10.

8.4.4 Mixed Strategies

We have seen that not every normal-form game has a solution in terms of dominance (SESDS), nor in terms of Nash equilibria in

FIGURE 8.9 Matching pennies game.

		Player B	
		s_{B1}	s_{B2}
Player A	s_{A1}	-1 $\ \ \ $ 1	1 $\ \ \ $ -1
	s_{A2}	1 $\ \ \ $ -1	-1 $\ \ \ $ 1

		Player 2		
		s_{B1}	s_{B1}	s_{B3}
Player 1	s_{A1}	0 $\ $ 1	0 $\ $ 0	1 $\ $ 0
	s_{A2}	0 $\ $ 0	1 $\ $ 1	0 $\ $ 0
	s_{A3}	1 $\ $ 0	0 $\ $ 0	0 $\ $ 1

FIGURE 8.10 2-person 3-strategy normal-form game with unique Nash equilibrium that is unsolvable with SESDS.

pure strategies. Returning to the matching pennies game introduced above, we may therefore ask how rational agents will decide in this situation and by extension if a rational decision is possible in this and similar situations. Another example is the well-known *Rock-Paper-Scissors game* (Figure 8.11).

Of course, a rational decision is possible. However, the *pure strategies* rock, paper, and scissors are no good candidates: All of them are exploitable by another pure strategy. Humans engaging in this game will therefore never decide to always play the same pure strategy but try to be as incomputable as possible. And so do rational agents; the game theory concept is called mixed strategies.

Let a *mixed strategy* formally be defined as a vector of probabilities. Any available pure strategy is assigned a probability with which the agent will play this strategy; hence the number of elements the vector is composed of must equal the number of pure strategies of the underlying game. Hence, formally, a mixed strategy σ_i of player i contains any probabilistic combination of all x available pure strategies weighted with probabilities $p_1, p_2, \ldots, p_x$ to play these pure strategies. For the 2-strategy case (i.e., two pure strategies), the mixed strategy is thus

$$\sigma_i = \begin{pmatrix} p \\ 1-p \end{pmatrix}$$

The agents can now choose from a continuum of infinitely many strategies (defined as $p \in [0, 1]$)

and have to react to an equally defined continuum of strategies of the other player(s). Of course, best answers do still exist for any strategy combination of the other players. They are now conveniently written and illustrated as the *reaction function* to the combined strategy choices of the other agents $p_j(s_{-i})$ (where p_j is the vector of probabilities for choosing strategy j as above). In the 2-person 2-strategy case with probabilities p for player 1 and q for player 2 respectively to play their respective first strategies, the reaction functions are $p(q)$ and $q(p)$. This is illustrated for a matching pennies game in Figure 8.12.

8.4.5 Nash Equilibrium in Mixed Strategies

A Nash equilibrium in mixed strategies σ^* is a configuration of mixed strategies for all n players $\sigma^* = \{\sigma_1^*, \sigma_2^*, \ldots, \sigma_n^*\}$ such that

$$\Pi_i(\sigma_i^*, \sigma_{-i}^*) \geq \Pi_i(\sigma_i, \sigma_{-i}^*) \quad \forall \sigma_i \ \forall i$$

Intuitively, this is where the reaction functions of all players intersect; see again Figure 8.12 for an illustration.

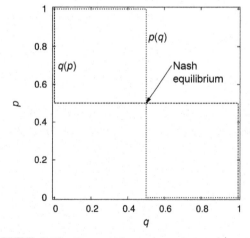

FIGURE 8.12 Reaction functions and mixed strategy equilibrium in a matching pennies game (corresponding to the matrix in Figure 8.9).

		Player B		
		Rock	Paper	Scissors
Player A	Rock	0 / 0	1 / -1	-1 / 1
	Paper	-1 / 1	0 / 0	1 / -1
	Scissors	1 / -1	-1 / 1	0 / 0

FIGURE 8.11 Rock–Paper–Scissors game.

Proposition (2): A mixed Nash equilibrium strategy σ_i^* must always yield the same expected payoff (against all other agent's corresponding mixed Nash equilibrium strategies σ_{-i}^*) as every pure strategies $s_{i,j}$ of player i played with a positive probability $p_j > 0$ in this mixed strategy Nash equilibrium

$$\sigma_i^* = \begin{pmatrix} p_1 \\ \vdots \\ p_j \\ \vdots \\ p_x \end{pmatrix}$$

thus,

$$\Pi_i(\sigma_i^*, \sigma_{-i}^*) = \Pi_i(s_{i,j}, \sigma_{-i}^*) \quad \forall j : p_j > 0$$

Proof: Assume the proposition did not hold. First, assume the mixed strategy Nash equilibrium strategy σ_i^* would yield a lower payoff than $s_{i,j}$,

$$\Pi_i(\sigma_i^*, \sigma_{-i}^*) < \Pi_i(s_{i,j}, \sigma_{-i}^*)$$

This is a direct contradiction of the definition of Nash equilibria, i.e., it would follow that $\sigma_i^*, \sigma_{-i}^*$ is not a Nash equilibrium as defined in the proposition. This can therefore never happen.

For the second case, assume σ_i^* would yield a higher payoff than $s_{i,j}$,

$$\Pi_i(\sigma_i^*, \sigma_{-i}^*) > \Pi_i(s_{i,j}, \sigma_{-i}^*)$$

The expected payoff Π_i computes as

$$\Pi_i(\sigma_i^*, \sigma_{-i}^*) = (p_1 \quad \cdots \quad p_j \quad \cdots \quad p_x) \begin{pmatrix} \Pi_i(s_{i,1}, \sigma_{-i}^*) \\ \vdots \\ \Pi_i(s_{i,j}, \sigma_{-i}^*) \\ \vdots \\ \Pi_i(s_{i,x}, \sigma_{-i}^*) \end{pmatrix}$$

$$= p_1 \Pi_i(s_{i,1}, \sigma_{-i}^*) + \cdots + p_j \Pi_i(s_{i,j}, \sigma_{-i}^*) + \cdots + p_x \Pi_i(s_{i,x}, \sigma_{-i}^*)$$

The expected value of the jth pure strategy of this term is smaller than the overall result. Hence a combination of the remaining strategies

(the weight relation among them remaining equal) without strategy $s_{i,j}$, thus a mixed strategy

$$\sigma_i^\sim = \frac{1}{(1 - p_j)} \begin{pmatrix} p_1 \\ \vdots \\ p_{j-1} \\ 0 \\ p_{j+1} \\ \vdots \\ p_x \end{pmatrix}$$

must yield a better payoff than σ_i^* (note that the factor $(1/(1 - p_j)) > 1$)

$$\Pi_i(\sigma_i^\sim, \sigma_{-i}^*) > \Pi_i(\sigma_i^*, \sigma_{-i}^*)$$

σ_i^* is in this case strictly dominated by $\sigma_i^\sim$ and can therefore not be the best answer to $\sigma_i^\sim, \sigma_{-i}^*$. This proves the above assumption wrong.

Further, this must hold for any positive element p_j of a mixed Nash equilibrium strategy where $s_{i,j}$ shall be the set of pure strategies played with positive probability as a part of the mixed Nash equilibrium strategy by player i. Consequently it follows that

$$\Pi_i(\sigma_i^*, \sigma_{-i}^*) = \Pi_i(s_{i,j}, \sigma_{-i}^*) \quad \forall j : p_j > 0$$

and even that all possible mixed strategy combinations of the j strategies $s_{i,j}$ yield the same payoff.

Proposition (3): Every finite n-person normal-form game G (with a finite number of strategies for each of the n players) has at least one Nash equilibrium in pure or mixed strategies.

Outline of proof: Either G does have a Nash equilibrium in pure strategies or it does not. In the first case, Proposition (3) is always true; therefore, it remains to be shown, that for games G that do not have a Nash equilibrium in pure strategies, there is always at least one in mixed strategies. We proceed by eliminating any strategy $s^\sim$ in G that does not constitute a best answer to any of the remaining players' strategy configurations s_{-i} to construct a modified game G' (which is a subgame of G) and repeat the process until no $s^\sim$ is left to be eliminated in G'. Further we eliminate all players with only one strategy left as their choice does not affect the outcome of the game and they do obviously have only one strategy they can rationally play in G or any of its subgames G'. Call the resulting game G'', n the number of players in G'', and x_i the number of strategies player i has in G''. Since no best answer strategy has been effected, mutual best answers (Nash equilibria) in pure strategies cannot exist in G'' either as they did not in G. However, all players will now rationally play all of their remaining strategies s_i with positive probability if all combinations of strategies of the other players s_{-i} occur with positive probability. This condition is fulfilled exactly if all players play all remaining strategies with positive probability. The expected payoff for any of the strategy configurations of the remaining players σ_{-i} and player i using her mixed strategy

$$\sigma_i = \begin{pmatrix} p_1 \\ \vdots \\ p_{x_i} \end{pmatrix} \text{ is}$$

$$\Pi_i(\sigma_i, \sigma_{-i}) = p_1 \Pi_i(s_1, \sigma_{-i}) + p_2 \Pi_i(s_2, \sigma_{-i}) + \cdots + p_{x_i} \Pi_i(s_{x_i}, \sigma_{-i})$$

It follows that for each agent i, there is a combination of mixed strategies for all other players σ_{-i} such that

$$\Pi_i(s_1, \sigma_{-i}) = \Pi_i(s_2, \sigma_{-i}) = \cdots = \Pi_i(s_{x_i}, \sigma_{-i})$$

in which case i is indifferent between all possible mixed (and pure) strategies in G''. This is possible if there are different best answers for each combination s_{-i}, i.e., $\Pi_i(s_j, \sigma_{-i})$ is the sum of both low and high payoffs resulting from strategy s_j weighted with the mixed strategy probability values of the other players. This follows from the nature of G'' without dominant strategies as analyzed above; therefore, there are valid solutions for each agent. Now, we have the solutions that fulfill the above

condition for all agents simultaneously. This results in a system of n equations (one for each remaining agent) to assert

$$\Pi_i(s_1, \sigma_{-i}) = \Pi_i(s_2, \sigma_{-i}) = \cdots = \Pi_i(s_{x_i}, \sigma_{-i})$$

for all agents. The equations contain $\sum_i x_i - n \geq n$ independent variables—the probabilities of the mixed strategy vector for each agent minus one to fulfill the condition that the probabilities sum up to 1. As the number of equations is at most the number of independent variables, there is at least one solution with

$$\Pi_i(s_1, \sigma_{-i}) = \Pi_i(s_2, \sigma_{-i}) = \cdots = \Pi_i(s_{x_i}, \sigma_{-i}) \quad \forall i$$

in G''. That is, a combination of mixed strategies σ^* exists to which any mixed or pure strategy of any agent is a best answer in G'' including the mixed strategies that are part of the combination σ^*. Hence, σ^* is a combination of mutual best answers and thus a Nash equilibrium in G''. Since the strategies that are additionally part of G (but not of G''; those removed above) do not add best responses, they do not affect the structure of Nash equilibria and σ^* must also be a Nash equilibrium in G.

Note that there is a more elegant proof by Nash (1950) using the so-called fixed point theorem of Kakutani. Showing that the space of mixed strategies in G is convex (any linear combination of two mixed strategies is also a mixed strategy) and compact (the space is bounded and closed (between 0 and 1 for any probability to play a pure strategy as part of a mixed strategy)), the proof proceeds to demonstrate that the global best answer function (the combination of best answer functions of all players) is quasi-concave. Kakutani's fixed point theorem applied to this yields that the global best answer function must have a fixed point. In other words, there must be a subset of the strategy combinations for which the global best answer function maps the strategy combination into itself (i.e., the strategy combination is a best answer to itself.)

8.4.6 Computation of the Nash Equilibrium in Mixed Strategies

Let the game for an agent with x possible pure strategies and y possible pure strategies of her opponent be further defined as an $x \times y$-matrix $\mathscr{A}$, the elements of which are the payoffs of just the first player, not her opponent. In the rock−paper−scissors case

$$\mathscr{A} = \begin{pmatrix} 0 & -1 & 1 \\ 1 & 0 & -1 \\ -1 & 1 & 0 \end{pmatrix}$$

Note that this notation is convenient for an easy and straightforward computation of expected payoffs by a simple matrix multiplication (see Section 8.7.2).

$$\Pi_1 = \sigma_1^T \times \mathscr{A} \times \sigma_2$$

$$\Pi_1 = \begin{pmatrix} 0.4 & 0 & 0.6 \end{pmatrix} \begin{pmatrix} 0 & -1 & 1 \\ 1 & 0 & -1 \\ -1 & 1 & 0 \end{pmatrix} \begin{pmatrix} 1/3 \\ 1/3 \\ 1/3 \end{pmatrix} = 0$$

And the corresponding computation of payoffs, in this case for the first player (symmetry implies, however, $\Pi_1 = \Pi_2$).

For an abstract (symmetric) 2-strategy case, this comes down to the game shown in Figure 8.13.

$$\Pi_1 = \begin{pmatrix} p & 1-p \end{pmatrix} \begin{pmatrix} a & d \\ b & c \end{pmatrix} \begin{pmatrix} q \\ 1-q \end{pmatrix}$$

$$\Pi_1 = apq + dp(1-q) + bq(1-p) + c(1-p)(1-q)$$

$$\Pi_1 = ((a-b)+(c-d))pq + (d-c)p + (b-c)q + c$$

	Player 2	
	s_{B1}	s_{B1}
s_{A1}	a	b
	a	d
s_{A2}	d	c
	b	c

FIGURE 8.13 Abstract symmetric 2-person 2-strategy normal-form game.

The strategy choice p: $\sigma = \begin{pmatrix} p \\ 1-p \end{pmatrix}$ may subsequently be optimized by maximizing the payoffs, thus

$$\frac{\partial \Pi_1}{\partial p} = ((a-b)+(c-d))q + (d-c)$$

Further, to any point that for this derivative yields

$$\frac{\partial \Pi_1}{\partial p} = ((a-b)+(c-d))q + (d-c) = !0$$

$$q^* = \frac{(c-d)}{(a-b)+(c-d)}$$

i.e., changing the mixed strategy does not result in any change of the resulting payoffs, every possible mixed strategy is a best answer. Computing a strategy configuration such that this is true for both players yields a Nash equilibrium in mixed strategies.

Taking the above matching pennies game (see also Figure 8.12) as an example

$$\Pi_1 = \begin{pmatrix} p & 1-p \end{pmatrix} \begin{pmatrix} -1 & 1 \\ 1 & -1 \end{pmatrix} \begin{pmatrix} q \\ 1-q \end{pmatrix}$$

$$\Pi_1 = -4pq + 2q + 2p - 1$$

$$\frac{\partial \Pi_1}{\partial p} = -4q + 2 = !0$$

$$q = 0.5$$

$$\Pi_2 = \begin{pmatrix} q & 1-q \end{pmatrix} \begin{pmatrix} 1 & -1 \\ -1 & 1 \end{pmatrix} \begin{pmatrix} p \\ 1-p \end{pmatrix} = -\Pi_1$$

$$\Pi_2 = 4pq - 2q - 2p + 1$$

$$\frac{\partial \Pi_2}{\partial q} = 4p - 2 = !0$$

$$p = 0.5$$

This yields the mixed strategy Nash equilibrium

$$\sigma^* = \left\{ \begin{pmatrix} 0.5 \\ 0.5 \end{pmatrix}, \begin{pmatrix} 0.5 \\ 0.5 \end{pmatrix} \right\}$$

8.4.7 Properties of the Nash Equilibrium in Mixed Strategies

The idea to use mixed strategies at least in cases without dominant option in pure strategies is not new. In fact, von Neumann and Morgenstern (1944) considered the matching pennies game and theorized that the optimal strategy choice for both players may be the "saddle point" at $p = 0.5, q = 0.5$. The expected payoffs of both players over the product space (for the two-dimensional closed interval $(p; q) = ([0, 1]; [0, 1])$) as depicted in Figure 8.14 illustrate why von Neumann and Morgenstern termed this Nash equilibrium a saddle point. Though the Nash equilibrium as a concept was not yet known, their description features the crucial property of the Nash equilibrium in mixed strategies, namely that for specific opponent strategies (in this case $q = 0.5$) the expected payoffs are always the same (in this case, zero) and do not depend on p (or vice versa for the other player, $p = 0.5$ leads to payoffs independent of q). The saddle point shape, however, is specific to the symmetric Matching Pennies

game. Nash's description of his equilibrium concept (Nash, 1950) was abstract and not specific to pure strategies. The detailed analysis of Nash equilibria in mixed strategies was achieved only in the course of the subsequent decades, notably due to the work of Harsanyi (1973) and later Aumann (1985). The concept was heavily criticized as it relies on the heroic assumption of an exact computation of the mixed strategy on the part of the agents. Further, a mixed strategy is by definition never strictly dominant. Though mixed strategies are always a best answers, the agents are still indifferent between employing the mixed strategy, any of the involved pure strategies, and any other mixed strategy obtained through combination of these pure strategies.

Aumann's defense of the concept views mixed strategies not as a conscious randomization of agents' pure strategies but (drawing on a model by Harsanyi, 1973) rather as how players believe their opponents and observers believe players to act (Aumann, 1985). In this model, players may reconsider their strategies (making the game effectively a repeated game,

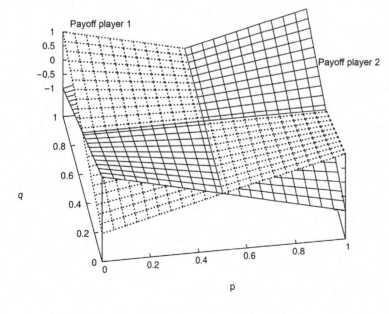

FIGURE 8.14 Payoffs of both players in a matching pennies game depending on the mixed strategies of both players; at the Nash equilibrium ($p = q = 0.5$), both players are indifferent between all feasible strategies.

see section 8.6 below) but the observation of other players' choices is imperfect leading the players to construe (their perturbed observations of) the other players' pure-strategy choices as random distributions. Another interesting defense of mixed strategy equilibria results from the stability analysis in evolutionary settings, as in some games such as matching pennies and hawk-dove games only mixed strategy equilibria are stable (see section 8.7 on evolutionary stability).

8.4.8 Further Refinements: Trembling-Hand Equilibrium and Proper Equilibrium

The critique as directed to Nash equilibria in mixed strategies does also apply to Nash equilibria in pure strategies. Consider for example the game G as shown in Figure 8.15, a subtype of the coordination game with $a = b > c > d$.

In order to achieve a mutually beneficial optimum state (a, a), the agents have to contribute by both playing their first strategy. Thus, the game retains some properties similar to the prisoners' dilemma game, though the agents will not be able to exploit the opponent by defecting ($a = b$, which makes (a, a) a Nash equilibrium).

Though $(a, a) = (2, 2)$ is indeed a Nash equilibrium, the players ought to be heroically optimistic and trusting in order to arrive at this point. What if they err about the goodwill or only the faithfulness of the other player? What even, if one of the players has imperfect control of her own strategy (may be imagined as a "trembling hand," Selten, 1983)? Contributors

will lose, while strategy 2 players face no risk at all.

Two particularly promising but closely related refinements of the Nash equilibrium as a solution concept for 2-person normal-form games have been proposed: *Selten's trembling hand perfect equilibrium* (Selten, 1975, 1983) and *Myerson's proper equilibrium* (Myerson, 1978).

The set of trembling-hand perfect equilibria σ^{**} of a game G in mixed or pure strategies is a subset of G's Nash equilibria σ^* with the property

$$(1 - \varepsilon) \Pi_i(\sigma_i^{**}, \sigma_{-i}^{**}) + \varepsilon \Pi_i(\sigma_i^{**}, \sigma_{-i}) \geq (1 - \varepsilon)$$

$$\Pi_i(\sigma_{i,j}, \sigma_{-i}^{**}) + \varepsilon \Pi_i(\sigma_{i,j}, \sigma_{-i}) \quad \forall \sigma_{i,j} \; \forall \sigma_{-i} \; \forall i$$

If the opponent(s) play the trembling-hand perfect strategies σ_{-i} with a high probability $(1 - \varepsilon)$ and any other strategy σ_{-i} with an arbitrarily small probability ε than for any player i, the expected result of the strategy σ_i^{**} that leads to the trembling-hand perfect equilibrium σ^{**} (with probability $1 - \varepsilon$) is to be higher than the expected payoff of any other strategy $\sigma_{i,j}$.

For G, there are two nonvanishing Nash equilibria $(a, a) = (2, 2)$, $(c, c) = (0, 0)$. The third, mixed strategy Nash equilibrium vanishes, its computation yields again (a,a)

$$p^* = q^* = \frac{(c - d)}{(a - b) + (c - d)} = \frac{(0 + 1)}{(2 - 2) + (0 + 1)} = 1$$

$$\Rightarrow \sigma^* = (M, M) \text{ with } M = \begin{pmatrix} 1 \\ 0 \end{pmatrix}$$

Investigating the trembling-hand stability of the two Nash equilibria, we find for (a, a)

$$2(1 - \varepsilon) - \varepsilon \neq 2(1 - \varepsilon) \pm 0\varepsilon$$

$$2 - 3\varepsilon \neq 2 - 2\varepsilon$$

Hence (a, a) (corresponding to contributing to the production of the public good) is not trembling-hand perfect, while (c,c) is

$$0(1 - \varepsilon) + 2\varepsilon \geq -1(1 - \varepsilon) + 2\varepsilon$$

$$2\varepsilon \geq 3\varepsilon - 1$$

Player 1	Player 2			
	s_{B1}		s_{B1}	
s_{A1}		2		2
	2		−1	
s_{A2}		−1		0
	2		0	

FIGURE 8.15 Example: unperturbed game.

Mathematically, for every game with *perfect information* (i.e., the agents are informed about the game and its properties, including all their and their opponent's payoffs), there is a sequence of *perturbed games* $G^\varepsilon_{\text{Selten}}$ where the rational strategy choice of the agents with respect to the unperturbed game G is perturbed with (an arbitrarily small) probability ε. A trembling-hand perfect Nash equilibrium of the unperturbed game G is the limit for $\varepsilon \to 0$ of the sequence of Nash equilibria of the games $G^\varepsilon_{\text{Selten}}$.

In the example considered above, the Nash equilibrium (c, c) is such a limit of a sequence of Nash equilibria of $G^\varepsilon_{\text{Selten}}$, while (a, a) is an isolated Nash equilibrium for G. This is because the perturbed game $G^\varepsilon_{\text{Selten}}$ of G is not a coordination game but a prisoners' dilemma (where the second strategy is of course strictly dominant) (see Figure 8.16).

Another variant of stability sensitive solution concepts, the *proper equilibrium*, has been introduced by Myerson (1978) This concept is very similar to Selten's trembling-hand perfectness. Instead of considering an abstract "arbitrarily small" probability that any other than the Nash equilibrium strategy is chosen, it assigns specific relations according to their respective expected payoff to the different options. Specifically, the game's strategies for each player are ordered with respect to the expected payoffs (in turn depending on the mixed or pure strategy assumed for the other player(s)). Any pure strategy s_A with a strictly lower expected payoff than another strategy s_B is played with a probability $p_{s,A}$ that is at most

ε times the probability $p_{s,B}$ for strategy s_B to be played, hence $p_{s,A} \le \varepsilon p_{s,B}$ with $1 > \varepsilon > 0$. Again as with trembling-hand perfectness, any Nash equilibrium of the unperturbed game G that is the limit for $\varepsilon \to 0$ of the sequence of Nash equilibria of the perturbed games $G^\varepsilon_{\text{Myerson}}$ is a *proper equilibrium*.

8.5 EXTENSIVE FORM GAMES

8.5.1 Extensive Form Notation

Games including normal-form games may as well be written in *extensive form*. In this case, the sequence of decisions is the basis for the illustration. States are depicted as the nodes of a decision tree. For each state, the player who is to make a decision at this stage is named as well. Possible decisions are written as the edges of the tree. Usually the tree is written from top to bottom or (sometimes) from left to right. Usually, it is convenient to assume *perfect information*, i.e., the agents are aware of the game, its properties and its exact course to the current state. However, there are cases in which agents might not be able to distinguish two particular states which is denoted by a dashed line between the vertexes representing the respective states. For example, to write a simple 2-person normal-form game with simultaneous choice of strategies in extensive form, it is necessary to ensure that the second to choose has no information about the choice of the first agent. (It does however not matter which of the two agents is assigned the position to be the first.)

It is immediately obvious that the extensive form is a more powerful technique to illustrate a greater variety of games: it is straightforward to write games for more than two agents (while in matrix form a third dimension would be necessary), the *information sets* of the agents are part of the illustration (at least their ability to distinguish the states), and games with sequential or repeated decision making are

		Player 2	
		s_{B1}	s_{B1}
Player 1	s_{A1}	2−3ε 2−3ε	2−2ε 3ε−1
	s_{A2}	3ε−1 2−2ε	ε2 2ε

FIGURE 8.16 Example: perturbed game corresponding to the game in Figure 8.15.

representable relatively conveniently. It is generally impractical if not impossible to write games with sequential decision making in matrix form; the matrix form is specifically useful for games with exactly two agents and simultaneous strategy choice. A two stage game with the second agent lacking (at stage 2) any knowledge about the first agent's action (at stage 1) is mathematically equivalent to simultaneous strategy choice. (See the normal-form prisoners' dilemma written as an extensive form game in Figure 8.17.) For greater ease of analyzing agent-specific strategy profiles, finding equilibria, and investigating other aspects of the interdependent structure of simple 2-person normal-form games, the matrix notation is generally favored for this type of games.

8.5.2 Complete Strategies

A *complete strategy* in a sequential game is considerably less simple than a strategy in a 2-person normal-form game. Let V be the set of states in the extensive game G^E; further let V_A be the set of player A undistinguishable states in which it is A who has to decide for an action for the next move. Then a complete strategy of player A contains an instruction for each element of the set V_A (even for vertices that are unreachable due prior moves of A specified in the same strategy).

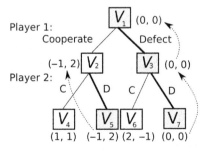

FIGURE 8.17 Extensive form prisoners' dilemma with solution by backward induction.

8.5.3 Backward Induction

Sequential games (as conveniently depicted in extensive form) do not contain coordination failure problems caused by simultaneous uncoordinated decisions. Therefore, with perfect information (perfect knowledge of both the game and the current state), it is possible to predict the actions of rational agents. At the time of the last decision made in the game, there is no uncertainty at all; the last agents choice of his expected payoffs is not subject to any other agents actions. Hence, the next-to-last agent is able to predict the last agents actions; given that her rationality assumption is correct, her uncertainty is eliminated as well. This in turn enables the previous agent to predict her action. Thus tracing the decision making of perfectly rational agents from the last turn to the start of the game gives an exact solution; this method is called *backward induction* (see Figure 8.17).

The conditions required for a Nash equilibrium are still applicable for sequential games, they are however more difficult to assess than in normal-form games and do often lead to the same set of solutions. This is however not always the case. Consider the game in Figure 8.18.

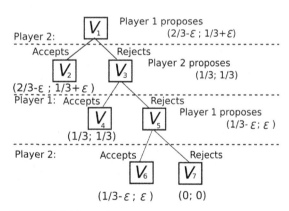

FIGURE 8.18 Rubinstein Bargaining game in extensive form. (Simplified; any splitting of the good may be proposed, depicted are only the strictly rational ones that result from backward induction, i.e., just above the reservation price.)

Both players setting their reservation price equal to the entire good that is bargained for (1 in the first period, 2/3 in the second, 1/3 in the third period, 0 thereafter) satisfies the conditions of the Nash equilibrium: none of the players gains by unilaterally deviating from this strategy, hence it is a mutually best answer.

8.5.4 Subgame Perfectness

The difference between the Nash equilibrium and the sequential equilibrium derived by backward induction is that the latter is always *subgame perfect* while the former is not. A subgame is a part of a game that is composed by a nonempty subset of any player's possible strategies. Imagining subgames in extensive form, they are what remains from the strategy tree if one or more (but not all) edges representing one of the strategy options of one of the players (and any options of the same or other players that follow this option) is severed. Subgame perfectness states that an equilibrium of the game must always also be an equilibrium of any subgame as long as the equilibrium is contained in that subgame.

Considering the sequence of choice the rejection of an offer of more than the maximum payoff of the subsequent period is not credible, hence an *incredible threat*. As shown, subgame perfectness of equilibria can easily be implemented using backward induction. This however is usually only possible if the respective game specifies perfect information for all agents and is finite. Obviously backward induction is only applicable for games with a true last period (finite games) are; further with imperfect information it is not always certain which subgame we are in thus leading to problems with the subgame perfectness of the derived solutions (if any).

8.6 REPEATED GAMES

8.6.1 Repeated Games and Supergames

Consider the coordination game in Figure 8.7 in the normal-form specification. You are to choose one of two options; if your choice matches that of your opponent, you win, otherwise you lose. What choice do you make? How would you rate the likelihood winning given that the opponent does not have a dominant strategy and no way to predict your choice either? Note that the setting is a *one-shot game*: The players choose their strategies simultaneously and only once. There is no opportunity for corrections or reactions to the opponent's choice. Once the decisions are made, the game is over—for the better or for the worse of the agents.

From the viewpoint of game-theoretic modeling with the purpose to explain real-world phenomena, the answer is simple: You will not have a chance significantly surpassing 0.5 to successfully coordinate in a one-shot coordination game. One-shot games, however, are arguably relatively rare in real-world systems. The one-shot Nash equilibrium considerations for instance are better perceived as practical simplifications of specific repeated games. Hence, the agents get the opportunity to reconsider their strategy and thus to coordinate and settle on a common choice. Once the strategy of the opponent is revealed, decision making becomes much easier and coordination is easily accomplished. The eventual solution will be one of the Nash equilibria of the one-shot game as the repeated setting matches the condition for a Nash equilibrium: No agent must have an incentive to unilaterally deviate from the Nash equilibrium.

To briefly clarify the notation, a repeated normal-form game *G* is considered a *sequence of repetitions* of the same one-shot game *G*. Agents are able to retain their memory for at least the last few interactions but usually (and if not specified otherwise) perfectly from the beginning of the interactions to their eventual end (if there is one). We call $\mathcal{G}$ a *supergame*. Supergames may be finite or infinite.

Why then do we not generally consider repeated games if it is so obviously more appropriate as a modeling framework of the phenomena we want to deal with? For infinitely repeated games, the now unrestricted set of strategies is incredibly large and incredibly rich. In fact, a single strategy itself could contain an infinite number of instructions, for instance one for each repetition. Strategies can further take the history of the game into account, thus reacting to past interactions. In short, the situation is far more complex than for one-shot games. For a finitely repeated supergame $\mathcal{G}$, the number of possible nonmixed strategies is of course finite as well, restricted by the number of iterations, say T, and the number of strategy combinations (including the strategies of all involved agents) possible in each state, say $|S|$. As the game is not an irregular sequential game but rather a repeated normal-form game, it follows that the number of possible distinguishable states of the game is

$$V = \sum_{t=1}^{T} |S|^t$$

out of which

$$V_{\text{nf}} = \sum_{t=1}^{T-1} |S|^t$$

are nonfinal distinguishable states, i.e., states in which the agents have to make a decision. (Distinguishable means in this case that the starting points of the decisions of individual agents in the same interaction are not counted separately.) The maximum possible number of strategies of an individual agent i is the number of states in which she has to make a decision (V_{nf}) times the number of options (strategies) among which she can choose, $|s_i|$.

$$|s_i^{\mathcal{G}}| = V_{\text{nf}}|s_i|$$

This is more easily understood when written in extensive form; however, it comes down to the sum over the number of strategies i can choose at each time she has to make a decision, namely T times. Those in turn are greater in a repeated game than in a single-shot game as the history of the game, namely, the prior decisions may be taken into account and multiplied by the number of options.

In repeated games as in other sequential games, the information set differs from that of normal-form games as agents may react to their opponent's strategy choices in subsequent rounds. Finitely repeated games are therefore also conveniently solved by backward induction (see above). However, for finite sequential games, there is a last period in which this option does not exist. Agents may in this period choose as if it were a simple nonrepeated game. Since agents in the second-to-last period are perfectly able to predict which choices rational opponents will make in the last period, they can choose as if the second-to-last period was the last one. This argument also applies to all prior periods until the first period is reached. This method allows perfectly rational behavior in finite sequential games; it is known as *backward induction*.

Finite supergames are conveniently solved by backward induction and are in no way different from other finite sequential games. For infinite supergames, this is not valid. Usually the payoffs of infinite supergames are discounted because they would otherwise, if positive, say a value $a > 0$ with each interaction, sum up to ∞ no matter the exact value of a. For the same sequence, discounting with a rate δ generates the finite present value of

$$\Pi = a + \delta a + \delta^2 a + \cdots = \frac{a}{1-\delta}$$

Generally, the discounted payoffs of rational players of an infinite supergame $\mathscr{G}$ can never be less than the infinite sum of the discounted maximin payoffs a_{Maximin} of the underlying one-shot game G. This is because any agent can ensure a_{Maximin} for each interaction. If a strategy s_i of G that leads to at least a_{Maximin} can further inflict damage on an opponent (reducing her payoffs for all possible strategies), $s_{i,\text{Maximin}}$ can be used to construct a *trigger strategy* $s_{\text{trigger}}^{\mathscr{G}}$ in the supergame $\mathscr{G}$. The maximin property guarantees that the trigger strategy is *subgame perfect*, i.e., the strategy stays a rational (not dominated) option at any point in time no matter how the game evolved to this point (i.e., any *subgame*). Threatening to employ $s_{\text{trigger}}^{\mathscr{G}}$ if a specific expectation was not matched by the opponent and employing it often enough to strip the opponent of any gains she might have made by deviating from the expectation is a called a *credible threat*. That is, it must be rational (not dominated) to exercise the punishment when an opponent deviated from the expected behavior (i.e., the threat did not work), which is a specific subgame of $\mathscr{G}$. A trigger strategy can be used to force the opponent to accept mutually beneficial agreements that do not constitute a Nash equilibrium in a one-shot game (the so-called *folk theorem*). For example in a prisoners' dilemma, defection satisfies the property required for $s_{i,\text{Maximin}}$ as it ensures a minimum payoff of a_{Maximin} (the payoff of mutual defection for the prisoners' dilemma) and also punishes the opponent by reducing her payoff no matter what her strategy is. As an example, consider the trigger strategy *tit-for-tat* (for a detailed discussion of this strategy, see Chapter 3) that starts with cooperation and then adheres to the rule

$$s_{\text{trigger}}^{\mathscr{G}} = \begin{cases} \text{cooperate} & \text{if} -i \text{ cooperates} \\ \text{defect}(s_{i,\text{Maximin}}) & \text{if} -i \text{ deviates from} \\ & \text{cooperation} \end{cases}$$

As for the opponent $-i$ not conforming to the expected behavior (cooperation), thus defecting, is no best answer to $s_{\text{trigger}}^{\mathscr{G}}$ (tit-for-tat), while $s_{\text{trigger}}^{\mathscr{G}}$ is a best answer to itself, so mutually playing $s_{\text{trigger}}^{\mathscr{G}}$ is a Nash equilibrium in the supergame $\mathscr{G}$. The infinitely repeated prisoners' dilemma has two types of Nash equilibria, the first being mutual defection ($s_{i,\text{Maximin}}$) in all periods, the other mutually playing trigger strategies like tit-for-tat. For details on the repeated prisoners' dilemma, see Chapters 3 and 13 or Axelrod (1984); for details on trigger strategies, the maximin strategies in repeated games, see Rubinstein (1979).

Trigger strategies are not possible in finite games. From the point at which the time of the end of the game is known they are dominated by the backward induction considerations—known in game theory as *endgame effect*.

8.6.2 Rubinstein's Proof of the Folk Theorem

The maximin criterion (see Section 8.3.2) maximizes the minimum payoff an agent can guarantee for herself by her own (and only her own) actions. Analogously, Rubinstein (1979) defined a minmax payoff Π_{Minmax} such that an opponent can prevent the agent from ever receiving more than this payoff value. This may be useful for a trigger strategy to punish the agent in question. Finding the minmax payoff (of agent j) and the corresponding minmax strategy s_{Minmax} (of opponent i) is straightforward (and analogous to the maximin criterion):

$$\Pi_{\text{Minmax},i,j} = \min_i \max_j \Pi_i(s_j, s_i, s_{\text{other agents}})$$

Rubinstein (1979) was able to prove that in an infinitely or indefinitely repeated game any strategy may be a best answer strategy (hence a viable choice for rational agents) if it—as long as all agents adhere to it—guarantees a payoff higher than Π_{Minmax} and if such a strategy exists for all agents. All agents will play a more cooperative strategy s_C which awards their opponents a payoff higher than Π_{Minmax} as long as the respective opponent adheres to the same rule. If she does not, agents will punish her by playing s_{Minmax}. This is, in fact, a trigger strategy

$$
s_{TR,i} = \begin{cases} s_{C,i} & \text{if } j \text{ played } s_C \text{ in every previous} \\ & \text{round} \\ s_{\text{Minmax},i,j} & \text{otherwise} \end{cases}
$$

As deviating from cooperation s_C results in lower payoffs, playing s_C is the only best answer to the opponent playing s_C; as this holds for all agents, it satisfies the conditions of a Nash equilibrium.

This holds for any game that contains a minmax strategy for all agents. The threat (of playing s_{Minmax}) may, depending on the payoff structure, however, be credible or incredible. For instance, in hawk-dove games, the resulting trigger strategy—punishing the opponent for playing hawk by responding with hawk—is not subgame perfect, as $\Pi(D, H) > \Pi(H, H)$, thus an incredible threat. For a repeated prisoners' dilemma, the threat is credible.

8.7 POPULATION PERSPECTIVES AND EVOLUTIONARY GAMES

8.7.1 Evolutionary Approaches to Game Theory

The most important goal of game theory is the modeling of social interactive situations. It is convenient, as in the concepts discussed so far, to simplify reality to obtain a single game (one-shot or repeated) with the interaction rules, players, and information sets specified and proceed analyzing this game. Depending on the number of actors, the repeatedness, information sets, etc., even these approaches may lead to overly complex

mathematical problems. Still, they may be considered insufficient in their scope as they are unable to cover the dynamics present at a larger scale. How are social interactions related in a dynamic population? What can game theory contribute to the prediction of population dynamics if single interactions are modeled as games? Applying game theory to population settings enables the branch to take the step from a distinctly microeconomic technique to a generalized method. It becomes possible to consider the meso- and macrolevels and most importantly to offer a convenient bridge between different scales, to gain an integrated view of complex socioeconomic problems including their micro, macro, and intermediate aspects, to provide macroeconomic theories with proper micro foundations, an old dream of especially neoclassical economics that the general equilibrium theories were never able to fulfill (see Chapters 5 and 6).

As seen in the previous sections, game theory is able to predict rational behavior in interactive situations whether repeated or nonrepeated, whether between two agents or in large groups (an *n*-person game), whether with perfect or imperfect information. Assuming that all agents in a population are strictly rational, it follows that the whole population will, if possible, play dominant strategies or at least Nash equilibrium strategies (or strategies leading to Nash equilibria). For repeated games, as discussed in Section 8.6, we may also assume that the population will eventually arrive at a Nash equilibrium even if there is more than one. However, this is merely the application of the solution concepts of a single game to another setting reasoning that what is impossible at the small scale (irrational behavior) will not occur at the large scale either.

There is another somewhat different approach to games in populations, *evolutionary game theory*. This approach involves some further assumptions:

1. the population consists of a number of distinguishable and specified types of agents
2. the composition of the population (of agents of the various types) develops according to the performance of these types in games played in this population.

It is convenient to explicitly specify this evolutionary performance of a type of agents as a variable, usually called the *evolutionary fitness f_i* of type *i*. Note that it is not necessary to measure this quantity or even to specify it explicitly for the model to function, it is merely a concept adopted from evolutionary biology that may be helpful for predictions. Also note that the evolutionary fitness may (and usually does) change with the composition of the population which is also analogous to evolutionary biology.

The three most important solution concepts for evolutionary game theory will be discussed in this textbook (two of them in this section, the third, simulation, in Chapter 9).

Evolutionary stability (developed by Maynard Smith and Price, 1973) is a refinement of the Nash equilibrium to evolutionary settings. A population of *n* agents playing *symmetric (usually 2-person) normal-form one-shot games* is considered. The agents are matched randomly; the possible types of agents correspond to the mixed strategies of the underlying game the types are playing. As evolutionary stability as a general game, theoretic solution concept must be a general property of the strategies (thus the types) it is independent of any specific composition of the population. Rather, it considers which strategies (i.e., which types) are generally able to prevail in the population.

Replicator dynamics is a mathematical specification of the dynamic development of a population of *n* agents playing *sequential n-person games*. Dynamic processes may or may not

contain equilibrium points with various properties with respect to stability, a question addressed with methods of *dynamic systems theory*.

1. *Simulation of dynamic populations in evolutionary game theory* is the computational study of well-specified dynamical systems representing population settings of evolutionary game theory of various kinds. Simulation is not an exact mathematical method (which is a major disadvantage); however, it is a very flexible and powerful technique to conveniently analyze systems of great complexity. The idea is to study the behavior of a dynamic system for a broad range of possible initial states in order to identify regular patterns in its development. Simulation is most attractive for the most complex settings, in game theory especially those with heterogeneous agents, in which case the situation is modeled to represent each individual agent separately (*agent-based modeling*). For details, see Chapter 9.

8.7.2 Evolutionary Stability

The standard Nash equilibrium is—by definition—the combination of mutual best answers. We may be inclined to deduce that Nash equilibria are also stable states in population settings: As the dynamic development of the players of a Nash equilibrium strategy (i.e., a strategy leading to the Nash equilibrium) follows their performance in the underlying game against the rest of the population, it should be the best possible performance against a population of actors aiming at the same Nash equilibrium. However, there are two major issues with this intuition. Firstly, in order to apply to both the population and the single game, a Nash equilibrium should involve only one strategy that in turn is the best answer to itself. These are the Nash equilibria located on the main diagonal in the game matrices, other Nash equilibria would imply a configuration of two (for 2-person games) strategies with the specific shares of the strategies not defined. Secondly, the application to population dynamics requires a robust analysis of stability for any equilibrium concept.

As a refinement of the Nash equilibrium for population settings, the concept of evolutionary stability formulated by Maynard Smith and Price (1973) is used. A strategy σ^* is called evolutionary stable if a population dominated by σ^* is not invadable by any other strategy $\sigma^\sim$. That implies that once the population is dominated by σ^*, this situation will remain stable. It does not explain how the population comes to be dominated by σ^*. Note that while both the Nash equilibrium and the evolutionary stable strategies are equilibrium concepts, the Nash equilibrium refers to a combination of strategies in a game while the evolutionary stable strategy refers to a particular strategy or rather a stable situation in a population (which is, the population is completely dominated by the evolutionary stable strategy).

Let $\mathscr{P}_{\mathscr{G}\mathscr{V}}$ be an evolutionary population setting with the underlying one-shot normal-form game $G_{\mathscr{G}\mathscr{V}}$. $G_{\mathscr{G}\mathscr{V}}$ shall be a symmetric game, i.e., all players face the same options of strategy choice including the same payoffs and information sets. The game may be represented as a matrix $\mathscr{A}$ containing the payoffs of just one of the (identical) players—most intuitively the row player; an example is given below. Note that expected payoffs are again computed as a simple matrix multiplication of the form

$$\Pi_{\sigma_1/\sigma_2} = \sigma_1^T \mathscr{A} \sigma_2$$

in this case computing the expected payoff of a strategy σ_1 against σ_2. The agents are matched randomly to play $G_{\mathscr{G}\mathscr{V}}$ employing their predefined strategies, in turn represented as mixed

strategies σ. According to their performance, the composition of the population changes which may be seen as forced switching of strategies in case of poor performance or—to put it more cruelly—as a birth–death process. The population is assumed to be large and—in the limit—infinitely divisible.

To formalize the above description of evolutionary stability, consider the strategy σ^* in a population primarily composed of σ^*-players with a small invading group playing a strategy $\sigma^\sim \neq \sigma^*$. Call the share of invaders ε; ε being arbitrarily small. A share $1 - \varepsilon$ close to encompassing the total population continues playing σ^* resulting in an expected composition of the population(in terms of the shares of strategies expected to be played)

$$(1 - \varepsilon)\sigma^* + \varepsilon\sigma^\sim$$

where σ^* is evolutionary stable if and only if it yields a higher expected payoff in this population than the invading strategy $\sigma^\sim$, thus

$$\sigma^{*T}\mathscr{A}((1-\varepsilon)\sigma^* + \varepsilon\sigma^\sim) > \sigma^{\sim T}\mathscr{A}((1-\varepsilon)\sigma^* + \varepsilon\sigma^\sim)$$
$$\sigma^{*T}\mathscr{A}(1-\varepsilon)\sigma^* + \sigma^{*T}\mathscr{A}\varepsilon\sigma^\sim > \sigma^{\sim T}\mathscr{A}(1-\varepsilon)\sigma^*$$
$$+ \sigma^{\sim T}\mathscr{A}\varepsilon\sigma^\sim$$

$$(8.1)$$

As ε is arbitrarily small, the inequality must also hold for $\varepsilon \to 0$ which yields the *first condition of evolutionary stability* (though it does not necessarily have to hold strictly, thus replacing the "greater than" with a "greater or equal")

$$\sigma^{*T}\mathscr{A}\sigma^* + 0 \geq \sigma^{\sim T}\mathscr{A}\sigma^* + 0$$

Indeed, this means that σ^* must be a best answer to itself in turn requiring the strategy configuration composed of σ^* for every player, in the 2-person case (σ^*, σ^*), to be a symmetric Nash equilibrium of the underlying game $G_{\mathscr{G}\mathscr{V}}$.

The first condition as stated above is a necessary condition for evolutionary stability; as ε is arbitrarily small, however, it is not just the necessary but also the sufficient condition if it holds strictly.

$$\sigma^{*T} \mathscr{A} \sigma^* > \sigma^{\sim T} \mathscr{A} \sigma^*$$

If it does not, however, i.e., if

$$\sigma^{*T} \mathscr{A} \sigma^* = \sigma^{\sim T} \mathscr{A} \sigma^*$$

we may substitute $\sigma^{\sim T} \mathscr{A} \sigma^*$ with $\sigma^{*T} \mathscr{A} \sigma^*$ in Eq. (8.1), resulting in

$$(1 - \varepsilon)\sigma^{*T} \mathscr{A} \sigma^* + \varepsilon\sigma^{*T} \mathscr{A} \sigma^\sim > (1 - \varepsilon)\sigma^{*T} \mathscr{A} \sigma^*$$
$$+ \varepsilon\sigma^{\sim T} \mathscr{A} \sigma^\sim$$
$$\varepsilon\sigma^{*T} \mathscr{A} \sigma^\sim > \varepsilon\sigma^{\sim T} \mathscr{A} \sigma^\sim$$
$$\sigma^{*T} \mathscr{A} \sigma^\sim > \sigma^{\sim T} \mathscr{A} \sigma^\sim$$

which is the *second condition of evolutionary stability*. Note that the second condition is to be considered only if the first condition holds with equality.

As an example consider a population setting with the following hawk-dove game $G_{\mathscr{HD}}$ as the underlying game-theoretic structure as shown in Figure 8.6. As explained above, the game may be completely represented by a game matrix

$$\mathscr{A} = \begin{pmatrix} 2 & 1 \\ 3 & 0 \end{pmatrix}$$

containing only the payoffs of the row player (player 1) since it is a symmetric game.

Using the first condition of evolutionary stability, we know that only Nash equilibrium strategies may be evolutionary stable. The game $G_{\mathscr{HD}}$ has three Nash equilibria, in pure strategies (H, D) and (D, H) and in mixed strategies $(M, M) = \left(\begin{pmatrix} 0.5 \\ 0.5 \end{pmatrix}, \begin{pmatrix} 0.5 \\ 0.5 \end{pmatrix} \right)$. Hence, we have three strategies that may be evolutionary stable, $D = \begin{pmatrix} 1 \\ 0 \end{pmatrix}$, $H = \begin{pmatrix} 0 \\ 1 \end{pmatrix}$, and $M = \begin{pmatrix} 0.5 \\ 0.5 \end{pmatrix}$.

Testing H and D against each other, we can easily show that they fail to fulfill the first condition, for H

$$H^T \mathscr{A} H < D^T \mathscr{A} H$$

$$(0 \quad 1)\begin{pmatrix} 2 & 1 \\ 3 & 0 \end{pmatrix}\begin{pmatrix} 0 \\ 1 \end{pmatrix} < (1 \quad 0)\begin{pmatrix} 2 & 1 \\ 3 & 0 \end{pmatrix}\begin{pmatrix} 0 \\ 1 \end{pmatrix}$$

$$0 < 1$$

and for D

$$D^T \mathscr{A} D < H^T \mathscr{A} D$$

$$(1 \quad 0)\begin{pmatrix} 2 & 1 \\ 3 & 0 \end{pmatrix}\begin{pmatrix} 1 \\ 0 \end{pmatrix} < (0 \quad 1)\begin{pmatrix} 2 & 1 \\ 3 & 0 \end{pmatrix}\begin{pmatrix} 1 \\ 0 \end{pmatrix}$$

$$2 < 3$$

What remains to be tested is the mixed strategy M. In order to prove M evolutionary stable, it must be shown that no mixed or pure strategy $M^\sim = \begin{pmatrix} m \\ 1 - m \end{pmatrix}$ with $m \neq 0.5$ (that would be M itself) that would be able to invade M does exist.

$$M^T \mathscr{A} M = M^{\sim T} \mathscr{A} M$$

$$(0.5 \quad 0.5)\begin{pmatrix} 2 & 1 \\ 3 & 0 \end{pmatrix}\begin{pmatrix} 0.5 \\ 0.5 \end{pmatrix} = (m \quad 1 - m)$$

$$\begin{pmatrix} 2 & 1 \\ 3 & 0 \end{pmatrix}\begin{pmatrix} 0.5 \\ 0.5 \end{pmatrix}$$

$$1.5 = (3 - m \quad m)\begin{pmatrix} 0.5 \\ 0.5 \end{pmatrix}$$

$$1.5 = 1.5$$

Thus the first condition holds. All possible strategies perform equally against M. Proceed with the second condition

$$M^T \mathscr{A} M^\sim > M^{\sim T} \mathscr{A} M^\sim$$

$$(0.5 \quad 0.5)\begin{pmatrix} 2 & 1 \\ 3 & 0 \end{pmatrix}\begin{pmatrix} m \\ 1 - m \end{pmatrix} > (m \quad 1 - m)$$

$$\begin{pmatrix} 2 & 1 \\ 3 & 0 \end{pmatrix}\begin{pmatrix} m \\ 1 - m \end{pmatrix}$$

$$(2.5 \quad 0.5)\begin{pmatrix} m \\ 1 - m \end{pmatrix} > (3 - m \quad m)\begin{pmatrix} m \\ 1 - m \end{pmatrix}$$

$$2m + 0.5 > 4m - 2m^2$$

$$m^2 - m + 0.25 > 0$$

Except for the point $m = 0.5$, the function $m^2 - m + 0.25$ is indeed always larger than 0. Thus M must be evolutionary stable.

Note that alternatively it could also be shown that the two conditions for evolutionary stability hold for M against the pure strategies D and H. With this proven, and keeping in mind that M is the strategy against which both pure and all mixed strategies perform the same, it can be seen that the expected payoffs of any mixed strategy other than M would be a combination of the expected payoffs of M and a pure strategy, the former equal to the performance of M, the latter worse. Hence, showing that the conditions of evolutionary stability hold against H and D would also prove M evolutionary stable. Testing M against D yields

$$M^T \mathscr{A} M = D^T \mathscr{A} M$$

$$(0.5 \quad 0.5) \begin{pmatrix} 2 & 1 \\ 3 & 0 \end{pmatrix} \begin{pmatrix} 0.5 \\ 0.5 \end{pmatrix} = (1 \quad 0) \begin{pmatrix} 2 & 1 \\ 3 & 0 \end{pmatrix} \begin{pmatrix} 0.5 \\ 0.5 \end{pmatrix}$$

$$1.5 = 1.5$$

Thus, the second condition must be tested and proves to hold as well.

$$M^T \mathscr{A} D > D^T \mathscr{A} D$$

$$(0.5 \quad 0.5) \begin{pmatrix} 2 & 1 \\ 3 & 0 \end{pmatrix} \begin{pmatrix} 1 \\ 0 \end{pmatrix} > (1 \quad 0) \begin{pmatrix} 2 & 1 \\ 3 & 0 \end{pmatrix} \begin{pmatrix} 1 \\ 0 \end{pmatrix}$$

$$2.5 > 2$$

Testing M again with H as opponent gives similar results:

$$M^T \mathscr{A} M = H^T \mathscr{A} M$$

$$(0.5 \quad 0.5) \begin{pmatrix} 2 & 1 \\ 3 & 0 \end{pmatrix} \begin{pmatrix} 0.5 \\ 0.5 \end{pmatrix} = (0 \quad 1) \begin{pmatrix} 2 & 1 \\ 3 & 0 \end{pmatrix} \begin{pmatrix} 0.5 \\ 0.5 \end{pmatrix}$$

$$1.5 = 1.5$$

$$M^T \mathscr{A} H > H^T \mathscr{A} H$$

$$(0.5 \quad 0.5) \begin{pmatrix} 2 & 1 \\ 3 & 0 \end{pmatrix} \begin{pmatrix} 0 \\ 1 \end{pmatrix} > (0 \quad 1) \begin{pmatrix} 2 & 1 \\ 3 & 0 \end{pmatrix} \begin{pmatrix} 0 \\ 1 \end{pmatrix}$$

$$0.5 > 0$$

8.7.3 Asymmetry in Evolutionary Game Theory

To allow a glimpse of the richness of the field of evolutionary game theory, consider the following: The result of an evolutionary hawk-dove game changes dramatically if we change the evolutionary setting such that the players are able to distinguish row player and column player. Note that the game is not symmetric any more even though the payoff structure has not changed and is technically still symmetric: players are aware of their position and have thus a larger evolutionary strategy space since a strategy can define different actions for different roles. It must thus be "symmetricized" before it can be used in an evolutionary setting. This is accomplished by requiring the agents to chose a strategy for both cases, the case in which they are row player and the case in which they are column player—and it does not have to be the same strategy. Now the actors have four possible pure strategies:

1. Chose D if being row player, D if being column player (DD)
2. Chose D if being row player, H if being column player (DH)
3. Chose H if being row player, D if being column player (HD)
4. Chose H if being row player, H if being column player (HH)

The resulting normal-form game matrix (see Figure 8.19) has $4 \times 4 = 16$ fields, it is symmetric if we sum up the payoffs to obtain an average[2] for both cases (first player is row, second column and vice versa) in every field.

Note that this method can be used as well for games with an asymmetric payoff structure such as matching pennies (which could not be used in evolutionary game theory without "symmetrication").

---

[2]Here we assume that players are drawn equally often as row and column player. Otherwise, probability weights would have to be applied.

| | Player 2 | | | |
	DD	DH	HD	HH
DD	4 / 4	5 / 3	5 / 3	6 / 2
DH	3 / 5	4 / 4	2 / 2	3 / 1
HD	3 / 5	2 / 2	4 / 4	3 / 1
HH	2 / 6	1 / 3	1 / 3	0 / 0

(Player 1 labels the rows)

FIGURE 8.19 Games in which players are aware of their position as row or column players have a substantially larger strategy space (hawk-dove game example).

The analysis of evolutionary stability can rapidly grow rather complicated. For the sake of simplicity, this four strategy settings shall not be analyzed exhaustively. However, the differences from the setting discussed above shall briefly be outlined. It is immediately evident that both the strategy DH and the strategy HD are the only best answers to itself. Thus, the first condition of evolutionary stability holds is sufficient for those strategies, both are evolutionary stable. Considering the unique evolutionary stable strategy of the setting above, M, which corresponds to

$$M = \begin{pmatrix} 0.5 \\ 0 \\ 0 \\ 0.5 \end{pmatrix}$$

in the current situation, testing M against DH (or HD) shows that the first condition holds with equality

$$M^T \mathscr{A} M = DH^T \mathscr{A} M$$

$$(0.5 \quad 0 \quad 0 \quad 0.5) \begin{pmatrix} 4 & 3 & 3 & 2 \\ 5 & 4 & 2 & 1 \\ 5 & 2 & 4 & 1 \\ 6 & 3 & 3 & 0 \end{pmatrix} \begin{pmatrix} 0.5 \\ 0 \\ 0 \\ 0.5 \end{pmatrix}$$

$$= (0 \quad 1 \quad 0 \quad 0) \begin{pmatrix} 4 & 3 & 3 & 2 \\ 5 & 4 & 2 & 1 \\ 5 & 2 & 4 & 1 \\ 6 & 3 & 3 & 0 \end{pmatrix} \begin{pmatrix} 0.5 \\ 0 \\ 0 \\ 0.5 \end{pmatrix}$$

$$3 = 3$$

Proceeding to test the second condition however reveals

$$M^T \mathscr{A} DH < DH^T \mathscr{A} DH$$

$$(0.5 \quad 0 \quad 0 \quad 0.5) \begin{pmatrix} 4 & 3 & 3 & 2 \\ 5 & 4 & 2 & 1 \\ 5 & 2 & 4 & 1 \\ 6 & 3 & 3 & 0 \end{pmatrix} \begin{pmatrix} 0 \\ 1 \\ 0 \\ 0 \end{pmatrix}$$

$$< (0 \quad 1 \quad 0 \quad 0) \begin{pmatrix} 4 & 3 & 3 & 2 \\ 5 & 4 & 2 & 1 \\ 5 & 2 & 4 & 1 \\ 6 & 3 & 3 & 0 \end{pmatrix} \begin{pmatrix} 0 \\ 1 \\ 0 \\ 0 \end{pmatrix}$$

$$3 < 4$$

which means that the former evolutionary stable strategy M is now invadable by DH or HD. To outline an intuitive explanation, both M and the more complex strategies DH and HD aim at the Nash equilibria of the underlying game (H, D) and (D, H). However, while the allocation of the roles as exploiter (H) and exploited (D) is accomplished using a stochastic mechanism in M which leads to occasional worst-case results (H, H), the roles are well-defined social rules (or institutions) using the position as row player or column player as markers in DH and HD.

8.7.4 Replicator Dynamics

Contrary to evolutionary stability, replicator dynamics does not envisage the abstract stability properties of a strategy but rather the development of the population as a dynamic system. Dynamic systems are discussed in more detail in Chapters 10 and 11; for now, it shall be sufficient to say that dynamic systems generally describe the development of a set of z state variables in time. Assume the state variables written as a vector

$$\theta_t = \begin{pmatrix} \theta_{1,t} \\ \theta_{2,t} \\ \vdots \\ \theta_{z,t} \end{pmatrix} = (\theta_{i,t})_{i=1,\ldots,z}$$

The development is independent of the time the system is initialized, t_0. For the sake of simplicity, let us however assume the nomenclature $t_0 = 0$, in other words the system starts at time index 0. Though the development is independent from t_0 it does depend on the initial values of the state variables θ_0 and, of course, the (system of) development equations, which in turn are either difference equations of the form

$$\theta_{t+1} = F_{\tilde{D}}(\theta_t)$$

(where $F_{\tilde{D}}(\sim)$ is a function) or differential equations of the form

$$\frac{d\theta(t)}{dt} = F_{\tilde{d}}(\theta(t))$$

Specifically in the case of replicator dynamics, the state variables are the shares of specific types of agents $i = 1, \ldots, z$ in the population, hence

$$\sum_i \theta_{i,t} = 1 \quad \forall t$$

According to the agent types' evolutionary potential, described above as evolutionary fitness $f_{i,t}$, the share of the population increases or decreases over time. Note, however, that models of replicator dynamics have nothing to do with misanthropic ideologies of the so-called social Darwinism. In fact, there are a number of different evolutionary mechanisms apart from the "survival of the fittest" which is an extreme special case (for a detailed discussion see Nowak, 2006, Chapter 2). Further the example considered below shows that evolutionary systems (both biological and other) are much more complicated with the global state

of the system (the ecology, so to speak) having a profound impact on the individual fitness values and with the globally stable state the system converges to being a combination of different populations (types of agents in the system). From the individual fitness values, it is straightforward to define an average fitness of the population

$$\phi_t = \sum_i \theta_{i,t} f_{i,t}$$

As evolutionary performance of the agent types is determined by the relation of their individual fitness and the average fitness in the population, the development equation functions ($F_{\tilde{D}}(\sim)$ and $F_{\tilde{d}}(\sim)$) may be specified more conveniently to include $f_{i,t}$ and ϕ_t to yield

$$\theta_{i,t+1} = F_D(\theta_{i,t}, f_{i,t}, \phi_t)$$

or respectively as a differential equation

$$\frac{d\theta_i(t)}{dt} = F_d(\theta_i(t), f_i(t), \phi(t))$$

The central question of replicator dynamics is which situations (state variable configurations $(\theta_{i,t})_{i=1,\ldots,z}$) are equilibria and which of these are stable. Of course, an equilibrium θ^* is any state from which the system does not change any more, in other words the development equation maps the state into itself and if the equilibrium is reached at time t', then the state of the system is at this equilibrium point for all times after t', hence

$$\theta_t = \theta^* \quad \forall t \geq t'$$

For difference equation systems, the equilibrium condition is

$$\theta_{t+1}^* = F_D(\theta_t^*, f_{i,t}, \phi_t)$$

and for differential equation systems, it is

$$\frac{d\theta_i^*(t)}{dt} = F_d(\theta_i^*(t), f_i(t), \phi(t)) = 0$$

Compared to other methods of game theory, it is rather easy to assess the stability properties of these solutions (equilibria) since they are determined by continuous functions, the development equations. Specifically, we have to consider the eigenvalues λ and determine whether the dynamic process is contractive in the neighborhood of the equilibria. For systems of difference equations, this is the case if the dominant eigenvalue, the eigenvalue with the largest absolute value, is smaller than 1, which means that all eigenvalues are smaller than one, $|\lambda| < 1$. In the case of differential equations, the dominant eigenvalue, here the eigenvalue with the largest real (as opposed to imaginary) part, is negative, hence all eigenvalues are negative $Re(\lambda) < 0$. (For details on eigenvalues, see Box 11.1.) The systems of replicator dynamics we investigate in this section do not usually have constant eigenvalues; the eigenvalues depend on the position in the phase space (the state variables). Hence we have the eigenvalues typically as functions of the type

$$\lambda = \lambda(\theta_t)$$

For a more detailed discussion of replicator dynamics, see Nowak (2006); for an assessment of the role of models of replicator dynamics for microeconomic theory, see Kirman (1997).

Consider the following case as an example: Two types of enterprises offer mobile phone contracts in an economy (or region). Every agent maintains her own mobile phone network in which calls are offered at marginal costs, thus without profits. Their profits result entirely from intra network communication, where both involved networks share the profits. One type of enterprise (D) offers equal sharing of profits, while the other type (H) tries to exploit other networks by charging higher network access costs. Assume that connections between networks occur randomly and uniformly. Assume further that the network access costs between two H-type networks are prohibitive, hence no profits are generated, while otherwise there are revenues

of 4 monetary units per customer. The allocation of these profits follows the scheme shown in Figure 8.8.

Further, the agents are matched randomly a large number of times such that the distribution of opponents each agent meets is representative for the composition of the population. The payoffs are normalized to those in the matrix above (thus divided by the number of encounters), yielding payoffs for type D and H of

$$\Pi_D = (1 \quad 0) \begin{pmatrix} 2 & 1 \\ 3 & 0 \end{pmatrix} \begin{pmatrix} \theta_D \\ \theta_H \end{pmatrix} = (1 \quad 0) \begin{pmatrix} 2 & 1 \\ 3 & 0 \end{pmatrix}$$

$$\begin{pmatrix} \theta_D \\ 1 - \theta_D \end{pmatrix}$$

$$= (2 \quad 1) \begin{pmatrix} \theta_D \\ 1 - \theta_D \end{pmatrix} = \theta_D + 1$$

$$\Pi_H = (0 \quad 1) \begin{pmatrix} 2 & 1 \\ 3 & 0 \end{pmatrix} \begin{pmatrix} \theta_D \\ \theta_H \end{pmatrix} = (0 \quad 1) \begin{pmatrix} 2 & 1 \\ 3 & 0 \end{pmatrix}$$

$$\begin{pmatrix} \theta_D \\ 1 - \theta_D \end{pmatrix}$$

$$= (3 \quad 0) \begin{pmatrix} \theta_D \\ 1 - \theta_D \end{pmatrix} = 3\theta_D$$

respectively. Assume the payoffs to be the individual fitness

$$f_D = \Pi_D = \theta_D + 1$$
$$f_H = \Pi_H = 3\theta_D$$

and the development equation to be the following differential equation

$$\frac{d\theta_i(t)}{dt} = \theta_i(t)(f_i(t) - \phi(t)) i = D, H$$

As the state vector has just two elements, one of them depending on the other due to the requirement that shares sum up to one

$(1 - \theta_D = \theta_H)$, it is sufficient to consider just one development equation (for example that of θ_D)

$$\frac{d\theta_D(t)}{dt} = \theta_D(f_D - (\theta_D f_D + (1 - \theta_D)f_H))$$

$$= \theta_D(1 - \theta_D)(f_D - f_H)$$

Proceeding to substitute the fitness values in the development equation yields

$$\frac{d\theta_D(t)}{dt} = \theta_D(1 - \theta_D)(- 2\theta_D + 1) = 2\theta_D^3 - 3\theta_D^2 + \theta_D$$

There are three equilibria:

$$\theta_{D,1}^* = 0$$

$$\theta_{D,2}^* = 0.5$$

$$\theta_{D,3}^* = 1$$

The eigenvalue of this one-dimensional system (system of only one equation) is the first derivative of the development equation with respect to the state variable. (For larger systems, the eigenvalues would have to be computed using the Jacobi matrix J of the development equations to fulfill $\lambda J = \lambda v$ as explained in Box 11.1.)

$$\lambda = \frac{\partial^2(d\theta_D(t)/dt)}{\partial \theta_D} = 6\theta_D^2 - 6\theta_D + 1$$

Consequently the eigenvalue assumes for the fixed points the values

$$\lambda(\theta_{D,1}^*) = \lambda(0) = 1$$

$$\lambda(\theta_{D,2}^*) = \lambda(0.5) = -0.5$$

$$\lambda(\theta_{D,3}^*) = \lambda(1) = 1$$

It follows that $\theta_{D,2}^* = 0.5$ is the only stable equilibrium. This is not surprising as the game used to construct this population setting is a hawk-dove game. In fact, it is the very hawk-dove game used as an example in Section 8.7.2 and $\theta_{D,2}^*$ corresponds to the evolutionary stable mixed strategy M computed there.

8.8 RATIONALITY IN GAME THEORY

Before getting to the conclusions, a few words about conceptions of rationality in game theory are in order. As mentioned in the context of formal concepts of game theory, agents are required to be perfectly rational in order to apply game theory concepts. This may seem an unrealistically heroic assumption not unlike those used in neoclassical theory, especially in the light of empirical findings from behavioral and experimental economics (see, for instance, Tversky and Kahneman, 1973). However—in contrast to Walrasian general equilibrium theory—game theory allows for imperfect and incomplete information and with certain extensions also for bounded rationality, i.e., the agents apply a heuristic as considered for instance in evolutionary game theory (see Chapters 1–3). It is impractical to drop every concept of rationality, this would lead to the impossibility to predict anything. Any heuristic approach will again make the assumption that agents adhere to the defined heuristic, i.e., in effect, they are rational within the limits of the setting under investigation. Reality is complex and real agents (humans) do not have the processing capacity to be perfectly rational (and do not even try to be); there are, however, approaches that explicitly include complex modeling and heuristics (see Chapters 9–11).

8.9 CONCLUSION

This section provided a formal introduction to game theory drawing on the basic game-theoretic concepts already introduced in Chapter 1 as well as on the extensive discussion of the context which makes game theory a necessary and valuable tool for microeconomics. The current chapter added the formal conventions of notation and a discussion of the basic solution concepts of game theory (the Nash equilibrium and dominant strategies). Further, several extensions to both the setting and the solution concepts have been discussed, including mixed strategies and repeated games. These extensions are among many others especially valuable to push the extent to which game theory is able to approximate real-world systems. Finally, the last part of the chapter introduced basic conceptions of evolutionary game theory which in turn forms the basis for many of the models discussed in Chapters 3, 7, 10, 13, and 14 (among others).

In short, game theory provides a rich toolkit for economics that leads to important insights both for analyzing the models and predictions of neoclassical general equilibrium theory (which was discussed in Chapter 5–7), assessing their explanatory scope and constructing a different kind of models. Many authors have analyzed game theory representations of neoclassical perfect market systems (Albin and Foley, 1992; Kirman, 1997) with the result that the neoclassical world is possible—as a limit case of a large variety of systems with very different results. (However to go into detail about these discussions, especially that presented by Albin and Foley, an extensive discussion of graph theory and the theory of games on networks would be required. For an introduction on this topic, see Easley and Kleinberg, 2010). As Chen (2002) describes it, neoclassic theory works by defining heterogeneity away—using the argument of general rationality—and arriving at a one-body problem. Evolutionary models (with a game theory micro foundation) however allow heterogeneity and construct multi-body problems, while physics taught us that three-body problems may already be sufficiently complex to lead to deterministic chaos and make predictions very difficult. However, certain mechanisms (discussed in more detail in Chapters 10 and 11), e.g., emergence, may still lead to stable patterns being produced in complex systems. Arguably, evolutionary game theory explains some of the

most important and powerful mechanisms of emergent stability. It is this field microeconomic theory should turn to in order to find more plausible explanations for the many phenomena of a complex world. In fact, many of the models discussed in Chapter 13 are part of this tradition.

Commented Game Theory Textbook References

– Shaun P. Hargreaves Heap and Yanis Varoufakis (1995, 2004) *Game Theory: A Critical Introduction.*
  Hargreaves Heap and Varoufakis give an extensive yet critical introduction to game theory including the discussion of concepts and assumptions as well as the verbal and formal presentation of methods and demonstrative examples. The textbook covers the basics of game theory as well as the extensions to repeated and evolutionary games, and non-normal-form games.
– Herbert Gintis (2000) *Game Theory Evolving: A Problem-Centered Introduction to Modeling Strategic Behavior.*
  Gintis' textbook takes the term "game theory" literally: the introduction to game theory is a commented collection of games as practical examples. Nevertheless, the book spans a large field starting with the very basics, discussing all facets of game theory including repeated games, Bayesian games, stochastic games, evolutionary game theory, replicator dynamics, as well as an introduction to probability and decision theory.
– Herbert Gintis (2009) *The Bounds of Reason: Game Theory and the Unification of the Behavioural Sciences.*
  This textbook offers comprehensive introductions to decision theory, game theory, and evolutionary game theory. All the major concepts are introduced—but they are always contrasted with evidence from various behavioral sciences and real-world examples. It is therefore not only a game theory textbook but also a critical and balanced introduction.
– Alexander J. Field (2001) *Altruistically Inclined?: The Behavioral Sciences, Evolutionary Theory, and the Origins of Reciprocity.*
  Field provided an institutional economic introduction to game theory. The textbook covers simple, repeated, and evolutionary game theory. Game theory is discussed in context of institutional concepts such as norms, institutions, and culture.
– David Easley and Jon Kleinberg (2010) *Networks, Crowds, and Markets: Reasoning About a Highly Connected World.*
  Easley and Kleinberg pursue an interdisciplinary approach discussing game theory, repeated and evolutionary game theory as well as graph theory and

applying the field of games on networks to a number of social, economic, and technical fields.

- Martin A. Nowak (2006) *Evolutionary Dynamics: Exploring the Equations of Life.*

  Nowak's textbook focuses on the evolutionary perspective of game theory. It provides a comprehensive mathematic introduction illustrated with a variety of examples from different fields but with a focus on evolutionary biology.

- Ross Cressman (2003) *Evolutionary Dynamics and Extensive Form Games.*

  Cressman provides a game theory textbook with special attention to extensive form games (not discussed in this section), evolutionary game theory, and other advanced topics.

- Fernando Vega-Redondo (2003) *Economics and the Theory of Games.*

  Vega-Redondo gives a broad introduction to game theory including all important concepts from the very basics to replicator dynamics and incomplete information games. The book explores also the economic implications and applications of the discussed concepts.

- Samuel Bowles (2006) *Microeconomics: Behavior, Institutions, and Evolution.*

  Bowles provides a general introduction to microeconomic theory; instead of following the usual neoclassical market approach, he does this from a game theory perspective.

Chapter References

Albin, P.S., Foley, D., 1992. Decentralized, dispersed exchange without an auctioneer. J. Econ. Behav. Organ. 18 (1), 27–51.

Aumann, R., 1985. What is game theory trying to accomplish? In: Arrow, K., Honkapohja, S. (Eds.), Frontiers of Economics. Basil Blackwell, Oxford, pp. 909–924.

Axelrod, R., 1984. The Evolution of Cooperation. Basic Books, New York, NY.

Bowles, S., 2006. Microeconomics: Behavior, Institutions, and Evolution. Princeton University Press, Princeton, NJ.

Chen, P., 2002. Microfoundations of macroeconomic fluctuations and the laws of probability theory: the principle of large numbers vs. rational expectations arbitrage. J. Econ. Behav. Organ. 49 (3), 327–344.

Cressman, R., 2003. Evolutionary Dynamics and Extensive Form Games. MIT Press, Cambridge and London.

Easley, D., Kleinberg, J., 2010. Networks, crowds, and markets: reasoning about a highly connected world. Cambridge University Press, Cambridge, New York, Melbourne, Madrid, Cape Town, Singapore, Sao Paolo, Delhi, Dubai, Tokyo, Mexico City.

Fehr, E., Fischbacher, U., Gächter, S., 2002. Strong reciprocity, human cooperation and the enforcement of social norms. Hum. Nat. 13 (1), 1–25.

Field, A.J., 2001. Altruistically Inclined? The Behavioral Sciences, Evolutionary Theory, and the Origins of Reciprocity. The University of Michigan Press, Ann Arbor, MI.

Finne, T.D., 1998. The three categories of decision making and information security. Comput. Secur. 17 (5), 397–405.

Gintis, H., 2000. Game Theory Evolving: A Problem-Centered Introduction to Modeling Strategic Behavior. Princeton Univ. Press, Princeton, NJ.

Hargreaves Heap, S.P., Varoufakis, Y., 2004. Game Theory: A Critical Introduction. Routledge, London, New York.

Harsanyi, J., 1973. Games with randomly disturbed payoffs: a new rationale for mixed-strategy equilibrium points. Int. J. Game Theory. 2 (1), 1–23.

Hurwicz, L., 1953. What has happened to the theory of games. Am. Econ. Rev. 43 (2), 398–405.

Kirman, A.P., 1997. The economy as an interactive system. In: Arthur, B.W., Durlauf, S.N., Lane, D.A. (Eds.), The Economy as a Complex Interactive System. Addison-Wesley, Reading, MA, pp. 491–531.

Maynard Smith, J., Price, G.R., 1973. The logic of animal conflict. Nature. 246, 15–18.

Myerson, R.B., 1978. Refinements of the Nash equilibrium concept. Int. J. Game Theory. 7 (2), 133–154.

Nash, J., 1950. Equilibrium points in n-person games. Proc. Natl. Acad. Sci. 36 (1), 48–49.

Nelson, R., Winter, S., 1982. An Evolutionary Theory of Economic Change. Harvard University Press, Cambridge, MA.

Neumann, J.V., Morgenstern, O., 1944. Theory of Games and Economic Behavior. Princeton University Press, Princeton, NJ.

Nowak, M.A., 2006. Evolutionary Dynamics: Exploring the Equations of Life. Belknap Press of Harvard University Press, Cambridge, London.

Rubinstein, A., 1979. Equilibrium in supergames with the overtaking criterion. J. Econ. Theory. 21 (1), 1–9.

Savage, L.J., 1951. The theory of statistical decision. J. Am. Stat. Assoc. 46 (253), 55–67.

Selten, R., 1975. A reexamination of the perfectness concept for equilibrium points in extensive games. Int. J. Game Theory. 41, 25–55.

Selten, R., 1983. Evolutionary stability in extensive two-person games. Math. Soc. Sci. 5, 269–363.

Simon, H.A., 1956. Rational choice and the structure of the environment. Psychol. Rev. 63 (2), 129–138.

Tversky, A., Kahneman, D., 1973. Availability: a heuristic for judging frequency and probability. Cognit. Psychol. 5 (2), 207–232.

Vega-Redondo, F., 2003. Economics and the Theory of Games. Cambridge University Press, New York, NY.

Further Reading—Online

For further reading, see the textbook website at http://booksite.elsevier.com/9780124115859

EXERCISES

1. Consider the following 2-person normal-form games.

I   Player 1

	Player 2 s_{B1}	s_{B1}
s_{A1}	2 / 2	3 / 0
s_{A2}	0 / 3	1 / 1

II   Player 1

	Player 2 s_{B1}	s_{B1}
s_{A1}	3 / 3	2 / 0
s_{A2}	0 / 2	1 / 1

III   Player 1

	Player 2 s_{B1}	s_{B1}
s_{A1}	3 / 3	0 / 2
s_{A2}	2 / 0	1 / 1

IV   Player 1

	Player 2 s_{B1}	s_{B1}
s_{A1}	0 / 0	3 / 2
s_{A2}	2 / 3	1 / 1

a. Can these games be solved using SESDS?
b. Which strategy configurations are Nash equilibria in pure strategies in these games?
c. Are there further Nash equilibria in mixed strategies? If so, compute the Nash equilibrium strategy for both players for each game.
d. Assess the evolutionary stability for each of the pure and mixed strategy Nash equilibria.
e. Assess, whether or not each of the equilibria in pure strategies is trembling-hand perfect.
f. Discuss for each of these games whether or not there are trigger strategies of a supergame consisting of an infinite sequence of repetitions of the respective normal-form game.

2. In the vicinity of an illegal rave, the police arrests two persons, T.H. Cunning and L.S. Deedful; they are accused of having been involved in organizing the party. Both are presented with the following deal: Confess and testify against the other and you will be released immediately if the other person denies having been involved (0 months in prison), while the other is convicted of creating public disorder (12 months in prison); if the other person confesses as well, the punishment for both is reduced (10 months in prison). Should both refuse to testify, the prosecutor lacks convincing evidence and both are released from prison after 1 month detention for questioning.

   Write this game in matrix notation and discuss its properties. Which of the solution concepts introduced in this chapter are appropriate to derive a solution? To which equilibrium do the respective solution concepts lead? What changes if this game is repeatedly played (say the rave takes place annually and the two above-mentioned persons are always the unlucky ones that get arrested)?

3. Kim, a first-year economics undergraduate, while eating a big tub of ice cream at the beach during her/his summer vacation, is approached by a party of extraterrestrial invaders who demand a share of the ice cream. As both Kim and the extraterrestrials

are both reasonable and strictly rational beings, they engage in a bargaining game with the extraterrestrials starting to propose a division of the remaining amount of ice cream. If Kim rejects, it is Kim's turn to propose a split. The bargaining process takes 1 min per offer (and rejection). As the sun is burning hot, the ice cream melts slowly but steadily one-tenth of the original amount per minute (i.e., nothing is left after 10 min).

a. Which outcome of the bargaining process is to be expected?

b. Suppose, the extraterrestrials—being unfamiliar with earth food—are unaware of the fact that the ice cream melts. How does the bargaining process and its outcome change?

c. Suppose, the encounter occurs not during summer vacation but during Christmas break when it is cold and the ice cream does not melt. How does the bargaining process and its outcome change?

4. Consider the game matrices in exercise 1 again. Suppose these games are played in an evolutionary population setting.

a. Which evolutionary stable strategies are there in each of the games?

b. Which equilibria are derived in a replicator dynamic model constructed from these normal-form games using the same approach used for the hawk–dove game in Section 8.7.3?

LIST OF SYMBOLS

G	A one-shot game
$G_0, G_1, G_2,$ $G_n, G_m, G', G'', \ldots$	Particular one-shot games
S	Set of possible strategies in a game G
i, j	Index variables for the agents (i) and strategies (j) involved in a game G
n	Number of agents involved in a game G
S_i	Set of possible strategies of agent i in a game G
s_i	A strategy of agent i in a game G
s_{-i}	A combination of strategies of all n agents except i in a game G
Π_i	Payoff of agent i in a game G
a, b, c, d	Payoffs in a 2-person 2-strategy normal-form game
I_i	Information set of agent i in a game G
s^*	Equilibrium combination of strategies, e.g., Nash equilibrium
s_i^*	Agent i's equilibrium strategy, element of the equilibrium combination of strategies s^*
$s_i^{\sim}$	Particular strategy of agent i, especially in contrast to an equilibrium strategy s_i^*
A, B	Particular agents
$s_{B1}, s_{B2}, s_{Bx}, \ldots, s_{Ax}, \ldots$	Particular strategies (of player A and B respectively)
$s^S = \{s_1^S, s_2^S, \ldots, s_n^S\}$	Particular dominant strategy equilibrium configuration
$s^N = \{s_1^N, s_2^N, \ldots, s_n^N\}$	Particular Nash equilibrium strategy configuration
$E(\sim)$	Expected value function, especially expected values of payoffs $E(\Pi)$
$H(s)$	Decision value of the Hurwicz decision rule (depending on the strategy)
α	Parameter for optimism in the Hurwicz decision rule
$L(s, Z)$	Opportunity costs of the Savage minimax regret decision rule
Z	State of the system in Savages minimax regret decision rule
σ_i	Particular mixed strategy of agent i
σ_{-i}	Particular combination of mixed strategies for all n agents except i
$\sigma^* = \{\sigma_i^*, \sigma_{-i}^*\}$	Equilibrium configuration in mixed strategies (e.g., Nash equilibrium in mixed strategies)
P	Probability for the row player to choose her first pure strategy playing a mixed strategy $\sigma = \begin{pmatrix} p \\ 1-p \end{pmatrix}$
q	Probability for the column player to choose her first pure strategy playing a mixed strategy $\sigma = \begin{pmatrix} q \\ 1-q \end{pmatrix}$

x	Number of pure strategies an agent i has
p_x	Probability to choose pure strategy x while playing a mixed strategy σ
$s_{i,x}$	Pure strategy x of player i
$\tilde{\sigma_i}$	Particular mixed strategy of agent i, especially in contrast to an equilibrium strategy σ_i^*
p^*, q^*	Mixed strategy Nash equilibrium specified by the mixed strategy probabilities
$\mathscr{A}$	Game matrix of a normal-form game
ε	Arbitrarily small probability
$M, \tilde{M}$	Particular mixed strategies
m	Probability for an agent i to choose her first pure strategy playing a mixed strategy $M = \begin{pmatrix} m \\ 1-m \end{pmatrix}$
$G_{\text{Selten}}^\varepsilon, G_{\text{Myerson}}^\varepsilon$	Selten-type and Myerson-type perturbed games as modified versions of the game G
$p_{s,A}, p_{s,B}$	Perturbing probabilities for the strategy choices of players A, B in a Myerson-type perturbed game $G_{\text{Myerson}}^\varepsilon$
G^E	Particular extensive game
V	Set of states of an extensive game G^E
V_A	Subset of V in which player A (and not any other player) has to choose her next move

$\mathscr{G}$	Particular repeated game
V_{nf}	Set of nonfinal states of a repeated or extensive game
t	Time index
T	Number of iterations of a finitely repeated game $\mathscr{G}$
s_i^G	Strategy of an agent i in a repeated game $\mathscr{G}$
δ	Discount factor
a_{Maximin}	Discounted maximin payoffs of a supergame $\mathscr{G}$
$s_{i,\text{Maximin}}$	Maximin strategy of an agent i
$s_{\text{Trigger}}^{\mathscr{G}}$	Trigger strategy of an agent i in a supergame $\mathscr{G}$
$\mathscr{P}_{\mathscr{G}\mathscr{V}}$	Evolutionary population setting
$\mathscr{G}_{\mathscr{G}\mathscr{V}}$	Underlying game of an evolutionary population setting $\mathscr{P}_{\mathscr{G}\mathscr{V}}$
z	Index for the number of state variables
$\theta_t, \theta(t)$	State variables at time t
$\theta_{i,t}$	Element i (for agent type i) of the state variable vector θ_t at time t
θ^*, θ_t^*	Equilibrium, fixed point of the dynamic system (specific dynamically static state variable values)
$f_{i,t}$	Individual fitness of agent type i at time t
ϕ_t	Average fitness of the population at time t
$\tilde{F_D}(\sim), \tilde{F_d}(\sim),$ $F_D(\sim), F_d(\sim)$	Functions
λ	Eigenvalue

Tools III: An Introduction to Simulation and Agent-Based Modeling

Cartoon by Randy Glasbergen

9.1 INTRODUCTION

Simulation as a method is both much more powerful and less exact than deterministic methods. It may reveal information about a system under investigation, which could not be obtained by deterministic computation either because the system is not analytically solvable or because we lack the computation power and resources to do so. The fundamental difference from exhaustive deterministic analysis of the whole system is that simulation does not attempt to investigate any possible state, let alone the possible relations between the states of the system. Rather, for a finite set of valid states, the behavior is traced to establish a general idea of the resulting trends. The initial state can be modified slightly to derive knowledge about the consequences of particular modifications, particular influences, or particular patterns in the system's state. Nevertheless, the system under investigation still has to be well-specified in order to compute its future behavior.

While manual simulation (with pen and paper) is basically possible, it is convenient to employ computers, as only large computation power enables both, to deal with highly complex systems and to derive sufficient data for sufficiently many different settings to investigate a system of greater complexity. This is also why simulation as a scientific method was not widely used and developed before the advent of computers.

This chapter gives an overview of basic techniques, common problems, and the resulting advantages and disadvantages of computer simulation. It further provides an example of the use of computer simulation in a microeconomic context and thereby offers an introduction to the discussion of models of direct interdependence in the following chapters of the textbook.

Note that simulation is not an exact method in a formal-analytical sense, as there is always the possibility that the results of the simulation do not or only partly match the true behavior of the system under investigation. Therefore, simulation should only be employed if other scientific techniques are not available. Moreover, the weaknesses of this method have always to be taken into account, focusing especially on the typical errors arising from these weaknesses (as discussed in Section 9.3).

However, if a system is indeed highly complex[1] so that deterministic analysis is not feasible or not economic, simulation may be very useful. This is especially the case, if

- a system's solution or dynamics is not exactly solvable in a formal-analytical way;
- a system is basically computable but would take an unacceptably long computation time;
- a system does not show regular convergent behavior. That is, if the trajectories diverge, not only the system's future variable values, but also its future behavior depend on the initial values, and, if present, stochastic shocks.

Simulation has come to be widely used in economics especially in the form of *agent-based simulation*: a large number of entities with similar but heterogeneous characteristics are simulated as if they were independent in their decision making. This allows to construct models with a much more generic microfoundation than it is the case for general equilibrium models. The systems are, however, also much larger, which makes deterministic analysis unfeasible.

Simulation is also a constructive method. It does not only allow to show that a solution of a type of behavior is theoretically possible, but it also shows how it can actually occur and offers specific predictions about the necessary conditions. One may think of it as a type of a mathematical proof: We prove something by doing it. An analysis of the probability of

the occurrence of a certain situation is also possible.

As mentioned, simulation could also be done with pen and paper and without a computer. In fact, the history of simulation goes back to a time long before modern computer technology.[2] Its first recorded use was by the French mathematician Comte de Buffon who managed to approximate the number π with a mechanical experiment and some computation in the late eighteenth century. While he did not intend to establish a novel method and probably thought of it as a simple experiment, his study clearly has characteristics of simulation in that he did not try to measure or analyze but rather to approximate making use of statistics and a large number of observations. Similar approaches were taken by other scientists later on—notably William Sealy Gosset who derived the Student's t-distribution by simulation in the early 1900s. But it was not until the 1940s when simple computation technology was already around that the method was properly and extensively described and studied by a group of mathematicians who saw its full potential: John von Neumann, Stanislaw Ulam, and Nicholas Metropolis. Simulation was used more and more commonly first in natural sciences and engineering but had made the jump to the social sciences only by the 1970s when agent-based simulation was more widely employed for the first time by Richard Nelson, Sidney Winter, and other evolutionary economists. Some of the resulting models will be presented in Chapter 13.

This chapter introduces the method (Section 9.2), addresses a number of specific problems of the method (Section 9.3), and analyzes advantages and disadvantages (Section 9.4) before giving an example for a simulation study

---

[1]For a formal definition of the term also in the context of feasibility or unfeasibility of deterministic and simulation methods, see Chapter 11.

[2]For a short overview over the history of simulation, see Goldman et al. (2009).

in Section 9.5. The final section is a practical introduction using the programming language Python and showing how the example from Section 9.5 can be programmed as a simulation model. It should be noted that this chapter can only give a brief overview. However, some suggestions of introductions dedicated to the topic of simulation are added at the end of the chapter.

9.2 METHOD

While it is possible to compute targeted approximations for not exactly computable values, the usual application of computer simulation is to study the general behavior, or aspects of that behavior, of systems. Simulation provides a powerful tool to investigate not only results but also development paths. The following procedure will typically be employed:

1. *Identify the system under investigation.* At this stage, it has to be determined what will be included in the system and what will not. The scope of the system has to be chosen such that the complexity is kept as small as possible, however without neglecting important influences in order to be able to derive meaningful results that resemble the real-world structures after which the system is modeled.
2. *Formalize the system under investigation.* A mathematical model has to be developed; the components of the system have to be transformed into variables and equations.
3. *Determine whether simulation is a viable and effective method* to investigate the system. Is, for instance, deterministic analysis feasible (so that it is not necessary to resort to simulation)? On the other hand: Is sufficient information about the system available to allow the construction of a simulation model with which one could hope to reproduce real-world patterns?

4. *Formalize the mathematical model as a computer program.* Note that this is the most important stage; the behavior of the model is shaped by the program. While the mathematical formalization is a great simplification of the real world, the program formalization differs again fundamentally from the mathematical model. There are considerable limitations to numerical computation that will be discussed in detail later, which is why this stage is the main source of errors. Specifically, it is defined how data is to be shaped and how it is to be transformed. That may include *constants*, which are unchangeable, *parameters*, set at the beginning of the particular simulation run, and *variables*, which may change through the process of the simulation. Of course, the program specifies also when and how a variable is changed.
5. *Define the input value or value range for each parameter*, i.e., determine which part of the system is to be investigated and how deeply it is to be studied. First, several evenly or randomly distributed points of the state space may be chosen to monitor the general behavior. Second, to eliminate volatility (if stochastic variables are included), the simulation may be run several times for the same input values. Third, to study the sensitivity of the results, a particular state and several points of its "close neighborhood" (in terms of variable values) may be investigated. These may of course be set for each variable independently.
6. *Run the simulation.*
7. *Analyze the results.* This includes determining whether the model is indeed a representation of what was to be investigated (validation), and if the results are reliable (verification).

A simulation model is said to be valid if it resembles the problem it was designed to simulate, i.e., if the data it produces resembles the behavior of the real-world structure it simulates. (In other words, the model is valid if its formulation is correct.) It is called reliable if the behavior it generates is reproducible in subsequent simulation runs, i.e., if it does not change widely and randomly. A valid simulation model may or may not be reliable.

No simulation model can be completely valid and perfectly reliable. An unreliable or invalid model may produce data that is not related to the real-world behavior at all (arbitrary/random data generated by the model). Models may further produce data that is correlated to the real-world behavior, but shows other systematic influences that do not resemble the real world—these models are said to be biased. A systematic bias represents an invalidity in the formulation of the model.

9.3 PARTICULAR ISSUES IN COMPUTER SIMULATION

9.3.1 Computability

Computers are discrete machines; they consist of some type of memory to hold data and at least one processing unit to perform operations on the data held in memory—one at a time. In order to run a simulation of a model on a computer, the model must be computable and it must be possible to slice the data necessary for the simulation into finite entities on which the computer can perform operations. A computable problem is one that could be solved on hypothetical computer with infinite memory—called a *Turing machine.* The Turing machine, named after the English mathematician Alan Turing is not a real computer but a concept used in mathematics to demonstrate or disprove the computability of certain problems. Computability requires that the model can be transformed into a well-defined sequence of algorithms. Computer

simulations do therefore always work with either discrete problems or with discretizations of continuous problems as opposed to, for instance, general equilibrium models which are sometimes infinite dimensional and generally neither finite nor discrete. Note that this is also the source for some of the major criticisms of computer simulation as a method.

9.3.2 Entities

A model of a system is by definition a simplification of the real system which it therefore only approximates. This is not a particular issue of computer simulation, but is an extraordinarily important one. The model usually has to be *finite* which for the real-world system is not necessarily the case. Thus, the model will consist of a finite number of well-defined (often similar, nearly identical) entities with well-defined (often heterogeneous) behavior, representing substantially more complex structures in the real world. Entities that are modeled to behave as if they were autonomous decisions makers are called *agents*. Other entities (e.g., goods exchanged by the agents) may also be present.

9.3.3 Numbers

Computers cannot deal with irrational numbers and will perform better for rational numbers the easier they are *representable* as fractions of integers. Numbers will be approximated by easier representable numbers, if necessary. This happens at the expense of exactness, but there are benefits in terms of storage space and computation time. This has considerable consequences, as rounding errors may sum up over time. But there are even more problems. Computers employ specific number types, able to store a defined range of numbers each. If a value that is to be stored does not fall into the range of the type the corresponding variable is defined as, there are three possible behaviors of the program that may result from this: the variable type might be changed, the program might fail, or (worst of all) the variable might "overflow." (An "overflow" of a variable is the transgression of the maximum value it can hold. All bits of the variable are 1 at this point; further "increment" by 1 will change all bits to 0 such that the variable takes its lowest possible value and the program will return wrong results.)

9.3.4 Time

Time has to be *discrete* in computer simulation. To work with continuous time, the computer would have to be either infinitely fast, or able at least to deal with irrational numbers (for a variable representing continuous time). Continuous time systems can be approximated, but the approximations will actually always be time-discrete. Of course, not every simulation needs time as a feature, but dynamic systems are usually the most complex ones, for which computer simulation is required. The simulation's frequency will be different from the computer's processor frequency, as there are usually several to many necessary arithmetic operations per time step—therefore the simulation will need its own clock, its own internal time variable.

9.3.5 Randomness

A special problem is how to generate stochastic influences, i.e., random numbers and stochastic distributions. This is an unsolvable problem, as computers work deterministically and computably and are therefore not able to generate true randomness but only pseudorandom numbers.

As mentioned earlier, some numbers are more easily representable than others, all distributions will therefore be discrete, and all values are of finite complexity. Hence for each level of complexity, there is only a finite number of representable values. Partly because of this, partly as the complexity of the computer itself is finite, each sequence of random numbers generated by a computer is repetitive from a certain point on—called the *period* of the random number generator.

Pseudorandom number generators usually work with the *modulo operation* (denoted by the % character—the remainder of a division), but may be extended using other operations or constantly changing globally available variables, such as the computer's system clock. The most common basic pseudorandom number generator, also employed in the programming language C++'s rand()- and srand()-functions, is the linear congruential generator:

$$X_{n+1} = (aX_n + c)\%m \tag{9.1}$$

where X_n is the sequence of the random numbers, a, c, and m are integers, a and m positive, c at least nonnegative.

9.3.6 Simplicity

The more complex a simulation model is, the more difficult is the interpretation of the obtained results. With a vast number of parameters, it becomes more challenging to identify the crucial influence for a certain observed behavior; a more complicated program makes it more difficult to find and correct errors and complex interrelations of variables may lead to genuinely chaotic behavior of the system itself. It is therefore a crucial principle to keep simulation models (as well as formal models) as simple as possible. However, it is also important to retain descriptiveness in order not to diverge too far from the system to be simulated. This second principle conflicts with the former one (simplicity) to some degree.

9.3.7 Monte Carlo Simulations

As mentioned in Section 9.1, there are many reasons to conduct simulations. A widely used technique for instance is the approximation of mathematical quantities, functions, or distributions that are difficult to compute analytically. This technique is called Monte Carlo simulation or Monte Carlo method, reportedly named after the casino where Stanislaw Ulam's uncle used to gamble because Ulam described the method formally in the context of approximating stochastic probabilities in games of chance in a resource-efficient way. Note that the earliest recorded uses of simulation including Buffon's experiment and Gosset's approximation of the student's t-distribution may be seen as examples for Monte Carlo simulations. This chapter will not specifically go into detail on this technique as the focus lies on the more explorative technique of agent-based simulations that is more widely used in evolutionary, institutional, and complex systems branches of economics. However, since every simulation does by definition correspond to a well-defined mathematical algorithm, every simulation may be seen as a Monte Carlo approach in that it tries to determine certain properties of that algorithm—what differs is rather the perspective in that explorative simulation is usually not interested in any particular quantity but in the possibility to generate certain behavioral patterns or to explain certain observations with a particular set of assumptions.

9.4 ADVANTAGES AND DISADVANTAGES OF SIMULATION

As was already mentioned earlier, consideration should be given to whether simulation is the appropriate method for the problem in question. The ease and convenience of computer simulation is counterweighted by several considerable disadvantages. The advantages include:

- Simulation as a scientific technique enables approximation of some otherwise incomputable results.
- Highly complex systems become, if modeled appropriately, predictable within the technical limits such as reasonable computation time.
- Sufficiently modeled systems (i.e., given the model is valid) allow quite flexible investigations; it is possible to study each element of the system, each modification in this element, and it is possible to change the scale of the variables (e.g., to contract or expand space and time).
- A great variety of possible states and dynamics may be studied; therefore, it is much easier to identify complex mechanisms and constraints of the system.
- Preliminary testing prior to more in-depth analysis is possible, which may save time and other resources.
- Simulation may constitute a bridge to behavioral economics. Particularly agent-based models allow behavioral algorithms to be integrated much easier than this is the case with, e.g., systems of equations, since behavioral algorithms follow a structure similar to computational algorithms.
- Simulation models are easy to calibrate using empirical data. Simulations may therefore also be suitable for comparative analysis for, e.g., assessing the effects of policy changes. In fact, in other fields such as engineering or computer science the use of simulation to test certain models before using them is widely established practice.

The particular disadvantages on the other hand are:

- Simulation results in general are to some degree unreliable, and may not be treated as certain data.

- The results might be difficult to understand and to interpret, which is another source of error.
- The capacity of computation in general is limited and (given the capacity) also restricted to certain types of values and operations. This may influence the quality of the result. There is, e.g., no guarantee that a discrete-time model will behave in the same way as a real-world system with continuous time.
- Unawareness of these limitations or of the functioning of specific tools may lead to further errors.
- The chosen scale of variables and parameters may bias the results.
- Finally, there is (as yet) no unified structure for comparative analysis of simulation models and results.

9.5 MICROECONOMICS AND COMPUTER SIMULATION

9.5.1 Computer Simulation in Microeconomics

Simulation as a method is particularly useful when dealing with systems that are inherently complex. This is especially the case for economics and other social sciences where even the basic elements—humans—are complex and indeed incomputable systems. This forces general analytical models such as the neoclassical equilibrium theory as discussed in Chapter 5 to make a number of greatly simplifying assumptions—among others the homogeneity of agents to which we get back to in Section 9.5.2. Computer simulation does however allow the analysis of more complex settings though some degree of simplification is required to keep the simulation models simple enough for a conclusive interpretation of the results. Most importantly, simulation as a method in economics helps to bridge the gap

between microeconomic and macroeconomic models.

Most simulation models in microeconomics follow a common pattern. They contrast a micro-level of similar but not usually homogeneous agents with the aggregate level of the simulation, in turn representing the system or sector level. In turn, there are *macro-* (i.e., system level) and *micro-variables* respectively describing the system or one agent. *Macro- and micro-state variables* describe the entire variable set of the system or the agent at one point in time and *macro- and micro-parameters* refer to the basic values or properties of the system or an individual agent beyond that entity's "control." The simulation program usually cycles through the agents letting them behave as if they were making independent decisions and taking the appropriate actions. According to specified (homogeneous or heterogeneous) decision rules, the agents manipulate their micro-variables while their control over macro-variables and their own micro-parameters is minimal. Those change as a result of all actions of all agents but have significant effects on the individual agent's decisions. This modeling approach is called *agent-based modeling*, the distinctive property being that such programs behave as if micro-level agents were acting independently. As with all simulations, agent-based modeling uses discrete (or quasi-continuous) time (the timesteps being called iterations). Note that agents follow defined rules, thus implying a concept of bounded rationality. The accuracy of such a model in mapping the real world is limited; for details on this question, see Chapters 1 and 8.

9.5.2 Homogeneous Versus Heterogeneous Agents

The assumption of homogeneity among agents (the "representative agent") was of course most radically developed in neoclassical microeconomics. It reduces, like the assumption of independence of these actors, the complexity of the system to such an extent that it becomes computable by deterministic means.

Let N agents be represented by the state vectors $a_{1,t}, \ldots, a_{N,t}$ at time t. Furthermore, P shall denote a vector of global variables or parameters, which might represent environmental conditions, or in standard neoclassical microeconomics, most importantly, prices. The system is then described by equation (9.2) (f denotes a function that is for this setting homogeneous for all agents).

$$a_{n,t+1} = f(a_{n,t}, P) \quad n = 1, \ldots, N \quad (9.2)$$

However, as argued repeatedly in this book, both assumptions are unsuitable for many questions. Real-world actors are neither homogeneous in their incentives nor in their properties, though microeconomic modeling may start with relatively homogeneous settings in order to keep complexity moderate. But first and foremost, the agents are interdependent and interacting. By this, the system becomes highly complex. First, the assumption of homogeneity is abandoned:

$$a_{n,t+1} = f_n(a_{n,t}, P) \quad n = 1, \ldots, N \quad (9.3)$$

While Eq. (9.3) is doubtlessly more complex, it is presumably still computable and predictable as a whole, as will be shown. This, however, changes if the assumption of independence is dropped:

$$a_{n,t+1} = f(d_1 \times a_{1,t}, d_2 \times a_{2,t}, \ldots, d_N \times a_{N,t}, P)$$
$$n = 1, \ldots, N \quad (9.4)$$

where $d_n = \{0, 1\}$ are N dummy variables, indicating whether the state of agent a_n depends on the previous state of the agent a_m or not. Note that this implies a network structure between the agents where positive dummy variables ($d_n = 1$) are indicating edges (links). Also note that this formulation includes the aforementioned standard neoclassical setting: For the neoclassical system, for any agent n all dummy variables, except d_n, are zero.

9.5.3 Simulating Games on Networks: The Example of the Prisoners' Dilemma

Consider a system of 100 interactive agents playing repeated prisoners' dilemma games in pairs, three repetitions with each opponent in each iteration. They are either cooperative players, employing the tit-for-tat (TFT) strategy (see Chapter 3), or noncooperative, defecting always (All-D). Initially, there are 30 cooperative and 70 noncooperative agents. The numerical payoff structure of Figure 9.1 is chosen as in a similar but more extensive simulation study by Axelrod (1984).

Those whose aggregated payoff exceeds the mean of the payoffs of their interacting partners will "reproduce" their habit. One among their less lucky interacting partners adopts their strategy (unless all of their interacting partners are either already playing the same strategy or have already adopted another strategy in the same iteration).

The strategies and the switching behavior can equivalently be described as the functions f_n. If, however, all agents have the same interaction partners, i.e., if each agent interacts with every other agent (*total connectivity*), the system can be deterministically computed with the current strategy shares as global variable P:

$$a_{\text{TFT},t+1} = f_{\text{TFT},t}(P)$$

$$a_{\text{All-}D,t+1} = f_{\text{All-}D,t}(P)$$

Specifically, the payoff each defector gets is:

$$3(n_{\text{All-}D} - 1) + (5 + 2)n_{\text{TFT}} = 417$$

		Player B	
		Strategy 1	Strategy 2
Player A	Strategy 1	3 3	5 0
	Strategy 2	0 5	1 1

FIGURE 9.1 Prisoners' dilemma with the incentive structure as in Axelrod (1984).

(A)   (B)

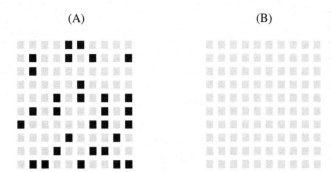

FIGURE 9.2 Network game on a complete network. TFT players (dark) and defectors (light) in a network game (repeated prisoners' dilemma) on a complete network (total connectivity): (A) initial state (30% TFT players) and (B) after one iteration (0% TFT).

($n_{\text{All-}D}$ and n_{TFT} denoting the number of All-D and of TFT players, respectively) while the TFT players get

$$3 \times 3 \times (n_{\text{TFT}} - 1) + 2n_{\text{All-}D} = 401$$

As the average is $(417 \times 70 + 401 \times 30)/100 = 412.2$, the All-D players finish all above this average; hence, the system will switch all 30 TFT players to defective behavior in the very first iteration (see Figure 9.2).

If there is no total connectivity, this is not that obvious any more. Let the actors be arranged on a two-dimensional 10×10 lattice where the interacting partners are their direct horizontal, vertical, and diagonal neighbors (*Moore neighborhood*).

The simulation of both a system with total connectivity in Figure 9.2 and a system with Moore neighborhood in Figure 9.3 shows that while the above prediction of the total connectivity system is correct, its behavior is hence trivial and predictable, the Moore neighborhood system shows complex and maybe chaotic patterns. Models of the emergence of cooperation are explored in more detail in Chapters 3, 13, and 14.

9.6 SIMULATION IN PRACTICE: AN EXAMPLE

9.6.1 Some Preliminary Considerations

Having presented the method on an entirely theoretic level so far, we conclude the chapter with a short glimpse at the practice of simulation. The purpose of this section is to illustrate what was presented so far and to allow the interested reader a "quickstart" in using the technique. It should be noted, however, that this is no detailed introduction; we strongly advise the consultation of textbooks on the subject, a selection of which will be recommended at the end of the chapter.

The first thing to do when conducting a simulation study (even before the process shown in Section 9.2) is to select the proper tools, most importantly the *programming language* to be used. There is a substantial number of alternatives; in the first sections we have mentioned C++, which is a good choice for resource-intensive simulations. It is fast and efficient in computation but less flexible and more difficult to program; it also is a *compiled language*, i.e., the program has to be compiled for the specific system before execution. Other common languages of this category include Fortran, Pascal, Lisp, and Haskell. A more accessible but less efficient alternative are *scripting languages* that are run in a *virtual machine* which compiles and executes the program on-the-fly. Scripting languages are often also more intuitive and perform many routine operations (such as memory allocation) automatically in the background. Popular scripting languages include Perl, PHP, Tcl, and Python. Some few compiled languages exist that are still executed using a virtual machine and are thus still platform independent—this includes Java. All those are general-purpose programming languages as opposed to

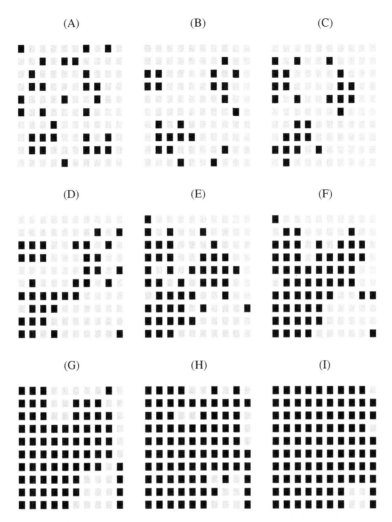

FIGURE 9.3 Network game on a lattice network. TFT players (dark) and defectors (light) in a network game (repeated prisoners' dilemma) on a lattice network with Moore neighborhood: (A) initial state (30% TFT players), (B) after one iteration (22% TFT), (C) after two iterations (26% TFT), (D) after three iterations (36% TFT), (E) after four iterations (46% TFT), (F) after five iterations (57% TFT), (G) after six iterations (73% TFT), (H) after seven iterations (84% TFT), and (I) after eight iterations (94% TFT).

special purpose programming languages for statistics (R), for algebra (Mathematica, MATLAB), and even agent-based modeling (NetLogo). Specialization also facilitates programming while using general-purpose languages gives more flexibility and efficiency.

Our example will use the open source general-purpose scripting language Python. In order to run the example scripts given in this section, a virtual machine is required; for editing the code it is recommended to use a development environment. The standard open source Python virtual machine (including the standard programming libraries) can be downloaded from python.org; a recommendable free and open source development environment is Spyder which can be found at http://code.google.com/p/spyderlib; both are available for all major operating systems.[3] Note that you can either save the scripts as plaintext .py files and execute them directly with the virtual machine or run them from the development environment.

9.6.2 General Programming Concepts and Python Commands

The programming language Python is mostly straightforward. Each command is usually given on a separate line without indent. (Indentation is interpreted as changing the level of the code block; see the code listings below.) Variables are defined and assigned values at the same time with an = operator; the identifier (the variable name) is on the left-hand side, the assigned value on the right. Comments—whatever follows on the same line after a # character—are ignored by the interpreter and can be used to add explanations. Output is controlled by the print() function. The following defines two variables a and b and prints the result of the addition of the two:

```
a = 12          #assignment (right to left, i.e. 12 is assigned to a)
b = 6           #another assignment
c = a + b       #addition
print(c)        #print function
```

The code obviously results in the following output

```
18
```

Other simple arithmetic operations are equally straightforward. The following code:

```
c = b - a       #subtraction
print(c)
c = a*b         #multiplication
print(c)
c = a/b         #division
print(c)
c = a**b        #power
print(c)
```

gives the output:

```
-6
```

```
72
2.0
2985984
```

If the value is assigned to the same variable, i.e., if we for instance want to increment a variable a by 1, we can shorten the statement a = a + 1 to a + = 1 (or for multiplications a* = 1, subtractions a- = 1, etc). There are different types of variables. Different from C++, however, variables are not explicitly defined as being of a certain type, the virtual machine is able to assign an appropriate type depending on the assignment:

```
a = 12          #assigns a integer value
print(type(a))
a = 12.0        #assigns a real-valued number
```

[3]For some operating systems, packages are available that include both the virtual machine, the integrated development environment, and additional resources for scientific computing with python; one of those (also free and open source) is Python(x,y) which is available at https://code.google.com/p/pythonxy/. Also note that more advanced techniques may require further programming libraries not included with the virtual machine from python.org. Notable packages commonly used for scientific simulation in Python are Numpy, Scipy, and Matplotlib. All of these are free, open source, and can conveniently be obtained from the open source package repository Sourceforge (http://sourceforge.org); they are also already included in the Python(x,y) package. For the examples included in this chapter, however, no additional modules are needed and the standard package from python.org suffices.

```
print(type(a))
a = 'text'       #assigns a string of text
print(type(a))
    <class 'int'>
    <class 'float'>
    <class 'str'>
```

There are functions for transforming variable types, `str(a)` for instance transforms a (int or float or ...) variable `a` into string. We can also define an array (or list) of values gives the output:

```
a = [0.5,1.0,1.7,12.0]
print(type(a))
        <class 'list'>
```

the individual elements of which can be accessed with an index number in square brackets (numbering starts at 0, not at 1)

```
print(a[0])
print(type(a[0]))
        0.5
        <class 'float'>
```

There are some general functions that can be performed on lists. `sum()` for instance returns the sum of a numeric list; `append()` adds one more element to the list; for examples see the code listings at the end of the current section and in section 9.6.3. For multidimensional lists (arrays of arrays), we use multiple index brackets, e.g., `a[3][1]` returns the second element (index 1) of the array which is the fourth (index 3) element of `a`.

Further, we can state conditions usually by using comparison operators $<$, $>$, $<=$, $>=$ (smaller than, larger than, smaller or equal, and larger or equal), as well as != (not equal) and == (equal); note that for the latter we have to use two = characters in order to distinguish the comparison from the assignment operation. To control the program flow we can make use of if-statements which define a code block that is only executed if the condition holds true.

```
if a == b:              #if statement
    print('a == b is true')
else:
    print('a == b is false')
    a == b is false
```

Indentation blocks (and thus also if-statements) can be nested. Further, we can define loops if code blocks are to be executed repeatedly. The following loop is repeated 9 times and thus computes stepwise 2^{10}:

```
a = 2
for i in range (0,9):
    a = a*2
print(a)
    1024
```

Code blocks that are needed several times in different parts of the program can be defined as a function (the definition of which is preceded by `def`). Consider the following function; it accepts exactly two numeric arguments (input variables) and returns the product of the two.

```
def my_function(x,y):
    z = x*y
    return(z)
```

We would call the function as follows:

```
a = my_function(7,10)
print(a)
    70
```

Finally, we can define custom data structures (variable types) as classes which may have attributes (variables) and methods (functions that are specifically designed for the class and may be run on an instance of it). Every class has a constructor method—a function that is executed whenever an instance of this class (i.e., a variable of this type) is created; the constructor is always named __init__(self) where the self is a reference to the instance of the class that is being created. All methods (functions of classes) are handed their instance of the class as an input variable and must therefore accept this (self) argument. The following defines a class which has two variables, one list, one float and a method that adds a new element to the list and assigns the other variable the list's sum.

```
class my_class():
    def __init__(self):
        self.v = 0.0
        self.m = [0.9,0.1,0.1]
    def my_method(self,z):
        self.m.append(z)
        self.v = sum(self.m)
```

Now we have to create an instance of the class. Having done that we can access the instance's attributes and methods by calling the instance name and the attribute (or method) name separated by a dot, i.e., if the instance is named a, we can access the method by calling (not forgetting to provide the required input, in this case 5.0) a.my_method(5.0). Thus we create an instance and call it as:

```
a = my_class()
a.my_method(10.0)
print(a.v)
    11.1
```

Of course we can also create large arrays of instances of a class:

```
a = []
```

```
for i in range (0,10000):
    a.append(my_class())
```

This is the advantage of object-oriented[4] programming for agent-based modeling: We can define the agents as a class of which we then can create as many instances as we like.

Finally, from time to time, we need functions or classes that are predefined in separate modules. In this case we tell the virtual machine to include these by using the import statement. The following example imports the random module and obtains an observation of a uniform distribution between 0 and 1:

```
import random
a = random.uniform(0,1)
print(a)
```

9.6.3 Implementing a Simulation in Python

The concepts of Python programming introduced in Section 9.6.2 are sufficient to conduct some simple and even moderately complicated simulations including the simulation the results of which were presented in Section 9.5.

First we list the complete program; after this we will go into detail on how it is structured and why:

```
import random
class agent():
    def __init__(self):
        global agentnumber
        self.id = agentnumber
        agentnumber += 1
        if random.uniform(0,1) < 0.3:
            self.strategy = 1
        else:
            self.strategy = 0
```

[4]Classes for instance are objects but the concept is broader. Programming languages that make heavy use of such concepts are called object-oriented; this includes virtually all newer programming languages.

```
                self.payoff = 0.0
                self.neighbors = []
                self.memory = []
                self.lidx = []
        def evaluate_strategy(self):
                number_of_neighbors = len(self.neighbors)
                neighbor_average_payoff = 0
                for n in self.neighbors:
                        neighbor_average_payoff+=n.payoff
                neighbor_average_payoff/= number_of_neighbors
                if self.payoff < neighbor_average_payoff:
                        maximum = 0
                        oldstrategy = self.strategy
                        for n in self.neighbors:
                                if n.payoff > maximum:
                                        maximum = n.payoff
                                        self.strategy = n.strategy
                        if not oldstrategy == self.strategy:
                                for i in range (0,len(self.memory)):
                                        self.memory[i] = 1
def mn(agent1,agent2):                #make neighbors function
        agent1.neighbors.append(agent2)
        agent2.lidx.append(len(agent1.memory))
        agent1.memory.append(1)
        agent2.neighbors.append(agent1)
        agent1.lidx.append(len(agent2.memory))
        agent2.memory.append(1)
def play(agent1,agent2,idx1,idx2):
        if agent1.strategy == 1 and agent1.memory[idx1] == 1:
                agent2.memory[idx2] = 1
                if agent2.strategy == 1 and agent2.memory[idx2] == 1:
                        agent1.memory[idx1] = 1
                        agent1.payoff+=3
                        agent2.payoff+=3
                else:
                        agent1.memory[idx1] = 0
                        agent1.payoff+=0
                        agent2.payoff+=5
        else:
                agent2.memory[idx2] = 0
                if agent2.strategy==1 and agent2.memory[idx2]==1:
                        agent1.memory[idx1] = 1
                        agent1.payoff += 0
                        agent2.payoff += 5
                else:
                        agent1.memory[idx1] = 0
```

III. FURTHER TOOLS AND THE ANALYSIS OF COMPLEX ECONOMIES

```
                            agent1.payoff += 1
                            agent2.payoff += 1

agentnumber = 0
grid_size = 10
iterations = 10

agent_arr = []                    #create agent array
for i in range (0,grid_size):
      agent_arr.append([])
      for j in range (0,grid_size):
            agent_arr[i].append(agent())

for i in range (0,grid_size):
      for j in range (0,grid_size):
            if not i==0:
                  if not j == 0:
                        mn(agent_arr[i-1][j-1],agent_arr[i][j])
                  mn(agent_arr[i-1][j],agent_arr[i][j])
                  if not j+1 == grid_size:
                        mn(agent_arr[i-1][j+1],agent_arr[i][j])
            if not j == 0:
                  mn(agent_arr[i][j-1],agent_arr[i][j])

for t in range(0,iterations):
      for i in range (0,grid_size):
            for j in range (0,grid_size):
                  for k in range (0,len(agent_arr [i][j].neighbors)):
                        agent1 = agent_arr [i][j]
                        agent2 = agent_arr [i][j].neighbors[k]
                        idx2 = agent_arr [i][j].lidx[k]
                        idx1 = agent_arr [i][j].neighbors[k].lidx[idx2]
                        play(agent1,agent2,idx1,idx2)
      for i in range (0,grid_size):
            for j in range (0,grid_size):
                  agent_arr[i][j].evaluate_strategy()
      for i in range (0,grid_size):
            for j in range (0,grid_size):
                  agent_arr[i][j].payoff = 0.0
      print('Iteration ',t)
      for i in range (0,grid_size):
            printstring = ''
            for j in range (0,grid_size):
                  printstring += str(agent_arr[i][j].strategy)
            print(printstring)
input()
```

The program starts with the import of the random module and the definition of the agent class as well as two functions, `mn()` and `play()`. According to the class definition,

```
def __init__(self):
    global agentnumber
    self.id = agentnumber
    agentnumber += 1
    if random.uniform(0,1) < 0.3:
        self.strategy = 1
    else:
        self.strategy = 0
    self.payoff = 0.0
    self.neighbors = []
    self.memory = []
    self.lidx = []
```

agent objects have five attributes, three of which are list variables (`neighbors` holding links to the agent's neighbor agents, `memory` holding her memory of the neighbor agent's actions in the same sequence as well as a third variable[5]). The other two attributes are variables, one recording the agent's strategy `strategy` with 1 for TFT, 0 for defection, and the other for recording the agent's payoff. Note that the random function ensures that 30% of the agents initially are cooperators while 70% are initially defectors. Further note that the lists initially are empty; the grid structure will be established in the `mn()` function.

The class also defines a method `evaluate_strategy()` which consists of three parts. In the first five lines it computes the average payoff of the neighbor agents:

```
def evaluate_strategy(self):
    number_of_neighbors = len(self.neighbors)
    neighbor_average_payoff = 0
    for n in self.neighbors:
        neighbor_average_payoff += n.payoff
    neighbor_average_payoff /= number_of_neighbors
```

After this, the method checks whether the agent performs good or bad compared to her neighbors:

```
if self.payoff < neighbor_average_payoff:
```

Then, if the performance is not good, the strategy of the neighbor with the highest payoff is chosen and the agent switches to this strategy:

```
maximum = 0
oldstrategy = self.strategy
for n in self.neighbors:
    if n.payoff > maximum:
        maximum = n.payoff
        self.strategy = n.strategy
```

Finally, if the agent's strategy has changed, her memory is also cleared. This is necessary to ensure that agents who have switched to TFT start with cooperation.

```
if not oldstrategy == self.strategy:
    for i in range(0,len(self.memory)):
        self.memory[i] = 1
```

The following functions define the creation of the neighborhood structure `mn()`, and the assignment of payoffs in the game `play()`. The `play()` function simply specifies a differentiation between the four possible outcomes. The outcomes are chosen according to the agent's strategy choice and, as detailed in

---

[5]For the technical purpose of recording the agent's list index in the other agent's memory.

Chapter 3, agents cooperate only if they play TFT and even then only if their memory about their counterpart suggests that she is a cooperator as well (technically if the agent's strategy variable is 1 and not 0 and if the appropriate element in the agent's memory list is also 1 and not 0). For all four cases, the agent's payoffs are accordingly incremented, and the agents record their opponent's action into memory.

```
def play(agent1,agent2,idx1,idx2):
        if agent1.strategy == 1 and agent1.memory[idx1] == 1:
                agent2.memory[idx2] = 1
                if agent2.strategy == 1 and agent2.memory[idx2] == 1:
                        agent1.memory[idx1] = 1
                        agent1.payoff += 3
                        agent2.payoff += 3
                else:
                        agent1.memory[idx1] = 0
                        agent1.payoff += 0
                        agent2.payoff += 5
        else:
                agent2.memory[idx2] = 0
                if agent2.strategy == 1 and agent2.memory[idx2] == 1:
                        agent1.memory[idx1] = 1
                        agent1.payoff += 0
                        agent2.payoff += 5
                else:
                        agent1.memory[idx1] = 0
                        agent1.payoff += 1
                        agent2.payoff += 1
```

The next part of the script is where the main program starts and where the computer begins executing the simulation.

```
agentnumber = 0
grid_size = 10
iterations = 10
```

A global counter variable for agent objects is defined,[6] the desired number of iterations is set to 10, and the grid size is defined. Since this simulation operates with square grids it is sufficient to set one side length; in this case the grid is 10×10 agents. Following this, the grid is populated with agents by looping through the rows and columns and creating an agent object for each position. To be able to access the objects later on, they (or rather references to them, so-called pointers) are recorded into a two-dimensional array, agent_arr.

```
agent_arr = []                #create agent array
for i in range (0,grid_size):
        agent_arr.append([])
        for j in range (0,grid_size):
                agent_arr[i].append(agent())
```

[6]This variable is incremented every time an instance of class agent is created; it also serves to give the agents unique ID numbers. See the first three lines of the constructor function of class agent.

Then the Moore neighborhood structure is created. To do this we have to go through the grid again and call the function for each pair of agents that are to be neighbors. The function requires to be given the two agents as arguments.

```
for i in range (0,grid_size):
    for j in range (0,grid_size):
        if not i == 0:
            if not j == 0:
                mn(agent_arr[i-1][j-1],agent_arr[i][j])
            mn(agent_arr[i-1][j],agent_arr[i][j])
            if not j + 1 == grid_size:
                mn(agent_arr[i-1][j + 1],agent_arr[i][j])
        if not j == 0:
            mn(agent_arr[i][j-1],agent_arr[i][j])
```

The program structure might—with nested loops and if-statements—seem rather complicated at this point. There is unfortunately no simpler way to establish a Moore neighborhood structure in a finite grid. However, we could have the program print the neighborhood structure for debugging purposes if we were not convinced that the way the program does it is the correct one. The following code block would conveniently do this.

```
for i in range (0,grid_size):
    for j in range (0,grid_size):
        print('Agent ',agent_arr [i][j].id,' grid position ',i,j)
        print('has the following neighbors:')
        printstring = ''
        for n in agent_arr [i][j].neighbors:
            printstring += ' ' +str(n.id)
        print(printstring)
```

Having created the agents, established the neighborhood structure and defined all required functions, we are now ready to start the actual simulation. The simulation is to be iterated as often as defined above in the iterations variable

```
for t in range(0,iterations):
```

In each iteration we let any two neighbors play the prisoners' dilemma at hand exactly twice such that using TFT—which relies on recording the opponents action and reacting accordingly—has an effect. This is done by looping through the entire grid, hence going from agent to agent, and there again looping through the agent's list of neighbors. For every agent, the play function is then called for every one of her neighbors (with the appropriate arguments, the two playing agents and their index numbers in each other's memory):

```
for i in range (0,grid_size):
    for j in range (0,grid_size):
        for k in range (0,len(agent_arr [i][j].neighbors)):
            agent1 = agent_arr [i][j]
```

```
agent2 = agent_arr [i][j].neighbors[k]
idx2 = agent_arr [i][j].lidx[k]
idx1 = agent_arr [i][j].neighbors[k].lidx[idx2]
play(agent1,agent2,idx1,idx2)
```

Also, all agents have to reevaluate their strategy in each iteration, thus enabling the strategy choices of the group to evolve. For this, the agent object's `evaluate_strategy()` function is called.

```
for i in range (0,grid_size):
    for j in range (0,grid_size):
        agent_arr[i][j].evaluate_strategy()
```

Then, the agent's payoffs have to be reset to zero for the next iteration:

```
for i in range (0,grid_size):
    for j in range (0,grid_size):
        agent_arr[i][j].payoff = 0.0
```

And we finally want to create some output. Specifically, the entire grid's strategy choices (still 0 for defection and 1 for TFT) are arranged into strings row by row. Thus, for each iteration, we obtain as output a field of 1s and 0s representing the current strategies on the grid. This could easily be turned into the form presented in Figures 9.2 and 9.3.

```
print('Iteration ',t)
for i in range (0,grid_size):
    printstring = ''
    for j in range (0,grid_size):
        printstring + = str(agent_arr[i][j].strategy)
    print(printstring)
```

Finally, the last line (`input()`) of the program is merely to avoid that the output window is closed after the program finishes the simulation.

9.7 OUTLOOK

This chapter has given an overview of methodology and common issues and errors of simulation. An example illustrated how to use the particular advantages of simulation. Simulation was applied to acquire a prediction of the behavior of a system that would have been both difficult and resource-intensive to solve analytically. A set of independently acting agents, described by a number of equations of the same order as the set itself is difficult to solve, but easy to compute for particular sample values. Thus, even for very complex systems a prediction of the dynamics can be obtained quickly. However, the reliability of that prediction has to be studied by careful analysis of the volatility and the sensitivity of the results and possible different predictions for other values.[7]

[7]This is one of the aspects that could not be discussed at length in this brief introduction; interested readers are advised to consult one of the simulation textbooks and guides referenced below.

Simulation and agent-based modeling are still not widely used methods in economics though their potential is recognized more and more widely. They may continue to develop rapidly and will likely offer many challenges and opportunities that cannot yet anticipated. The role of agent-based modeling and simulation in economics will be taken up again in the following chapters. Specifically, Chapter 11 will give a formal introduction to complexity and address simulation as one of the methods suitable for the analysis of complex systems. Chapter 13 will present several instructive models from the literature many of which either rely on computer simulation or provide techniques for simulation modeling. Simulation is used to explain special segregation patterns as a general structure in complex populations, to model potentially impeding technological lock-ins as well as the phenomenon of the emergence of cooperation—the latter model similar to the simple example discussed in Sections 9.5 and 9.6.

Commented Textbook and Introductory Guide Reference

— Andreas Pyka and Giorgio Fagiolo (2005) *Agent-Based Modelling*.
  Pyka and Fagiolo give a short but comprehensive introduction to agent-based modeling, discussing concepts, techniques, and economic applications.
— Alan G. Isaac (2008) *Simulating Evolutionary Games*.
  Isaac provides a 40-page introduction to simulation modeling in evolutionary game theory with extensive examples in the programming language Python.
— John Stachurski (2009) *Economic Dynamics*.
  Stachurski's textbook is an advanced guide to dynamic theory and its economic applications. It gives many simulation program examples in the written programming language Python and also includes an introductory chapter on computer simulation. There is also a complementary introductory course on the author's homepage.
— Louis G. Birta and Gilbert Arbez (2007) *Modelling and Simulation*.

Birta and Arbez' textbook is a generic computer simulation textbook. It therefore does not provide examples from economics but is extensive on the method and techniques of computer simulation.
— Jeffrey Elkner, Allen B. Downey, and Chris Meyers (2012) How to Think Like a Computer Scientist.
  Elkner et al. provide a very detailed and accessible introduction to the programming language Python and to methodological aspects of programming in general. Though they do not place any particular focus on either simulation or the use of programming techniques in economics, the interested student of economic simulation may find their text (which is available online and for free) very useful as an introduction to the technique of programming.

Chapter References

Axelrod, R., 1984. The Evolution of Cooperation. Basic Books, New York, NY.

Birta, L.G., Arbez, G., 2007. Modelling and Simulation: Exploring Dynamic System Behavior. Springer, London.

Elkner, J., Downey, A.B., Meyers, C., 2012. How to Think Like a Computer Scientist: Learning with Python. Available online as <http://openbookproject.net/thinkcs/python/english2e/> (as of February 2014).

Goldman, D., Nance, R.E., Wilson, J.R., 2009. In: Rossetti, M.D., Hill, R.R., Johansson, B., Dunkin, A., Ingalls, R.G. (Eds.), Proceedings of the 2009 Winter Simulation Conference. Available online: <doi:10.1109/WSC.2009.5429341>.

Isaac, A.G., 2008. Simulating evolutionary games: a python-based introduction. J. Artif. Soc. Social Simul. 11 (3), <http://jasss.soc.surrey.ac.uk/11/3/8.html>.

Pyka, A., Fagiolo, G., 2005. Agent-based modelling: a methodology for neo-Schumpeterian economics. In: Hanusch, H., Pyka, A. (Eds.), The Elgar Companion to Neo-Schumpeterian Economics. Edward Elgar, Cheltenham.

Stachurski, J., 2009. Economic Dynamics: Theory and Computation. MIT Press, Cambridge, London.

Further Reading

Further Texts on Simulation

Banks, J. (Ed.), 1998. Handbook of Simulation. John Wiley & Sons, New York, NY.

Gould, H., Tobochnik, J., Christian, W., 2007. An Introduction to Computer Simulation Methods. Addison-Wesley, San Francisco, CA.

Robinson, S., 2004. Simulation. Chichester. John Wiley & Sons.

Simulation Models in Economics

Axelrod, R., 1984. The Evolution of Cooperation. Basic Books, New York, NY.

Epstein, J. (Ed.), 2007. Generative Social Science. Princeton University Press, Princeton, NJ.

Nelson, R., Winter, S., 1974. Neoclassical versus evolutionary theories of economic growth: critique and prospectus. Econ. J. 84 (336), 886–905.

Tesfatsion, L., Judd, K.L. (Eds.), 2006. Handbook of Computational Economics Volume 2: Agent-Based Computational Economics. Elsevier, Amsterdam.

See also Chapter 13.

Particular Problems of Computer Simulation and Agent-Based Models in Economics

Epstein, J., 2008. Why model? J. Artif. Soc. Social Simul. 11 (4), <http://jasss.soc.surrey.ac.uk/11/4/12.html>.

Edmonds, B., Hales, D., 2003. Replication, replication and replication: some hard lessons from model alignment. J. Artif. Soc. Social Simul. 6 (4), <http://jasss.soc.surrey.ac.uk/6/4/11.html>.

Galán, J.M., Izquierdo, L.R., Izquierdo, S.S., Ignacio Santos, J., del Olmo, R, López-Paredes, A., Edmonds, B., 2009. Errors and artefacts in agent-based modelling. J. Artif. Soc. Social Simul. 12 (1), <http://jasss.soc.surrey.ac.uk/12/1/1.html>.

Richiardi, M., Leombruni, R., Saam, N., Sonnessa, M., 2006. A common protocol for agent-based social simulation. J. Artif. Soc. Social Simul. 9 (1), <http://jasss.soc.surrey.ac.uk/9/1/15.html>.

Tesfatsion, L., 2003. Agent-based computational economics: modeling economies as complex adaptive systems. Inf. Sci. 19 (4), 262–268.

Thompson, N.S., Derr, P., 2009. Contra epstein, good explanations predict. J. Artif. Soc. Social Simul. 12 (1), <http://jasss.soc.surrey.ac.uk/12/1/9.html>.

Simulation, Economics, and Society

Buchanan, M., 2009. Meltdown modelling. Nature. 460, 680–682.

Epstein, J., 1999. Agent-based computational models and generative social science. Complexity. 4 (5), 41–60.

Programs, Tools, and Platforms for Computer Simulation

Nikolai, C., Madey, G., 2009. Tools of the trade: a survey of various agent based modeling platforms. J. Artif. Soc. Social Simul. 12 (2), <http://jasss.soc.surrey.ac.uk/12/2/2.html>.

Prechelt, L., 2000. An empirical comparison of C, C++, Java, Perl, Python, Rexx and Tcl. IEEE Comput. 33 (10), 23–29.

Further Reading—Online

For further reading, see the textbook website at http://booksite.elsevier.com/9780124115859

EXERCISES

1. Obtain the Python virtual machine and the integrated development environment Spyder from the websites given in Section 9.6.1. Download the scripts given in this chapter from the textbook's companion website http://booksite.elsevier.com/9780124115859. Run each of the short scripts explained in Section 9.6.2. Feel free to try combinations of the concepts that are illustrated by these scripts.

2. Run the longer script discussed in Section 9.6.3. Verify the result given in Section 9.5.2.

3. Append the script from exercise 2 to give additional output which would allow the observer to verify that the neighborhood structure has been arranged correctly. (Hint: The code block given for this purpose in Section 9.6.3 may be used.)

4. The simulation conducted using the script in exercise 2 contains stochastic components. As seen earlier in this chapter, it is necessary to verify simulation results, especially if the simulation makes use of random numbers. Suggest a way to do this in the case of the script from exercise 2.

5. The number of agents considered in the script in exercise 2 is very low compared to realistic models of economic reality. Increase the number of agents and rerun the

script. Do the results change? (Hint: The number of agents in the script is defined by the size of the grid.)

6. The script from exercise 2 models only the second setting discussed in Section 9.5 (Moore neighborhood), not the first one (total connectivity, every agent being the direct neighbor of every other agent). Make the appropriate changes to the script to model the first setting. The following code block is the one that has to be altered:

```
for i in range (0,grid_size):
    for j in range (0,grid_size):
        if not i == 0:
            if not j == 0:
                mn(agent_arr[i-1][j-1],agent_arr[i][j])
            mn(agent_arr[i-1][j],agent_arr[i][j])
            if not j + 1 == grid_size:
                mn(agent_arr[i-1][j+1],agent_arr[i][j])
        if not j == 0:
            mn(agent_arr[i][j-1],agent_arr[i][j])
```

Make further modifications and study the behavior of the simulation program. For instance, try other neighborhood structures or run the simulation with other underlying games (e.g., a coordination game instead of a prisoners' dilemma). Feel free to write other simple simulation programs and to conduct your own simulation studies.

10

A Universe of Economies: Interdependence and Complexity, System Trajectories, Chaos, and Self-Organization*

"It turns out to be a major mathematical tour de force to add even a small degree of institutional complexity to the general equilibrium model, and there has been absolutely no progress in providing a dynamic to a generalized model of production and exchange. Most embarrassingly, attempts to formalize the Walrasian tatônnement process have led precisely to complex nonlinear dynamics in which prices are, unlike in observable economies, generically chaotic." **Herbert Gintis**[1]

*This chapter is widely based on Duncan Foley's introduction chapter to "Barriers and Bounds to Rationality" (Foley, 1998), a collection of works by Peter Albin edited by Foley. The authors would like to thank Foley for comments on this chapter.

[1]In a review of "The Origin of Wealth" by Eric D. Beinhocker, *Journal of Economic Literature*, **44.4**, 2006, pp. 1018–1031, p. 1028.

10.1 SOME BASICS OF COMPLEXITY ECONOMICS VERSUS NEOCLASSICAL ECONOMICS: TOPOLOGY, EVOLUTIONARY PROCESS, AND BOUNDS AND BARRIERS TO PERFECT RATIONALITY

As we have shown in the previous chapters, economies are complex, with many bilateral relations and with different possible types of relations, as soon as we allow for a most basic characteristic of real economies, namely, *direct interdependence* and subsequent *direct interactions*, among each two agents in a population.

10.1.1 The General Equilibrium Once Again

We have also mentioned the general idea of *neoclassical* "mainstream" economics that excludes such direct interdependence through the assumption of perfectly informed agents who can *maximize* their objective functions in complete *isolation*, being dependent only on one type of external factor, namely, the *price* vector (see Chapters 5 and 6). This ideal decentralized decision structure in a pure price-quantities world is called a *market*. Under this condition, agents can decide in full autonomy and isolation and are only *indirectly dependent* on each other, in the sense of being dependent only on the *sums of the quantity decisions* of all suppliers and demanders in all "markets." Aggregated supplies and demands on a particular market will equalize, i.e., so-called *excess demand* becomes zero, it is assumed, at a certain price. This is the equilibrium price of that partial market which leads to market clearing in that market.

The interrelations among the different market-clearing prices and the quantity effects in the different partial markets that need to lead to a *simultaneous equilibrium* in all partial markets (the "general equilibrium"), however, remain a complex thing to solve (as shown in Chapter 6) logically and mathematically, since all agents have to recalculate their quantities (supplies and/or demands) for *all* partial markets if the price for only one partial market changes. This means that *all* prices and quantities in all partial markets will change if not all partial markets are in equilibrium simultaneously. They can only be cleared simultaneously. This is why *General Equilibrium Economics* (or GET) is both the basis and crown of neoclassical economics—only considering all partial markets allows to analyze cross-effects between them. Its research program was to prove that a general pure "market" economy is feasible and the optimal thing in human history. There is nothing else needed in the economy except a "market," if "perfectly" instituted and left alone, particularly by the state and other societal entities. However, as explained in Chapter 6, the interconnected quantity/price decisions of a great number of agents in a great number of partial markets may become a highly complex thing, and to ensure its feasibility at all may require a number of very specific presumptions.

The indirect interdependence mentioned is equivalent to the assumption of neoclassical "market" economics that the *number of agents* is always so *large* that no one's decision has any realizable impact on the decision parameters of anyone else so that agents can ignore each other and pretend to be isolated maximizers. The assumption of a very large number of agents, in turn, is equivalent to the perspective of a *spot market* where all are present at the same time and same location, thus being always very many, an anonymous crowd.

The isolated maximizers also are perfect maximizers as they have everything they need for a perfect decision, particularly *perfect information*. They completely know both their "inner" givens (their ordered objectives, costs or "preferences") and the "outer" givens, i.e., all prices. And if we include *intertemporal optimization*, e.g., of a given initial stock of wealth to be consumed over the span of a lifetime, or

of *investment* of a stock of capital, agents also need to know all *future prices* in order to make optimal decisions, and to have a complex process come to a stable unique and optimal equilibrium. We will go into more detail below.

Finally, perfectly "rational" agents need to be *all the same*, i.e., knowing one individual you know them all. The neoclassical agent thus is the *representative individual*. Their preferences may even be different, if this cancels out at the aggregate level and does not interfere with its optimality. But the *functional forms of the objective functions* (utility functions of the consumers and profit functions of the suppliers) need to be the same, namely, such that they can unambiguously be maximized. Particularly, they need to be *convex*. And optimality then basically refers to the marginal condition that all agents end up with the same marginal rate of substitution among the goods in their portfolios, given equilibrium prices (see again Chapters 5 and 6).

10.1.2 Agents in Real Space: Proximity and Distance, and the Neighborhood Structure

In contrast to that paradigm, we have introduced directly interdependent economies which immediately imply *initial strong strategic uncertainty*. The subsequent interactions, nevertheless, need to be analyzed and explained, and related complex models to be specified.

For instance, real-world agents do not live in a "spot market" but in *time* and *space* with local interactions among two or more agents. This has fundamental implications.

First, they are *located* somewhere in a *relation* to each other, *close* or *distant* from each other, in a *geographical* and/or a *functional* sense. We may consider a *lattice* (a grid, web, or net) where agents have their positions relative to each other, typically in a continuum of *overlapping localities* or "regions." Thus, some have proximity, some have distance, some are *direct neighbors*, some are *indirect neighbors* (having someone in between). It is obvious that *neighbors would interact more frequently* than indirect neighbors and/or that the behaviors of her closer neighbors are weighted higher by an agent than those of more remote neighbors. The influence of indirect neighbors on an individual may nevertheless exist, although indirectly through the decisions of her direct neighbors only (who, in turn, are directly dependent on *their* neighbors' decisions, etc.).

Considering "functional," or *economic proximities*, we may say that *direct competitors* may be "closer" to each other (even though geographically distant) than noncompetitors. In the same way, noncompetitors who have a *supplier* relation with each other may also be economic neighbors (although maybe geographically distant). Also, a *specialized professional group*, say those collaborating on a global interfirm R&D project, or the top ranks of a global industry, or a group of economics professors of a specialized field, may be said to be functionally close even while dispersed over the globe.

Finally, while an agent may react to the action of a close competitor in some way (say, an expansion of supply), she may react to the same action of an (also close) supplier in a different way. Thus decisions may not be fully determined by direct neighborhood in a *functional* sense.

In social and economic systems, the topology is not necessarily a *Euclidian* space with an unambiguous *geographical distance* among agents (see Foley, 1998, 18ff.). In human socioeconomies distance/closeness can be "functional" in addition to geographical. Two agents, as said, may be *functionally close* (e.g., in the value-added chain) but at the same time geographically distant. There are also potential asymmetries involved: If A is a neighbor

to B because A's sales create demand for B upstream in the value-added chain, this is typically not true in reverse: B's sales will not normally create demand for A. In the economy, or human society in general, therefore, an agent may react asymmetrically toward the same actions (say, a price increase) of his neighbors on two sides, B and C. Finally, economic distance may *not be additive*. The distance between A and C must not be the sum of the distances of A to B and B to C as economic distance may be non-Euclidian.

Second, agents rarely are "very many" on a spot, but *few*, typically—an oligopolistic structure rather than a polypolistic one (as assumed in "perfect markets"). However, agents in an oligopolistic structure are directly interdependent. We have applied that general characteristic of real-world economic interaction systems to the *typically oligopolistic structures of real-world "markets"* in Chapters 4 and 7.

In Chapter 13, we will explain a number of complex models based on defined lattices or neighborhood structures, or what is called a *topology*. While the term topology denotes both topological spaces (structures with spatial properties) and the field of study of such structures as a branch of mathematics, we use the term here to specifically refer to the social structure of interaction as a spatial structure. The social structure consists of the relations between the agents. If a topology is assumed, agents do directly interact, but not randomly but engage in structured interactions.

10.1.3 Knowledge, Rationality, Time: General Equilibrium and Evolutionary Process

As shown in Chapter 1, *initial strong strategic uncertainty* leads to somehow "imperfect" rationality, as, e.g., in different coordination and anti-coordination games. For instance, agents logically cannot know in the beginning of a repeated interaction (or in a definite one-shot interaction) the action the other one will take. As is immediately obvious from the neighborhood structure mentioned (and was discussed in Chapter 8), manifold simultaneous bilateral interactions on a topology may generate a complex process throughout a whole population. In fact, this process, if not a one-shot, will be *time-dependent* and *dynamic* in the sense that different agents may score differently in an interaction or a supergame and thus will *learn*, *imitate*, or somehow else *adapt* differently, including having different *replication rates* over generations in a biological sense, dependent on their different payoff scores. In a word, the processes implied will be *evolutionary* and the research program of economics going beyond the special case of neoclassical economics mentioned may be labeled *Complexity Economics*. The latter coincides in large parts with evolutionary mechanisms and processes which mostly are also complex. Thus, complexity economics largely converges with the older tradition of *Evolutionary-Institutional Economics* (see Chapter 11 for more detail).

In such an evolutionary process, it appears already intuitively, there are *limits to perfect "rationality"* which exist beyond the initial strong strategic uncertainty mentioned. They stem from properties of the resulting complex dynamic. First, there are *"computational complexity"* and *"bounds to rationality"* (Foley, 1998, 34, 46), i.e., the fact that *computation costs* may be disproportionately high as compared to the resources available (in terms of time and calculation capacity), the classical case of *"bounded rationality"* as mentioned already in Chapter 1. Second, the system's dynamics may be so complex as to make the *calculation of a "rational" behavior* even *logically* (i.e., mathematically) *infeasible*. An absolute *"barrier to rationality,"* as termed by Foley, is where the problem at hand is

"undecidable" or *"intractable,"* as no computer is able to come up with a solution within a finite time. We will explain and illustrate such situations later.

Note that this applies, first, to the economic researcher, being an "impartial spectator" of a system under investigation, trying to explore the problems of "optimal" behavior of individual agents involved as well as of the dynamics and a potential "optimal" equilibrium of the system, and, second, to the hypothetical agents involved whose informational "equipment" and calculation capabilities are investigated.

We will illustrate in the remainder of this chapter that with direct interaction the "optimal rationality" as postulated by neoclassical "market" economics is impossible to maintain—unless one sets such restrictions as to make a complex system very simple. This is not at all the end of economics but the beginning of a more relevant, substantial, realistic, and also formally analyzable economics.

In contrast to the perfect representative individual mentioned earlier, we have already explained in Chapter 2 that the agents in a directly interdependent economy have *different options to behave* and different options to develop a *strategy*, which typically is equivalent to *different conceptions of rationality*. This already led us to argue that, with *individual interaction histories*, i.e., individual past *experiences* and related future *expectations*, *agents* easily may become *heterogeneous*—even if they started out as (a worst-case) homogeneous short-run hyper-rational maximizers.

So far this chapter repeated some aspects from earlier chapters, which are central to complexity economics. They are listed as issues (1)–(3) in Table 10.1 below; the other issues in the table, (4) and following, will form the thread, and may also serve as a checklist for the student reader, for the remainder of this chapter.

TABLE 10.1 A Universe of Economies: The Market-Equilibrium Special Case and a Universe of More Complex Economies Compared

Complexity Economics	Neoclassical Economics (General-Equilibrium Economics)
(1) Direct interdependencies (between any two agents), entailing "strategic" interactions, depending on their spatial (or economic) proximity.	(1) No direct interdependence (only indirect interdependence) through equilibrium prices based on the sum of all individual excess demands (equivalent to the assumption that the number of agents is so large that none has a realizable effect on others; thus agents can ignore each other and pretend to be isolated).
(2) "Strong (strategic) uncertainty," with "bounded rationality" or absolute "barriers to rationality" in a resulting complex process.	(2) Perfect information (i.e., the equilibrium price vector is known, including present and future prices) and unrealistically large computation capacity.
(3) Heterogeneous individual agents, possibly developing different strategies, depending on their individual past experiences and related future expectations.	(3) The "representative individual": all agents are the same, all are perfectly "rational," perfectly maximizing their objective (utility or profit) functions.
(4) Most information is "local," emanating from interactions with their spatial (or economic) "neighborhood."	(4) Information is completely "global" (same perfect information available to all).
(5) Local information spreads through many decentralized bilateral interactions which takes time; memory and monitoring efforts required to increase one's information ...	(5) Global information is costless and instantaneous, provided by a central and powerful agency, i.e., the "auctioneer" (preventing exchange at nonequilibrium prices; no two-party bargaining or exchange; at equilibrium prices, decentralized, bilateral exchange is senseless: a central collective action at a spot market realizes the equilibrium).
(6) ... and to generate specific, though preliminary, expectations.	(6) "Rational expectations."
(7) Time-dependent action, dynamic and evolutionary system motions ("orbits").	(7) Time-independent action and system state, timeless system motion.
(8) Resulting in complex evolutionary processes with search, learning, imitation, adaptation, differential replication ...	(8) Resulting in a static general equilibrium, i.e., a unique global attractor of the system.
(9) Specific system states unpredictable; inherent instability.	(9) System state is predictable; inherent static stability.
(10) Agents are (act and react) at least as complex as their environment, deploying experience, calculation, expectations and anticipation, search, creativity, and experimentation; pursuing survival and evolutionary effectiveness rather than maximization.	(10) Agents are not complex, (re)act the same way, toward equilibrium; simplified trajectory.
(11) System states and orbits dependent on initial conditions.	(11) Existence of a unique equilibrium independent of initial conditions.
(12) High complexity: "complex adaptive systems"; high "computational complexity" and often logical infeasibility of a solution ("undecidability") ("bounds" and "barriers" to "rationality").	(12) Low inherent complexity; systems made simple by restrictive assumptions.

(Continued)

TABLE 10.1 (Continued)

Complexity Economics	Neoclassical Economics (General-Equilibrium Economics)
(13) Even simple structures may generate complex trajectories; many different dynamics possible; a whole universe of levels of complexity opens up.	(13) Complex trajectories and different dynamics excluded by very specific assumptions.
(14) The policy "solution": third-party (exogenous) intervention, introducing some global information; does not generate a simple stable system, though.	(14) The auctioneer is total policy (in neoclassical terms: the perfect market does not need any policy intervention).
(15) The institutional "solution": evolutionary-institutional emergence may stabilize processes based on complex decision structures; some self-organization as problem-solving (morphogenesis, autopoiesis) and some homeostasis become possible; particularly at "meso"-sized platforms (populations or groups).	(15) The auctioneer also represents the social rules required for problem-solving, particularly when allowing or prohibiting "market" exchange.

10.2 LOCAL AND GLOBAL INFORMATION, THE NEOCLASSICAL AND THE COMPLEXITY ECONOMICS APPROACHES, AND COMPLEX SYSTEM DYNAMICS

10.2.1 Local and Global Information and Their Implications

In real-world direct-interaction systems located in time and space, information primarily emanates from identification of other agents in the neighborhood and from *interactions with* those *neighbors*. These can be own interactions, past and present (the information on past ones depending on the agent's *memory* length), and interactions between two other agents in one's neighborhood (depending on the agent's capability to *monitor* a certain number of third-party interactions). Most *information is local* this way. And it also diffuses through countless decentral bilateral interactions. The basic difference between such local and a fully global (or collective) information is that local information is not necessarily uniform. Depending on factors of *diversification* such as search, experimentation, etc. and thus on

heterogeneous experience from different local interactions, spreading information on cooperative behavior in some location may encounter spreading information on defective behavior emanating from some other locality. Thus, local information is unlikely to be homogeneous throughout the whole system (or population). Correspondingly, such heterogeneous experience will trigger heterogeneous *expectations* which cannot be qualified as being "true" or "false." At best, they can be proper or improper for an agent in her specific environment when it comes to maximizing her long-run success. And the *algorithm* for an agent to utilize her experience with own and others' interactions in the neighborhood to *translate* it into her expectation and appropriate *behavior* needs to be specified in any model.

Note that with this already both individual action and system behavior are *time- and path-dependent*, and also inherently *unstable*, characterized by *complex evolutionary moves*, and often *unpredictability*. Individual behavior obviously cannot be predetermined, given the heterogeneous information, but agents will have to be assumed as searching for further and more clear-cut information, as learning, comparing themselves with others, perhaps imitating, and adapting in different ways. This is equivalent to saying that *information provision is costly*, in terms of time, effort, and continuing uncertainty.

It also appears plausible already that such *agents* could easily be conceptualized as being (i.e., acting and reacting), *at least as complex as their social environment*. Such agents would clearly not maximize a one-dimensional objective function and be "efficient." In complex models, agents often have to struggle for mere *survival* in the short-run or for *long-run relative success*, improving one's relative position in the population or increasing one's evolutionary success (issues (4)–(10) in Table 10.1).

Compare the characterization above with the assumption of the neoclassical perfect "market economy" of the *"market" providing full and cost-less information to everyone*. In fact, the information about prices would be *genuinely collectively* generated with the help of a genuinely collective agency (the "auctioneer") that first generates and then spreads the news about the equilibrium price vector. Since action is either formally forbidden or is not in the agent's interest, or just does not take place, at nonequilibrium prices (depending on specific assumptions of the model), and thus bilateral decentralized bargaining does not occur, processing this information is quite an easy task for the agents. *Complexity* and, thus, *computation costs are low* for them, in fact zero. A solution of their optimization problem may be feasible with no costs. And their exchange action virtually will become a central and simultaneous action. These assumptions drastically simplify the trajectory from any initial starting point of the system. As equilibrium prices are determined and called out, all (re-)act the "right" way, toward equilibrium. At the equilibrium price, the same total quantity of any good will be offered and demanded, purchased and sold, meaning zero excess demand on any partial market. A static general equilibrium will result as the unique global attractor of the system.

And since, in an intertemporal model, the auctioneer also determines future prices (or, as

is equivalent, the price of credit, or the "true" real interest rate or discount factor) every agent must have true or *"rational expectations,"* i.e., perfect knowledge about the future. In this way, both individual behavior and system behavior virtually are *time- (and path-) independent*. Individual behaviors and the system are inherently *stable*, their trajectories and final states *predictable*, complex trajectories excluded by assumptions (see issues (4)–(13) in the right-hand column of Table 10.1).

10.2.2 Dynamics of a Linear System

Now, if we, in contrast to the specific neoclassical assumptions for a general equilibrium, consider and acknowledge some of the real-world properties of decentralized, multiagent interaction systems, such as just *time dependence* (dynamics), even *simple model structures* may generate rather *complex system trajectories* (see section 1.1 in Foley, 1998), i.e., different dynamics, qualitatively different from stable equilibrium. Consider a dynamic system of the form:

$$x_{t+1} = F(x_t) \qquad (10.1)$$

representing the *state of a system* at time $t + 1$, where x_t is the *vector* at time t with, say, n components, changing through *time*, in a data space, or *state space* X. Each component may be in one of two possible states, say 1 for an agent who has cooperated at a certain point of time and 0 for an agent who has defected. F is an *operator* on the state space subject to important parameters of the system (for instance, certain conditions under which individual agents cooperate or defect or switch between these states).

Consider the *linear case* first. Here, F is a transformation matrix $\mathscr{A}$ so that

$$x_{t+1} = \mathscr{A} x_t \qquad (10.2)$$

The movement of this system depends on a crucial property of this matrix, i.e., its *eigenvalue* (see Box 10.1).

BOX 10.1

EIGENVALUES

The behavior of a *linear transformation* $\mathscr{A}$ is governed by its *eigenvalues* λ. If $\mathscr{A}$ is to transform an n-dimensional state vector x_t into an n-dimensional state vector x_{t+1} (t denoting the time),

$$x_{t+1} = \mathscr{A}x$$

$\mathscr{A}$ takes the form of an $n \times n$ matrix. The eigenvalue λ together with a corresponding nonzero *eigenvector* v is defined as a scalar such that

$$\lambda v = \mathscr{A}v$$

$\mathscr{A}$ has n (n is the dimension) *single eigenvalues,* of which several may take the same value (double, triple, ... eigenvalues). The number of nonzero single eigenvalues is equal to the *rank* of $\mathscr{A}$ (its number of independent row vectors).

An eigenvalue with $|\lambda| < 1$ causes contractive motion, one with $|\lambda| > 1$ expansive motion. A complex eigenvalue (with nonzero imaginary part) causes a circular or spiral motion according to its angle from the positive real axis. A real negative eigenvalue without imaginary part (180° from the positive real axis) therefore causes an oscillation.

As an example, consider a simple *Lotka– Volterra difference equation system*:

$$x_{1,t+1} = x_{1,t} + x_{2,t}$$
$$x_{2,t+1} = -x_{1,t} + x_{2,t}$$

Therefore,

$$\mathscr{A} = \begin{pmatrix} 1 & 1 \\ -1 & 1 \end{pmatrix}$$

This matrix is of rank 2 and must have two single nonzero eigenvalues λ. We compute these as

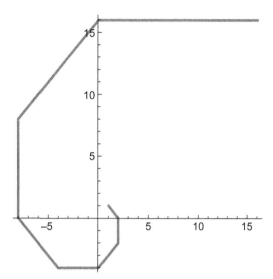

FIGURE 10.1 Two-dimensional development of the dynamical system $x(t)$.

$$\lambda v = \mathscr{A}v$$
$$0 = \mathscr{A}v - \lambda v$$
$$0 = (\mathscr{A} - \lambda I)v,$$

where I is the unit matrix. Since $v \neq 0$,

$$0 = \mathscr{A} - \lambda I$$
$$0 = \det(\mathscr{A} - \lambda I)$$
$$0 = \det\begin{pmatrix} 1 - \lambda & 1 \\ -1 & 1 - \lambda \end{pmatrix}$$
$$0 = (1 - \lambda)^2 + 1$$
$$\lambda = 1 - \sqrt{-1}$$
$$\lambda_{1,2} = 1 \pm i.$$

Then we can derive the eigenvectors $v_{1,2}$ for the two eigenvalues and check whether the computation was correct with the definition of

---

BOX 10.1   (cont'd)

---

eigenvalue and eigenvector above. The eigenvectors are:

$$v_1 = \begin{pmatrix} 1 \\ i \end{pmatrix} \text{ for } \lambda_1 = 1 + i \quad \text{and}$$

$$v_2 = \begin{pmatrix} 1 \\ -i \end{pmatrix} \text{ for } \lambda_2 = 1 - i.$$

Since both eigenvalues have a nonzero imaginary part, they yield a spiral motion, and since their absolute values are $|(1 \pm i)| = \sqrt{2} > 1$, their motion is expanding, therefore divergent.

This result is true as we can see for an example computation of the first eight steps of such a system, starting with the initial values $x_0 = \begin{pmatrix} 1 \\ 1 \end{pmatrix}$ (see also Figure 10.1):

$$x_1 = \begin{pmatrix} 2 \\ 0 \end{pmatrix}; \quad x_2 = \begin{pmatrix} 2 \\ -2 \end{pmatrix}; \quad x_3 = \begin{pmatrix} 0 \\ -4 \end{pmatrix}; \quad x_4 = \begin{pmatrix} -4 \\ -4 \end{pmatrix}$$

$$x_5 = \begin{pmatrix} -8 \\ 0 \end{pmatrix}; \quad x_6 = \begin{pmatrix} -8 \\ 8 \end{pmatrix}; \quad x_7 = \begin{pmatrix} 0 \\ 16 \end{pmatrix}; \quad x_8 = \begin{pmatrix} 16 \\ 16 \end{pmatrix}.$$

Each eigenvalue (see Box 10.1) governs a component of the behavior of the system. If an eigenvalue of $\mathscr{A}$ is a *real*, *positive* number, the system will *expand* (if the value >1) or *contract* (if <1) along an arrow (which, in turn, is the corresponding eigenvector of $\mathscr{A}$, i.e., x). The action of that matrix on that (positive, nonzero) vector then changes its magnitude but not its direction. If an eigenvalue of $\mathscr{A}$ is a *real*, *negative* number, the system will "flip" from one side of the origin to the other, back and forth.

The third case possible is a more complicated one, in terms of numerics. For any complex value in the matrix (consisting of a *real* and an *imaginary* component) there is a pair of eigenvalues that are also *complex numbers*, where the imaginary component may, however, have either a positive or a negative sign. In the case of complex eigenvalues, it has been shown in Box 10.1 that the system will *spiral inward* or *outward*.

Across these three cases of the system's motion, some specific *magnitudes of the eigenvalues* determine the stability of the motion: Only when the *absolute eigenvalues* are *smaller than 1* will the system be stable and move toward the origin, a *stable equilibrium* (either directly or while flipping, as explained). However, if the absolute eigenvalue is *greater than* 1, the system will *move away from the origin* (again either directly or while flipping), i.e., no stable equilibrium. (The special cases are: With the eigenvalue being equal to +1, the system will remain at any initial state. If it equals −1, the system will oscillate around the origin at a stable distance. If a pair of complex eigenvalues has magnitude 1, the system will rotate around the origin on a stable circle through the starting point.)

All eigenvalues define a different dynamic motion of the system. For eigenvalues with absolute value smaller than 1, the motion is contracting. In the presence of eigenvalues with larger absolute values, contracting dynamics will after some time not play any significant part in determining the position of the system any more. The eigenvalue with the largest absolute value is also called the *dominant eigenvalue* of the system.

While eigenvalues with absolute value larger than 1 does indicate divergence (toward $\pm \infty$), it is not necessarily an indicator for complex dynamics. The motion of the system may, in fact, be much less predictable in the presence of different contracting and expanding dynamics, perhaps circular movements, and particularly if the system has different stable and unstable equilibria. This does, however, require the system to be nonlinear and the eigenvalues to change over the state space so that they could all be very small (close to 0) at one point making the system contract toward that point but very large at another point, making it diverge. For details on this as well as on concepts of complexity and chaos, see Sections 10.2.4 and 10.2.5 and Chapter 11.

In sum, you can see that even from a simple system structure complex dynamics can easily emerge, and that a *single stable equilibrium* is to be considered a *special case* in the range of possible dynamics of such a simple structure.

10.2.3 Dynamics of a Nonlinear System

Linear systems have the convenient property that they behave proportionally in all regions of the state space. However, this is not the case for nonlinear dynamic systems which behave *differently in different regions of the state space.*

The easiest way to proceed from a linear to a nonlinear system is to consider a nonlinear system as a so-called *perturbation* of the linear system (see Foley, 1998, 7ff.), i.e., adding a "small" term to the more easily describable (initial) linear formulation, in terms of a so-called *power series*. A power series is an infinite series of the form:

$$F(x) = \sum_{n=0}^{\infty} a_n(x-c)^n = a_1(x-c)^1 + a_2(x-c)^2 + \cdots$$

A power series typically is used to approximate a not exactly solvable problem, or a not exactly describable function, by starting from the exact description of a solvable problem, i.e., from an exactly describable function, by adding successively less important deviations

from that exactly describable function. Here, a_n is a coefficient of the nth term, c a vector of constants, and x a vector around c. Often the problem is evaluated at $c = 0$ where the power series takes the simpler form:

$$F(x) = \sum_{n=0}^{\infty} a_n x^n.$$

In the case of the representation of a function as a power series, the added terms are calculated from the values of the known function's derivatives evaluated at a certain point. More specifically, a_n is the nth derivative of the function which we will approximate, evaluated at the point around which we approximate, $a_n = F^{(n)}(c)$. In this case the power series assumes the form of a so-called *Taylor series*. The Taylor series is the following power series:

$$F(x) = \sum_{n=0}^{\infty} \frac{[F^{(n)}(c)](x-c)^n}{n!} = \frac{F(c)}{0!} + \frac{[F'(c)](x-c)}{1!} + \frac{[F''(c)](x-c)^2}{2!} + \cdots$$

It approximates the value of the function $F(\cdot)$ at point x which lies close to point c. A Taylor series of a function $F(\cdot)$ evaluated for $c = 0$ is also called a *Maclaurin series*. Consider a system as in Eq. (10.1) where the operator F is not linear. The motion of this nonlinear system in the neighborhood of the origin, can be approximated using the Taylor series:

$$F(x) = \frac{[F(0)]}{0!} + \frac{[F'(0)](x_t)}{1!} + \frac{[F''(0)](x_t)^2}{2!} + \cdots$$

(10.3)

If the system starts at x_t, a point close to the origin, the system's state in the next period is approximated as x_{t+1} in Eq. (10.3). This functional form illustrates that the motions of the system change as the system moves in the state space.

However, contrasting to the linear systems, the eigenvalues of the system are not necessarily static. The eigenvalues are again the eigenvalues of the transformation matrix consisting of all partial derivatives of all components of the transformation equation (10.3) (the equation has one component for each component of the vector x_{t+1}) with respect to all components of the vector x_t resulting in a quadratic matrix. In the case of a linear system, all derivatives are scalars, and therefore all components of the transformation matrix are scalars. In the nonlinear case, the equivalent to the transformation matrix (specifically, the Jacobian matrix) contains functions. Therefore, the eigenvalues will in most cases also not be constant scalars but will differ between different points of the state space. They have to be obtained from the linearized Jacobian matrix at the specific state (represented by state vector x_t). If this linearization yields (for given x_t) a number with an absolute value smaller than 1 (for every single eigenvalue), the system will behave like a stable system, if not the system will be unstable. Therefore, the behavior of the system itself depends on the state vector. A stable system may become unstable and vice versa. For an example and some details of the theory of chaos and bifurcation, see Section 10.2.5.

The system may wander indefinitely, *never exactly repeating* its earlier orbit. The system's movement then is *unpredictable*. This is called a *chaotic* behavioral pattern.

10.2.4 Chaotic and Complex Dynamics

Generally, *chaos* can be *generated deterministically* by relatively simple systems, particularly simple *nonlinear difference* or *differential equations* (Eq. (10.3) is an example of the latter). A more simple case than the Taylor series described earlier, in fact, a Taylor series truncated to its first two terms, is the following quadratic difference equation (the much used "logistic function" of biological growth under a resource constraint):

$$x_{t+1} = a(x_t - x_t^2). \tag{10.4}$$

For certain values of the parameter (or matrix) a, the variable (or vector) x may exhibit equilibrium-growth ("steady-state"), or periodic behavior, for other values of a, x may show an extremely complicated dynamics. Thus, chaotic fluctuations can all be produced deterministically through this function (see also, e.g., Jarsulic, 1998). Chaotic systems have *asymptotic trajectories* (or "attractors") *only in parts* of their state space while these are absent in others. This does not imply that they are not locally predictable or have no statistical regularities at all. We define "chaotic" trajectories more exactly and illustrate such behavior in greater detail in Section 10.2.5.

From Eq. (10.4) we see that, for instance, if the linear part of the function is destabilizing, corresponding to $a > 1$, the nonlinear element may become stabilizing as the system moves further away from the origin, thereby increasing x^2 which is part of the negative term of the development equation. If the two effects are perfectly balanced, we obviously have an equilibrium. However, for larger a (as will be shown Section 10.2.5) the equilibrium becomes unstable, giving rise to a limit cycle (attractor) which cycles over a number of periods but does so predictably and always hits the same values. With a further increasing the cycle length grows longer and the system finally reaches a regime of deterministic chaos. Again, trajectories starting at different points will diverge so that "*initial conditions*" (i.e., their "starting points" or initial parameter values) *matter*, and such divergence would lead to ever larger "errors of prediction" if one would predict trajectories in terms of "stability" and "equilibrium."

Chaotic systems may have some regular stochastic behavior, but their stochastic regularities also may be very complex. The dynamical behavior of a chaotic system cannot be reduced or broken down into disjoint subsets of its domain. It has been said that chaotic systems "mix" over time, which implies that periodic orbits, if they occur, cannot be stable (see, e.g., Jarsulic, 1998, p. 60).

Note that we have introduced so far four types of complex dynamic behavior emerging from linear or nonlinear system structures (see Foley, 1998, 50ff.):

- stability of (or toward) a unique, globally attracting equilibrium state;
- stability of (or toward) regular motions (*periodic oscillations or orbits*, with possibly very long distances and with complicated and even varying paths between two periodic attractors);
- chaotic behavior, where trajectories are nonrepeating patterns, small changes in initial conditions have large effects, statistical regularities can be observed in the evolving patterns;
- behavior at the edge of chaos, where trajectories are nonrepeating patterns, small changes in initial conditions spread out at first but eventually contract, statistical regularities cannot be observed.

As argued before, direct interdependence and direct interactions among agents are one condition of complex dynamics (see also, e.g., Brock, 1988, p. 82).

10.2.5 General Properties of Dynamic Systems

In this chapter, we concentrate on one of several cases of dynamic systems, namely, on linear systems of difference equations. For nonlinear systems and systems of differential equations, see Chapter 11. Every *dynamic system* consists of a *state vector* x_t of degree (number of *components*) D and dependent on the time t and a *transformation function* F

(see Eq. (10.1)). From this transformation function, a *transformation matrix* $\mathscr{A}$ is constructed containing the marginal effects of all components of the current state vector x_t on each component of the future state vector x_{t+1}. These effects are equal to the first derivatives; therefore, the transformation matrix $\mathscr{A}$ is equal to the *Jacobian matrix* of F:

$$
\mathscr{J} = \begin{pmatrix}
\dfrac{\partial x_{t+1,1}}{\partial x_{t,1}} & \dfrac{\partial x_{t+1,1}}{\partial x_{t,2}} & \cdots & \dfrac{\partial x_{t+1,1}}{\partial x_{t,D}} \\
\dfrac{\partial x_{t+1,2}}{\partial x_{t,1}} & \dfrac{\partial x_{t+1,2}}{\partial x_{t,2}} & \cdots & \dfrac{\partial x_{t+1,2}}{\partial x_{t,D}} \\
\vdots & \vdots & \ddots & \vdots \\
\dfrac{\partial x_{t+1,D}}{\partial x_{t,1}} & \dfrac{\partial x_{t+1,D}}{\partial x_{t,2}} & \cdots & \dfrac{\partial x_{t+1,D}}{\partial x_{t,D}}
\end{pmatrix}.
$$

For a linear dynamic system, all the derivatives are scalars; therefore, $\mathscr{J}$ only contains scalars and is a simple transformation matrix $\mathscr{A}$ (see Box 10.1). The *eigenvalues* of the linear transformation are computed by the equation

$$
\lambda v = \mathscr{A}v
$$

where

$$
v \neq 0
$$

are the *eigenvectors* corresponding to the eigenvalues λ. This yields

$$
0 = \mathscr{A} - \lambda I
$$

and the characteristic equation

$$
0 = \det(\mathscr{A} - \lambda I)
$$

from which λ may be computed. For an example see again Box 10.1. For a *nonlinear system*, the components of $\mathscr{A}$, as well as its eigenvalues are likely not static but functions of x_t. Since the behavior of the system is governed by the eigenvalues, the behavior is dependent on the state vector x_t and may change, and may even switch from stability to instability and vice versa as the system develops. For an

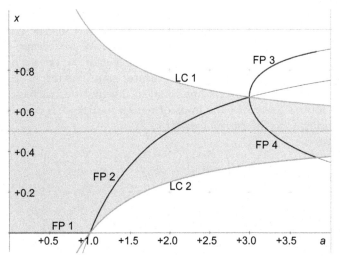

FIGURE 10.2 State space of the logistic map depending on the parameter a (bifurcation diagram), with the fixed points FP 1–FP 4, the upper and lower boundaries of the stable area LC 1 and LC 2, and the stable area shaded.

introduction to the analysis of nonlinear systems, see Chapter 11.

The state space of the system is characterized by the *fixed points*, especially the stable fixed points (attractors) and the distribution of the *stable areas*. A fixed point in the state space is a particular value x_t with

$$x_{t+1} = x_t$$

i.e., the system remains at this point, once it has reached the point. (Note that a valid set of eigenvalues for this transformation would be a set of eigenvalues that are all $\lambda = 0$.)

An *attractor* is a fixed point or (for complex attractors) a set of points (i) that the system remains in forever once the set is reached (by definition, this is true for fixed points) and (ii) that is surrounded by a stable area from which the trajectories contract toward the attractor.

The distribution of stable areas is determined by the eigenvalues. Every eigenvalue governs a motion of the system. The behavior is contracting if the absolute value of all eigenvalues is $|\lambda| < 1$, expansive if it is $|\lambda| > 1$. As the *trajectories* converge in the contracting case, the system tends to be stable for

eigenvalues $|\lambda| < 1$. Contracting motion approaches an attractor (a stable fixed point). If an eigenvalue is $|\lambda| = 1$, the corresponding motion is neither contracting nor expanding, but a so-called *limit cycle*; the motion of the system maintains a constant distance from the attractor.

If the eigenvalues are continuous functions of x_t, the stable area is bordered by the limit cycles $|\lambda| = 1$ for all eigenvalues.

A *bifurcation* is a point in continuous parameters (or even in endogenous variables) where the properties of the system change qualitatively, e.g., if one attractor becomes unstable and gives rise to a new, different attractor; in the example below a pitchfork bifurcation is shown, that replaces a stable fixed point with an attractor consisting of two period-2 fixed points.

The behavior of a system is said to be *deterministically chaotic* if no regularities, e.g., similarities of the behavior for different, at least for similar initial values are present. The direct consequence is the impossibility to make any forecast for particular initial values without exact simulation of the system for these values. There are various approaches as to how to define and consequently how to detect deterministic chaos. The most widely used are those using the *Lyapunov exponents* and *autocorrelations*. The Lyapunov exponent is a measure of the change of the distance of trajectories in time. If this distance is generally growing in a system, the system is said to be chaotic. The *autocorrelation function* for a certain time lag τ correlates values of timeseries of a dynamic variable with the same value τ time units later. The falling apart of the autocorrelation functions, i.e., the vanishing of a regular stable autocorrelation is also used as an indication of the presence of deterministic chaos.

The concept of *complexity* is broader than, but related to, deterministic chaos. The complexity of a dynamic system may be seen as the information needed for a complete description of the system. A system with maximal complexity is therefore a system that cannot be described with less information than that necessary to represent the system itself (this tends to be the case for deterministically chaotic systems); but a system can of course be much less complex. For more on this, see Chapter 11.

As an example, we consider again the nonlinear, one-dimensional logistic map (see Eq. (10.4)):

$$x_{t+1} = a(x_t - x_t^2).$$

This function depends on a parameter $0 \leq a \leq 4$ and maps a state space $0 \leq x_t \leq 1$ into itself. The properties of the system depending on the parameter a can therefore be depicted in a two-dimensional plot (see Figure 10.2). Although it is a one-dimensional map and thus a very simple nonlinear system, it exhibits for different values of a a number of different behaviors ranging from entirely stable to a periodic system with an attractor consisting of two points with

$$x_{t+2} = x_t$$

through deterministic chaos.

We start by computing the fixed points (for simplicity neglecting the indices)

$$x = ax - ax^2.$$

The first solution is obvious $x_{FP1} = 0$. To compute a second solution different from the first one, we can divide by x:

$$1 = a - ax$$

yielding

$$x_{FP2} = \frac{a-1}{a}.$$

For $a < 1$, only the first fixed point is in the valid state space, for $a = 1$ the two fixed points are equal $x_{FP1} = x_{FP2} = 0$, and for $a > 1$, the fixed points are different and both valid solutions. So which of them is stable for which values of a?

The Jacobian matrix of this system is one-dimensional:

$$\mathscr{A} = \frac{\partial F(x)}{\partial x} = a - 2ax.$$

The single eigenvalue (depending on x and a) of this system is therefore also easily computed from

$$a - 2ax - \lambda = 0$$

since

$$\lambda = a - 2ax.$$

This equation is a continuous, linear, and strictly decreasing function of x. Strictly speaking, the eigenvalue of the current system is not the function but rather its linearization, its values corresponding to any valid values of a and x. The linearization of nonlinear dynamic systems such as these is addressed in more detail in Chapter 11. Since the function is continuous, there must be an upper boundary of the stable area $\lambda_{LC1}(x) = -1$ and a lower boundary of the stable area $\lambda_{LC1}(x) = 1$ (with $\lambda_{LC1} > \lambda_{LC2}$) for each value of a. The region of the state space between the two is governed by contractive motion and will approach one of the two fixed points provided they fall into this region.

The two boundaries are easily computed as

$$x_{LC1} = \frac{a+1}{2a}$$

and

$$x_{LC2} = \frac{a-1}{2a}.$$

The first fixed point is stable for $a \leq 1$, otherwise unstable, the second one is stable for a larger than or equal to 1 but smaller than or equal to an a for which the fixed point leaves the stable area crossing the upper boundary. As may be computed by setting the second fixed point equal to the upper boundary, this point is $a = 3$. For $a > 3$, both fixed points are unstable and a bifurcation occurs. A stable period-2 solution emerges (thus a pair of period-2 fixed points) that are computed by

$$x = F(F(x)) = a(ax - ax^2) - a(ax - ax^2)^2,$$

which yields two period-2 fixed points

$$x_{FP3/4} = \frac{a+1}{2a} \pm \sqrt{\frac{a^2 - 2a - 3}{4a^2}}.$$

The lower one of the period-2 fixed points (x_{FP4}) enters the stable area again, only to cross the lower boundary toward the lower unstable area at $a_c = 1 + \sqrt{8} \approx 3.8284$. The system of x_{FP3} and x_{FP4} however becomes unstable even earlier (for a smaller a) since the eigenvalues of the period-1 system are not valid any more for the period-2 system. For a range below a_c, stable solutions for different even periods emerge (period 4, period 6, period 8, etc.); starting at a_c however, as, e.g., May (1976) puts it, there are cycles with every integer period, as well as an uncountable number of asymptotically aperiodic trajectories. This situation in turn was proven to be chaotic by Li and Yorke (1975) (see Figure 10.2 for illustration).

10.2.6 Social Systems and Economic Space — A Local- and Direct-Interaction General Equilibrium?

As mentioned earlier, the neoclassical perfect-equilibrium "market" economy restricts the real world, among others, to a representative individual. One of the neoclassical ideal settings is a *pure exchange economy* where every individual agent is *initially endowed* with a *stock of wealth* (in terms of exchangeable goods). Every agent then is supposed to be both buyer and seller, supplier and consumer, with no distinctive producers in the narrow sense. The market economy equilibrium requires a price vector such that all partial markets are in equilibrium, i.e., in states of market clearance. Every partial market then needs to exhibit a net demand (or net supply), i.e., an excess demand of zero.

One consequence of assuming homogeneous (identical, i.e., identically endowed) agents is that agents must also have the same excess demand and that there, consequently, is *no actual exchange at all* (see Foley, 1998, 21f.).

Therefore, Albin and Foley (1988) have modeled a decentralized exchange system *without an auctioneer* instead and in a world of *direct interaction*. Agents are still identical in their tastes and utility functions, but have *different endowments* and thus *different excess demand functions in prices*. The assumption of a spot market with a global public market price announced is relaxed, but the agents are *arrayed in a topology* and do directly *exchange with their neighbors only*. In this way, the various geographical (local) submarkets are indirectly linked. As agents are allowed to exchange directly, they consequently are also allowed to *exchange at nonequilibrium prices*.

Particularly, n agents are located on a *one-dimensional topology*, i.e., a *circle* where each has $k = 1$ neighbors on each side (a "radius-1 neighborhood"), i.e., *two neighbors* (the radius, however, may be a parameter in the model, with higher values given, e.g., two, three, or more neighbors on each side). Since each agent has two possible states (the info bits "on/off," "buy/sell," or "Cooperate/Defect," indicated as "0/1"), each of the interconnected local sub-markets of three agents (i.e., radius 1) may have eight possible configurations (three-digit bytes: 000, 001, 010, 011, 100, 101, 110, 111) depending on an adaption algorithm (to be determined), based on one's own and one's two neighbors' actions. (The full description of the state of an agent in a certain period includes the quantities of the goods she holds and the memory of the neighbors' supplies and demands in terms of quantities and prices.) As said, agents just interact locally and have different initial endowments. In this way, even while agents are kept largely identical in terms of their objective (utility) functions, they do not have the same global information and do not behave the same way. In fact, agents have bounded rationality this way.

As said, agents have initial endowments $\{x_1, x_2\}$ of the two goods x_1 and x_2 which they can trade with their neighbors. Let their identical utility functions be $U = x_1 x_2$. At an *indifference curve* where utility is constant and thus $U' = 0$ (equivalent to the first-order condition of utility maximization), $U' = x_1 \partial x_2 + \partial x_1 x_2 = 0$ so that agents' exchange rate of the goods (their marginal rate of substitution, or their willingness to pay for a good in terms of giving a quantity of the other good, or the relative price of the goods) is

$$\frac{\partial x_2}{\partial x_1} = \left| \frac{x_2}{x_1} \right|,$$

where ∂x_1 is the partial derivative of the utility function with respect to x_1.

Trade is motivated now by *differences in the initial endowments* of the agents i, e_{1i} and e_{2i}. The agents only know about their own endowments, though. The total endowment of the two goods in the economy is assumed to be

such that the market equilibrium price will be unity, which, however, the agents do not know either. While the individual endowments are different, they are subject to the condition that the individual's wealth at the equilibrium price would be the same for all individuals, $e_1^* + e_2^*$. But the initial offer prices will differ because of the different (initial) portions of e_1 and e_2. This will motivate the agents to trade in order to improve their endowments (and utilities). Each agent, in fact, must find out about the possibilities of trading with his neighbors, about offering and buying prices and quantities.

Obviously, a very complex process of revealing the willingness to trade and the prices offered and demanded will start to evolve. Nevertheless, a simulation of such a setting could mimic the ideal neoclassical textbook model of the perfect market in equilibrium (Foley, 1998, 16, 22, 58−61, and Chapter 5). Model simulations have shown that agents in this model indeed may achieve a Pareto-efficient allocation of goods where no further mutually advantageous trading opportunities exist. A perfect "market" can be reproduced under certain conditions on that direct-interaction basis, working, as it is supposed to, to redistribute initial endowments and to even out the proportions in which agents hold the two goods. In this way, agents may attain their household optima where their consumption structures reflect their identical preferences and the economy-wide goods supplies of x_1 and x_2 (the total endowments). This decentralized system of a "market" thus may meet the criterion of marginal efficiency where the marginal rate of substitution of the goods

$$\frac{\partial x_2}{\partial x_1} = \left| \frac{x_2}{x_1} \right|$$

becomes the same across all agents and equals the economy-wide rate, so that the equilibrium price may indeed be determined in a decentralized direct-interaction process with only local information and exchanges at nonequilibrium prices. Note that this is a specific result that is *one* possibility emerging under specific conditions in that model of a market, based only on direct local interactions.

We do not delve deeper here into the details of the model, the process, and the system trajectory emerging (for more details, see Foley, 1998, section 1.6.4, and Chapter 5). You have learned on the *marginal conditions of efficient equilibrium* in the conventional neoclassical "market" economy in Chapter 5.

However, a notable, and unavoidable, by-product of direct interdependence, exchange at disequilibrium prices, and uneven initial distribution of wealth, is that while this "market" may be marginally efficient it also creates a *systematic inequality of wealth* endowment. This applies in spite of the careful design of the model that would create an even wealth distribution if the system would jump to equilibrium in one step, i.e., if it were a conventional neoclassical model with an auctioneer. This effect is not much considered in mainstream economics. Mainstream economics does not care about *distribution* since this is not part of its efficiency conditions which are purely *marginal* conditions (while wealth distribution is not an object of marginal analysis, as reflected particularly by the *Pareto* criterion). However, as soon as we *allow for trade taking place at disequilibrium prices*, as is necessarily the case in a really *decentralized system with only local direct interactions* and information, agents *redistribute wealth* while trading and at the same time evening out their marginal rates of substitution of the goods and determining the global equilibrium price.

How does this come about? Agents with initial endowments very different from $x_2/x_1 = 1{:}1$ and thus with very different price offers for the goods (for instance, very high price offers for goods they have very little quantity of) will have to make most of their *exchanges at rather unfavorable prices*, since they

are in particular need of one of the two goods. By paying such unfavorable prices, they in fact transfer wealth to those agents whose endowments are closer to the economy-wide structure of goods and thus the prices they pay are closer to the final equilibrium prices.

Note again that this model reflects some effective "market" that may generate a specific Pareto-optimal allocation of goods at the equilibrium prices detected. But since it is *not a Walrasian market* where agents are barred from exchange at nonequilibrium prices (the one we have introduced earlier and explained as the usual neoclassical "mainstream" model in more detail in Chapter 5), the result is less a support for the conventional neoclassical mainstream model of the "perfect market," but rather a first indication of the *possibility of self-organization* of agents in a complex system based on local interaction and local information only (see also Foley, 1998, 60f.). The latter is a possibility of a complex system trajectory. We will get back to this "institutionalized self-organization" solution at the end of this chapter.

10.3 A QUASI-NEOCLASSICAL PERFECT-EQUILIBRIUM MODEL BASED ON GLOBAL INFORMATION AND DIRECT INTERDEPENDENCE

Generating a unique stable equilibrium through agents who perfectly rationally maximize given objective functions over time requires a considerable *reduction of complexity* such that the reality content of the setting may disappear. Two crucial assumptions of this "rational choice" program are, first, *excluding any direct interaction* between agents (supposing none of them has any measurable impact) and, second, supposing that the *informational endowments* of agents are given as *public goods*, i.e., as *full global information*.

Well-known problems of this program with its isolated individualistic perfect maximization are, first, the fact that the objective function is "inherently unobservable, so that it is not clear what explanatory advantage its presence in the theory confers" (Foley, 1998, 24), and, second, "the hypothesis of rationality puts no observational restrictions on an agent's actions. We can always rationalize behavior by positing an appropriate objective function" (Foley, 1998, 23).

As already discussed in Chapters 1 and 3, some rule-based behavior, although apparently "irrational" as viewed through a neoclassical lens, may be better explicable and even better predictable than such rational behavior, if more realistic conditions are assumed.

The issue at hand in this chapter, however, is to consider the *limited computability* as existing in the real world, i.e., *boundaries to rationality*, or even the logical infeasibility of a mathematical solution to an optimization problem, i.e., absolute *barriers to rationality*, both connected to certain degrees of complexity of system behavior (Foley, 1998, 25; again, see definitions of complexity in Chapter 11). As we have explained, simple structures may lead to very complex system behaviors, where already finding some solution may imply considerable computational complexity and even computational infeasibility—and an "optimal" solution can hardly be determined.

We will consider now how bounds and barriers to neoclassical "rationality" may emanate even from the strict neoclassical setting.

10.3.1 An Optimal Lifetime Consumption Problem

We consider a simple neoclassical model, the decision problem of an isolated single agent—a restricted initial setting (Foley, 1998, section 1.3.3). Assume an isolated agent with a finite lifetime of T periods (known to him) and

with an initial stock of wealth of W_0 of which she has no reason to spare something beyond her lifetime. W can be invested at an interest rate r. Alternatively, parts of W can be consumed in the magnitude C, where the following holds at any period:

$$W_{t+1} = (1 + r)(W_t - C_t). \qquad (10.5)$$

For the sake of simplicity, we assume that the agent's utility function is the sum of the natural logarithms of her consumption over his lifetime, where future utility is discounted with $0 < \beta < 1$.

Thus, the agent's decision problem is to choose the *optimal consumption vector over time* $(C_0, C_1, C_2, \ldots, C_T)$—which is assumed to take logarithmic form (to model decreasing marginal utility in a simple way) so that

$$\max(\log(C_0) + \beta \log(C_1) + \beta^2 \log(C_2) + \cdots + \beta^T \log(C_T)) = \max \sum_{t=0}^{T} \beta^t \log(C_t) \qquad (10.6)$$

where $W_{T+1} = !0$ in an optimal lifetime consumption path (no bequests are made).

The *Lagrange* algorithm, of which you have learned the details in Chapter 5, transforms this problem of optimally "rational" decision-making on consumption into a dynamical system. Basically, the Lagrange function reformulates the original (objective) function (Eq. (10.6)) by subtracting the condition, or constraint (Eq. (10.5)). The latter is, first, set zero and, second, multiplied with the so-called Lagrange multiplier (called P in our case). The Lagrange algorithm is used for maximization under a given constraint (a maximum or minimum limit). Instead of the original function, this Lagrange function will be maximized. The Lagrange function $\mathcal{L}$ in the case at hand is the following:

$$\max \mathcal{L}\left(\{W_t + 1, C_t, P_t\}_{t=0}^{T}\right)$$
$$= \sum_{t=0}^{T} \beta^t \{\log(C_t) - P_t[W_{t+1} - (1 + r)(W_t - C_t)]\} \qquad (10.7)$$

Maximizing the Lagrange function requires calculation of the first-order conditions of $\mathcal{L}$, i.e., the partial derivatives with respect to all three variables are to be set to zero:

$$(\beta^{-t})\frac{\partial\mathcal{L}}{\partial C_t} = \frac{1}{C_t} - (1+r)P_t = !0 \qquad (10.8)$$

$$(\beta^{-t})\frac{\partial\mathcal{L}}{\partial W_{t+1}} = -P_t + \beta(1+r)P_{t+1} = !0 \qquad (10.9)$$

$$(\beta^{-t})\frac{\partial\mathcal{L}}{\partial P_t} = -W_{t+1} + (1+r)(W_{t+1} - C_t) = !0. \qquad (10.10)$$

Since Eqs. (10.8)–(10.10) have to hold for all periods t, $0 \le t \le T$, this gives us a system of $3(T+1)$ equations which have to hold simultaneously. The first condition (Eq. (10.8)) informs us that

$$(1+r)P_t = \frac{1}{C_t} \qquad (10.11)$$

and equals the marginal utility of consumption in each period, but is not a dynamic structure. The other two conditions, however, form a dynamic system which consists of

$$\beta(1+r)P_{t+1} = P_t \qquad (10.12)$$

$$(1+r)(W_t - C_t) = W_{t+1} \qquad (10.13)$$

Inserting Eqs. (10.5) and (10.11) into Eq. (10.13) we get:

$$W_{t+1} = (1+r)\left(W_t - \frac{1}{(1+r)P_t}\right). \qquad (10.14)$$

The optimal, or "rational," decision (or series of decisions, or "strategy," "policy," or decision path) must be one of the many trajectories of this dynamic system. Setting P_T as a parameter initially and in this way determining the whole path of P_t, and inserting this into Eq. (10.14) would determine the path of W_t. An optimal path must be based on such a P_T which makes $W_{T+1} = 0$.

Typically, there are many feasible trajectories, and the agent's decision problem would

be to sort out the one with the highest value of utility over her life span. When the dynamical system resulting from the intertemporal optimization problem becomes complex or even chaotic, sorting out the optimal consumption plan can become a problem where the agent (or the economist calculating this system representative of the agent) will face bounds or barriers to rationality (see Foley, 1998, 27f.).

10.3.2 A Quasi-Neoclassical "Market" with Consumption and Investment

Also, in the conventional neoclassical structure of isolated maximizing agents (the *Walrasian* model as shown in Chapter 5), the resulting system behavior may become quite complex, as already the *individual excess demand functions* in the prices may be *complex nonlinear functions*. Therefore, neoclassical economics needs to strongly *simplify* in order to meet the objective of its research program, i.e., to demonstrate the equilibrating tendencies of "market" economies. Among these simplifications is the requirement to make *agents fully identical* in preferences, technology, and initial endowment (see Section 5.4.2 and Chapter 6). But as said above, it has the paradoxical implication that at equilibrium prices, no exchange takes place at all, i.e., the specific case of a situation where all individual excess demand vectors in all partial markets need to be zero. This is an extreme simplification required to prove the historical superiority of the "market." But even here some degree of complexity can be found.

Consider the following model of intertemporal equilibrium determination (see Foley, 1998, 29 ff.). The economy has two goods, corn, K, and steel, S. To produce 1 K next period requires a_{SK} units of steel (in terms of agricultural tools and machines). Similarly, to produce 1 S requires a_{KS} units of corn (in terms of food for steel workers). The stocks of both goods depreciate at the discount rate δ each period. The *representative agent* starts with an initial endowment of K_0 and S_0. She *consumes* only corn each period, C_t, but in order to produce more corn, she needs to produce steel (i.e., to *invest*) first. So the rational decision problem is to decide how much to invest and how much to consume.

We assume the same utility function to be maximized as in the previous example, with the same discount factor β for future utility (future consumption) as before. The utility maximization problem then is to choose $\{C_t, S_{t+1}, K_{t+1}\}_{t=0}^{\infty}$ so that

$$\max \sum_{t=0}^{\infty} \beta_t \log(C_t)$$

given the technological constraints

$$a_{SK}[K_{t+1} - (1 - \delta)K_t] \leq !S_t$$

and

$$a_{KS}[S_{t+1} - (1 - \delta)S_t] \leq !(K_t - C_t).$$

Again, the problem is solved by maximizing the objective function under the restrictions given (two technological restrictions and endowment restrictions in this case), i.e., the Lagrange function:

$$\max \mathcal{L}(\{C_t, S_{t+1}, K_{t+1}, P_{St}, P_{Kt}\}_{t=0}^{\infty})$$
$$= \sum_{t=0}^{\infty} \beta^t \log(C_t)$$
$$- \sum_{t=0}^{\infty} \beta^t P_{St}\{a_{SK}[K_{t+1} - (1 - \delta)K_t] - S_t\}$$
$$- \sum_{t=0}^{\infty} \beta^t P_{Kt}\{a_{KS}[S_{t+1} - (1 - \delta)S_t] - (K_t - C_t)\}$$
$$(10.15)$$

The first-order conditions are:

$$\beta^{-t}\frac{\partial \mathcal{L}}{\partial C_t} = \frac{1}{C_t} - P_{Kt} = !0 \qquad (10.16)$$

and analogously

$$\beta^{-t}\frac{\partial \mathcal{L}}{\partial K_{t+1}} = !0, \quad \beta^{-t}\frac{\partial \mathcal{L}}{\partial S_{t+1}} = !0,$$
$$\beta^{-t}\frac{\partial \mathcal{L}}{\partial P_{St}} = !0, \quad \text{and} \quad \beta^{-t}\frac{\partial \mathcal{L}}{\partial S_{t+1}} = !0.$$

Since this is an infinite horizon problem we have an infinite number of first-order conditions, and methods from dynamic programming have to be used to solve this system. These methods would require a lengthy treatment and will not be discussed here.

From Eq. (10.16), we get $C_t = (1/P_{Kt})$ and we can substitute $(1/P_{Kt})$ for C_t in the equation to be formed for $\beta^{-t}(\partial \mathcal{L}/\partial P_{Kt})$. In this way, we get a nonlinear dynamical system from the first-order conditions for an extremum of the Lagrange function:

$$P_{St} = \beta \left[\left(\frac{1}{a_{SK}}\right)P_{Kt+1} + (1 - \delta)P_{St+1}\right]$$

$$P_{Kt} = \beta \left[(1 - \delta)P_{Kt+1} + \left(\frac{1}{a_{KS}}\right)P_{St+1}\right]$$

$$S_{t+1} = (1 - \delta)S_t + \left(\frac{1}{a_{KS}}\right)\left(K_t - \frac{1}{P_{Kt}}\right)$$

$$K_{t+1} = (1 - \delta)K_t + \left(\frac{1}{a_{SK}}\right)S_t.$$

As in the previous example of optimal lifetime consumption, the *optimal joint consumption and production plan* of any individual agent must be one of the trajectories of this dynamical system. (There typically is no unique equilibrium in the neoclassical general equilibrium setting.) There are some possibilities to reduce the set of possible candidates for the optimal consumption and production path, but that does not fundamentally change the problem.

Generally, as in the previous "optimal consumption" example, the agent's problem is to not to set the initial so-called "*shadow price*" of corn (i.e., the *opportunity costs* of its consumption in terms of the quantity of the steel production foregone) too low or too high. In the first case, consumption would be too high so that the stock of corn would be exhausted and eventually become zero. In the second case, consumption would be too small, steel production thus too high, which never would increase the agent's consumption because of the high depreciation costs of the high steel stock.

The rational agent is required to calculate all trajectories of this system in order to sort out suboptimal and infeasible plans. This simplified "market" structure is, as Foley (1998, 32) mentioned,

> fairly simple and exhibit(s) only a small range of the possible spectrum of (the) dynamical repertoire of nonlinear systems. In these cases it is possible (...) that the discovery of the market equilibrium is computationally feasible for highly motivated and clever agents, who might use methods of trial-and-error extrapolation to determine the consistent current prices of assets.

Note again that the clever auctioneer who calls out the current prices, consistent with current and future market clearings, can be substituted by the clever economist who runs the model or by the clever agent himself who calculates her optimal infinite behavioral sequence. If any of them is able to solve the problem, all of them are. But note also that the conventional neoclassical "market equilibrium" wisdom, with its implicit auctioneer, particularly gives no way in which "the" market equilibrium (let alone complex equilibrium paths) would be arrived at. The Lagrange algorithm thus represents the representative individual's potential optimal decision. It has been illustrated earlier that even this setting (isolated individuals) leads to a dynamical system that may generate complex trajectories and prohibit any unique and stable equilibrium.

But even more so, such intertemporal rational choice models can exhibit very complex trajectories as soon as we loosen even the slightest restriction, as has been shown by, e.g., Boldrin and Montrucchio (1986) and Benhabib and Day (1981). Any complex dynamical system may arise from an intertemporal identical-agent optimal-consumption model as soon as,

for instance, several capital goods are allowed for (see Foley, 1998). Trajectories arising then may be chaotic, for instance.

It is well known that chaotic behavior can arise in a wide range of economically relevant intertemporal models (see Section 10.2.4 above). "These mathematical facts raise serious questions for the methodological plausibility of the Walrasian equilibrium concept that underlies these models (...)". And, therefore, "what warrant do we have for regarding Walrasian equilibrium as a relevant model of real market interactions?" (Foley, 1998, 33).

10.4 A POLICY SOLUTION AND THE EMERGENT-INSTITUTIONS SOLUTION

Within the wide range defined by the extremes of pure local information emerging exclusively from neighborhood interaction and pure global knowledge provided by some central agency (the "auctioneer"), system stability and trajectory predictability might emerge from "some" global information in a decentralized direct-interaction system. Some global information may be either generated and provided through an *exogenous agency* (a *policy* agent, a neutral advisor or a public policy agent), i.e., the "policy solution," or through the emergence of a social rule (or institution) from a process of interactively and informally solving the complex stability and coordination (or often cooperation) problem through interactively learning to behave rule-based and to follow a long-run and thoughtful rationality rather than "autistic" short-run maximization (for a detailed explanation of policy implications, see also Chapter 17).

10.4.1 Emergent Institutions with Policy

Albin and Foley (Foley, 1998, 18, and Albin and Foley, 1988) have modeled the "exogenous-agent"/third-party idea within a direct-interdependence topology. They model a public agent (a central bank, for instance, in the case of monetary policy), the measures of which are common knowledge available to each private agent. Such global information is considered "weak" in the sense that it does not replace the local information but comes on top of it. They introduce into the topology of private agents a *public agent* at a special site (on a different plane) which is a *neighbor to all private agents*. In this way all private agents receive some same, common and public, information. The informational unit is of the same dimension and size as the information that the individuals receive as a result of their decentralized interactions in their neighborhoods.

Consider that agents can assume the states $+1$ and -1 only (or C = cooperate and D = defect) and will do so according to an algorithm based on their current own, their memorized own, and their monitored third-party interactions in a neighborhood, past and present. Then the public policy agent can add another informational unit (confirmation or challenge of the state an agent has assumed on that informational basis, i.e., a "procyclical" or "anticyclical" policy) by adding another " $+1$ " or " -1 " to each agent's information stock, which somehow has to be processed by the agent, who will then have to reconsider her latest decision.

Depending on the algorithm governing that transformation of experienced and perceived local interactions into individual decisions, simulations of this model yield the result that the impact of policy is not at all clear and uniform. Complexity levels can be reduced but also increased by the public information supplement. Therefore, "solutions" in terms of equilibrating and stabilizing tendencies may become easier or more difficult.

Obviously, an issue here is the relative weight the public decision has for the decisions of the individuals, be it either the same

weight as any private interaction or any greater weight (say, the value of 100 private interactions), i.e., the degree of the weakness or strength of the global compared to the local information. Foley concludes that still "we have very little feel for the impact of weak global interactions in these contexts (of direct-interaction systems — WE)" (Foley, 1988, 18).

Note that in the conventional neoclassical "market"-equilibrium world the *auctioneer* in fact represents also a *strong policy*, i.e., full information provision. Agents do not need to collect information from interactions with others. Since the auctioneer metaphor has not been considered by neoclassical economists to be also a metaphor of strong policy, the prevailing way to view the "market economy" by the economic "mainstream" (and the everyday consciousness) has been that the (perfect) "market" does not need any policy intervention or frame setting and regulation (see Table 10.1, issue 14).

10.4.2 An Evolutionary Solution with Emergent Institutions Again

In the real world, interactions are always somehow *local*, with *information* consequently generated also locally only, i.e., with a *limited number of agents* rather than "very many" agents on a spot simultaneously, and, thus, with always some *scope for bargaining* on price, quantity, quality, and other dimensions of a transaction or relation between agents.

Living organisms and the social systems of human beings rarely exhibit full-fledged chaotic behavior. They typically have some *stabilizing*, particularly *structure-generating* ("*morphogenetic*" or "*autopoietic*") and self-reproducing ("*homeostatic*") properties. This is a "behavior qualitatively different both from simple stability and chaos" (Foley, 1998, 14; see also Chapter 11). As human beings do perceive, interpret, explore, consciously reflect, imitate, learn, expect, plan, anticipate, and adapt in manifold ways social systems are called *complex adaptive systems*. Their trajectories can exhibit extremely high *computational complexity* and thus *computational costs*, and often even a computational *infeasibility* and *logical insolvability* (see, e.g., Foley, 1998, 13ff.). Again, high computational complexity delineates "bounds" to rationality while logical infeasibility is equivalent to absolute "barriers" to rationality.

The research program to demonstrate how exactly the behavior of a large system converges on some asymptotic trajectory (i.e., an "attractor" in a complex system trajectory), in the sense of *self-organization* as described above, while the number of agents can be arbitrarily large, is connected with game theory, particularly evolutionary game theory. This has already been introduced in Chapter 8. We have applied this research program to real-world markets with few agents and with some scope for bargaining in the Cournot–Nash oligopoly in Chapter 7. We will get back to this in Chapters 11 and 13. As already explained, complexity is inherent in evolutionary modeling, and simplistic rationality impossible to maintain therein.

A *fully elaborated strategy* for a supergame would explicitly tell what the agent would do in every single interaction, depending on what has been done so far in the game. Developing an *"optimal" strategy choice in advance* would imply considerable *computational complexity* and, in fact, computational infeasibility. Strategies will typically be some *truncated version* of an ideal full strategy, i.e., a *more simple rule* to calculate and behave. This already indicates that there is no ideal rationality since agents have a smaller brain and memory capacity already than that required for a complete strategy for every individual interaction to come—which, in turn, relates to the bounded computational capacity of the human brain which is "biological" in this respect.

As mentioned, real human beings basically are at least as complex as their surrounding social interaction systems; they may be capable of very *complex reasoning*, but at the same time may also display a quite *simple behavior*.

In typical and recurrent complex situations, agents often need to, and in fact tend to, *reduce complexity*. They often have to reduce complexity in order to make undecidable problems (i.e., computationally infeasible solutions of systems) tractable. The simplest example of this was the 2×2 Prisoners' Dilemma supergame and the paradigm of its institutionalized cooperative solution, as explained and applied in Chapters 1 and 3.

While game theory provides basic devices for mathematical modeling, system trajectories of a certain level of complexity are no longer tractable in deterministic mathematical ways (see, e.g., Foley, 1998, 50ff.). They then require complex computation, i.e., model *simulation*, as introduced in Chapter 9.

We have seen already, in a rudimentary form, in Chapter 3 that, and how, *complexity reduction* through the agents themselves is a *prerequisite of problem-solving* in typical complex multipersonal decision settings such as a Prisoners' Dilemma, a coordination game, and other games. Problem-solving here does not mean that agents realize a predetermined unique stable system equilibrium as suggested by the "optimal market economy." On the contrary, they enter a complex process of experiencing and learning where they develop *social institutions* as less complex ways of behavior and as alternatives to recurrent counterproductive short-run rationality. This is to solve a problem, perceived as individual, in a rather egoistic way, just because they have to realize that they are not isolated individuals, that the problems at hand typically are collective ones, and that they have to consider the others if they want to improve their very own payoffs and status in the long run. Our introduction to complexity and related fields will continue with formal definitions and a broader set of applications in Chapter 11.

Evolutionary-institutional economics in this way may provide "an explicit theory of the ways in which agents achieve simplified representations of complex social interactions" (Foley, 1998, 67) as needed in these contexts. And in the complex social and economic contexts described typically "optimization of an objective function (is) less important than avoidance of disaster" (Foley, 1998, 67), as can easily be seen by considering a Prisoners' Dilemma or Coordination supergame. Thus, the perspective and "vanishing point" of complexity analysis is agents rationally developing some (somehow evolving) "equilibrium" (or attractor area), i.e., some stable *self-organization*, through proper behavioral regularities (see also Foley, 1998, 67ff.).

In contrast, as mentioned in Table 10.1 above (see issue (15)), the implicit auctioneer of the neoclassical interpretation of the classical idea of the invisible hand not only would implicitly represent, and thus explicitly redundantize, a policy agent (as mentioned earlier), but also the set of social rules as a required problem-solving device in complexity economics. In complex modeling, institutions emerge in a process of morphogenesis (or autopoiesis), i.e., self-organization, and the structure emerging often exhibits properties of homeostasis. That is, socioeconomic systems often display some stability, even after some circumstances have changed, or return to their paths even after some external shock.

The contemporary crises, particularly the financial "markets" crisis, have revealed most complex system properties and trajectories, i.e., an evolution with often changing behavioral regimes (bifurcations, see Section 10.2.5), rather than smooth deterministic or simply distributed stochastic motions (as in option-price or hedge theories). One of the problems of, and reasons for, the financial markets and their meltdowns may be that both financial economists and agents in the financial "markets" perceive and model them with lower complexity levels, such as systems with periodic orbits or of the chaotic type, amenable to analyses based on statistical regularities (see, e.g., Foley, 1998, 71).

To sum up, a universe of complex economies and processes exists—but this is not a situation where economic agents are "lost in complexity" or economic science would have to become agnostic. On the contrary, a new world of analysis and praxis is to be learned.

10.5 CONCLUSION

Following a systematic introduction to game theory and replicator systems (Chapter 8) and simulation (Chapter 9), this chapter presented the technique of dynamic modeling using difference equation systems. The relevant methods were briefly introduced and it was shown (based on Foley) how a neoclassical equilibrium system (see Chapters 5 and 6) would have to be modeled in a real-world way, e.g., with local direct interaction. This also showed that general-equilibrium models represent only an extreme point in the field of possible ways to model economies using dynamic systems, most of which would yield models with very different characteristics and results.

The central concepts, dynamics, evolution, and complexity, introduced in this chapter will be further explored in Chapter 11. There, we will also address the connections of these fundamental issues of economic systems with game theory and simulation, and include a number of definitions and examples that serve to clarify those most fundamental issues of all modern scientific disciplines.

Chapter References

Albin, P.S., Foley, D.K., 1988. Decentralized, dispersed exchange without an auctioneer: a simulation study.

In: Albin, P.S., Foley, D.K. (Eds.), Barriers and Bounds to Rationality. Essays on Economic Complexity and Dynamics in Interactive Systems. Princeton University Press, Princeton, NJ, pp. 157–180.

Benhabib, J., Day, R., 1981. Rational choice and erratic behavior. Rev. Econ. Stud. 48, 459–471.

Boldrin, M., Montrucchio, L., 1986. On the Indeterminacy of capital accumulation paths. J. Econ. Theory. 40 (1), 26–39.

Brock, W.D., 1988. Nonlinearity and complex dynamics in economics and finance. In: Anderson, P.W., Arrow, K.J., Pines, D. (Eds.), The Economy as an Evolving Complex System. The Proceedings of the Evolutionary Paths of the Global Economy Workshop, vol. 5. Addison-Wesley, Redwood City, CA, pp. 77–97. Santa Fe Institute Studies in the Sciences of Complexity.

Foley, D.K., 1998. Introduction. In: Albin, P.S., Foley, D.K. (Eds.), Barriers and Bounds to Rationality. Essays on Economic Complexity and Dynamics in Interactive Systems. Princeton University Press, Princeton, NJ, pp. 3–72.

Jarsulic, M., 1998. Chaos in economics. In: Davis, J.B., Hands, D.W., Maeki, U. (Eds.), The Handbook of Economic Methodology. Edward Elgar, Cheltenham, Northampton, pp. 59–64.

Li, T.-Y., Yorke, J.A., 1975. Period three implies chaos. Am. Math. Mon. 82 (10), 985–992.

May, R.M., 1976. Simple mathematical models with very complicated dynamics. Nature. 261, 459–467.

Further Reading—Online

For further reading, see the textbook website at http://booksite.elsevier.com/9780124115859

EXERCISES

1. Consider a difference equation model $x_{t+1} = ax_t(1 - x_t^2)$ (with $0 \le x_t \le 1$)

  a. Depending on parameter a, which fixed points do exist? Are they stable?

  b. Does the model undergo any bifurcations or other phase transitions? If so, at which point or parameter setting?

  c. Based on the analysis of the logistic map in this chapter, would you assume that the current system shows chaotic behavior?

2. Consider the following difference equation models. Determine if there are fixed points and (if so) which of them are stable.

  a.

$$x_{t+1} = x_t$$

  b.

$$x_{t+1} = x_t + 1$$

  c.

$$x_{t+1} = x_t$$
$$y_{t+1} = y_t$$

  d.

$$x_{t+1} = y_t$$
$$y_{t+1} = x_t$$

  e.

$$x_{t+1} = ax_t$$

  f.

$$x_{t+1} = x_t^2$$

3. What is a Taylor series? What can it be used for in economic models?

11

Dynamics, Complexity, Evolution, and Emergence—The Roles of Game Theory and Simulation Methods

"Complexity is like dark energy: It doesn't go away." **Sergey Bratus**[1]

[1]At the 29C3 Congress, Hamburg, 2012.

The Microeconomics of Complex Economies.
DOI: http://dx.doi.org/10.1016/B978-0-12-411585-9.00011-7

11.1 INTRODUCTION

Innovation is one of the most important elements of our economy. While small and steady incremental innovations occur all the time, it is not the small changes that develop economic systems but the radical innovations. Introducing new concepts, new innovative ways of looking at things, or new forms of organizations, wherever this introduction takes place, is what leads the economy to making progress. It is also highly risky. The innovator faces great uncertainty and again and again the risk of bankruptcy. There have been a number of well-known inventors and innovators in economic history, people who were lucky and who got used to taking the risk. However, they are few and the number of their unlucky counterparts is far larger. The stories of tragic geniuses, of the innovators that failed at some point do, however, mostly not go down in history. Successful innovations are scattered through time and over all regions of the world, though some were at certain times luckier than others. One might say, where they occur is complex and difficult to predict. Complex?

The phenomenon can be modeled using Christiaan Huygens' (a seventeenth century Dutch mathematician) *gambler's ruin problem*. A gambler engages in a series of bets with a 50% chance of winning and a 50% chance of losing an equal amount of money; she continues until she has gambled away her entire money (i.e., gambler's ruin)—how long does that take? If we observe several gamblers (or potential entrepreneurs), how is the time distributed it takes them to go bankrupt, what is the average and the variance of that distribution?

Mathematically, the process at hand is simply a random walk[2] starting at a positive value (say, 1 unit of money), and with each period randomly losing or gaining 1 unit; the process ceases when it reaches 0. The resulting distribution of the time of ruin over a large number of observations has surprising properties. Low values are very common, i.e., usually the game comes to a very quick end, but some incredibly high values occur in rare cases. Plotting the distribution in a log-log diagram, a diagram with a logarithmic scale on both axes, results in a straight line; see Figure 11.1. The distribution is also *scale-free* and self-similar. Each sufficiently large subsample (for instance, if we take only the observations exceeding a number of 20 successful gambles

---

[2]A random walk is a stochastic process that in each time step either increases or decreases its value by 1 (both with a probability of 50%). Random walk processes are common elements of stochastic models in financial and economic systems.

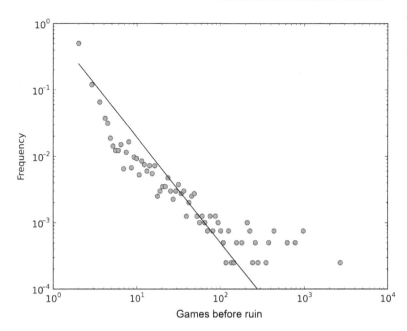

before bankruptcy occurs) mirrors the general distribution. The shape of the distribution is very stable—what is less stable is the average value and the variance we observe: they keep growing with the size of the sample. It is not immediately obvious why such a simple process would lead to such—to avoid using the term *complexity* again before we define it later on in this chapter—comprehensive and intricate phenomena. At the end of this chapter, we will shed some light on this question.

This chapter addresses the question of how complexity and related concepts are to be defined. It shows how methods like game theory, evolutionary game theory, general equilibrium theory, and simulation relate to this concept and, in a way, also to each other.

The first part of the chapter starts with models of the type that was introduced in Chapter 8, extends them gradually in order to explain and applies the concept of complexity using an example already introduced in Chapter 8 (Section 11.2). Section 11.3 addresses some formal aspects before we return to the question of

the origin of complexity in economic systems (Section 11.4) and briefly what this means for modeling in economics (Section 11.5).

11.2 THE PICTURE BECOMES COMPLEX

11.2.1 Increasing Complexity: A Sequence of Models

Consider the following situation: Two companies fight for dominance in an industry, a fight similar to the one we currently witness between Facebook and Google Plus in the social media sector of the Internet economy. Similar situations have been and will be mentioned a number of times in this book (see, e.g., Chapters 4, 8, 13, or 15)—the defining characteristic is that the competitors do not compete in the market (as addressed by oligopoly models, see Chapter 7); they compete for the market because they will be able to gain much larger profits once they dominate its technological standards.[3] This is particularly the case in industries with network externalities—where the users have an incentive to choose the technology that is used by the majority.

This example is similar to the one in Section 8.7.4. There, we used replicator dynamics to model the situation. A dynamic system with a single state variable θ_1 and a single development equation $\frac{d\theta_1}{dt} = -2\theta_1^3 + 3\theta_1^2 - \theta_1$ was defined. For the current example the development equation is slightly different; see equation below 11.1. The model is obviously a very simple one and indeed a tremendous simplification of reality. The entire system is reduced to one variable, the market share of one of the commercial competitors (with that of the second competitor implied as $1 - \theta_1$), the number of competitors has been limited to 2, their interaction has been reduced to a generalized one that can be captured in a single equation, and, most importantly, the independence, interdependence, and heterogeneity of the customers has been defined away.

There are good reasons for applying some simplifications. A nonsimplified model of reality would have to be as complex as reality itself (and can therefore not be both smaller than the entirety of reality and contained in reality). The general goal of developing models is to identify stylized mechanisms that are as simple and as simplified as possible but do still describe the original system as good as possible and can be used to make predictions that are as accurate as possible. Obviously, models can have different degrees of simplification; for instance the above model is not necessarily wrong, it is just unable to capture certain aspects of the system it was designed to investigate. We will now gradually extend the model to allow more and more

		Player B			
		P		G	
Player A	P		3		1
		3		1	
	G		1		3
		1		3	

FIGURE 11.2   Coordination game.

details of the system to be reflected in the model. It will become obvious that while the explanatory power of the model increases, the model itself becomes more and more difficult to handle and to analyze.

Model 0: Let us define Model 0 as the basic model: two competitors with market shares θ_1 and $1 - \theta_1$, hence only one state variable, θ_1 the development of which is given by a single differential equation $(d\theta_1/dt) = F(\theta_1)$. θ_1 is constrained to lie between 0 and 1 (since it denotes a market share)—for every possible value of θ_1, the continuous function F assigns a corresponding dynamic development, either growing, or decreasing, or, in case of a fixed point, an equilibrium, constant. Depending on F, there can be different equilibria of which at least one will be stable since the function is continuous. Other than in Chapter 8, we are not dealing with an underlying hawk-dove game. There, the hawk-dove game was used to describe the pricing for internetwork communications on the part of the networks. Here, we have a simple network externality: users benefit from using the same competitor's standard as many as possible other agents, the underlying game being a coordination game (Figure 11.2). There are two strategies, P (Facebook) and G (Google Plus). For a structured introduction to the method used here, consult Section 8.7.4.

---

[3]In sectors with large entry barriers as they are created by network externalities, competitors may have sufficient incentive to engage in costly price wars in order to drive their opponents out and then be able to appropriate monopoly profits. For details on this example, see Chapter 15.

The expected payoffs (used as fitness terms in this model) are:

$$\Pi_P = (1 \quad 0)\begin{pmatrix} 3 & 1 \\ 1 & 3 \end{pmatrix}\begin{pmatrix} \theta_1 \\ 1 - \theta_1 \end{pmatrix}$$

$$= (3 \quad 1)\begin{pmatrix} \theta_1 \\ 1 - \theta_1 \end{pmatrix} = 2\theta_1 + 1$$

$$\Pi_G = (0 \quad 1)\begin{pmatrix} 3 & 1 \\ 1 & 3 \end{pmatrix}\begin{pmatrix} \theta_1 \\ 1 - \theta_1 \end{pmatrix}$$

$$= (1 \quad 3)\begin{pmatrix} \theta_1 \\ 1 - \theta_1 \end{pmatrix} = -2\theta_1 + 3$$

As in Chapter 8, a replicator equation of the form

$$\frac{d\theta_i(t)}{dt} = \theta_i(t)(\Pi_i(t) - \phi(t)) \quad i = P, G \quad (11.1)$$

where $\phi(t)$ is the average fitness or average payoff at time t, hence $\phi(t) = \sum i \, \theta_i(t)\Pi_i(t)$, shall be used. Substituting the expected payoffs and average payoff into the replicator equation yields

$$\frac{d\theta_1(t)}{dt} = \theta_1(1 - \theta_1)(4\theta_1 - 2) = -4\theta_1^3 + 6\theta_1^2 - 2\theta_1$$

for θ_1(or equivalently for $\theta_2 = 1 - \theta_1$). The system has the equilibria

$$\theta_{1,1}^* = 0$$
$$\theta_{1,2}^* = 0.5$$
$$\theta_{1,3}^* = 1$$

the stability of which is conveniently assessed by linearizing the Jacobi matrix and computing the eigenvalue(s) of the corresponding linearized Jacobi matrix. In this case, the Jacobi matrix has only one element, the first partial derivative of the single replicator equation with respect to the only state variable, which gives us the basis for the linearization and the computation of the single eigenvalue as

$$\lambda = \frac{\partial d\,\theta_1(t)/dt}{\partial \theta_1} = -12\theta_1^2 + 12\theta_1 - 2$$

Linearizing for the three fixed points gives

$$\lambda(\theta_{1,1}^*) = \lambda(0) = -2$$
$$\lambda(\theta_{1,2}^*) = \lambda(0.5) = 1$$
$$\lambda(\theta_{1,3}^*) = \lambda(1) = -2$$

Thus, the first and the third fixed points are stable while the second one, the market sharing fixed point, is not. The stable fixed points correspond to the complete monopolization of the market with either of the two competitors as monopolist. This result is not surprising for cases with network externalities and corresponds to the introduction to the modeling of network externalities in Chapters 3, 4, and 8 as well as to Arthur et al.'s (1983, 1987) seminal model as presented in more detail in Section 13.6.

Note that the single eigenvalue of model 0 is always real,[4] never imaginary or complex, and that, no matter the specific form of the function F, at least one equilibrium is always stable. The stability is, however, not constant over the phase space and since there are at least two equilibria and the dynamic is continuous, there will also be one or two unstable equilibria. For details see Section 11.3.5.

Model 1: Consider model 0 with *three or more competitors*: what if—again considering the example of social networks—one of the distant third competitors, say, the free, distributed, and user-

---

[4]Real numbers are mathematically the numbers that arranged along a continuous line together with ordinary integers. Some arithmetic operations on such numbers—notably roots of negative numbers—do however lead to results which are not on this line. Specifically, imaginary numbers, usually denoted i, $-i$, etc., are those numbers on a continuous line orthogonal to the line of the real numbers and intersecting with it at 0. Complex numbers, conveniently denoted as sums of real and imaginary numbers $(1 + i)$, are the generalization of the two including the plain generated by them.

owned social network Diaspora, were to catch up? The market share vector would change to

$$\begin{pmatrix} \theta_1 \\ \theta_2 \\ 1 - \theta_1 - \theta_2 \end{pmatrix}$$

or, in case of multiple (n) competitors to

$$\begin{pmatrix} \theta_1 \\ \theta_2 \\ \vdots \\ \theta_{n-1} \\ 1 - \sum_{j=1}^{n-1} \theta_j \end{pmatrix}$$

Hence, the system now has $n-1$ state variables, which implies also $n-1$ development equations:

$$\frac{d\theta_1(t)}{dt} = \theta_1(t)(\Pi_1(t) - \phi(t))$$

$$\frac{d\theta_2(t)}{dt} = \theta_2(t)(\Pi_2(t) - \phi(t))$$

$$\vdots$$

$$\frac{d\theta_{n-1}(t)}{dt} = \theta_{n-1}(t)(\Pi_{n-1}(t) - \phi(t))$$

corresponding to replicator equation (11.1), as well as $n-1$ eigenvalues. The last share variable θ_n is always fully determined by the others and does therefore not have an independent dynamic development. Like in model 0, the eigenvalues of the Jacobian and consequently the stability properties are not constant over the phase space. Further, in this setting, the eigenvalues can become complex and therefore the dynamic may exhibit circular movements, possibly sustained cycles, instead of simply approaching an equilibrium. This does, however, not imply the impossibility to analytically study such dynamics.

Model 2: It has often been argued that profits and reinvestment are not the only aspect that

has an impact on a firm's fitness. There may be issues related to *routines, institutions, human capital, tacit knowledge*, and more. Taking this into account will make the fitness f_i a complicated function but most importantly it will be cumulative or, more generally, time-persistent. It becomes a state variable in its own right instead of being a simple transformation of the current market shares. In a simple implementation of this idea, the model becomes

$$\frac{d\theta_i(t)}{dt} = \theta_i(t)(f_i(t) - \phi(t)) \quad \forall i$$

$$\frac{df_i(t)}{dt} = F(f_i, \theta_i) \qquad \forall i$$

thus a system with $2n$ state variables, $2n$ development equations, and $2n$ eigenvalues. Moreover, only the market share variables θ_i are constrained while the fitness terms f_i can take any real value. Also, the fitness terms are structured differently: they do not directly depend on the entire system but the dynamic development of agent i's fitness only depends on her current fitness and her current market share while the dynamic developments of the market shares depend globally on all state variables of all agents. In turn, the Jacobi matrix becomes larger, has more eigenvalues, and consequently more different independent dynamics. The same goes for the following extensions of the model.

Model 3: In the models considered so far, only the firms were included as distinct entities with state variables and corresponding development equations representing them. The *consumers* supposed to decide for one or another technology were, however, implicitly reduced to a homogeneous type, the collective influence of which is included in one of the development equations. Considering the technological decisions d_j by all m consumers $j \in M$ (in this example, the decisions are made depending on the market shares of the n firms), the model as described above is complemented by m further development equations:

$$\frac{\mathrm{d}d_{ij}(t)}{\mathrm{d}t} = F_i(d_{ij}, \theta_1, \ldots, \theta_n) \quad \forall i \ \forall j$$

will naturally give a more accurate representation of reality. The number of state variables, development equations, and eigenvalues of the resulting system is now $(2 + m)n$.

Model 4: However, since the issue at hand is communication technology, customers may make different decisions for contacting different members of their peer group. For instance, a college student may regularly talk to her grandparents on the phone while preferring social media systems, internet chats, or voice over IP to communicate with her friends. That is, d is now a state variable on the level of links between customers j and $k \in M_j$, where M_j denotes the set of direct contacts of j.[5]

$$\frac{\mathrm{d}d_{i,j,k}(t)}{\mathrm{d}t} = F(d_{i,j,k}, d_{i,j,h}, d_{i,k,l}, \theta_1, \ldots, \theta_n)$$

$$\forall i \ \forall h \in M_j \ \forall l \in M_k \ \forall j \in M_j$$

This increases the number of state variables (and consequently also that of development equations and eigenvalues) to[6]

$$2n + \frac{k^2 n}{2} - kn$$

Model 5: Considering model 4 again, there are not necessarily $(k^2 n/2) - kn$ active connections since every consumer is only in communication with her direct peer group. The *network*

structure may also be subject to change over time. This does not decrease the number of state variables since the information if any two customers are connected or not must be represented in the model. It may be included as a special value in the variables $d_{i,j,k}$ or in a separate adjacency matrix.[7] It does, however, introduce further asymmetry since some variables are now mostly dependent on the local—peer group—level while others continue to be global variables. Depending on how closely or loosely the subsystems are interconnected, there may or may not be distinct and independent local developments, e.g., the local neighborhood may be mostly stable in a quickly changing global market or a stable structure in the global system may develop in spite of considerable variation on the peer-group levels—something that is described by the concept of emergence.

Model Extensions

Further possible extensions may add specific network structures between consumers—i.e., do some people have more friends or are likely to acquire more friends than others? And is this affected by their technology choices? They may include limited knowledge about existing technological alternatives on the part of the customers. They may extend the model to represent advertisement campaigns by the producers targeted at increasing the knowledge about their product or technology. Birth and death of customers may be included in the model as may entrance of newcomers to the market and exit of less successful competitors. Further, the market size and growth may be given in explicit

---

[5]These sets must obviously be symmetric, i.e., $k \in M_j \Leftrightarrow j \in M_k$.

[6]Because the matrix $D_i = \langle d_{i,j,k} \rangle_{\forall j \forall k}$ must be symmetric as well such that $d_{i,j,k} = d_{i,k,j}$ and because the main diagonal (i.e., $d_{i,j,j}$) does not contain meaningful elements.

[7]An adjacency matrix is in network theory a matrix that describes which nodes of a network are connected by direct edges. The rows and columns of the matrix correspond to the network's vertices. If two vertices j and k are connected than the element $ADJ_{j,k}$ (as well as element $ADJ_{j,k}$) are 1, otherwise it is 0.

terms instead of shares; it may be subject to a capacity constraint. There are numerous other possibilities.

What distinguishes each of these models from the models before (models 0 through 5) is that they are more detailed and more complex. The sequence gradually introduces more details, makes the models more and more difficult to analyze, and potentially increases the accuracy of their descriptions of reality. It also requires more and more information to describe the model exhaustively, and fewer and fewer simplifying assumptions have to be made for using the model. This fits the term and concept of *complexity* as we defined it in Chapter 1: complexity is what results from an interdependent situation with large numbers of heterogeneous and independent agents.

The reader may notice that complexity can be understood as an *ordinal* measure—here specifically when noting that each model above is more complex than the previous one. In other contexts, complexity may be seen as a *property* that may or may not be there. This raises the question of where exactly to draw the line: How detailed does a system have to be to be called complex? How many different features does it have to represent, how many variables does it have to have? How many interdependent agents have to be present in an agent-based model to justify that we call it a complex agent-based model—and how interdependent do they have to be? To be sure, we do not want to dismiss this property-like understanding of complexity entirely (nominal measures). It allows us to describe systems with particularly low *ordinal complexity* as *not complex*.

For instance, basic game theory setups—a 2-person-2-strategy normal-form game, two agents, two strategies each, four outcomes with payoffs for each of the agents, and easily inferable sets of Pareto optima and Nash equilibria

etc., see Chapters 2 and 8—are not particularly complex. The same is true for general equilibrium models with representative agents and without friction as detailed in Chapter 5; they are not very complex either. The real-world economy on the other hand is. Hence, while both game theory and general equilibrium economics can conveniently illustrate and reproduce certain aspects of economic reality, more complex models are needed to model other aspects. Note that it is also disputable if model 0 above (the basic model from Chapter 8) is particularly complex since it is effectively limited to two agents with all heterogeneity on the part of the customers assumed away. That does however change in the extensions in models 1 through 5.

As said, complexity can be defined in a number of ways. The remainder of this section will introduce a selection of the more important ones before returning to the aforementioned models in order to assess their complexity in a more systematic way.

11.2.2 Defining Complexity

Common usage of the term complexity follows a large number of concepts of which some may be useful while others are probably not. The list encompasses size, variety, difficulty, improbability, unexpectedness, and many more. Apart from everyday language, the concept is also widely used in a variety of scientific disciplines which gives rise to an even larger number of scientific definitions. The term was introduced into the scientific debate only 65 years ago by the American mathematician Warren Weaver (1948). While in social sciences the usage of the term tends to be more fuzzy—sometimes defined by a list of properties to be taken into account—natural sciences tend to resort to one of many[8] formally computable measures.

---

[8]A list of more than 40 such measures is given by Lloyd (2001).

The lists of necessary properties of complex systems as commonly used in social sciences[9] and sometimes in natural sciences often include the following:

- composition out of huge numbers of similar entities (such as cells, animals, people, or even groups of humans or machines),
- simple patterns of interaction between the entities on the micro-level in connection with the
- adaptiveness of the entities,
- limited predictability of future and reconstructability of past states of the system by means other than those involving exact representations of the system,
- nonergodicity,
- emergence of structure, patterns, and behaviors that are
- stable on the macro-level but
- which (the emergent macro-level properties) are not explicitly and trivially encoded into the systems' micro-level (basic entities).

Of course, a number of variations exist. For instance, such systems are sometimes called complex adaptive systems if adaptiveness is present and just complex systems if the micro-level entities are not strictly adaptive in the sense that entities react more or less consciously to other agents. For instance, a star system—composed of one or more stars and usually several planets and other celestial bodies—doubtlessly fulfills the other listed properties but the celestial bodies do not make decisions (if gravitational interaction is not seen as a kind of "decision"). That basic entities and their micro-level interaction should be simple is usually in relative

terms compared to the system's macro-level, for instance social systems are composed of humans which are in no way—neither physiologically nor psychologically—simple. Finally, emergence seems to be the most important of the commonly accepted characteristics of a complex system. If micro-level dynamics and macro-level dynamics are clearly distinct and not mediated by simple aggregation or something similar, then it becomes difficult if not impossible to describe local subsystems without explaining the macro-level and the rest of the system. This warrants that the system is described as an integrated whole and not just an agglomeration of parts. How this may happen is discussed in the context of the term emergence in the following Section 11.3.3.

This qualitative definition of complexity is sometimes called the *semantic definition* of complexity (Standish, 2006) as it concentrates on the meaning,[10] consequences, and implications of something being complex while quantitative measures are sometimes named *syntactic*[11] because they yield a specific value which may even be used as one of the bases of the qualitative, semantic assessment.

As mentioned, there are also many quantitative measures of complexity.[12] Some, however, are more commonly used and more important than others.

Information complexity is defined as the amount of information needed to describe a system exhaustively (or to a certain detail). For instance, a system composed of h elements each of which may take ℓ different states (microstates) has

$$\Omega = \ell^h \qquad (11.2)$$

---

[9]See, e.g., Standish (2006), Mitchell (2009), or Omerod (2009).

[10]The ancient Greek translation of the word "meaning", σημαντικός (semantikos) is the origin of the word "semantics."

[11]From ancient Greek σύνταξις (syntaxis), "arrangement."

[12]See, e.g., Bar-Yam (1997), Standish (2006), or Mitchell (2009).

different *macrostates*. This in turn implies the amount of information $\mathscr{C}$ needed to describe the system (in bits) as

$$\mathscr{C} = \log_2 \Omega \qquad (11.3)$$

Further, complexity is often linked to *entropy*. Entropy is a concept from physics, which captures the disorder of a system, more specifically, in how many different ways it could be arranged without being distinguishable from the current arrangement, technically how many different microstates exist for the current macrostate. Entropy of a system is defined as proportional to the probability of its current macrostate which, in turn, is the combined probability of the microstates of the elements and their arrangement, divided by the number of indistinguishable macrostates. Specifically, the *Shannon entropy* is defined as

$$H = E(-\ln P(\mathscr{M})) \qquad (11.4)$$

with $E(\sim)$ denoting the expected value and $P(\mathscr{M})$ being the probability weight of the macrostate $\mathscr{M}$. While systems tend to the most entropy-rich state, the complexity of a system is thus higher, the lower its entropy is, and the less likely the random occurrence of its current macrostate is.

Computational complexity of an algorithm is defined as the computation power required to compute that algorithm. Of course, the system the computational complexity of which is to be assessed needs to be an algorithm first—hence the measure cannot be used for observed phenomena that are not completely understood. Usually computational complexity is used as a theoretical construct to evaluate the complexity in relation to another system, i.e., whether they belong to the same or different complexity classes, if they were computed on a theoretical computer with infinite resources (a Turing machine, see Chapter 9). More illustratively, *Kolmogorov complexity*, one of a number of measures of computational complexity, is the

length of the shortest possible program that computes a given string.

Note that the basis for the computation of information complexity as introduced earlier is the uncompressed information, i.e., a string of 50 times the letter "a" would be evaluated as having the same complexity as a random string of 50 different characters. Kolmogorov complexity is in a way an extension to this since it allows the use of compression algorithms.

One final quantitative measure of complexity to be addressed in the current section is the *fractal dimension* or *Hausdorff dimension* of objects (particularly geometric structures or networks). A certain number $\mathscr{N}$ of regular geometric shapes of scale ζ (such as circles or balls with radius ζ, squares, cubes, or hypercubes with edge-length ζ) are needed to cover the object completely. The complexity of the object may be seen as higher, the higher its Hausdorff dimension. This can be used to define a dimensionality measure; the general definition is more complicated but for purposes of this textbook the simplified definition shall suffice. The fractal dimension is given by:

$$D_H = \lim_{\zeta \to \infty} \log_\zeta \mathscr{N} = \lim_{\zeta \to \infty} \frac{\log \mathscr{N}}{\log \zeta} = \lim_{\zeta \to \infty} -\frac{\log \mathscr{N}}{\log \frac{1}{\zeta}}$$

$$(11.5)$$

Note that the fractal dimension is always constrained by the dimension of the space it resides in, i.e., an object in d-dimensional space never has a fractal dimension larger than d because the maximum number of N at scale ζ progresses as a function of degree d (of ζ), $\mathscr{N}_{max} = \zeta^d$, hence

$$D_{H,max} = \lim_{\zeta \to \infty} \frac{\log \mathscr{N}_{max}}{\log \zeta} = \lim_{\zeta \to \infty} \frac{\log \zeta^d}{\log \zeta}$$

$$= d \lim_{\zeta \to \infty} \frac{\log \zeta}{\log \zeta} = d$$

Further note that every object with positive area (in two-dimensional space) has a fractal

(A)

(B)

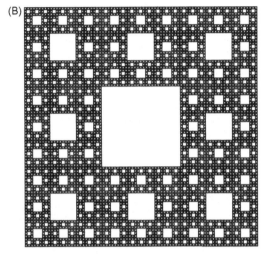

FIGURE 11.3 Examples for objects with (A) nonfractal (triangle) and (B) fractal (Sierpinski carpet) dimension.

dimension of 2, every object with positive volume (in three-dimensional space) has a fractal dimension of 3. Consider as an example a two-dimensional object that encompasses a share of exactly $0 < \alpha < 1$ of the total area (for instance the triangle in Figure 11.3A covers $\alpha = 0.5$ of the area). In this case, it follows that $\mathcal{N} = \alpha \zeta^d$, thus the fractal dimension is:

$$D_H = \lim_{\zeta \to \infty} \frac{\log \alpha \zeta^d}{\log \zeta} = \lim_{\zeta \to \infty} \frac{\log \zeta^d + \log \alpha}{\log \zeta}$$

$$= d \lim_{\zeta \to \infty} \frac{\log \zeta}{\log \zeta} + \lim_{\zeta \to \infty} \frac{\log \alpha}{\log \zeta}$$

$$= d + \lim_{\zeta \to \infty} \frac{\log \alpha}{\log \zeta} = d$$

Note that

$$\lim_{\zeta \to \infty} \frac{\log \alpha}{\log \zeta} = 0$$

since

$$\lim_{\zeta \to \infty} \log \zeta = \infty$$

while $\log \alpha$ has a constant (negative) value.

Fractional fractal dimensions remain for two-dimensional objects with zero area but infinite perimeter, for three-dimensional ones of zero volume but infinite surface, etc. Consider as an economic example the following simple model of industrial clusters in space: for every large square (say, starting with 1000 km by 1000 km) a cluster of innovative businesses builds up which occupies the 1/9th in the middle (1/3 length and 1/3 width). Now we have 1 developed square-shaped region and 8 undeveloped square-shaped regions. We repeat the same for each of the 8 undeveloped regions, giving us a further 8 (smaller) developed and $8 \times 8 = 64$ undeveloped regions. Infinite repetition yields the so-called *Sierpinski carpet* (Figure 11.3B). Computing the fractal dimension of the remaining undeveloped area we note that here $\mathcal{N} = 8^{\log_3 \zeta}$ and obtain the fractal dimension as

$$D_H = \lim_{\zeta \to \infty} \frac{\log 8^{\log_3 \zeta}}{\log \zeta} = \lim_{\zeta \to \infty} \frac{\log 8 \log_3 \zeta}{\log \zeta}$$

$$= \lim_{\zeta \to \infty} \frac{\log 8 \log \zeta}{\log 3 \log \zeta} = \lim_{\zeta \to \infty} \frac{\log 8}{\log 3} \approx 1.89379$$

There are many more measures for complexity; the one to be used depends obviously on the context, such as the object to be evaluated (Can it be represented as a geometrical shape? Is it a finite string of data? Do we have to deal with empirical measurements?). Often, we are faced with constraints regarding the scale to which we can represent or compute the object or to which we have data about the object. Sometimes, the object has to be transformed in order to be able to use specific measures. For instance, the systems of equations given in Section 11.2.1 do not have a geometrical form (hence the fractal dimension is not applicable to the system as such). They are also not data strings. However, the states can be and are generally stated as strings of data—i.e., the list of state variables at a given point in time. Though this is not an adequate representation of the system either since the basic characteristic of the system is to be dynamic and possibly adaptive, it may potentially be the case (and is sometimes claimed in the literature) that a system generates complex patterns, i.e., not only the system is complex but also the states the system assumes for certain points in time. Such a claim could conveniently be verified by assessing the complexity of the (possibly very large) data strings that represent the state of the system for a specific point in time. Depending on which measure is used, not only the number and variety of different values (which would dominate measures such as informational complexity) but also their *arrangement, symmetry*, and *recurrence* can be assessed. If a changing network of agents is part of the system as in model 5 above, this is of course a geometrical figure, the complexity of which may be assessed using its fractal dimension or other measures.

Evaluation of the complexity of the dynamics of the system, however, requires an intertemporal representation of its development. Phase portraits, diagrams of the change of (some of) the state variables in time (see Section 11.3.1), for instance, are often used. Since these do have a geometrical shape, the fractal dimension may be an adequate measure of their complexity, e.g., for nontrivial attractors (see Section 11.3.1), their fractal dimension is used as one of their defining characteristics. Other measures also remain valid.

11.2.3 Complexity in the Sequence of Models

Returning to the models 0 through 5 as discussed in Section 11.2.1, we may now return to evaluate their complexity. The difficulty with assessing the complexity of a dynamic model lies in defining the basis of this assessment. As mentioned in Section 11.2.2, the complexity of patterns generated by a system such as a network structure or a specific market structure is substantially different from the complexity of the dynamics of the system. While the network may have a complex scale-free small-world (see Section 13.10) shape, the development of the system might have led straight to a monopoly with no more changes occurring after that or vice versa (complex dynamics, regular network). However, the two are subject to mutual influencing and certain features of the model facilitate the development of complex properties in both structure and dynamics.

One such characteristic has already been addressed in detail in Section 11.2.1: the number of state variables. Since each of the state variables corresponds to a dynamic equation, their number is equal to the number of development equations. The number is also an upper boundary of the number of independent dynamic influences, represented by the eigenvalues of the transformation matrix of the (corresponding linearized) system. Cyclical behavior, for instance, is only possible if we have at least two state variables (and hence two development equations and two eigenvalues) as presented in more detail in Section 11.3.5. The symmetry of the system of equations is another characteristic: if each variable depends on every other variable, the system is less likely to develop locally different characteristics and multiple layers. This result is typical for agent-based models which consist of global variables on the one hand and of local variables on the other hand. The local variables depend only on some few variables that correspond to the same agent and its immediate environment as well as potentially the global variables while the global variables directly depend on the entire system. If the local subsystems were completely independent but similar to each other, the system would still be symmetric and it would likely result in a collection of systems that show the same dynamic. Weak connectivity between the subsystems, however, can give rise to qualitatively different dynamics. Then the system is asymmetric in the sense that (i) some variables have an impact on substantially more variables than others and that (ii) the dependence of variable B on variable A does generally not imply the reverse. Influences between subsystems is thus limited to indirect influences via the global layer—whether this will indeed lead to complexity depends on a number of things but it becomes more likely the more the symmetry of the system decreases.

While complexity measures as introduced in Section 11.2.2 corresponding to the models from Section 11.2.1 will thus depend on the details of the respective models for which we did not make any assumptions, the potential complexity can be rated using the number of development equations, the symmetry properties, and potential cyclicity. An overview is given in Table 11.1.

The technical details of the linearization of nonlinear models like these and the consequences for cyclicity etc. are discussed in Section 11.3.5. Also, an illustrative example of cyclical models in economics and their consequences for the system's stability will follow there alongside with an introduction to more complex structures that may result in dynamic systems. First, however, a structured introduction to a number of formal aspects will be required.

Note that simple neoclassical models are by comparison generally less complex. Assuming perfect market properties and homogeneous agents reduces the system essentially to a few macro-level equations with only a couple of independent equations (apart from the fact that such neoclassical systems are assumed to be static, not dynamic, and thus do not have development equations). With the numerous extensions that general equilibrium theory has produced over the years, this is, however, not necessarily the case. For instance, the infinite horizon optimization problems introduced in the last sections of Chapter 5 and analyzed in more detail in Chapter 10, are much more complex. They include a potentially independent restriction for every one of the infinitely many time steps. Further, the dynamic stochastic general equilibrium models mentioned in Chapter 5 recognize that there may be dynamic disturbances around a theoretical equilibrium. For these models, development equations do, of course, exist.

TABLE 11.1 Potential for Complexity in Models 0 Through 5

Model Number	Model Type	Number of Development Equations	Symmetry	Cyclicity
0	Basic evolutionary competition model	1	Yes	No
1	Multiple competitors	$n - 1$	Yes	Yes
2	Cumulative fitness	$2n - 1$	Partially	Yes
3	Heterogeneous customers	$(2 + m)n$	Partially	Yes
4	Direct interactions between customers	$2n + \dfrac{k^2 n}{2} - kn$	Partially	Yes
5	Changing neighborhood structure	$2n + \dfrac{k^2 n}{2} - kn$	No	Yes

11.3 FORMAL ASPECTS OF DYNAMIC AND COMPLEX SYSTEMS

Having introduced the basics of dynamic (evolutionary) game theory in Chapter 8 and the basics of dynamic systems in general in Chapter 10 (Section 10.2.5) we proceeded to apply the concept of complexity to these fields in Section 11.2. A number of technical aspects have been mentioned without going into detail. At this point, a couple of formal definitions and considerations is in order before the discussion of the relation of complexity, evolution, and economic systems will be continued in Section 11.4.

11.3.1 Dynamic Systems, Attractors, Ergodicity, Chaos, Path Dependence, and Other Concepts

Dynamic Systems

A dynamic system (for a definition, see Chapter 10) is a system of *state variables* given in the form of a state vector x_t at time t and *development equations* for each of the state variables given as the function $F(x_t)$. The development equations are generally given as either *differential equations* $(\mathrm{d}x_t/\mathrm{d}t) = F(x_t)$ or *difference equations* $x_{t+1} = F(x_t)$; the dynamic system is respectively called a system of differential equations or a system of difference equations. It may or may not be *time-invariant*, i.e., not directly dependent on time t so that the behavior of the system is not affected by the starting point t_0 but only by the *initial values* $x_0 = x_{t_0}$. And it may or may not be *linear* in the sense that F are linear functions of x_t. A linear dynamic system's properties are characterized by the *eigenvalues* of the *transformation matrix* $\mathscr{A}$, where $\mathscr{A}$ contains the coefficients for the linear transformation of the input variables into the output variables. For nonlinear systems, the properties change depending on x_t; for specific points they may be assessed by linearizing the *Jacobi matrix* $\mathscr{J}$ of F:

$$\mathscr{J} = \begin{pmatrix} \dfrac{\partial \mathrm{d}x_1/\mathrm{d}t}{\partial x_1} & \dfrac{\partial \mathrm{d}x_1/\mathrm{d}t}{\partial x_2} & \cdots & \dfrac{\partial \mathrm{d}x_1/\mathrm{d}t}{\partial x_n} \\[2ex] \dfrac{\partial \mathrm{d}x_1/\mathrm{d}t}{\partial x_1} & \dfrac{\partial \mathrm{d}x_2/\mathrm{d}t}{\partial x_2} & \cdots & \cdots \\[2ex] \vdots & \vdots & \ddots & \vdots \\[2ex] \dfrac{\partial \mathrm{d}x_n/\mathrm{d}t}{\partial x_1} & \dfrac{\partial \mathrm{d}x_n/\mathrm{d}t}{\partial x_2} & \cdots & \dfrac{\partial \mathrm{d}x_n/\mathrm{d}t}{\partial x_n} \end{pmatrix}$$

$$(11.6)$$

Note that for linear systems the Jacobi matrix only contains scalar numbers, no functions, thus $\mathscr{A} = \mathscr{J}$. The linearization for nonlinear systems and its consequences are addressed in Section 11.3.5.

The eigenvalues of the Jacobi matrix or transformation matrix are computed as the set of values λ that fulfill the following condition with an arbitrary corresponding eigenvector v:

$$\lambda v = \mathscr{A} v \qquad (11.7)$$

For an illustrative example and details on the computation, see Box 10.1 and Section 10.2.5. Every eigenvalue defines a separate property of the behavior of the dynamic system which may be expanding or contracting and cyclic or noncyclic; see Table 11.2. A dynamic system has the same number (n) of state variables, development equations, and eigenvalues.

Phase Space

The phase space—or for discrete systems also *state space*—R_x of the system is the space formed by the domains (possible values) of the state variables x; hence, the phase space of a system with n state variables is n-dimensional. For instance, if the domain of every state variable are the real numbers $\mathscr{R}$ then $R_x = \mathscr{R}^n = \prod_n \mathscr{N} = \mathscr{N} \times \mathscr{N} \times \mathscr{N} \times \cdots$.

TABLE 11.2 Dynamic Characteristics Resulting from Specific Eigenvalues

Dynamic Characteristics Defined by Eigenvalue λ	Systems of Differential Equations	Systems of Difference Equations
Contracting	Negative real part, $Re(\lambda) < 0$	Modulus smaller than 1, $|\lambda| < 1$
Expanding	$Re(\lambda) > 0$	$|\lambda| > 1$
Marginally stable	$Re(\lambda) = 0$	$|\lambda| = 1$
Cyclical	Nonzero imaginary part, $Im(\lambda) \neq 0$	$Im(\lambda) \neq 0$
Definition of the dominant eigenvalue λ_D	$\lambda_D = \lambda$: $\max(Re(\lambda))$	$\lambda_D = \lambda$: $\max|\lambda|$

Trajectories

The development of a system starting from a particular starting point is called a trajectory. Since there are (generally) infinitely many possible starting points, there are infinitely many trajectories. Trajectories never cross.[13] The dynamic development of a system may be assessed using the *phase portrait* which is a graphical depiction of a selection of trajectories in (some dimensions of) the system's phase space.

Fixed Points

A fixed point x_B is an equilibrium point of a dynamic system in the sense that the system will, if it ever reaches that point (say at time t_B), remain there forever:

$$x_{t_B} = x_B \Rightarrow x_t = x_B \quad \forall t > t_B \qquad (11.8)$$

The necessary and sufficient condition for fixed points is, in case of differential equations:

$$\frac{dx_t}{dt} = 0 \qquad (11.9)$$

or, in case of difference equations (compare Section 10.2.5):

$$x_{t+1} = x_t \qquad (11.10)$$

Note that the conditions (11.9) and (11.10) are vector equations and have to be fulfilled component-wise, i.e., for all state variables. Fixed points are important because they may allow predictions about future values of the state variables. If a fixed point is stable, i.e., if it is approached by the trajectories in its immediate environment (see Figures 11.4A and 11.5A), the probability for the system to be in that fixed point for any given point in time is substantially higher than for arbitrary other points. This is, of course, even more true for stochastically disturbed dynamic systems in which small stochastic shocks can cause the system to leave the equilibrium and end up somewhere in the immediate vicinity (thus falling back into the fixed point if and only if the fixed point is stable). In order to assess the stability of a fixed point, the eigenvalues of the system (in case of nonlinear systems of the linearized system in that point) have to be evaluated. If (and only if) the dynamic represented by the dominant eigenvalue (and thus also those represented by any other eigenvalue) is contractive, then the fixed point is stable. It may be *marginally stable* if it is neither contractive nor expansive or unstable if the dominant eigenvalue defines an expanding dynamic. Unstable fixed points are called *repellers* or *repulsors* (see Figure 11.4B).

---

[13]This holds only for systems that are not stochastically disturbed; otherwise, it holds for the trajectories of the corresponding undisturbed system.

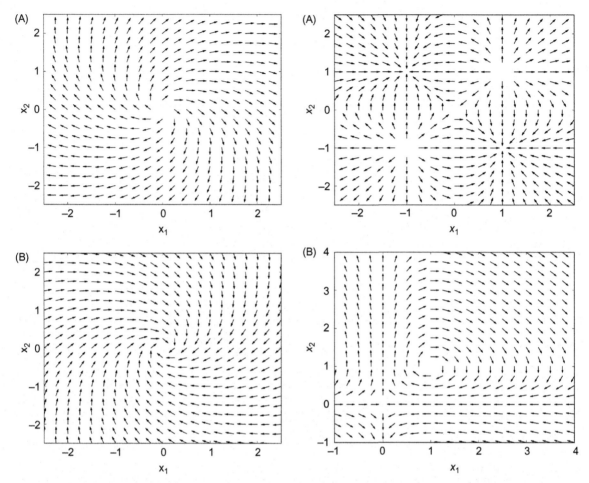

FIGURE 11.4 Phase portraits showing an attractor (A) and a repeller (B).

FIGURE 11.5 Phase portraits showing a path dependent system with two attractors, two repellers, and a saddle point (A) and a limit cycle attractor (visible in the upper right part) (B, the system from Eq. (11.17)); the dynamic here forms a perfect cycle.

Attractors

Stable fixed points are called attractors but the concept of attractors extends beyond fixed points. An attractor is every set of points $B \in R_n$ such that if the system reaches one of the points in the set at a time t_B the trajectory is absorbed by B, i.e., it never leaves B again:

$$x_{t_B} \in B \Rightarrow x_t = x_B \quad \forall t > t_B \qquad (11.11)$$

and the trajectories from an immediate vicinity of B converge toward B (see Figures 11.4 and 11.5). As with stable fixed points, the identification of

attractors may help making predictions since the probability of ending up in an attractor B is strictly positive while this is not the case for other points of the phase space (that are not part of attractors). The probability for the system ending up in B increases the larger the area in the phase space is from which the trajectories converge toward B. This area is called B's *basin of attraction*. If the basin of attraction encompasses the entire phase space with the exception of isolated repellers (or sets or repellers), then B is called a *global attractor*; otherwise, it is called a *local attractor*.

Limit Cycles

A closed circular dynamic in continuous dynamic systems whether it attracts trajectories from its surroundings or not is called a limit cycle. Inside a limit cycle is always at least one (stable, unstable, or often marginally stable) fixed point (see Figure 11.5B).

Ergodicity and Nonergodicity

A system is said to be ergodic if the time distribution of the system's states matches its distribution of microstates (its ensemble distribution). As mentioned earlier, the microstates are the product space of the possible states of all the state variables. In our case, they are equivalent to the system's phase space but the concept also holds for representations that see several state variables[14] as indistinguishable. In this case, macrostates (ensembles) that can be generated by more different microstates are more likely to occur and have larger probability weight in the system's ensemble distribution and—if the system is ergodic—also in its state's time distribution. To put it in simpler terms, a system is said to be ergodic if every point in its phase space will be reached. Systems with attractor structures for instance are nonergodic since the attractor absorbs the system's trajectories and the system will then not any longer be able to reach points outside the attractor. As it is difficult to formally show that a system is strictly ergodic, the assessment is in practice often limited to show that the mean and variance of time distribution and ensemble distribution match (weak ergodicity). For the systems under consideration here, ergodicity can often immediately be ruled out since we are often faced with attractors.

Deterministic Chaos

A dynamic development is said to be characterized by deterministic chaos if the trajectories diverge. For the formal evaluation of this, we select two trajectories of a dynamic system which take the values x_t and $\tilde{x}_t$ at time t and the values x_{t+T} and $\tilde{x}_{t+T}$ at time $t + T$. If for any two such trajectories, the *Lyapunov function* $V(x_t, \tilde{x}_t)$ gives a however defined distance between the two trajectories, the *Lyapunov exponents* are defined as the function $\Lambda(T)$ fulfilling

$$V(x_{t+T}, \tilde{x}_{t+T}) = e^{\Lambda(T)} V(x_t, \tilde{x}_t) \qquad (11.12)$$

Positive Lyapunov exponents indicate diverging trajectories. This is important because it limits the system's predictability up to the point where it is impossible to make any predictions if (i) the state of the system is not precisely known or (ii) the system is subject to stochastic disturbance. Note that the system is perfectly predictable if neither of the two holds, which makes systems showing deterministic chaos conveniently analyzable. Further note that deterministic chaos is fundamentally different from both perfect randomness (in which case, the Lyapunov exponents should be $\Lambda(T) = 0$ for all T) and convergent dynamics which occur in the presence of, for instance, stable fixed points. For an example, see Section 10.2.5.

Phase Transitions and Bifurcations

Spontaneous or, via infinitesimally small parameter changes, exogenously introduced sudden changes in the characteristics of the system, its behavior, or the structural patterns it generates in its state variables are called phase transitions. A phase transition that changes the structure of the phase space such that a fixed point becomes unstable and/or gives rise to two (or more) new fixed points is called a bifurcation. An example for a bifurcation in a system of difference equations was given in Section 10.2.5

---

[14]For instance binary properties of agents: the agent has adopted technology An or she has adopted technology B.

(which includes a bifurcation diagram of the discrete logistic map).

Path Dependence

A system is called path dependent if the outcome of two different, and perhaps only slightly different, states leads to a persistently different development path, for instance, the convergence to two different attractors (see Figure 11.5A). The implication for stochastically disturbed systems is, of course, that the path the system will take and that will then be impossible to be changed may depend on small random influences. Implications of this concept for real-world systems are addressed in the examples and models for technology choice in Chapters 4, 13, and 15, among others.

11.3.2 Complex Dynamic Systems

So far we have extensively discussed both dynamic systems and complex systems in this chapter. While dynamic systems may or may not be complex, the question if the reverse is also true has not yet been considered. However, the concepts of complex and dynamic systems are inextricably linked.

A dynamic system is called a *complex system* if one of the many well-founded definitions of complexity as reviewed in Section 11.2.2 can reasonably be applied to it, the dynamics it generates, or the states (the configurations of values of the state variables) that result from it. Note that while some definitions allow such characterizations (semantic definitions), others are quantitative and would rather assign a specific complexity value to the system (syntactic definition) and/or allow only assessments like the one that the system is more or less complex than another system compared with it (also semantic). Note that semantic definitions of the term complexity usually involve a number

of characteristics often including adaptiveness, limited predictability, and—most importantly—emergence and nonreducability of the characteristics of the macro-level to the characteristics of the micro-level. Some of these are also partially quantifiable in that they are partially captured in one of the quantitative measures of complexity.

A complex system does also imply a dynamic development particularly if the behavior (dynamics) of the system are claimed to be complex. While this is not necessarily true for complex patterns, every pattern can also conveniently be characterized by describing the process of its generation, i.e., it can be transformed into a dynamic system.

To model systems that change in time, however, one or another type of dynamic equations (or, less conveniently a combination of both) has to be used. This in turn means that dynamic systems (either systems of differential or of difference equations) are among the most straightforward models that could be considered for any type of complex systems—for many types (those that are inherently dynamic) there are not even feasible alternatives to this way of modeling.

11.3.3 Emergence

Historic Debates on Emergence and Reductionism

The most important and defining among the characteristics of complexity is, as described earlier, emergence. This concept is rooted in an old philosophical debate[15] that revolves around nothing less than science, religion, and the nature of the universe. *Reductionism* has over much of the past 200 years been perceived as the essence of the scientific method: Out of which elements is an object of study composed,

---

[15]Aristotle's writings on the concept of emergence survive and are testament to an already ongoing philosophical discussion on such issues.

how do they work, how do they interact? Naturally there has been some resistance against this view motivated by ideological and religious reasons, but some traditions of philosophy have also argued that a radical reductionist program means throwing out the baby with the bath water. Their argument was that while it is feasible to use a reductionist methodology in order to understand the elements of a system, some properties of a system are qualitatively different from those of the elements and cannot be anticipated from an analysis of the elements only. The idea does obviously depend on how the ability to anticipate is defined—this was a major point of contention in height of the scholarly debate on emergence in the late 1920, with other issues being free will, life, evolution, the universe, consciousness, and religion. While the concept of emergence was defended by, among others, biologist Lloyd Morgan, philosopher C. D. Broad, and mathematician Bertrand Russell, it was broadly attacked by biologists Oscar Riddle, Hans Driesch, and others. An overview is given in Ablowitz (1939). In a way, the debate anticipated the later discussion revolving around the concept of complexity mirroring many of its arguments.

The earlier 1920s debate faded slowly into history with the next generations of scholars being strong advocates of reductionism. The concept was revived only in 1972 when an article by physicist Philip Anderson—without even once mentioning the term "emergence"—reiterated some of the earlier debates arguments and offered a formal explanation (Anderson, 1972), something the 1920s debate had failed to do. Anderson contended that a central feature in the behavior of simple systems is their symmetry (in space and time); the symmetry is broken under certain conditions in their macroscopic arrangements of simple elements. Anderson offered examples from particle physics, including ferromagnetism, crystals, and dipole molecules,[16] but held that it probably works in a similar way on other levels such as cells, organisms, or societies.

Definitions and Conditions of Emergence

The concept has by now been widely accepted in many disciplines as well as interdisciplinary approaches (mostly under the label of "complex systems"). Since in other fields even the symmetry of the elements is at best questionable, a number of other criteria have been introduced and are used alongside with broken symmetry. Among those are the impossibility to infer the system's macro-level and characteristics from its micro-level elements (*irreducibility*), its impact on the micro-level elements' behavior (*downward causation*), the robustness of the macro-level patterns compared to variation and turbulence on the micro-level (*dissipativity*), and a few less common others. For an overview, also discussing the more recent debate, see Corning (2002). While irreducibility is largely intuitive equivalent to the argument from the earlier debate covered earlier, the other two warrant a few more words of explanation.

Downward causation is the idea that not only the system's micro-level has an impact on the emerging macro-level, but there is a *feedback loop* that, in turn, makes the behavior of the micro-level dependent on what happens on the macro-level. Note that this is not an additional assumption but merely another way to put the general idea since the macro-level does not exist independently from the

---

[16]In particle physics, persistent dipole moments cannot exist; simple dipole molecules like ammonia invert their orientation at breathtaking speed, thus still being symmetric with respect to electric charge, but for much larger molecules, say, proteins such inversion is no longer possible "in finite time compared to, say, the age of the universe" (Anderson, 1972, p. 394).

micro-level and it only has characteristics that somehow also exist on the micro-level. If for instance a solid metal structure develops ferro-magnetic properties, this is only due to the fact that the magnetic polarity of its elements is perfectly aligned. For the first or the first few elements that align themselves, this is a random alignment, but the arrangement of the structure leads to this first aligned element having an impact on the alignments of the surrounding elements (as modeled in physics with the *Ising model*). The same is true for a group of people developing over the centuries into a consistent language group and then forming a nation state. It also holds for the universal acceptance of technological standards and institutions or moral codes. There are plenty of other examples.

Dissipativity is the ability of a structure to exist in and on top of a turbulent environment by avoiding to absorb the inflowing entropy. In effect this typically means structures that organize their elements but exist independently of specific elements. The structure persists while elements and entropy flow in and out. In effect it is a subsystem that conserves a certain kind of information while not conserving the information it is exposed to in its environment.

One of the striking features of emergence is that it defines in a generic way an aggregated level complete with its own properties, characteristics and laws of behavior. This is different from the common macro-level which usually is defined as simply the entire system or the reference level of the data under investigation (e.g., a country if the respective analysis works with data compiled by that country's government). The usual macro-level is therefore context specific. An emergent layer is different and may exist independently of context, region and era. An example are the groups of cooperators that form on a specific (meso) level in the model introduced in Chapter 3 and developed in more detail in Chapter 14.

11.3.4 The Surprised Observer

Much confusion with regard to both complexity and emergence has arisen from a common misconception which results from some of the less elaborate accounts of both concepts: If the defining characteristic lies in a subjective term like irreducibility or unpredictability, is not then the concept as such subjective? If a given observer fails to deduce the characteristics of an object from analyzing its parts, this does not infer the general impossibility to do so. The critique is not new; in fact Ablowitz (1939) discusses it as one of the main points of contention in the old debate on emergence. There are several variants that involve other concepts which rest on either the subjective perception or the personal ability or inability to do or anticipate something. They include novelty, surprise, anticipation, and predictability.

Note that even the quantitative concepts are potentially vulnerable to this critique: The Kolmogorov complexity introduced earlier, certainly one of the most elaborate quantitative measures, states that the complexity is given by the shortest possible program required to construct a string (or pattern, or other object). While the theoretical definition involves the shortest possible program which is not subject to change with the programming skills of different observers, any possible empirical measurement is—unless it involves a mathematical proof that no shorter program is possible.

The critique shows that both emergence and complexity as a semantic term (in the sense that something is or is not complex) are fuzzy concepts. This is probably why no unique and commonly accepted definition of either complexity or emergence has yet emerged. However, most of the measures and definitions introduced earlier allow to take more objective measures and characteristics into account. And while some of the subjective properties—say, irreducibility—may be important for the definition of the concept, they should be approached carefully when it comes to its application while others— say, surprise—should obviously be avoided altogether.

11.3.5 Assessing the Stability of Nonlinear Systems: Linearizing Jacobians

After introducing some of the central concepts of the study of complex systems we conclude this section by addressing a very different but also formal aspect. Section 11.2 discussed linear and nonlinear dynamic systems and made several contentions about their different properties. A formal demonstration of these is given in the following; this demonstration will also provide an example for an economic model generating a stable cyclical dynamic instead of a simple fixed point attractor (like in most of the systems considered so far).

However, to make the example more illustrative we start with a linear model: Consider the linear system of equations:

$$\frac{dx_1}{dt} = 0x_1 + 1x_2 = x_2$$

$$\frac{dx_2}{dt} = -1x_1 + 0x_2 = -x_1$$

(11.13)

Recall that the fixed points of a dynamic system are defined by condition (11.9) and note that the only fixed point of this system is $x_1 = x_2 = 0$. The transformation matrix is:

$$\mathscr{A} = \begin{pmatrix} 0 & 1 \\ -1 & 0 \end{pmatrix}$$

(11.14)

Note how the elements of the matrix correspond to the coefficients in the system of equations above. For linear systems of differential equations or difference equations, the transformation matrix is identical to the Jacobi matrix. The Jacobian matrix is defined

as the matrix of partial derivatives of the system of equations, namely:

$$\mathscr{J} = \begin{pmatrix} \dfrac{\partial dx_1/dt}{\partial x_1} & \dfrac{\partial dx_1/dt}{\partial x_2} \\ \dfrac{\partial dx_1/dt}{\partial x_1} & \dfrac{\partial dx_2/dt}{\partial x_2} \end{pmatrix}$$

(11.15)

Consequently, the eigenvalues for system (11.13) are computed by applying Eq. (11.7) from which it follows that (I being the unit matrix of the same order):

$$\det(\mathscr{A} - \lambda I) = 0$$

(11.16)

The transformation is explained in more detail in Box 10.1. We obtain:

$$(0 - \lambda)(0 - \lambda) + 1 = 0$$

$$\lambda^2 = -1$$

$$\lambda_{1/2} = \pm\sqrt{-1} = \pm i$$

As both eigenvalues are purely imaginary (zero real part), it follows that the system is marginally stable and induces cyclical dynamics. As the system is linear, this is true for the entire phase space including the single fixed point.

Now consider a nonlinear dynamic system:

$$\frac{dx_1}{dt} = x_1 x_2 - x_1 = x_1(x_2 - 1)$$

$$\frac{dx_2}{dt} = -x_1 x_2 + x_2 = x_2(-x_1 + 1)$$

(11.17)

Assume the two variables are macro-level characteristics of an economy, specifically let x_2 be a function of the employment rate (1—unemployment) while x_1 is a function of the employees' share of the total output. Note that the two are not identical to but functions of the employment rate and the employees share of income respectively—this means that they are not constrained between 0 and 1. The dynamic development of both functions does, of course, depend on their current value and also on the (multiplicative) interaction term with the other one. Specifically, if the employment rate is higher than some specific value (1 in this case), the bargaining power of the trade unions increases which also leads to higher wages, i.e., x_2 has a positive effect on x_1. However, if the wage share is too high, employment drops, specifically, if x_1 is higher than some value (again 1 in our case), x_2 falls, if it is lower, x_2 increases. The model is a simplification of Richard Goodwin's (1967) growth cycle model. The historic relevance of this model was that it was one of the first economic models that could—together with a production function that is left out here for the sake of simplicity—generate realistic growth cycles. Since its theoretic foundations is rooted in Marxian theory—class struggle dividing worker's and "capitalist's" share of output—with a Keynesian macroeconomic framework, it is sometimes also called the *Marx–Keynes–Goodwin* or *MKG model* or Goodwin's class struggle model. In Chapter 13, later evolutionary growth theories will be presented, theories that partly share a common approach with the MKG model but are built around a much more sophisticated evolutionary agent-based micro-level. For more details on Goodwin, see also Chapter 12.

The fixed points have to fulfill condition (11.9); the two obvious solutions are easily obtained by setting both factors in one of the equations equal to 0, thereby obtaining the first variable and substituting the same into the second equation. Choosing the first equation the condition requires that either $(x_2 - 1) = 0$ (i.e., $x_2 = 1$) or $x_1 = 0$. Both can be substituted into the second equation. The first ($x_2 = 1$) gives $x_1 = 1$; the second ($x_1 = 0$) yields $x_2 = 0$. Hence, we have two fixed points:

$$(x_{1,1}^* = 1, x_{2,1}^* = 1)$$
$$(x_{1,2}^* = 0, x_{2,2}^* = 0)$$
(11.18)

The Jacobian as defined in Eq. (11.15) is obtained as:

$$\mathcal{J} = \begin{pmatrix} x_2 - 1 & x_1 \\ -x_2 & 1 - x_1 \end{pmatrix}$$

Now, in order to compute the eigenvalues, the system has to be linearized for the fixed points. This is accomplished by substituting the fixed points into the Jacobian (which gives an ordinary linear transformation matrix) or the other way around by deriving the formula for computing the eigenvalues as a function of x_1 and x_2 and linearizing afterward. The first method is generally more straightforward.

For the first fixed point, $x_1 = x_2 = 1$, linearizing the Jacobian we obtain the same linear transformation matrix as we computed for the linear system (11.13). The eigenvalues are therefore also identical. This reveals that the behavior of the current nonlinear system around the first fixed point is approximated by the linear system analyzed above. The fixed point is marginally stable and the system behaves cyclical in the immediate surroundings—in turn, we will find a group of limit cycles (see Section 11.3.1) orbiting the fixed point; the system, if it arrives in this region of the phase space, will neither diverge from nor further approach the fixed point, instead it will orbit around it.

For the second fixed point $x_1 = x_2 = 0$, the linearized Jacobian is the transformation matrix:

$$\mathcal{A} = \begin{pmatrix} -1 & 0 \\ 0 & 1 \end{pmatrix}$$

which yields the eigenvalues

$$(-1 - \lambda)(1 - \lambda) = 0$$

$$\lambda^2 = 1$$

$$\lambda_{1/2} = \pm 1$$

In this case, the dominant eigenvalue is positive, leading to the conclusion that the fixed point is unstable. Further, the two eigenvalues are both real. Therefore, there is no cyclical dynamic in the surroundings of this fixed point.

Note that while the stability properties of linear dynamic systems are global, for nonlinear systems they change from one point in the phase space to another. This allows a system to have both stable and unstable fixed points.

Further note that one-dimensional linear or nonlinear systems can never be cyclical because their single eigenvalue is always purely real. Only for higher dimensional systems, the computation of eigenvalues may involve roots of negative numbers which can give rise to imaginary or complex values. Cyclical dynamics may add nontrivial features to dynamic systems: they break the phase space's ergodicity without leading to a stable situation. Rather, trajectories may be captured into a limit cycle orbit leading to sustained circular motion of the system's variables (see Figure 11.5B).

11.4 THE ORIGINS OF ORDER, TURBULENCE, AND COMPLEXITY

11.4.1 How Does Complexity Emerge?

In this chapter, we have discussed all kinds of definitions, measures, and examples of complexity. We have introduced many related concepts and provided an overview of the mathematics applicable to this field. What has remained unaddressed is the question where complexity actually comes from.

Granted, we see complex structures everywhere: we see intricate networks of institutions that make our economy work; we see people engaging in complicated rituals knowing that society as we know it would simply not work without many of those; we see all kinds of fractal patterns when we look out of the window, in trees, in clouds, in mountain ranges. But why? Why does it have to be that way? Could it not just be simple? Maybe plants would want to maximize the amount of

sunlight they can absorb in order to extract energy? Fine, that is a simple optimization problem which would be conveniently solved by a flat surface inclinable to match a certain angle with respect to the sun. Nothing is complex about that. Maybe plants would want to achieve other ends—access to water, stability—as well? No problem, we will take it into account in our optimization. You would like to organize the economy to grant a maximum of wealth to your society or to the world as a whole and maybe to reduce poverty and inequality to a certain target level? That is just another optimization problem, is it not?

Well, the world does not work that way. The world is about energy and turbulence. The world is a ball of mostly molten iron in an endless void with deadly radiation of which it is protected by the magnetic field generated by the molten iron. It is not a static world, it is subject to rapid and sometimes unforeseeable changes. Life emerges in such an environment not by extreme optimization but by extreme resilience. Structures to be found on such a world in general will be one of two things: Either likely to emerge at random or able to influence the likelihood of their emergence. Technically, the requirement for the second category is the definition of a *von Neumann machine*, a machine that is able to reproduce itself. If an entity is able to do that, its existence becomes self-enforcing since it will continue to create more of itself. No matter how many instances will then be destroyed by destructive environmental conditions, if the reproductive process happens fast enough, their number will still be growing. By some definitions, dead objects fall into the first category while living organisms fall into the second. There are some points of contention about this. For instance, following this categorization, computer viruses would qualify as living organisms. Like some—not all—computer viruses, simple von Neumann machines are bound to consume and destroy their own environment, since the process of reproduction requires matter and energy and both is most likely finite, hence self-limiting and also in a way fragile. If the environmental conditions under which they thrive, do not exist anymore, the ability to reproduce ceases as well, and the von Neumann machine "species" dies out.

To develop *resilience*, another essential ingredient—apart from the ability to reproduce—is required: the "species" must be able to react to environmental conditions. It needs a mechanism to create diversity, in a way imperfect reproduction, among which dire environmental conditions will enforce selection of the ones best adapted to the current conditions. Since these are not the ones that consume their own basis of existence, the mechanism gives rise to not only different competing species but to an ecosystem that is mostly able to keep itself from destroying itself. Indeed, there are various cooperative and noncooperative ways in which elements of an ecosystem interact. The key to understanding this is that evolution does not act only on the level of species but on multiple levels, most importantly that of genes (Dawkins, 1976), but also that of groups (Henrich, 2004), groups of species in symbiotic relationships and so-called quasi-species, related species that share a higher or lower compatibility and thus a higher or lower level of genetic exchange brought about by a higher or lower rate of mutation or diversity generation (Eigen, 1993).

11.4.2 Fractals, Complexity, and Emergence in the Real World

It is a misconception that nature always forms a balance or self-sustaining equilibrium—consider a viral disease that kills the infected organism[17]—but the evolutionary mechanisms do act self-organizing in another way: they form structures. If the structures are to be self-organizing, they have to work in different contexts, on different levels, and on different scales; they have to be self-similar much like the fractals considered in Section 11.2.2. When we introduced the fractal dimension we treated the scale of the consideration as arbitrary. This was because fractals do not have a scale, they are scale invariant, they are and look exactly the same on any scale and so is the design of the fractal dimension as a measure. Technically that means the following: Consider structures of a certain size $z = (1/\zeta)$ in the fractal (i.e., for instance, straight lines from vertex to vertex in the perimeter of a figure or developed squares in the above Sierpinski carpet example, see Figure 11.2B). The frequency (number) of these structures is distributed according to

$$f(z) = Cz^{-\alpha} \qquad (11.19)$$

This is a *power law distribution* or *scale-free distribution*, where C is a scaling factor and α is the power law exponent of the distribution. Drawing the distribution in a log-log plot results in a straight line of slope $-\alpha$. Such distributions have certain remarkable, if not, unsettling properties: for $\alpha < 2$ the mean of the distribution is infinite, for $\alpha < 3$, the distribution has infinite variance, etc. In fact one example for such a distribution has already been given in the gambler's ruin example in Section 11.1 (see Figure 11.1). It turns out that in this case the exponent is $\alpha \approx 1.6$, which was why we could not find a fixed average and variance. However, power law distributions occur frequently both in nature and in economic and social systems. For instance, the rank distribution of the size of certain groups (such as the groups of speakers of the world's languages) is power law distributed (see Figure 11.6), the relative price changes of bonds

---

[17]This is, however, not for every virus the case. In fact, a substantial part of higher organism's DNA is made up of viral elements, so-called endogenous retroviruses (Löwer et al., 1996).

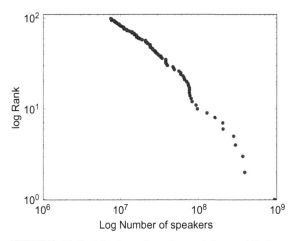

FIGURE 11.6 Number of speakers of the world's languages versus rank of the language (in terms of the number of speakers) in a log-log plot.

and commodities are power law distributed, and so is the relative change of their trading volume (Mandelbrot, 2001); the oldest such distribution in economics has already been recognized in the nineteenth century by Vilfredo Pareto (1897): the income distribution—it also turns out to be quite robust across regions in time. (For more on Pareto, see also Chapter 12.)

Such self-organizing structures, while certainly complex, exhibit a remarkable stability. In effect, complex systems are thus more stable than simple non-self-organizing systems even if this does not mean that every part of them is robust. The persistence of the structure holds only on an aggregated level but does not prevent the in- and outflow of elements, it—thus the way in which the current elements are arranged—simply forces them to organize in a certain way in relation to the system.

11.5 MODELING COMPLEXITY

Having established that economic reality is—in a certain sense—complex the final question we need to ask is how to integrate it into our models. The question is tricky in the sense that complexity is by definition something that is difficult to represent and to analyze, perhaps even something irreducible. The implication is that an accurate model of the complex reality could only be the complex reality itself. And if we simplify a bit so that our model is smaller than reality but still complex, we will still have a hard time analyzing it.

In essence, if the goal is to build a model that we indeed are conveniently able to analyze in every way, we are back to the models of neoclassical economics as seen in Chapters 5–7, to those of game theory as considered in Chapter 8, and to those of replicator dynamics as presented in the first sections of the current chapter. To be sure, each of them makes a very important contribution to understanding economic processes. They mostly allow an exhaustive analysis which leads to some conclusions that can be applied to reality and if we are not mistaken with the assumption that the essence of the real system we wanted to investigate was not assumed away in the model, our conclusions may actually be useful. It is reasonable to assume that we are sometimes right and sometimes wrong with that assumption.

However, there is another alternative; an alternative that does not require us to solve the models analytically. That alternative—simulation—was already introduced in Chapter 9. To be sure, it still requires some degree of simplification, but we are able to relax that requirement significantly while still being able to probably make a complete analysis and good forecasts of the system. The method—especially agent-based simulation—is particularly well-suited when dealing with microfounded social systems. The micro-level can then be explicitly modeled by conveniently defining the agents as the basic entity and applying heterogeneous properties in this definition as needed. Over the past decades, many economists have successfully made use of this method, sometimes with far-reaching and surprising results. We will go into detail on some of these models (by Brian Arthur, Robert Axelrod, Thomas Schelling, Richard Nelson, Sidney Winter, and Kristian Lindgren) in Chapter 13.

11.6 WHY DOES IT MATTER: THE AGENT'S STRUGGLE WITH HER COMPLEX ENVIRONMENT

For individual agents, being in a complex world may not always be beneficial. Their limited capacity to perceive their environment and generate solutions, strategies, and decisions is very limited compared to the complexity of the system. If this were not so, the unsteadiness and unforeseeability of financial markets would pose much less of a problem both for investors and policy makers. This is also part of the reason why real-life agents do not—or only in a rather crude approximation—behave according to ideas of rational optimization: if it is impossible to perceive the problem as a whole there is no way to compute an optimal solution for it.

However, humans are not unprepared for this challenge. Thousands and millions of generations of ancestors were confronted with the very same problem and have developed quite efficient strategies to cope with it. One of them is the use of simple heuristics which allow to pay attention to only part of the problem and nevertheless take a—likely successful—action. It may not even be necessary to understand why the heuristic works, it is sufficient to evaluate its success correctly and discontinue the use of less successful heuristics, something called trial and error and sometimes modeled in evolutionary models as *reinforcement learning*. Another one is the creation of subsystems of which the behavior is known, which essentially make it easier to apply heuristics. Examples for this are plenty, many have also already been discussed in this textbook. This personal complexity reduction

strategy could in other words be described as uncertainty reduction, as the creating of informal (and later formal) institutions, or as learning and habituation of cooperative behavior as discussed in Chapters 1, 3, and 14 among others. (For more on policy implications resulting from the complexity perspective, see Chapter 17.)

11.7 CONCLUSION

In this chapter we have provided a structured and partly formal introduction to complexity as well as related concepts like emergence, deterministic chaos, ergodicity, fractals, dissipativeness, path dependence, and others. Though there is no universally accepted definition, we have introduced many qualitative and quantitative definitions as well as the—as yet unresolved—historic debates surrounding the concepts in question. A number of economic examples, starting with evolutionary game theory but extending far beyond that have been given and recent lines of research and scientific debate have been briefly mentioned.

With the concept of complexity as well as the formal methods and theories studied so far in mind, it is now time to turn our attention to more specific questions. The following part of the textbook (Part IV) will give an overview over influential theories of complex, evolutionary, institutional, and interactive economics starting with the classics and extending the review almost to the current date. Many of the models—particularly the recent ones—draw heavily on the concepts presented in this part of the textbook.

Chapter References

Ablowitz, R., 1939. Theory of emergence. Philos. Sci. 6 (1), 1–15.
Anderson, P.W., 1972. More is different. Science. 177 (4047), 393–396.
Arthur, W.B., Ermoliev, Y.M., Kaniovski, Y.M., 1983. A generalized urn problem and its applications. Cybernetics. 19 (1), 61–71 (Translated from Russian *Kibernetika* **19** (1), 49–56).

Arthur, W.B., Ermoliev, Y.M., Kaniovski, Y.M., 1987. Path dependent processes and the emergence of macrostructure. Eur. J. Oper. Res. 30 (3), 294–303.

Bar Yam, Y., 1997. Dynamics of Complex Systems. Addison-Wesley, Reading, MA.

Corning, P.A., 2002. The re-emergence of emergence: A venerable concept in search of a theory. Complexity. 7 (6), 18–30.

Dawkins, R., 1976. The Selfish Gene. Oxford University Press, Oxford.

Eigen, M., 1993. Viral quasi-species. Sci. Am. 269 (1), 42–49.

Goodwin, R.M., 1967. A growth cycle. In: Feinstein, C.H. (Ed.), Socialism, Capitalism and Economic Growth. Cambridge University Press, Cambridge, pp. 54–58.

Henrich, J., 2004. Cultural group selection, coevolutionary processes and large-scale cooperation. J. Econ. Behav. Organ. 53 (1), 3–35.

Lloyd, S., 2001. Measures of complexity: A non-exhaustive list. IEEE Control Syst. 21 (4), 7–8.

Löwer, R., Löwer, J., Kurth, R., 1996. The viruses in us: Characteristics and biological significance of human endogenous retrovirus sequences. Proc. Natl. Acad. Sci. USA. 93 (11), 5177–5184.

Mandelbrot, B.B., 2001. Scaling in financial prices: I. Tails and dependence. Quant. Finance. 1 (1), 113–123.

Mitchell, M., 2009. Complexity: A Guided Tour. Oxford Univ. Press, Oxford.

Ormerod, P., 2009. Keynes, Hayek and complexity. In: Faggini, M., Lux, T. (Eds.), Coping with the Complexity of Economics. Springer, Milan, pp. 19–32.

Pareto, V., 1897. The new theories of economics. J. Polit. Econ. 5 (4), 485–502.

Standish, R.K., 2006. Theory of Nothing. Booksurge, Charleston, SC.

Weaver, W., 1948. Science and complexity. Am. Sci. 36 (4), 536–544.

Further Reading

Bak, P., 1996. How Nature Works: The Science of Self-Organized Criticality. Springer, New York, NY.

Faggini, M., Lux, T. (Eds.), 2009. Coping with the Complexity of Economics. Springer, Milan (pp. 19–32).

Foley, D.K., 1998. Introduction. In: Foley, D.K. (Ed.), Barriers and Bounds to Rationality: Essays on Complexity and Dynamics in Interactive Systems, by Albin, P.S., with an Introduction by Foley, D.K.. Princeton University Press, Princeton, NJ, pp. 3–72.

Gandolfo, G., 1997. Economic Dynamics. Springer, Berlin.

Gatti, D.D., Gaffeo, E., Gallegati, M., Giulioni, G., Palestrini, A., 2008. Emergent Macroeconomics: An Agent-Based Approach to Business Fluctuations. Springer, Milan.

Mandelbrot, B.B., Hudson, R.L., 2004. The (mis)Behavior of Markets. Basic Books, New York, NY.

Miller, J.H., Page, S.E., 2009. Complex Adaptive Systems: An Introduction to Computational Models of Social Life. Princeton University Press, Princeton, NJ.

Prigogine, I., Stengers, I., 1984. Order Out of Chaos. Bantam Books, New York, NY.

Santa Fe Institute, 2013. Complexity Explorer. Available online at: <http://www.complexityexplorer.org> (as of October 2013).

Further Reading—Online

For further reading, see the textbook website at http://book site.elsevier.com/9780124115859

EXERCISES

1. Consider a dynamic system with a single repeller (say $x_{t+1} = x_t + y_t$; $y_{t+1} = -x_t + y_t$).
   a. Could such a system be characterized as a complex system?
   b. Are complexity and divergence separate phenomena?

2. Consider the following model of the formation of innovative clusters in the economy Triangulum (see Figure 11.7). Triangulum is located on an island shaped like an equilateral triangle; the first and

FIGURE 11.7 Developed and undeveloped regions in exercise 2.

largest cluster (the capital) encompasses a smaller triangle, the three corners of which are exactly in the middle of the three sides of the island. This splits the island into four smaller equilateral triangles: one developed and three undeveloped regions. In the undeveloped regions, smaller clusters are formed in the same way as before on the whole island, a process that then continues infinitely. The prime minister of Triangulum claims that the undeveloped region in that will remain in his country is a complex structure.

a. How can the prime minister's statement be verified? Which measures of complexity do you know? Are they well-suited to assess the complexity of the undeveloped region?

b. Compute the fractal dimension (Hausdorff dimension) of the undeveloped region as it will remain after an infinite number of steps of the cluster-formation process.

c. What is the area and what is the perimeter of the undeveloped region?

d. Assume that the process ceases after x iterations. What is the fractal dimension (Hausdorff dimension) of the undeveloped region in this case? What is the difference to the situation in b?

3. Consider an industry with many small and no large firms (think of bakeries) using two competing types of technology. The firms "reproduce" by former employees founding start-ups using the same technology at a constant rate. Demand is, however, limited and if too many firms are in operation, not all of them can cover their production costs and some are forced out of business. Let the system be represented by the following

system of equations (demand limit is normalized to 1):

$$\frac{dx_1}{dt} = x_1(1 - x_1 - x_2)$$

$$\frac{dx_2}{dt} = x_2(1 - x_1 - x_2)$$

a. Derive the fixed points of the system and assess their stability.

How would the dynamics change if one of the technologies would allow to serve a larger customer base, i.e., the limit of demand is increased to, say, 2 with one of the equations now consequently being (in this case the second one)

$$\frac{dx_2}{dt} = x_2(2 - x_1 - x_2)$$

4. Consider again the MKG model example given in Eq. (11.17).

a. What would change if the tipping point level (from which on the dynamic is growing) were increased in both equations? That is,

$$\frac{dx_1}{dt} = x_1 x_2 - 2x_1 = x_1(x_2 - 2)$$

$$\frac{dx_2}{dt} = -x_1 x_2 + 2x_2 = x_2(-x_1 + 2)$$

b. Explain how the system and the solution would change if the system was a system of difference equations instead of a system of differential equations (note that for this system, the original economic interpretation does not apply any more), i.e.,

$$x_{1,t+1} = x_{1,t} x_{2,t} - x_{1,t} = x_{1,t}(x_{2,t} - 1)$$

$$x_{2,t+1} = -x_{1,t} x_{2,t} + x_{2,t} = x_{2,t}(-x_{1,t} + 1)$$

PART IV

HISTORY OF THOUGHT AND CONTEMPORARY MODELS IN COMPLEXITY ECONOMICS

Themes of Complexity in the History of Economic Thought: Glimpses at A. Smith, T.B. Veblen, J.A. Schumpeter, and Others

"After Samuelson, who needs Adam Smith?" **Kenneth E. Boulding**[1]

"Economics [. . .] has a useful past. A past that is useful in dealing with the future." **George J. Stigler**[2]

[1]*History of Political Economy*, **3.2** (1971), pp. 225–237.

[2]"Does Economics have a useful past?," *History of Political Economy*, **1.2** (1969), pp. 217–230, p. 229.

The Microeconomics of Complex Economies.
DOI: http://dx.doi.org/10.1016/B978-0-12-411585-9.00012-9

12.1 INTRODUCTION

12.1.1 The Use of Dealing with the History of Economic Thought

There has been a long and ongoing debate in economic science about the relevance and benefit of a systematic dealing with the history of economic thought (HET), i.e., with past (and dead) economists, their conceptions and theories. In the neoclassical mainstream, the dominant position for a long time was that everything we need to know is contained in current cutting-edge models. This position does no longer appear to be the dominant one even in the mainstream—while "heterodox" economic paradigms have mostly considered HET as a most important source of a variety of ideas and approaches, useful to promote best pluralistic debate and, thus, scientific progress in the discipline. Nowadays, HET appears to be widely acknowledged as a fund for inspiration, cognition, and deeper insight that systematically must be used and exhausted by any economic researcher, in order to prevent reinventing the wheel again and again, to receive inspiration and knowledge to better help solving current and future economic problems (see, e.g., Kates, 2013; see also the reference of the quote of G. Stigler above).

Notably, this is not well reflected yet in the usual economics or business studies curriculum, which nowadays usually does not contain HET again as it was the case in earlier times. For a full (micro-) *economics curriculum*, however, HET is indispensable. This gap will be closed by the present chapter.

In particular, it has been argued in a longer debate about the development of the economic science and in a wider epistemological and paradigmatic perspective, that in a historical sequence of *"paradigms"* with Kuhnian *"scientific revolutions"* (Kuhn, 1970), the newer paradigm, basically a closed scientific system, may be superior to an older one in terms of solving some "puzzles" that older ones could not solve. However, it usually is the case, according to the Kuhnian epistemology of sequences of scientific paradigms, that a newer paradigm cannot include all knowledge that was present in the older ones. Thus there typically exist what has been termed *Kuhnian losses*, which in turn not only justify but require a *systematic recourse* to older world views, conceptions, approaches, theories, and models, and a systematic exploration and exploitation of HET to improve the current knowledge fund for the benefit of current problem-solving. This is particularly important in an *ongoing multi-paradigmatic situation* of a *contested discipline*, where concurrent paradigms may display *mutual "knowledge losses"* or knowledge deficits (for a comprehensive discussion of the paradigmatic development of economic science, see, e.g., Elsner, 1986).

12.1.2 Complexity in HET: The Example of Unintended Consequences and the Scottish Enlightenment

The HET has, in fact, dominantly been a history of *complex social thinking* about the economy as a *system of interdependent agents* and *open process*, as you will see in this chapter (for an overview, see, e.g., Colander 2000, 2008).

Modern complex social systems thinking was present in a rough stage already as early as in *Bernard Mandeville's "The Fable of the Bees: or, Private Vices, Publick Benefits"* (1714) where the author articulated an early version of the idea of *unintended consequences*, particularly of the later so-called invisible hand: Individual "vices" such as selfishness may turn into a collective benefit *if working within a proper socioeconomic arrangement*, i.e., set of behavioral rules. This was articulated by Mandeville, in a rather rough way, and even applied to the most brutal selfishness of the rich and powerful of his time, which allegedly is triggering benefits for all, as Mandeville claimed. This resembles the recent social conception of *neoliberals*, where it is the mechanism of making the super-rich even richer so that their speculative/investment activities leave something for improving the conditions of the general public.

As you see, the idea of "unintended consequences," usually as positive unintended consequences (the invisible hand idea) is a most general and virulent idea and metaphor of social economic thinking.

The basic idea was refined, "civilized," and cleaned from the odor of rough, brutal, and untamed selfishness, during the eighteenth century, particularly through the so-called *Scottish Enlightenment* (Francis Hutcheson, David Hume, Adam Smith, Adam Ferguson, and others). In its socioeconomic thinking, the socially more acceptable idea of the *invisible hand* was born. The conception applies to any individual action that has unplanned, *unintended beneficial consequences*, particularly actions that are not coordinated by a central command, but nevertheless have a systematic beneficial collective effect. According to most representatives of the Scottish Enlightenment, the mechanism requires a *decentralized social organization* and some degree of *individualism*, i.e., the preservation and advancement of the self and the rational pursuit of self-interest as norms.

Francis Hutcheson (1694–1746), the academic teacher of Adam Smith, further developed the idea by basing it not just on crude, untamed selfishness but on an *intrapersonal capability*, which he called a *moral sense*, i.e., the capability of individuals to develop rules, institutions, and norms through *introspection* and *reflection of own and others' behaviors*. We might think here of what we have called *interactive or social learning*.

12.1.3 Unintended Consequences Within a System of Emerged Social Institutions, and the Importance of Formal Institutional Arrangements: Adam Smith

Against this background, Adam Smith (1723–1790) developed an advanced, and in fact surprisingly modern version (regarding both modern complexity economics and modern psychology) of that general principle of decentralized interactive learning of coordination in complex decision structures with dominant incentives to be selfish and hyperrational in the short run. He did this in his first book, a most basic work of modern social science, *The Theory of Moral Sentiments* (TMS, 1759).

We will explain this approach as our core example from the history of complex economic thought in Section 12.2.

But first, in Part VII of the TMS, which deals with "Systems of Moral Philosophy," and particularly with "licentious" systems (section II, chapter IV), Smith straightforwardly *criticizes Mandeville*:

> There is, however, another system which seems to take away altogether the distinction between vice and virtue, and of which the tendency is, upon that account, wholly pernicious; I mean the system of Dr. Mandeville (p. 308).

Smith rejects Mandeville's interpretation that human beings are generally motived exclusively by selfish motives and that this, in the aggregation, would yield a beneficial outcome for society as a whole. On the contrary, he rejects the perception of humans as selfish, or, in the language of modern mainstream economic theory, utility maximizers:

> It is the great fallacy of Dr. Mandeville's book to represent every passion as wholly vicious, which is so in any degree and in any direction. It is thus that he treats every thing as vanity which has any reference, either to what are, or to what ought to be, the sentiments of others; and it is by means of this sophistry that he establishes his favorite conclusion, that private vices are public benefits (pp. 312–313).

For Smith, there is more than one motive for human action, and a complex social interaction and internal reflection process is involved in any of our actions, as we will explain below.

Contrary to a broad mainstreamy misconception that tacitly prevails until today, Smith did not assert that all individuals are selfish maximizers, and that self-interested behavior necessarily benefits society. His approach was, rather, that in a *proper institutional arrangement* and incentive structure, people *usually learn* to behave in non-hyperrational but *socially informed, "prudent" ways*. Both the TMS and

"An Inquiry into the Nature and Cause of the Wealth of Nations" (WN) are filled with analyses, considerations, recommendations, and policy prescriptions to "socialize" untamed selfishness. Recommendations and policy prescriptions typically contain provisions and measures against untamed selfishness and for proper institutional arrangements to control individualistic behavior and incite "prudent" behavior. Particularly, a market, if not properly regulated, controlled, and made transparent for everyone, provides numerous opportunities and incentives for maximizing one's own profit at the expense (rather than for the benefit) of others.

Adam Smith's whole work is an attempt at a complete system of social science, a comprehensive, synoptic, and synthetic theory of *psychology, society, economy,* and *policy* (see, e.g., Samuels, 1994). Any theoretical generalization or policy implication based on those few parts of the WN that might be read as a simplistic view of a predetermined, unique, and stable equilibrium of a perfect market economy, therefore, are extremely problematic. His whole system, rather, is tripartite and encompasses *morals*, i.e., the emergence of basic social rules and norms, the *economy*, and *jurisprudence*, i.e., the science of formal rules, institutional design, and control. The market economy as dealt with in the WN cannot be comprehended without the other two, i.e., the theory of informal institutional emergence and the theory of proper formal public regulations. Particularly, interactively learned basic social rules as laid down in the TMS are prior to and a precondition of any reasonable and socially beneficial working of a market.

As put down in the TMS, human nature encompasses the capabilities and potentialities of both *selfishness* and *benevolence*, but also of *sympathy*, which at its core is the ability of man to *put oneself in the place of another* one and to imagine how he feels (i.e., how one would feel being in his place) toward one's own actions. The agent thus may assume some distant position from his very own immediate interests, i.e., the position of some *Impartial Spectator*. Through this process of "mirroring," or *empathy*, and subsequent "moral" *approval or disapproval*, crude self-interest may be tamed, informed, civilized, self-controlled, and transformed into a *"prudent" pursuit of one's (long-run) interest*. As we will illustrate below, such "prudent" behavior will be, and can only be, *rule-based, or institutionalized, behavior*, i.e., *internalized* and *habituated*. The very fact and the strength of the emergence of these informal and basic social institutions is most critical also to the functioning of the economy, since both the *market* and the *state* are not "neutral" but *may be corrupted* in favor of certain particular interests, in Smith's view (see, e.g., Samuels, 1994, 289).

In this way, the TMS established a complex *system and process perspective* in economics. The WN, in comparison, is a more detailed analysis of the effects of, and of arrangements and measures to regulate and control such complex structures and processes. The WN is thus not mainly an early (general) equilibrium approach toward the market economy, but may be considered an early development of an *evolutionist* and *institutional* approach (see also Samuels, 1994, 290; see also, e.g., Rosenberg, 1960; Clark, 1990; Aguilera-Klink, 1994; Song, 1995; Witztum, 1998).

We will explain in the next section how Smith developed an early instance of a modern view of emergent institutions in a decentralized economy of interdependent agents with collectivities and dilemma structures—a view consistent with the modern complexity approach as introduced in the previous chapters of this textbook.

In all, Smith was able to show that a *decentralized society* would not automatically drift into *Hobbes*ian chaos but would *create a minimum level of order*. In doing so, he offered an answer to what was an important *political and philosophical*

question of his day, in the system transition from a locally controlled feudal system to the early, liberal phase of bourgeois society.

12.2 ADAM SMITH: THE CLASSICAL MODEL OF THE ORIGINS AND EMERGENCE OF INSTITUTIONS, AND THE MODERN SIGNIFICANCE OF THE CLASSICAL APPROACH

12.2.1 The Alleged Adam Smith Problem

For many decades, mainstream economists and many other social scientists have contended that there exists a so-called Adam Smith Problem, a strict contradiction between an alleged "altruistic" perspective in the TMS and an alleged "egoistic" perspective in the WN, i.e., two incommensurable works. For mainstream economists, this meant that the WN represented the "true" Adam Smith, while the TMS was just some moralistic philosophy, good for philosophers, but to be ignored by economists. With the increasing importance of institutional economics in the last four decades, however, many mainstream economists have started reading, and dealing with, the TMS—and to find that the emergent social institutional order that Smith explains in the TMS is far more than just a general precondition and remote framework for the economy, for economics, and a price mechanism. The basic social coordination and dilemma problems that the TMS deals with, and the interactive process of the individual development of a problem-solving institution in face of dominant incentives to defect that Smith developed in the TMS, in fact, form the kind of informal behavioral structure that in particular has to be presupposed for a "market economy" to become workable at all. This is at the core of the behavioral structure of any workable "market economy." But nevertheless, the WN does not straightforwardly trust that this structure is invulnerable under any conditions. Informal social coordination through learned cooperation may be vulnerable and break down under increasing incentives to defect. Therefore, a market economy, for appropriate working, must be embedded in a proper set of formal regulations, rules, institutions, and state measures. This is what the largest parts of the WN are about, beyond just the story of the ideal market, the "natural price" and its perfect adjustment—a "political economy."

Many writers have suggested in the last decades (particularly after the bicentenary of Smith's WN in 1976) that a careful rereading of Adam Smith yields valuable insights for today (see, e.g., Coase, 1984; but see already the early approach of Samuels, 1964). Hutchison (1984), for instance, has argued that Smith's *theory of institutions* incorporates the notions of (strong) *uncertainty* and "imperfect knowledge" that we have introduced and defined in the previous chapters. Also Buchanan (1976) has pointed out that Smith pursued a *historical-genetic*, rather than a contract-theoretic, static or equilibrium-oriented, approach to the development of institutions (see also, e.g., Clark, 1990).

In fact, Smith assumed a basic social situation involving *direct interdependence* and *strong uncertainty* as the basis of his social theory. Within a social setting of this kind, the problem of the *spontaneous emergence* of institutions was the main question Smith addressed in the TMS. And he developed a theory of the emergence of *basic institutions* that is surprisingly modern in character and of relevance to modern evolutionary-institutional analysis.

The TMS was typically regarded, particularly by mainstream economists, as a theory of "altruistic" behavior that has little bearing on economic theory, except, perhaps, as a general ethical presupposition and framework for the neoclassical modeling of "perfect markets."

Contrary to this view, the TMS provides an indispensable foundation of Smith's economic theory. Thus the problem of the emergence of institutions turns out to be, in fact, the starting point of classical economics.

12.2.2 Competing Motives

Smith's social theory begins, in a logical sequence, with the assumption of two competing basic "motives" of individuals—the "egoistic motive" and what we shall call the "motive of being socially approved."

The *egoistic motive*, in its unsophisticated version, is clearly very negatively evaluated by Smith. To unrestrained selfishness, he links terms like "rapacity" (Smith, 1759, IV.i.10, 184; further citations of Smith refer to Smith, 1759). In his view, this involves a basic kind of behavior that aims at the *enrichment of the individual through redistribution*, i.e., without developing the productive forces of the economy and thereby increasing the wealth of the nation. Unrestrained selfishness, rather than leading to productive effort, is more likely to lead to a pursuit of the easiest means by which one may enrich oneself, including harmful predatory practices. Unrestrained selfishness on the part of all individuals would result in a fight for redistribution rather than increasing the common wealth. As a result, *all individuals taken together would be worse off*, at least in the long run—after a process of mutual negative sanctioning and in a general culture of *mutual exploitation*—than they possibly could be and, in fact, than they expected to be. In Smith's view, the power of the selfish motive is always latent. Nonlegal social control of selfishness, therefore, is Smith's main subject here (e.g., TMS: Smith, 1759, II.ii.1, p. 83; III.3.4, p. 137; see also, e.g., Samuels, 1964).

The second *motive of being socially approved* becomes important as a conceivable counterbalance to the egoistic motive. To the degree that they are seeking approval for their actions, agents can be expected to abstain from undertaking actions that might prove harmful to others, where purely egoistic motives might not have stopped them. Smith's formulations here reflect the typical natural-law bias of his time:

> Nature, when she formed man for society, endowed him with an original desire to please, and an original aversion to offend his brethren. She taught him to feel pleasure in their favourable, and pain in their unfavourable regard. She rendered their approbation most flattering... for its own sake; and their disapprobation most mortifying and most offensive (TMS: Smith 1759, III.2.6, 116; see also, e.g., III.1.4, 111).

Beyond this "desire to please," to gain approval for one's actions from others, Smith points to one more general tendency in people that can help to keep a check on unrestrained selfishness. This is the ability to share in others' emotions. He assumes this to be a basic human trait, positing a

> general fellow-feeling which we have with every man merely because he is our fellow creature (TMS: Smith 1759, II.ii.3.10, 90).

This might refer—in modern terms—to real historical processes of *bio-cultural group formation*. These processes would include the formation, existence, and change of such instrumental traits, together with the better performance of social groups carrying these traits and thus being positively selected. Within the relevant group of humans, relatively homogeneous criteria of approval/disapproval must indeed be effective so that individuals can receive more or less unequivocal information of social approval/disapproval over actions and people feeding back to them.

We may assume that the basic criteria of evaluation (i.e., of approval/disapproval) prevailing within a relevant group are connected to the different economic performance individuals and society at large can achieve through the different basic kinds of traits they have developed. The basic evaluations of approval or disapproval might be explained against the background of some historical experience of the individuals concerning the different economic outcomes of different kinds of behavior. Interdependent individuals might thus actually experience, or at least suspect, that their basic situation is of the Prisoners' dilemma (PD)-type and accordingly might form their basic evaluations of the different behavioral options given. Thus, crudely speaking, those groups who have developed more socially favorable motives or traits and with this perhaps have attained more favorable economic outcomes may have been positively selected in an evolutionary process (see, e.g., Cordes, 2007a,b; for the naturalistic approach to the emergence of institutional cooperation, including group selection, see Chapter 14).

To be sure, given this motivational setting, "Adam Smith would not have thought it sensible to treat man as a rational utility-maximiser" (Coase, 1976, 545) in the limited sense of economic maximizing.

In order to apply formal analysis, particularly *game-theoretic analysis* based on the assumption of calculating and maximizing agents, a theoretical foundation of our analysis at least requires *broader agency capacities* (such as risk-taking, non-enviousness, memory, memorizing, and partner selection) *beyond just maximizing* to make emerging structure and coordination feasible—as we will see particularly in Chapters 13 and 14.

12.2.3 Prisoners' Dilemma Type Situations

Tullock (1985) already pointed out that a *PD* is indeed the social situation that Smith had in mind. He not only argued (consistent with our explanations in Chapters 1, 3, and 7) that almost all interactions between human beings, including those in real-world markets, can be drawn as PDs because it is always possible for any individual to make a one-time gain by cheating, but also that Smith knew well the working of recurrent PD-situations underlying markets, assuming somehow a "cooperative equilibrium" when he wrote in the WN about "the discipline of continuous dealings." We will consider in the following in which sense Smith's approach can be considered a forerunner of, and thus properly reflected by, a modern game-theoretic treatment.

As said, in Smith's approach, *two kinds of behavior*—a *selfish* one and a more *sophisticated* one yet to be defined—are related to the two *competing motives*. While there is a one-to-one relation between the selfish motive and selfish behavior—the negative benchmark, so to speak—the more elaborate behavior rests upon both motives in a more sophisticated way to be explained. This obviously is a richer conceptualization of the individual than just the maximizing agent that governs neoclassical modeling, but also is the starting point in game theory.

With these two kinds of behavioral motivations, individuals and society may indeed face alternative individual and collective social and economic payoffs that are distributed according to the structure of a PD. With unrestrained selfishness, then, all individuals would be worse off individually and collectively than they could be, and of course also expected to be. It takes that dual set of motives that includes the desire of being approved by one's peers, or the *ability and incentive to see the world through another one's eyes* that allows even the maximizing agent to further the wealth of himself, other individuals, and the community. Considering a *longer time horizon* and a *long-run sequential process* of actions, we can introduce an ability to learn and contemplate the outcomes of different behaviors, and to search for institutions that help to reach a (new local) social and economic equilibrium—not so much in combination with an emotional

component in the utility function but simply through the different outlook that curious and learning agents may adopt.

12.2.4 Ability of, and Inclination to, Self-Approbation: The Impartial Spectator

Smith's conception of *sympathy* in the first instance is, as mentioned, the ability of the individual to *place her into the situation of others* by imagination (see, for instance, TMS: Smith, 1759, I.i.1.2, 9). The context here is the question of the *propriety of individual behavior*, i.e., whether in principle it should be approved by the others or not. The individual tries to judge the propriety of the behavior of others by imaginative *changing places in the fancy* (TMS: Smith, 1759, I.i.1.3, 10).

First, he brings to his mind the objective *results* of the behavior in question, the objective *circumstances*, and the *motivation* (intentions) of the other agent. She asks herself:

How would I have decided?

An external spectator, however, will never achieve perfect certainty concerning the propriety of behavior of another agent because he can never be certain about the true motivational structure of that agent and he could even be deceived by him about that.

Second, the individual will achieve a better (more exact) evaluation of the propriety only by using his ability of "changing places in the fancy" in order to *evaluate his own behavior* from the point of view of an *impartial spectator* in another agent (TMS: Smith, 1759, III.2.3, 114). The criterion for this evaluation is:

How would I evaluate my own behavior if I were an impartial spectator?

This "reflexive" impartial spectator cannot be left uncertain or deceived concerning the motivation that underlies the individual's behavior.

The individual is not only able but also *inclined* to develop that inner "reflexive" impartial spectator. It is not only a means of getting qualified knowledge on human behavior, its circumstances, and consequences, but it is also a means of evaluating, forming, regulating, and *adapting* the individual's behavior *ex ante* in order to *achieve approval* and to avoid disapproval by others (see, e.g., TMS: Smith, 1759, III.i.4.4, 111).

This *principle of self-approbation* will supply information only on whether the behavior of the individual *deserves* approval or disapproval, judged by a criterion that is, preliminarily, valid only for this individual. It does not supply information on whether the other individuals actually will approve or disapprove. It thus may even be *independent of some actual reputation mechanism*. This initial criterion for the evaluation of the individual's behavior we call the individual's *initial normative rule*. It phrases (just like the Kantian Imperative of reciprocity):

> Behave in a way that you could approve your behavior as another one's impartial spectator!

Since the evaluation of the behaviors of others may always remain somewhat ambiguous, even for an individual with a trained "impartial spectator" if confronted with a trained cheat, there will always be *room left for cheats* when situations are somewhat opaque (which would translate into some kind of *"incomplete information"*). However, these agents might have to lead a *costly life* if *permanently cheating* others trying *not to get detected*—and perhaps *lose their reputation* anyway. But as said, typically they will behave *independent of external (dis-) approval*. We will get back to this issue below.

12.2.5 Recurrent Interaction, Experience, Social Learning, and the Development of an Institution

Endowed with that *initial normative rule*, the individual enters the social interchange i.e., a *recurrent-decision* process during which his own actions as well as the actions of others are mutually evaluated and approved of or disapproved (TMS: Smith, 1759, II.ii.3.6, 87). This, thus, is a process of exchange of information on actions and reactions (and on the corresponding outcomes) and their approval or disapproval. This exchange of information on actions and approvals is of course intimately connected to economically relevant transactions (including the "market" exchange of goods and services).

In that process, the individual increasingly experiences which actions are approved and which are disapproved. In this way, the criterion for evaluation will develop and become clearer. The sanction mechanism, or, as Smith puts it, the mechanism of reward and punishment, influences the concrete behavior of the individuals through the motive of social approval (see Smith, 1759, part II). "Successful" behavior in this sense will presumably have a greater chance of being *learned* and *reinforced*, whereas disapproved behavior presumably induces a *search* for alternatives or an *imitation* of observed approved behavior—or might be negatively *selected* in some other way. Iterated experience of this kind induces the formation of *positive knowledge* on *action—reaction sequences* and *action—approval sequences*.

Depending on the length of the individual's memory and on the concrete history of the process, an institution may evolve and corroborate. Its normative formulation may be put this way:

> Behave in a certain way *if you* want to induce, or to avoid, certain kinds of behavior of others, i.e., certain sanctions (reactions, approvals or disapprovals, respectively)!

Following this rule, the individual may expect, with normally increasing probabilities, certain kinds of actions/reactions, i.e., certain kinds of sanctions and approvals by the others. Based on his growing experience, the individual further develops his behavior:

> Every day some feature is improved; every day some blemish is corrected (TMS: Smith, 1759, VI.iii.25, 247).

As the individual is inclined to adapt his kind of behavior ex ante, he will accordingly further develop his initial normative rule. A more *sophisticated normative rule* thus may evolve. It phrases:

> Behave in such a way that you can approve your behavior as another one's impartial spectator while taking your experience into account!

A sophisticated normative rule of a "reflexive" impartial spectator then works for the individual as "the tribunal of their own consciences, [...] the great judge and arbiter of their conduct" (TMS: Smith, 1759, III.2.32, 130).

The information this rule provides is not mainly what actually is approved of or disapproved of, but *what* deserves *being approved of or disapproved of* (see, e.g., TMS: Smith, 1759, II.i.1., 4., 5., and III.2, 113). The individual in this way avoids disapproval on the basis of *his own criterion* of evaluation of behavior, *even if no other individual actually should disapprove* or should have the information needed to be able to disapprove. The institution then has become a fully internalized, *habituated norm*. Such a norm is reflected in the agents' own evaluation of the outcomes of actions in terms of utility, thus weakening the link between the economic result of a particular decision and the decision-making itself.

In the course of continuous social interaction, the sophisticated normative rule may further "condense" in a way that specific kinds of behavior are strictly postulated and specific kinds of behavior of others (i.e., approving/disapproving sanctions) can be *anticipated* with increasing certainty (see, e.g., TMS:

Smith, 1759, III.5.2, 163). All elements of a socially valid *normative* institution then have come to a full existence. It phrases:

> Behave in a way so that you fulfill the expectations of the others so that they fulfill your expectations with their kinds of behavior and so that you avoid negative sanctions!

In the decision structures, we have referred to in more detail in, e.g., Chapter 3 and will return to in, e.g., Chapters 13 and 14, this informational and "expectational" content of the institution still embraces the *connection with the economic outcome* so that everyone is aware that he will be better off than with mutual defection (and mutual disapproval). But, as indicated above, that rational, calculating embrace of economic outcomes need not be maintained if an agent's mere habituation dominates all rational, calculating considerations.

In an economic context, Smith calls that longer-term oriented habituation *prudent behavior*. With this he characterizes an *industrious, frugal, circumspect, forward-looking*, long-run, and *investing* kind of behavior (see, e.g., TMS: Smith, 1759, VI.i.6, 213) in the sense that the individual pursues *his own interest* in a way that fosters the productive forces of the society and the wealth of the nation, i.e., the development of an economy in which goods are produced and *exchanged under the condition of some basic mutual trust*, rather than one in which agents are striving for a short-run redistribution of the wealth already produced.

Note that Smith in this way envisages some *sophisticated, and long-run, rationality* which alone can *Pareto-improve* the individual's socioeconomic (including "moral") position. It appears to be consistent with what we have learned as the *single-shot* condition in Chapter 3 and what you will learn within a proper *process story* for an application area in, e.g., Chapter 14. Note also that in Smith's reasoning, *both original motives combine* in the process that leads to that sophisticated behavior.

In the short run, however, given *incentives* to "defect" that are strong enough, or some *opacity* of the action—approval connectivity, the purely *selfish inclination* may still be *dominant*. And in some *fiercely competitive market* situation, it can easily come to the fore.

Therefore, the process not only requires some *recurrence* but, for the time being (until full internalization, habituation, and social validity), also some *transparency* of the *action—approval—outcome chain* (note again *complete information* in game-theoretic terms), so that the causal chain can be experienced, the social *reputation mechanism* made effective, and agents can interactively learn.

Anyway, the individual will have a *normative rod* to know *what he ought to do*, at least *in the long run*. And, as mentioned, recurrent defection over a long period, while trying to maintain one's reputation, may cause a strenuous life of hiding and cheating. And "knowing better" and having the "morally just" norm internalized while actually defecting may cause pain from *cognitive dissonance*.

Again, this conveys a richer picture of the agent than the *one-dimensional/one-motive agent* that underlies neoclassical economics and also might serve as a starting point in the *game-theoretic perspective*. Some game-theoretic models have *integrated "moral" approvals/disapprovals into an individual's utility/payoff function*, thus influencing strategy choices and their respective socioeconomic outcomes. Payoffs then include "moral" or emotional portions. Also, in a game-theoretic *population approach*, Smith's second motive and his "moral" approval mechanism might explain the building of a *"moral" stock of individual good will*, i.e., what we know as a *reputation mechanism* (see, e.g., Chapter 14).

12.2.6 A General Rule as a Positive Institution

The normative institution at first provides a mechanism to be applied to each individual case only. At this stage of the process, the individual would still have to decide in each individual situation whether to obey the rule or to disobey. The institution that has emerged so far is still a deficient mechanism, as mentioned. Again, *selfishness*, in Smith's view, still is a powerful impulse that should not be underestimated. The "violence and injustice of our own selfish passions" (TMS: Smith, 1759, III.4.1, 157) is sometimes able to invalidate the mechanism of the institution (that has emerged so far) by distorting our perception of the real circumstances and consequences of our behavior (misrepresentations of "self-love" and "self-deceit" in Smith's terms). In the "heat and keenness" of an action, the individual might expect the payoff of untamed selfishness to be very high, whereas the future disapproval might be neglected so that a kind of behavior might be exerted that will be *regretted afterward* (TMS: Smith, 1759, III.4.2-4, 157—158).

However, individuals learn also from that. Experiencing "false" actions of this kind, and related disapproving reactions, and the regret the actor may feel afterward, individuals further develop the moral norm into a *general rule of behavior* (TMS: Smith, 1759, III.4.7, 159). An ever more *habituated and routinized* behavior will be adopted in order to *reduce the probability of "false" behavior* even in those tempting situations mentioned. The experience contained in the normative institution will increasingly be *transferred into a schematic pattern* of behavior (full habituation) (see TMS: Smith, 1759, III.4.8, 159) so that eventually even in most tempting situations a "prudent" kind of behavior can be applied, using most simple criteria. *General rules of conduct* thus will evolve (TMS: Smith, 1759, III.4.12, 160). It is the *practice* and habituation in an ongoing process that forms it. As Smith puts it:

> Exercise and practice [...] without these no habit can ever be tolerably established (TMS: Smith, 1759, III.3.36, 152).

With such fully habituated institutional behavior, there will no longer be a cost-utility-calculus applied in each individual case. The institution has emerged as a fully developed positive institution. It may reduce the initial strong *uncertainty* to virtually *zero* and thus *save transaction costs* compared to cost-utility calculations and expensive other alternatives in each individual case (information costs, expenditure of time, costs of cheating others to avoid sanctions, psychic costs of acting in a state of cognitive dissonance, etc.). The *fully habituated* norm that has developed out of behavior leading to a (local) optimum at some point in the past then serves as a heuristic in decision making, resulting in "satisficing" rather than an "optimizing" by the agent (see Section 12.12 and Chapter 13). Again, this may result in economic considerations playing a minor or no role at all in decision-making processes. In that case, not only the "rules of the game" may be changed, as, for instance, the adoption of the longer time horizon and a subsequent change of the underlying problem structure (*from a PD to a Stag Hunt*, see Chapter 3) would indicate, but also "the way the game is played" may be affected, if the norm contained, for instance, certain behavioral taboos.

Positive institutions then may become most *basic social facts* for the behavior of individuals who often consider them of the *same strength as legal decisions* or laws (TMS: Smith, 1759, III.4.11, 160). Their emergence from historical processes of recurrent interactions in PD-type situations then may no longer be realized by the individual. They precede people coming "into the game" after the institutions have emerged and in this way they may become a normal part of individual behavior (for a modern institutional–anthropological description of this, see, e.g., Alverson, 1986, 676–677). The institution has become a *macro-social factor*.

Note also that Smith has made many further considerations for the prudent individual and a fully developed personality to *escape the conformism* obviously inherent in such habituation (see below).

12.2.7 Some Implications for, and Comparisons with, a Game-Theoretic View

As we have seen, Smith's approach contains a specific moral mechanism—a *motive* (additional to selfishness) to be socially *approved*, and the *ability* (and because of that motive also a *propensity*) to *develop an impartial spectator*. As mentioned, this would go beyond the standard game-theoretic conception of maximizing agents, even if approval and disapproval are reflected in increasing or decreasing payoffs.

However, arguing in game-theoretic terms, we might integrate the *moral sanction* as a part of "just" action. Selfish behavior is negatively socially sanctioned because the individuals know from experience—and normally perceive immediately—that it is a kind of rapacious and redistributive behavior at their expense and does not foster the wealth of the group or nation. They know from experience, or at least suspect, that all would be worse off in the long run if everyone behaved this way. The reverse applies to "prudent" behavior. They may realize a PD problem structure.

Also, the moral mechanism of approval/disapproval may be interpreted as *building a moral stock* for the individual, i.e., a reputation mechanism as may be used in a game-theoretic population setting in supergames.

Further, the moral sanction mechanism might even be considered to work alone, i.e., without the sanctions of the normal iterated PD. It might be seen as conveying certain negative or positive payoffs (of each selfish or prudent kind of behavior) on its own. An initially favorable payoff (or small opportunity cost) of selfish behavior might be changed by additional social disapproval so that the cooperative kind of behavior might come out to be more favorable.

An *additional moral sanction mechanism* might have the advantage over the normal iterated-PD action-based sanction mechanism that agents may sanction noncooperative behavior *without destroying the institution*—i.e., "morally" reducing the payoffs of defectors relative to the payoffs of cooperators without having to deviate from the institution of cooperation and to perform selfish behavior on their part that might cause cumulative negative economic effects. The additional moral mechanism thus might stabilize the institution in a specific way, while a PD structure may continue to exist or be transformed into some coordination game depending on other parameters shaping the game (for a class of game-theoretic lab experiments with sanction, see, e.g., Ostrom et al., 1994; see also Section 13.13 below).

However, a theoretical weakness of the additional moral sanction mechanism may be seen in the fact that a kind of private good (individual approval) is employed in order to explain the change of individual decisions in favor of the public good. If, however, moral approval/disapproval is another collective good with opportunity costs, we enter an endless regress. Rational agents would have no incentive to engage in costly punishment since it results in a lower payoff for both the punisher and the punished agent. An argument for withholding social approval as costly punishment is made for example in Brennan and Pettit (2000).

A final consideration on a "moral" sanction mechanism: The information content of the *usual endogenous sanction* in a PD supergame may be *more ambiguous* than the Smithian moral mechanism. A reactive deviation from coordinated behavior might be interpreted by the partner as a normal behavior rather than a sanction that would be terminated if he changed his behavior. Interpreting it as a normal behavior, the partner would possibly feel confirmed to defect further on (for this "echo effect," see, e.g., Axelrod, 1984, 36—39 and 62—63).

Note that in all these respects (e.g., the reputation mechanism), Smith turns out to be very *modern*. He often comes close to the views

of, for instance, the modern psychologist. In his case for a voluntary approvable behavior even in the *absence of formal external control*, he employs surprisingly modern concepts such as *cognitive consonance*, as mentioned.

However, supergames, starting from the simple single-shot solution of the PD, both in analytical models and computer simulations, may show that such a transformation of payoffs by an additional moral sanction mechanism is not necessarily required for the emergence of an institution. Even relatively small changes of payoffs or other critical parameters may help generate and stabilize an institution once agents consider the effects of their behavior in settings with repeated interactions, and "the situation may change from one in which cooperation is not stable to one in which it is" (Axelrod, 1984, 134; see also, e.g., Schotter, 1981; see the models in Chapter 13). In that case, a PD may be transformed into a more simple coordination game, namely a stag hunt. We have discussed this in Chapter 3 and will further elaborate on this in Chapter 13 (with the approaches of A.K. Sen, A. Schotter, and R. Axelrod), and in Chapter 14.

12.2.8 Informal Institutions and Formal Institutional Design by the State

Smith's argument implies that only when basic institutions have emerged will people be able to form systems consisting of more specific institutions, with specific property rights, contractual rights, etc., including, for instance, markets (see also, e.g., Samuels, 1964). In fact, Smith's work includes a considerable amount of analysis for a *deliberate construction* of specific institutions, mainly contained in the *WN* (see also, e.g., Buchanan, 1976). The basic informal social institutions, in his view, are not sufficient to place the individuals into such incentive—sanction structures that they develop with sufficient certainty prudent kinds of behavior, particularly in fierce market competition, so that the productive forces would be developed in the best way (see, for instance, TMS: Smith, 1759, III.6.9, 174). In fact, most of the WN can be considered "comparative institutions" and "institutional design" analyses.

12.2.9 Socialization, Anti-Conformism, and Prudently Deviating Behavior

The individual is born into a family and other (secondary) social reference groups and systems to which he is more or less indissolubly and more or less emotively related. This has several implications: First, existing institutions are more effectively transmitted, learned, and stabilized. Institutions then are normally prior to the individual and an analysis would have to start also with what the individual in his early enculturation learns he institutionally *has* to do in addition to what he *prefers* to do (see, e.g., Dugger, 1984). In the course of his life, however, the individual may sometimes be compelled to *redefine the set of reference groups* with which he identifies *and institutions* he (more or less) wants to adhere to.

Smith's *moral anti-opportunism*, in fact, allows for some rule-deviating (innovative) behavior, particularly if the received rules imply selfishness, hyperrationality, and defection. He explicitly deals with *sub- and anticultures* in the TMS (see, e.g., Smith, 1759, VI.ii.1.9, 221) including criminal cultures (see, e.g., Smith, 1759, VI.ii.1.17, 224), which have their own institutions. Also, in Smith's model, as has been mentioned, there is always room for cheating. The rule breaker thus may be both the anti-opportunist and the cheat who attempts to deceive the others with respect to his intentions.

In general, "prudent," informed anti-opportunism may be considered properly *innovative behavior*, when a *new strategy opportunity* has emerged (e.g., through some technological change), promising higher payoffs if a new

coordination on this strategy can be attained (see, e.g., Heinrich and Schwardt, 2013).

With some *partner selection* given in a population setting, the social process may produce a group of "outlaws" with whom everyone deals only on a selfish basis, if at all, or any other *minority culture* (see, e.g., Tullock, 1985). There may be agents indeed applying the strategy of defecting/exploiting with a resulting bad reputation (see, e.g., Axelrod's simulations with different defecting strategies; Axelrod, 1984/2006). In fact, also people of very high virtue, in Smith's view, may only be a minority group in society. We will explain the *relative ("meso") size of the carrier group* of an institution, with a minority of defecting/exploiting agents or actions remaining, in more detail in Chapter 14. However, depending on the parameter settings, the "meso"-group carrying the institution may easily be a (stable) minority while defectors may form a majority culture.

12.2.10 A Final Remark

It has been pointed out in this section that the question of *spontaneous emergence* of basic social institutions from a basic social exchange process was the *first and the main question of the classical economics* of Adam Smith. This turned out to be a highly modern approach and can be reconstructed in modern game-theoretic terms. In addition, it provides further interesting aspects for modern institutional theory with its theoretical elements of competing motives, different *behavioral options and potentialities*, a *reputation mechanism*, the ideas of the costs of *cognitive dissonance* and cheating, the indication of the relevance of *peer groups*, enculturation, the emotive dimension, and the (additional) *moral sanction mechanism*. At the same time it raises, with these broader issues, many questions open for further analysis.

We will find in the next section that the basic themes of the founding father of modern economics reoccurred as central themes, in many variations, in the works of the other great founding fathers of what nowadays is considered complexity microeconomics.

12.3 THOMAS R. MALTHUS: INTRODUCING BASIC BIOLOGICAL PRINCIPLES—THE "PRINCIPLE OF NATURAL SELECTION" AND THE DANGER OF "BIOLOGISM"

As should have become clear already in the preceding chapters, the *biological analogy* of evolutionary process is at the core of complexity economics. But what is the theoretical core of "biological evolution" and its analogy in economics? A widespread understanding is that evolutionary and complexity economics took their analogies from biology, namely from *Darwinism*, and its famous starting point, Darwin's *On the Origin of Species* (1859). However, in fact, *Charles Darwin* (1809–1882) was largely influenced by the "complexity" economists of his time who had developed the ideas and principles of *unintended consequences* and *emerging "spontaneous" complex order* derived from many decentralized individuals who pursue their self-interest, with no common intention or central deliberate design— the idea of Mandeville, the Scottish School, and Smith. Darwin's notebooks show that he had intensively studied them and drew upon them exactly when he had his own theoretical breakthrough on the conception of biological evolution (see, e.g., Hodgson, 1994a).

While the "civilized" version of the invisible hand (Smith) suggested a teleological message of a final good order (at least, that was its dominant reading over two centuries), there was another economist who went beyond any naïve positive connotation of "social order and wealth" connected with emergent structure. This was Thomas Robert Malthus (1766–1834)

who had published his important *Essay on the Principle of Population* in 1798. And, in fact, Darwin drew heavily upon Malthus—which was important in the end to make Darwinian evolution fully *non-teleological*.

With Malthus, *variety* and *diversity of agents* did not just mean favorable *specialization* and productive *division of labor*, as in the Scottish School, and Smith, but "the infinite variety of nature" included lasting *inferiority*, *failure*, and the *death* of many. The "struggle for existence" and the "principle of population" was not only connected to permanent generation of variety (i.e., some *diversification mechanism*) but also the "natural selection principle" (some *selection mechanism*), i.e., the selection of those inferior to others, measured at the same environmental conditions. The latter, in turn, not only include the relatively stationary and *static physical environment* and the *biological environment*, but also the *permanently changing social environment*, i.e., the changing population structure of the very own species.

Malthus addressed a quite modern issue with a model according to which the resources provided by the natural environment (namely *food*, generally put in units of *energy*) would grow more or less *linearly*, while *human population*, as being relatively relieved from evolutionary pressure, might easily increase *geometrically*, and the amount of energy humans will actually consume might increase even faster than the population, as the technology to extract that energy will improve. Therefore, inevitably there will be a *point of crisis*, i.e., *relative overcrowding*, followed by a "struggle for existence" and "natural selection."

These are the driving forces of a *dynamic of selection*, where the diversification of the species includes *improved forms* and thus provides the raw material not only for some for selection but also some, according to Malthus, *overall improvement* through selection.

In Malthus' view, there is just an *open-ended* dynamic, with *no suggestion of a teleological equilibrium* or optimum attained (see also, again, Hodgson, 1994a). This is exactly what influenced Darwin's idea of *evolutionary population thinking* in biology which has largely been corroborated in modern biology: *Fitness* as an extremely *relative* conception (see also Kauffman's model in Section 13.9 below) relative to the ever moving environmental conditions of the individual among even its own species and of a species among other species—an ever *moving fitness surface*, conditioned to ongoing diversification and selection, which renders the idea of a unique and unambiguous progress toward some predetermined equilibrium senseless. This is common sense in all modern sciences of complex systems. Particularly, in a social environment, any action of any member of the population will contribute to permanent change of that very social environment through relative advantage, selection, and *differential replication*, and thus a new composition of the population which may require or support different traits than in the previous period.

Thus, there is nothing like some plain "survival of the fittest" in a complex world that leads to some socioeconomic "optimum." Rather, there are many instances in all areas of the real world, i.e., cases analyzed in all modern scientific disciplines, according to which *positive feedbacks* may *lock in* systems on *inferior paths* for a long time (see also, e.g., Hodgson, 1994b). And as we have seen in, e.g., Chapters 9 and 10, much depends on sometimes very little variation of *"initial" conditions*.

With his non-teleological approach, Malthus was quite modern both in terms of the modern real-world dynamics of global resources and climate crises and with respect to the modern theoretical non-teleological, anti-equilibrium understanding in complexity sciences, i.e., a permanent motion and transformation of complex systems. In economics, this non-teleological view has later been stressed and further developed into the notion of *cumulative causation*

by Thorstein *Veblen* (see below). The late twentieth and early twenty-first centuries have indeed seen the return of some of Malthus' themes, including issues like the *growing energy extraction*, global ecological degradation, and again increasing portions of the world population starving or dying from famines.

However, the *Malthusian direct biological analogy* nevertheless appears somewhat simple and *biologistic*. We do know much more nowadays about food and energy supply and population development with both social diversification generation and selection. Both the population and agricultural production/development mechanisms are by far more than just biologically determined. They are *dominantly culturally, socially, and economically determined* and largely *politically* influenced if not often consciously *designed*. We do nowadays know more about why in the socioeconomy an individual has to die or will be selected out from certain supplies or chances. And we would have the technological and organizational knowledge to prevent the worst consequences of the biological "population principle." In this sense, mankind indeed has *overcome "blind" biological laws* through *cultural* development. In fact, we would have the technical and organizational knowledge and organizational and financial power to prevent that a billion people (i.e., nearly 15% of the world population) starve and another billion of the "working poor" live at the existence minimum today. What is still lacking is a broad organizational knowledge of *generating rational collective action capability* through emergent coordination and cooperation—one of the red threads of complexity microeconomics and certainly a common thread of this textbook.

That is, in order to attain some *progress* and some *stability* on a path toward some betterment mankind cannot just trust in systems and their structures as they are—which might or might not generate some "self-organized" and "favorable" outcomes (i.e., reach some favorable attractor area). Rather, mankind should also become a *deliberate, conscious, planning, and reflexive agent of its own history*. This would require reducing *the systems' complexity, stabilizing and channeling its path* through informal *and* formal institutions of coordination and cooperation. And as said, this, in turn, requires *building collective action capacity*, generate *proper organizational collective and public forms*, including state-like forms, and exert proper policies for *proper design of framework conditions* (see Chapter 17 for an "institutional policy" conception).

This will go beyond the theoretical realm of noncooperative game theory modeling, but will rather imply *discourse, agreement, contracting*, and perhaps cooperative game-theoretic modeling. We will deal with related *policy options* in a broad sense at the end of this textbook in Chapter 17.

The idea of changing the conditions and structures of complex systems, and thus channeling their historical paths, through generating deliberate collective action capability leads over to the understanding of the "dialectics" of system motions, process analyses, and policy action in Marx.

12.4 KARL MARX: PRINCIPLES OF HISTORICAL SYSTEM EVOLUTION, AND COLLECTIVE ACTION CAPACITY

Karl Marx (1818–1883) was a classical economist, historian, and social scientist in a broad sense who, in his philosophical basis, rejected the idea of the existence of a simple socioeconomic system tending to some stable equilibrium which would be the end of history. Elaborating on the classical philosophy, as received through *G.W.F. Hegel* (1770–1831), he analyzed the socioeconomic history as an *ongoing process* driven by a *"dialectical" process* where *contradictions unfold* through a "thesis" provoking its "antithesis" which, in turn, may lead to some "synthesis"— which will establish again as a new thesis on a higher level, which provokes the emergence of a new antithesis, etc. Particularly *contradictions of*

interests between the main *social classes* stemming from their relations to the *means of production* (owners versus nonowners, exploiters versus exploited, etc.) are considered to drive human socioeconomic dynamics.

Darwin's then new theory of the evolution of biological systems was particularly appealing to Marx and he appreciated it as *the* new natural-scientific basis of history (see also, e.g., Hodgson, 1994c). A dialectically moving history (with the antithesis as a diversification vis-á-vis the thesis and both being "selected" and at the same time somehow retained in the synthesis which provokes another diversification, etc.) indeed appears to have some structural similarity with evolution based on variation and selection, since antithesis and synthesis may easily be considered specific forms of variation and selection.

Particularly the *capitalist mode of production*, centered around the compulsion to invest capital for production and profit generation and— because of the *rivalry among capitals*—to increase its amount, value, profit rate, and socioeconomic *power* (over laborers, smaller capitals, the state, the media, societal values, foreign countries, etc.), is considered not only to be a *most dynamic system*, but also a *most contradictory system* and a *most complex system*. The fundamental contradiction of the capitalist system is less some obvious class conflict but the contradiction between the dynamic *"socialization" of the means of production* (into global hub&spoke production nets nowadays) and the *still private ownership of ever larger concentrated and centralized capitals* (i.e., formal, legal, and hierarchical entities of money value, production, and command over labor—a value and a social relation in one), the legal ownership structure called "superstructure." In this way, the capitalist system ironically "socializes" itself at its very foundations and would prepare its takeover by some future, more rationally and collectively acting mode of production. That basic contradiction comes to a culmination in late capitalism where these tensions reach a maximum (where, e.g., today some few multibillionaires own as much as half of the world population—the most *uneven income and wealth distribution* that has ever existed in world history).

The contradiction triggers so many different measures to deal with, and in fact neutralize, these tensions and to protect the system so that late capitalism becomes an *overly complex system* with particular deficiencies, backlashes, cycles, crises, and breakdowns resulting. The "super-structure" or its acting representatives, of course, will try to resist the necessary change.

The particular crises mechanism of the capitalist structure is at the core of Marx' economic theory. With s the surplus value (profit), c the constant (nonliving) capital, and v the working capital (labor), this has to do with the *tendency of the profit rate*

$$\pi = s/(c + v) = (s/v)/[(c/v) + 1]$$

to fall with the ongoing *capital accumulation* (disproportionately increasing c, while v tends to relatively decrease through increasing productivity, cheaper commodity prices for consumption, i.e., lower reproduction costs for labor, and pressure on labor through unemployment and on wages in a general redistribution struggle).

Subsequent countermeasures of the capitalists, trying to increase s and increase the *exploitation rate* (s/v), cutting wages and laying off laborers (decreasing v), employing capital-saving technologies to improve the capital structure, or the *organic composition of capital*, (c/v), and taking over other capitalists and appropriating their c, v, and s, may help increasing the profit rate again.

In a cyclical crisis, after a downswing of the profit rate and an over-accumulation of c (or under-consumption from v), c will also depreciate, and make the profit rate increase again.

There is an *ongoing struggle for redistribution*, with *no end*, *no equilibrium*, and no predetermined result, with a tendency toward cyclical (relative) overproduction and (relative) under-consumption crises, large (cyclical) capital destruction, mechanisms of planned obsolescence, and moral deterioration (short term fashions, etc.). This all was laid down in Marx' most famous work, *The Capital*, volume 1 of which appeared in 1867.

Marx' epistemological stance as a philosopher, historian, economist, and social scientist was that the world was not just to be analyzed but to be changed. So another major dialectic of his work was the *interrelation between* (scientific and societal) *knowledge and (collective) action*. Collective action of the classes who (allegedly) had nothing to lose except their chains might change the so far "blind" evolutionary path of history and, for instance, generate a more collective socioeconomic system with a less (over-) complex structure and thus less turbulence, less contradictory interests, less domination and authority, and a more societally controlled and stable path of economy and society.

The most enigmatic conception of future "communism" has often been misinterpreted as a system gaining stability by requiring total homogeneity and sameness of agents. At least, Marx' own description included the enhanced liberty for more *variety* and *diversity* through liberation from ubiquitous private authority and domination. In this, he was informed by Darwin's new biology and systems approach: Only a diverse system will be a robust and resilient one vis-á-vis the inescapable eventualities and changes. It remains open, in which sense such a basically planned but diverse and free system would be less complex and more stable than capitalism. (See also Section 12.15.1 below.)

12.5 CARL MENGER: THE EARLY AUSTRIAN INDIVIDUALISTIC EVOLUTIONARY APPROACH—AN ORGANIC ANALOGY OF MARKET EVOLUTION

The Austrian economist Carl Menger (1840–1921) has usually been praised in mainstream accounts of the HET as one of the founders of neoclassical equilibrium economics in the early seventies of the nineteenth century, developing methodological individualism, marginal utility, and marginal production analyses as preconditions of "optimal" and stable market equilibrium (together and parallel with L. Walras and W. St. Jevons). In fact, he was methodologically individualistic in the sense that he defined [in his main books *"Grundsaetze der Volkswirtschaftslehre"* (principles of economics), 1871, and *"Untersuchungen ueber die Methode der Socialwissenschaften und der Politischen Oekonomie insbesondere"* (investigations on the method of the social sciences and particularly of political economy), 1883] the *origin and emergence of "unreflected"* (unconsidered, nondeliberate, unplanned, spontaneous) *social structures from the interactions of individual agents* who only pursue their individual interests as the major issue of economics. Those "unreflected social formations" he termed *organic institutions* as distinct from those formal institutions based on agreement and conscious common will. In this way, Menger was a founder of neoclassicism who, however, was in the tradition of Mandeville, Hutcheson, Smith, and Ferguson with the conception of *unintended consequences*. Prominent examples of such institutions for Menger were language and money, but also the *market as a system of institutions*, and, thus, market prices as reflections of such institutions.

The *emergence of money* was his prominent example. Starting from the ideal situation of a pure barter economy, he "rationally reconstructed" a process where innovative agents, in pursuit of their individual interests, "discovered" that they could surmount the tediousness of barter exchange by exchanging less "marketable" goods for more "marketable" goods. This discovery brought them success and advantage. The idea was imitated, diffused, and brought to ever more perfection until the *most marketable, fluid, and most comfortably wearable*

goods eventually became the most attractive "intermediate" goods that were most easily and most frequently exchanged against the other goods. These "intermediaries" less and less became the object of final need, use, and consumption, based on general use and trust in the issuers, legitimized by personal relations, a more and more abstract value and numéraire— and its increasingly *unquestioned, habituated, and "trusting" use* finally generated the full-fledged *institution of money*.

Obviously, this reconstruction rests on rather parsimonious presumptions and thus can easily be modeled as a game-theoretic process (see, e.g., Schotter, 1981, 35ff.). With this, Menger was not just a straightforward forerunner of mainstream neoclassicism, but another early evolutionary economist with a core interest in evolving institutions (see, e.g., Vanberg, 1994).

Was Menger considering a "perfect," "optimal" process leading to a unique stable equilibrium? Apparently he was not mainstream in this respect either. As, for instance, R. Arena has repeatedly pointed out (see, e.g., Arena and Gloria-Palermo, 2008), Menger's extensive theorizing on money was such that a path-dependent learning process took place at many centers of civilization simultaneously, leading to different degrees of "generality" of the intermediary goods in different times and places and, thus, different forms of money "and the idea of an optimal monetary system is therefore completely alien to Menger" (Arena and Gloria-Palermo 1997, 5, see also Arena and Gloria-Palermo, 2001).

Also, it appears that the human agent for Menger was not the hyperrational calculator, but erring, ill-informed, uncertain, with hopes and fears, incapable of making perfect decisions. And there is no clear indication that in Menger's view there is a high-capacity market that conveys fragmented pieces of information among imperfectly informed agents in such a way to generate "perfect" "spontaneous order" as was later contended by *F.A. von Hayek*.

Considered this way, Menger was not only an early institutional economist but also an evolutionary, complexity, and *nonequilibrium* economist. Unintended consequences, if not put in the static optimal-market-equilibrium model that formalizes and simplifies the "invisible hand," typically requires some complexity conceptualization of the socioeconomic system.

However, Menger was not an evolutionary economist in the Darwinian, "phylogenetic" or population-theoretic sense. As indicated by his own coining of "organic institutions," his conceptualization of the socioeconomic system was in fact an "organic" ("*ontogenetic*") biological analogy—as was the case also in the Mandeville-Scottish School-Smith tradition—in the sense that *individuals were taken as given*, with an *enduring "genetic" quality*, as Hodgson (1994c) has pointed out. As in the basic conception of the *invisible hand*, agents are not molded, no diversity permanently generated in the system and, thus, also no selection. The *organism*, i.e., the economic system, just evolves from given "genetic material" (motivated individuals), and "the emphasis is on the development of a single 'organic' institutional setup, rather than an unceasing process of cumulative causation in which the 'genetic' elements themselves are changed" (Hodgson, 1994c, p. 221).

In this way, the "organic" analogy is a conceptualization where the unintended consequences virtually tend to generate some *predetermined entity*, a working *organism*. The positive connotation is affine with the optimistic view of the invisible hand rather than with ongoing coordination or dilemma problems, unceasing complex and path-dependent system orbits, and potential lock-ins. However, the optimistic, virtually heroic view of the capacities of the deregulated market came to dominate in the later "Austrian" tradition only, with Hayek's conception of a spontaneous market order—but not so much with Menger yet. Menger was rather somewhat "in between" evolutionary-institutional and complexity economics on the one hand and "mainstream," "teleological" market idealization on the other.

12.6 ALFRED MARSHALL: "ECONOMIC BIOLOGY" AS THE "MECCA" OF ECONOMICS

Alfred Marshall (1842–1924) brought *neoclassical economics*—from the theories of its three separate founding fathers, Jevons, Walras, and Menger—into its basic form that students are still taught today: marginal analysis with marginal utility, demand theory, marginal costs and supply, microeconomic partial market equilibrium as price determination, etc. With this, he was considered the leading economist of his time, and with his basic book, the *Principles of Economics* (1890, 8th ed., 1920), he shaped mainstream economic thought for more than four decades. The fact that two of his most famous students were such diverse economists as the neoclassicist A.C. Pigou and the anti-neoclassical macroeconomist J.M. Keynes (for Keynes, see below) is indicative of the *diverse paradigmatic potentials in his work*.

His aims indeed were broader than just building the comprehensive system of neoclassical (partial) equilibrium economics. In socioeconomic and policy terms, his prime interest was in the causes of poverty and the policy tools to overcome it (see, e.g., Jensen, 1994). This led him to the inquiry of the *evolution of the key institutions* that caused the permanence and reproduction of poverty with the same people and classes. He endeavored to comprehend this complex socioeconomic phenomenon by developing a *theory of the human nature*. Its kernel was neoclassical-utilitarian, a neoclassical unchanging utility function. But also curiosity, learning, and habituation were human capacities he dealt with. So human nature was pliable in his view, and with this are social institutions as based on learned coordinated behavior. In policy terms, as engaged in the socioeconomic tools to remedy poverty, he even considered himself a "socialist." (Note that the German economic society founded at the end of the nineteenth century named itself "Verein fuer Socialpolitik," "association for social policy.")

However, Marshall increasingly came to be *in favor of a biological analogy*, and this has gained renewed interest at the end of the twentieth century. His famous statement that *"the Mecca of the economist lies in economic biology"* has been the starting point of a reconsideration of Marshall in "heterodox," particularly evolutionary-institutional economics. Although Marshall, as said, started from, and in fact fully developed, the mechanistic analogy of neoclassical partial equilibrium, the "vanishing point" of his life work, and the focus of his increasing interest was some evolutionary and biological analogy. However, while the static-equilibrium theory of the first volume of the *Principles* was well elaborated and became *the* textbook of his times, with eight editions between 1890 and 1920, the planned second volume, to be based on the biological and evolutionary analogy, was never completed. In fact, Marshall was—of course—unable to reconcile neoclassical equilibrium and evolution, in fact two contrasting economic paradigms—although he endeavored hard to build bridges (see also, e.g., Hodgson, 1994c, 218, 222). "While Marshall is associated with the popularization of the mechanical equilibrium metaphor in economics, his own writings suggest that the application of biological analogies represented the best way forward" (Hart, 2003, 1140).

Besides societal poverty, Marshall had another field of interest that required complex theorizing and modeling: the *spatial dynamics of industry* systems, particularly the dynamics of *industrial agglomerations and clusters* which included the mechanisms working in industrial districts to increase collective performance over isolated firms that (in a neoclassical view) ideally would have been evenly distributed over space (according to the balancing of marginal productivity). His analysis also included the *social, cultural, and informational relations* relevant in such districts. This subject field played a role not only in the *Principles*, but already in his early book *Economics of Industry* (1879).

Marshall's lifelong theoretical struggle between neoclassical equilibrium and evolutionary conceptualizations "arose from an unsuccessful attempt to construct an equilibrium concept that could be used to shed light on the outcomes of processes that are recognized as being continuous and irreversible in time" (Hart, 2003, p. 1140). He struggled with some logical inconsistencies and the *opacity of the neoclassical equilibration process*, where, for instance, all firms need to be the same, while on the other hand partial market equilibrium adaptation suggested that only *some* firms exit or enter. Thus, even while the industry as a whole may be in equilibrium, *some firms should be considered in disequilibrium*. In fact, Marshall's efforts remained an "incomplete journey into economic biology" (Hart, 2003, p. 1140)—partly due to the more limited formal capacities at his time.

Marshall's famous "Mecca" quote is from the preface of the latest edition of his *Principles* (Marshall, 1920). It marked his somewhat ambiguous stance between a more Smith-like, Menger-like, and perfect market and equilibrium-prone *"organic" analogy*, influenced by the politically rather conservative *"social organism"* metaphor of Herbert Spencer that was widespread at that time. This worldview was used in conservative, apologetic social theory to tell people that everybody is at his "right" place in society. It also could easily be combined with a *reductionist Darwinism* to lead to either a *"Panglossian"* view that everything that is "right," just because it has "survived," or even the misconceived and simplistic "Social Darwinism" that, in turn, led to the world view of an unlimited war of all against all, the survival of the most powerful (or brutal) in these wars of "races" and "nations," thus, a justification of later imperial wars.

Marshall himself, of course, was neither kind. He was intimately familiar with the *German Historical School* and its dominant social reform implications, but also with *scientific evolutionary Darwinism*. While the "organic" analogy often turned out to be mechanistic and, thus, prone to equilibrium thinking—which obviously was appealing to the neoclassicist Marshall (see, e.g., Hodgson, 1993a)—he also explored the *genuine evolutionary analogy* for economics for which he found rich material in *industrial-spatial dynamics* (agglomerations, districts, clusters), as said, with its *ongoing, non-teleological motions* and life cycles of coordination and improvement, but also potential oligopolization, "hierarchization," sclerotization, and lock-in, but then again potential *breakout* mechanisms. Marshall tried to combine the idea of "division of labor" and "specialization," bound together in the organic analogy of an industrial organism, with the idea of the "struggle for existence" and "selection."

Finally, he became interested in two critical economic phenomena that are most challenging, if not destructive, for the neoclassical way to model the economy: *externalities* and *increasing returns*. Both signify a larger complexity than the simple neoclassical world view of a perfect general equilibrium could grasp and process. At the end of his career, Marshall did understand that consequently the economy was a continuous and non-teleological "process of change and reorganization, entailing the principles of 'survival' (competition), 'differentiation,' and 'integration' that [he] understood to be fundamental" (Hart, 2003, 1149). Since he did not succeed in elaborating a consistent economic complexity approach, his life work "simply reflects the opposing forces of equilibrium and evolution" (ibid.).

With its underlying presumption of change as a teleological process and an ameliorative trend, Marshall largely remained pre-Darwinian. A complexity paradigm in economics, and particularly evolutionary economics, still had to be elaborated. (For a further development in neoclasscial economics, see also Section 12.15.4 below.)

12.7 THORSTEIN B. VEBLEN: THE FOUNDING OF EVOLUTIONARY-INSTITUTIONAL ECONOMICS

The evolutionary-institutional complexity paradigm was in fact founded by Thorstein Bunde Veblen (1857–1929). With his radical critiques of both the dominant "predatory" *business culture* which causes an inefficient economy, and the received "teleological" equilibrium economics which justifies and thus perpetuates its operation, Veblen was one of the most radical and provocative economists in the history of economics, comparable in this respect to Marx. No wonder that his academic career remained tenuous and he never made it to a full professor, although he taught at renowned universities (Johns Hopkins, Yale, Cornell, University of Chicago, University of Missouri, and the New School for Social Research) and allegedly was offered presidency of the American Economic Association in his late years.

His first book, *The Theory of the Leisure Class. An Economic Study of the Evolution of Institutions* (1898), is a most important work in social theory, going beyond just a theory of consumption, a critical analysis of the *institutions of everyday (consumptive) behavior*, of fashions, ceremonials, emulation, invidiousness, conspicuous behavior, and rivalry. And although his style generally was worse than baroque and most demanding to the reader (and most offensive to many), it attracted millions of readers and made him a national celebrity in the USA (see, e.g., Ramstad, 1994).

Besides the *Leisure Class* Veblen's work included such important books and broad and diverse themes as *The Theory of Business Enterprise* (1904), a theory of the modern economy dominated, and, in fact, "sabotaged," by giant oligopolies and financial corporate superpowers, furthermore *The Instinct of Workmanship and the State of Industrial Arts* (1914), a work on issues of human behavior and social organization, *Imperial Germany and the Industrial Revolution* (1915), an inquiry of the cultural implications of the "machine process," *An Inquiry into the Nature of Peace and Terms of its Perpetuation* (1917), contending contradictions between the system of imperial (transnational) business enterprise and a lasting peace, *The Higher Learning in America* (1918), a critique of the domination of US universities by big business, *The Engineers and the Price System* (1921), with the argument that the engineers would carry the "revolution" in favor of instrumental service, workability, and efficiency of industrial business against obstructive pecuniary interests, and, finally, *Absentee Ownership and Business Enterprise in Recent Times* (1923), another variation on the *sabotage* of industry and serviceability by dominating and vested *pecuniary interests*.

In Veblen's view, received neoclassical economics of his time was not a modern science, since pre-Darwinian. His earliest important analysis on this was titled *Why is economics not an evolutionary science?* (1898). In fact, he contended, received economics was an apologetics of the vested interests of the system. And it was *premodern*, based on *preconceptions* about the human agent with an outmoded *hedonistic psychology* and its alleged forms of a "preference" function, based further on all kinds of *general laws*, and on a teleological, equilibrating, and *meliorative* tendency assigned to the economic process. In this way, it has to end up in a *taxonomy* of disturbing factors that prevents the system from attaining its predetermined final equilibrium state. *Teleological*

economics always assumed, if not a straightforward equilibrium, a "meliorative" trend, and even if referring to Darwin and "evolution," reduced evolution to some *optimal selection* according to some exogenously imposed (normative) selection criterion. The narrow focus on the ideal "market" prevented received economics from investigating the *endogenous matter-of-fact causal sequences*. "Veblen saw this account, in which change was extra-systemic but beneficial, as a teleological defense of the status quo" (Jennings and Waller, 1994, 109). And he had derived his central notion of *cumulative causation*, i.e., the research objective of investigating the inherent and *endogenous motions* of the system without fixed external preconceptions, directly from Darwin (see, e.g., Hodgson, 1994a, 128).

Following the research objective of endogenous, systemic, matter-of-fact explanations of causal sequences, there was no room in Veblen's view for a neatly isolable range of activities, processes, and institutions to be defined as purely "economic," since behavior always was both rational and habituated, purposeful and rule-based, *action* and *valuation*, furthermore interconnected, *systemic* through man's *strive for meaning* and *contextual understanding*. The economy, i.e., the *social provisioning* process comprehensively understood, thus, is related to the entire institutional complex, and exchange is not just "market" but a much more comprehensive *variety of behavioral expressions and institutional arrangements* (see, e.g., Jennings, Waller, 1994, p. 110; Waller, 2007).

Referring to both Darwinian complex process and recent anthropological and psychological knowledge he conceptualized the human agent in an *activist* and *experience-based* sense, driven by some basic propensities and "instincts" that finally shape realized behavior in the form of *institutions*, i.e., *habits of thought common to the generality of man*. Really scientific economics, a non-predetermined, non-preconceptual theory, must be evolutionary in his view, capable of explaining the process following complex structure, to be explained in terms of matter-of-fact sequences, a process of *cumulative causation.*

Critical for Veblenian evolutionary economics is the anthropologically and psychologically informed view of the human nature. With some similarity to Adam Smith's approach, Veblen saw the human agent endowed with quite different drives and propensities. The implicit benchmark here, however, is not untamed selfishness but, rather, the "positive" *instincts* of *parental bent, idle curiosity,* and *workmanship.* They foster *industrious labor, creativity, provisioning* the community with goods and services, the *betterment of the general human condition, peacefulness,* and *caring for each other,* contributing to the common good and providing for the next generation—in all *long-run real problem-solving* (for the full Veblenian theory of human social behavior, see, e.g., Cordes, 2007b; Dutraive, 2012). On the other hand, there are instincts of *predation, invidious distinction,* and of *emulating the higher social ranks.* These hinder comprehensive and sustainable human development, cause *ceremonialism* and the preservation and increase of *status and power differences,* "hierarchization," "petrifaction," and *inhibiting or distorting real innovation.* These drives conduce to the impairment of human welfare, with stronger *redistribution* and usually greater enrichment of single individuals (Ramstad, op. cit., 366).

Veblen considered the first set of drivers the main force of human history, supporting technological development, challenging established positions and practices, and giving rise to an *instrumental value criterion* and "warrant": Does a behavioral practice help solving a realized societal problem? Does an institution contribute to more *serviceable* ways of *consumption* and more *industrious* ways of doing *business,* i.e., increasing provision rather than maximizing pecuniary surplus of a few? The second set of urges induces agents to develop and apply a *ceremonial criterion of value judgment:* Is a new practice consistent with the preservation of

vested interests, established ways of invidious distinction, status and power differences, predation, ways of redistributing wealth, maximization of pecuniary success, etc.?

Veblen's diagnosis of modern-day economic life was that it was a system of inefficiency and waste. The *pecuniarization* and *financialization* of the industrial process led to predatory practices, and useless *absentee owners* ("financial investors"), maximizing their short-run *financial returns* even at the expense of their own future profits, but mainly at the expense of the industrial process of real provisioning, i.e., a *"sabotage" of the economy* and society through the vested financial interests, the super-rich, and the organizations of "financial investment."

For obvious reasons, thus, Veblen's theories became highly relevant already shortly after their publication, in the imperial clashes of WWI and in the first Great Depression. And they continue to be of high relevance in furthering our understanding of the cumulative crises of finance, industry, resources, food, and climate in the beginning twenty-first century (see, e.g., Ramstad, 1994, p. 367; Brown, 1998).

Veblen's conceptualization of the human agent and its behavioral and social valuation implications have been reflected in the so-called *Veblenian institutional dichotomy.* The distinction between the "instrumental" (Veblen himself used the term "technological") and "ceremonial" dimensions of institutions and valuations has been crucial for Veblenian evolutionary institutionalism. Veblen discussed ways of behavior that were legitimized by outdated habits of thought and behavior legitimized by matter-of-fact knowledge. The idea was first elaborated in the *Leisure Class* where he made the distinction between *conspicuous consumption* and *serviceable consumption,* further in the *Business Enterprise* where he distinguishes between *making money (business)* and *making goods and services (industry)* (see also, e.g., Waller, 1994).

Against this background it appears obvious that Veblen refuted the presumption of mainstream social theory (which was "reductionist" Darwinian) that evolutionary selection was something optimizing. *Ceremonial valuations* and deformed "imbecile institutions" can too easily dominate and *encapsulate* technological progress and prevent new instrumental practices (see the institutionalist core model of Bush, 1987, in Chapter 13, Section 12). Vested interests and conformist "conventions closed off so many possibilities for social improvement" (Jennings and Waller, 1994, p. 110) that Veblen saw a "blind drift" rather than an inherent progress in modern economy and society.

After a long discussion and by integrating the so-called instrumentalist philosophy, evolutionary and institutional economists in the tradition of Veblen have come to agree that institutions are always past-bound in the sense that they reflect condensed past experience, but at the same time are the required guidelines that may lead strongly uncertain agents to stabilize their expectations and to act regarding the future, by empowering them to overcome complex decision situations in a coordinated way—as we have explained in Chapters 1 and 3. The dichotomy in this way is prevented from becoming a static dualism. Institutionalized behavior in the sense of a coordinated behavior once learned to overcome a coordination or dilemma problem in this way is *instrumentally warranted*. Predatory urges may deform an instrumental practice, in a life cycle of that institution, to subordinate it to status, hierarchy, power differentials, "animistic" folktales and folkways, etc., i.e., values that provide a *ceremonial warrant* of an institutions. The ceremonial dimension of an institution may even come to dominate lastingly. Again, we will explain the modern, more elaborated institutionalist *model of institutional change* (Bush, 1987) based on the Veblenian institutional dichotomy as one

of the modern key models of complexity economics in Section 13.12.

The institutional dichotomy has indeed developed into a concrete research program for empirical social research. It is not just a reflection of complex structure and path-dependent, open-ended process, and it not only makes sure that "what is" (namely an institution) is not just "good" because it has survived and passed an "optimal" selection process, but it is also an operational guideline for empirically "inquiring into the warrant for a particular aspect of behavior" (Waller, 1994, 369).

In fact, Veblenian evolutionary economics today is a lively interdisciplinary paradigm in the social sciences with much influence on other complexity approaches in economics (see, e.g., Edgell, 2001; Knoedler et al., 2007; see also Section 12.15.2 below).

12.8 JOHN M. KEYNES: COMPLEX MICROFOUNDATIONS OF MACRO-PRICE LEVEL, INTEREST RATE, AND EMPLOYMENT UNDER UNCERTAINTY—AND THE POST-KEYNESIAN FINANCIAL INSTABILITY HYPOTHESIS

12.8.1 Genuine Macro, with Complex Microfoundations

John Maynard Keynes (1883–1946) has revolutionized the *micro—macroeconomic relation*, i.e., the *composition* or *aggregation* problem as explained already in Chapter 1. There was no understanding of a genuine macro level in neoclassical economics till then, but just perfect micro-behavior, i.e., maximization, and simple static *summing-up aggregation* to some medium level, the partial market equilibrium. This, however, always takes place under the tacit assumption "that each household and firm makes its maximization decisions as if it were in a general equilibrium macro economy and that all the decisions add up to produce that general equilibrium economy" (Cohn, 2007, 71). Thus the genuine macro level was represented, or, in fact, replaced, in neoclassical economics by the conception of a *general equilibrium*, which we have introduced in Chapter 5, and which is exclusively considered to be micro in mainstream textbook economics rather than macro.

12.8.2 Defanging Keynes' Impact: A "Neoclassical Synthesis"

Neoclassical economics had no, or only wrong answers, to the *Great Depression* of the 1930s with its lock-in in a lasting "equilibrium" with long-run mass unemployment. In that situation, Keynes came up with a new understanding of the economy, i.e., with a different microeconomic and a new genuinely macroeconomic analysis, implying, in turn, a new role for the state and a new policy conception. And neoclassical mainstream economics had to respond and develop a stance to the new economic reality and a new genuine macroeconomics. Neo- and later so-called New Classical (see also Section 12.8.5) efforts typically came up with demonstrating that, even if agents may be insufficiently informed and take "wrong" decisions in the short run, "in the long run" they are optimally informed and the (perfect market) economy always returns to a full-employment equilibrium. Keynes was reported to have replied his famous statement: "In the long run we are all dead"—which meant that an equilibrium that does not realize itself within verifiable time spans simply is irrelevant. In addition, a so-called neoclassical synthesis emerged already in the 1940s and 1950s that purportedly integrated the main Keynesian insights into the neoclassical structures (J.R. Hicks, P.A. Samuelson). However, the basic Keynesian insights of the inherent instability of capitalist economies were ignored. Keynesianism was reduced to an economics

solely to be applied to recession or depression, a special case that could be integrated into the neoclassical framework, that offers the tools to lead the economy back to its (natural) equilibrium state after an external shock (preferably in the form of wage increases) had temporarily derailed it.

12.8.3 Rediscovering Keynes' Microfoundations: Uncertainty, "Animal Spirits," and Emerging Institutions in Post-Keynesianism …

That interpretation conveniently ignored fundamental elements of Keynes' own writings; namely, all those not compatible with the equilibrium-based, mechanistic world view of neoclassical economic models. Keynes had a thorough understanding of *uncertainty* in the economy and was trained in mathematics. His first major publication was *A Treatise on Probability* (1921). His understanding of the complexity of the economy and the course of events therein was such that his understanding was built on the notion of true or *strong uncertainty*, the *absence of any probabilistic knowledge*, again different from mainstream notions of uncertainty as still calculable probabilistic risks: "Keynes without uncertainty is something like Hamlet without the Prince" (Minsky, 1975 (2008), 55). For critical economic situations, processes, or actions, "there is no scientific basis on which to form any calculable probability whatever. *We simply do not know*" (italics added—W.E.). Therefore, even regular economic actions like *investment* have no fixed and certain basis and require *expectations* to be formed, explicitly or implicitly, from past experience. However, these past experiences cannot necessarily be expected to go a long way into the past, or, as Minsky put it, "As recovery approaches full employment… soothsayers will proclaim the business cycle has been banished (and) debts can be taken on."

The weight of the financial sector in modern capitalist societies, the massive debt-financing of investment lay the foundation for a new crisis, as high leverage increases profits but also can result in relatively minor disappointments starting a chain reaction in financial markets with serious repercussions in the real sector. And as the economic outlook is good for any individual agent, the value of current liquidity decreases, and leveraging gets more attractive, reducing the desire for the margin of safety that liquidity embodies (see, e.g., Minsky, 1975 (2008)).

Additionally, for each individual agent, yesterday's conditions are the best guide to formulate expectations for today, with their combined decisions then prone to establishing the conditions for a new macro-level crisis (another example of the "fallacy of aggregation"). Even more so, behavior based on expectations will be deeply habituated and *institutionalized*, adopting some *instinct* quality. In his main work, *The General Theory of Employment, Interest and Money* (1936) Keynes speaks of *animal spirits*:

> Most [...] of our decisions to do something positive, the full consequences of which will be drawn out over many days to come, can only be taken as the result of animal spirits [...] and not as the outcome of a weighted average of quantitative benefits multiplied by quantitative probabilities (Keynes, 1936, 161f.).

So both micro behavior of agents and macro behavior of aggregates will be crucially dependent on the conditions, status, levels, and course of institutionalized "spirits" and expectations. Of course, agents will try to take out insurance to protect themselves against uncertain and unexpected events. This has made the insurance industry one of the dominating industries of the economy. But also, a spontaneous reaction of agents, according to Keynes, will be to increase their action flexibility by *holding liquidity*. So money demand is directly connected to one of the most basic facts of the economy, (true) uncertainty, expectations, and

habits. Therefore, the (macro-) economy cannot be understood in real terms only as in neoclassical economics, but the capitalist economy indeed has a *genuinely "monetized" nature* (see also, e.g., Cohn, 2007, 137ff.). Given certain conditions of uncertainty and expectations, individual agents may generate even an infinitely high *liquidity preference*, i.e., hoarding of money, and thus *stop most of their real-economic actions*, i.e., consumption of durable goods, new investment, and hiring workers. Real aggregate "effective demand" then may be so small that it causes a severe economic depression (the famous *Keynesian case* of the *liquidity trap* causing a *lasting unemployment equilibrium*): "It is not the rigidity of wages or prices, but rather the natural preference of households, firms, and even banks, for liquidity in conditions of uncertainty over future conditions which explains unemployment" (Kregel, 1994, 45). In fact, for Keynes the liquidity preference was "the prime determinant of the money rate of interest" (ibid.), with its fundamental implications for investment and consumption, prices and wages.

As another side of the same coin, the liquidity preference also signals expectations the agents form regarding economic prospects. As investment is financed by taking on debt, a contractual obligation to service this debt is entered into. These obligations consist of nominally fixed amounts of money payments. This is, incidentally, why an adjustment mechanism of falling prices and wages, supposedly paving the way for the return to equilibrium, may in reality prove disastrous, as the cash flows needed by debtors to meet their obligations are reduced in parallel, thus in fact threatening a downward spiral in real economic activity. And when expectations regarding future developments are taking on a negative outlook, cash is needed to guarantee the ability to continue servicing one's debt.

In this way, behavior is contingent on expectations, and institutions and habits ("spirits") to overcome blockages of action and stabilize expectations are idiosyncratic and dependent on *micro—macro-constellations* to be within certain bounds. "Outside these bounds, their fragility is explicitly revealed and this may well sow the seeds of crisis" (Harcourt, 1994, 444). This then may explain certain pathologies of the financial markets, as, for instance, improper (e.g., highly uneven) income and wealth distribution may, in a depression, prevent the interest rate to fall and become a barrier to full employment (see ibid.).

So it is the course of macro conditions that shape micro behavior, and micro behavior to influence macro conditions: "[…] a Keynesian model has continuous feedback between the micro and macro levels […] the macro level infuses the micro level, which constructs the macro level" (Cohn, 2007, 71). The result is a complex interrelationship of *micro and macro* with both being *"foundations" for each other*.

Also, Keynes had realized already in his early work, the *Treatise*, that the *whole is more than the sum of its parts*, the case for a *fallacy of aggregation* (or fallacy of composition) (see, e.g., Harcourt, 1994). Having been a student of Alfred Marshall, he was aware of the theoretical split between the neoclassical, only "real-economic" equilibrium approach where money is neutral, just a "veil" (Marshall's volume I of the *Principles*, see above), and the evolutionary approach that should have been more systemic, macro, include the price level and money—but never was realized. Keynes tried to avoid those Marshallian dichotomies.

Uncertainty, expectations, and money have indeed formed a complex distinguishing feature of Keynes' theory (see, e.g., Kregel, op. cit., 42f.). As said, "liquidity preference" and speculative urges may under particular micro and macro conditions (related to uncertainty and unfavorable expectations) prevent the interest rate to fall even in a depression. Given a low real rate of return on capital investment, or *"marginal capital efficiency"* in a depression,

the nominal interest rate (kept rather high by the "speculation motive" or liquidity preference) may be too high for investors to invest in real capital.

And since workers are focused mainly on nominal wages, the price level would be required to rise in order to get real wages down and thus perhaps increase labor demand. But there is not much room for raising prices in a downturn either.

Finally, increasing the money supply would be incapable of lowering the interest rate, given a constellation of expectations so that the speculative demand for money will lead to any additional money supply being *hoarded*.

Similar to Marx's approach, income distribution is a critical factor of macroeconomic conditions, particularly for effective domestic demand, in Keynes' theory. In (later elaborated and formalized Post-) Keynesian modeling, the *ratio of prices to costs* are given by strongly *imperfect competitive* conditions where *oligopolies* can *set prices* through some *markup* over costs. Overproduction or under-consumption then may cause not only a cyclical downturn but even combinations of inflationary push and supply restrictions ("stagflation"), fostered by backlogs in both consumption and, subsequently, investment.

Thus, in *price formation*, *income determination*, and *interest rate* (price of money) *formation*, we find complexity theorizing in Keynes in the sense of a dominant role of uncertainty, expectations, institutionalized behavior (sometimes more "instrumental," but often more "ceremonial," depending on the whole micro—macro-constellation), and even dynamics of social struggle. Complexity in micro, in micro—macro interrelations, and in macro cause complex process and the system property of *non-ergodicity* (as already explained in Chapters 1 and 11), "where future values cannot be predicted from knowledge of past conditions" (Kregel, 1994, p. 45).

Kregel has stressed a "money theory" of price formation, i.e., money is endogenous also to price formation:

> Since money rates of interest are ratios of present and future prices, if liquidity preference determines interest rates it also determines intertemporal prices. [...] Since changes in interest rates must reflect changes in asset prices relative to changes in expected returns to investing in capital goods, any increase in investment [...] due to lower interest rates must also represent a process of price adjustment. [...] there must be a [...] price adjustment process in [...] economic expansion (Kregel, op. cit., 45f.).

12.8.4 ... and the Post-Keynesian Financial Instability Hypothesis

In all, *money* is no longer "neutral" and just a numéraire as in neoclassical economics but a major *inherent source of instability*. Production and financing together determine supply and prices. This would imply that the interwoven money and capital markets, i.e., the *financial markets* in total, with their ever higher leverages, often unaccountable risk taking, and increasing domination of the "real" industry, the whole economy, of government, and even large states, need a careful and tight institutional embedding through public design (regulation)—as we can confirm from recent experience.

It is only too obvious how up-to-date and topical Keynes' analysis and theory is in face of another global financial (and real economic) crisis in recent years, with similarities to the first Great Depression. No wonder that Keynesianism and Post-Keynesianism have gained renewed theoretical interest as evolutionary economics (see, e.g., Cornwall and Cornwall, 1996) and more recently in face of the fundamental global crises caused by the neoclassical–neoliberal regime within only 30 years of its domination (see again *Minsky's "Financial Fragility Hypothesis"* that has identified the debt-financing of investment

in capitalist society, in combination with uncertainty and the importance of expectations in determining actions, as an *endogenous* source of instability in modern capitalist systems, as indicated above). For Minsky, see Section 12.15.3 below.

12.8.5 Dealing with Keynes' Legacy: Neo-Keynesian, New Keynesian, and Post-Keynesian

As indicated earlier with the "neoclassical synthesis," there have been many approaches to deal with, and "mitigate," Keynes' not easy-to-handle microfoundations. What is called nowadays *Neo-Keynesian economics* has its intellectual root in that earlier attempt of John Hicks (mentioned above) of synthesizing Keynes work and the standard neoclassical model of general equilibrium (the "neoclassical synthesis"), which resulted in the well-known macroeconomic IS-LM (investment and saving, liquidity demand and money supply), and AS-AD (aggregate demand and supply) models, with the "Keynes constellation" (liquidity trap and equilibrium with unemployment) as a special case, still taught as Keynesianism in the macro-curricula. These models lack most of Keynes central concepts like uncertainty or "animal spirits" and were designed to make Keynes' theory compatible with the standard neoclassical general-equilibrium models. Apart from John Hicks, Paul Samuelson was the most famous contributor to this branch of economics. Neo-Keynesian models received a harsh critique from different sides (neoclassical and "neoliberal" economics as well as heterodox Post-Keynesians) during the 1970s and 1980s as they were accused of having led to the stagflation period of the 1970s by making false policy prescriptions and having wage-push–profit-push spirals institutionalized.

Later, also *New Keynesian economics* tried to explain macroeconomic phenomena with a sound neoclassical microfoundation. These economists try to explain macroeconomic phenomena through the behavior of *intertemporally utility-maximizing agents*: They generally use a *representative* household, a representative firm, and a central bank for their models. In contrast to Neo-Keynesian models, New Keynesian models incorporate *"market frictions"* such as *incomplete competition*, for instance, as in the *Dixit—Stiglitz model* (which you have encountered in Chapter 7). Important contributors include Paul Krugman, Joseph Stiglitz (although current publications of these two economists are more in the realm of Post-Keynesian economics, see next), and Gregory Mankiw.

Post-Keynesian economics reject both New and Neo-Keynesian models and their neoclassical microfoundations. Instead, as indicated, they focus on *uncertainty*, "animal spirits" and *institutions*, on income and wealth *distribution* and often also related class conflicts. Remarkably, the intellectual father of both Neo- and New Keynesian economics Hicks (1981) made a very critical survey of the work of Neo-Keynesians in the *Journal of Post-Keynesian Economics*. Post-Keynesian economics cannot only be regarded as one of the important fields of heterodox economics today, but also as the true intellectual succession of the complex microfoundations of Keynes' theory. Important contributions were made inter alia by *Michael Kalecki, Nicholas Kaldor, Hyman Minsky*, and *Paul Davidson* (see Section 12.15.3 below).

12.9 JOSEPH A. SCHUMPETER: COMPLEX PROCESS THROUGH "ENTREPRENEURIAL" INNOVATION—BRIDGING NEOCLASSICAL MAINSTREAM AND EVOLUTION

Joseph Alois Schumpeter (1883—1950) developed an economic approach that was somehow between the *Walras*ian general-equilibrium type

of neoclassical mainstream and "Austrian" (particularly *Menger*ian) evolution—and in this way somehow seemed to fulfill the older *Marshall*ian aspiration. For the evolutionary perspective, he developed a specific approach through a *novel theory of innovation* and, in fact, a novel broad *theory of economic development* of market economies through innovation (see, e.g., Cantner and Hanusch, 1994; Arena and Gloria-Palermo 1997, 2001, 10ff.). His main work in this respect was *The Theory of Economic Development* which appeared in German in 1912 already in its first edition, 1926 in a second edition (Schumpeter, 1926), and 1934 in its famous English edition.

As we have seen throughout the history of complex economic thought so far, complexity often comes into economics through (at least two) *different complexes of motives* or urges ("instincts," "rationalities"). This was also the case with Schumpeter.

One urge he called *hedonistic egoism* and identified it with neoclassical behavior (utility maximization and the equalization of relative prices with relative marginal utilities—see Chapter 5), which he primarily referred to the Walrasian GET model. This was the approach of *static equilibrium* which he termed *circular flow*, where the economy repeats itself with a *constant structure*.

However, even here his comprehension of behavior was broader. Perhaps because he was not particularly well trained, or not interested, in mathematics, his real-world understanding of this behavior was a more rule-based, customary, institutionalized behavior, largely beneath the threshold of consciousness. This conception of hedonism thus was less "optimal behavior" but routinized behavior under given conditions, a rationality *adaptive to conditions that constantly recur*, the static "circular flow" mentioned. We might also say a "culture of individualistic rationality."

The other urge he termed *energetic egoism*. This one he assigned to those few people he called *entrepreneurs*, i.e., creative, imaginative, and *innovative* "leaders" who do not optimize either, but behave "voluntaristically," following their *"will* to conquer." They differ drastically from the hyperrational neoclassical agent. Since they are preoccupied with a *strongly uncertain future*, they cannot perfectly calculate, cannot predict, but have to guess, being forced and propelled forward by their *vision*. "Entrepreneurs" basically do no longer adapt to given conditions but adapt conditions to their own ideas and visions rather.

Schumpeter did never fully break with the neoclassical mainstream, though. Rather, he considered his *Theory of Economic Development* a supplement and extension of, or a broader framework for, the neoclassical mainstream. The dream Marshall could not realize was realized in Schumpeter's work in the sense that he *left neoclassical economics*, be it in Walrasian or Marshallian terms, *undisputed "on its own ground."* Although its assumptions were far from reality, he considered its logical scheme a valid principle that could be adapted to reality (through econometric modeling, which Schumpeter was very interested in) by specifying "frictions," time lags, etc. However, he considered the "own ground" of neoclassical modeling smaller than commonly supposed, and was convinced that the whole economic process cannot be properly described by neoclassical economics. Neoclassical modeling applies to a world of constant conditions, "static equilibrium" or identically recurring "circular flow," as said—and where change and development (itself a more complex conception than "growth") can only come into the picture through an exogenous change of conditions.

Schumpeter's aspiration in this respect was to *explain the driving forces of economic development endogenously*. In this way, he largely approached an evolutionary understanding of the economic process. *Time* in his understanding was definitely *historical*, i.e., "real" and *irreversible*, and equilibrium did not make much sense to him and played no major role in

his understanding of development (see, e.g., Cantner and Hanusch, 1994, p. 274).

The "microeconomics" of that more "evolutionary" comprehension of development is that "entrepreneurs" create and successfully implement *innovations*. The latter, in turn, are understood in a broad sense: *new products, new processes, new markets, new sources*, and/or *new organizational forms*. Entrepreneurs are motivated by gaining *differential profit* and power, i.e., a *monopolistic position* ("quasi-rents"), at least for some limited time. What was the need for capitalists to regularly devalue capital, to prematurely wear out machinery and produced goods ("moral depreciation," nowadays also known in the variant of "planned obsolescence") in Marx' system (see above) is a strictly positively appreciated phenomenon in Schumpeter's system, *creative destruction*, inherent in competition and exerted by entrepreneurs.

Thus, also competition is something broader and more complex than in neoclassical models, not only price competition but *competition by innovation*—and catch up *imitation* by followers (who are more or less innovative, depending on the length of lag behind the innovative first movers). "[...] for this kind of competition the chances for yielding profits are not signaled solely by prices and market relations but are also to be seen in the imagination and creativity of single actors" (Cantner and Hanusch, 1994, p. 275).

Obviously, the innovation and imitation process as a whole generates some *cyclical motion* of the system. In his later book *Business Cycles* (1939), Schumpeter thought of cycles of appearing entrepreneurs and basic innovations triggering upswings and of imitators triggering diffusion, standardization, and—if only imitators dominate—downswings of products, technologies, industries, and thus perhaps even whole economies. The *wave idea* as elaborated by Schumpeter is well established nowadays: upswing, recession, depression, recovery. The whole process thus also cyclically comes close to some ideal neoclassical "equilibrium," if transitionally only. Schumpeter, in fact, has identified *empirical cycles* of different length, depending on the breadth and depth of innovations. Well known are the Kondratieff cycles (50–60 years of length), long waves assigned to major innovations like the steam engine, electricity, railroads, or telecommunication technologies.

The *late Schumpeter* definitely was less optimistic about the dynamics of the market economy. In his book *Capitalism, Socialism and Democracy* (1942), he painted a picture of *inherent changes* of the market economy where innovative success itself generates *large bureaucratic oligopolistic hierarchies* that *undermine individual entrepreneurs*. Innovation are generated in huge laboratories, managed, routinized, and impersonal. Competition among those dominating entities will change compared to earlier polypolistic competition and, in fact, decrease. SMEs will be more and more dependent on the large hub corporations and the formers' profits redistributed to the latter in many ways. Schumpeter thus envisaged—resembling Marx' argument—an endogenous deformation of the capitalist market economy, a long-run stagnation for capitalism and some objective preparation of socialism within capitalism, through some socialization of what Marx called the forces of production.

With this, Schumpeter not only gave another example of his integrative perspective on theory and history, but also an example of his approach to *institutional change*—what he called "economic sociology."

Schumpeter's evolutionism has been much debated. Some say its core was that both entrepreneurial *innovation* and the business *cycles* as the process of absorbing the impact of innovation with a response mechanism have been *made endogenous* and economic development conceived of as the *destruction of equilibrium* (see Shionoya, 1998). Schumpeter himself was referring to a *zoological analogy*, rather than explicitly elaborating on a Darwinian

analogy. While he referred to *Walras* for the "pure logic" of economic decision-making, as mentioned, he referred to *Marx* for his vision of evolution. However, the *occurrence of entrepreneurial activity* (which in itself appears as somewhat of an *idealization* and a leader myth) "cannot be explained endogenously by his theory; it remains in a 'black box' " (Shionoya, 1998, p. 437).

In all, Schumpeter did develop some theory of the *evolution of capitalist institutions*, did consider the boundaries between the economic and noneconomic domains blurred and changing, and did envisage a potential path of the market system to deform and suspend itself. With the construction of the entrepreneur, there appears to be some *diversification mechanism* working, and there also appears some *selection mechanism* attached to the imitation and emulation process. And while some have reconstructed such *Darwinian mechanisms in Schumpeterian evolution* (see, e.g., Kelm, 1997, 111–127), others argue that there is some "evolutionary flavor" in Schumpeter, though not in a Darwinian (population biology) sense, but rather as a disturbance of existing structures in a "series of explosions" (i.e., the appearance of swarms of entrepreneurs), rather than incessant evolutionary transformation (Arena and Gloria-Palermo 1997, 13; Hodgson, 1993b, chapter 10).

No wonder, therefore, that Neo-Schumpeterianism today is a broad domain of approaches of evolutionary, institutional, and complexity economics with different perspectives on the market, on entrepreneurship, and on policies (see, e.g., Hanusch and Pyka, 2007).

12.10 KARL POLANYI: THE "MARKET" ECONOMY, THE DISEMBEDDING OF THE MARKET AND ITS DOWNSIDE

Karl Polanyi (1886–1964) studied the *historical* foundations of the modern "market" economy, or what he called the *Market Society*, particularly how the "market" economy became *disembedded from*, but still *unavoidably dependent on*, and, nevertheless, *dominating society*. He studied earlier systems in order to provide a benchmark and perspective for his analysis of that "market society." All systems prior to the "market society" were characterized by the principles of *centricity* and *symmetry*, where the former relates to *redistributive* processes and the latter to *reciprocal* processes. In fact, they were based on three, normally concurrent and interrelated, allocation mechanisms: first, redistribution through some central instance, second reciprocity, i.e., any kind of exchange that is beyond short-run accountable equivalence, including *gift giving*, and third, *householding*, i.e., subsistence economies for individual households, family units, and larger communities.

But then a "great transformation" came. Polanyi's main work, in fact, was called *The Great Transformation. The Political and Economic Origins of Our Time* (1944). His historical, sociological, anthropological, and economic work showed that *Market Society* was not a spontaneous outcome of the working of some "natural forces," but a *political-bureaucratic*, mostly *violent revolution from above*, a "progress" reinforced against the domains of stable and integrated societies. Marx had already described the primitive or original, or first wave of, accumulation, a comprehensive expropriation of the (then still mostly commonly used) land and houses of the rural population through the feudal and early bourgeois castes, an early *private annexation of the commons* to create critical minimum sizes of capitals for more systematic profit-making. This is what Polanyi then further analyzed, showing, for instance, that this required a stronger and larger, and in the end *nationwide, state* in order to both exert the power required and *mitigate the markets' worst social impacts*, such as mass displacement and pauperism.

Thus, the neoliberal account of the "natural path" to ever greater efficiency through "the market," is turned upside down in Polanyi's historical account: First, *laissez-faire was planned* by accountable forces and their state agencies, and second, the *counter* or *double movement*, i.e., forms of (self-) *protection of society* against the negative impacts of increased complexity, uncertainty, exposition, and vulnerability of people through the unchecked "market," in contrast, was a more unorganized, *spontaneous reaction*.

In a word, "precapitalist societies had no separate economic sphere with a distinct and explicit set of motives and functions. [...] Instead, [...] acquisitive self-interest was negatively sanctioned by the fabric of religious, familial and political life" (Stanfield, 1994, 166). In contrast, in the Market Society, the position of an individual within society is determined by selfish pecuniary urges, behavior, and career making.

However, the *disembedded, deregulated "market" does not work*, according to Polanyi's analysis. It is a utopia in a negative sense, and dangerous for society: It "leaves social life open to disruption by the disturbances of an uncontrolled market process. Economic or material provisioning is an integral part of social reproduction. The inherent instability and insecurity of the self-regulating market threatens that reproduction. The market mentality also [...] undermine[s] social cohesion. The bargaining mentality [...] erode[s] social bonds and generate[s] [...] distrust [...]" (Stanfield, op. cit., 167). The excessive complexity and turbulence, the failures, and social costs of deregulated "markets" may disrupt learned instrumental institutional patterns, the reproduction of which requires a *different dimension of time* than "market" transactions, and it wears down what we nowadays would call the *social capital* of a society (on this, see also, e.g., Chapter 14).

This explains that double movement, the second part of which, as said, is a more or less spontaneous *counter movement against that*

Great Transformation, i.e., some regulations to mitigate the worst consequences of the "market" or hide them from the public eye. Instances here are some regulations to protect children against severe exploitation, some workday hours regulations, some land use planning, some consumer product safety regulation, old-age care, labor market regulations, including the long tradition of poverty laws and workfare, i.e., making the unemployed and displaced work for any wage, etc.

And even the corporate economy, creating *large hierarchies* and hub&spoke networks, is an indication that capital has to *protect itself* against inordinate complexity, turbulence, and the imponderability of the "market" (see already Chapter 4). Thus, the state and the capital side itself have to contain the impacts of the "market" economy on society.

Nevertheless, the *"market" economy* remains to be an *open system* in Polanyi's view in the sense that its metabolism profits from permanent inflows of "raw material" from society (e.g., freshly educated economics and business graduates) and from outflows of "waste" such as ill or old people.

This leads to a final theoretical issue of Polanyi: The Market Society is a complex, contradictory system with that permanent and unsettled double movement. This is most obvious with regard to the three crucial "commodities" of the "market," the three important resources of most economies: *labor, land,* and *money*. These definitely have to be *regulated* in a counter movement since they are what Polanyi has termed *fictitious commodities*, i.e., they have qualities and are subject to behaviors and causations that can never made fully consistent with the "laws" of the "market." We will not delve into the details of the individual fictitious commodities, but just note that these quite obviously are the main areas of state regulations which indicate that they are most *inconsistent with* the requirements of a (disembedded) *market*. And

they are even highly *regulated* under the auspices of neoliberalism, and often against neoliberal rhetoric.

No wonder, thus, that in *theoretical* terms Polanyi was a critic of neoclassical mainstream economics. For instance, taking an individual agent with his preferences and capacities as a given entity and black box would run counter to his view of the formation and evolution of individuals in the whole of society.

Finally, in political terms, Polanyi was a "reformer" rather than a "revolutionary." But, of course, he had to emigrate from the Nazis. Remarkably, his wife was declared a communist and thus was not permitted immigration in the USA. He was much like the American Institutionalists (such as, e.g., John R. Commons) and philosophical pragmatists or instrumentalists (such as Charles Pierce and John Dewey) advocating a more collectively rational, *collective-bargaining* and *indicative-planning* style of socioeconomic decision-making, where prices, rents, interest rates, and wages are to be collectively influenced in order to reflect *reasonable value* relations agreed upon in a transparent, participatory, public decision-making process (see also Section 12.15.2 below). Nevertheless, like Marx and Schumpeter, he saw the future as objectively and necessarily becoming some kind of socialistic.

No wonder as well that Polanyi with his theory of the continuous tensions of the *mutually open* subsystems *economy* and *society* has regained high interest within the ranks of evolutionary-institutional and critical complexity economics in the last two to three decades and a *Karl Polanyi Institute* was founded in 1987 at Concordia University in Montreal, Canada, where he and his wife had lived. Last not least 2014 was a year of a twofold commemoration of Polanyi, with the 50th anniversary of his death, and the 70th anniversary of the publication of *The Great Transformation*.

12.11 GUNNAR MYRDAL: PATH-DEPENDENT DEVELOPMENT OF COMPLEX SYSTEMS—CIRCULAR CUMULATIVE CAUSATION

Gunnar Myrdal (1898–1987) was one of the most important figures of the twentieth century in economics and economic policy contributing both to economic theory and methodology and assuming responsible positions in public policy. He had been a trained neoclassical economist at the outset, interested in monetary theory and policy in the early 1930s—and soon developed, through his empirical research, into one of the leading institutionalists. He also was an early Nobel Prize laureate in economics (1974) and received other prizes such as the Veblen-Commons Award of the Association of Evolutionary Economics—AFEE (1975) or the Indian governmental Nehru Prize for international understanding (1981). With his famous studies on America and Asia, he was one of the founding fathers of *development economics*; furthermore he was Swedish minister of trade (1945–1947) and the first director of the United Nations Economic Commission for Europe (1947–1957).

In the early 1930s, he worked on the monetary theory of economic cycles building on the work of the famous Swedish economist Knut Wicksell. Wicksell already had rejected the earlier simple neoclassical monetary theory (the so-called quantity theory of money) and focused, for instance, on the importance of the difference between the real and monetary rates of interest to explain *cumulative process away from equilibrium*. Myrdal further elaborated on the conception of (strong) *uncertainty* in investment, *expectations*, and cumulative process in the financial markets, and in this way paved the way for *Keynes'* "General Theory." Some even have contended that the Keynesian revolution in economics and policy had been fully prepared by Myrdal's work of that time (see, e.g., DeGregori and Shepherd, 1994, 108).

The major theoretical-methodological book of Myrdal was *The Political Element in the Development of Economic Theory* (1953), where Myrdal develops an epistemology of inescapable valuing and an appropriate *methodology of value judgments* in measuring, analyzing, theorizing, and modeling (see, e.g., Myrdal and Streeten, 1958). Here he caught up, for economics, with modern natural sciences and their recognition of the inescapability of value judgments in any measurement design or experimental setup (the famous Duhem-Quine thesis, on which the modern philosophy and sociology of science has built, according to Thomas Kuhn (see Section 12.1.1, or Imre Lakatos); for more detail, see Chapter 18). The purportedly *"positive"* economic theory of neoclassicism was demonstrated to be in fact value-laden, based on outmoded hedonistic psychology and eighteenth century natural-law philosophy, thus being teleological and metaphysical rather than empirically verifiable. Generally, any economic analysis and any conclusions from economic theory, recommendations for action, reform, and politics should be forced, according to Myrdal, to explicitly reflect its value premises and the social objectives and the values chosen.

The full reorientation of Myrdal (1944) from a believing neoclassicist came with his first big empirical investigation *An American Drama: The Negro Problem and Modern Democracy* which he had begun in 1937 and which was finished and published in 1944, a multivolume study that became world famous and strongly influenced thinking and policies of national development. Here he found that economic analysis can only become complete when embedded in the wider *social context*. He found that only the analysis of the whole *institutional setup* of a socioeconomy, the rules, conventions, customs, mores, folkways, norms, and belief systems could explain major socioeconomic problems, such as lasting racism in the USA. Economic and social factors and variables turned out to be in an evolutionary interaction and typically *mutually reinforcing* to push a system on a cumulative path with some lock-in at the end.

Thus, his *holistic*, rather than individualistic, partial, or marginal, methodological approach lead him to realize that for complex systems, such as the interrelated economic and social subsystems, the unique and stable equilibrium conception was too simple, and that not negative but *positive feedback* and *cumulative causation* was the crucial mechanism in large parts of the system's motions: "[C]hanges moving through the system will accumulate, causing changes in one or another direction through the whole system" (DeGregori and Shepherd op. cit., 110). Similarly, not the *pendulum* was the appropriate metaphor but the shifting circle, i.e., the *spiral*. This insight could only come about when the economy was investigated as an open system and, thus, allegedly noneconomic areas, factors, and variables were considered. Typically then the analysis would come to conclusions contrary to what narrow and simplistic, "purely economic," neoclassical analysis would have predicted.

Myrdal further elaborated on his empirical insights in his major book on development and regional economics, *Economic Theory and Underdeveloped Regions* (1957), later published as *Rich Lands and Poor: The Road to World Prosperity* (1958) where he presented the core socioeconomic mechanism of *circular cumulative causation* (CCC). With typical spatial development cases, he showed that *initial changes*, while working through all variables of a system, rather than triggering automatic negative equilibrating feedbacks, would often trigger secondary reactions – *positive feedbacks* – that push the system further on in the *same* direction (see, DeGregori and Shepherd, op. cit., 111; see also, e.g., Berger and Elsner, 2007). Typically, rich and expanding regions, on *local, national, and global levels*, when having profited from, e.g., trade surpluses, can mobilize further factors, the so-called *backwash effects*, through mechanisms like *income multipliers, tax*

income, public social expenditure, public investment, capital movements, and *labor migration* into that region, so that their distance from the lagging regions will be *reinforced*. Myrdal also found that while rich nations and areas may mobilize the so-called *spread effects* from the growth centers into their wider hinterland, poorer regions (subnational, national, or continental) will not be able to generate such dynamics to trigger spread effects, but the backwash effects still will dominate.

Myrdal's analyses and theory have become particularly relevant in the current deregulated, *neoliberal globalization* process, which has caused, contrary to the rhetoric of neoliberalism and globalization, extreme uneven developments worldwide. But active development policy, in a dimension capable of attacking the problems, that Myrdal with his work had promoted in the 1950s and 1960s, is no longer a part of world politics under the neoliberal global regime— again, contrary to usual pious orations.

At least, Myrdal himself has gained renewed theoretical interest (see, e.g., Berger, 2009) and his name today decorates international prizes in evolutionary, institutional, ecological, and development economics.

12.12 HERBERT A. SIMON: COMPLEXITY, BOUNDED RATIONALITY, AND "SATISFICING"

Herbert A. Simon (1916–2001), the 1978 Nobel laureate in economics, was trained and published in disciplines as diverse as computer science, systems research, sociology, decision theory, psychology, and philosophy, and it was from all these angles that he became a complexity economist. Starting from both empirical and logical analyses, modeling, and simulations of systems in different areas, the complexity of any system became a most fundamental fact to him. As we have seen in Chapter 10, the calculation effort required to determine "globally optimal equilibria" even of a rather simple complex system can be considerable and, in fact, often even infinite. Such systems, as seen, can be described by differential equations of the form $[(d/dt)y - f(y)]$, where the dependent variable is a function of the independent variable t, and of its own.

Such complexity of human agency systems, i.e., of the environment surrounding an individual decision maker, mostly *exceeds the ability of humans* to process information and calculate in order to solve decision problems of "global" maximization over the whole solution space. This refers to limitations of both knowledge (information) and *cognitive capacity* (taking on, processing, computing information). This is what Simon coined *bounded rationality*, a term and conception that have induced major reformulations of whole economic areas since his work became known in the late 1950s (an early major book out of his many books was *Models of Man*, 1957).

The logical and at the same time real-world behavioral consequences of bounded rationality, which is always bounded relative to the objective computational requirements to "optimize" within complex systems, is that agents try to *draft reduced, partial mental models* and *identify recurrent patterns* of motions that they can oversee and manage.

One of the capacity limitations of the human agent is his *short memory*. And also *foresight*, which might require consideration of conflicting objectives and other complex interrelations of goals and means, will be reduced by the agent to a degree that appears manageable to him. Thus, agents "rationally" adopt a "[m]ental tunnel vision and myopia" (Earl, 1994, 285) so that they can filter out so much information that they avoid information overload.

Simon has rejected the neoclassical interpretation of "rational non-knowledge"—a *"second-order" optimization* when information is costly, i.e., an optimal decision about the relative quantities of *costly information* acquired and non-knowledge remaining—since this would lead into an *infinite regress*: Agents would have to "grapple with the question of how to discover the best way of checking that they are doing the best thing" (ibid.). The problem they face in that case is how much information they have to acquire in order to be able to make the optimal decision about the proportion of costly information acquired and non-knowledge remaining.

Simon's conception of human economic behavior has been coined *satisficing* rather than optimizing. Agents do decide and act referencing to that reduced, partial model they have of the real system they are in. And rather than finding a "global optimum" of the system, they would be satisfied with attaining some *local optimum*, since they never can know where in the solution space of the system they are located. Specifically, their objectives or *aspiration levels* are *limited* compared to a global optimum. For instance, they might be satisfied, according to Simon, if improving 10% above last year's yield, not losing more than 5% from last year's yield, and the like.

Technically, Simon proposed a "utility function" with a codomain $\{0, 1\}$ or $\{-1, 0, 1\}$, which correspond to {unacceptable, acceptable} or {reject, draw, accept}. The decision problem for the agent then is reduced to the search for actions yielding only acceptable (but not necessary optimal) states. Thus, climbing a "local hill" rather than the "global peak" they deploy *simplifying behavioral rules* to attain a "satisfying" rather than "optimal" state. Sometimes this objective may be as humble as just surviving in a turbulent and hostile environment. Simon proposed other simplifications for the individual decision problem, such as for information gathering processes and for the consideration of the environment by the agents. He ended up with a decision problem, which has sound psychological foundations and is decidable for real human beings.

Not only will there be no global optimum realistically feasible, also attaining some "local" improvement does not imply anything like equilibrium. Since the complex system probably is in a permanent motion agents will have to "muddle through," adapting their aspiration levels and *rules of thumb* all the time. *Search, experimentation, adaptation, simplification, routinization*, etc., all much in consistence with evolution, will be endless, not necessarily improving, *non-teleological*, and will relate to both alterable objectives and behavioral rules.

With his more than thousand much-cited publications, many of them founding modern scientific domains, Simon has become not only one of the most influential scientists, in fact, a polymath, but also has revolutionized micro-economics. He had started with industrial orga-nization and found that neither internal nor external organizational behavior of firms could fruitfully be explained by neoclassical rational decision-making. In fact, the modern conception of (strong) uncertainty, with neither perfect nor complete information (as defined in Chapter 1), has been further elaborated and applied by Simon. And he was one of the founding fathers also of complex modeling and *computer simula-tion*, the best way he considered to study com-plex systems and decision situations.

No wonder that all strands of institutional, evolutionary, behavioral, and other complex economics today refer to bounded rationality as one of their crucial theoretical ingredients. The internet resources on Simon today are virtually infinite. Both more mainstream and more het-erodox economics associations dignify his work by naming prizes and awards after him.

But his contributions were far more than just the concept of bounded rationality: He was also a precursor in the field of *artificial intelli-gence* and designed the first computer program which was able to proof fundamental theorems of mathematical logic. He figured out that there were striking similarities between the way the program addressed logical problems

and human beings. He therefore advocated to model the decision-making process of human beings not by utility functions, but with pro-grams, or algorithms (his simple "utility func-tion" mentioned is consistent with this approach), which paved the way for the com-puter simulation of decision problems. Also of major importance was his explication of the so-called *power law distributions* (e.g., of economic wealth) through the process of preferential attachment ("The rich get richer" or the so-called Matthew Effect). For the latter, see also Section 12.15.4 on V. Pareto, who first studied power law distributions, and Section 13.11 below. Nowadays, for instance, the European Association for Evolutionary Political Economy regularly awards a Herbert Simon Prize.

12.13 NICOLAS GEORGESCU-ROEGEN: THE ECONOMY AS AN OPEN SYSTEM, AND ITS ENTROPY

Nicolas Georgescu-Roegen (1906–1994) is another of the great economists who were not born or trained as "dissenters" from the main-stream or as heterodox economists. On the con-trary, he was one of the big representatives of the trend toward the "mathematization" of neo-classical economics from the 1930s on, with obvious first-class perspectives at Harvard then. After praised contributions to mathematical neoclassical theory, he developed into "one of the most profound and prominent dissenters in economics" (Seifert, 1994, 277). "Profound" here includes that he knew neoclassical standard theory as well as anyone, being invited by Schumpeter for coauthoring on growth, busi-ness cycles, and econometrics during the 1930s and 1940s, later praised by, for instance, Paul Samuelson for his contribution to the neoclassi-cal theory of consumer behavior.

But during the 1950s, he increasingly broke up with the neoclassical mainstream and became the founding father of what he termed

Bioeconomics, which has grown into an important part of nonconventional economics since the 1980s. Since also his criticism of neoclassical economics still was based on the most intimate knowledge of its mathematical structures and (mathematical) inconsistencies and shortcomings, he had never been criticized or his approach and theory challenged by the mainstream—but rather was ignored from the 1960s on. He blamed the mainstream for a simplistic *arithmomorphism*, a tendency to subordinate the conceptualization of the economic problems to the mathematical tools at hand, in this way trivializing much and even abusing mathematics.

His major critique of the mainstream centered on the *ignored relation between the economy and the natural environment*. He criticized the neoclassical production function for leaving most fundamental things out and started his positive theory of the economy as a system open toward the natural environment with agrarian economics: His book *Economic Theory and Agrarian Economics* (1960) was a decisive break with neoclassical economics. He criticized the mainstream for its *mechanical analogy* (see also Chapter 6 above), ignoring *historical time* and the *irreversibility* of real economic processes, and for its conception of a closed economy, presuming a self-reproducing circuit among production, income, demand, and prices.

No wonder then that he increasingly considered himself an "original" *evolutionary-institutional economist* in the Veblenian tradition.

In his most famous work, *The Entropy Law and the Economic Process* (1971), Georgescu-Roegen developed the applicability of natural-science knowledge to the economic process with its tight metabolism with the natural processes through consuming natural resources of all kinds and storing waste in all forms into nature, without paying the price for the reproduction of these natural functions and services. Particularly, he was the first to apply the second law of *thermodynamics*, the so-called *entropy law*, to economics.

First, he saw the economic process embedded in, framed and shaped by, and an *extension of, biological evolution*. However, with the tools mankind has developed in a cultural evolution, they can change their very own natural living conditions. These changes often are "qualitative" ones and as such cannot be depicted by "arithmomorphism."

Second, the economic process is not mechanical but *entropic*, since economic activity requires energy, transforms available or "free" energy into unavailable or bound energy. The economy is thus a main application of the thermodynamic entropy law that explains increasing and *irreversible energy degradation*. The economy is that subsystem that is most advanced in ever further *increasing its own complexity* at the expense of the degradation (entropy, *disorder*) of the energy resources of the planet. (The economic system, however, may try to consume other planets as sources of energy, as waste sites, or even as living spaces, in order to keep it going, as soon as technologies will make this economically feasible.)

Georgescu-Roegen applied the same idea to matter rather than energy only. Particularly, he developed the insight "that a closed system—i.e., a system that can exchange only energy (not matter) with its environment, as in the case, approximately, of the Earth—cannot produce mechanical work forever at a constant rate" (Seifert, op. cit., 280).

Obviously, this all is most relevant today to understand how the endless number of economic, both production and consumption, processes that diffuse "dead," inappropriate, and often toxic matter into nature and the atmosphere in this way cumulatively cause the current resource, energy, food, and climate crises. Also, naïve early "green" hopes for *recycling* and nowadays revived beliefs of solving the problems through a *greening* of the global capitalist "market" economy are undermined by Georgescu-Roegen's informed, truly interdisciplinary (physical, biological, mathematical, economical), and incorruptible analyses. As long as this economy needs to "grow," both in output and in complexity, there is no way out of entropy and downgrading the resources of the earth.

The implications of this analysis, and Georgescu-Roegen did dare to draw them, are most radical in terms of *policies* and "Western" lifestyles: There is *little hope for* a "Prometheusian," endlessly *viable technology*, a technology that would have *no* far-reaching impacts "in the back," that would further absolve economy and society from the obligation to *change and reduce themselves, their ways, styles, institutional arrangements* and organizations first and fundamentally: "stop growth in consumption, production, population, stop overheating, overcooling, overlighting, overspeeding, and so on; i.e., do everything to conserve" (ibid. 281), so that mankind can survive as long as possible with this one planet. However, whether this world, the economy, the corporations, businessmen, frequent fliers, financial speculators, real estate investors, consumers, car drivers, leisure activists, etc. will be able to change their culture, institutions, objectives, and organizational forms in order to *reduce both quantities and complexity*, would appear more than doubtful after 40 years of greening discussion that had little real consequences.

Georgescu-Roegens life work has had its implications on heterodox economics at least (see, e.g., Dragan and Demetrestu, 1991; Arestis and Sawyer, 1992, who even speak of a *new paradigm* that he developed) and still is a plentiful source of most relevant, serious, profound, and critical analyses and theorizing today.

12.14 KARL W. KAPP: OPEN-SYSTEMS APPROACH, ENTROPY, AND THE "SOCIAL COSTS OF PRIVATE ENTERPRISE"

Karl William Kapp (1910–1976) was another founding father of modern economic "heterodoxies," particularly of evolutionary-institutional complexity economics and, within

this frame, of *modern ecological economics* from a truly interdisciplinary perspective. Besides *Georgescu-Roegen*, he was the second pioneer to analyze the economy as an *open system* in its relation to nature and to apply the then new *thermodynamic knowledge* to it. His focus, though, was on both *nature* and *society* with the economy sustaining and expanding itself at the expense of the societal *and* natural environment. Society, however, in parts may convey its "burden" onto nature again, and in this way the entropy of the whole system of the planet will accelerate. Thus, going beyond Georgescu-Roegen, Kapp considered possible *societal deterioration* together with and parallel to natural entropy.

Going further beyond Georgescu-Roegen, he also considered the *institutional arrangement of the capitalist market economy* and its core institutional set, the *business enterprise*, particularly prone, if not designed, to intense and accelerated exploitation of nature (and society) with its comparatively *limited accountability* for the costs (in both nature and society) that it causes, the so-called *social costs*. So Kapp was perhaps more the institutional economist who came to develop an open-systems economics rather than, as Georgescu-Roegen, the formal systems economist who came to become an institutionalist.

As Schumpeter, Polanyi, and Georgescu-Roegen, Kapp was a European evolutionary-institutional economist who made his most important contributions to complexity economics in the USA during the 1930s through 1950s, but somehow "wandered" between Europe and the USA. Kapp in particular, as many of the most profiled German economists and social scientists (the Frankfurt School of sociology, philosophers, psychologists, art scientists, and economists like *G. Colm, E. Heimann, E. Lederer,* and *A. Lowe*), was forced to escape from Nazi-Germany in 1933. He found his first exile, though, in Switzerland where he finished his doctoral dissertation, before joining most of the other emigrants mentioned in New York. After later stays in India and the Philippines

(1957–1964), Kapp returned to Europe not before 1965. While he found a professorship in Switzerland (Basle) again, rather than in Germany, and was already an international expert (also for the UN) on environment and development, he remained an outsider in mainstream academic economics. However, other than Schumpeter, Myrdal, and Georgescu-Roegen, Kapp has not only been more or less ignored by the mainstream but it also took a particularly long time for him to become recognized as a major contributor to modern evolutionary-institutional economics in heterodox ranks (see, e.g., Elsner et al., 2006; Ramazzotti et al., 2012). Today after all, for instance, the European Association for Evolutionary Political Economy—EAEPE—awards a Kapp-Prize.

His doctoral dissertation, written in Switzerland before leaving for New York, already contained his later main themes: a *critique of valuations in terms of market prices* and of the neoclassical *dichotomy between the "individual" and the common good*.

Both from his teaching and publication of a major New York based project on the emergence and making of contemporary capitalist civilization and from his stays and work in *developing countries* he early developed the *holistic perspective* that an interconnected system of institutions, norms, and beliefs makes up a socioeconomy. Thus, for students to get aware of the objectives, ideas, belief systems, folk views, and functioning of their socioeconomy they had "to liberate themselves from preconceptions, projections, dogmas, obsolete traditions and ideologies of the past" (Steppacher, 1994, 435). Both problems and their collective responses, more or less instrumental or ceremonial institutions, thus, can only be understood, and reformed, if considered and analyzed as a part of the whole. Socioeconomic change and reform is a particularly complex and holistic enterprise, particularly because the process of enculturation and institutional

emergence "provides at the same time the axiomatic values which serve to explain, rationalize, and justify the same [...] process. This closing-down mechanism of circular causation is value-laden [...] and to a large extent unconscious" (Steppacher, op. cit., 439). In a Veblenian sense, we might talk of the ceremonially warranted dimension of institutions that have a tendency to become abstract norms, if the ceremonial warrant dominates, i.e., when power and status differences have become dominant (as has been explained already in Chapter 1 and will be further elaborated in the Bush model in Chapter 13, Section 12).

That complexity of culture of course undermines, according to Kapp, any cultural colonialism, imperialism or intervention that strives to impose specific cultural ways on other cultures—which typically entails long-run negative repercussions in the subordinated culture, if not in the same field and immediately, then in other sometimes remote functional areas and in the long run.

Also Kapp, as others presented above, came to criticize the mechanical worldview of neoclassical economics and its typical "Western-culture" conception of reduced formal (hyper-) rationality which reduces humans (and organizations) to stimulus-response mechanisms, like a pinball globule (a similar picture was used already by Veblen in 1898). Kapp's critique here was informed and influenced by the social sciences and thus was broader than with most critical economists. It included the antagonisms of values versus facts, unconsciousness versus consciousness, substance versus formalism, quality versus quantity, and emotions versus deliberation. If the broader perspective would be suppressed, *"shadow aspects of modern civilization"* (Steppacher, op. cit., 436) could not be made open. Among these, Kapp saw colonialism and imperialism, fascism, war, *social deterioration*, *underdevelopment*, and, most of all, *ecological disruption*. His intimate knowledge of developing countries led him to recognize early that also they bear the problems of social and ecological deterioration, rather than a simple and straightforward "upward" development.

Kapp's main book *The Social Costs of Private Enterprise* was published in 1950 already (Kapp, 1950). And here several strands of his thinking already flowed together: modern *biological knowledge*, modern *physical knowledge*, i.e., the *entropy* and *open-systems* issues, the *evolutionary* and complexity perspectives, the specific *institutional* analysis of the capitalist "market" economy and its core institution and agent, the *business firm*, individual psychology, and others (see also, e.g., Heidenreich, 1998; Berger and Elsner, 2007). He analyzed not only the reduced accountability and *cost shifting* to society and nature of the capitalist firm but also its consequences in the macro measures of *national accounting*. In this way, he also anticipated the discussions on the *limits and desirability of growth* and the *critique of the national product* as a measure of well-being that came up more than two decades later only.

From his experience in underdeveloped countries, he developed a theoretical, methodological, and practical approach of substantive rationality, as an alternative of "market"-price and "market"- income-based national accounting, the *basic needs* and *existential minima* approach, based on a substantial description of *social indicators* as well as *thresholds* and measures of minima of a "good life." With this, he also anticipated already in the mid-1960s what UN development reports from the 1990s on operationalized with indicators and data on a comprehensive substantial and a global scale. Also, he much anticipated of what *Amartya K. Sen* later developed as the positive freedom and *human capabilities approach*, which has been taken on by the UN development conception nowadays, and which earned Sen the economics Nobel prize in 1998 (given, among others, for welfare economics and measurement), and which caused a lasting discussion and reflection

in the social sciences on modeling human agency and individualism that still is going on. As seen, Kapp was an early founding father of such *developmental economics and policies* which included his *social needs* approach and "a critical evaluation of those institutional arrangements that [...] inhibit the self-actualization process" (Steppacher, op. cit., 439).

With his 1961 book *Towards a Science of Man in Society*, Kapp (1961) finally presented his full-fledged comprehensive theory of system openness, complexity, entropy, institutional man, and of a critical institutional analysis of the social and natural costs of the capitalist business firm. His openness approach went beyond the more general (and more formal) one of Georgescu-Roegen that was meant to apply to the economy–nature interrelation only. Kapp covered several levels of complex systems: inanimate nature, biology at large, human beings, human society, and the whole economy–society–nature interaction system. In general, *living organisms* are able to keep themselves in a steady state and even evolve to *higher complexity* by taking in low-entropy energy and discarding high-entropy waste, in this way *avoiding the increase of entropy for themselves* for some time of their lives (see for this, e.g., Steppacher, op. cit., 438–440). Thus, human agents inevitably are double-bound with nature: Their lives have an impact on nature and changing nature impacts their lives, which in turn forces them to adapt.

But human agents have implications beyond that. *Man is particularly open* as a biological structure. Being *born in a quasi-embryonic state* and highly dependent on external support from other human beings for many years, man's biological condition is fundamentally *sociobiological*, extremely vulnerable and *uncertain, dependent on* communication and *cooperation* with others, and thus highly *undetermined in their individual potentials* which may be conditioned and "encultured" in most constructive or destructive ways.

In this way, our modern understanding of *institutions* as basically problem-solving devices to *stabilize* expectations and thus *empower* and enlarge interdependent human action capacity has received an early underpinning by Kapp's *biologically informed theory of human enculturation*. Institutions particularly "stabilize the unstable structure of human drives and needs, open to being channeled into the most diverse directions [. . .]" (Steppacher, op. cit., 439).

Thus, the circle of Kapp's theory, approach, or perhaps even "paradigm," closes, going through a comprehensive theory of openness and entropic process and critical analysis of institutional arrangements, and against that background resuming the idea of social costs of private enterprise (perhaps deliberately) designed with its business accounting system and legally encouraged not to bear the real social and natural costs of its expansion, but to shift them onto the socially and naturally generated commons, if only to be borne by geographically remote populations or by future generations (see also Chapters 1 and 3 for an explanation of the "commons").

This also is about "economic rationality'" versus "ecosocial reason" (Steppacher, op. cit., 440), a *system of irresponsibility* and *nonaccountability*. And, of course, nowadays it is not only the private enterprise that systematically shifts costs, but under conditions of neoliberal deregulation and privatization cost shifting has become an even more ubiquitous principle. And the new "business" metaphors and behavior of politicians and public administrations make also public agencies to cost shifters, generating social costs.

Kapp was not only a founding father of institutional development and ecological economics in this way, but he also came down-to-earth in development policy with minimum thresholds, indicators, measures, and data. Similarly, he helped developing *ecological economics* with detailed environmental minimum standards, thresholds, indicators, and critical

interrelations between, e.g., different substance concentrations. In his last years, he published a whole bunch of specific papers with high relevance for concrete environmental policies.

Thus, a most comprehensive work, and perhaps more than a "theory" or an "approach" was developed by a critical evolutionary-institutional economist who took the journey into the fundamental interrelations among an open capitalist "market" economy, society, and nature.

12.15 FURTHER CONTRIBUTIONS TO COMPLEXITY MICROECONOMICS

There is no perfect and ultimate list of selected themes, ideas, approaches, and great economists for a reconstruction of the history of complexity economics. Colander (2000), for instance, in a "thumbnail sketch of the history of thought from a complexity perspective" listed—together with Adam Smith, Thomas Malthus, Karl Marx, Alfred Marshall, and John Maynard Keynes—also *David Ricardo, John Stuart Mill, Léon Walras,* and *Friedrich von Hayek.* There would certainly be something to say, under a complexity perspective, on these economists as well. We will try to bring the picture, "down to a round figure" by looking at some *specific major twentieth century figures,* who may complete the picture of some major "schools of thought" or paradigms. (Note that another candidate for this exercise, not considered here, might have been the Austrian School after Menger, particularly von Hayek.). Among those figure the following.

12.15.1 Further Developing Classical and Marxian Modeling: Piero Sraffa

Piero Sraffa (1898–1983) was a mathematical economist and published his most influential book *Production of Commodities by Means of Commodities* (Sraffa, 1960) only late, after he had made, from the mid-1920s on, several important contributions to criticize and substitute neoclassical modeling, such as exploring the untenability of neoclassical modeling under *increasing returns* and under serious consideration of the *economic circuit of continuously changing prices, incomes, distribution, consumption structure, and sectoral production structure* (for the basics of his model, see Chapter 6), under which condition an equilibrium would simply be impossible. In that sense, his microeconomic analysis and model considered the macroeconomic circuit as well. In fact, *Keynes* had invited the Italian economist to Cambridge University, where Sraffa for some years contributed to Keynes' research on his *General Theory* (see above).

Sraffa's work has also been taken as founding a so-called *Neo-Ricardian* economics. In fact, Sraffa's main book (see above) developed a model to formalize the classical *(labor) theory of value*, as developed by *David Ricardo* and Marx. He criticized the neoclassical theory of value and developed a model of aggregating capital as "dated inputs of labor" (which led to a famous debate known as the *Cambridge capital controversy*).

12.15.2 Further Developing Veblenian Evolutionary Institutionalism: John Commons and Clarence Ayres

Commons

John R. Commons (1862–1945) was after Veblen and together with *Wesley C. Mitchell*, one of the founding fathers of American (evolutionary) Institutionalism (evolutionary-institutional economics). He probably was the one who, with his "Wisconsin School of Institutionalism", was most responsible for making institutionalism the leading school of *policy* advice in the 1920s and 1930s, when several states, and the federal government during Franklin D. Roosevelt's "New Deal," established basics of a welfare state in the USA. While Mitchell established Institutionalism in empirical economic research and national accounting (the founding father of the NBER—National Bureau of Economic Research), Commons was the practical and pragmatist economist who best knew about formal institutions and labor and social welfare laws.

His first major work was accordingly *The Legal Foundations of Capitalism* (Commons, 1924). Other major works include the two-volume book *Institutional Economics. Its Place in Political Economy* (Commons, 1934) and *The Economics of Collective Action* (Commons, 1950). Commons had studied the historical development of jurisdiction, common law, and state laws on the background of conflicting interests of the parties, of institutions with their distributions of rights and duties, and of balancing interests—as a living part of the behavioral structures of a socioeconomy.

He was the first to develop the later Coasian *idea of transactions* as the basic socioeconomic unit in 1934, i.e., 3 years before *Coase's* famous article (Coase, 1937), instead of the neoclassical "equivalent" exchange in the "market," with their *institutionally determined sets of rights and duties* and their continuing evolutionary change. He thus is also the proper founder of the modern field of *law and economics*.

Commons has always stressed the *collective character* of economic solutions and defined *institutions* "as collective action in control, liberation, and expansion of individual action." He clearly stated the importance of *futurity* in the *expectations* of agents for attaining superior socioeconomic solutions. His pragmatistic approach is reflected also in his reform conception, which were based on the ideas of *going concerns* (as institutionalized interests, mainly of firms), of *working rules* (as institutions bargained for balancing of interests), and of prices, profits, and wages as *reasonable values*, which are to be transparently bargained in order to balance conflicting social interests. His idea of man, thus, focused on a *negotiational psychology*, social discourse, and controlled evolution of institutions. His idea of a *negotiated economy*, a transparently bargained economy, has not only shaped the institutionalist vision of a pragmatist social reform, but also received some revival, from the 1990s on, in conceptions to further develop the Scandinavian variety of capitalism.

Ayres

Clarence E. Ayres (1891–1972) was a student of Veblen. He refined the *dichotomy of ceremonial institutions and technology* that Veblen had formulated by introducing more nuance into the concept. According to him (and later developed further, culminating in P.D. Bush's contribution to a theory of institutions and institutional change, see Section 13.12 below), we continue to find a past-binding component of institutions but at the same time also a, more or less pronounced, instrumental (problem-solving) component. This has been laying the ground for our understanding of institutions serving as coordinating, and hence more or less problem-solving, devices for agents, stabilizing their mutual expectations and enabling interdependent decision making (for applications of this perspective on institutions, see, e.g., Chapters 14 and 15).

Technological change is still the principal driver of institutional change, according to Ayres, as far as the institutions as such are concerned. However, the recognition that rules contain ceremonial as well as instrumental components allows for a second dimension, along which institutions can change, namely, the instrumental-ceremonial dimension. A loss of relative problem-solving capacities, as potentially available better solutions, are not adapted, due to status-driven motivations, signifies an increasingly ceremonial content of institutions. Status-driven motivations by influential agents in a group are important influences in this process. However, as individuals are *socialized within a certain institutional framework*, which is typically supported by an *ideological narrative for justifying it*, and a subsequent emotional attachment of agents to these rules and overall framework (see, e.g., Ayres, 1996, Foreword to the 1962 edition), even agents that are not profiting from an existing societal structure may be found to *oppose change*. The degree to which an existing institutional framework limits curiosity, workmanship, and parental bend as individual motivators for action improving the overall group situation has a significant impact on the dynamics a system can take.

Ayres also contributed significantly to our understanding of *technology* as a combination of skill and equipment. Something becomes a tool when it is applied in an act of skill, and skill, in turn, requires equipment *to be exercised, acquired, and absorbed*. This leads to a different view on economic problems, not just in matters of development, since a focus on investment in machines is obviously not enough, as the possibility and potential to develop further skills has to be in place. The latter requires a *supportive institutional framework*. (See also the neo-Schumpeterian perspective as given in the Nelson-Winter model in Chapter 13). It also concerns the view on scarcity, as in this reading it depends on the level of skill and available tools, which material and matter can be used in economic processes; or, in de Gregorio's words, "resources are not; they become" (de Gregorio, 1988).

12.15.3 Further Developing Macroeconomics and Keynesianism: Michal Kalecki, Nicholas Kaldor, Luigi Pasinetti, Richard Goodwin, and Hyman Minsky

Kalecki

Michal Kalecki (1899–1970), a Polish macroeconomist, concurrently with Keynes worked on a *genuine macroeconomic theory of nonequilibrium, unemployment, and crisis*. He worked at the London School of Economics, University of Cambridge, University of Oxford, and the Warsaw School of Economics, as well as an economic advisor to governments of Cuba, Israel, Mexico, and India.

Kalecki developed many of the same ideas as Keynes, even before Keynes; however, since he published in Polish, he remained less known to the English-speaking world. He integrated *Marxist class analysis* and the then new literature on *oligopoly theory*, and his work had a significant influence on both Marxian and Post-Keynesian economists. He was also one of the first macroeconomists to apply mathematical models and statistical data to economic questions.

In 1933, Kalecki wrote an essay that brought together the issues, which would dominate his theory ("An Essay on the Theory of the Business Cycle"), in which Kalecki was able to develop a comprehensive theory of business cycles. In 1936, he learnt about the publication of Keynes's *General Theory*. This was his motive for traveling to England. He first visited the London School of Economics and afterward went to Cambridge. Here began a friendship with *Joan Robinson* and *Piero Sraffa*. In 1937, he met *Keynes* upon intermediation by Joan Robinson. In fact, two thinkers, from different political and theoretical starting points, came to the same conclusion. In 1939, Kalecki wrote one of his most important works, *Essays in the Theory of Economic Fluctuations* (Kalecki, 1939).

While Kalecki was generally enthusiastic about the Keynesian revolution, he predicted that it would not endure. He predicted that the *full employment* delivered by Keynesian policy would eventually lead to a more assertive working class and weakening of the social position of business leaders, causing the elite to use their political power to force the *displacement of Keynesian policy* even though profits would be higher than under a laissez-faire system: The erosion of social prestige and *political power* would be unacceptable to the elites despite higher profits. In 1944, Kalecki published an article with a theory of *business cycles caused by political events*.

In 1946, he accepted the Polish government's invitation to become head of the Central Planning Office of the Ministry of Economics, later he accepted the position offered him in the Economic Department of the United Nations Secretariat. He remained there until 1954, allowing him to develop his work as a political advisor. However, McCarthy's witch hunt depressed him, as many of his closest friends were directly affected. In 1955, he returned to Poland. In Poland, Kalecki and *Oskar Lange*, another great Polish economist of the time, collaborated in economic seminars. In 1957, he was appointed chairman of the Committee for the Perspective Plan. The plan had a horizon covering 1961 to 1975, and was a reflection of Kalecki's theory of growth in socialist economies. The last years of his life he devoted to advising the Polish Government.

Kalecki's most famous contributions were his *profit equation*, the *determinants of investment*, and a theory of *socialist planning*, and his work has inspired *Post-Keynesians*, including Robinson, Kaldor, Goodwin, and, in the recent two decades also younger heterodox economists, Post-Keynesians, Marxian, and Institutionalist (macro-) economists.

Kaldor

Nicholas Kaldor (1908–1986) was another famous Cambridge economist in the post-WWII period. He developed the famous *compensation criterion* called *Kaldor–Hicks efficiency* for *welfare comparisons* (1939), derived the famous cobweb model, and developed some regularities of economic growth, Kaldor's growth laws.

He also worked alongside with *Gunnar Myrdal* to develop the concept *Circular Cumulative Causation* (see above), a recursive, multi-causal, and cumulative mechanism of market-based economic development. Myrdal received the basics of the concept from one of his Swedish teachers, *Knut Wicksell*, and developed it alongside with Kaldor, when they worked together at the *United Nations Economic Commission for Europe*. While Myrdal concentrated on the social provisioning aspect of development, Kaldor focused on demand–supply relationships to the manufacturing sector. In the collaboration with Myrdal, Kaldor displayed some theoretical proximity to *institutionalism*.

Kaldor's contribution to growth theory, in a *Keynesian* but also largely in a *Marxian* tradition, was basically a *two-class model* of different consumption propensities of workers and capitalists, which implies that the *income and wealth distribution* between the two basic classes becomes a critical parameter for approaching aggregate consumption/ saving and investment, which, in turn, better informed the Keynesian growth model of the Harrod–Domar type. Finally, in that context, Kaldor developed a *technical progress function* connecting the growth rates of labor productivity (y/v) (with y = output) and capital intensity (c/v).

In all, Kaldor displayed a "trilateral" integrative perspective between institutionalism, Keynesianism, informed by Marxian economics.

Pasinetti

Luigi L. Pasinetti (born 1930) is one of the most influential Post-Keynesian theorists and a student (as well as later colleague) of Keynesians *Joan Robinson*, *Piero Sraffa*, and *Nicholas Kaldor*. Similar to Goodwin's focus (see next section), Pasinetti's research program may be seen as devoted to deriving an *integrated theory of capital, prices and macroeconomics* in general. To accomplish this, he also turned to *dynamic systems*. A central result of his research is that, although the macroeconomic system is modeled in an integrated way following clearly defined equations, many variables have a higher degree of freedom than previously thought, i.e., they are determined by the model but are not directly correlated to other variables. For instance, the price system has two degrees of freedom, one for its absolute value and one for its intertemporal development, since prices are only determined in relation to one another for any point in time (Pasinetti, 1993; for details of Pasinetti's theory, see, e.g., Baranzini, 2000).

Goodwin

Richard M. Goodwin (1913–1996) devoted much of his professional life to the study of *nonlinear dynamics in economic systems*, particularly in macroeconomics. One of his most influential accomplishments was to derive a framework for the modeling and a series of models of growth cycles. Doing so, he fused *Marxian* and *Keynesian* but also *Schumpeterian* influences. Goodwin employed dynamic systems in his economic variant of a *Lotka–Volterra model* (which has been presented in a simplified version in Section 11.3.5). He also followed the mainstream debates on, and joined the heterodox criticism of, general-equilibrium theory, but he continued to work on dynamics, complex systems, and, eventually also, chaos (see, e.g., Goodwin, 1967, 1990).

Minsky

As already indicated in Section 12.8.4, Hyman P. Minsky (1919–1996) worked on the deep and hidden causes and characteristics of *financial crises*, in an increasingly leveraged and thus fragile and vulnerable financial system. He worked largely in both the *Keynesian* and the *evolutionary-institutionalist traditions*. As such, he also was a social reformer, supported government intervention in financial markets, opposed deregulation, stressed the importance of the Central Banks as lenders of last resort, and argued against the explosion of private debt and credit. Minsky argued that a key mechanism that pushes an economy toward a crisis is the accumulation of debt by the nongovernment sector.

His theory links financial market fragility, in the normal life cycle of an economy, with speculative investment bubbles endogenous to financial markets. In prosperous times, when corporate cash flow rises beyond what is needed to pay off debt, a speculative euphoria develops, and eventually debts exceed what borrowers can pay off from their incoming revenues, which in turn produces a financial crisis. As a result of such speculative borrowing bubbles, banks and lenders tighten credit availability, even to companies that can afford loans, and the economy subsequently contracts (the much-cited "Minsky moment").

His model of the credit system, the *financial instability hypothesis* (FIH) mentioned above, incorporates much knowledge that was present in the HET for long, such as with John Stuart Mill, Alfred Marshall, Knut Wicksell, or Irving Fisher, but was denied by the "neoliberal" turn of supply-side economics and monetarism and their dominant influence in politics from the 1970s on, namely that the financial system swings between robustness and fragility and these swings becomes an integral part the business cycle. These booms and busts are inevitable in a deregulated "market economy"—unless governments and central banks step in to control it. His views were laid out in two books, *John Maynard Keynes* (Minsky, 1975) and *Stabilizing an Unstable Economy* (Minsky, 1986), and more than a hundred academic articles. Minsky's theory has become most relevant during the crisis 2007ff., but obviously still has little influence in mainstream economics or central bank policy.

Minsky stated his theories verbally and did not build mathematical models. Another excuse for the fact that his theories have not been incorporated into mainstream macroeconomic models, which do not include private debt as a factor. *Post-Keynesian* economists such as *Steve Keen* have developed models of endogenous economic crises based on Minsky's theory.

12.15.4 Developing Neoclassical Economics into Greater Complexity: Vilfredo Pareto

Vilfredo F.D. Pareto (1848–1923) was one of the most influential economists of his time. He was also both one of the most brilliant economists and one of the most radical social Darwinists and political right-wingers in the history of economics.

On the one hand, the antidemocratic mockery and the misogynic rants, which his writings are riddled with, made him one of the Italian fascists' favorite scholars: Mussolini appointed him a Senator upon his ascension to power. However, Pareto died already in 1923.

On the other hand, some of Pareto's contributions were revolutionary. In fact, while his *general-equilibrium theory* was immediately acknowledged by his contemporaries, the full potential of his most important ideas was only realized decades later. Pareto was the first to introduce a modern concept—what we today call *Pareto efficiency* and *Pareto optimum*—of the comparison of groups of values (such as bundles of goods and income of different persons) and to recognize its importance for economics. He was also the first to understand the persistent stability and *self-perpetuating nature of the distribution of income* (Pareto, 1897), he derived the corresponding *power distribution function* and suggested that it resulted from *evolutionary processes* (although he described an oddly brutal and hostile world, see, e.g., Pareto (1971/1906)). That such distributions actually occur very frequently in economic systems was observed only decades later by Mandelbrot (2001) (on the relevance of power law distributions, see also Section 12.12 above and Section 13.11 below).

12.16 CLUSTERING ECONOMISTS IN DIVERSE ECONOMIC PARADIGMS, AND A FINAL REMARK

Obviously, it is most tempting to sort and cluster the multiplicity, plurality, and diversity of leading economists into a smaller and better manageable number of groups, clear-cut schools of thought, or better: paradigmatic systems of ontologies, axioms, core assumptions, core propositions, core models, and core examples—i.e., the so-called Kuhnian paradigms. There are many examples in the literature to do this (e.g., Colander, 2000; Radzicki, 2003; O'Hara, 2007). The complexity economics landscape, however, will never fit, and cannot fit by definition, into clear-cut boxes. Rather, the system is *overlapping* in manifold ways. Just to provide a first indication of this, we might start with the following overlapping listing:

Paradigmatic System	Original Representatives (those not introduced above are set in brackets)	Later Representatives (those not introduced above are set in brackets)
Classical Political Economy	Smith, Malthus, (Ricardo), Marx, (Mill)	Sraffa
Marxian Economics/ Radical Political Economy	Marx	Kalecki, Sraffa, Goodwin
(German) Historical School(s)	(Schmoller)	(M. Weber)
Evolutionary Institutionalism	Veblen, Commons, Ayres	Myrdal, Polanyi, Georgescu-Roegen, Kapp, Minsky, Simon
Keynes, Keynesian Economics, Post-Keynesian Economics	Keynes, Sraffa, Kalecki, (Robinson)	Kaldor, Goodwin, Pasinetti, Minsky
Developmental-Evolutionary, Schumpeterian, Neo-Schumpeterian Economics	Schumpeter	Polanyi, Myrdal, Kapp, Simon
Austrian Evolutionary Economics	Menger	(Hayek)
Complexity Turn in Neoclassical Economics	Marshall, Pareto	(. . .)

Note that we might not only *further extend* this list (by, e.g., the historical approach in economics, stemming from the German Historical School, and by "Austrians", namely v. Hayek), but also break it down ever more in sub- and sub-subsections until a huge mind map of names, groups, and schools, and their multiple relations emerge. This is not the place to pursue such exercises, though.

With all the great founders of complexity economics, we find that they were not only profound theorists but also *profound epistemologists*. Analyzing a complex real socioeconomy in a theory, approach, or paradigm of adequate degrees of both complexity and realism is impossible without such methodological and epistemological reflection. We will reflect this dimension of modern complexity economics in Chapter 18.

If we reconsider the forerunners of modern complexity economics, we may easily find *similar themes*, often *overlapping* themes conceptualized in overlapping ways with overlapping and *converging* results. Within this not so obvious dimension of the HET, we also find at least some upward sloped path of insight, a *growth in the ideal common "knowledge fund"* of complexity economics.

Most of these forerunners and founding fathers were particularly broad in their scope, if not fully *interdisciplinary* and well informed in economics, the social sciences, psychology, philosophy, and often the natural sciences, with focuses here mostly on biology but sometimes also beyond.

The *selection* of great economists presented above may be imperfect, and many more macroeconomists, political economists, Post-Keynesians, behavioral economists, industrial and regional economists, developmental economists, ecological economists, and others might have been mentioned. This, of course, is a micro-oriented and it is an evolutionary-institutionally oriented selection. It definitely is no full-fledged HET, and not even a history of "heterodox" economic thought. But it hopefully illustrated some core themes and perspectives of complexity economics.

We will find that those themes show up again in the modern core models of complexity economics in Chapter 13, cast there in more formal frames. And you will see that Chapters 6 (critique), 10 (the universe of economics systems), 11 (dynamics, complexity, and evolution), 12 (the present one on the historical development of these *great themes*), and 13 (*critical anchor models* of complexity economics of recent times) show some common thread. The well-trained economics, business, or social science student should not disregard any of the different perspectives provided in these chapters, their specific informational contents, and their specific potential contributions to a well-informed modern academically trained professional. Rather, one should enjoy the different perspectives and potential contributions to one's own knowledge fund and the social knowledge fund.

Chapter References

Aguilera-Klink, F., 1994. Some notes on the misuse of classic writings in economics on the subject of common property. Ecol. Econ. 9, 221–228.

Alverson, H., 1986. Culture and economy: games that "play people". J. Econ. Issues. XX, 661–679.

Arena, R., Gloria-Palermo, S., 2001. Evolutionary themes in the Austrian tradition: Menger, Wieser and Schumpeter on institutions and rationality. In: Garrouste, P.,

Ioannides, S. (Eds.), Evolution and Path Dependence in Economic Ideas: Past and Present. Edward Elgar, Cheltenham, Northampton (cited after an earlier mimeo presented at the annual conference of the EAEPE—European Association of Evolutionary Political Economy 1997: Arena, Gloria 1997).

Arena, R., Gloria-Palermo, S., 2008. Menger and walras on money: a comparative view. Hist. Polit. Econ. 40, 317–343.

Arestis, P., Sawyer, M. (Eds.), 1992. 'Nicholas Georgescu-Roegen'. In: A Biographical Dictionary of Dissenting Economists, Edward Elgar, Aldershot, UK, and Brookfield, VT, USA, pp. 179–187.

Axelrod, R., 1984. The Evolution of Cooperation. second ed. Basic Books, New York, NY (2006).

Ayres, C.E., 1996, The theory of economic progress. Available at: <http://cas.umkc.edu/econ/Institutional/Readings/Ayres/tep/TEP.html>. (accessed March 2, 2014).

Baranzini, M., 2000. Luigi Lodovico Pasinetti. In: Arestis, P., Sawyer, M. (Eds.), The Biographical Dictionary of Dissenting Economists, second ed. Edward Elgar, Aldershot, Brookfield, pp. 417–425.

Berger, S. (Ed.), 2009. The Foundations of Non-Equilibrium Economics. Routledge, London, New York.

Berger, S., Elsner, W., 2007. European contributions to evolutionary institutional economics: the cases of "Cumulative Circular Causation" (CCC) and "Open Systems Approach" (OSA). J. Econ. Issues. XLI, 529–537.

Brennan, G., Pettit, P., 2000. The hidden economy of esteem. Econ. Philos. 16 (1), 77–98.

Brown, D. (Ed.), 1998. *Thorstein Veblen in the Twenty-First Century. A Commemoration of "The Theory of the Leisure Class" (1899–1999)*. Edward Elgar, Cheltenham, Northampton.

Buchanan, J.M., 1976. Public goods and natural liberty. In: Wilson, T., Skinner, A.S. (Eds.), The Market and the State. Essays in Honour of Adam Smith. Clarendon, Oxford, pp. 271–286.

Bush, P.D., 1987. The theory of institutional change. J. Econ. Issues. XI, 1075–1116.

Cantner, U., Hanusch, H., 1994. Schumpeter, Joseph Alois. In: Hodgson, G.M., Samuels, W.J., Tool, M.R. (Eds.), The Elgar Companion to Institutional and Evolutionary Economics, vol. 2. Edward Elgar, Aldershot, Brookfield, pp. 273–278.

Clark, C.M.A., 1990. Adam Smith and society as an evolutionary process. J. Econ. Issues. XXIV, 825–844.

Coase, R.H., 1937. The nature of the firm. Economica. 4 (16), 386–405.

Coase, R.H., 1976. Adam Smith's view of man. J. Law E. 19, 529–546.

Coase, R.H., 1984. The new institutional economics. Zeitschrift für die gesamte Staatswissenschaft (Journal of Institutional and Theoretical Economics). 140, 229–231.

Cohn, S.M., 2007. Reintroducing Macroeconomics. A Critical Approach. M.E. Sharpe, Armonk, London.

Colander, D., 2000. A thumbnail sketch of the history of thought from a complexity perspective. In: Complexity and the History of Economic Thought. Perspectives on the History of Economic Thought, Routledge, London, New York (Selected papers from the History of Economics Society Conference, 1998, 2000, pp. 31–43).

Colander, D., 2008. Complexity and the history of economic thought, Middlebury College Economics Discussion Paper No. 08-04, Middlebury, VT (Retrieved March 1, 2014).

Commons, J.R., 1924. The Legal Foundations of Capitalism. Macmillan, New York, NY (repr. 2012).

Commons, J.R., 1934. Institutional Economics. Its Place in Political Economy. Macmillan, New York, 1934, repr. New Brunswick, N.J., London: Transaction Publishers, 1989.

Commons, J.R., 1950. The Economics of Collective Action. Macmillan, New York, NY.

Cordes, C., 2007a. Turning economics into an evolutionary science: veblen, the selection metaphor, and analogical thinking. J. Econ. Issues. XLI, 135–154.

Cordes, C., 2007b. The Role of "Instincts" in the development of corporate cultures. J. Econ. Issues. XLI, 747–764.

Cornwall, J., Cornwall, W., 1996. A Keynesian framework for studying institutional change and evolutionary process. In: Pressman, S. (Ed.), Interactions in Political Economy. Routledge, London, New York, pp. 170–185.

De Gregori, T.R., 1988. Resources are not; they become: an institutional theory. In: Tool, M.R. (Ed.), Evolutionary Economics I: Foundations of Institutional Thought. M. E. Sharpe, Armonk, London, pp. 291–314.

De Gregori, T.R., Shepherd, D.A., 1994. Myrdal, Gunnar. In: Hodgson, G.M., Samuels, W.J., Tool, M.R. (Eds.), The Elgar Companion to Institutional and Evolutionary Economics, vol. 2. Edward Elgar, Aldershot, Brookfield, pp. 107–112.

Dragan, J.C., Demetrescu, M.C., 1991. Entropy and Bioeconomics: The New Paradigm of Nicholas Georgescu-Roegen. second ed. Nagard, Rome.

Dugger, W., 1984. Methodological differences between institutional and neoclassical economics. In: Hausman, D.M. (Ed.), The Philosophy of Economics. An Anthology. Cambridge University Press, Cambridge, pp. 312–321.

Dutraive, V., 2012. The pragmatist view of knowledge and beliefs in institutional economics: the significance of habits of thought, transactions and institutions in the conception of economic behavior. In: Arena, R., Festré, A., Lazaric, N. (Eds.), Handbook of Knowledge and Economics. Edward Elgar, Cheltenham, Northampton.

Earl, P.E., 1994. Simon, Herbert Alexander. In: Hodgson, G.M., Samuels, W.J., Tool, M.R. (Eds.), The Elgar Companion to

Institutional and Evolutionary Economics, vol. 2. Edward Elgar, Aldershot, Brookfield, pp. 284–287.

Edgell, S., 2001. Veblen in Perspective. His Life and Thought. M.E. Sharpe, Armonk, London.

Elsner, W., 1986. Oekonomische Institutionenanalyse. Paradigmatische Entwicklung der oekonomischen Theorie und der Sinn eines Rückgriffs auf die oekonomische Klassik am Beispiel der Institutionenanalyse (Economic Institutional Analysis. The Paradigmatic Development of Economic Theory and the Meaning of a Recourse to the Economic Classics, Using the Example of Institutional Economics). Duncker&Humblot (in German), Berlin.

Elsner, W., Ramazzotti, P., Frigato, P. (Eds.), 2006. Social Costs and Public Action in Modern Capitalism. Essays Inspired by Karl William Kapp's Theory of Social Costs. Routledge, London, New York.

Georgescu-Roegen, N., 1971. The Entropy Law and the Economic Process. Harvard University Press, Cambridge, MA.

Goodwin, R.M., 1967. A growth cycle. In: Feinstein, C.H. (Ed.), Socialism, Capitalism and Economic Growth. Cambridge University Press, Cambridge.

Goodwin, R.M., 1990. Chaotic Economic Dynamics. Clarendon Press, Oxford, New York.

Hanusch, H., Pyka, A., 2007. Principles of neo-Schumpeterian economics. Cambridge. J. Econ. 31, 275–289.

Harcourt, G.C., 1994. Keynes, John Maynard. In: Hodgson, G.M., Samuels, W.J., Tool, M.R. (Eds.), The Elgar Companion to Institutional and Evolutionary Economics, vol. 1. Edward Elgar, Aldershot, Brookfield, pp. 442–445.

Hart, N., 2003. Marshall's dilemma: equilibrium versus evolution. J. Econ. Issues. XXXVII, 1139–1160.

Heidenreich, R., 1998. Economics and institutions: the socioeconomic approach of K. William Kapp. J. Econ. Issues. XXXII, 965–984.

Heinrich, T., Schwardt, H., 2013. Institutional inertia and institutional change in an expanding normal-form game. Games. 4, 398–425.

Hicks, J., 1981. "IS-LM": an explanation. J. Post. Keynes. Econ. 3 (2), 139–154.

Hodgson, G.M., 1993a. The Mecca of Alfred Marshall. Econ. J. 103, 406–415.

Hodgson, G.M., 1993b. Economics and Evolution. Bringing Life Back into Economics. Polity Press, and University of Michigan Press, Cambridge, MA.

Hodgson, G.M., 1994a. Darwinism, Influence of Economics on. In: Hodgson, G.M., Samuels, W.J., Tool, M.R. (Eds.), The Elgar Companion to Institutional and Evolutionary Economics, vol. 1. Edward Elgar, Aldershot, Brookfield, pp. 125–129.

Hodgson, G.M., 1994b. Evolution and optimality. In: Hodgson, G.M., Samuels, W.J., Tool, M.R. (Eds.),

The Elgar Companion to Institutional and Evolutionary Economics, vol. 1. Edward Elgar, Aldershot, Brookfield, pp. 207–212.

Hodgson, G.M., 1994c. Evolution, theories of economic. In: Hodgson, G.M., Samuels, W.J., Tool, M.R. (Eds.), The Elgar Companion to Institutional and Evolutionary Economics, vol. 1. Edward Elgar, Aldershot, Brookfield, pp. 218–224.

Hutchison, T.W., 1984. Institutionalist economics old and new. Zeitschrift fuer die gesamte Staatswissenschaft. 140, 20–29.

Jennings, A.L., Waller, W., 1994. Cultural hermeneutics and evolutionary economics. In: Hodgson, G.M., Samuels, W.J., Tool, M.R. (Eds.), The Elgar Companion to Institutional and Evolutionary Economics, vol. 1. Edward Elgar, Aldershot, Brookfield, pp. 108–114.

Jensen, H.E., 1994. Marshall, Alfred. In: Hodgson, G.M., Samuels, W.J., Tool, M.R. (Eds.), The Elgar Companion to Institutional and Evolutionary Economics, vol. 2. Edward Elgar, Aldershot, Brookfield, pp. 53–55.

Kalecki, M., 1939. Essays in the Theory of Economic Fluctuations. George Allen & Unwin, London, repr. London, New York: Routledge, 2003.

Kapp, K.W., 1950. The Social Costs of Private Enterprise. Harvard University Press, Cambridge, MA.

Kapp, K.W., 1961. Towards a Science of Man in Society. A Positive Approach to the Integration of Social Knowledge. M. Nijhoff, Den Haag, NL.

Kates, S., 2013. Defending the History of Economic Thought. Edward Elgar, Cheltenham, Northampton.

Kelm, M., 1997. Schumpeter's theory of economic evolution: a Darwinian interpretation. J. Evol. Econ. 7, 97–130.

Keynes, J.M., 1921. A Treatise on Probability. Dover Publications, New York, NY.

Keynes, J.M., 1936. The General Theory of Employment, Interest and Money. Macmillan and Cambridge University Press, Cambridge.

Knoedler, J.T., Prasch, R.E., Champlin, D.P. (Eds.), 2007. Thorstein Veblen and the Revival of Free Market Capitalism. Edward Elgar, Cheltenham, Northampton.

Kregel, J., 1994. Macroeconomic theory (II). In: Hodgson, G.M., Samuels, W.J., Tool, M.R. (Eds.), The Elgar Companion to Institutional and Evolutionary Economics, vol. 2. Edward Elgar, Aldershot, Brookfield, pp. 42–47.

Kuhn, T.S., 1970. The Structure of Scientific Revolutions. second ed. The University of Chicago Press, Chicago, IL.

Mandelbrot, B.B., 2001. Scaling in financial prices: I. Tails and dependence. Quant. Finance. 1 (1), 113–123.

Marshall, A., 1920. Principles of Economics. Macmillan and Co, London, UK.

Minsky, H.P., 1975. John Maynard Keynes. McGraw Hill, New York, NY (repr. 2008).

Minsky, H.P., 1986. Stabilizing an Unstable Economy. Yale University Press, New Haven and London (repr. 2008).

Myrdal, G., 1944. An American Dilemma: The Negro Problem and Modern Democracy. Harper & Brothers Publishers, New York, London.

Myrdal, G., 1953. Conference of the British sociological association 1953. Ii. Opening Address: the relation between social theory and social policy. Br. J. Sociol. 4 (3), 210–242.

Myrdal, G., 1957. Economic Theory and Under-Developed Regions. Gerald Duckworth, London.

Myrdal, G., Streeten, P., 1958. Value in social theory, a selection of essays in methodology. Econ. J. 69 (274), 365–367.

O'Hara, P.A., 2007. Principles of institutional-evolutionary political economy – converging themes from the schools of heterodoxy. J. Econ. Issues. XLI.1, 1–42.

Ostrom, E., Walker, J., Gardner, R., 1994. Rules, Games, and Common-Pool Resources. Michigan University Press, Ann Arbor, MI.

Pareto, V., 1897. The new theories of economics. J. Polit. Econ. 5 (4), 485–502.

Pareto, V., 1971/1906 Manual of Political Economy, translation of the 1927 edition, Augustus M. Kelley, New York, NY.

Pasinetti, L.L., 1993. Structural Economic Dynamics—A Theory of the Economic Consequences of Human Learning. Cambridge University Press, Cambridge.

Polanyi, K., 1944. The Great Transformation. Beacon Press, Boston, MA.

Radzicki, M.J., 2003. Mr. Hamilton, Mr. Forrester, and a foundation for evolutionary economics. J. Econ. Issues. 37 (1), 133–174.

Ramazzotti, P., Elsner, W., Frigato, P. (Eds.), 2012. Social Costs Today. Institutional Analyses of the Present Crises. Routledge, London, New York.

Ramstad, Y., 1994. Veblen, Thorstein. In: Hodgson, G.M., Samuels, W.J., Tool, M.R. (Eds.), The Elgar Companion to Institutional and Evolutionary Economics, vol. 2. Edward Elgar, Aldershot, Brookfield, pp. 363–368.

Rosenberg, N., 1960. Some institutional aspects of the wealth of nations. J. Polit. Econ. LXVIII, 557–570.

Samuels, W.J., 1964. The classical theory of economic policy: non-legal social control. South. Econ. J. 31, 1–20, 87–100.

Samuels, W.J., 1994. Smith, Adam. In: Hodgson, G.M., Samuels, W.J., Tool, M.R. (Eds.), The Elgar Companion to Institutional and Evolutionary Economics, vol. 2. Edward Elgar, Aldershot, Hants, Brookfield, pp. 287–291.

Schotter, A., 1981. The Economic Theory of Social Institutions. Cambridge University Press, Cambridge.

Schumpeter, J.A., 1926. Theorie der wirtschaftlichen Entwicklung: Eine Untersuchung über Unternehmergewinn, Kapital, Kredit, Zins und den

Konjunkturzyklus. Duncker & Humblot, Berlin (repr. 1994).

Schumpeter, J.A., 1939. Business Cycles: A Theoretical, Historical, and Statistical Analysis of the Capitalist Process. Porcupine Press, Philadelphia, PA.

Schumpeter, J.A., 1942. Capitalism, Socialism and Democracy. Routledge, London and New York (repr. 1976).

Seifert, E.K., 1994. Art Georgescu-Roegen, Nicholas. In: Hodgson, G.M., Samuels, W.J., Tool, M.R. (Eds.), The Elgar Companion to Institutional and Evolutionary Economics, vol. 1. Edward Elgar, Aldershot, Hants, Brookfield, pp. 277–283.

Shionoya, Y., 1998. Schumpeterian evolutionism. In: Davis, J.B., Hands, D.W., Maeki, U. (Eds.), The Handbook of Economic Methodology. Edward Elgar, Cheltenham, Northampton, pp. 436–439.

Smith, A., 1759. In: Raphael, D.D., Macfie, A.L. (Eds.), The Theory of Moral Sentiments. Clarendon and Oxford University Press, Oxford (also: Indianapolis, IN: Liberty Fund, repr. 1976).

Song, H.-H., 1995. Adam Smith as an early pioneer of institutional individualism. Hist. Polit. Econ. 27, 425–448.

Sraffa, P., 1960. Production of Commodities by Means of Commodities. Cambridge University Press, London, repr. 1975.

Stanfield, J.R., 1994. Polanyi, Karl. In: Hodgson, G.M., Samuels, W.J., Tool, M.R. (Eds.), The Elgar Companion to Institutional and Evolutionary Economics, vol. 2. Edward Elgar, Aldershot, Brookfield, pp. 166–169.

Steppacher, R., 1994. Kapp, K. William. In: Hodgson, G.M., Samuels, W.J., Tool, M.R. (Eds.), The Elgar Companion to Institutional and Evolutionary Economics, vol. 1. Edward Elgar, Aldershot, Brookfield, pp. 435–441.

Tullock, G., 1985. Adam Smith and the Prisoners' Dilemma. Q. J. Econ. 100 (Suppl.), 1073–1081.

Vanberg, V.J., 1994. Carl Menger's evolutionary and John R. Commons's collective action approach to institutions. A comparison. In: Vanberg, V.J. (Ed.), Rules and Choice in Economics. Routledge, London, New York, pp. 144–163.

Veblen, T., 1898. Why is economics not an evolutionary science. Q. J. Econ. 12.

Veblen, T., 1899. The Theory of the Leisure Class. Oxford World's Classics, Oxford, NY (repr. 2009).

Veblen, T., 1904. The Theory of Business Enterprise. Charles Scribner's Sons, New York, NY (repr. 2011).

Veblen, T., 1914. The Instinct of Workmanship: and the State of Industrial Arts. Macmillan, New York et al.: (repr. 2006).

Veblen, T., 1915. Imperial Germany and the Industrial Revolution. Cosimo Classics, New York, NY (repr. 2006).

Veblen, T., 1917. An Inquiry into the Nature of Peace, and the Terms of its Perpetuation. Arc Manor, New York, NY (repr. 2008).

Veblen, T., 1918. The Higher Learning in America: A Memorandum on the Conduct of Universities by Business Men. B.W. Huebsch., New York, NY (repr. 2009).

Veblen, T., 1921. The Engineers and the Price System. Cosimo Classics, New York, NY (repr. 2006).

Veblen, T., 1923. Absentee Ownership: Business Enterprise in Recent Times: The Case of America. B.W. Huebsch, New York, NY (repr. 2009).

Waller, W., 1994. Veblenian dichotomy and its critics. In: Hodgson, G.M., Samuels, W.J., Tool, M.R. (Eds.), The Elgar Companion to Institutional and Evolutionary Economics, vol. 2. Edward Elgar, Aldershot, Brookfield, pp. 368–372.

Waller, W., 2007. Veblen's missing theory of markets and exchange, or can you have an economic theory without a theory of market exchange? In: Knoedler, J.T., Prasch, R.E., Champlin, D.P. (Eds.), Thorstein Veblen and the Revival of Free Market Capitalism. Edward Elgar, Cheltenham, Northampton, pp. 87–126.

Witztum, A., 1998. A study into smith's conception of the human character: Das Adam Smith problem revisited. Hist. Polit. Econ. 30, 489–513.

Further Reading

Canterbery, E.R., 2003. The Making of Economics. fourth ed. World Scientific, New Jersey.

Dopfer, K. (Ed.), 2005. The Evolutionary Foundations of Economics. Cambridge University Press, Cambridge.

Elsner, W., 1989. Adam Smith's model of the origins and emergence of institutions: the modern findings of the classical approach. J. Econ. Issues. XXIII, 189–213.

Foley, D.K., 2003. Unholy Trinity. Labor, Capital, and Land in the New Economy. Routledge, London, New York (Chapter 1).

Halteman, J., Noell, E., 2012. Reckoning with Markets. Moral Reflection in Economics. Oxford University Press, Oxford, New York.

Heilbroner, R., 1953. The Worldly Philosophers. The Lives, Times, and Ideas of the Great Economic Thinkers. Simon&Schuster, New York, NY (rev. seventh ed. 1999).

Hirshleifer, J., 1998. Stability of anarchic societies, The New Palgrave. Dictionary of Economics and Law, vol. III. Palgrave Macmillan, Basingstoke, 495–502.

Hollander, H., 1990. A social exchange approach to voluntary cooperation. Am. Econ. Review. 80 (5), 1157–1167 (ed. by P.K. Goldberg).

Hunt, E.K, 1992. History of Economic Thought. A Critical Perspective. second ed. HarperCollins Publ., New York, NY.

Rima, I., 2009. Development of Economic Analysis. seventh ed. Routledge, London, New York.

Sackrey, C., Schneider, G., Knoedler, J., 2004. Introduction to Political Economy. fifth ed. Economic Affairs Bureau/Dollars&Sense, Boston, MA, 2008.

Sherman, H.J., Hunt, E.K., Nesiba, R.F., O'Hara, P.A., Wiens-Tuers, B., 2008. Economics: An Introduction to Traditional and Progressive Views. seventh ed. M.E. Sharpe, Armonk, NY.

Further Reading—Online

For more further reading, further material, and updates, visit the textbook web site: http://booksite.elsevier.com/9780124115859

EXERCISES

Early Scottish Classical Economics and Adam Smith

1. Discuss the relations among the conceptions of "unintended consequences," "invisible hand," and "fallacy of aggregation." Refer to the historical optimism of the Scottish Enlightenment. Also refer to the vulgar apologetic version of Bernard Mandeville.

2. How may complex direct interdependence lead to unintended consequences in the sense of a fallacy of aggregation?

3. Explain how Adam Smith, in his Theory of Moral Sentiments, explained the emergence of basic social institutions through a consideration of others by the individual. Refer to his dual motivations and the mechanism of "changing places in the fancy."

4. Give a (nonformal) game-theoretic interpretation of the mechanism of "changing places in the fancy," using the one-dimensional approach of (long-run) maximizing agents.

Early Evolutionary Understandings in Post-Smithian and "Darwinian" Economics

5. Explain Malthus' conception of a periodically increasing selective pressure on humankind.

6. Explain Malthus' understanding of a "principle of natural selection." Why does it tend to be too "biologistic"?

7. Explain Marx' understanding of the historical evolution of the capitalist system. Why is capitalism a (over-) complex system in his perspective?

8. Explain Menger's "organic" analogy to the evolution of the market system. Why is it not Darwinian evolution?

9. Explain Menger's approach to the evolution of money.

10. Why did Marshall aspire for an "organic" analogy and consider biology as the "Mecca of the economist"?

11. What did Marshall learn for economic evolution from his industrial analysis?

Veblen, Keynes, Schumpeter

12. Explain Veblen's critique of neoclassical economics.

13. Explain Veblen's understanding of the evolution of social institutions. Why is it Darwinian and non-teleological?

14. Why does Keynes' understanding of aggregation and "macro" belong to the "fallacy of aggregation" side of economic theory, rather than the "invisible hand" side?

15. Explain Keynes' understanding of fundamental uncertainty, the investor's recourse to "animal spirits," and the agent's general reference to habits.

16. Why are money and prices complex phenomena in Keynes' theory?

17. What is the specific Schumpeterian approach to evolution?

18. How is Schumpeterian entrepreneurial innovation subject to a diversification and a selection mechanism?

Post-Veblenian Evolutionary-Institutional and Ecological Economics

19. Please explain K. Polanyi's conception of a "Great Transformation."
20. Why are land (nature), labor, and money not easily marketable commodities but complex economic factors?
21. Explain Myrdal's understanding of circular cumulative causations and processes.
22. Explain Simon's conception of "bounded rationality."
23. Explain how "bounded rationality" relates to complexity and causes "satisficing" behavior rather than maximizing.

24. Explain the complexity stemming from the economy as a subsystem open to, and exploiting, another subsystem (nature), in Georgescu-Roegen's theory.
25. Explain the tendency toward entropy of the economic system in Georgescu-Roegen's theory.
26. Explain Kapp's additional institutional analysis for the (capitalist) economy's tendency to exploit the other two subsystems, nature, and society, and toward entropy of the total system "earth."

SOLUTION KEYS

For solution keys of the exercises and other material on the subject of this chapter, visit the textbook website: http://booksite.elsevier.com/9780124115859

Recent Core Models of Complexity Microeconomics*

"[...] it reminded me of a lecture by the great mathematician Stan Ulam that I heard as a physics graduate student at UC Santa Cruz in 1977. The lecture was titled 'nonlinear mathematics'. Ulam began by saying that he was embarrassed by the inappropriateness of title: Since almost all of mathematics is nonlinear, he said, it is like calling an animal a 'non-elephant animal'. [...] Just as almost all mathematics is nonlinear, almost all economic phenomena are complex, and a discussion of which problems are illuminated by complexity economics is silly. A more tractable topic would be whether there are any problems it does not illuminate, or should not illuminate." **Doyne Farmer**[1]

*Some sections of this chapter have been contributed by Prof. Shuanping Dai, PhD, University of Essen-Duisburg, Yanlong Zhang, Claudius Gräbner, PhD candidates, University of Bremen, and Matthias Greiff, PhD, University of Giessen.

[1]"Economics Needs to Treat the Economy as a Complex System," Paper of his presentation at the INET conference *Paradigm Lost: Rethinking Economics and Politics*, April 14, 2012. http://ineteconomics.org/sites/inet.civicactions. net/files/farmer_berlinpaper.pdf.

The Microeconomics of Complex Economies.
DOI: http://dx.doi.org/10.1016/B978-0-12-411585-9.00013-0

13.1 INTRODUCTION

Having introduced many aspects of economic modeling, from game-theory and general-equilibrium models to simulation, evolutionary agent-based models and complexity, and after you have learned about the wealth of ideas, theories, and approaches to real-world economics in Chapter 12, one question remains: How can a powerful evolutionary-institutional and complexity microeconomics be derived without falling back onto the same heroic assumptions neoclassic theory forces its followers to make?

It is not too difficult to model single interactive situations and even complex societal phenomena. An integrated powerful general theory, however, is still lacking in spite of promising approaches by both evolutionary game theorists as discussed in Chapter 8 and complexity economists as discussed in Chapters 10 and 11. The present chapter shall serve to offer a few particularly inspiring building blocks, non-neoclassical models that are both striking in their relative simplicity and powerful in the scope of their explanatory potential and the impact they had in modern economics.

We are going to present A. Sen's isolation paradox, the models of institutional emergence by A. Schotter, R. Axelrod, and K. Lindgren, and models of the emergence of social segregation, by T.C. Schelling and R. Axelrod. Attendance coordination problems as studied by T.C. Schelling and W.B. Arthur will be

introduced as a simple example for self-organization in economics. This chapter will also further discuss path dependence in positive feedback processes such as technological standardization (following P.A. David and W.B. Arthur). R.W. Cooper and A. John's general model of coordination failures and potential coordination synergy will be introduced. Three models that focus on technological change, search patterns, and networks will also be presented, namely R.R. Nelson and S.G. Winter's theory of evolutionary change, S.A. Kauffman's technology landscapes, a model of technological progress under uncertainty, as well as D.J. Watts and S.H. Strogatz's and A.-L. Barábasi and R. Albert's approaches to the modeling of social networks (small-world networks and scale-free networks). The following section will introduce the more qualitative scheme of Veblenian institutional change by P.D. Bush. Finally, the last section of the chapter describes E. Ostrom's models of common pool resource problems.

13.2 A. SEN (1967) ON THE ISOLATION PARADOX AND ASSURANCE GAME, AND THE IMPORTANCE OF THE FUTURE

Amartya Sen's (1967) article "Isolation, Assurance and the Social Rate of Discount" is part of a then ongoing discussion that centered on the question of whether markets are generally able to produce socially desirable outcomes or not. Developing a model in which individual savings rates serve as the strategic variable, Sen shows that the likelihood of a coincidence of a market result and the social optimum is small, in fact, that this outcome is contingent on very specific, and limiting, assumptions.

But at first, he formulates a general setup that allows him to distinguish between two situations, the "isolation paradox" and the "assurance game" that were not always as clearly kept apart as is necessary. For both, we start with a group of N individuals. The agents have two behavioral choices, A and B. However, the preference settings of the agents differ in the two situations. In a preference setting that is leading to an N-person version of a *prisoners' dilemma (PD) game*, the corresponding choices would mean that everyone prefers everyone else to choose A, but has a dominant incentive to choose B herself. The result of an individual decision will hence be Pareto-inferior to the social optimum, as the individual rationality dominates the decision-making process. This situation describes what Sen calls the "isolation paradox." The Pareto-superior social optimum can only be reached if enforced by a collective agent external to the individuals.

With reference to this limit case, he constructs a second setting that is based on a slight change in the preference order; in this case, if everyone else chooses A, the individual actor has an incentive to do likewise. In all other cases, that is if some actors choose B, B continues to be the preferred choice. (We see that this setup corresponds to an N-person version of a coordination game, specifically a *stag hunt-type game*.)

As the strict dominance of behavior B no longer holds in the latter case, the expectations of the actors regarding the choices of all others now matter. If an actor expects all others to behave in a way that produces the socially optimal outcome, i.e., that they choose A, she has an incentive to behave accordingly, possibly leading to the Pareto-superior result (if her expectations are fulfilled). If she doubts or distrusts the others, her behavioral choice is likely to be B, leading to a Pareto-inferior result for the group. A substantial difference that emerges from the change in the preference order are the consequences for the collective external actor's behavior. It is no longer necessary to enforce a certain behavior of the agents; rather it is now sufficient to assure the agents that all others will choose the "right" behavior. Accordingly, Sen calls this situation the *assurance game*.

To address the question of the social optimality of results from individually optimal decisions, Sen has formulated the following model. Assume a group of N individuals, each facing the choice between behavioral option A, saving an extra unit, or option B, not saving an additional unit. The time horizon is two periods, present and future. Utility is generated by consumption. Saving means a reduced consumption capacity today in exchange for an increase of consumption k tomorrow ($k > 1$). Future consumption is, however, not enjoyed by the individual deciding on saving more or not, but by her heirs. The individual gains the following utility from consumption: utility 1 from her own current consumption, utility β from one unit of consumption by her contemporaries, utility γ from one unit of consumption by her heirs, utility α from consumption of one unit by the heirs of the other actors; with β, γ, and α taking values <1.

If a portion $0 < \lambda < 1$ of the agent's savings goes to her own heirs, and, accordingly, $(1 - \lambda)$ to the heirs of the other agents, then, taking the decisions of the other actors as given, the net gain from an additional unit of saving for one actor is

$$G(i) = [\lambda\gamma + (1 - \lambda)\alpha]k_i - 1. \qquad (13.1)$$

If this is above zero, the actor will save an additional unit. As we assume our starting point to be a situation of atomistic equilibrium, the additional gain from marginal extra savings should be zero, so that $G(i) = 0$.

Now, allowing for a *social contract* between the members of the group, stipulating one additional unit of savings by every one of them, we get the net gain for an individual from this social contract (with h as the proportion of future consumption from these savings that accrues to the heir of the agents under consideration) as

$$G(s) = [Nh\gamma + N(1 - h)\alpha]k_s - 1 - (N - 1)\beta. \quad (13.2)$$

For everyone to prefer saving by all others to not saving, $G(s) > 0$ has to hold; if $G(i) = 0$ at the same time, the preferences describe an isolation paradox.

Given these two conditions, we can approach the question of whether market outcome and social optimum coincide when agents make isolated optimizing decisions. In order to do so, we have to introduce more specific assumptions regarding the parameters used. First, we focus on the utility derived from the consumption of the different groups under consideration. In the second step, we will change the perspective and focus on the rates of discount that are implicitly included in the values that future consumption has to take for the conditions to hold.

Regarding the utility from consumption, one possibility is to assume that an individual does not differentiate between her own and other people's heirs so that $\gamma = \alpha$. Under that assumption, Eq. (13.1), equal to zero, reduces to $k = 1/\alpha$. Substituting this term in Eq. (13.2), $G(s) > 0$ can be rearranged to $\beta < 1$, certainly a reasonable result for the isolation paradox to hold. However, the assumptions made can of course be discussed.

Another set of assumptions that can be analyzed is $\lambda = 1$, $h = 1/N$, and $k = 1/\gamma$. The second condition now is reduced to $1/\gamma > \beta/\alpha$. There is no way of knowing whether this inequality holds or not. Nevertheless, we know that in the case where the inequality is

fulfilled, individual savings are too low from the social perspective. And when the inequality sign is turned around, we in fact find another version of the problem, namely that the individually optimal saving is too high from the social perspective. In both cases the *isolated individual decisions do not lead to the socially optimal outcome*. Only if $1/\gamma = \beta/\alpha$ is fulfilled, are atomistic savings allocations optimal from a social perspective as well. Sen now argues that, as soon as individuals show egoistic traits, the equality is a very strong assumption as it seems rather unlikely that an individual's egoistic preferences for consumption apply to the own heirs to the same degree that they apply to the individual with respect to her contemporaries and their heirs respectively.

More specific assumptions regarding the share that an individual's heir receives from the overall heritage in the coming period can also be made. The line of argument that Sen replies to only focuses specifically on the case of $\lambda = 1$. That assumption in itself is rather simplifying as it leaves out the possibility of taxation, among others; assuming $0 < \lambda < 1$ seems more reasonable. We arrive at the result that even for the case where we set $h = \lambda/N$, that means where an individual's heirs receive less than the proportionate share of savings in the future, the condition $\beta < 1$ is sufficient for the isolation paradox, the insufficiency of individual decisions in the production of socially optimal outcomes, to hold.

In a last change of perspective, the issue can also be approached looking at the rates of discount that are implied in Eqs. (13.1) and (13.2) as private and social *rates of discount* ($k_i = 1 + \pi$ and $k_s = 1 + \rho$, respectively), i.e., as the value of future relative to current consumption that private and public agents set. The different rates signal that the individuals' discount rate (the market interest rate) may not be the appropriate rate when considering social investments. For instance, it may be reasonable to assume that the public agent is more patient than the private agents and operates under a longer time horizon when considering courses of action.

Under the assumption that $h = 1/N$, where each heir receives the same share of the disbursed extra inheritance from the social contract, we get the private rate of discount from Eq. (13.1) (with $G(i) = 0$)

$$\pi = \frac{1}{\lambda\gamma + (1 - \lambda)\alpha} - 1 \qquad (13.3)$$

and from Eq. (13.2) results the social rate of discount

$$\rho = \frac{1 + (N - 1)\beta}{\gamma + (N - 1)\alpha} - 1. \qquad (13.4)$$

One obtains equality of private and social rate of discount under the specific assumption of $\lambda = 1$ and $\beta = \alpha/\gamma$, i.e., that all gains from saving accrue to the own heirs and that the ratio of the utility from current own consumption and consumption by contemporaries is equal to the ratio of utility derived from the consumption of one's heirs and that of the others' heirs (that, again, Sen argues, is a difficult assumption to justify as soon as individuals are assumed to show egoistic traits).

In more general terms, setting Eq. (13.3) equal to Eq. (13.4) shows that there are a number of combinations of λ and γ for which the equality holds; however, these would only result by coincidence, not because some underlying market mechanism produced them. That means, there is no reason to assume that the market outcome would be equal to the socially optimal outcome.

Again, the isolation paradox—or, reflecting the terminology of the preceding chapters, the isolation dilemma—is an N-person version of a PD game. As in that game, the individually maximizing decision—the strictly dominant strategy choice—results in a Pareto-inferior overall outcome. This is, obviously, the result of the assumptions regarding the preferences of the actors. In this situation, the socially desirable, the Pareto-superior, outcome would have to be enforced (which of course leads to numerous caveats).

Another option, however, that would mean less interference, would be attempts to alter the payoff structure the individuals face. In this case, that means to alter the underlying game from the N-person PD to an N-person stag hunt. Then, the agents would play an assurance game and would choose their strategy so as to produce the socially desirable outcome as long as they can trust in the other actors to make the same choice.

As we have seen already in earlier chapters in this book, such a change in the payoff structure can be the result of numerous changes in the situation the actors face (remember, markets, for instance, themselves are constructs and always depend on the rules and norms in place to define them). Possible changes we have seen earlier include changes in the time horizon under which decisions are formulated and expectations of repeated interactions with the same agents (for instance in Chapter 3, but also in Chapter 14), or maybe more direct alterations from payoffs using instruments such as taxes or other policy instruments (that will be taken up in Chapter 17).

13.3 A. SCHOTTER (1981), R. AXELROD (1984/2006), AND K. LINDGREN (1997) ON THE EMERGENCE OF INSTITUTIONS

13.3.1 Schotter

Andrew Schotter proposed a theory of institutional emergence that centers on the development of *mutually consistent expectations* of agents regarding their respective behaviors (in Schotter, 1981; especially Chapter 3, with Simeon M. Berman). He stressed the function of institutions as "informational devices... that help (the agents) place subjective probability estimates over each other's actions" (p. 109). More secure expectations enhance individuals' decision-making capacity because they make it easier to choose one's own behavior in situations characterized by interdependence and uncertainty (see Chapter 1). Focusing on this aspect in his model, the emergence of specific institutions depends on the *observed behavior* of agents. However, the agents' behavioral choices also include a stochastic element, and so the eventual institution is not determined from the outset; rather, from one initial situation we may see the development of different institutional settings.

For his analysis, Schotter chose a setup in which agents would meet repeatedly in strategic interactions, as can be described by *game-theoretic* tools. The agents thus can create a relationship and learn what behavior to expect from one another. They choose their own behavior according to their expectations about the others. Once all agents' expectations are correct, no more adaptations of expectations are needed and the individual behavioral choices no longer change. The expectations regarding the others' behavior are shaped by the common observations of behavior, as an action today influences expectations about behavior tomorrow and so on. To describe the emergence of institutions, Schotter employs a Markovian diffusion process to model the adjustment of the expectations of the agents (a process in which the state of a system in the subsequent period depends only on its state in the current period, or, more technically, where the conditional probability distribution of the future depends only on the current state). The absorbing points (where the probability distributions no longer change) are interpreted as corresponding to stable social institutions embodying the "behavioral modes" of the agents.

As institutions are devices to help the players move more securely in strategic interactions with others, they need to contain some reference to the other players' behaviors (even if that is, "continue doing what you did no matter what anybody else has been doing"). Realizing that this is an important part of the institutional content, we can understand why Schotter based his model on supergame strategies—only in the repetition (the memory of the agent) do we find the basis for references to the others' behaviors.

To illustrate the model, we limit ourselves to four strategies to describe the behavioral modes of the agents. These strategies can be very basic ones (play a^1 as long as the other one plays a^1, play a^1 as long as the other one plays a^2, etc., where a^j is a pure strategy in the constituent game). In fact, rather simple formulations of strategies/behaviors are seen as sensible choices insofar as for institutions to be established, it seems reasonable to assume that they do not consist of overly complicated behavioral rules. In the case of a 2×2 normal-form game, the strategy set S_i, including the supergame strategies σ_i, for a player i is given by

$$S_i = \left(\sigma_i \begin{bmatrix} a_i^1 \\ a_j^1 \end{bmatrix}, \sigma_i \begin{bmatrix} a_i^1 \\ a_j^2 \end{bmatrix}, \sigma_i \begin{bmatrix} a_i^2 \\ a_j^1 \end{bmatrix}, \sigma_i \begin{bmatrix} a_i^2 \\ a_j^2 \end{bmatrix} \right). \quad (13.5)$$

As said, in the example, these are the four behavioral modes the players choose from.

In the next step, Schotter defined a *convention* as including the compatible strategies of two players. The two strategies in such a convention are called a *pair* b^k. Thus, if the convention

$$\sigma = \left(\sigma_i \begin{bmatrix} a_i^1 \\ a_j^1 \end{bmatrix}, \sigma_j \begin{bmatrix} a_j^1 \\ a_i^1 \end{bmatrix} \right)$$

is observed we call the pair $b^1 = (a_i^1, a_j^1)$. The purpose of the model is to account for the process through which agents arrive at such conventions—mutually compatible behavioral decisions (social rules, in the terminology introduced in Chapter 1).

Now, instead of assuming that the agents formulate expectations regarding the others' behavior based on the payoff matrix alone, Schotter chose a different approach. The agents start by assigning a uniform probability vector to the pure strategies in the game which Schotter calls a *norm p*, giving them a uniform norm $p_i^u = \left(\frac{1}{4}, \frac{1}{4}, \frac{1}{4}, \frac{1}{4}\right)$ as the starting point ($1/n$ for each of the n strategies). Based on this probability distribution each agent calculates her own optimal mixed strategy $s_i = (s_i^1, s_i^2, s_i^3, s_i^4)$ for the first interaction with another player. These mixed strategies assign the probabilities that govern the choice of a pure strategy in an interaction so that based on the mixed strategies we can calculate the probability for each pair b^k to occur.

As an example for a probability of a supergame strategy, take $s_1(\sigma_1[a_1^1/a_2^2])$. This instructs player 1 to play strategy 1 as long as player 2 plays strategy 2 and attaches a weight s to it in the optimal mixed strategy calculated. The probability that a player chooses a supergame strategy starting with his strategy 1 is given by $\sum_{j=1}^{2} s_1(\sigma_1[a_1^1/a_2^j])$ and analogous for his second strategy and the strategy options of player 2. That means the probability q of observing a strategy pair b^k that for example consists of both players choosing strategy 1 is given by

$$(a_1^1, a_2^1) = \left[\sum_{j=1}^{2} s^1(\sigma^1[a_1^1/a_2^j]) \cdot \sum_{i=1}^{2} s^2(\sigma^2[a_2^1/a_1^i])\right]$$
(13.6)

At any moment, there may thus be a positive probability for any strategy pair to be chosen.

For the process of institutional emergence, we now define a rule according to which the agents update the norm p for the calculation of their optimal mixed strategy before each interaction. For this update, we let the agents assume that the strategies they observed in their previous interaction represent a pair b^k. Such a pair is then translated into the corresponding supergame strategy. In the updated norm, the probability assigned to this convention is increased (the probabilities for the others are reduced accordingly). Specifically, in the example given here, the agents increase the probability for one convention by an amount ε and decrease the probabilities for the other three conventions by $\varepsilon/3$. Then, the *best mixed strategy* against this updated norm is calculated.

The solution procedure, the *iterated adjustment* of the probability vectors, lets players adjust expectations until the same equilibrium probability n-tuple is continuously prescribed. In the eventual equilibrium, one strategy is chosen with probability one (as values less than one in one interaction would lead to an altered probability vector in the following interaction). At that point, the agents arrive at a *stable rule or institution* for their, *mutually consistent, behavior*. The process is historical insofar as the changes in probabilities in the current norm depend on the observed strategy choice(s) of the opponent(s) in the preceding round. The stochastic element results from the fact that *optimal strategies are mixed strategies* during the process of emergence. That is, a pure strategy chosen in one encounter may be any of the (in the example, four) pure ones included in the strategy set, as long as each one is included in the optimal set with a positive probability.

If you choose a PD as the constituent game of the supergame, there are two attractors. The institution may thus prescribe mutual cooperation or defection (in this case it is just a social rule in our defintion, see Chapter 1) as the behavioral mode of the agents. A combination of cooperation/defection in a population is effectively not possible, as that would mean a mixed population in which every players' expectations are always fulfilled, meaning that every player is always matched with a player of the other type, something that is not going to happen in groups larger than two.

In his model, although based on game theory, Schotter did not employ any of the usual solution concepts for finding equilibria in games. Instead, he formulated a rule for the continuous adaptation of expectations regarding the other agents' behavior. As a result, there are a number of attractors in the system (as many as pure strategies in the constituent game, in fact). Additionally, because in Schotter's model, the process of institutional emergence includes a stochastic element, it is not determined at the beginning, which of the behavioral modes eventually results.

13.3.2 Axelrod

Robert Axelrod (1984/2006) has also investigated the possibility of the emergence of institutions on the basis of *iterated PD* games. However, while in Schotter's approach, the process leading to the behavioral prescription (i.e., institution) is historical as well as stochastic, Axelrod, in turn, based his approach solely on the *payoffs* different strategies would achieve against each other in a supergame to see which one would prove advantageous for the players. For this, he held two tournaments in which a number of strategies were entered (a smaller one with 14 entries first and subsequently a second, larger one where 62 strategies were entered). All strategies played against all others, and then their respective average payoffs were calculated to see which one fared best. As this was not a theoretical approach to model the process of institutional emergence, but rather a lab experiment to see the returns strategies would generate against each other in supergames, the strategies considered are more complex than the four that have served as the basis for Schotter (where it was unnecessary to include more, or more complicated strategies, to make the point).

In the first tournament interactions were fixed at 200 rounds to make it large enough to at least limit if not completely avoid endgame effects from dominating the results (backward induction as a solution concept is a theoretical concept that agents do not apply if enough repetitions can be expected). In the second tournament, this setup was altered slightly, as interactions continued with a given probability, $P = 0.99654$. This leads to an expected 200 interactions in each round and eliminates endgame effects entirely as the number of interactions per game is unknown to the agents. The payoff matrix was the same both times awarding 3 points to each agent for mutual cooperation, 1 point to each agent for mutual defection, and 5 points to a defecting agent exploiting cooperative behavior, with the cooperating agent receiving 0 points in that case.

After all strategies played against each other (including playing against itself and a random strategy that was cooperating and defecting with a 50% probability respectively), the average results of their interactions were calculated. At the end, strategies were ranked according to the average points scored. The winning strategy was the same both times, the simplest of all strategies entered, tit-for-tat (TFT).

Given this result, Axelrod tested the strategy specifically over a number of additionally constructed tournaments with a variety of distributions of strategies, to see whether TFT was a robust strategy, or depended significantly on specific environments for its success. For the construction of these altered tournaments, Axelrod used the fact that in the second tournament, a group of 5 out of the 62 strategies had actually proven sufficient to predict the overall results in the tournament with very high accuracy. He then let all strategies play against these five, increasing the number of rounds played with one of the five in turn, thus increasing their weight in the calculation of the overall returns achieved by all strategies in the respective altered tournaments. In all those additional trials, TFT proved remarkably successful as well.

Based on these tournaments, Axelrod also constructed repeated tournaments in which updating rules for strategy choices were included — these were meant to reflect the fact that highly unsuccessful strategies would in all likelihood not be chosen again whereas the more successful ones should be chosen more frequently. The shares of strategies in subsequent tournaments were assumed to correspond to their relative payoffs (if strategy A's average payoff is twice as large as B's, A's share will be twice as high). Again TFT proved quite successful, representing the plurality of the population (with one-sixth of the population).

The results of the tournaments show, underlining the argument of Schotter to focus on simple strategies, that strategies in games involving complex decision problems (particularly social dilemma games), and hence the institutions reflected in them, should not be too complicated so that agents can understand them easily and are able to adapt their behavior without excessive effort. Additionally, Axelrod, based on the large dataset from the results of the tournaments, was able to formulate more detailed requirements for successful strategies in PD-based supergames. They should be *friendly* (nice), thus avoiding unnecessary conflict as long as the opponent cooperates, embody a *sanctioning mechanism* should the opponent cease to cooperate, in order to punish defections immediately (retaliation), but also show a capacity to *forgive* in case a deviating opponent returns to cooperative behavior (forgiving).

As the results further show, *cooperation* can emerge in a "world of egoists without central authority." The central aspect upon which its eventual emergence depends is the *likelihood of repeated interactions*, the probability that agents will meet again in the future. In the case that the probability of future interactions is sufficiently high, cooperation based on reciprocity can be established between individual agents; and, once established, in this setup a cooperative strategy is actually able to defend itself against an invasion by less cooperative strategies (see Chapter 3).

In fact, in the tournaments, "nice" strategies, those that did not have an option of defecting first, did significantly better than those that were not nice (with the first half of the ranking in the final tableau being taken by "nice" strategies and the bottom half by the "not-nice" ones). Among the nice strategies, those that were forgiving (like TFT that punishes only once and then possibly reverts to cooperation) did better than the less forgiving ones (in fact, as Axelrod points out, an even more forgiving strategy than TFT, namely tit-for-two-tats, would have won had it been entered into the first tournament). However, the punishment of an unprovoked defection was also a necessary characteristic of a successful strategy. Finally, those that attempted more complicated patterns did not do nearly as well as the simpler ones even if the underlying rationale of the more complicated strategies seemed compelling at first sight.

13.3.3 Lindgren

In a next step, Kristian Lindgren (1997) further extended Axelrod's analysis by allowing for a number of variations in the games. He introduced the possibility that agents make *mistakes*, and for *mutation* possibilities (that may serve to model some types of learning as well). When mistakes are allowed (meaning that with a certain probability a player may execute an action he had not intended—say, to choose "defect" instead of "cooperate"), the advantageous strategies turn out to be some variant of TFT (nice, forgiving, retaliatory) but with an additional provision that lets them recover a cooperative relationship in case of accidental mistakes in the execution of a strategy by one of the players in an interaction.

However, if simulations run long enough, given the option for mutations (where Lindgren uses a provision that leads to an increased memory length of strategies), strategies may emerge that are capable of exploiting the error correction mechanism of a previously successful strategy. The *arbitrary endpoint* of simulations (as in Axelrod, for instance) only allows making statements regarding a *temporary advantage* of one specific strategy; for instance, in some runs, Lindgren finds strategies dominating a population for 10,000 generations (repetitions of the underlying game) only to then be replaced by another one dominating for 15,000 generations. Given such long dominance in combination with subsequent changes, there is no possibility of determining a possible stable equilibrium that may or may not emerge eventually. Nevertheless, the (temporarily) dominant strategies are generally *variants of TFT*, somewhat more elaborate for sure, but, as mentioned above already, respecting the same principal concepts with the differences lying in the details of length of retaliation period and the error correction mechanism (where strategies may eventually be distinguished by their ability to react to mistakes that are made in the process of correcting prior mistakes).

Finally, specifically including neighborhood structures in the analysis, in simple iterated PD games, where All-D would become dominant in a so-called mean-field setup (especially in large groups where all interact with all), a lattice structure (where interactions are limited to the direct neighborhood, meaning smaller groups; see also Section 13.4) usually leads to cooperation (TFT) being able to at least stay present in the population—either as the strategies change in waves of ascent and retreat, or due to the establishment of stable islands of cooperation in parts of the lattice.

13.4 T.C. SCHELLING (1978) AND R. AXELROD (1984/2006) ON SEGREGATION

Many common instances of segregation are caused by gender, such as restrooms, showers, changing rooms, sports matches, or even schools sometimes. However, from a broader perspective, the phenomenon of segregation often has more to do with individual choices. Though agents only have a preference for a certain minimum level of agents of their own type in the composition of their neighborhood, this may cause a strong degree of segregation as a collective result. And furthermore, neighborhood structures likewise lead to distinct patterns of interaction—the process of developing different topologies on which interactions take place has been the focus of some of the seminal works of Nobel laureate Thomas C. Schelling (1971, 1978) and Robert Axelrod (1984/2006).

13.4.1 A Spatial Proximity Model

In a first approximation to the segregation phenomenon, Schelling (1971, 1978) applies two models. One is a linear and the other is a two-dimensional neighborhood, in which agents are divided into two groups that are observable for everybody. Agents' preferences simply consist of a minimum requirement regarding the number of their own group's members in their neighborhood. If anyone is dissatisfied with her neighborhood composition, she can move and find a satisfying place. For these moves, different rules are formulated to compare the resulting neighborhood structures.

Under the *linear distribution* condition, there are 40 agents, 20 stars, and 20 zeros, randomly distributed on a line (Figure 13.1). All are concerned with their neighbors and want at least half of them to be like themselves. The neighborhood extends to four neighbors

0 + 000 + +0 + 00 + +00 + + + 0 + +0 + +00 + +00 + +00 + +000 +

FIGURE 13.1   The initial distribution of agents.

000000 +0000000000 0000

FIGURE 13.2   Segregation in a linear distribution.

in each direction (fewer to one side, obviously, for those on either end). Figure 13.1 shows a possible initial random distribution. In the case depicted there, 13 individual agents (marked with dots) can be found whose neighborhood does not meet their demands.

Now, anyone dissatisfied with her neighborhood can move in order for her preferences to be met. Starting from the left, the dissatisfied group members move to the nearest spot that meets their demands regarding the neighborhood composition. In Figure 13.1 that means, the first to move is the first star, on the second from the left, followed by the second star, on the sixth from the left, and so on.

After a few more rounds, while agents seek new positions in order to find satisfying neighborhoods, we eventually arrive at a situation where no agent wants to change her position any longer. As depicted in Figure 13.2, the stable endpoint that we arrive at the following rules as set out above shows a segregated pattern with three clusters.

The determining elements for arriving at the result are the neighborhood size, the required percentage of one's own type in the immediate neighborhood, the share of different types of agents in the total population, the rules governing movement, and the original configuration. These mechanisms and conditions do, however, only shape the specific endpoint reached; the general pattern of a development toward segregation holds more broadly.

Another possible formulation for analyzing segregation dynamics is not to choose a linear pattern, but an *area distribution* in a two-dimensional space instead. Divide a space up into squares (imagine a chess board) and let

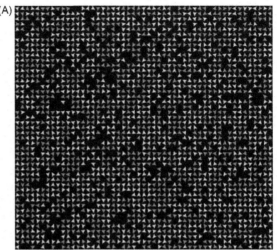

FIGURE 13.3   Segregation model in an area distribution.

some of those squares be occupied by agents, with one agent per square. Some squares stay empty to allow agents to move if necessary. Neighborhoods are defined as a set of squares (e.g., 3×3, 5×5) in which the agent under consideration occupies the center position. No fewer than 60% of an agent's neighbors are to be of the same type as she is. For those whose current position does not meet that specification, the moving rule used in the succession shown in Figure 13.3 is specified as follows: An agent has to move to the nearest vacant square meeting her demands regarding the composition of her neighborhood, crossing horizontally or vertically through other squares.

Figure 13.3A shows a possible initial random *area distribution*. There are 2000 agents (two kinds of color of agents, 50 to 50), of the occupying agents, initially 66.6% are discontent and move as the above assumption requires 60% of the neighborhood to be of the same type for the agent to be satisfied. A first round of movement will leave new agents behind unsatisfied, and moving will continue until eventually all agents have settled in neighborhoods that leave them content. The models are thus open to social or spatial interpretations, for instance, as different cultures (strategies, institutions, or social rules subpopulations may settle upon). Figure 13.3B shows the final stable segregation state after a number of rounds via simulation. For details, see also, e.g., Wilensky (1997, 1999).

13.4.2 A Bounded-Neighborhood Model

Another variation of a segregation model is the bounded-neighborhood model. Again, each agent is concerned with the ratio of agents in her neighborhood. We have two types of agents, blue and green. The more tolerant an agent is, the higher the share of members of the other group she is willing to accept in her neighborhood. Again, when the limits are crossed, agents leave and move to a neighborhood that satisfies their preference setting.

The different ratios R that agents are willing to tolerate allow us to draw a *distribution of "tolerance."* An example of a linear distribution schedule is shown in Figure 13.4A. For the greens, the vertical axis presents the *upper tolerance limits* measured by the ratio of blues B to greens G. The horizontal axis is the amount of greens, 100 in total. If the median green can live with an equal number of blues in her

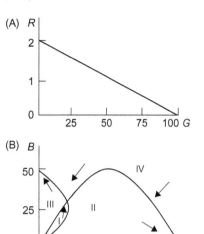

FIGURE 13.4 Distribution of tolerance. After Schelling (1978, p. 104).

neighborhood, the ratio is 1:1. In the example, the most tolerant green is willing to accept a ratio of blue to green of 2:1, and the least tolerant green only tolerates all-green groups.

Suppose now that the tolerance of blues is identical to that of greens. The total number of blues is 50, half that of the greens. We can translate the straight-line tolerance schedules for the single groups into a parabola, respectively, translating the shares agents are willing to accept into absolute numbers (with blues on the vertical and greens on the horizontal). The resulting parabolas divide the quadrant into four areas. The figure allows us to graphically depict the direction that the changes of compositions of neighborhood populations take starting from all possible initial combinations, as indicated by the arrows. Already a first glance shows that there are strong forces pulling toward equilibria in which fully segregated neighborhoods will have resulted. For almost every agent that means that, due to the heterogeneity of preferences regarding the neighborhood population ratio, they live in a much more segregated environment than they would have been willing to live in.

The direction of the population movement given a composition of a neighborhood is marked by the arrows in each area. In the overlapping area, area I, the numbers of greens and blues will both be increasing until the schedules cross. That point would mark an equilibrium composition for the neighborhood, however, an unstable one, for any change pushing the composition into areas II or III would lead to substantial changes. In area II, greens would be entering, while the blues are departing. The process would continue until the lower right is reached, leaving an all-green neighborhood. Within area III, the opposite dynamic would be playing out, leaving an all-blue neighborhood. Finally, in area IV, outside both curves, the motion depends on the initial ratio between blues and greens. From area IV, the dynamics of segregation lead to two stable equilibria, of which one is formed of all greens and no blues, the other vice versa.

The detailed results are attributable to the specific *tolerance schedule* and the *size of population*; if we change them, a different outcome can be arrived at. Figure 13.5A shows the situation of two colors with the same tolerance schedule and equal numbers (of 100 agents each). The median green (or blue) agent can tolerate a ratio of 2.5 blues to greens (vice versa). In this case, a linear tolerance schedule runs as a straight line with a vertical intercept at 5.0, which is the upper limit. As the graph shows, there are two stable equilibrium states at 100 blues or 100 greens respectively in a neighborhood, and a stable equilibrium at a mixture of 80 blues and 80 greens.

Leaving the tolerance schedule unchanged while reducing the number of blue agents produces the situation depicted in Figure 13.5B. Due to a change in the size of population, one curve now lies within the other one, and the stable mixed equilibrium disappears, leaving only the two equilibria of complete

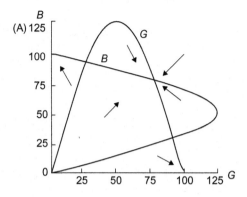

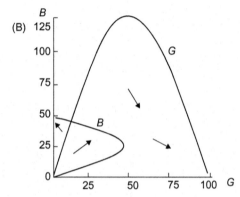

FIGURE 13.5   Alternative instances of tolerance distribution. After Schelling (1978, p. 173).

segregation. From this situation, we can further alter conditions in order to be able to produce a stable mixed neighborhood again.

13.4.3 A Territoriality Model

Axelrod (1984/2006) dedicated some space to an analysis of the stability of strategies in territorial social systems as compared to his baseline case of social systems in which everyone can meet everyone else. In social systems of total connectivity (everyone, at least potentially, interacting with everyone), a TFT strategy can be stable, meaning that it cannot be invaded by an All-D agent. This, Axelrod calls *collectively stable* strategies. An interesting question that follows is whether conditions change when agents are confined to interacting with their neighbors only. In other words, are collectively stable strategies *territorially stable* as well?

In general, we see that a collectively stable strategy is territorially stable as well. To see why, imagine a structure in which every agent interacts with four neighbors (north, east, south, west). If one of these neighbors does better on average than the others, the direct neighbors subsequently copy his strategy. The strategies under consideration are All-D and TFT. If TFT is collectively stable that means that TFT against TFT does better than All-D against TFT in a PD supergame. In a neighborhood structure in which one agent plays All-D, the All-D player may do better than the TFT players with which he interacts. But it also follows from this that the average result achieved will be below the result of a TFT player playing against TFT players only. If only one All-D agent invades, then no other agent has a reason to copy the All-D strategy, because there will always be direct neighbors playing TFT who are more successful. If a strategy is collectively stable, it will thus always be territorially stable as well. For an illustration of a very similar model, see Figure 9.3 in Chapter 9.

13.5 T.C. SCHELLING (1978) AND W.B. ARTHUR (1994) ON ATTENDANCE COORDINATION

13.5.1 Schelling: Simple Attendance Dynamics

Minimum Attendance

Thomas C. Schelling, in his book *Micromotives and Macrobehavior* (1978), tells a story about a certain seminar format, which was planned to take place on a regular schedule. At first, many interested people attended the sessions, but little by little the number

of attendants shrunk. Eventually, the seminar had to be abandoned. Schelling states that a lot of people, in fact, were interested, however nobody came. An explanation is that the individual willingness to attend falls with a lower general participation. If you do not expect enough people to meet and talk to, you will prefer to stay off. Schelling, thus, refers to some expected *critical mass* required for a successful event. An event, such as a regular seminar, needs a certain minimum number of attendants to make it a success. (For a *minimum critical mass* as a general requirement for success in a population, see also Chapter 14.) But agents are *heterogeneous* in their preferences. One would like to see 10 visitors in a seminar; others would like to meet perhaps 100.

Schelling's question now is how much attendance it needs for a sustained success of the repeated event, i.e., the quest for the critical mass to be self-perpetuating, or for the threshold beyond which there will be *increasing returns* in terms of a growing attendance.

Interdependent Attendance Decisions

Schelling, of course, immediately considered that individual behavior in social situations such as that seminar is *dependent on others' behaviors*. Typically, if more people are engaged in an activity, others may easily follow. But with two exceptions: First, there will always be some agents who will *never* attend, and second, there will always be some who will *always* attend, independently of others. In general, though, while the individual *expectation of future attendance* is based on the *attendance in the past*, this will supposedly shape the individual's decision to attend next time. Particularly, *when actual attendance is above (below) expectations in a recent social event, it will increase (decrease) next event.*

The Dynamics of Attendance

For a first illustration of actual attendance depending on expected attendance, see

Figure 13.6. It represents a *cumulative process* (an s-shaped curve), which is based on a bell-shaped distribution of the numbers of actual attendants dependent on the number of expected attendants.

As an example, assume a population size of 100 per seminar meeting. The dashed diagonal line serves as the usual reference, indicating equality between expectations and actual behavior. The illustration displays *multiple equilibria*, one (instable) equilibrium at around 40% attendance expectation, one with zero attendance (0/0), and one with a high attendance (85/85), the latter two are stable. The high-attendance equilibrium is at 85 only rather than at 100, because, as said, a certain share of the relevant population will never attend.

On the other hand, below the instable middle equilibrium, if, for instance, 25 people were expected, only 10 would actually attend. And these would be disappointed. Therefore, next time, when informed agents, based on their last experience, expect only 10 people to attend, according to the sigmoid relation, nobody will actually show up. The *dropout zone*, within which the dynamics always tends toward the stable *nonattendance* situation (0/ <10), runs until the unstable equilibrium (40/40). Above this point, the *drop-in zone* runs up to the stable *maximum-attendance* situation (85/ >85). For instance, if 50 are expected, 60 people will attend, and so on. (40/40) obviously is unstable as any small divergence from (40/40) will trigger a process away from (40/40), with actual attendance either declining to zero or increasing to 85.

Alternative Expectation/Attendance Relations

For potential alternative relations between expected and actual attendance, see Figure 13.7.

For instance, consider *curve C* and its group of people, who will attend independently of others' decisions to attend. The attendance of that dozen people will attract others. Three equilibria occur again: (16/16—stable);

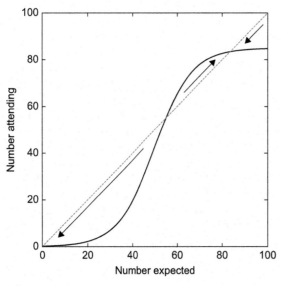

FIGURE 13.6 Attendance depending on expected attendance. *After Schelling (1978, p. 104).*

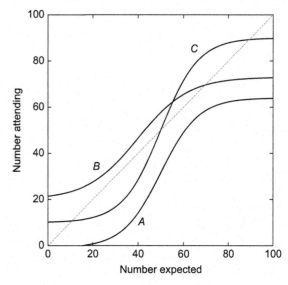

FIGURE 13.7 Further examples of expectation/attendance relations. *After Schelling (1978, p. 106).*

(50/50—unstable); (85/85—stable). But there will always be a positive minimum in this case.

With *curve A*, in contrast, a critical mass will never occur. Only 60 people would attend even if 100 were expected. This actual attendance would be too small for a self-sustaining level of attendance. So it will be an unstable situation and the only equilibrium (and a stable one) will be at zero attendance.

Finally, *curve B* has just one stable equilibrium (70/70), and attendance will never be below 25.

Curve B may serve as an example to illustrate the *multiplier effect* working on actual attendance in relation to expectations. Schelling considers an example with a dozen people incidentally and independently of each other were unable to show up again in the future. In this case, curve B would shift downward by 12 units. The new equilibrium would be at an actual attendance of 25 only, i.e., 45 agents less would attend compared to the earlier equilibrium. Thus, the initial 12 would induce 33 more not to attend through a new expectations/attendance relation. A multiplier effect of 3.75 would occur, i.e., 45 people less attending in total based on the initial 12 people unable to attend.

While Schelling has given more interesting examples that further analyze curve forms and their related dynamics and effects, he has not dealt with the phenomenon of *congestion*. In that case, people would not attend, because *too many* others are expected to attend. This is an aspect that W.B. Arthur has investigated.

13.5.2 Arthur: The El Farol Bar Problem

W. Brian Arthur, in his article "Inductive reasoning and bounded rationality" (1994), considers situations that are "ill-defined," i.e., complex interactive situations without a rigid deductive solution. Agents have to generate an *inductive model and strategy* for problems like these and have to change them by learning, if they have not fulfilled their expectations.

Arthur considers an example that he called The El Farol Bar Problem: In Santa Fé, New Mexico (where he is a fellow at the famous "Santa Fé Institute" for complexity sciences), is a bar, in which Irish folk music will be played every Thursday. But the bar is small and only 60 people (of a whole relevant population of 100) will comfortably fit. The bar is enjoyable only, if not overcrowded (i.e., not more than 60% of the relevant population attends). If 60 people or less attend, they will have fun. If there are more than 60 people, they would have preferred to stay away. Everyone has to decide simultaneously and independently, whether he/she will go to the bar or not. If everyone applied the same strategy ("go" or "stay away"), the El Farol would be going to be either overcrowded or completely empty. If agents assume the bar will not be overcrowded, everyone will go, but if agents assume the bar will be crowded, nobody will go. This is a complex interdependent situation, because decisions and expectations of agents depend on the others. In order to optimize one's utility, each agent would have to predict what everyone else will do. However, any mental model of the situation that is shared by the other agents would trigger what Schelling referred to as a self-destroying prophecy: If all believe few will go, all will go, and vice versa.

Arthur sets up a model of the situation by having each agent decide on her strategy based on a number of "predictors" (randomly available to her from a given fund) of the number of attendants next Thursday, given past data, e.g., the past n periods (weeks) attendance figures, with n being a given memory. Each person then simultaneously and independently employs a prediction rule

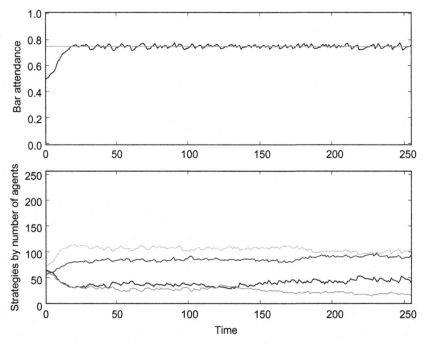

FIGURE 13.8   Interactive "El Farol" attendance and strategy dynamics (own simulation with threshold 75%).

to estimate how many people will appear at the bar next event. Typical predictors may be:

- the same number as last event;
- around 50% of last event's attendance;
- the average of attendances over the past two (three, four, ..., *n*) events;
- the same number as two previous periods, etc.

Each period each agent evaluates these rules against the past data and considers exchanging her prediction rule for one that has performed better for her next attendance decisions. She will attend if the prediction is 60% or less and will stay off if it is more than 60%. As agents have different suitable predictors (out of a larger fund) in their individual sets, in the end, some will turn up at the bar and others will not. A new attendance figure is available and everyone updates their predictors.

Arthur chooses his values (100 as the limit and 60 as the optimum) to keep the argument

simple. *Computer simulations* of models based on the above approach with all kinds of value sizes, however, have confirmed the basic results. Figure 13.8 shows the simulation results of a system similar to that studied by Arthur. In this case, the attendance threshold is set at 75% and there are—for simplicity— only four possible predictors. The system adapts to the 75% level pretty quickly after which there are only small variations though there are continuing changes in which strategies are employed by the agents.

What we see here is the result of a *complex adaptive system* with continuous learning and rule updating. The system is adaptive as well-functioning strategies are generated by a learning process—however, of course, not for the whole population, but in an individual way by inductive reasoning, with no opportunity for rational collective action or collective communication and decision-making. It is also complex, because the rules and hypotheses of agents depend on the others' behaviors. There is *no optimal strategy*.

Like Schelling's model, also Arthur's model is not and *cannot be deterministically (deductively) solved*. In both cases, the adaptive learning processes of the agents are not based on absolute (once-for-all) rationality; they are based rather on processes of "trial and error."

Arthur's model of limited resources reveals how *unstable behavior* is yielded in repeated interactions (in fact modeled as a *repeated multi-person game*), with two specific patterns emerging.

First, the number of people who attend fluctuates around the optimal level, with a *mixed strategy*, in a "game of predicting" (Arthur, 1994, p. 410), of forecasting above 60% attendance with probability 0.4 and below 60% with 0.6 would be the Nash equilibrium, which, in fact, is selected through the computer simulations. It is learning that allows the bounded-rational agents to approach this equilibrium strategy.

Second, the *dynamics appear random*, despite the fact that *no random component* determines the dynamics. Each agent is applying a different predictor at any one time, with varying degrees of success. Globally and in the longer run, however, they appear quite homogeneous. The only "random" part of the model is the high complexity of the setting, stemming from the number and heterogeneity of the agents, the number and heterogeneity of rules they apply, and the interdependence and period-wise learning interaction among agents' behaviors. Thus, once the game is set, the output basically is deterministic and rather stable, as the individual rule update is predictable and stabilizing. The result is deterministic as deterministic chaos is deterministic. (For details on complexity, randomness, chaos, and computer simulations, see Chapters 9 and 11).

13.6 W.B. ARTHUR ET AL. (1982), W.B. ARTHUR (1989), AND P.A. DAVID (1985) ON INCREASING RETURNS, POSITIVE FEEDBACK IN TECHNOLOGY CHOICE PROCESSES, AND LOCK-IN

13.6.1 Standardization and Technology Choice in Economic Systems

Economic systems, such as value-added chains for production, require a certain level of coordination in order to function properly (see Chapters 4 and 7). The types of coordination in practice range from unified measures to standardized intermediate products to common technologies and to universally agreed communication systems. Contrary to the assumptions needed for neoclassical microeconomic optimization, this leads to increasing returns to the number of users of such standards (network externalities). As a consequence, there is no optimal share of users that should use a standard but the largest benefits are realized if the standard is used by the entire economy. This in turn brings about new problems such as the realization of technological progress: Given the entire economy uses the currently best possible option and a new and better technology is developed, there is no feasible way to switch to this technology which of course has no user base and therefore does not generate network externalities. Hence, technological progress is hampered in a standardized economy (lock-in); further, in the case of several competing standards, there is not necessarily a way to predict which one of the standards would eventually be the socially best option to establish.

Paul A. David (1985) was among the first scholars to study this phenomenon in detail using the case of the QWERTY keyboard as an example. At the time when the QWERTY keyboard was developed, keyboard layouts were still mainly physical devices (i.e., mostly mechanical typewriters) that could not be changed. Almost everyone in the English-speaking world and certainly the major corporations adhered to the QWERTY standard that continues to dominate the default layout of today's computer keyboards. Yet David discussed evidence that the alternative but rarely used DVORAK keyboard layout would have significantly increased the average typing speed in turn generating noticeable efficiency gains (though the credibility of this evidence was later contested, see Liebowitz and Margolis, 1990). Network externalities and the (not surprising) failure to achieve a coordinated switching to the better standard with a significant share of the population prevented the economic system from leaving the lock-in, the inefficiency trap it was caught in. With various collaborators, David (David and Bunn, 1988; David and Steinmueller, 1994) continued to analyze similar historical cases in other industries, including the dominance of alternating current over direct current in today's electricity grids and the success of the VHS videotape standard over several better alternatives. David has emphasized the role of expectations in the emergence of the lock-in; the outcome does therefore always have a social component regardless of the underlying structure being institutional or technological in nature.

13.6.2 A Formal Model of Technology Choice and Lock-In

The formal approach to model such cumulative feedback processes, however, is by Arthur et al. (1982). Arthur and David were mutually aware of each other's work and worked together to some degree. Arthur later applied the purely theoretical work of 1982 to more illustrative examples of network effects in economic systems (Arthur, 1989); other game-theory models (for instance, Katz and Shapiro, 1985) follow similar lines.

The core of the formal approach is the feedback loop inherent in these standardization processes that allow for path-dependent cumulative development of the technological or organizational system, i.e., a state variable (the usage share x of a standard) as a function of itself:

$$x = f(x). \tag{13.7}$$

This, however, is to be the consequence of individual technology choice. Let A and B be two competing technologies generating utilities u which are composed of an intrinsic utility r and a network utility $v(n)$ the latter one being a strictly increasing function of the number of users n. In turn

$$u_A = r_A + v(n_A). \tag{13.8}$$

Further, let δ be the difference in the intrinsic utility $\delta = r_A - r_B$ and $v(n)$ be a linear function. The decision problem consequently comes down to

$$u_A - u_B = \delta + v(n_A - n_B), \tag{13.9}$$

which is either positive or negative; the agent adopts standard A or B accordingly. Adoptions occur sequentially; the agents choose one after another. They are perfectly informed about the state of the system. Consequently, the direction of the path-dependent development is determined by the values and distribution of δ for the agents and by the sequence in which the agents get to choose a technology. In a theoretical homogeneous case, i.e., δ is identical for all agents, the process—given as the probability that an agent chooses technology A—comes down to

$$p(A) = \begin{cases} 1 & \text{if } u_A - u_B > 0 \\ 0 & \text{if } u_A - u_B < 0 \end{cases}. \tag{13.10}$$

As all agents are identical and $v(n)$ is strictly increasing, all agents would follow the decision of the first adopter reducing the process to a one period process. The more interesting

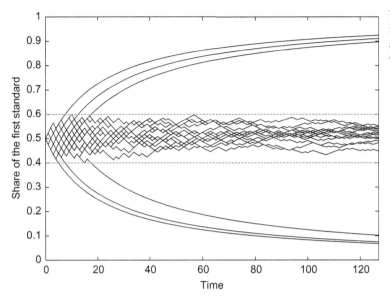

FIGURE 13.9 Simulation of a technology choice process with two homogeneous groups; network utility in absolute user numbers.

case of two distinct homogeneous groups (1 and 2), one preferring A, the other one B, exhibits absorbing barriers at which the behavior of the system changes abruptly: Once the network effect $v(n)$ for one technology favored by one group has grown large enough to surpass the intrinsic preference of the other group for the other technology, everyone will make the same choice. Before the absorbing barrier is reached, the process follows the distribution of agents among the two groups (assuming a uniform 0.5:0.5 distribution for the further considerations here):

$$p(A) = \begin{cases} 1 & \text{if } u_{A,1} - u_{B,1} > 0, \ \text{if } u_{A,2} - u_{B,2} > 0 \\ 0.5 & \text{if } u_{A,1} - u_{B,1} > 0, \ u_{A,2} - u_{B,2} < 0 \\ & \text{or } u_{A,1} - u_{B,1} < 0, \ u_{A,2} - u_{B,2} > 0 \\ 0 & \text{if } u_{A,1} - u_{B,1} < 0, \ u_{A,2} - u_{B,2} < 0 \end{cases}$$

(13.11)

We simulate this process (20 runs) to illustrate the behavior of the system; the simulation result is given in Figures 13.9 and 13.10. The dynamic properties of this process depend on the scale of δ with respect to the slope of the linear net utility function $v(n)$, shifting

the absorbing barriers outward or inward (see Figure 13.9). Note that the absorbing barriers are constant if the net utility is a function not of the absolute user numbers n but of the usage shares $x_A = n_A/(n_A + n_B)$ (Figure 13.10).

Considering truly heterogeneous agents, the probability function $p(A)$ becomes a continuous function:

$$p(A) = f(n_A - n_B)$$

(13.12)

or, using usage shares instead of absolute numbers,

$$p(A) = f\left(\frac{n_A}{n_A + n_B}\right) = f(x_A)$$

(13.13)

which, in effect, is the positive feedback function (13.10). The system is thus given by a stochastic recurrence equation that shares the same dynamic properties and equilibria (fixed points) with its corresponding non-stochastic form (i.e., the function $f(x)$ is not treated as a probability distribution but rather a deterministic function):

$$x_{A,t+1} = f(x_{A,t})$$

(13.14)

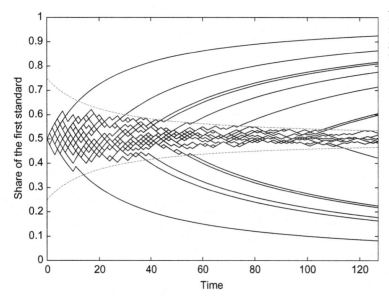

FIGURE 13.10 Simulation of a technology choice process with two homogeneous groups, network utility in usage shares.

the fixed points of which are the points for which the function crosses the 45°-line, i.e.,

$$f(x_{A,t}) = x_{A,t}. \qquad (13.15)$$

For a graphical illustration using a typical (s-shaped) network externality function as an example, see Figure 13.11. Specifically the fixed points are stable (attractors) if the crossing occurs from below the 45°-line, i.e.,

$$\frac{\partial f(x_A)}{\partial x_A} < 1 \qquad (13.16)$$

and unstable otherwise. Arthur et al. (1982) showed that if the set of stable fixed points of such a positive feedback function is nonempty (i.e., there is at least one attractor), the process converges to one of the attractors with certainty.

Arthur emphasized that positive feedback processes, in other theory traditions also known as circular cumulative causation (see Chapter 12 on Veblen and Myrdal), are a central feature in economic systems especially when considering technological progress. While such processes are difficult to

account when using neoclassical theory and its methods, it is relatively straightforward when applying dynamic systems as discussed in more detail in Chapters 10 and 11.

13.7 R.W. COOPER AND A. JOHN (1988) ON SYNERGIES AND COORDINATION FAILURES

Cooper and John (1988) offer a model that allows analyzing the conditions that are necessary for coordination failures to occur in a broad set of situations. The basis for their analysis is an abstract game; the results that can be derived here can, however, serve to illustrate a number of economically relevant situation. The focus they choose in their examples is on macroeconomic outcomes, specifically inefficient macroeconomic equilibria resulting from individual agents' inability to coordinate their actions so as to reach possible better results. For coordination failures to occur, you need more than one possible outcome (multiple equilibria) among which you can make a

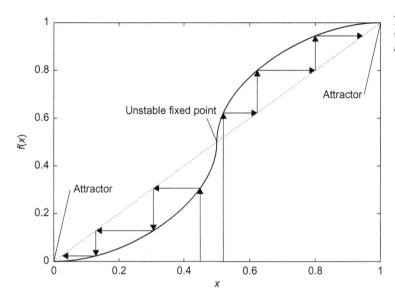

FIGURE 13.11 S-shaped Arthurian technology choice function (without absorbing barriers).

welfare-based distinction (that can be Pareto-ranked). The necessary condition are strategic complementarities meaning a higher effectiveness of others' actions in general following from agents' behavioral decisions, combined with positive external effects. This is not sufficient, however, as some more technical conditions have to hold as well (as we will momentarily see).

The basic game is described by the following features. There are N agents, indexed $n = 1, 2, \ldots, N$. The strategic variable for an agent n is $e_n \in [0, 1]$. The payoff for an agent n is given by $\sigma(e_n, e_{-n}, \theta_n)$. Here, e_{-n} is the vector of the strategy choices by the other agents and θ_n is a parameter in the payoff function. If $\theta_n = \theta$, the payoff functions for all agents are symmetric (and so is the game). Payoff is assumed to be continuously differentiable, with $\sigma_{11} < 0$ and $\sigma_{13} > 0$, meaning payoffs are strictly concave in e_n and marginal returns to effort are increasing in θ.

Let $e_n^*(\bar{e})$ be the optimal response to the actions by all other agents. The natural solution for the kind of game under consideration is a symmetric Nash equilibrium (SNE). If all

other agents choose e, then so will agent n, so that $e_n^*(\bar{e}) = e$. The SNE is defined by $S = \{e \in [0, 1] \mid \sigma_1(e, \bar{e}, \theta) = 0\}$.

Assume that $\sigma_1(0, 0, \theta) > 0$ and $\sigma_1(1, 1, \theta) < 0$, implying that the best response in the first case is $e_n > 0$ and in the second case is $e_n < 1$, so that if all agents choose effort levels at one of the extremes, the remaining agent's best response differs and lays in the interior of the interval. This assumption also assures that there is at least one interior Nash equilibrium as σ was defined as continuous. Whether there are in fact multiple symmetric equilibria depends on the precise shape of the best response function. As can easily be appreciated from Figure 13.12, the best response function has to cross the 45°-line (where $e_n = \bar{e}$) in one point with a slope larger than 1 for multiple equilibria to exist (for a proof see, for instance, Cooper, 1999; the other possibility is that the best response function lies on the 45°-line which would give a continuum of equilibrium points).

The upward sloping best response function (equivalent to $\sigma_{12} > 0$) signals a positive relation between own effort and that of other

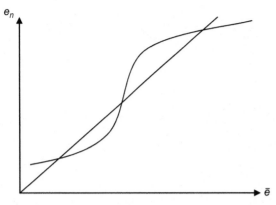

e_n

$\bar{e}$

FIGURE 13.12   Strategic complementarity and multiple equilibria.

agents (strategic complementarity). In this case, the resulting equilibria can be Pareto-ordered, their respective rank depending on the level of e. As we focus on SNEs, we immediately see that there is no mechanism in the model (game) that would move the system to a higher equilibrium once it has settled on one outcome. However, even the highest ranking Nash equilibrium is not the Pareto-optimal outcome of the game (as in other approaches such as the Nash–Cournot duopoly model, Chapter 7). The coordination problem is thus that agents may not reach the highest ranking Nash equilibrium. But assuming positive external effects over the whole range of the game, the highest ranking Nash equilibrium will still be Pareto-dominated by a cooperative solution.

In terms of a macroeconomic application, strategic complementarity and multiple equilibria are the key conditions for the transmission of shocks. If, for instance, due to an external shock, the other agents were to reduce their effort (economic activity), the best response for the nth agent would be to do likewise. A Pareto-inferior equilibrium would result, characterized by demand constraints for all those willing to sell (and hence showing a result that the Walrasian world, where supply is assumed

to always create sufficient demand to avoid constraints for the supply side, cannot account for). No single agent has an incentive to change her strategy, a coordinated effort would be required.

13.8 R.R. NELSON AND S.G. WINTER (1974, 1982) ON THE EVOLUTIONARY THEORY OF ECONOMIC CHANGE

Since the 1960s the state of the art of neo-classical theory regarding economic growth had been growth models with an endogenous investment decision leading to a notion of rationally optimized technological change. In contrast, the *Schumpeterian* approach—which was presented in more detail in Chapter 12— had long argued that technological change was not due to rational optimization but was rather driven by the innovative and risk-taking behavior of the entrepreneur in truly uncertain environments. Schumpeter argued that this was also the driving force behind growth cycles. Growth cycles are very difficult to explain from a rational optimization point of view. There are some attempts to do so, most importantly the real business cycle theory presented at the end of Chapter 5 above, still, Schumpeter's approach is much more direct. It does require to include the micro-level, the entrepreneurs, into the model, thereby extending the model's size and complexity to a point where deterministic analysis is only feasible in a few uninteresting special cases.

13.8.1 Evolutionary Approaches to Economics

This problem is not specific to Schumpeter's theory, it holds for the entire evolutionary economics. As mentioned in Chapter 12, Marshall had already argued almost a century ago that methods from evolutionary biology might be beneficial in economics but that the complexity such a model would necessarily have would make it impractical to handle.

In the early 1970s, Nelson and Winter (1974) offered a first formulation to tackle this problem. They turned to agent-based modeling and simulation to study a model of economic growth and technical change that included, and was driven by, a multitude of heterogeneous agents and their decisions. In another paper together with Herbert Schuette, they discussed details of the simulation (Nelson et al., 1976) and in a later monograph (Nelson and Winter, 1982) they presented a much broader variety of more or less similar evolutionary models. Here, they also discussed theoretical considerations on these models' interpretation, on their relation to classical, neoclassical, Marxian, Austrian, and specifically Schumpeterian theory as well as future research prospects using evolutionary modeling. They claimed to be able to explain US growth data better than contemporary neoclassical models could. But what was really innovative about their model was that they were able to do what was not possible for Marshall in 1920: They developed an economic model that relied on mechanisms similar to evolution in biology thereby strengthening the foundations of evolutionary economics. Their model does—for certain parameter ranges—also lead to a cycle pattern (or wave pattern) in output growth: An entrepreneur would devise a revolutionary innovation which enables her to produce in a much more efficient way. This is followed by subsequent diffusion of the innovation through the economy with more and more agents imitating the new technology. The initial discovery of the new technology and the more rapid growth the first movers are able to sustain while their competitive advantage lasts constitutes the upswing of the growth cycle. The downswing is the following period of rather slow innovation and

the diffusion of the technology to the last producers who were still using outdated technologies.

13.8.2 An Evolutionary Approach to the Theory of the Firm

In later works, Nelson and Winter (1982) partly reinterpreted their earlier model in order to integrate an understanding of technology that allows investigations of firms. Agents do not operate with perfect information and their capacities for processing information are limited. Decision-making processes are shaped by heuristics and rules that serve to reduce problems agents face to manageable proportions. In fact, decision-making in firms generally shows a "by the rules" character (this is the case in many areas, not only choice of production techniques, but also pricing decisions, inventory management, advertising policies, etc.).

The evolutionary-institutional theory of the firm that Nelson and Winter developed rests on the decision rules of the firm as the basic operational concept. Behaviors that are repeated and show a regular pattern are called routines. Routines are captured in rules and institutions. The key role of routines in the evolutionary approach to the firm means that the framework applies best to organizations that provide goods and services over longer periods of time and that are large and complex.

Firms that have developed routines that are better suited to the prevailing conditions have better chances of succeeding in competition with other firms. However, note that "better routines" does not imply "optimal routines." Firms pick the rules that seem best among those they know; at the same time, they can learn and find new ones. But they cannot constantly assess and change the rules they have decided on, or do so abruptly for the whole set of rules characterizing them at any given moment. At any moment, the rules governing the decision-making in a company are the historically given set that has developed up to that moment:

- There is no reason to assume that they would be in any sense optimal for addressing current problems.

The *selection mechanism* that is proposed is the *profitability of firms*. More successful firms will be driving less successful ones out of the market. As success is defined by current profits at the firm level, there is no reason to expect the technology that dominates to be the most desirable from the point of view of society as a whole, under a different time horizon, etc. In combination with the learning processes referred to above, this means:

- There is no reason to believe that market processes would produce the socially most desirable result.

Organizations remember by doing. This includes the development of an internal "code" for the transmission of messages and the knowledge regarding which routine is to be followed in a given situation. They are seen as a set of routine operations engaging a constant flow of messages, each of which may be triggering responses. The internal code introduces a notion of knowledge that is specific to the company. The so-called tacit knowledge may constitute an important part of the relevant knowledge. The term tacit knowledge is used to refer to concepts and information that are difficult or impossible to communicate (resulting from learning-by-doing processes, for instance):

- The transfer of routines and techniques from one company to another is not easily possible given tacit knowledge.

Firms operate a vast *number of routines simultaneously*:

- The targeted change of a selected few may then be difficult to accomplish as they are

always embedded in a wider structure of interlocking routines.

Given all these different aspects of routines and their changes, it is unlikely that the same routines (routines fulfilling the same function) will be chosen for modification in different firms at a given moment, or that the changes implemented would be the same. All of this makes the convergence of behavioral patterns between organizations extremely difficult to accomplish as there is no complete blueprint that could describe the whole set of routines constituting one specific production technology. Still, in the evolutionary economic models homogeneous structures tend to result, as usually a monopoly will eventually come to dominate.

13.8.3 An Evolutionary Growth Model

The central model of Nelson and Winter's contributions is composed of a production function, a demand function and stochastic research and diffusion processes.

First, consider a simplified version of the model: The agents are at any time t characterized by a set of technologies (or routines) available to them $A_{i,t} = \{a_{K1}, a_{K2}, \ldots\}$ and their capital stock $k_{i,t}$. They choose one (the current best) of their technologies, $a_{i,K,t}$, and produce according to a production function

$$q_{i,t} = \frac{1}{a_{i,K,t}} k_{i,t}. \tag{13.17}$$

The economy is subject to a strictly decreasing aggregated demand function assigning a market price p_t to the aggregated production of all firms i at time t

$$p_t = F\left(\sum_i q_{i,t}\right). \tag{13.18}$$

The firm's capital at time $t + 1$ is thus

$$k_{i,t+1} = (1 - \delta)k_{i,t} + I(q_{i,t} p_t) \tag{13.19}$$

where δ is the depreciation rate and I is an investment function that is essentially governed by the profits $q_{i,t}p_t$. Further, the firm may engage in innovative research (the model's *innovation* mechanism) and imitative research (the model's *diffusion* mechanism). The former has a very low success probability but gives the firm a much better technology (i.e., a lower value a_{Kx}) if successful. Innovation is in accordance to what we observe in reality assumed to be cumulative, i.e., the new technology constitutes an improvement of the best technology known to the agent. Imitative research has a higher success probability. If successful, it gives the firm access to a technology not previously available to it but known to one (or more) of the competitors. It is obvious that for the technologically leading firms, there is no point in engaging in imitative research while it can lead to vast improvements in the position of less technologically advanced firms. Both innovative and imitative research require an investment on which the success probability also depends. Of course, this reduces the capital the firm can use for its production (that flows into the above production function). Firms may thus decide how to allocate the capital available to them between production, research (innovative research), and industry espionage (imitative research).

Nelson and Winter's original model is slightly more complicated; here, technology is a two-dimensional variable and each technology is composed of two elements that govern its capital productivity (a_{Kx}) and its labor productivity (a_{Lx}), respectively. The set of available technologies of firm I thus becomes

$$A_{i,t} = \{\{a_{K1}, a_{L1}\}, \{a_{K2}, a_{L2}\}, \ldots\} \qquad (13.20)$$

and the production function (13.17) is now subject to additional labor cost which is determined by an—again aggregated—labor market equilibrium depending on the firms' aggregated labor demand $\sum_i (a_{i,L,t}/a_{i,K,t})k_{i,t}$. Nelson and Winter add a technology search function governing innovative research that is based on a "genetic" distance measure between the technologies. Stuart Kauffman and others have later developed more elaborate approaches along these lines; see the following section. Nelson and Winter also offered a number of extensions including, for instance, a banking sector that allows the firms to exceed their current budget with their research and production activities—at least temporarily.

One important aspect of the model is that it changes the industry structure; some competitors will grow larger and may eventually develop into a monopoly. Those who command a larger capital stock in the present will not only be able to produce more, they will also be able to conduct more research. It depends on the models parameters, how likely this effect is.

Figure 13.13 shows the results of a simulation along the lines of the Nelson–Winter model. The first panel shows the development of total output with the wave pattern in output growth clearly visible. The second panel shows technological development, namely it shows the economy's average capital–output ratio ($1/a_{i,K,t}$, recall that the technology is more efficient the lower the capital–output ratio is). The last panel shows a measure of the economy's monopolization, the normalized Herfindahl–Hirschman Index[2] (a value of 1 indicated monopolization, values close to 0 indicate almost equal market shares of all firms).

The central aspect of Nelson and Winter's models is that a stable and realistic pattern of industry dynamics results from an evolutionary model. As shown, the model is also able to

---

[2]With θ_i being the market shares of the n firms indexed by $i = 1, \ldots, n$, the normalized Herfindahl–Hirschman index is computed as $HHI = \frac{\sum \theta_i - (1/n)}{1 - (1/n)}$.

generate a stable growth path. Finally, though Nelson and Winter do not explicitly take credit for being able to reproduce growth cycles with their model (and though this is only a marginal aspect of the model), this seems to be one of its most interesting features. Other evolutionary economists quickly realized this (Conlisk, 1989) and have attempted to follow up on this research program (see, e.g., Conlisk, 1989; Silverberg and Lehnert, 1993; Heinrich, 2013). The crucial mechanisms in Nelson–Winter-type models are:

- Heterogeneity and stochastic research success (otherwise, the model would be a representative agent model that would practically remain on the macro-level, similar to the models of the general-equilibrium theory presented in Chapter 5).

- Persistent scarcity either in the form of finite demand or of a finite labor force (otherwise capacity extension would dominate the technological change mechanism and the model would grow toward infinity along an exponential function with a slight drift in the market shares toward more effective firms).

- Open diffusion of technologies, i.e., the technologies become available to the rest of the economy at some point. It is not important if this happens through industrial espionage as in this model, through inappropriability of knowledge (see Chapter 4), or through deliberately sharing of technologies (as for instance in open source approaches, see Chapter 15). Diffusion generates the characteristic wave pattern in economic growth (Figure 13.13).

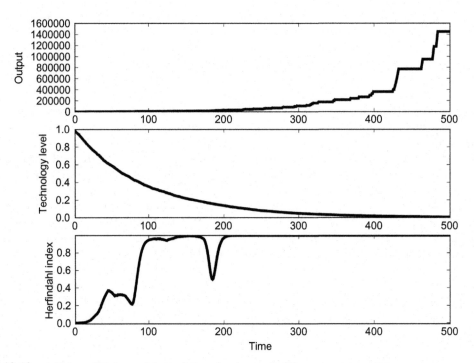

FIGURE 13.13 A Nelson–Winter model simulation: development of the economy over time.

13.9 S.A. KAUFFMAN (1993) ON SEARCH ON FITNESS LANDSCAPES

Evolutionary processes describe, among others, the change in the traits of an organism through successive generations. Change comes about by recombination or mutation. In evolutionary-institutional economics, a technology was always understood as a combination of different tools. Innovation can then be conceived as the recombination of existing tools (Ayres, 1944, chapter VI).

A landscape visualizes all different combinations of traits the organism can have. Associated with each point on the landscape, there is a fitness level, which can be thought of as the height of the landscape at that particular point. If the landscape is simple and has only one peak, like a mountain in the middle of the desert, then this peak can easily be found. But if the landscape is very rugged having multiple peaks, like the Alps, finding the highest peak is more difficult. Figure 13.14 illustrates the difference between simple and complex landscapes. Although we can easily find the highest peak on the complex landscape (lower graph) if we look from above, finding the highest peak can be very difficult for agents who do not have this bird's-eye view but are situated on the landscape.

13.9.1 Illustrative Example

In order to model the search for better technologies in a complex environment, we choose a so-called *NK landscape*, where N and K are two parameters. As we will see below, N is related to the size of the landscape and K is related to its complexity. By choosing an NK landscape we follow Kauffman (1993) and Kauffman et al. (2000). This section will present an illustrative example and the next section will provide a more formal representation of NK landscapes.

As an example assume that a homogeneous good is being produced by the combination of N different tasks. Let us assume that we produce coffee by combining three tasks: (i) picking the beans, (ii) roasting the beans, and

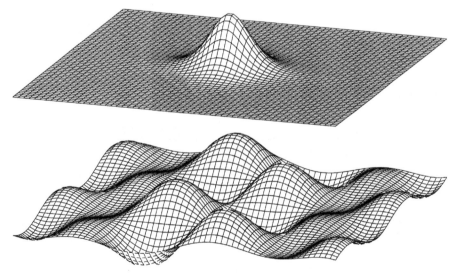

FIGURE 13.14   A simple fitness landscape (upper graph) and a complex fitness landscape (lower graph).

(iii) grinding the beans. Further we may assume that each task can be done in one of two ways. Picking the beans can be done manually or automatically, the roasting can be done for either 10 or 20 min, and grinding can be coarse or fine. We codify the two alternatives for each task by 0 and 1. A technology for producing coffee can then be codified as a unique combination of the 0 or 1 states of each task. In total we have $2^3 = 8$ technologies for producing coffee, (000); (001); (010); (100); (011); (110); (101); (111). The quality (fitness) of our finished product coffee depends on which tasks are used. But, and this is the crux of *NK* landscapes, the contribution of one task might depend on the state of other tasks. Fine grinding might improve the quality tremendously but only if the beans were roasted for 20 min. If the beans were only roasted for 10 min fine grinding might not improve the quality at all, etc.

13.9.2 NK Landscapes

In an *NK* landscape, *N* corresponds to the number of tasks and *K* corresponds to the number of other tasks on which the contribution to overall fitness depends. For $K = 0$, each task's contribution to overall fitness depends only on the state of the task. For $K > 0$, each task's contribution to overall fitness depends on the state of the task as well as the state of the *K* other tasks. By changing the parameter *K*, we are able to vary the *complexity* of the landscape and the corresponding search problem, as the number of local optima increases with *K*.

More generally, an *NK* landscape is a metaphor for modeling an environment of varying complexity characterized by two parameters *N* and *K*. Each point on the environment is specified by *N* coordinates. Associated with each point on the landscape is a fitness level. In search models, one or more agents navigate through the landscape with the goal of finding

higher peaks, where local peaks correspond to local optima and the highest point on the landscape corresponds to a global optimum. In our example from above, the environment is a technology consisting of $N = 3$ different tasks and the quality of coffee corresponds to fitness.

Keeping as an example the landscape as a technological environment in which agents search for a better technology, the *technology landscape* is defined as the set of all possible technologies and the associated fitness levels. A step uphill on the landscape is then a metaphor for finding a better technology.

We call the *N*-dimensional vector $v = (v_1, \ldots, v_N)$ a technology. A technology assigns a state to each of its elements (tasks) where each element can assume one of *S* states. The variable v_j thus indicates the state of task *j*. For simplicity, we assume that $S = 2$ and

$$V_{j \in \{1, \ldots, N\}} \in \{0, 1\} \qquad (13.21)$$

which allows us to represent each technology as a binary string (a vector of 0 and 1) of length *N*. The space of all possible technologies is then given by $V = \{0, 1\}^N$ and the size of the *technology space* is given by 2^N. We can represent the technology space as an undirected graph. A specific technology $v \in V$ is represented as a vertex and is connected to its $d = 1$ neighbors. A *d*-neighbor is a technology that differs exactly by *d* tasks, i.e., *d* tasks have to be changed to turn one technology into another. Using the *Hamming distance* (to be explained below) as a metric allows us to measure the *distance between technologies* where distance refers to similarity, not spatial distance. Formally the set of neighbors of technology $v \in V$ is

$$N_d(v^{i'}) = \{v^i \in \{V - v^i\} : \Delta(v^i, v^{i'}) = d\}. \qquad (13.22)$$

For $N = 3$, the technology space is an undirected graph which can be visualized as a 3-bit binary cube (Figure 13.15). The $d = 1$ neighbors

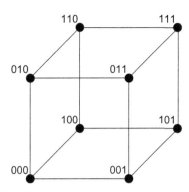

FIGURE 13.15   A 3-bit binary cube.

of technology (000) are the technologies (010), (100), and (001). The Hamming distance is just the number of bits that have to be changed, so for example, the Hamming distance between (100) and (111) is 2 since the last 2 bits have to be changed. From the cube, we see that there are $2^N = 2^3 = 8$ different technologies, each represented by a vertex of the cube. By increasing N, the technology space grows rapidly. If we take, e.g., $N = 15$, there are 32,768 possible technologies in total. Firms do not know these technologies and searching the complete space of technologies would be too costly and time-consuming. Thus, firms try one technology after another, as we will see later.

13.9.3 Fitness Levels

Next we link the positions on the landscape to fitness levels. With each possible technology $v \in V$, a specific level of efficiency or fitness $e(v) \in [0, 1]$ is associated. A *fitness function e* transforms the state space into a fitness landscape. In our case, this is a mapping

$$e : v \in V \to \mathbb{R}^+ \qquad (13.23)$$

which associates a specific level of efficiency to each technology. The levels of efficiency are drawn from the set of positive real numbers.

The contribution to efficiency by task j depends on the state of the task v_j, as well as on the state of K other tasks $v_{j1}, \ldots, v_{jk}$. For the simplest case, $K = 0$, there are no connections between individual tasks, i.e., no intranalities (Kauffman et al., 2000, p. 145; by intranality we mean a task has an externality, i.e., the performances of two tasks affect each other. For the technology, however, this effect is not external. Some authors, e.g., Frenken and Nuvolari (2004), use the term epistatic relation instead of intranality). The value of each bit v_j is independent of every other bit for a particular state. For $K = 0$, we have the simplest possible landscape with only one maximum. If we increase K, the complexity of the landscape increases and with it the number of local optima increases. This means that search becomes more complicated.

To every bit, we assign a value $e_j(v_j)$ which is drawn from a $0-1$ uniform distribution. We generate a value for $e_j(0)$ and for $e_j(1)$ for $j = 1, \ldots, N$, so we generate $2N$ values in total. Then, overall efficiency is given by

$$e(v) = \frac{1}{N} \sum_{j=1}^{N} e_j(v_j). \qquad (13.24)$$

If we move to a more general cases, we have $0 < K \leq N - 1$. The efficiency of process j depends not only on v_j but also on K other values $v_{j1}, \ldots, v_{jK}$, i.e., $e_j = e_j(v_j, v_{j1}, \ldots, v_{jK})$. Overall efficiency e for state v is then given by

$$e(v) = \frac{1}{N} \sum_{j=1}^{N} e_j(v_j, v_{j1}, \ldots, v_{jK}). \qquad (13.25)$$

The number of random values we have to generate is $2K + 1N$. Table 13.1 illustrates this for $N = 3$ and $K = 2$.

13.9.4 Search

Search can be modeled in a number of ways. In general, search algorithms are used.

TABLE 13.1 Fitness Levels Associated with Technologies and Fitness Contributions of Each Task, for $N = 3$ and $K = 2$

V	e_1	e_2	e_3	$e(v)$
(0,0,0)	0.6	0.3	0.5	0.47
(0,0,1)	0.1	0.5	0.9	0.5
(0,1,0)	0.4	0.8	0.1	0.43
(0,1,1)	0.3	0.5	0.8	0.53
(1,0,0)	0.9	0.9	0.7	0.83
(1,0,1)	0.7	0.2	0.3	0.4
(1,1,0)	0.6	0.7	0.6	0.63
(1,1,1)	0.7	0.9	0.5	0.7

Adapted from Kauffman (1995, p. 172).

The algorithm is a set of rules. Following the rules, the agent navigates through the landscape. One particularly simple search algorithm is the *adaptive walk* or *hill-climbing* (Kauffman, 1995). Agents, which are firms in our example, start at their initial position and change one randomly chosen task. For $N = 3$ and initial position $v(t) = (1, 0, 1)$, the new position on the technology landscape could be $v(t + 1) = (0; 0; 1)$. That is, *the firm tries one technology out of the set of neighboring technologies with distance one*:

$$v(t + 1) \in N_1(v(t)). \qquad (13.26)$$

If fitness at the new position is higher, i.e., if the new technology is better, the firm moves to the new position. Otherwise it stays at the old position. Regardless of the efficiency of the new position, firms have to pay the *cost of search*. A problem with this search algorithm is that it gets stuck at *local optima* since only $d = 1$ neighbors are considered. To overcome this problem, more sophisticated algorithms have to be devised. The example of a firm's search for a better technology is only one particular example illustrating the characteristics of *NK* landscapes. In principle, it is possible to model a wide range of phenomena as landscapes and let agents search on it. The *NK* model illustrates that if technologies are complex (*N* and *K* are large), the best technology cannot easily be found. Here it is assumed that agents do not have perfect information about the technology, i.e., they do not know the landscape in advance. Boundedly rational agents might easily get stuck at *suboptimal outcomes* since there are no simple rules for finding the global optimum. Instead of trying to find the global optimum, which implies searching the whole landscape, with high costs in terms of time and effort, agents could change their approach and try to arrive at a *local optimum* without searching too long. Taking this perspective, which obviously becomes relevant for boundedly rational agents engaging in costly search in complex environments, the next step would be to find efficient search algorithms.

13.10 D.J. WATTS AND S.H. STROGATZ (1998) ON SMALL-WORLD NETWORKS

"The world is small" is a common saying for many people to describe a somewhat surprising phenomenon: We may meet a complete stranger and are surprised to find we share a mutual friend, or, more generally, everybody in the world can be reached on average with only six steps of relationships. This is commonly referred to as the small-world phenomenon, the name already suggests its intriguing characteristic within social networks, which has been explored in many scientific experiments by Milgram and others (see Milgram, 1967; Mitchell, 1969; Korte and Milgram, 1970). After a number of explorations, for instance, by Pool and Kochen (1978), Skvoretz (1985), and Kochen (1989), who theoretically investigated the small-world phenomenon, Watts and Strogatz (1998) provided the first model of the small-world phenomenon, appearing widespread in the social and natural sciences. In this section, we explain what the small-world phenomenon is, and how it has been formalized by Watts and Strogatz (1998).

13.10.1 The Small-World Phenomenon

In an experimental study in the 1960s in the USA, Milgram (1967) asked more than 300 people in Kansas and Nebraska to send letters to targets in Boston (i.e., people randomly chosen in Boston). Each sender was only given the name of target—no address. If the targets were complete strangers to them, they could have intuitively sent the letter to whoever of their friends, who might possibly know the target. This procedure was repeated several times. Finally, each process of transfer generated a chain from the sender to the recipient. Statistically, Milgram found that 60 persons out of 300 finished the tasks, of which the average number of links in the chain was six. The same results were also found in experiments by researchers such as Mitchell (1969) and Korte and Milgram (1970). From a series of experimental results, it may be concluded that the small-world phenomenon exists, namely that we are connected by a series of short links, or, in other words, we can connect any persons in the world over several acquaintances, even those vastly separated.

Of course, research specific to the small-world phenomenon had a considerable history after Milgram's (1967) experiment, but none of these works before Watts and Strogatz's (1998) succeeded to provide a comprehensive model. In reality, many phenomena, such as the spread of diseases, rumors, technologies, and fashion, are based on contacts between individuals. More importantly still, if many other large, sparse networks such as biological networks and neural networks have this deep feature—that an element can connect with any other in a network over several elements— new discoveries would be made. Therefore,

it is necessary for an effective model to be built to improve the understanding of related areas.

13.10.2 Formalization of the Small-World Phenomenon

Before going further, it is best to understand the following definitions to simplify explanations.

Definition 1: *Characteristic path length (L)*, for a given graph, is defined as the average number of edges that must be traversed in the shortest path between any two pairs of vertices in the graph (Watts, 1999a).

Often the small-world phenomenon is described as "everybody in the world can be reached by only six steps." Roughly, "six steps" here would be characteristic path lengths. Concretely, L would be the average chain length from any sender to the recipient (in the edge set), which appeared in Milgram's (1967) experiment, or, in other words, the *shortest path length* between m and j. In other words, it is the median of the means of the shortest path lengths connecting each vertex $m \in G$(graph) to all other vertices and, specifically, we first calculate $d(m,j)$ $\forall j \in G$ and find mean d_m for each m, then L is defined as the median of $\{d_m\}$(Watts, 1999a).

Definition 2: *Clustering coefficient (C)* is a measure of the local graph structure (Watts, 1999a). Specifically, C measures the degree to which vertices in a graph tend to cluster together.

That is, assuming vertex v having m_v as immediate neighbors, then the immediate neighbors of m_v form a subgraph where $m_v(m_v - 1)/2$ edges exist if every neighbor is connected. If the number of actual connections in the neighborhood (subgraph) is k, C_v is $2k/m_v(m_v - 1)$ then C is this fraction over all vertices in the graph.

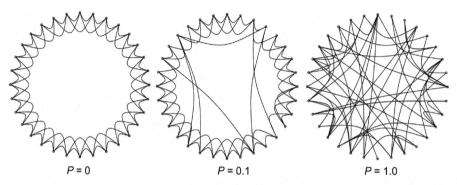

$P = 0$ $P = 0.1$ $P = 1.0$

FIGURE 13.16   Regular ring network ($P = 0.0$), a Watts–Strogatz small-world network ($P = 0.1$), and a random graph ($P = 1.0$).

To form a model of the small-world phenomenon, Watts and Strogatz (1998) proceeded in the following way.

Firstly, recognizing that while the real world is a rather large, sparse, and decentralized structure, this is impractical for creating a simple model. In order to reduce complexity, a minimal and simplified structure is required for the graph; no vertex should be special. For instance, in star networks, there is a central node; chain networks have endpoints. A topological ring structure (Figure 13.16), however, fulfills this requirement. Starting from such a regular geometric shape allows us, as will be discussed below, also to control and quantify the reduction of such regularity, and thereby the transition to a random network as well as the corresponding clustering and path length properties.

Secondly, Milgram's (1967) experiment showed that we are connected by a series of short links in the world. Hence alongside the ring structure, there should also be some short links connecting different parts of the ring.

Starting with a regular ring network, Watts and Strogatz (1998) use a probability p to rewire nodes randomly. If $p = 0$, the ring network is unchanged, for $p = 1$ all vertices are changed randomly, resulting in a random graph.[3] Then let $0 < p < 1$ represent the real world case. Watts (1999b, Chapter 4) gives the following algorithm to simulate the features above: Each vertex i in the ring connects, in a clockwise sense ($i, i + 1$), to its nearest neighbor. It ensures formation of an ordered world first.

A random deviate $r (0 < r < 1)$ is generated (it will be created by computer). If $r > p$, connections ($i, i + 1$) are unchanged. If $r < p$, ($i, i + 1$) is deleted and rewired to a vertex which is chosen at random from the ring. Thus, if $p = 0$, r is always greater than p, resulting in an ordered graph, and when r is always smaller than p, creating a random graph. When $0 < p < 1$, r is smaller than p in some cases and greater than p sometimes so that the formation of connections lies somewhere between randomness and order.

[3]When referring to a random graph here we mean an Erdős–Renyi random graph. Paul Erdős and Alfréd Rényi were the first scientists studying random graphs in detail and their model created a graph by starting with a fixed number of nodes and then adding edges to the nodes at random with a probability of p (Erdős and Rényi, 1959). Their model was of particular importance because it showed that real-world networks have properties very different from random networks and there are some organizing processes, which are to be explained, at work. Note that generally the term random graph is used in a broader sense and includes all graphs with some random element (see Section 13.11).

Finally, the three graphs in Figure 13.16 are created by simulating the algorithm above (for the simulation method in general see Chapter 9). Watts and Strogatz (1998) found the graph was highly clustered when $0 < p < 1$ (clustering coefficient), yet the characteristic path lengths were small, and called it a "small-world" network, in reference to the small-world phenomenon. In fact, this model not only simulates the real world by combining a topological ring and formation of social connections, but also simulates "small" by small characteristic path lengths. It therefore is an approximation of the small-world phenomenon.

13.10.3 Properties of Small-World Networks

Small-world networks are an important contribution to the modeling of economic reality not only because they seem to resemble real-world structures better than other types of networks but also as a consequence of their distinct properties. The network structure shapes the communication of agents, the spreading of epidemics, and, most importantly for our context of interactive economies, the diffusion of ideas, fashion, and innovations, of attitudes and strategies. Small-world graphs combine relatively high clustering with relatively short path lengths. Clustering gives rise to a number of distinct closely connected subgraphs that provide a protected environment for the development and evolution of new ideas and strategies; yet the distances in the graph are short enough to allow a rapid spread through the network once the time is right.

Consider as an example a population playing PD supergames in networks as discussed in Section 9.5. In a two-dimensional environment, only the two limit cases ($p = 1$, total

connectivity and $p = 0$, regular grid network) were considered; Watts and Strogatz (1998) did a more extensive analysis in their (one-dimensional) random graph context. Using a computer simulation, they found that when p was increased from 0 to 1 the fraction of cooperation decreased. This result suggests that *small-world networks can support cooperation* (although random networks cannot). Furthermore, from this result, we can also see that, in reality, choices of people are often constrained by the networks they belong to.[4]

13.11 A.-L. BARABÁSI AND R. ALBERT (1999) ON SCALE-FREE NETWORKS

The idea behind the Watts–Strogatz model was to model the real world phenomenon that networks often show small average shortest path length between nodes (the "small-world property") but also large cluster coefficients.

Barabási and his student Albert presented another model, which aimed to capture another important property of real world networks, namely, that there are few nodes with a very large number of adjacent nodes but that the number of neighbors decreases exponentially. More precisely, the degree distribution of most networks follows a power-law distribution. Barabási and Albert proposed a generative model of network growth, i.e. a model that explained the fact of this particular degree distribution by providing a mechanism of how this structure emerges in the real world.

13.11.1 The Distribution of Node Degrees

When investigating a particular network it is of interest to see what the average path

---

[4]If you are interested to study network and graph theory in more detail, consider the literature recommendations at the end of Section 13.11.

length is between different nodes and to what degree nodes form clusters. These properties were of particular importance in the Watts–Strogatz model. What did not play an important role was the degree distribution of the networks:

Definition 3: The *degree of a node v* is the number of edges incident with this node and is denoted by $\delta(v)$.

In social networks for example a node with a very high degree represents an individual (or a firm, etc.) of particular importance and with considerable power inside the network as it is connected with many other nodes. Where nodes represent humans and there is a connection between two humans who know each other well, a high node degree shows that the person represented by it has many acquaintances. It might therefore be illuminating to study how the degrees of different nodes are distributed in the network under investigation. This means to study the degree distribution of this network. One generally approaches this issue by deriving the probability $P(k)$ that a node in the network has k edges and then to study the probability distribution of $P(k)$.

It turns out that in almost all real-world networks, e.g., networks of individuals or organizations, of business firms, of scientific publications, of web sites in the world wide web or nerve cells and axons in the central nervous system, the node degrees are distributed in a particular way: There are very few nodes with a very high node degree and the value of the node degree decreases exponentially along the nodes in the network. This means that $P(k)$ follows a power-law distribution, i.e., $P(k) \sim ck^{-\gamma}$ with c being a factor ensuring that $\int_0^\infty P(k)dk = 1$ (see Chapter 11 for more information about power-law distributions).

An interesting feature of the power-law distribution is that if one considers only a very small part of the distribution and scales it up, it looks the same as the entire distribution,

i.e., the *distribution is self-similar*. The same is true for the network as such: If one transforms the network by joining several adjacent nodes into one, the degree distribution of the resulting network will still follow a power law. Therefore networks with a degree distribution following a power law are also called *scale-free networks*, as the scale for the degree distribution does not matter. The fact that so many networks in so many different areas exhibit this kind of degree distributions suggests that a process of self-organization common to real world networks is present. What Barabási and Albert did was to propose a process of network growth that yields this kind of degree distribution.

13.11.2 A Model of Network Growth

Barabási and Albert suggest that for understanding why scale-free networks are so common in the real world, one has to study the process of how they come to existence. According to their model, this process is characterized by two fundamental features, namely *network growth* and *preferential attachment*.

This means that in contrast to the Watts–Strogatz model, the Barabási–Albert model is a model of network growth: It starts with a small random graph and then adds more and more nodes to this graph.

The exact process goes as follows:

i. Start with a small random graph G_0 with node set V_0. At each time step t, a new node v_t gets added to the actual node set V_{t-1} to create the node set V_t.
ii. Add m edges to the graph; all of the new edges are incident with v_t and one of the nodes in V_{t-1}. The probability that a node $v^* \in V_{t-1}$ is chosen to be incident with the new edge is given by

$$P(v^*) = \frac{\delta(v^*)}{\sum_{w \in V_{t-1}} \delta(w)}.$$

Because the probability that a node gets an additional edge is proportional to its current node degree δ, this process is called *preferential attachment*: The more edges a node already has, the higher the probability it gets another one. It is therefore a *cumulative process of network growth.*

The resulting graph then exhibits a degree distribution that follows a power law, a relatively small clustering coefficient and remarkably small average shortest path length.

The Barabási–Albert model is of particular relevance for economists because many economic variables are distributed according to a power law and the process of preferential attachment is frequently used to explain this fact by showing that it yields network structures which then cause the variables of interest to be distributed according to a power law.

In Chapter 12, we introduced the *Pareto distribution* of income and Herbert Simon (1955) explained how such a distribution might have emerged due to preferential attachment. In Chapters 4 and 7, we have dealt with the fact that in many sectors there is a tendency toward monopolization, i.e., to structures in which there are very few huge corporations and many very small firms (see also Chapters 4 and 15 for a monopolization bias based on network externalities). Thanks to the Barabási–Albert model we can model the underlying topological network structure and provide an adequate explanation. In Chapter 17, we are going to deal with a policy implication of the fact that the size of firms in a given sector may be distributed according to a power law.

13.11.3 Scale-Free Networks, Small-World Networks, and the Real World

At this point it might be fruitful to compare the Watts–Strogatz model, the Barabási–Albert model, and network structures common in the real world: Both Watts and Strogatz and Barabási and Albert describe a probabilistic process and the resulting graphs belong to the family of random graphs. While Watts and Strogatz provide an algorithm, which builds graphs starting with a regular lattice and then adds edges according to a particular random process, the Barabási–Albert model is a model of network growth in which the number of nodes and edges is increasing.

Real world networks generally exhibit (i) a small average shortest path length, (ii) a large clustering coefficient, and (iii) a degree distribution, which follows a power law. Watts–Strogatz graphs exhibit (i) and (ii) but lack (iii) while Barabási–Albert graphs exhibit (i) and (iii) but lack (ii).

So the two models try to address different aspects of reality. Both models are of the generative type, i.e., they try to explain a real-world phenomenon by providing a mechanism according to which the phenomenon could have come to existence.

In reply to the pioneering work of Watts–Strogatz and Barabási–Albert, several models were developed which combine the properties of Watts–Strogatz and Barabási–Albert graphs: Klemm and Eguíluz (2002) proposed a model of network growth which yields graphs showing both a power-law degree distribution and the small-world behavior of the Watts–Strogatz graph. Today, the study of small-world and scale-free networks is a very active area of research and the network structures of interactive situations are used to explain a variety of economic phenomena.

If you wish to study graph and network theory in a more rigorous way, we especially recommend the following literature:

Goyal (2009) is the standard textbook on network analysis with a particular focus on economics. Easley and Kleinberg (2010) is a textbook particularly well suited for beginners and might be a very good starting point.

Van Steen (2010) focuses on the mathematical analysis of graphs and has a more general perspective than the other two books. He, Easley, and Kleinberg provide free pdf versions of their books in the Internet.

Other interesting sources of information are the (long) papers of Newman (2003) who gives a very compressed introduction and Boccaletti et al. (2006) who provide a good introduction into the state-of-the-art models in network analysis from a more general perspective. A collection of the most important articles published in this field is provided by Jackson and Zenou (2013). The introduction to this volume is also worth reading to get an idea about the current stage of research.

13.12 THE VEBLENIAN EVOLUTIONARY-INSTITUTIONALIST MODEL OF INSTITUTIONAL CHANGE (P.D. BUSH, 1987)

In Chapters 1 and 3, institutions were presented as solutions of complex social dilemma problems and an introduction to the Veblenian conception of institutional theory was given. This approach, starting with T.B. Veblen (see Chapter 12), furthered by C.E. Ayres and J.F. Foster, and during the 1980s advanced by Bush (1983, 1987) to constitute a theory of institutional change, has been termed the Veblen–Ayres–Foster–Bush model (Elsner, 2012). Different from the formal models for the emergence of institutions as presented in the first sections of this chapter and in a particular model frame in Chapter 14, the present section deals with the dynamics of existing institutions between their instrumental and ceremonial potentials, following Bush's more qualitative, but schematized, approach in the Veblenian evolutionary-institutionalist tradition.

13.12.1 Veblenian Evolutionary Institutionalism Today

As indicated in Chapter 12, T.B. Veblen was the founder of a whole economic paradigm, which has been called *American Institutionalism*, or OIE, Old or *Original Institutional Economics*, but which we would prefer to call *Evolutionary-Institutional Economics*. A whole number of leading figures in economics, which we have introduced in Chapter 12, are close to this major paradigm—such as K. Polanyi, G. Myrdal, N. Georgescu-Roegen, K.W. Kapp, H. Simon, J.K. Galbraith, and H. Minsky (in addition to the older institutionalists J.R. Commons and C.E. Ayres). Veblenian's Evolutionary-Institutional Economics has become a revivified paradigm since the 1980s, after some downturn since the 1940s, when it had to step behind Keynesian and neoclassical, later supply-side, monetarist and "neoliberal" issues. At that time, a new interest of the discipline in evolutionary, institutional, and complexity issues and perspectives came to the fore on a broad, comprehensive basis, and not only in the usual "heterodoxies" but in the "mainstream" as well (O'Hara, 2007; Elsner, 2011). A major starting point in the 1980s was *Geoffrey Hodgson*'s book (Hodgson, 1988), rightly called a manifesto in its subtitle, *Economics and Institutions*, which was followed by more than a dozen other path-breaking books by the same author, who has become one of the leading figures of evolutionary institutionalism from the 1990s on. Besides many other approaches since the 1940s to trace the history of evolutionary-institutional thinking and sort their central themes (Dorfman, 1959/1969; Gruchy 1947/1967), O'Hara (2007) has made a continuing effort to elaborate central and converging themes among major "heterodox" and complexity "schools of thought"—(Veblenian) evolutionary-institutional economics, (Marxist) radical political economy in a classical tradition, socioeconomics (engaged in value and ethical questions), ecological economics, feminist economics, and developmental economics—which might eventually form an "Institutional-Evolutionary Political Economy," as he has put it. Related associations and journals have spread accordingly.

Among other things, O'Hara identifies different, overlapping, interacting, and possibly converging orientations and themes within those major "heterodox" paradigms:

— besides the academic grandchildren of the founders and fathers generations (Veblen, Commons, Ayres, W. Hamilton, J.M. Clark, D. Hamilton, and "pragmatist" philosopher J. Dewey) themselves (such as L.F. Junker, W. Gordon, M.R. Tool, W. Samuels, P.D. Bush, A. Mayhew, R. Tilman, W. Waller, or James Galbraith), we find
— the more radical institutionalists with their focus on power and ceremonialism (J.R. Stanfield, W.M. Dugger, S. Bowles, P.A. O'Hara);
— Post-Keynesian institutionalists with focuses on uncertainty, endogenous money, distribution, circular cumulative causation, or financial instability (P. Davidson, M. Sawyer, P. Arestis, F. Lee, M. Lavoie, L.R. Wray);
— institutional Marxists with their focuses on capital circuits, cycles and waves, social/institutional arrangements of reproduction and regulation (H.J. Sherman, D.M. Gordon, S. Bowles, H. Gintis, R. Wolff, M. Aglietta, R. Boyer);
— social economic institutionalism with a focus on the theory of individual behavior, values, norms, and ethics, trust and community, structure and agency (K.E. Boulding, J. Davis);
— institutional Schumpeterians with a focus on institutions, innovation, and change, long waves, industrial ecologies, endogenous growth, and path dependence;
— plus radical/institutional feminist economics and ecological economics.

They would converge, O'Hara argues, on overarching themes such as complexity and uncertainty, dynamics, evolution, and institutions, structural emergence, systems theory and path dependence, circular cumulation, open process and non-equilibrium, and in methodological terms on systemic/holistic perspectives (see, for instance, F.G. Hayden's institutionalist *Social Fabric Matrix Approach*; M.J. Radzicki's institutionalist *Social Dynamics Approach*) and *"critical realism"* (T. Lawson) in search of prima facie invisible structures explaining prima facie visible system motions.

O'Hara lists converging contributions:

— from Veblenian themes "converging heterodoxers" look at habits, instincts, and institutions;
— from neo-Marxian themes, they look at the circuit of social capital and "social structures of accumulation" (SSA);
— from feminist themes, they link class, gender, and ethnicity;
— from neo-Schumpeterian themes, they focus on long waves, cycles, and the technology—institutions interface;
— from Post-Keynesianism, demand, uncertainty, and a monetary theory of production are provided;
— social economics provides themes such as trust, ethics, and morality;
— from ecological economics, converging themes are sustainability, ecological capital, and systemic thermodynamics; and, finally,
— from global political economy, one would look at hegemonic power relations, uneven development, and varieties of capitalism and other systems.

O'Hara elaborates on what he considers the overarching principles of a broad evolutionary-institutional convergence, such as:

— methodological "Critical Realism";
— complexity;

- the interrelation of "structure" and "agency," with emergent system properties such as institutions or "social capital," trust, and "community" size (for examples of models of emergent institutions, see this chapter above, and on emergent size, see also Chapter 14);
- heterogeneous agents;
- process and history ("historic specificity"; for this, see the lock-in model of David and Arthur above), together with circular cumulation and an interest in long waves;
- a systemic or holistic or circuit perspective of capital (physical, money, and social capitals);
- general reproduction (social structures of accumulation), and, last but not least;
- an interest in *institutional change*, based on the institutional dichotomy, with a basic accessibility to the idea of "progress" and *"progressive institutional change"* with its governance and policy dimension.

It is the latter, which has played a prominent role throughout most of the history of evolutionary-institutional economics. This has led to one of the few condensed schemes (if not models) in this paradigm (if we disregard the applications of institutionalism through the methods of the Social Fabric Matrix and System Dynamics (see above). This scheme, therefore, will be picked out in the following to provide a core model of the paradigm of Veblenian evolutionary-institutional economics.

13.12.2 The Institutionalist Definition of Institutions

Bush (1987, p. 1076) first defines an institution as *"a set of socially prescribed patterns of correlated behavior."* The term "socially prescribed" in this definition stresses the fact that institutions mostly appear as received preexisting normative phenomena to individual

agents, having emerged earlier and being received in a process of "reconstitutive downward causation." They may be objectively either still instrumental, i.e., problem solving, or already fully abstract and detached from the original problem, thus ceremonial, i.e., mostly preserving power and status differentials, with regard to the agents. In the latter case, the original instrumental context of their emergence usually has faded away.

This is often not just a "social behavioral rule (plus endogenous sanction)" as conveyed by social conditioning and enculturation, but above that, an explicit feeling of individuals of a "must" or "must not" of behavior, similar to semiconscious habituation, as explained in Chapters 1 and 3.

Further, as the definition quoted above states, institutions require *correlated* behavior. In our instrumental derivation of institutional emergence, behaviors are correlated first between two agents who learn to correlate their behaviors in recurrent interaction to solve a problem at hand, particularly correlated (or reciprocal or mutual) cooperation learned in a PD supergame. "Correlation" may also be any coordination in a broader sense, including both institutionalized cooperation and some repeated mutual defection, carried out as a rule. Such "correlated" behavior, therefore, can not only be correlated cooperation in an instrumental sense, but also defection in a ceremonial sense, as we will explain below. Repeated (mutual or one-sided) defection, in fact, may in this way have become established as a certain individualist, hyperrational, ceremonial "culture." And while in a PD supergame defection typically will be mutual among hyperrational agents, under some particular assumptions, there may also be power and status exertion by one agent and corresponding acceptance by the other one. This would be a continuous, institutionalized exploitation.

Furthermore, any such behavior is correlated not only among agents, but also over time, since it emerged as a recurrent, repetitive, just rule-based behavior. In fact, a rule would be no rule (a "strategy" in game-theoretic terms) if this behavior were not somehow correlated with itself over time. Thus, a set of correlated behaviors may refer to a set of *coordinated agents* carrying the institution and/or a set of repetitions of coordinated behaviors, i.e., a set of *coordinated interactions over time*.

Finally, according to the institutionalist conception, different institutions can be correlated among each other to form larger *institutional sets* and whole institutional arrangements or cultures. However, they cannot actively correlate themselves but will be correlated by agents through the values that motivate agents' behaviors and thus warrant individual institutions or sets of—then, and by this—correlated institutions.

13.12.3 Values Correlating Patterns of Behavior

The central aspect of determining the character of institutions (predominantly instrumental or ceremonial) and correlating different institutions (and determining the character of those together) in the institutionalist approach, which has not explicitly been accounted for in the game-theoretic treatment so far, is *values*. As Bush puts it, "*Values function as the 'correlators' of behavior within and among patterns of behavior*" (Bush, 1987, p. 1077). That is "*two behaviors [...] [are] correlated by a value*" (Bush, 1987, p. 1077). In a game-theoretic perspective, for instance, cooperative behavior in a PD—and also, basically, coordinated behavior in a coordination game, particularly if coordinated on a superior Nash equilibrium in a stag hunt game—are correlated among agents and over time through the "instrumental value" (or valuation or motivation) of problem solving, which seems quite obvious. Defection, aimed

at unilateral exploitation and the often resulting mutual defection, on the other hand, is justifiable—also in game theory—through the value of Veblenian "invidious distinction," i.e., the striving for superior power and status, in a word, ceremonial value. This dual characterization of institutions by instrumental or ceremonial warrant is called the *institutional dichotomy*, as originally introduced by Veblen.

Those motivations (values, valuations) may simultaneously determine the characters of, and thus correlate, different institutions coexisting in different arenas. The basic scheme of this institutionalist argument is

$$B - V - B$$

with V for the correlating values and B for the patterns of behavior or institutions. V correlates behaviors B, again either *interpersonal* or *intertemporal* or *inter-institutional*.

The characters of and relationship between the B's are fundamentally determined by the type of V. Therefore, first, all kinds of constellations, including conflicting ones, between instrumental and ceremonial V's and their determined institutions have to be expected, and, second, institutional change must entail (or require, presuppose, or just go along with), basically, a change of the value correlating the behaviors.

13.12.4 The Asymmetry in the Institutional Dichotomy, Ceremonial Dominance, and Ceremonial Encapsulation

Again, behavior warranted by ceremonial values is based on invidious distinction and differential status and power. The logic of ceremonial warrant is, as Veblen has already put it, one of "sufficient reason," which means that ceremonial values refer to tradition, received authority, and suitable myths, and are beyond critical scrutiny and scientific inquiry. The *operative criterion* for such behavior is thus "ceremonial adequacy," i.e., just conformity with the myths of differential power and status, without any proof of real efficacy—conformity is just sufficient.

Instrumental values, on the other hand, are bound to some specified problem solving, and thus their logic is that of "efficient cause" rather than just "sufficient reason." The operative criterion by which instrumentally warranted behavior is judged, therefore, is that of "instrumental efficiency" (rather than "ceremonial adequacy"), i.e., efficacy. Typically, with new "technological" knowledge (in the broadest sense), instrumental behavior would have to be scrutinized and properly adapted.

Several qualifications are to be made here:

- First, there are two *pure forms* of behavior that can be expressed in the values–behaviors scheme:

$$B_c - V_c - B_c \text{ and } B_i - V_i - B_i$$

where c and i stand for ceremonial and instrumental, respectively.

- Second, it is most important in the institutionalist approach to institutional change that most behavior is *dialectical* in the sense of having *both ceremonial and instrumental* characteristics or potentials. These are patterns of behavior to be symbolized by B_{ci} (or equivalently, B_{ic}), which are ambivalent and open, and in their final significance depend on the type of values that warrants them. Thus, there can be added the following forms:

$$B_{ci} - V_c - B_{ci} \text{ and } B_{ci} - V_i - B_{ci}$$

and, of course, also

$$B_c - V_c - B_{ci} \text{ and } B_i - V_i - B_{ci}.$$

Both ceremonial and instrumental values can warrant and correlate either "dialectical" patterns of behavior or a "pure" form of their own kind with a "dialectical" or ambivalent form.

- Third, there is a *fundamental asymmetry* between instrumental and ceremonial modes of valuation, as already apparent from the two different logics and operational criteria given above: The instrumental logic and operational criterion of efficient cause and instrumental efficiency are inapplicable to purely ceremonial behavior: "Instrumental valuation cannot rationalize purely ceremonial behavior" (Bush, 1987, p. 1083). The ceremonial logic and operational criterion of sufficient reason and ceremonial adequacy, on the other hand, are limitless in principle: Any behavior, including instrumental behavior, may be "rationalized," absorbed (mis-)used, or occupied, so to speak, by ceremonial valuation, since its logic is weaker and its operational criterion less demanding. In game-theoretic terms, we might think, as a potential equivalent, of the exploitation constellations in the upper right and lower left cells of a PD normal form, where instrumental (cooperative) behavior of some agents is dominated by the ceremonial (defective) behavior of others (to their own benefit).

In cases of *ceremonial enclosure* of purely instrumental or "dialectical" patterns of behavior, institutionalists speak of *encapsulation*: "In these instances, instrumental behavior is 'encapsulated' within a ceremonially warranted behavioral pattern, thereby incorporating instrumental behavior in a ceremonially prescribed outcome" (Bush, 1987, p. 1084).

The forms of ceremonial encapsulation are manifold, first, with pure behaviors, where purely instrumental behavior is warranted, correlated with purely ceremonial behavior, and in this way subordinated to ceremonial behavior, i.e., "encapsulated," by ceremonial valuing:

$$B_c - V_c - B_i$$

and the "weaker" form (or rather a stronger assumption?) of purely instrumental behavior warranted, correlated with "dialectical" behavior, and encapsulated by ceremonial valuation, where even "dialectical" and purely instrumental behaviors can be encapsulated to serve a ceremonially prescribed outcome:

$$B_{ci} - V_c - B_i.$$

And, of course, also

$$B_{ci} - V_c - B_{ci} \quad \text{and} \quad B_c - V_c - B_{ci}$$

are forms of ceremonial encapsulation.

Note that $B_i - V_c - B_i$ is no possible constellation, as ceremonial values cannot justify pure instrumental behaviors. For instance, general mutual cooperation, in our sense of problem solving for all, cannot be considered ceremonially warrantable, although one-sided cooperative behavior can easily be ceremonially encapsulated. Similarly, as indicated, no constellation $B_c - V_i - B_c$ is possible. Furthermore, because of the asymmetry explained, instrumental values cannot even justify *any* purely ceremonial behavior, so no constellations

$B_i - V_i - B_c$ and $B_{ci} - V_i - B_c$ are feasible. See Figure 13.17 for an overview of forms.

The *asymmetry* between the two logics of the ceremonial and the instrumental easily combines with the general comprehension of institutions in the Veblenian tradition according to which institutions are always and unavoidably past-bound and thus prone to a *ceremonial dominance* anyway. However, specific cultures and nations, in fact, differ in the "permissiveness" of their institutions vis-à-vis new technological knowledge (or an "increase of the social knowledge fund"), of allowing for a change toward more instrumentally warranted behavioral patterns.

So this is about graduality and degrees. A related *index of ceremonial dominance* can then be derived from a specific network of correlated institutions, according to the relative numbers of (instrumental vs. ceremonial) dominance relations existing in that specific institutional structure of an economy (Bush, 1983). It will be inversely related to the degree of permissiveness: The higher that index, the lower is the permissiveness of the institutional structure of an economy.

According to what we have learned (mainly through the single-shot solution in Chapter 3), we would assume in a game-theoretic

	Ceremonially warranted patterns of behavior	Instrumentally warranted patterns of behavior
"Pure pure" forms	$B_c - V_c - B_c$	$B_i - V_i - B_i$
Pure "dialectical" forms	$B_{ci} - V_c - B_{ci}$ (involving some ceremonial encapsulation)	$B_{ci} - V_i - B_{ci}$
Mixed "pure" and "dialectical" forms	$B_c - V_c - B_{ci}$ (involving some ceremonial encapsulation)	$B_i - V_i - B_{ci}$
Pure "encapsulation" forms	$B_c - V_c - B_i$ $B_{ci} - V_c - B_i$	–/–

FIGURE 13.17 A scheme of the variants of ceremonially and instrumentally warranted and correlated patterns of behavior. *After Bush (1987, p. 1082).*

perspective that the *degree of permissiveness* is related to both the payoff structure and the learned importance of the common future δ in the considerations of the agents. While this may appear a bit "technical," it may nevertheless combine with the valuing aspect: The more "permissive" the value structure of the agents in those games would be, i.e., the more the agents will be after long run and broad (common and collective) "problem solving" having recognized their interdependence, the more a behavioral adaptation toward the superior solution would appear feasible.

13.12.5 A Reflection of Ceremonial Dominance and Encapsulation: The Degeneration of Instrumental Institutions into Ceremonial Ones

The Different Benchmarks: The Institution as Enabler Versus Ceremonial Dominance

As we have seen already in Chapter 3 (and will be explained in more detail in Chapter 14), in a *game theory perspective*, the institution emerges in a complex evolutionary process, from a defined particular common and collective problem. In that way it helps individuals to solve situations that otherwise would not be solvable in a decentralized "market" economy with individualistic culture. Based on a simple *single-shot solution*, the exact *definition of an institution* is *instrumentalist* (as introduced, for instance, by Schotter, 1981), as given in a short version in Chapter 3 already:

> An institution is a *habituated social rule* for the decision/behavior of individual agents in *recurrent* multipersonal (social) situations (*SGs*), with coordination problems involved (particularly collective-good problems/*social dilemmas*), that has gained, through an *evolutionary process of interaction and social learning*, a *general approval* so that it can *inform agents* about *mutual expectations* (beliefs) of cooperative behavior, and about the fact that with *unilateral deviation* from

the rule other agents also will *deviate in the future* so that eventually *all will be worse-off with mutual defection than with mutual rule-conforming behavior* (a *sacrifice*; thus, an *endogenous sanction* mechanism).

In consistence with this view, it has long been argued by institutionalists that the institution is not just a restriction to some ideal, allegedly unrestrained, perfect maximization, as argued by neoclassical economics. It is also not just flatly past-bound, conservative, and inadequate, but in complex situations it also is an "enabler" of a qualified, as coordinated, behavior of agents (see, e.g., Neale, 1994). As such, it serves as an *empowerment* of agents in terms of improving information, reducing uncertainty, making expectations of agents consistent with each other and thus stabilizing them and enabling action—the instrumental dimension of institutions.

On the other hand, as has been shown, ceremonial dominance is rooted in the asymmetry of the logics of ceremonial versus instrumental warrants, where ceremonial valuation is more "permeable," *capable of encapsulating more ways of behavior* than instrumental valuation is capable of embedding. This very asymmetry parallels a *dominance of defective strategies* in the game theory (PD) perspective. Defective behavior, in fact, is *exploitative* in its *motivation*, "warrant," or *value base*, as it strives to attain the maximum by making the other(s) contribute to the collective good (cooperate), and it is aspiring for *invidious distinction* (Veblen): In a PD, an agent can get a maximum payoff only by making the other one receive the minimum payoff—*ceremonial behavior*.

Also, in the institutionalist tradition, the ceremonially warranted institution has mostly been the starting point, due to the *historical* approach of institutionalism, where more or less *predatory* societies and economies have been the received object of socioeconomic analysis and theorizing—a perspective that Veblen himself had established (see Chapter 12).

However, both the logical and historical accounts do not fully "genetically" explain how ceremonial dominance *endogenously emerges*, particularly from a benchmark of an instrumentally warranted institution.

Instrumentally warranted institutions—having emerged in a long, complex process resulting in a good solution to a problem—can indeed have an endogenous course of their own. This can be understood as some *life cycle* leading them from an instrumental (considered here, for simplicity, the "natural state" of the system) to a ceremonial entity, from problem-solving cooperation to a behavior that—while perhaps even formally unchanged—has essentially become inadequate in face of *new conditions*. The idea is closely related to the idea of an *(institutional) lock-in* as in the famous QWERTY analysis (see above)—where a new collective action capability would be required for a proper new institution to emerge.

Note that in a game theory perspective, a general *defective* (ceremonial) behavior may be a *"culture"* as well, in the sense of a learned *social rule of individualistic behavior*. The analogy is to the solution of a simple *coordination game* (see Chapter 3). The solution of a coordination game is in everybody's immediate individualistic interest, we have called it a social rule, as distinct to a social institution. As defection is in everybody's immediate individualistic interest, this ceremonial behavior, if generally applied, may be considered a ceremonial social rule.

In the frame of a normal-form game (PD), we may think of a case, when new conditions, some new technological knowledge, particularly if occurring in some hierarchical environment, may trigger an *uneven distribution of the gains of cooperative behavior*. This may be changing the payoff structure in a way to make the formerly superior common cooperation behavior, which remains unchanged, inferior now, compared to a new cooperative solution that has become feasible in the meantime.

Degeneration of an Instrumentally Warranted Institution in a Hierarchical Environment: The Career Motive and the Motive of Identity and Belongingness

The idea applies when, for instance, a fresh economics MA or MBA joins a firm with his/her new ideas and new knowledge, but his/her suggestions are refused by a superior who is arguing, "We have always done it like this, we have been successful with it, and we will continue doing it like this." This would be a symbolic indication of an institution formerly successfully established to solve the specific problem of cooperation, by which a group became a cooperating one, thus successfully coordinated and highly performing. With the *successfully cooperating group "plus hierarchy,"* however, the group leaders and higher ranks of the cooperating team establish and tighten their own positions, promote their individual careers, and perhaps climb up the hierarchical ladder.

Differential hierarchical status and power in societies, economies, and organizations that are characterized by received power and status differences anyway, thus, becomes a particular *ceremonial motive* determining the future of that institution. That very ceremonial valuation may also provide *identity* and belongingness to the lower ranks of the team or division, which in turn may relieve their uncertainty in the turbulent environment they live in. These motives usually combine and may *transform* the character of the interaction system eventually into a *unilateral defection and exploitation*, where the superiors nevertheless still manage to keep their subordinates cooperating. *Habituation* of the old institution may explain why those receiving relatively less of the common gain still stick to the *same formal behavior*, although the character of the institution has tacitly changed.

In any case, the earlier instrumentally warranted situation has *transformed itself into a ceremonially dominated situation* of a $B_c - V_c - B_i$ type. A new *institutional cycle* may emerge. Note that "exploited" agents suddenly may perceive and reveal enviousness or relative deprivation vis-á-vis their superior or the new objective payoff opportunity.

Another Ceremonial Motive, Value, and Warrant: "Institutional Economies of Scale"—from an Instrumental Institution to a Ceremonially Warranted Abstract Norm (Institutional Lock-In)

Another factor supporting the process of collective cooperative success may be *transaction—cost reduction* or economies of scale of the application of an institution, with a learning curve, which ensures that sticking to the institution makes the average transaction costs of the single institutionalized decision ever more decrease. This is the classical case of *routinization* and, in fact, a *payoff argument* in favor of a prolonged habituation of the old institution, in face of new conditions suggesting a new cooperative behavior.

That senior manager who is referring to, and insisting upon, his past experience in the example above, thus, is of course not totally selfish, invidious, and ceremonial. She may rightly refer to a history of the institution that indeed has been successful. During that history, she and her interaction partners had successfully established the institution as an adequate instrumental device, with a lot of effort invested then, learning effort, risk-taking of being exploited, trial and error, non-invidiousness (see Chapter 3 and, with more detail, Chapter 14), and they still profit from routinization and low institutional transaction costs. They had to *invest* a lot in terms of *time, intellectual effort, uncertainty, risk-taking of getting exploited once, trial and error, non-invidiousness*, to make that institution eventually emerging in a long and fragile process. And as everyone who has invested such *high fixed and sunk costs*, she and her fellows aspire

to permanently high returns on their investment, by spreading their initial fixed costs over *as many applications as possible*. And, if possible, they do not wish to invest in a new learning process.

The argument in a population would be that such a learning process with cumulative reinforcement of cooperation may become ever more effective as the portions of cooperative agents in the population or of cooperative actions in all actions increases.

However, sticking to the old institution may still be consistent with the *instrumental* character of the institution and with instrumental warrant. While the institution may increasingly appear to the individual agents of the team, group, or organization as something external, an *exogenously given formal normative requirement*, or postulate, it still may be dominantly instrumentally warranted and still relate to the solution of the problem at hand. But *tacitly*, the motivation to maintain the institution may change from solving the original problem to (1) saving the careers of the leaders and thus making extra benefits from *unequal distribution* (see above) and/or (2) reducing *average institutional transaction costs*, i.e., just gaining through making their decisions as easy and smooth as possible, rather than properly solving the problems, particularly when there may have emerged a new problem in the meantime. A *norm*, thus, is not necessarily ceremonially warranted yet. The instrumentally warranted institution may have become a general prescription, or even become codified, and the connection to the basic problem has become somewhat opaque, but still may be an adequate behavioral pattern. We term this an *instrumentally warranted norm*.

We might either conceive the related behavior, earlier instrumental B_i, as tacitly becoming "dialectical," B_{ci}, and eventually ceremonial, B_c, as in the career motive of the superior above, while the subordinates stick to their cooperative behavior, which is now

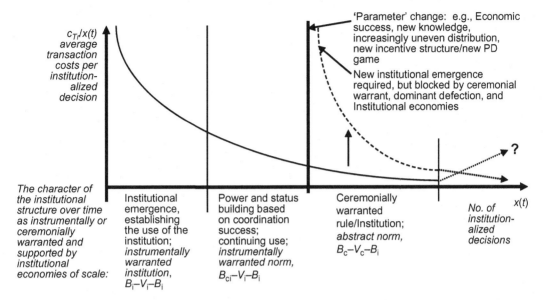

FIGURE 13.18   Average transaction costs and "Institutional Economies of Scale" supporting the degeneration into a ceremonially warranted abstract norm after some "Technological" change—illustration.

ceremonially encapsulated, or the whole institutional arrangement as changing its character, from instrumental to ceremonial warrant, as a new, superior, problem-solving institution is required (if not already available).

But only when some *external conditions change*—in game theory modeling: changing expectations and/or payoff structure through whatever increase of the social knowledge fund—the (so far instrumental) norm would turn out to be *fully disconnected* from the (new) problem setting, as the establishment of a proper new institution will be blocked by the now dominating ceremonial motives and warrant of differential career making and of continuing easy and smooth decision-making. The formally same behavior thus becomes ceremonially warranted, and in fact defective in terms of the potential new payoff structure. We call this an *abstract norm*.

The two cases of motives explain why interaction systems may stick to an institution for longer than instrumentally justified.

The institution may then eventually become "outdated," "petrified," "sclerotic," "ossified," or "locked-in." The ceremonial motivation and warrant will then *prevent* the interaction system to properly learn and gain the *renewed collective action capability* required.

Note that a new institution will facilitate lower average decision costs (on top of its superior payoff for reciprocal cooperation) in the long run. The abstract norm (note: formally the same behavior as before), on the contrary, may, for instance in the "career" case above, increasingly entail fight over unilateral exploitation or even mutual defection and its average *transaction costs* may thus *increase* again. Thus, the potential average transaction costs of a new institution may fall below those of the old norm. This, of course, as game theory analysis clarifies, does not guarantee that the system will easily regain anew a proper collective action capability, particularly not in the short run. And as long as the new institution will not be used, it will not be able to perform its superiority. See Figure 13.18 for an illustration.

In all, such *"endogenous" institutional degeneration* may help explain the *ceremonial domination* in an individualistic and hierarchical culture.

For a more elaborated model of Veblenian institutional change, in an evolutionary game theory framework and a sequence of PDs, when new superior solutions become periodically available, see Heinrich and Schwardt, 2013. While new institutionalized cooperation on the superior institution would increase everybody's payoff, it is an option for everybody to stick to the old one, in this way being able to exploit those who change over to the new one. In a model simulation, it is found that older (then ceremonial) and newer (instrumental) institutions always will coexist for a while—a heterogeneity of subcultures in larger groups (see also the model in Chapter 14).

13.12.6 The Process and Forms of Institutional Change

It follows from the above that *new knowledge* (technological change), together with related (newly learned or adapted) instrumental patterns of behavior, can become either encapsulated within still dominating ceremonially warranted patterns of behavior or "embedded" within a dominating instrumental value–behavior structure.

Basically, the asymmetry and ceremonial dominance restricts permissiveness: "(K)nowledge that cannot be reconciled with the need to justify existing patterns of status, power, and other forms of invidious distinctions would not be intentionally sanctioned" (Bush, 1987, p. 1091).

But new knowledge basically supports instrumental feasibility ("warrantability") of (newly learned or adapted) behavior. The index of ceremonial dominance (in a negative sense)

or the degree of permissiveness (in a positive sense), in fact, are indicative of the degree to which new knowledge is allowed to be used in the community's problem-solving process.

The asymmetric structure of feasibilities ("warrantabilities"), in sum, now defines an *institutional space*, within which we can not only define the different sectors (subspaces, cells) according to the value–behavior constellations (instrumental and ceremonial feasibilities and infeasibilities), but also can illustrate the motions of institutional change (Figure 13.19):

1. *Ongoing and enforced ceremonial encapsulation*: When (new) behavioral patterns are both *instrumentally feasible* (warrantable) and *ceremonially feasible* (warrantable), thus meeting both "efficient cause" and "sufficient reason," or both "instrumental efficiency" and "ceremonial adequacy," it is clear from the argument about asymmetry and ceremonial dominance that this is the case (and sector) of ceremonial encapsulation. Here, the institutional structure of an economy allows for benefiting from instrumentally warranted behavior that at the same time can be ceremonially justified, utilized, and encapsulated (upper left cell in Figure 13.19).

   In dynamic terms, if an increase of the knowledge fund would trigger an ongoing and even enforced ceremonial encapsulation, with no change in the degree of permissiveness, the system would remain in this sector (Case (1) in Figure 13.19).

2. Those behavioral patterns that are instrumentally feasible but ceremonially infeasible will typically be excluded under ceremonial dominance ("lost instrumental efficiency") (lower left cell in Figure 13.19). If, however, viewed dynamically, ceremonial dominance could be reduced through new knowledge and related potential of newly learned or adapted instrumental behavior, this would be indicative of *progressive institutional change*,

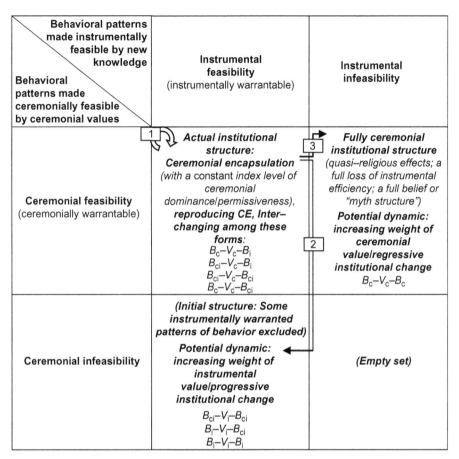

FIGURE 13.19   The institutional space in the interface of instrumental feasibility and ceremonial feasibility, and the basic movements of institutional change.

i.e., an increasing weight of instrumental over ceremonial values, and the economy could be thought of as moving from the sector of ceremonial encapsulation into the sector of increased instrumental problem solving, where instrumental patterns of behavior are no longer excluded but become dominant (a motion from upper left to lower left in Figure 13.19, case (2)).

3. Finally, if behavioral patterns were instrumentally infeasible and only ceremonially feasible, if they were purely ceremonial, a complete dominance of the "myth structure" and a full "loss of instrumental efficiency" (Bush, 1987, p. 1092) would occur, with instrumentally warranted patterns no longer existing (the upper right cell in the figure below). If, in response to new knowledge and potential new instrumental institutions, ceremonial dominance would even increase (through some counter movement) and the economy's institutional structure moved into this sector of ceremonial feasibility and instrumental infeasibility (excluding virtually all instrumental patterns of behavior), this

would be a *regressive institutional change*, i.e., an even greater dominance of ceremonial over instrumental values. This may be termed quasi-religious effects.

13.12.7 The Discretionary Character of Progressive Institutional Change: A Policy Perspective

Therefore, after all, progressive institutional change will normally not emerge, particularly when systemic crises and widespread uncertainty and fears may easily lead to enforced ceremonial encapsulation. The system may move perhaps from future-binding to past-binding encapsulation and from there even to regressive institutional change. Thus, progressive change would remain an issue of proper deliberate, discretionary policy action. In the institutionalist tradition, M.R. Tool developed the theory of instrumentalism and progressive institutional change into a theory of the so-called social value principle, which operationalized the institutionalist conception of public policy and its formation. For institutionalists, democracy and democratic policy are substantial in the sense that decisions will have to be found in a participatory democratic negotiation process with all interests involved (the "negotiated economy"). Thus it is not primarily about some formal majority rule but about the substantial "process by which majorities [...] are formed" (Bush, 1987, p. 1109)—and such process would be interconnected "with the process of inquiry upon which instrumental valuing depends" (Bush, 1987, p. 1109). In this way, substantial, participative, and discursive democracy would support collective long-run rationality and action capacity, and with this the dominance of instrumental values and instrumentally warranted patterns of behavior—i.e., progressive institutional change (for policy implications of evolutionary-institutional and complexity reasoning, see in more detail Chapter 17).

13.13 E. OSTROM (1990) AND E. OSTROM ET AL. (1992) ON THE GOVERNANCE OF COMMON POOL RESOURCES

13.13.1 General

A special focus in Nobel Laureate Elinor Ostrom's research lies on questions dealing with the joint use of (natural) resources by groups of individuals. Such common pool resources (CPRs) share one characteristic of *collective goods*, the difficulty to exclude agents from exploiting them, but they are distinguished from collective goods by their rivalry in use, at least once some degree of intensiveness in use is reached. For groups using CPRs that rivalry leads to problems regarding the coordination of individuals' degree of exploiting the CPR. The CPR typically already exists, being provided by nature (fisheries, forests, commons, etc.). An overexploitation is easily possible, in fact has often been identified as a likely result of the common use of resources when individual agents are not constrained but pursue an individually optimal behavior.

The core of the CPR problem lies in the fact that individually optimal (Nash) behavior produces a socially *and* individually suboptimal result. Hence, a useful approach for analyzing them is to formalize them as *social dilemma* games. An interesting question to address then is why some groups are able to give themselves rules that allow a prolonged joint use of the CPR at levels that are sustainable; in game-theoretic terms, how some groups are able to successfully prevent an inefficient Nash equilibrium (the overexploitation of the CPR).

In the 1990 book "Governing the Commons," Ostrom presents a number of case studies on CPR use, especially of successful groups avoiding the Nash outcome. The conditions under which successful coordination succeeded are in fact quite diverse (as regards the number of individuals involved, the discount rates applied by individuals within the groups, the interests of the group members involved, etc.). This makes it impossible to arrive at clear-cut results as to when and how groups are able to organize themselves to cooperate on issues of CPR use. However, some general aspects can be identified as influential. These include the general level of information available to the group members, capacities and willingness to communicate, as well as the possibility of the group to sanction and punish members for perceived misbehavior (see also, e.g., Gintis et al., 2005, for a number of studies on these issues in small groups in different cultural settings).

Ostrom and her collaborators Walker and Gardner then published an article in 1992, "Covenants with an without a sword," which contains a discussion of a series of experiments addressing issues of individual behavior when the use of a CPR by groups is concerned. They tried to set up the experiments so as to gain a structured overview over the distinct influences on individuals' behavior within groups sharing access to a CPR, especially how communication and enforcement mechanisms (punishment) on the group level influence individual behavior. (For an extensive textbook treatment of these issues see Ostrom et al., 1994.)

An important aspect when considering the mentioned influences is that it has been observed repeatedly that results in experiments consistently show behavior that is not reconcilable with the predictions derived on the basis of both neoclassical modeling and noncooperative game theory. For instance, allowing for *communication* significantly improves results from group interactions, even if there are *no* mechanisms for *punishing* deviation from an agreed-upon course of action. Also, in repeated interactions, individuals devote substantial time and resources to *monitoring* others' behavior (if the experimental setup allows this), even

if such behavior is not compatible with an optimal use of resources from the theoretical point of view. Hence, it also becomes an issue how different instruments for influencing the behavior of individual actors in groups are used and how their use may possibly be improved.

13.13.2 The Model

To set out the framework, the CPR game at the heart of the experiments conducted is specified as follows: We have a fixed number n of people with access to the CPR. Each agent i has an endowment e that she can invest in the CPR or in an outside activity that guarantees a safe constant marginal payoff w. The overall return from the CPR depends on the aggregate group investment in it. With x_i being the investment by an individual agent, the overall return from the CPR is a function $F(\Sigma x_i)$. Assume F to be a concave function with $F(0) = 0$, $F'(0) > w$, and $F'(ne) < 0$. The function shows an initially higher return from the CPR investment than from the safe private alternative, a point at which the return from the CPR reaches its maximum, when some but not all endowment is invested there, and thereafter falling marginal returns eventually even turning negative.

The individual agent receives a return from the CPR that is proportional to her investment share in the CPR. So, for an agent i, her return depends on whether she has invested in the CPR, and on the size of her investment relative to the overall amount invested. For $x_i = 0$, the agents receive $u_i = we$. If a positive amount is invested in the CPR by an agent (where investment maybe most easily interpreted as time dedicated to CPR exploitation), she receives

$$u_i = w(e - x_i) + \frac{x_i}{\sum x_i} F\left(\sum x_i\right). \qquad (13.27)$$

The first step is to try and find an individual equilibrium behavior (amount of investment) in order to compare it to the optimal allocation from the group perspective (for this approach, see also, e.g., Sen's model presented in Section 13.2). In the Nash equilibrium, every individual makes her own best decision given the behavior of all other agents. A maximizing investment schedule has to include some investment in the CPR, as the marginal return from that investment is initially higher than in the safe alternative. So, we are looking for an optimal allocation x_i given the allocations of the rest of the agents involved. To find the optimal individual allocation in that case, maximize Eq. (13.27) with respect to x_i. The first order condition is

$$-w + \frac{x_i}{\sum x_i}F'\left(\sum x_i\right) + \frac{\sum x_i - x_i}{\left(\sum x_i\right)^2}F\left(\sum x_i\right) = 0$$

(13.28)

Theoretically, we now have n first-order conditions for the n agents that would need solving—to circumvent this rather extensive exercise, we introduce a symmetry assumption and set $\sum x_i = n x_i^*$, where the asterisk denotes every agents' Nash equilibrium allocation to the CPR. Substituting in Eq. (13.28) yields

$$-w + \frac{1}{n}F'(nx_i^*) + \frac{n-1}{n^2 x_i^*}F(nx_i^*) = 0. \quad (13.29)$$

Now, we can compare this equilibrium allocation to the investment that would maximize the overall group yield from private and collective investment. The overall output for the group is given by (with x as the vector of the individual allocations to the CPR)

$$u(x) = nwe - w\sum x_i + F\left(\sum x_i\right). \quad (13.30)$$

There is a unique solution maximizing this expression, that can be found from the first-order condition,

$$-w + F'\left(\sum x_i\right) = 0. \quad (13.31)$$

Comparing Eqs. (13.31) and (13.29), we find that they give different results. This means that the agents' equilibrium behavior is not collectively optimal. If they found a way to coordinate their behavior and overcome the Nash behavior, they could improve their results.

13.13.3 The Lab Experiments

As said, for a structured analysis of which and how mechanisms allow groups to improve their results beyond a Nash outcome, a number of experiments have been carried out. Two mechanisms that were found to change the results in group interactions in experiments were incorporated into the experimental setups, namely communication between the agents and a possibility to punish other actors. Different ways to incorporate the mechanisms and different combinations of them were tested by comparing the average outcome achieved by different groups.

Now, even where those mechanisms are introduced, the Nash equilibrium, and hence model prediction, does not change—communication that does not yield any enforceable results does not change the underlying payoff structure and Nash behavior (cheap talk). Punishment, as soon as it is costly to implement, actually reduces the payoff to the punishing agent as well and is hence dominated by a strategy that refrains from meting it out (empty threat). So even if such additional mechanisms are included, the Nash prediction is not changed—however, both mechanisms seem to have a significant influence on individuals' behavior in lab reality.

A baseline experiment lets agents play the CPR game as shown above, in two settings that were differentiated by the endowments of the agents. One endowment gave agents only little more than the Nash contribution to the CPR (the Nash contribution does not depend on the size of the endowment, see Eq. (13.29)).

The second group received a substantially larger endowment—as a consequence, the return from the CPR would diminish substantially even if only few agents tried to exploit the CPR by investing a higher share of their endowment in it (think of the endowment as productivity enhanced labor, for instance). More specifically, in the low-endowment setting, around 90% of the overall endowment would have to be invested in the CPR to yield a 0% return, whereas in the high-endowment setting, less than 40% of the overall endowment invested in the CPR would achieve that outcome. In the baseline settings without communication (and thus no possibility of reaching agreements; or, covenants, hence the title) and without punishment (the sword in the title), the group results in both cases approached the aggregate Nash contribution. However, the results still fluctuated on the individual level, with Ostrom et al. reporting that no individual stabilization on the Nash contribution occurred. Overall, the individual agents were not able to solve the problem of collective action they were facing in the baseline experiment.

That changes once communication and punishment mechanisms were introduced. First, we will briefly present the results achieved by groups that could only communicate, then those by groups that could only punish, and finally those that were able to use both mechanisms.

Communication was either repeatedly possible or a one-off option. In the groups that were allowed to communicate repeatedly (with that option being introduced after a few rounds were played), returns from the CPR increased substantially, in the low- as well as in the high-endowment group. The low-endowment groups eventually got very close to 100% yields from the CPR. The high-endowment groups achieved only around 70%, however, from a much lower initial level. One-shot communication (where there was one possibility to communicate in the group after a few rounds of playing) also increased yields, but the effect was reduced again after a while, even though returns stayed substantially above those of the first rounds, when agents had not communicated to each other and had less experience in the game.

So, all settings in which communication was allowed managed to achieve a significantly higher yield than the Nash prediction would have suggested. Depending on whether communication was *one-shot or repeated*, outcomes varied, with higher returns being achieved in settings with repeated communication. As communication involved agreeing on a joint strategy (trying collectively not to invest too much into the CPR, where investment is resources dedicated to its exploitation), a possibility for defection came into play in that specific setup as well—but even without punishment mechanisms, repeated communication brought defection rates to extremely low levels.

The next experiments included a *punishment* only option (that was opened after a few rounds had been played). Individuals received data on the contributions of their fellow group members and could decide to put a fine on them (at a cost to themselves as well). Returns to the CPR increased significantly after the punishment mechanism was introduced. However, a lot of the gross gain was lost again in paying for the implementation of fines and the cost to those who were being punished. The overall willingness to punish infractions was significantly higher than predicted by theory. Additionally, a nontrivial amount of punishments occurred that were not related directly to previous high investments in the CPR, but rather seemed motivated by revenge on the side of agents receiving fines in earlier rounds or appear to simply be attributable to mistakes.

It would appear that without communication options, not only have people difficulties in solving a collective action problem. At the same time, the option of punishment is not used wisely but at too high a rate, leading to only slightly improved net outcomes for the group (over the first rounds).

The best results were achieved in those groups that could *communicate and punish*. Overall, the outcomes of the different experimental setups "suggest that some subjects can find yield-improving joint strategies, design a sanctioning mechanism, use the sanctioning mechanism, and achieve a high rate of conformance to their joint strategy" (Ostrom et al., 1992, p. 413). Frequently, agents will be able to deal with collective action problems, if they are given appropriate tools for formulating agreements, monitoring adherence to the agreements made, and punishing those group members who deviate from the agreed course of action. Such tools may hence initiate, accelerate, and/or stabilize emerging institutions of cooperation. Where internal group dynamics have not proven sufficient for establishing such tools, an external agent establishing conditions to facilitate cooperation among the agents may be able to structure situations in a way that supports private agents attaining improved results (see Chapters 14 and 17).

Chapter References

Arthur, W.B., 1989. Competing technologies, increasing returns, and lock-in by historical events. Econ. J. 99 (394), 116–131.

Arthur, W.B., 1994. Inductive reasoning and bounded rationality. Am. Econ. Rev. (A.E.A. Papers and Proc.). 84, 406–411.

Arthur, W.B., Ermoliev, Y.M., Kaniovskii, Y.M., 1982/1983. A generalized urn problem and its applications. Cybernetics. 19, 61–71.

Axelrod, R., 1984/2006. The Evolution of Cooperation. Basic Books, New York, NY.

Ayres, C.E., 1944/1978. The Theory of Economic Progress. New Issues Press, Western Michigan University, Kalamazoo, MI.

Barabási, A.-L., Albert, R., 1999. Emergence of scaling in random networks. Science. 284 (5439), 509–512.

Boccaletti, S., Latora, V., Moreno, Y., Chavez, M., Hwang, D.U., 2006. Complex networks: structure and dynamics. Phys. Rep. 424, 175–308.

Bush, P.D., 1983. An exploration of the structural characteristics of a Veblen–Ayres–Foster defined institutional domain. J. Econ. Issues. 17 (1), 35–66.

Bush, P.D., 1987. The theory of institutional change. J. Econ. Issues. 21 (3), 1075–1116.

Conlisk, J., 1989. An aggregate model of technological change. Q. J. Econ. 104 (4), 787–821.

Cooper, R.W., 1999. Coordination Games: Complementarities and Macroeconomics. Cambridge University Press, New York, NY.

Cooper, R.W., John, A., 1988. Coordinating coordination failures in Keynesian models. Q. J. Econ. 103 (3), 441–463.

David, P.A., 1985. Clio and the economics of QWERTY. Am. Econ. Rev. 75 (2), 332–337.

David, P.A., Bunn, J.A., 1988. The economics of gateway technologies and network evolution: lessons from electricity supply history. Inf. Econ. Policy. 3 (2), 165–202.

David, P.A., Steinmueller, W.E., 1994. Economics of compatibility standards and competition in telecommunication networks. Inf. Econ. Policy. 6 (3–4), 217–241.

Dorfman, J., 1959. The Economic Mind in American Civilization: 1918–1933. Viking Press, New York, NY.

Easley, D., Kleinberg, J., 2010. Networks, Crowds and Markets. Reasoning about a Highly Connected World. Cambridge University Press, Cambridge.

Elsner, W., 2011. Evolutionary institutionalism: sources, history and contemporary relevance of the association for evolutionary economics—AFEE, Intervention. Eur. J. Econ. Econ. Policies. 8 (1), 29–41.

Elsner, W., 2012. The theory of institutional change revisited. The institutional dichotomy, its dynamic, and its policy implications in a more formal analysis. J. Econ. Issues. XLVI1, 1–43.

Erdős, P., Rényi, A., 1959. On random graphs. I. Publicationes Mathematicae. 6, 290–297.

Frenken, K., Nuvolari, A., 2004. Entropy statistics as a framework to analyse technological evolution. In: Foster, J., Hoelzl, W. (Eds.), Applied Evolutionary Economics and Complex Systems. Edward Elgar, Cheltenham, Northampton, pp. 95–132.

Gintis, H., Bowles, S., Boyd, R.T., Fehr, E. (Eds.), 2005. Moral Sentiments and Material Interests: The Foundations of Cooperation in Economic Life. The MIT Press, Cambridge, MA.

Goyal, S., 2009. Connections. An Introduction to the Economics of Networks. Princeton University Press, Princeton, Oxford.

Gruchy, A., 1947/1967. Modern Economic Thought: The American Contribution. Augustus Kelley, Clifton, NJ.

Heinrich, T., 2013. Technological Change and Network Effects in Growth Regimes: Exploring the Microfoundations of Economic Growth. Routledge, Oxon, New York.

Heinrich, T., Schwardt, H., 2013. Institutional inertia and institutional change in an expanding normal-form game. Games. 4 (3), 398–425.

Hodgson, G.M, 1988. Economics and Institutions: A Manifesto for a Modern Institutional Economics. Polity Press and University of Pennsylvania Press, Polity Press and Basil Blackwell Press, Cambridge and Oxford.

Jackson, M.O., Zenou, Y. (Eds.), 2013. Economic Analyses of Social Networks. Edward Elgar, Cheltenham, UK.

Katz, M.L., Shapiro, C., 1985. Network externalities, competition and compatibility. Am. Econ. Rev. 75 (3), 424–440.

Kauffman, S.A., 1993. The Origins of Order. Oxford University Press, Oxford, UK.

Kauffman, S.A., 1995. At Home in the Universe. Viking Press, New York, NY.

Kauffman, S.A., Lobo, J., Macready, W.G., 2000. Optimal search on a technology landscape. J. Econ. Behav. Organ. 43 (2), 141–166.

Klemm, K., Eguíluz, V.M., 2002. Growing scale-free networks with small-world behavior. Physical Review E. 65, nb. 057102.

Kochen, M., 1989. Toward structural sociodynamics, in Manfred. In: Kochen (Ed.), The Small World. Ablex, Norwood, NJ, pp. 52–64.

Korte, C., Milgram, S., 1970. Acquaintance linking between White and Negro populations: application of the small world problem. J. Pers. Soc. Psychol. 15 (1), 101–118.

Liebowitz, S.J., Margolis, S.E., 1990. The fable of the keys. J. Law Econ. 33 (1), 1–25.

Lindgren, K., 1997. Evolutionary dynamics in game-theoretic models. In: Arthur, W.B., Durlauf, S.N., Lane, D.A. (Eds.), The Economy as an Evolving Complex System II. Addison Wesley, Reading, MA, pp. 337–367.

Milgram, S., 1967. The small world problem. Psychol. Today. 2 (1), 291–308.

Mitchell, J.C., 1969. The concept and use of social networks. In: Mitchell, J.C. (Ed.), Social Networks in Urban Situation. Manchester University Press, Manchester, UK, pp. 1–50.

Neale, W.C., 1994. Art. "Institutions". In: Hodgson, G.M, Samuels, W.J., Tool, M.R. (Eds.), The Elgar Companion to Institutional and Evolutionary Economics, vol. 1. Edward Elgar, Aldershot, Hants, UK, Brookfield, VT, USA, pp. 402–406.

Nelson, R.R., Winter, S.G., 1974. Neoclassical versus evolutionary theories of economic growth: critique and prospectus. Econ. J. 84 (336), 886–905.

Nelson, R.R., Winter, S.G., 1982. An Evolutionary Theory of Economic Change. Harvard University Press, Cambridge, MA.

Nelson, R.R., Winter, S.G., Schuette, H.L., 1976. Technical change in an evolutionary model. Q. J. Econ. 90 (1), 90–118.

Newman, M., 2003. The structure and function of complex networks. SIAM Rev. 45 (2), 167–256.

O'Hara, P.A, 2007. Principles of institutional-evolutionary political economy—converging themes from the schools of heterodoxy,. J Econ Issues. XLI (1), 1–42.

Ostrom, E., 1990. Governing the Commons: The Evolution of Institutions for Collective Action. Cambridge University Press, New York, NY.

Ostrom, E., Walker, J., Gardner, R., 1992. Covenants with and without a sword: self-governance is possible. Am. Polit. Sci. Rev. 86 (2), 404–417.

Ostrom, E., Walker, J., Gardner, R., 1994. Rules, Games and Common-Pool Resources. University of Michigan Press, Ann Arbor, MI.

Pool, I. de Sola, Kochen, M., 1978. Contacts and influence. Soc. Networks. 1 (1), 1–48.

Schelling, T.C., 1971. Dynamic models of segregation. J. Math. Sociol. 1 (2), 143–186.

Schelling, T.C., 1978. Micromotives and Macrobehavior. W. W. Norton, New York, London.

Schotter, A., 1981. The Economic Theory of Social Institutions. Cambridge University Press, New York, NY.

Sen, A., 1967. Isolation, assurance and the social rate of discount. Q. J. Econ. 81 (1), 112–124.

Silverberg, G., Lehnert, D., 1993. Long waves and "Evolutionary Chaos" in a simple Schumpeterian model of embodied technical change. Struct. Change Econ. Dyn. 4 (1), 9–37.

Simon, H.A., 1955. On a class of skew distribution functions. Biometrika. 42 (3–4), 425–440.

Skvoretz, J., 1985. Random and biased networks: simulations and approximations. Soc. Networks. 7 (3), 225–261.

van Steen, M., 2010. Graph theory and complex networks. An introduction. Available at: <http://www.distributed-systems.net/>.

Watts, D.J., 1999a. Networks, dynamics, and the small-world phenomenon. Am. J. Sociol. 105 (2), 493–527.

Watts, D.J., 1999b. Small Worlds: The Dynamics of Networks Between Order and Randomness. Princeton University Press, Princeton, NJ.

Watts, D.J., Strogatz, S.H., 1998. Collective dynamics of "Small-World" networks. Nature. 393 (4), 440–442.

Wilensky, U., 1997. *NetLogo Segregation Model*, Center for Connected Learning and Computer-Based Modeling. Northwestern University, Evanston, IL. Available at: <http://ccl.northwestern.edu/netlogo/models/segregation>.

Wilensky, U., 1999. *NetLogo*, Center for Connected Learning and Computer-Based Modeling. Northwestern University, Evanston, IL. Available at: <http://ccl.northwestern.edu/netlogo>.

Further Reading—Online

For further reading, see the textbook website at http://booksite.elsevier.com/9780124115859

The Size Dimension of Complex Economies—Towards a Meso-Economics: The Size of Interaction Arenas and the Emergence of Meso-Platforms of Institutional Coordination*

"Small is beautiful? Small is effective! (... a necessary condition of effective cooperation in complex economies)." **(Wolfram Elsner, Torsten Heinrich, Henning Schwardt)**

"[...] viable systems must be selectively connected, and [...] viable large systems are highly-decomposable assemblies of smaller systems." **Brian J. Loasby[1]**

*This chapter was coauthored by Claudius Gräbner.

[1]"Building Systems," Journal of Evolutionary Economics, **22.4** (2012), pp. 833–846, p. 833.

14.1 INTRODUCTION: WHY AGENTS MIGHT RATIONALLY STRIVE FOR SMALLER STRUCTURES

This chapter resumes the issue of the emergence of a social institution of cooperation as already well known by the reader from Chapters 1–3 and 13, and, in a more technical context, Chapters 8–11. The real world is not a unique economic interaction arena, where more than 7 billion human agents and millions of firms and other organizations exist together, evenly and completely connected and interacting to generate some basic collective decisions and behavior for the ubiquitous social dilemmas. It is formed, rather, by many different populations (called interaction arenas in the following) and by countless smaller and overlapping places, net structures (or lattice, or grid structures—termed *network* in the following), and subpopulations, i.e., spatially and/or socially defined entities such as clusters and networks, regions and localities. We may consider these overlapping subarenas.

Not only real-world agents, namely human agents, but also organizations, including firms, are usually incapable of taking coordinated decisions simultaneously together with billions, millions, or even just thousands of other agents. Cognitive, psychological, and organizational factors suggest that all kinds of agents, when trying to solve problems of direct interdependence, strive to make their relevant decision and action arenas, their relevant populations, their peer groups, and the carrier groups of emerging institutions (called interaction platforms in the following) smaller if possible, and thus more transparent and manageable for themselves. The critical factors related to the size dimension that we introduce in this chapter indicate that higher efficacy, related expectations, and eventually trust and thus the capability and willingness of behavioral innovation, problem solving, rule-based

behavior, and sustainable coordination and cooperation are more easily achieved in smaller platforms below the size of the initial larger populations relevant for particular interaction issues.

We refer to what we explained on the population perspective of analyzing emergent institutions already in Sections 3.2.2 and 3.2.3. Moreover, as has been explained in Chapter 4, firms in the real world tend to cluster and network—and increasingly so, the larger (more global), more obscure and more turbulent their environment is (on the counter movement of localism for preserving intangible cultural heritage against globalization, see Garon, 2012). In this way, the emergence of institutions, or more generally: of structure, will depend on some meso-sized group of institutionally coordinated agents (in fact, agents cooperating in face of social dilemmas; see Chapter 3) within a larger population. This most basic social fact of economics will be rationally reconstructed in an approach to a broader future meso-economics.

The general framework, within which the concepts in this chapter are introduced, still is an economy as a complex system, meaning a system consisting of a potentially large number of heterogeneous constituting elements (agents) interacting in nontrivial ways. The system therefore will show properties that cannot be inferred from the analysis of those single elements. We have some fundamental building blocks that interact in a way that the result cannot be described and analyzed by reference to these building blocks only, but require some additional elements. A crucial characteristic of such system is the ability for self-organization, i.e., the *emergence of structure* without external enforcement resulting in a stable final state or set of states (for the definition of emergence, see Section 11.2.2).

In the last sections of this chapter, we present mechanisms that are critical for the emergence of institutions from the interactions of individual agents. These rules that then are drawn on for stabilizing agents' expectations and structuring agents' interactions are in this setting the outcome of individual interactions, not following a particular design but, as said, emerging on a level beyond their constitutive microeconomic interactions.

14.2 TERMS AND OVERVIEW

14.2.1 Expectations

The (subjectively perceived) importance of the common future, i.e., expectations (as explained in Chapters 1, 2, 3, and 8) to meet

- either the same partner again,
- or an agent who knows about my earlier behavior through some channel,
- or an agent of a particular type (namely a cooperator, who starts cooperating without knowing about my earlier behavior),

in agents' subsequent interactions will be critical to the outcome they will achieve. This expectation will help to determine the individual's decision on her behavior and possibly the size of the emerging carrier group. Particularly, in a population perspective, the individuals need to form expectations about the population shares of those agents who apply certain strategies.

14.2.2 Agency Capabilities

Further, agency capabilities and mechanisms such as memory, monitoring, reputation building and the use of reputation chains, and particularly active partner selection based on knowledge gained through those mechanisms will be introduced. With continuing random encounters at the beginning of every round, agents are assumed capable of forming some expectations over time, based on their experience and empirically gained knowledge about agents. They then, using this knowledge, will

sometimes be able to reject the next interaction partner who they randomly encounter. In this way, agents will be able (within limits) to generate and sort out their individual relevant population of interaction partners, i.e., their peer group (see Section 14.6.4).

14.2.3 Expectations in Meso-Sized Groups

These mechanisms will allow relevant emerging group (platform) size to increase from very small into meso-sizes, while keeping expectations to meet a cooperator next round sufficiently high. Expectations then can be supportive to institutional emergence even in a meso-sized group, conserving cooperation as the superior strategy for the individual even after group size has increased.

14.2.4 Exhaustion of Cooperative Advantage

However, if these agency mechanisms for some reason lose power and efficacy with increasing use, or reach some limits, defectors may increasingly profit from the growing numbers of cooperators, and the institution will be carried by some maximum group size smaller than the whole population involved. For instance, reputation chains may generate decreasing net information gains when expanded into a larger distance. In this way, the arena and the platform disconnect, thus qualifying informal institutionalized coordination as a truly meso-economic phenomenon.

14.2.5 A Maximum Critical Mass

Nevertheless, some initial minimum critical mass of cooperators has to come into being through some motivation to diversify behavior (see Chapter 3), as, as a benchmark, we start from a world of common defection. In the end, this may lead to the takeover of the whole population by cooperators under ideal conditions. However, if the relative success of common cooperation, as supported by the agency mechanisms indicated above, should become exhausted with a growing share of cooperators, the process will yield the relevant cooperating group smaller than the whole population, the maximum critical mass.

14.2.6 Manifold Applications

This all may contribute to a general meso-economics, where meso-groups, platforms, or systems in manifold socioeconomic areas (regional, industrial, or professional clusters and networks, agglomerations, segregation and neighborhood structures, etc.) may become the theoretical locus of emergent structure. Coordinated systems of such sizes may have a specific capability of innovative collective action and thus eventually high macro-performance as well. Some areas of application, instances of relevance, and references, overlapping in manifold ways, have been:

- for the most prominent and largest field study of different interaction structures in small-scale societies (Henrich et al., 2004)[2];
- for a more general systems theory, according to which viable systems must be selectively connected and decomposable into smaller systems (Loasby, 2012)[3];
- for an ontological foundation and theoretical definition of institutions as meso-phenomena (Dopfer et al., 2004; Dopfer, 2007, 2012; for more details, see Section 14.3);

- for general theoretical considerations of the economic efficacy and innovation capacity of (smaller) size (Legum, 2007; Rose, 2011, Chapter 3);
- on industrial and firm applications (with firm clusters and networks of meso-size) (Huggins and Johnston, 2010; Chertow and Ehrenfeld, 2012, and the references given already in Chapter 4);
- for advantageous influences of a general spatial meso-scale and neighborhood (Batten, 2001, 89ff.; Jun and Sethi, 2007; McCann, 2007; Goldenberg, 2010; Nousala, 2010);
- for the greater effectiveness of smaller firm size, for cognitive limits and limits of informational transmission (Cordes et al., 2011);
- for knowledge workers, it has been found that the size of their professional network has an inverted U-shaped effect on their job performance, i.e., there is an optimal (smaller) network size that they can maximally effectively deal with (of around 10 in that case) (Chen and Gable, 2013);
- on the more recent issue of processes of decomposing (shrinking, balkanizing) the internet into smaller arenas (Ozcan and Santos, 2010; Wells, 2010; Waterman and Ji, 2011; Jones, 2012; Saunders, 2012; and the references given in Chapter 15);
- the topical issues of micro-finance and P2P-lending also reflect the criticality of small groups and nets that specifically can mobilize the critical factors and mechanisms of successfully overcoming opportunism

[2]In this study group size has been but one critical factor among others and interferes with other factors to form different interaction conditions and trigger different resulting degrees of institutionalized cooperation. The real societies explored have all been small scale (ranging between 75 and some 1200 members). In fact, size was found in this largest cross-cultural field experiment ever to be a good predictor (similar and related to anonymity and complexity) for payoffs to cooperation and group performance.

[3]On the new branch of the "economics of identity," according to which (conscious) group membership has (both theoretically and in lab experiments) consistently positive effects on cooperation and economic and social performance (Hermann-Pillath, 2011, 169ff.; Guala et al., 2013).

and defection in social dilemmas through trust, social capital, and cooperation (Lin et al., 2009);

- a specific application has become the issues of trust and size: both trust and size have been major and topical, but (so far) separate issues in broader socioeconomic and institutional research; it is rather obvious in both empirical observation and theoretical modeling that favorable expectations relate to smaller arena and platform sizes (Fukuyama, 1995, Chapter 3); for inter-firm cooperation and regional industrial districts (Farrell, 2009); for urban systems of culture, trust, and related social capital (Häkli, 2009); for general (spatial) proximity as fostering trust through interaction density and face-to-face interaction (Rocco, 2005; McCann, 2007; Huggins and Johnston, 2010; Nousala, 2010; Parlamis and Ames, 2010); for the learning and innovation effects of trust in manageable arena sizes (Lazaric and Lorenz, 1998); the evolution-of-cooperation approach has been a standard perspective here; we have discussed trust and arena size in more detail elsewhere (Elsner and Schwardt, 2013);
- attendance problems and segregation as examples: specifically, there has been a renewed interest in Nobel Laureate Schelling's (1969, 1973, 1978) early investigations in the emergence of stable coordination in attendance problems and in emergent spatial segregation (Vinkovic and Kirman, 2006; Aydinonat, 2007; Waldeck, 2010; see also Elster, 1989); the attendance coordination problem (see W.B. Arthur's *El Farol Bar* attendance coordination problem, Arthur, 1994) also has triggered research on coordination success and failure, which implies a meso-size issue (a stable equilibrium attendance will be smaller than the potential maximum attendance); we have explained the original segregation and attendance models in Chapter 13;

- agency, selectivity, and reputation: in particular, an emerging theory of the critical mass (see Marwell and Oliver, 1988, 1993 with a focus on big and powerful agents and coalitions that these can bring together) has clearly elaborated the critical roles of *selectivity* in interactions in populations and particularly on specific topologies of populations, i.e., networks, with a clear affinity to smaller size (neighborhood, proximity) (Spiekermann, 2009; Konno, 2010), and of deploying *reputation chains* (Phelps, 2012); in the present chapter, we will apply these (and other, like memory and monitoring) agency mechanisms.

For the great bulk of game-theoretic and network-analytic studies on the relevance of (smaller) size for overall economic and social efficacy, see the literature given in Section 14.3.

- Note also that earlier, nonevolutionary uses of the conception and term *"meso"*-economics have included more or less static or comparative-static approaches to the *large corporation* (big business) having come to dominate the economy (Holland, 1987), *industry or sector models* of representative behavior and adaptions to sector-relevant parametric demand shifts (Ng, 1986), for *oligopolistic competition* and cooperative *network forms of industrial coordination* (Ozawa, 1999), or just for *regions and industries* as "mid-sized" economic units and levels (Peters, 1990). All these usages appear to be somewhat simple, a-theoretic, outmoded, and far off an evolutionary emergent perspective of structures as developed and applied here.

14.2.7 Incomplete Information, Lacking Adaptive and Learning Pressure, and Other Caveats

Note, however, that a heroic presumption of most game-theoretic arguments is complete information. Agents are assumed to have a direct observable connection between actions and outcomes and thus intense incentives or pressure to learn. This transparency is rarely the case in reality where the direct connection of action to feedback and thus the pressure to learn typically is considerably weaker. Real societies, even "primitive" and small-scale ones, thus display a surprising variety of degrees of learned and institutionalized cooperation and reciprocity (Henrich et al., 2004). Empirically, even small groups sometimes show low levels of cooperation. They can afford certain levels of noncooperation and conflict. However, typically, the backup capacity of humans to improve their position with low levels of cooperation is exploiting the commons of nature and this, regrettably, does not immediately and transparently feed back to the agent, as the Commons tend to be more or less global and remote rather than local and immediately perceivable.

But, anyway, the capacity of learning of direct interdependence will increase ceteris paribus with a decreasing group size, and thus some logic and rationality of superior problem solving may push agents collectively into appropriately organizing their decision structures, including cogenerating (without conscious collective design) a proper platform size.

14.2.8 The Danger of Strong Ties, Lock-In, and the Potential Degeneration of Institutions

Another important caveat regarding formal analyses of the superiority of small-scale cooperation refers to the ubiquitous dangers of strong ties, lock-in of cooperation systems, and the related potential deterioration of institutions into ceremonial abstract norms rather than continuing adequate collective problem-solving rules (see Liet al., 2013 and also the discussion of the theory and model of Institutional Change of P.D. Bush in Chapters 1, 3, and 13). We will discuss this further below.

14.2.9 Break-Out from Lock-In: From Analysis to Application and Political Design

If meso-size is relevant, it can be used for political design to generate institutional emergence and high macro-performance (see Chapter 17). This is particularly relevant because, as we have explained in Chapters 1 and 13, institutionally coordinated systems may possibly also become petrified, sclerotic, ossified, or locked-in, through ceremonial dominance. This is particularly the case if, in the course of their life cycles, instrumental collective action capability cannot properly and timely be renewed to break the system out when necessary (for the classical formal model of technological lock-in, see Arthur, 1989, and the classic for institutional lock-in, see David, 1985, as explained in Chapter 13; for break-out, see Dolfsma and Leydesdorff, 2009; and for policy action to both help institutionalization and (later) break-out, see Chapter 17).

14.2.10 Micro-to-Macro Aggregation or Meso Emergence?—the Systematic Place of Meso

It has often been argued that the macro-level, conventionally understood as the national level of formal organization and public agency, has become less relevant in a (global) cultural emergence perspective. Thus, it is highly relevant, whether it still is appropriate to consider informal institutional emergence under a micro-to-macro perspective and terminology or to conceptualize meso as a socioeconomic level of its own (see Hodgson, 2000 on the conception of emergence (micro-to-macro); Ayres and Martinás, 2005; Foster, 2005). We will argue here that there are considerable theoretical and empirical reasons to envisage a specific level of informal cultural emergence below, and across, conventional macro-jurisdictions (which typically are the loci of enculturation).

Since an emergent structure is not reducible to its initial micro-components, it is of course above the micro-level. In all, what complex evolutionary institutional theorizing, modeling or simulation, and real-world clusters, networks and all kinds of group cultures are all about may require a theoretical space of its own—meso (Chen, 2008).

We have defined micro as the level of individual agents and their interactions. As soon as some structure (institution) has emerged that exists independently of any individual agent's action, we understand this to belong to the meso-level (see Chapter 11). A meso-sized group is defined as any relevant group smaller than the larger whole population involved. Finally, if the relevant group can be shown to be smaller than the whole population the latter may be considered to belong to the macro-level, mirroring perhaps the real-world national level.

14.3 SIZE AND MESO-SIZE OF POPULATIONS AND GROUPS IN THE LITERATURE

14.3.1 Ontological Foundation of "Meso"

As mentioned, some evolutionary economists have elaborated on meso and the process of the generation, adoption, diffusion, and retention of institutions as meso-rules (Dopfer et al., 2004; Dopfer, 2001, 2007, 2012; Dopfer and Potts, 2008, Chapter 4). They have argued that, and have theoretically described how, the origination, adoption, diffusion, and retention of a rule take place in a group of carriers with a population of actualizations of an ideal generic rule at some meso-level of the economy. However, they have not elaborated on specific causal mechanisms, by which such meso-entities come into existence in order to solve specific problems.

14.3.2 A Causal-Genetic Approach

In addition to that (more definitional/ontological) approach, it has been advocated "to bring interests back into our thinking about (...) routine production" (Gibbons, 2006, p. 381) referring to the emergence of institutions (evolution of cooperation) and the folk theorem (see Chapters 3 and 8): "one cannot analyze just the evolution of beliefs" (p. 385). In fact, the game-theoretic approach is about a complex interest structure in which results are reached through mutual adaptations of behaviors and expectations.

In the present chapter, thus, we will further explore (beyond what has been referred to in Chapter 3) a simple logic of relations among

- a problematic incentive structure,
- expectations to meet (again),
- the group size, and
- the institution as such.

14.3.3 Theoretical and Methodological Literature So Far

Many have paved the way for exploring critical size. Beyond the applications we have already mentioned in Section 14.2, we may sort the theoretical and methodological literature under a number of overlapping aspects:

- *A Pioneering Analysis—M. Olson*: Group size has been a more or less obvious issue of the collective-good problem since Olson's (1965) *Logic of Collective Action*, where the collective good has a better chance of being produced the smaller the relevant group, which is constituted to generate the good. Some have investigated critical masses in collective action along Olsonian lines (Marwell and Oliver, 1993; Dejean et al., 2008), mainly considering, in consistence with Olson's pessimistic static and non-evolutionary perspective, large contributors to the collective good.

The latter can either produce the good alone or mobilize a selected minimum producer group. The evolutionary emergent perspective that has been developed since then, however, does not follow the path of one major producer.

- *The Evolution-of-Cooperation Framework— Minimum Critical Masses and Segregation*: Robert Axelrod's 1980 approach to a quasi-evolutionary simulation of emergent cooperation with its applications to (spatial and/or social) segregation and its critical role of sufficiently stable expectations (i.e., little turbulence; see Chapters 3, 8, and 13), is still widely discussed (see Axelrod, 1984 and the citation statistics in R. Dawkins' foreword to the 2nd edition, 2006), and the iterated prisoners' dilemma (PD) approach of the evolution of cooperation, accordingly, is still much applied and further elaborated in an evolutionary context (Ostrom et al., 1994; Knudsen, 2002; Devezas and Corredine, 2002; Eckert et al., 2005; Goyal, 2005; Traulsen and Nowak, 2006; Mohlin, 2010). The evolutionary dynamics in a PD, when controlling for a broad range of initial conditions and allowing for a variety and an ongoing generation of ever more complex strategies, has been developed far beyond standard PD supergame equilibria or well-defined attractor solutions (Lindgren and Nordahl, 1994; Binmore, 1998). Furthermore, there is some indication that, in contrast to pure game-theoretic modeling, cooperation may emerge in evolutionary process even under finitely repeated PD (Lindgren et al., 2013). We have explained the Axelrodian approach in Chapter 13. In this chapter, we will deal in the larger framework of the evolution of cooperation as explained above.
- *Games on Networks*: Game theorists in general have found overwhelming confirmation recently of the relevance of (meso) group/platform/network size, both in modeling (Hargreaves Heap, 2008, 80ff.) and in lab experiments (Yamagishi, 1992; Zhang and Bolten, 2011). Generally, in the newly emerged research field of games on networks, *network size* and *network structures* as well as related critical factors such as high interaction density (frequent interactions per period), (stable) expectations and general stability (little mobility, turbulence, change) have been comprehensively investigated in order to explain effective institutional emergence of cooperation (Goyal, 1996; Foley, 1998; Watts, 1999, Chapter 8; Zelmer, 2003; Jun and Sethi, 2009; Carpenter et al., 2010; Jackson and Zenou, 2012; Zenou, 2012; for the conception of emergence used throughout this textbook, see Section 11.3.3). We have explained some examples of core models using games on networks in Chapter 13.
- *Network (or Group) Formation*: A branch of this research field also deals with the evolution of institutions in networks (including network size) and explores the critical factors (Demange and Wooders, 2005; Page and Wooders, 2007; Zenou, 2012, 7ff.).
- *Institutional(ist) Game Theory*: Institutionally oriented game theorists, such as A. Schotter, A.J. Field, S.P. Hargreaves Heap, or E. Ostrom, have built bridges between game theory and evolutionary institutional theorizing, and the size dimension has mostly played some role here, tacitly or explicitly (for an overview of the issues, see Dosi and Winter, 2000; Ostrom, 2007; for particular game-theoretic models reflecting the *Veblenian—Darwinian* tradition of evolutionary economics, see Hargreaves Heap and Varoufakis, 2004; Villena and Villena, 2004; Field, 2007; Hédoin, 2010; Watkins, 2010; Pelligra, 2011). In addition, many evolutionary institutionalist economists have elaborated on institutional emergence and group or

network conceptions of the individual (Hodgson, 2000, 2006; Davis, 2007, 2008). And some particularly have contended that institutions are meso, emerge at some intermediate level, and are effective in mid-sized groups, etc. (van Staveren, 2001, 179f.; Elsner, 2000). We have explained more on the approach of evolutionary institutional theorizing and the application of game-theoretic tools to it in Chapter 12 (Veblen) and Chapter 13 (The Theory of Institutional Change).

- *The Methodological Perspective—Proper Story-Telling, Embedding of Formalism, and Applications*: It has turned out in the last decades of developing and applying complex modeling that there is no complex formal modeling without a proper qualitative evolutionary process story (Dosi and Winter, 2000; Gruene-Yanoff and Schweinzer, 2008). This is very much in line with the qualitative-verbal methodological tradition of embedded pattern modeling, rather than pure formalism, of evolutionary institutional economics and other perspectives critical to the neoclassical mainstream. In this chapter, we will indeed embed a simple formal logic in such a frame.

- *The Naturalistic Perspective*: As should have become obvious, it is well established in the complexity economics literature from various theoretical and methodological perspectives and different fields of application that some smaller size (below the conventional national macro and national population) tends to support the emergence of institutionalized cooperation (culture) in ubiquitous (obvious or tacit) social dilemmas and that institutions of cooperation thus are to be considered some meso-sized entities. As already indicated, representatives of the transdisciplinary biological, anthropological, and behavioral perspectives, dealing with so-called cultural group selection or multilevel selection

(i.e., evolutionary process among both individuals and whole groups), in particular have argued that in the real world humans do in fact cooperate both in large-scale populations and one-shot interactions (Henrich, 2004; Boyd and Richerson, 2005). The group-selection approach has indeed established a reconstruction of the vast and rapid human development of widespread reciprocity and cooperation, which, in turn, requires explaining the particular interactions of biogenetic and cultural evolution through the very mechanism of group selection. On the level of the individual human brain, Dunbar (2011) has argued that the relative neocortex volume and, thus, cognitive capability of humans have led to social group sizes not above 150 agents, related to information flows and information processing capabilities. Furthermore, social groups are layered formations, starting from emotionally close and few kinship relations to groups of the above-mentioned size, with different degrees of interaction frequencies and, thus, information flows, experience, social learning, expectations building, and, finally, emerging cooperation intensities and socioeconomic performances. Anthropological records, considering the conditions of free-riding opportunities on nutrition available, show typical group sizes of around 30, which still could easily deal with restricting opportunism and free riding (Marlowe, 2005, pp. 57—60). Modern evolutionary—developmental (evo—devo) biology has made huge progress in analyzing the manifold processes of emerging institutionalized cooperation, from the molecular and genetic through the individual/brain/organic and inter-individual levels to the inter-group interaction level (Wilson, 2012), covering both genetic and cultural evolutions. The basic message here is that a whole range of cooperation levels may emerge in groups. These levels correspond with different performance and replication levels. Groups then, basically, are selected that display higher levels of cooperation (and thus performance and replication). These findings have contributed much to establish a modern transdisciplinary science of human social behavior and institutionalization (Bowles et al., 2003; Fehr and Henrich, 2003; Field, 2006, 2007; Hamilton et al., 2009). In most of this literature, game-theoretic modeling plays some helpful analytical role, and groups typically display some maximum size that still is manageable for human agents in terms of cognitive information diffusion and processing (and sometimes emotional capacity) and beyond which groups tend to split up (Bowles et al., 2003; Traulsen and Nowak, 2006). Early claims that game theory could not be helpful in explaining large-scale cooperation even with strangers, as early predictions of "pure" game-theoretic models would have predicted universal defection in social dilemmas as enforced Nash equilibria (Henrich, 2004, pp. 7–9), thus appear to be obsolete nowadays.

- *Toward an Integrated Perspective*: In fact, as said, properly embedded evolutionary game theory plays an important supportive in most studies (Field, 2006, 2007; Gintis, 2000, 2004), so that it has been suggested to be an integral part of the unification of the behavioral sciences (Gintis, 2007, 2008). Critical factors such as the incentive structure (payoff structure), interaction density, information flows in arenas and platforms of certain sizes and perhaps topologies (network/neighborhood structures), interaction experience and expectations, relative stability versus change (e.g., mobility/emigration/immigration; Bowles et al., 2003) appear to be rationally reconstructed in their relations to superior/

inferior performance within a game-theoretic evolution-of-cooperation perspective. The group-selection mechanism appears complementary to such an approach, properly embedded in an evolutionary institutional and also naturalistic interpretation (see Elsner, 2012, with proper story telling, Dosi and Winter, 2000 and also Hodgson and Huang, 2012), and itself also appears apt to modeling within this framework, this might do the job for the intra- and inter-group developments of cooperation. The generalization of institutionalized cooperation even for one-shot encounters and even in large populations thus appears to be a common ground of theorizing and modeling among naturalistic approaches and evolutionary institutionalism. In this context, the argument in the following will be that experienced reciprocation in a number of meso-sized platforms is both a necessary and sufficient condition for the spillover from one arena/platform to another and the generalization of institutions even for large-scale one-shot cooperation (for more details, see Elsner and Schwardt, 2013). The inner size structure (or deep structure) of a population (economy, society, or nation), and related issues such as reduced turbulence, thus, explicitly arises as a critical variable explaining high levels of general cooperation and macro-performance—and in the last instance it may even be policy relevant for generating effective system structures (see Section 14.7).

We will show that how particular expectations and agency capabilities are logically required and, step by step, need to come into the picture to facilitate effectively cooperating meso-platforms, many of which, in turn, then may overlap and make up for a general culture of always initial cooperation even in a large-scale population.

14.4 THE UBIQUITY OF THE DILEMMA PROBLEM AND EMERGENT STRUCTURE AGAIN

14.4.1 A Ubiquitous Everyday Problem Embedding Every Single and Simple Transaction

The prominent relevance and everyday ubiquity of the collective-good/social dilemma/PD problem, although one of most cited and used collective decision structures in modern economic literature, requires a careful explication.

There is in fact a collective-good problem involved in numerous economic decisions, however, individualistic, private, and separable it may appear to the individual. Social dilemmas can be involved even in the most simple supermarket purchase, but of course, also in any more demanding technological coordination problem in the fragmented value-added chain (see Chapter 4).

14.4.2 Dominant Incentives to Free Ride or Exploit—Technology Choice and Innovation in the Value-Added Chain

If a fully fledged emerged, learned, and habituated institution already exists, then typically agents actively contribute to the reproduction of this institution, and of the corresponding expectations (general trust) of others, through cooperative behavior.

However, if an agent may expect another agent to behave in a cooperative way next interaction, then there may exist, under certain conditions, a dominant incentive for the first agent not to contribute. By not contributing (s)he may take the opportunity of a potential short-run extra gain by, for instance, running away without paying, by somehow cheating, secretly avoiding own costs, secretly (or overtly) exploiting some Commons, exploiting positive externalities from the cooperative actions of others,

etc., as the reader has already learned in the introductory chapters of this book. For instance, in the fragmented value-added chain, the incentive to free ride by saving R&D expenses and profit from incoming knowledge spillovers, which are to some extent inappropriable by their creators, may become virulent. As we have seen (in a more applied context in Chapter 4 and in a formal model in Chapter 13), even in a random net-technology choice problem, agents may be dominantly incited to free ride by waiting until others have made their decisions, in this way avoiding later regret—if they can afford to wait, otherwise they may have to incur the loss and regret from misinvestment.

Generally, agents in a more or less individualistic behavioral culture and under individualistic conditions may be incited to defect in manifold situations and ways. And they will do so insofar as the situation is not fully governed by institutions (not considering formal hierarchical control and enforcement, private or public) and a number of critical factors preventing opportunism are lacking. So any socioeconomic (trans-)action is embedded in a larger dilemma problem and will, or will not, contribute to the production or reproduction of the general frame of expectations, which in turn allow for, or undermine, institutions to overcome that basic dilemma. Specifically, if the institution does not exist in a dilemma situation yet, the individualist agent will not contribute to its production and assume the free-rider position; if it does already exist, the agent will not contribute to its fortification (will free ride again) but exploit it rather, assuming an exploiter position.

14.4.3 Collective-Good Character of Basic Information

In accordance with a large applied literature, we have explained already in Chapters 1–4 and 13, and will further elaborate on this in Chapters 15 and 16, that any production, information, and innovation system, under conditions of fragmented value-added chains and of complex integrated products, of competing net technologies, and of the collective-good character of basic information, can be modeled as a system of direct interdependence, of mutual positive and negative externalities, of collectivities, and, in a process perspective, of cumulative action, such that it can be reconstructed as a PD-SG.

14.4.4 Proper Institutionalized Problem Solving and Other Solutions in Reality

However, the PD structure often is only tacit, exists only in the background, while the observable social surface, as perceivable to the average individual, is dominated by some solution, some form of institutionalized arrangement. Again leaving private or public hierarchical command systems, such as the firm, corporation, and the state, aside, in terms of institutionalized cultures, this may be a fully appropriate instrumental institution. It may also be some institutional or technological lock-in, or even a completely mutually blocked situation with general free riding and noninnovative action, i.e., some rule-based ceremonially defection (see Chapter 12 on Veblen), motivated by invidious distinction and fierce rivalry.

14.4.5 Degeneration of Problem-Solving Institutions and the "Social Surface"

In a life cycle of institutions, with emerging lock-in of earlier cooperation and with insufficient collective action capability to generate new problem-solving institutions, ceremonial institutionalized cooperation may assume the character of an abstract norm. This may be traced back to power and status positions established in the course of the repeated applications of that institution beyond the point of its due change. Such petrified application of the same institution may be particularly motivated by yielding further

economies of scale or extra benefits for some agents (e.g., superiors in a hierarchy) from the continuing use of an institutional behavioral form of decision making that originally was problem solving but eventually has seized to be—the Veblenian ceremonial dimension of the institution having come to dominate (Bush, 1987; Elsner, 2012; see Chapter 12 on Veblen and Chapter 13 on the Bush model).

Such existence of improper solutions may not even be realized as such by the agents who perhaps do not know better. The surface of institutionalized everyday arrangements typically is more easily visible (and considered as being without alternative) than the complex dilemma problem structure that always remains existing in the background and its more adequate potential solutions.

14.4.6 Complexity and Market Failure

Given ubiquitous dilemma problems, individualist decision making may lead to inferior results, and markets, particularly deregulated markets that foster a myopic culture of agents, and the prices resulting in them may fail to generate and diffuse the information, shared knowledge, and related expectations required for problem solving. A solution then may require the learning of a recognized broader social interdependence and more long-run calculation, than an individualistic and myopic market culture can provide.

14.4.7 Habituation

The shared knowledge and informal coordination cannot be comprehended other than as an institutionalization of cooperation through a habituated social institution, as explained in Chapter 1. This is because coordination has to assume the specific form of cooperation, i.e., coordination plus sacrifice, and the institution thus has to be a social rule plus endogenous sanction in order to condition agents to abstain from the potential short-run extra gain. In a dilemma-prone, decentralized system, the dilemma problem can be overcome, if not through formal and authoritarian command mechanisms, only by learned, habituated, and semiconscious behavior.

14.4.8 Micro-Foundation of Macro- and Meso-Emergence

Evolutionary institutional economics conceives the outcome of a complex system and process as emergent structure (Hodgson, 2000, 113ff.). Emergence implies an "entity (that) has properties which cannot be deduced from prior knowledge of the elements" (113f.). The meso-structure, emerging from micro-level processes, contributes to the century-old but still topical economic problem of the micro-foundation of macro (Akerlof, 2007). And insofar as an institution has gained a general social acknowledgement and exists independently of any individual and of its own generating interaction process, and will change the conditions of the microeconomic behaviors and interaction processes in a continuing interaction process of the micro, meso, and macro levels, it exerts a "reconstitutive downward causation" (Hodgson, 2002) of individual behavior, i.e., a macro-foundation of micro.

14.4.9 Basic Rules of the Game, Common Culture, Beliefs, and Agency Capacities...

This is, of course, not to suggest that a formal mechanism, modeling, and simulation of emergent process, through some obscure methodological trick, could generate something from nothing. On the contrary, some basic common culture, basic rules of the game, agents' beliefs, and agency capabilities (such as searching and learning, risk taking, being not too envious, monitoring, memorizing, and identifying others, expecting and anticipating, reputation building, and partner selection) may have to be assumed at the outset or at later logical steps of the analysis.

14.4.10 ... and the Resulting Complex Process—and Changes It Will Trigger

Nevertheless, in spite of those assumptions, the complex process remains path dependent, cumulative, nonteleological (open), idiosyncratic, nonergodic, nonequilibrating, nonefficient, morphogenetic, and open-ended. In this way, it may increase our understanding by directing our attention back to crucial properties of the initial structure, of the process as such, of the micro units and their agency capabilities, and of a number of critical factors.

Agents will start as short-run maximizers, which may be considered a worst-case condition. Improved outcomes in the problematic decision setting they face will require a change of perspectives, horizon, and behavior. If those initial myopic worst-case maximizers can change their behaviors and can create cooperation through establishing a social institution and a social carrier group, something seems to be gained.

This is distinctive of noncooperative game theory, as compared to, e.g., experimental behavioral games that deal with the whole set of pre-existing norms (e.g., an inequality aversion or a given preference for caring about others, etc.) and perceptional frames that real-world test persons bring into the lab.[4] Noncooperative game theory modeling, rather, establishes a logic that, in turn, requires successive analytical steps connected to stringent story telling.

---

[4]For example, Camerer and Fehr gave an overview of research on pre-existing norms that are always present in participants of laboratory experiments such as those by Henrich et al. (2004, 55ff.). For a more detailed critical view on behavioral economics, see for instance Berg and Gigerenzer (2010).

14.5 A STOCHASTIC ELEMENT, THE POPULATION PERSPECTIVE, AND THE MINIMUM CRITICAL MASS AGAIN

A true population perspective with a structured population requires a more stochastic element. Moreover, more agency needs to be considered, which allows for selective interactions by the agents, meaning the ability to refuse interacting with at least some other agents. In a first step, we will lay down some frame in a short qualitative process story. In this, we focus on individual motivations to change behavior; group-selection mechanisms, for instance, can complement and further add to our understanding of emerging behavior patterns.

First, considering the PD supergame solution in a sequence or process, the institutional solution cannot come about, if agents' time horizon is too short. Thus, as mentioned, an institution can only emerge through learned habituation based on recognized interdependence and learned long-run horizons. This has also been elaborated under the perspective of a horizonal effect, where individual (cognitive, planning) horizons are extended, if real agency is to be gained (cf. Jennings, 2005).

Second, an initial minimum critical mass of cooperators, in a population of defectors, may indeed emerge on the basis of the individual motivations (i) to escape repeated frustration from common defection and (ii) to learn and to increase knowledge, and particularly to explore what a different behavior, namely common cooperation, might bring about (idle curiosity or an instinct of workmanship as T. Veblen has coined it), to find a way to improve one's economic situation. The payoffs for common cooperation may not even be known (some incomplete information) and may then be explored by searching agents. The institution thus might emerge out of agents' vision that there is more to be gained than what is currently achievable. Agents who then contribute to cooperation need to be searching, experimenting, imaginative, explorative, and creative.

Third, the individual who then starts to search and experiment with a different behavior will have to contribute repeatedly to the change of expectations of others in favor of cooperation. The process, thus, is cumulative in the sense that a minimum critical mass (or share) of agents must repeatedly and interactively (sequentially) contribute to cooperation.

Fourth, these agents also have to be risk taking and not be too envious. The first to send a signal for a potential better common future will have to take the risk of being exploited, at least once. She will never be able to compensate for a first exploitation, as compared to the other, even if common cooperation starts in immediate response to her cooperative action. This agent thus needs to be focused on her own net gain, which she has to compare only with her own payoff under continued common defection. Compared to this, she clearly will be better off over time.

Fifth, with agents starting to learn, search, experiment, and diversify behavior (in our two-strategy world, this of course means starting TFT cooperation) we may justify the population perspective. Agents then will no longer be able to exactly tell the strategy of another agent whom they will meet next. Behavior thus may be considered random, and agents will have to form expectations about the population shares of the strategies. The pure expectation to meet again will be replaced by the expected probability to meet a cooperative agent next round.

Sixth, the initial minimum critical mass (or share) of cooperators then becomes crucial to make TFT cooperation viable. With such a minimum critical mass, institutionalized cooperation may expand in a population initially consisting only of defectors.

Seventh, agents no longer remain focused on just (the probability to meet) the same agent (next round). They will have to know about as many agents as possible. Thus, more agency capabilities will have to be considered. Instances of such agency will be memory, monitoring, building and transmitting reputation and using reputation chains, and some active partner selection based on the knowledge generated by these mechanisms.

Eighth, the individuals, through some active partner selection, may determine group size of the cooperating group then. Agents in this way may affect both the size and composition of their individual selected peer group of interaction partners. We may consider the meso-group size then to be co-determined by cooperating agents who actively adapt their relevant peer groups to a maximum size still bearable, or manageable, for them, and to a composition which still allows them (according to the underlying rationality) to contribute to institutional emergence.

Real life displays properties that indicate some partner selection, i.e., proximity, or neighborhood, as either spatially, socially, or professionally defined. Agents then may confine themselves to some group of interaction partners through moving/mobility, choice of localization, social exclusion/segregation, in an effort to keep the expectation of cooperation high (or increase it). It is a *calculative rationality of smallness* in the peer group of an individual that is effective here (with the danger, of course, of too great a cliquishness, early petrifaction or sclerotization of institutions, and a subsequent institutional lock-in on an inferior path).

Ninth, the system then would adopt an endogenous dynamic with different equilibria, the fully defective one and a cooperative one, being either the whole population or a carrier group smaller than the whole population, as we have already graphically illustrated in Sections 3.2.2 and 3.2.3.

In the following, we will, in addition, explain *agency*, specifically *information gathering* and *selection* capabilities.

14.6 ADAPTING GROUP SIZE: AGENCY MECHANISMS

14.6.1 Expectations

In the population perspective, i.e., in a structured population with portions of (representatives of) different strategies, agents can no longer focus on the same interaction partner only. Rather, they have to learn about as many potential partners as possible and about the distribution of strategies in the whole population. Their expectations to meet any cooperator with sufficient probability in their inter-round random partner changes become a critical component for the possibility of the institution of cooperation to emerge. Particular agency capacities are required for this process.

14.6.2 Memory and Monitoring

First, knowledge of others will increase by adding some memory capability. *Second*, agents should be considered capable of monitoring concurrent interactions between identifiable third parties (Elster, 1989, 40f.).

The memorizing capacity typically is different for different periods of the past, i.e., correct memorizing decreases with the increasing number of past periods from now. Also, correct memorizing typically decreases with the distance of monitored agents from oneself, i.e., the further away a third person is from herself, the less the capacity of the agent of correct memorizing over the memory periods.

14.6.3 Reputation Chains

In addition, reputation may further increase the knowledge about other agents, that is, it further increases the probability to meet a partner next round, who knows the agent's earlier behavior and/or whose (earlier) behavior the agent knows, in these cases through third persons.

In all, this should illustrate that these agency mechanisms, allowing the active acquisition of information about others, may easily lead us into a meso-size of subpopulations of known agents and known cooperators. Some individual expectation regarding the true composition of the whole population may be closer to its real composition consequently.

Devices and mechanisms known in economics, such as signaling or substitute indicators such as gender, race, language, age, living area, formal education, certificates, identity cards, corporate uniforms, ceremonial behavior, would not be needed in a transparent system of monitoring others' behavior.

14.6.4 Partner Selection and a Maximum Critical Mass Smaller Than the Whole Population

Monitoring, memorizing, and using a reputation chain can be considered informational preconditions for selecting agents. Interaction partners still may appear in some random sequence.

Selection by Distance/Proximity/Neighborhood

They may also appear subject to distance, that is, in a (cultural or spatial) neighborhood topology the probability of an appearance of potential interaction partners may decrease with decreasing proximity. Such proximity, in turn, may be generated in a process of partner selection, with either a (spatial or social) move to a proper neighborhood or the formation of a proper (social) peer group of interaction partners.

Agency Capacity in Theory and Lab Experiments

There is a considerable amount of operational literature in complexity economics or socioeconomics (in the wide sense) on the theoretical foundation of such agency capacity, as presumed here (Davis, 2007, 2008; Dolfsma and Verburg, 2008).

Also lab experiments have shown that agents indeed try to reduce the complexity of their nets through active selection and active building of neighborhoods (Harmsen-van Hout et al., 2008), and that network effects can be (better) attained by groups constituted through the selective interactions of individuals (Tucker, 2008). Also, any selection mechanism alone (i.e., actively choosing or excluding/rejecting partners) may already allow for the emergence of cooperation in an n-person public-good game (Spiekermann, 2009).

Building Peer Groups

The cooperator i will be able to increase the number of cooperators k_i among his/her potential individual interaction partners n_i, i.e., increase (k_i/n_i), the share of cooperators k_i within the subpopulation of his/her potential interaction partners n_i, with $n_i < n$. Thus, the agent may decouple k_i/n_i from the general k/n existent in the population (see Section 14.6.5). Note that the agent is not assumed to reject every defector.

Improving Cooperators' Outcomes

In this way, she will also increase her average outcome in a population of a given size and structure, and cooperators together, thus, can make cooperation increasingly more attractive. Cooperators can improve their payoff curves through selection until a certain point, as in the end cooperators' payoffs logically cannot exceed an upper limit given by the present value of the payoffs from their encounters.

Note that the cooperators' population share has increased through initial experimentation (see Section 14.4) and will further increase through selection among existing cooperators. This will make cooperation more attractive (see below).

Overlapping of Individual Selected Peer Groups

Overlapping individual partner selections of the cooperators may then constitute a relevant cooperating group (see also Oestreicher-Singer and Sundarajan, 2008; the issue is similar to the idea of a minimum network that still allows for institutional diffusion (the small-world issue), see Foley, 1998, 18ff., 38ff., 61ff.; Watts, 1999, 204ff.; Batten, 2001, 89ff.).

More Generally: Net Externalities, Synergies, Cumulative Learning in Economics

In order to theorize and illustrate the simple logic of such sorting out process, different non-linear cooperation payoff curves have often been considered in the literature.

- For instance, Schelling (1978, 104f., 239ff.) already referred to net externalities to explain progressively increasing cooperative payoff functions. This implies, for our case, an additional payoff from network (or group) size for members of a group of agents in a population using the same technology, or, in our case, the same strategy. It implies that the better the selection mechanism and the greater, thus, the share of cooperators in the cooperators' individual peer groups, the larger additional positive mutual externalities among cooperators, even above what cooperators would have gained on average in that mixed population.
- In the same vein, applied *Schumpeterian innovation* economists have argued in favor of a cumulative character, both

interpersonally (depending on the size of the knowledge-sharing group) and intertemporarily (depending on the agents' learning and ever better application and use of the new knowledge), of the process of generating new knowledge through interaction, so that, for our case, average cooperative payoffs may increase through some synergetic effect (Pyka, 1999, 98ff.).

- Specifically, S-shaped curves have been used in such contexts. For instance, in his technology choice model with increasing returns (or net effects), Arthur (1989, 123ff.) (see also Chapter 13) has made use of such a logistics curve. While a technology adoption function maps the probability of choice of a certain technology by the next choosing agent against the number of those who have chosen this technology so far, being equivalent to a payoff function depending on the number k of those who have chosen cooperation, some improvement function would mirror additional increasing returns to adoption. Particularly, he considered cumulative learning (by using) effects and "coordination externalities" (p. 126). In addition, he considered a bounded improvement function where effects eventually become exhausted. The population may split up then, in equilibrium, with the coexistence of more than one technology (or strategy), one portion of the population using the dominant technology and another one some minority technology.
- Cooper and John (1988) (see also Chapter 13) elaborated on economies with "strategic complementarities," or synergies. Going beyond simple positive externalities generated by agent A, which just increase the payoff of agent B, synergies imply that an increase in agent A's strategy in addition

increases the marginal return of agent B's own action. A's strategy thus is an increasing function of agent B's strategy and vice versa. Such a synergetic reaction function reflects some multiplier effect and is considered S-shaped (p. 445ff.). The economic examples that Cooper and John discuss include net externalities through coordination in supplier networks and demand coordination among multiple industries in the business cycle.

The sigmoid function thus reflects the idea of, at first, exponentially growing payoffs for cooperative behavior (cumulative learning, synergies, net externalities, particularly effective information collection and sharing, reputation building, and related partner selection), which later change into maturity and, finally, nongrowth, when those specific resources of cooperation somehow become exhausted (see Elster, 1989, 28f., 32−34 for a logistics curve in a "technology of collective action").

14.6.5 Revisiting and Expanding the Population Perspective

Recall the simple formal sketch of the PD supergame single-shot solution in Section 3.2, and the Axelrodian evolution-of-cooperation approach in the frame of evolutionary game theory, as explained in Chapters 8 and 13, respectively, according to which TFT can be an evolutionary stable strategy in a population, compared to All-D. Remember that, under a given incentive structure, agents' time horizon and their expectations regarding the other agent (in the resulting coordination game) have turned out to be the crucial factor for the

solution. Expanding this setting to two agents who are randomly drawn from a population to engage in a PD supergame ($b > a > c > d$, with a as the payoff for common cooperation, c as the payoff for common defection, b as the payoff for a successfully exploiting agent, and d as the payoff of an exploited agent) introduces their expectations regarding the composition of the population as an additional relevant factor (Section 3.3).

In this case, the expected payoffs for a TFT-/All-D world are given by (with $k/n = \kappa$ as the share of cooperators in the population and δ as the discount factor for future payoffs[5]):

$$\pi^e_{\text{TFT}} = \kappa \frac{a}{1 - \delta} + (1 - \kappa)\left(\frac{c}{1 - \delta} + d - c\right) \quad (14.1)$$

$$\pi^e_{\text{All-D}} = \kappa\left(\frac{c}{1 - \delta} + b - c\right) + (1 - \kappa)\frac{c}{1 - \delta} \quad (14.2)$$

Solving for κ gives the share of TFT cooperators for which the expected payoffs for both strategies are equal, the minimum critical share of cooperators in the population needed to establish a TFT environment:

$$\kappa^{\text{crit}} = \frac{c - d}{((a - c)/(1 - \delta)) + 2c - b - d} \quad (14.3)$$

Figure 14.1 shows the payoff schedules.

Agency Mechanisms and Partner Selection

We will illustrate the effect of partner selection (when the PD has not been solved, no intersection of the linear curves) in Figure 14.2 (again, see Section 3.2 for some detail on the basic formulations).

[5]The discount factor can be formulated in any number of ways to reflect a particular setting. For instance, we could integrate the notion of a possibility for successive supergames taken into account by the agents, in a way, that δ increases in the probability to meet the same agent again in the subsequently played supergame. That way, interactions in smaller populations became more valuable to the agents and the conditions permitting the emergence of cooperation were more easily met in smaller groups (shifting the intersection of the payoff schedules to the left in Figure 14.1).

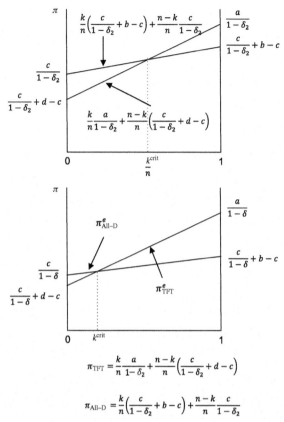

FIGURE 14.1 Expected payoffs in a TFT-/All-D environment.

$$\pi_{\text{TFT}} = \frac{k}{n}\frac{a}{1-\delta_2} + \frac{n-k}{n}\left(\frac{c}{1-\delta_2} + d - c\right)$$

$$\pi_{\text{All-D}} = \frac{k}{n}\left(\frac{c}{1-\delta_2} + b - c\right) + \frac{n-k}{n}\frac{c}{1-\delta_2}$$

Cooperative payoffs may quickly exceed the average defector's payoff now. The payoff functions with selection can be represented by

$$\pi_{\text{TFT}}^e = \kappa^{\alpha}\frac{a}{1-\delta} + (1-\kappa^{\alpha})\left(\frac{c}{1-\delta} + d - c\right) \tag{14.4}$$

$$\pi_{\text{All-D}}^e = \kappa^{1/\alpha}\left(\frac{c}{1-\delta} + b - c\right) + (1-\kappa^{1/\alpha})\frac{c}{1-\delta} \tag{14.5}$$

with $0 < \alpha < 1$. This α represents the strength of the ability of cooperating agents to select partners (more pronounced the smaller α) and

thereby increase the likelihood of interacting with like agents above their overall population share.

Note again that the cooperators' curve is set on top of the worst case, the PD not solved yet. This illustrates that the constitution of a meso-sized relevant cooperating group occurs where the PD has not been solved as the general time horizon of the agents and their expectations regarding the duration of their specific relations are too short or low. (If the underlying dilemma structure is transformed in the repeated interactions, the maximum critical mass is equal to the entire population.)

Institutions Do Carry Some Share of Defectors or Defecting Actions

As indicated earlier, this also reflects the fact that any established informal institution may carry some degree of defection, by making it more profitable to defect with increasing κ. Any institution, in fact, exists, and may survive, in the face of a certain number of defectors. These defectors do no longer endanger the institution as such, since, if their number increases above a certain share, they again will fare worse than the cooperators.

A Mixed Strategy Equilibrium

Also, of course, we must not necessarily, or even mainly, think of individuals being clear-cut cooperators or defectors, black or white sheep, at any given point in time, but may equivalently think of mixed strategies, that is, certain portions of cooperative and defective actions in the sets of actions of every single individual. In fact, as you will be aware, the solution is formally a Nash equilibrium in a mixed strategy in an evolutionary population setting (for details, see Chapter 8).

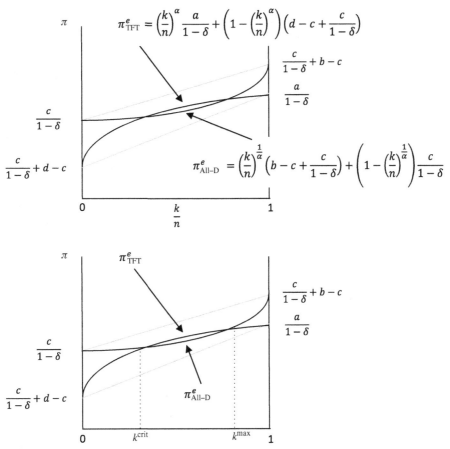

FIGURE 14.2 Illustration of the effect of partner selection on the payoffs from cooperation and defection, indicating the meso-sized area of the relevant cooperating group.

14.7 AN EMPIRICAL APPLICATION: HIGH GENERAL TRUST AND HIGH MACRO-PERFORMANCE IN MESO-STRUCTURED ECONOMIES—AN EXPLANATION OF PERSISTING VARIETIES OF CAPITALISM

14.7.1 Generalization from Expectations to Contextual and General Trust

As we have seen, cooperative behavior can emerge more easily, for a given incentive structure, when

- interaction arenas (populations) are relatively smaller;
- expectations to meet a cooperative agent again, within and across supergames, are higher and the time horizons of agents are longer;
- partner selection is stronger;
- therefore, required minimum critical masses are disproportionately smaller.

It is conceivable then that general behavioral predispositions of cooperation may emerge through habituation and generalization that support later cooperative behavior in other areas. Considering a population consisting of, and its members interacting in many different, and perhaps overlapping thematic fields and subarenas, the emergence of expectations and the institution of cooperation in a particular thematic (sub-)arena of a population, as discussed so far, is only a first step in the transfer of the model to real-world problems. Agents in new particular (thematic) arenas then will have to form a more general idea about how others will behave when they choose their actions beyond the platform in which they have learned institutionalized cooperative behavior first. On top of the agency assumptions and mechanisms already discussed (search and experimentation, nonenviousness, risk taking, workmanship, and curiosity as well as memory, monitoring, reputation building, and partner selection), some internal psychological generalization and spillover will support the process in real-world situations and thus will bring the formal argument closer to the real world.

We assume that every agent is interacting with many different others in different and potentially overlapping subarenas in one population (perhaps playing more than one game at a time). Subarenas may overlap in terms of interconnected themes, geographical overlap, or agents' overlap and different types of problem structures may characterize different thematic arenas.

Once a kind of cooperative environment has been established in a critical minimum number of platforms that an agent interacts in, the agent may follow a general learned behavioral pattern. That minimum critical mass of institutionalized cooperation, which is habituated and semiconsciously applied in each individual platform, may now facilitate a transfer, spillover, or generalization of institutionalized behavior and related contextual trust into other subarenas and eventually into a more general habit and into the broader setting of the whole population. The institutionalization of cooperation then may result in an embedding of trustworthiness as a desirable (since problem solving and successful) trait into the institutional structure of large parts of the population. This, eventually, may account for a general trustworthy behavior and a reflection of this in generalized trusting attitudes, which, in turn, may spill over to a general(ized) trust to meet a cooperator in any next interaction or round, even in subarenas and situations different from those, in which cooperation originally emerged.

Such a process may be equivalent with an "internalization of norms" as an "important prosocial psychological mechanism" supporting general cooperative behavior and general trust of cooperation (Gintis, 2003). Modern psychology, anthropology, and behavioral sciences are currently working on the details of such habituation/transfer/spillover/generalization and respective behavior selection, be it on an individual basis or as group selection, i.e., among groups that have differentially succeeded to develop critical levels of cooperation, as mentioned in Section 14.3.

14.7.2 High Levels of General Trust and Macro-Performance in Countries with Inner Meso-Structure

General trust levels empirically show high positive correlations with macro-performance levels: populations, or nations for that purpose, and even apparently similar countries that were supposed to converge, display different and even diverging trust levels, and these correlate with their different and diverging macro-performance levels in various economic, technological, and social areas. This indicates considerable systemic differences in their deep interaction structures of subarenas and platforms, with their different inner size structures as a new critical factor explained in this chapter.

Polls, nowadays carried out regularly in many countries with support of the World Bank and others major organizations such as the OECD and the EU (Knack and Keefer, 1997), namely the *World Value Survey*, include general trust questions such as "Do you think you can trust the next person you will encounter?" This is equivalent to the expectation to meet a cooperative agent next round.

Such polls have brought about surprising differences and even considerable divergence over time in trust levels among presumably similar and converging countries (e.g., leading OECD countries). Similarly surprising was the fact that such trust levels have turned out to be highly correlated with high macroeconomic and macro-social performance in broad areas (O'Hara, 2008).

Up until now, economists have often stressed disadvantages and volatility of small countries (Alesina and Spolaore, 2003). Others have generally argued in favor of advantages of smaller countries (Kuznets, 1960; Easterly and Kraay, 2000), particularly their superior adaptability, learning and cooperation conditions as dependent on proximity and interaction density (Cantner and Meder, 2008).

According to the explanations in this chapter, we would not just look at small countries per se, but consider countries, which have developed, in a path-dependent historical process, a proper inner meso-sized structure of interaction arenas and platforms. It appears that the principle of smallness is not mainly relevant in terms of the outer size but has successfully been internally generalized by some countries (through cumulative historical process rather than deliberate political design, of course), so that they in fact can make use of meso-sized arenas and platforms in their socioeconomic interaction processes. Still, smaller countries might have some advantages to do so.

This particularly applies to Scandinavian countries, given not only their small overall sizes but also their meso-scale residential

structures, enterprise size structures, dominant interactive workplace organization, degrees of general organizational membership and participation, informal networks structures—notably under some specific policy frame setting (particularly safeguarding some level of social integration, social stability, and social security).

There is a rich literature on these particular properties of their internal interaction structures (see, e.g., the material on the *Danish* case in Jørgensen, 2002; Lundvall, 2002; Edquist and Hommen,2008; Christensen et al., 2008; Holm et al., 2008). According to this empirical evidence, even a country of 5.5 million population might be sufficiently interconnected through overlapping meso-sized arenas and platforms to mobilize reputation chains and the other agency mechanisms explained in this chapter in order to generate high levels of expectations (general trust), commitment, thus institutionalized cooperation and socioeconomic performance.

While the usual explanation for the high empirical evidence of those countries on trust, subjective well-being, commitment, cooperation, innovativeness, flexibility, and performance refers to welfare-state explanation, we can add another critical set of factors, on the background of the explanations of this chapter, i.e., the size dimension of the interaction structures. Since in many respects also the Netherlands, Austria, Iceland, Switzerland, and some others belong to that group with similar empirical properties, the Scandinavian welfare-state explanation alone does not appear to be a sufficient explanation of the persistent varieties (and divergence) of capitalisms in that respect. The meso-size explanation thus appears to be a critical microeconomic foundation for future economic analyses of countries' macro-performances.

Note that the Scandinavian countries are not only leading in particular social areas, such as little poverty, a more even distribution, little unemployment, high education, social security, social upward mobility, and subjective well-being, but also in the leading groups with innovation rates, GDP pc, speed of structural change, labor market mobility, globalization rates, positive future expectations, etc.

The World Bank, the OECD, EU, and others, therefore, may have to adopt a more complex explanation of such phenomena than just international jurisdictional competition for "market" conform institutions (global competitiveness index, and the like). Particularly, the theoretical framework of institutional emergence, with its dimensions of trust (future expectations) and meso-sized platforms, should play a more important role in this field in the future.

14.8 CONCLUSION: TOWARD MESO-ECONOMICS

Against the background of an evolutionary approach to the emergence of meso-structures, meso-platform size, futurity (expectations), and institutional emergence of cooperation, given the incentive structures, will have to be further theorized, formalized, quantified in simulations, and backed by empirical evidence, in order to generate a more general economic theory of the size dimension of complexity microeconomics. The critical factors here are:

1. the incentive structure;
2. an initial distribution of strategies in a population and a minimum critical mass of cooperators;
3. agency mechanisms such as monitoring, memorizing, reputation building, and reputation chain using, as well as partner selection, based on related information;
4. possibly, potential additional mutual externalities of cooperation, cumulative learning, or synergies, typically justifying a degressively growing payoff curve;

5. the relevant cooperating group, typically smaller than the whole population and in this sense meso-sized. This may include (spatial, social, etc.) segregation patterns (for segregation models, see Chapter 13);
6. finally, additions include aspects such as a distribution of a population in a topology, i.e., proximity and neighborhood structure, with the corresponding rules of interaction (e.g., mobility).

The process, logic, and critical factors explained in this chapter may allow for a class of complex models and simulations focusing on size and particularly meso-size.

A more general meso-economics might be envisaged, that is, the economics of the emergent mid-size level for coordination in complex economies that have to solve complex decision problems, that generate higher innovation, that are capability-increasing and improving macroeconomic and macro-social performance of a population. Its applications, such as cultural emergence, production and innovation standardization, shared information governance and open source in a fragmented and interconnected economy, spatial industrial organization and agglomeration (see Chapter 4), general trust and macro-performance, all have high practical relevance. We will deal more with those applied aspects in Chapters 15 and 16.

Of course, we cannot expect a nontrivial, automatic emergence of an always stable, self-sustaining, Pareto-efficient institutionalized equilibrium, i.e., no deliberation-free, hierarchy-free, or state-free private self-organization or spontaneous order. For instance, the initiation, stabilization, and accelerated generation of a minimum critical mass may require considering the role of public policy (Schelling, 1978; Cooper and John, 1988; Elster, 1989, 31ff.). This may lead to a new interactive public policy design focused on specific frame setting to trigger the causal factors for institutional emergence

(Elsner, 2001, 2008). This may particularly give room for the emergence of the capability, inclination, and efforts to learn and innovate, where otherwise too much volatility and turbulence would undermine such capability, inclination, and efforts. Thus, innovation may emerge through the very stabilization of expectations and behaviors, attained by institutionalized coordination (Boudreau et al., 2008). We will deal more with policy issues in Chapter 16 and particularly with the model of interactive policy in Chapter 17.

The approach to meso-economics explained here still is a young field of complexity economics and still far from being fully understood and sufficiently elaborated. Although group or platform size has already been a dimension of many socioeconomic approaches and complex models, further strengthening relevant, applied, empirical, and policy-oriented economic research, such as the topical research on general trust and macro-performance, not least requires further elaboration and simulation of the logic and process of meso.

Chapter References

Akerlof, G.A., 2007. The missing motivation in macroeconomics. Am. Econ. Rev. 97 (1), 5−36.

Alesina, A., Spolaore, E., 2003. The Size of Nations. MIT Press, Cambridge, MA.

Arthur, W.B., 1989. Competing technologies, increasing returns, and lock-in by historical events. Econ. J. 99, 116−131.

Arthur, W.B., 1994. Inductive reasoning and bounded rationality (The El Farol Problem). Am. Econ. Rev. 84, 406−411.

Axelrod, R., 1984. The Evolution of Cooperation. Basic Books, New York, NY (revised edition 2006).

Aydinonat, N.E., 2007. Models, conjectures and exploration: an analysis of Schelling's checkerboard model of residential segregation. J. Econ. Methodol. 14 (4), 429−454.

Ayres, R.U., Martinás, K., 2005. On the Reappraisal of Microeconomics. Edward Elgar, Cheltenham, Northampton.

Batten, D.F., 2001. Complex landscapes of spatial interaction. Ann. Reg. Sci. 35 (1), 81−111.

Berg, N., Gigerenzer, G., 2010. As-if behavioral economics: neoclassical economics in disguise?. <http://ideas.repec.org/p/pra/mprapa/26586.html> (accessed 28.03.13).

Binmore, K., 1998. Review of Axelrod, R., the complexity of cooperation. JASSS. 1 (1).

Boudreau, K.J., Lacetera, N., Lakhani, K.R., 2008. Parallel search, incentives and problem type: revisiting the competition and innovation link. Harvard Business School Technology and Operations Management Unit Research Paper No. 1264038.

Bowles, S., Choi, J.-K., Hopfensitz, A., 2003. The co-evolution of individual behaviors and social institutions. J. Theor. Biol. 223, 135−147.

Boyd, R., Richerson, P.J., 2005. The Origin and Evolution of Cultures. Oxford University Press, New York, NY.

Bush, P.D., 1987. The theory of institutional change. J. Econ. Issues. XXI, 1075−1116.

Cantner U., Meder, A., 2008. Regional and technological effects on cooperative innovation. Jena Econ. Res. Papers, 014-2008.

Carpenter, J., Kariv, S., Schotter, A., 2010. Network architecture and mutual monitoring in public goods experiments. Institute for the study of labor. IZA DP 5307.

Chen, P., 2008. Equilibrium illusion, economic complexity and evolutionary foundation in economic analysis. Evol. Inst. Econ. Rev. 5 (1), 81−127.

Chen, P., Gable, G.G., 2013. Larger or broader: performance implications of size and diversity of the knowledge worker's egocentric network. Manage. Organ. Rev. 9 (1), 139−165.

Chertow, M., Ehrenfeld, J., 2012. Organizing self-organizing systems. Toward a theory of industrial symbiosis. J. Ind. Ecol. 16 (1), 13−27.

Christensen, J.L., Gregersen, B., Johnson, B., Lundvall, B.A., Tomlinson, M., 2008. An NSI in transition? Denmark. In: Edquist, C., Hommen, L. (Eds.), pp. 403−441.

Cooper, R., John, A., 1988. Coordinating coordination failures in Keynesian models. Q. J. Econ. CIII (3), 441−463.

Cordes, C., Richerson, P., McElreath, R., Strimling, P., 2011. How does opportunistic behavior influence firm size? An evolutionary approach to organizational behavior. J. Inst. Econ. 7 (1), 1−21.

David, P.A., 1985. Clio and the economics of QWERTY. Am. Econ. Rev. 75 (2), 332−337.

Davis, J.B., 2007. Complexity theory's network conception of the individual. In: Giacomin, A., Marcuzzo, M.C. (Eds.), Money and Markets. A Doctrinal Approach. Routledge, Abingdon, New York, pp. 30−47.

Davis, J.B., 2008. Complex individuals: the individual in non-euclidian space. In: Hanappi, G., Elsner, W. (Eds.), Advances in Evolutionary Institutional Economics: Evolutionary Mechanisms, Non-Knowledge, and Strategy. Edward Elgar, Cheltenham, Northampton, pp. 123−142.

Dejean, S., Penard, T., Suire, R., 2008. Olson's paradox revisited: an empirical analysis of filesharing behavior in P2P communities. CREM, Univ. of Rennes, F, mimeo. <http://papers.ssrn.com/sol3/papers.cfm?abstract_id=1299190> (accessed 26.03.13).

Demange, G., Wooders, M. (Eds.), 2005. Group Formation in Economics. Networks, Clubs, and Coalitions. Cambridge University Press, Cambridge, New York.

Devezas, T.C., Corredine, J.T., 2002. The nonlinear dynamics of technoeconomic systems. An informational interpretation. Technol. Forecast. Soc. Change. 69, 317–357.

Dolfsma, W., Leydesdorff, L., 2009. Lock-in & break-out from technological trajectories: modeling and policy implications. Technol. Forecast. Soc. Change. 76 (7), 932–941.

Dolfsma, W., Verburg, R., 2008. Structure, agency and the role of values in processes of institutional change. J. Econ. Issues. XLII (4), 1031–1054.

Dopfer, K. (Ed.), 2001. Evolutionary Economics: Program and Scope. Kluwer Academic Publishers, Boston, Dordrecht, London.

Dopfer, K., Hanusch, H., Pyka, A. (Eds.), 2007. The Elgar Companion to Neo-Schumpeterian Economics. Edward Elgar, Cheltenham, Northampton.

Dopfer, K. (Ed.), 2012. The origins of meso economics. J. Evol. Econ. 22, 133–160.

Dopfer, K., Potts, J., 2008. The General Theory of Economic Evolution. Routledge, London, New York.

Dosi, G., Winter, S.G., 2000. Interpreting economic change: evolution, structures and games. LEM Working Paper Series 2000/08, Pisa, Italy. <http://ideas.repec.org/p/ssa/lemwps/2000-08.html> (accessed 26.03.13).

Dunbar, R.I.M., 2011. Constraints on the evolution of social institutions and their implications for information flow. J. Inst. Econ. 7 (3), 345–371.

Easterly, W., Kraay, A., 2000. Small states, small problems? income, growth, and volatility in small states. World Dev. 28 (11), 2013–2027.

Eckert, D., St. Koch, J. Mitloehner, 2005. Using the iterated prisoner's dilemma for explaining the evolution of cooperation in OS communities. In: Scotto, M., Succi, G. (Eds.), Proceedings of the First International Conference on OS Systems, Genoa.

Edquist, C., Hommen, L. (Eds.), 2008. Small Country Innovation Systems. Globalization, Change and Policy in Asia and Europe. Edward Elgar, Cheltenham, Northampton.

Elsner, W., 2000. An industrial policy agenda 2000 and beyond—experience, theory and policy. In: Elsner, W., Groenewegen, J. (Eds.), Industrial Policies After 2000. Kluwer Academic Publishers, Boston, Dordrecht, London, pp. 411–486.

Elsner, W., 2001. Interactive economic policy: toward a cooperative policy approach for a negotiated economy. J. Econ. Issues. XXXV (1), 61–83.

Elsner, W., 2008. Art. Market and state. In: O'Hara, P.A. (Ed.). International Encyclopedia of Public Policy. <http://pohara.homestead.com/Encyclopedia/Volume-3.pdf>.

Elsner, W., 2012. The theory of institutional change revisited. The institutional dichotomy, its dynamic, and its policy implications in a more formal analysis. J. Econ. Issues. XLVI (1), 1–43.

Elsner, W., Schwardt, H., 2013. Trust and arena size. expectations, general trust, and institutions co-evolving, and their critical population and group sizes. J. Inst. Econ. 9, Available from: http://dx.doi.org/10.1017/s1744137413000179. Published online: 28 May 2013.

Elster, J., 1989. The Cement of Society. A Study of Social Order. Cambridge University Press, Cambridge.

Farrell, H., 2009. The Political Economy of Trust. Institutions, Interests, and Inter-Firm Cooperation in Italy and Germany. Cambridge University Press, Cambridge.

Fehr, E., Henrich, J., 2003. Is strong reciprocity a maladaptation? On the evolutionary foundations of human altruism. <http://ideas.repec.org/p/iza/izadps/dp712.html> (accessed 27.03.13).

Field, A.J., 2006. Group selection and behavioral economics. In: Altman, M. (Ed.), Handbook of Contemporary Behavioral Economics. M.E. Sharpe, Armonk, London, pp. 165–182.

Field, A.J., 2007. Beyond foraging: behavioral science and the future of institutional economics. J. Inst. Econ. 3 (3), 265–291.

Foley, D.K., 1998. Introduction to "Barriers and Bounds to Rationality".. In: Foley, D.K. (Ed.), Barriers and Bounds to Rationality: Essays on Economic Complexity and Dynamics in Interactive Systems, by P.S. Albin, with an Introduction by D.K. Foley. Princeton University Press, Princeton, NJ, pp. 3–72.

Foster, J., 2005. From simplistic to complex systems in economics. Cambridge J. Econ. 29, 873–892.

Dopfer, K., Foster, J., Potts, J., 2004. Micro–meso–macro. J. Evol. Econ. 14, 263–279.

Fukuyama, F., 1995. Trust. The Social Virtues and the Creation of Prosperity. The Free Press and Penguin Books, New York, NY.

Garon, J.M., 2012. Localism as a production imperative: an alternative framework for promoting intangible cultural heritage. In: Pager, S.A., Candeub, A. (Eds.), Transnational Culture in the Internet Age. Edward Elgar, Cheltenham, Northampton, pp. 346–369.

Gibbons, R., 2006. What the folk theorem doesn't tell us. Ind. Corp. Change. 15 (2), 381–386.

Gintis, H., 2000. Game Theory Evolving. A Problem-Centered Introduction to Modeling Strategic Interaction. Princeton University Press., Princeton, NJ.

Gintis, H., 2003. The Hitchhiker's guide to altruism: gene-culture coevolution, and the internalization of norms. J. Theor. Biol. 220 (4), 407–418.

Gintis, H., 2004. The genetic side of gene-culture coevolution: internalization of norms and prosocial emotions. J. Econ. Behav. Organ. 53 (1), 57–67.

Gintis, H., 2007. A framework for the unification of the behavioral sciences. Behav. Brain Sci. 30 (1), 1–61.

Gintis, H., 2008. Five principles for the unification of the behavioral sciences. <http://www.umass.edu/preferen/gintis/NewUnity.pdf> (accessed 27.03.13).

Goldenberg, J., 2010. Local neighborhoods as early predictors of innovation adoption. <http://papers.ssrn.com/sol3/papers.cfm?abstract_id=1545245> (accessed 27.03.13).

Goyal, S., 1996. Interaction structure and social change. J. Inst. Theor. Econ. 152 (3), 472–494.

Goyal, S., 2005. Learning in networks. In: Demange, G., Wooders, M. (Eds.), pp. 122–167.

Gruene-Yanoff, T., Schweinzer, P., 2008. The roles of stories in applying game theory. J. Econ. Methodol. 15 (2), 131–146.

Guala, F., Mittone, L., Ploner, M., 2013. Group membership, team preferences, and expectations. J. Econ. Behav. Organ. 86, 183–190.

Häkli, J., 2009. Geographies of trust. In: Häkli, J., Minca, C. (Eds.), Social Capital and Urban Networks of Trust. Ashgate, Farnham, Burlington, pp. 13–35.

Hamilton, M.J., Burger, O., DeLong, J.P., Walker, R.S., Moses, M.E., Brown, J.H., 2009. Population stability, cooperation, and the invasibility of the human species. PNAS. 106 (30), 12255–12260.

Hargreaves Heap, S.P., Varoufakis, Y., 2004. Game Theory. A Critical Text. Routledge, London, New York.

Hargreaves Heap, S.P., 2008. Individual preferences and decision-making. In: Davis, J.B., Dolfsma, W. (Eds.), The Elgar Companion to Social Economics. Edward Elgar, Cheltenham, Northampton, pp. 79–91.

Harmsen-van Hout, M.J.W., Dellaert, B.G.C., Herings, P.J. J., 2008. Behavioral effects in individual decisions of network formation. Maastricht Res. Sch. Econ. Technol. Organ.RM/08/019.

Hédoin, C., 2010. Did Veblen generalize Darwinism (and why does it matter)? J. Econ. Issues. 44 (4), 963–989.

Henrich, J., 2004. Cultural group selection, coevolutionary processes and large-scale cooperation. J. Econ. Behav. Organ. 53 (1), 3–35.

Henrich, J., Boyd, R., Bowles, S., Camerer, C., Fehr, E., Gintis, H., 2004. Foundations of Human Sociality. Economic Experiments and Ethnographic Evidence from Fifteen Small-Scale Societies. Oxford University Press, Oxford.

Hermann-Pillath, C., 2011. The Economics of Identity and Creativity. A Cultural Science Approach. Transaction Publishers, New Brunswick, London.

Hodgson, G.M., 2000. From micro to macro: the concept of emergence and the role of institutions. In: Burlamaqui, L., et al., (Eds.), Institutions and the Role of the State. Edward Elgar, Cheltenham, Northampton, pp. 103–126.

Hodgson, G.M., 2002. Reconstitutive downward causation: social structure and the development of individual agency. In: Fullbrook, E. (Ed.), Intersubjectivity in Economics: Agents and Structures. Routledge, London, New York, pp. 159–180.

Hodgson, G.M., 2006. What are Institutions? J. Econ. Issues. XL (1), 1–25.

Hodgson, G.M., Huang, K., 2012. Evolutionary game theory and evolutionary economics: are they different species? J. Evol. Econ. 22 (2), 345–366.

Holland, S. t., 1987. The Market Economy. From Micro to Mesoeconomics. Weidenfeld and Nicholson, London.

Holm, J.R., Lorenz, E., Lundvall, B.A., Valeyre, A., 2008. Work organisation and systems of labour market regulation in Europe. <http://vbn.aau.dk/files/16278109/HolmLorenzLundvallValeyre_EAEPE08.pdf> (accessed 26.03.13).

Huggins, R., Johnston, A., 2010. Knowledge flow and inter-firm networks: the influence of network resources, spatial proximity, and firm size. Entrepreneurship Reg. Dev. 22 (5), 457–484.

Jackson, M.O., Zenou, Y., 2012. Games on networks. To appear. In: Young, P., Zamir, S. (Eds.), Handbook of Game Theory, Vol. 4. Elsevier Science, <http://papers.ssrn.com/sol3/papers.cfm?abstract_id=2136179> (accessed 26.03.13).

Jennings, F.B., 2005. How efficiency/equity tradeoffs resolve through horizon effects. J. Econ. Issues. 39 (2), 365–373.

Jones, P.L., 2012. The impact of belonging on the acceptance of online interactions. University of West London. <http://papers.ssrn.com/sol3/papers.cfm?abstract_id=2150807> (accessed 25.03.13).

Jørgensen, H., 2002. Consensus, Cooperation and Conflict. The Policy Making Process in Denmark. Edward Elgar, Cheltenham, Northampton.

Jun, T., Sethi, R., 2007. Neighborhood structure and the evolution of cooperation. J. Evol. Econ. 17, 623–646.

Jun, T., Sethi, R., 2009. Reciprocity in evolving social networks. J. Evol. Econ. 19, 379–396.

Knack, S., Keefer, P., 1997. Does social capital have an economic payoff? a cross-country investigation. Q. J. Econ. 112 (4), 1251–1288.

Knudsen, T., 2002. The evolution of cooperation in structured populations. Constit. Polit. Econ. 13, 129–148.

Konno, T., 2010. A condition for cooperation in a game on complex networks. J. Theor. Biol. 269 (1), 224–233.

Kuznets, S., 1960. Economic growth of small nations. In: Robinson, E.A.G. (Ed.), Economic Consequences of the Size of Nations. Macmillan, London, pp. 14–32.

Lazaric, N., Lorenz, E., 1998. Introduction: the learning dynamics of trust, reputation and confidence. In: Lazaric, N., Lorenz, E. (Eds.), Trust and Economic Learning. Edward Elgar, Cheltenham, Northampton, pp. 1–20.

Legum, M., 2007. What is the right size? Post-Autistic Econ. Rev. 44, 75f.

Li, W., Veliyath, R., Tan, J., 2013. Network characteristics and firm performance: an examination of the relationships in the context of a cluster. J. Small Business Manage. 51 (1), 1–22.

Lin, M., Viswanathan, S., Prabhala, N.R., 2009. Judging borrowers by the company they keep: social networks and adverse selection in online peer-to-peer lending. <http://papers.ssrn.com/sol3/papers.cfm?abstract_id=1355679> (accessed 27.03.13).

Lindgren, K., Nordahl, M.G., 1994. Evolutionary dynamics of spatial games. Physica D. 75, 292–309.

Lindgren, K., Nordahl, M.G., Verendel, V., 2013. Evolutionary exploration of the finitely repeated prisoners' dilemma—the effect of out-of-equilibrium play. Games. 4 (1), 1–20.

Loasby, B.J., 2012. Building systems. J. Evol. Econ. 22 (4), 833–846.

Lundvall, B.A., 2002. Innovation, Growth and Social Cohesion. The Danish Model. Edward Elgar, Cheltenham, Northampton.

Marlowe, F.W., 2005. Hunter-Gatherers and human evolution. Evol. Anthropol. 14, 54–67.

Marwell, G., Oliver, P.E., 1988. Social networks and collective action: a theory of the critical mass. III. Am. J. Soc. 94 (3), 502–534.

Marwell, G., Oliver, P.E., 1993. The Critical Mass in Collective Action. A Micro-Social Theory. Cambridge University Press, Cambridge.

McCann, P., 2007. Sketching out a model of innovation, face-to-face interaction and economic geography. Spat. Econ. Anal. 2 (2), 117–134.

Mohlin, E., 2010. Internalized social norms in conflicts: an evolutionary approach. Econ. Governance. 11 (2), 169–181.

Ng, Y.-K., 1986. Mesoeconomics. A Micro-Macro Analysis. Wheatsheaf Books, Brighton.

Nousala, S., 2010. Emergent structures and geographical scales: what it means for practical policy application. In: International Symposium on Urban Futures and Human Ecosystems Wellbeing, Shanghai, China.

<http://papers.ssrn.com/sol3/papers.cfm?abstract_id=1868828> (accessed 27.03.13).

Oestreicher-Singer, G., Sundarajan, A., 2008. The Visible Hand of Social Networks in Electronic Markets. Mimeo. New York University, New York, NY. Available at: <http://papers.ssrn.com/sol3/papers.cfm?abstract_id=1268516> (accessed 15.04.13).

O'Hara, P.A., 2008. Uneven development, global inequality and ecological sustainability: recent trends and patterns. GPERU Working Paper, Curtin University, Perth, Australia.

Olson, M., 1965. The Logic of Collective Action. Harvard University Press., Cambridge, MA.

Ostrom, E., 2007. Challenges and growth: the development of the interdisciplinary field of institutional analysis. J. Inst. Econ. 3 (3), 239–264.

Ostrom, E., Walker, J., Gardner, R., 1994. Rules, Games, and Common-Pool Resources. University of Michigan Press, Ann Arbor, MI.

Ozawa, T., 1999. Organizational efficiency and structural change: a meso-level analysis. In: Boyd, G., Dunning, H.J. (Eds.), Structural Change and Cooperation in the Global Economy. Edward Elgar, Cheltenham, Northampton, pp. 160–190.

Ozcan, P., Santos, F.M., 2010. The market that never was: clashing frames and failed coalitions in mobile payments. IESE Business School Working Paper No. WP-882. <http://www.iese.edu/research/pdfs/DI-0882-E.pdf> (accessed 25.03.13).

Page, F., Wooders, M., 2007. Strategic basins of attraction, the path dominance core, and network formation games. Center for Applied Economics and Policy Research, Working Paper 2007-020. <http://papers.ssrn.com/sol3/papers.cfm?abstract_id=1019244> (accessed 26.03.13).

Parlamis, J., Ames, D., 2010. Face-to-Face and email negotiations: a comparison of emotions, perceptions and outcomes. <http://papers.ssrn.com/sol3/papers.cfm?abstract_id=1612871> (accessed 27.03.13).

Pelligra, V., 2011. Intentions, trust and frames: a note on sociality and the theory of games. Rev. Soc. Econ. LXIX (2), 163–187.

Peters, H.-R., 1990. Meso-economics and structural policies. Jahrbuch fuer Sozialwissenschaft. 41 (1), 71–88.

Phelps, S., 2012. Emergence of social networks via direct and indirect reciprocity. Autonomous agents and multi-agent systems. <http://link.springer.com/article/10.1007%2Fs10458-012-9207-8#page-1> (accessed 26.03.13).

Pyka, A., 1999. Der Kollektive Innovationsprozess: Eine Theoretische Analyse Informeller Netzwerke und Absorptiver Fähigkeiten. Duncker & Humblot, Berlin.

Rocco, E., 2005. Trust, distance and common ground. In: Bijlsma-Frankema, K., Woolthuis, R.K. (Eds.), Trust under Pressure. Empirical Investigations of Trust and

Trust Building in Uncertain Circumstances. Edward Elgar, Cheltenham, Northampton, pp. 186–205.

Rose, D.C., 2011. The Moral Foundation of Economic Behavior. Oxford University Press., Oxford, New York.

Saunders, K.W., 2012. Balkanizing the internet. In: Pager, S.A., Candeub, A. (Eds.), Transnational Culture in the Internet Age. Edward Elgar, Cheltenham, Northampton, pp. 107–123.

Schelling, T.C., 1969. Models of segregation. Am. Econ. Rev. 59 (**2**), 488–493.

Schelling, T.C., 1973. Hockey helmets, concealed weapons, and daylight saving: a study of binary choices with externalities. J. Conflict. Resolut. XVII (**3**), 211–243, Reproduced in Schelling, 1978.

Schelling, T.C., 1978. Micromotives and Macrobehavior. W. W. Norton, New York, London.

Spiekermann, K.P., 2009. Sort out your neighbourhood. Public good games on dynamic networks. Synthese. 168, 273–294.

Traulsen, A., Nowak, M.A., 2006. Evolution of cooperation by multilevel selection. PNAS. 103 (**29**), 10952–10955.

Tucker, C., 2008. Social interactions, network fluidity and network effects. NET Institute Working Paper No. 08-30. Available at: <http://ideas.repec.org/p/net/wpaper/0830.html> (accessed 15.04.13).

van Staveren, I., 2001. The Values of Economics. An Aristotelian Perspective. Routledge, London, New York.

Villena, M.G., Villena, M.J., 2004. Evolutionary game theory and Thorstein Veblen's evolutionary economics: Is EGT Veblenian? J. Econ. Issues. XXXVIII (**3**), 585–610.

Vinkovic, D., Kirman, A., 2006. A physical analogue of the Schelling model. PNAS. 103 (**51**), 19261–19265.

Waldeck, R., 2010. Segregation in social dilemmas. <http://litis.univ-lehavre.fr/~bertelle/epnacs2010/epnacs2010-proceedings/waldeck4epnacs2010.pdf> (accessed 25.03.13).

Waterman, D., Ji, S.W., 2011. Online vs. Offline in the U.S.: are the media shrinking? Inf. Soc. 28 (**5**), 285–303.

Watkins, J.P., 2010. Mainstream efforts to tell a better story—natural selection as a misplaced metaphor: the problem of corporate power. J. Econ. Issues. 44 (**4**), 991–1008.

Watts, D.J., 1999. Small Worlds. The Dynamics of Networks between Order and Randomness. Princeton University Press., Princeton, Oxford.

Wells, P.A., 2010. Shrinking the internet. N. Y. Univ. J. Law Lib. 5 (**2**), 531–580.

Wilson, E.O., 2012. The Social Conquest of Earth. Liveright Publishing/W.W. Norton, New York, NY.

Yamagishi, T., 1992. Group size and the provision of a sanctioning system in a social dilemma. In: Liebrand, W.B.G., Messick, D.M., Wilke, H.A.M. (Eds.), Social Dilemmas. Theoretical Issues and Research Findings. Pergamon Press, Oxford, pp. 267–287.

Zelmer, J., 2003. Linear public goods experiments: a meta-analysis. Exp. Econ. 6, 299–310.

Zenou, Y., 2012. Networks in economics. To appear in: International Encyclopedia of the Social and Behavioral Sciences. <http://ideas.repec.org/p/cpr/ceprdp/9021.html> (accessed 26.03.13).

Zhang, Y., G.E. Bolten. 2011. Social network effects on coordination: a laboratory investigation. <http://papers.ssrn.com/sol3/papers.cfm?abstract_id=2000974> (accessed 26.03.13).

Further Reading—Online

For further literature on the subject field, please visit the textbook website: http://booksite.elsevier.com/9780124115859

FURTHER APPLICATIONS: INFORMATION, INNOVATION, POLICY, AND METHODOLOGY

15

The Information Economy and the Open-Source Principle

"I'm going to ask you to open up your data. Give it away." **Aaron Swartz**[1]

[1]*Aaron Swartz's A Programmable Web: An Unfinished Work* (2013/2009), Morgan & Claypool, p. 28.

The Microeconomics of Complex Economies.
DOI: http://dx.doi.org/10.1016/B978-0-12-411585-9.00015-4

15.1 INTRODUCTION

One morning in September 1983, the astonished readers of the net.unix-wizards Usenet newsgroup[2] were surprised by a message announcing "a new Unix distribution."[3] The author, signing rms@mit-oz, to some of the readers better known as the MIT Artificial Intelligence lab programmer Richard Stallman, informed his audience that

> (s)tarting this Thanksgiving I am going to write a complete Unix-compatible software system called GNU (for Gnu's Not Unix), and give it away free to everyone who can use it. Contributions of time, money, programs and equipment are greatly needed. (Stallman, 1983)

Stallman was at the time an already well-known programmer who had developed the then popular editor EMACS as well as many other programs both with MIT and on his own. He was also known to be a vocal critic of the emerging software industry for not making the source code of their programs available to the users thereby preventing users from modifying the program applying their own improvements. One story is more well known: Stallman modified his lab's shared printer's software to send an email to the user when her printing job was finished or when the printer was jammed. When MIT obtained a new printer, the vendor was unwilling to provide the software's source code so that the advantages of Stallman's improvement on the old machine were lost. Though it had for many years been common practice for programmers

to share their code with anyone who was interested and in turn also to benefit from other programmer's work, this practice had a major disadvantage for commercial software vendors. If the source code of a program is distributed to everyone, everyone will be able to develop and sell their slightly modified version of the software thus competing with the original developer. As a consequence, the free and productive sharing of the 1960s and 1970s declined, more and more programs would not allow the users access to the source code, and Stallman was forced to find a way to deal with this development. Finally, in late 1983, he had had enough. He resigned from MIT in early 1984 and started developing his own, free computer operating system which was designed to pave the way for a new way of programming where software would be free and users would be free to modify it according to their needs and skills, where the culture of sharing of the 1960s and 1970s continued.

Thirty years later, development on the GNU operating system is still under way and technically still not finished—it lacks one crucial part, the kernel.[4] However, together with the Linux kernel, developed by Linus Torvalds since 1991, the operating system is well established and by now one of the major players in the industry. The combined operating system is called GNU/Linux, often referred to as simply Linux, though GNU developers insist that this is incorrect. Stallman is still part of the project and—more than ever—a well-known figure among programmers. The movement advocating the production and use of free and

---

[2]Usenet newsgroups and mailboxes were the dominant ways of online communication before the inception of the graphical world wide web.

[3]The history of the GNU Project as presented in this section follows the detailed account of Williams (2002).

[4]There is no stable version of the GNU HURD kernel. The other parts of the operating system are indeed ready and form a part of the GNU/Linux system, basically GNU with the Linux kernel, developed by Linus Torvalds since 1992, at its core. Had the Linux kernel not been developed, it is likely that much more effort had been put into GNU's own HURD kernel.

open-source software is commonly called the open-source movement with its major actors being the Free Software Foundation (FSF) and the Open-Source Initiative (OSI). GNU comes with its own license called GPL (GNU General Public License) which specifies that and how the software and any software derived from it must always be free and open. Today, a large number of other software packages are also released under GPL or other open-source licenses. Some of the more successful ones include the Apache web server, the MySQL database management system, the web browsers Firefox and Chromium,[5] as well as the compilers, libraries, and virtual machines of the programming languages Java, PHP, Perl, and Python. All of these software sectors (web servers, database management systems, web browsers, and scripting languages) are today largely dominated by these open-source programs with open-source competitors to commercial sellers also developing rapidly in other sectors.

The emergence of open-source communities is naturally a mystery to rational choice theories and social sciences dominated by such approaches, including neoclassical economics. Why would anyone possibly work for free? Why would a—highly skilled—programmer invest her time in a project which she will never be able to sell for a profit? Resourceful adherents of rational choice came up with a number of rational explanations for this seemingly irrational behavior: if the labor market is intransparent it makes sense to build a reputation to show one's skill in code that is openly available, even to use signaling strategies, i.e., to invest huge amounts of time as sunk costs into open-source programming in order to deter competitors from doing the same as an employment seeking strategy.[6] Open-source programmers themselves, however, have always emphasized that the primary motivation lies in the desire to and enjoyment in fixing things, in the immediate need of a certain tool (which if not available otherwise is just written as an open-source program without the desire to make profits), and in the belief that software should "be free" and that the community as a whole including themselves will benefit from such a cooperative culture (Stallman, 1985; Raymond, 1998).

Chapter 4 presented an introduction to the economic developments of the recent decades and the contemporary IT economy. As detailed in that chapter, software and information are different from traditional goods in that the related variable production costs are negligible and in that the coordination on common standards is particularly important. This gives rise to different types of social and economic problems, to very asymmetric industry structures,[7] to peculiar selling and marketing strategies, and to previously unknown options for policy makers. The current chapter not only focuses on the economic properties and specifics of open-source software and the principle of open source in general but also includes considerations on the economics of knowledge and information, the emergence of the IT economy and its specifics, particularly the economic consequences of network externalities, as well as an analysis of policy options.

---

[5]Chromium is related to but not the same as the Google Chrome browser.

[6]Some of these arguments are reiterated in Lerner and Tirole (2002) and in Lakhani and von Hippel (2003) even though these authors are aware that there are alternative explanations.

[7]Consider the operating system sector dominated by Microsoft or the fields of online search engines and social media that are equally cornered by Google and Facebook.

15.2 THE ECONOMICS OF INFORMATION, KNOWLEDGE, AND SOFTWARE

15.2.1 Data, Information, and Knowledge as Club Goods

One of the most notorious buzzwords of the recent years is *big data*. Since recently, the technological means for exhaustive recording of, say, a day's online activities of everyone in a city or the connection data of all phone calls in a country over a day exist. While for decades social scientists and marketing agents alike had to contend themselves with small sample sizes, everyone wants the whole of the data today even though a sample would do for most purposes. In the quest for big data, a subtle distinction seems to have been blurred: having data is not the same as having information—which, in turn, is not the same as having knowledge. Information needs to be extracted from data using statistical methods; knowledge is generated by understanding information. However, in their economic properties the three concepts have one thing in common (with the possible exception of certain types of knowledge): the marginal cost (variable cost) resulting from their production is negligible. Copying datasets, technical reports, ebooks, or educational resources costs almost nothing compared to the huge fixed costs incurred in the creation of the database or in the scientific project behind the report. Nonrivalry[8] is another common property of such goods as

they are not destroyed in the consumption process.

As a consequence, consumers do not have a dominant incentive to guard such goods against unauthorized access and copying by others. Producers, on the other hand, do. They may therefore try to design the goods as club goods rather than public goods (for more on the taxonomy and detailed definitions, see Chapter 1), ensuring that they are able to exclude unauthorized consumers.[9] They may then set an arbitrary price which they collect from all consumers and which then covers the fixed costs incurred in the production of the good. Given that they have the option to exclude unauthorized consumers, they may, however, also choose the price to be much higher than the value that would be sufficient in order to cover their fixed costs thereby securing gigantic rents. What is more, they may *ex ante* not know nor be able to estimate the number of customers. They could, of course, set an arbitrary price, collect revenue until the production costs are covered and then release the good into the public domain giving it away for free.[10] There is, however, no dominant reason for the producer why she should give up the revenue she could appropriate from a successful product.

From a social perspective, this strategic setup is rather unfortunate. A good with zero marginal cost could benefit the entire society; however, it is reserved for the group of those who are able and willing to pay for it. The degree to which this is the case depends on

---

[8]In certain cases it is possible that people with access to a certain information or knowledge might want to keep that information from the general public in order to be able to either sell their expertise or enjoy advantages in trading. This, however, is not generally true for information and knowledge, particularly if network externalities are involved as explained later in this section.

[9]This commonly includes the development of intricate technological mechanisms to prevent copying of data and to exclude the general public from information or knowledge. See Chapter 4 for more on exclusion technologies.

[10]This is a practice known to the open-source community as *delayed open-sourcing*. Note that this also generates a social dilemma for the users: once the costs are covered the latecomers are able to free-ride on the contributions of other users.

the—entirely arbitrary—price set by the producer. Taking into account that knowledge (in the form of learning resources, not full education programs) belongs to this type of goods, it follows that the skills, the human capital, and by extension the productivity of the society as a whole are also affected. In a way, the restrictive licensing on the part of the vendor cripples economic growth and development in the long run. While in order to encourage the production of goods with zero marginal cost, it is in most cases genuinely necessary to allow the producer to cover her costs somehow, it may be desirable to curb her power to hold the once finished good hostage for extended periods of time after this has been accomplished.

15.2.2 Network Goods, Network Technologies, and Network Externalities

Some goods do not only have no significant marginal cost, they are also subject to network externalities. This aspect has already been mentioned in Chapters 3, 8, 11, and 13. While it may also occur for information if the information in question is to form the basis for major projects or political decisions, it is more obvious in cases that involve a component that is used by the consumer in communication processes with other users, in cases such as software. Consumers benefit from using the same software standard; if their word processing software is compatible, they can exchange text documents; if they use the same instant messaging protocol, they can connect using a chat client; if their operating systems are compatible, they can use similar software, and are therefore able to combine learning efforts and share improvements.

The downside of this becomes obvious when considering communication barriers that arise from different standards used by different groups in the same population or indeed in the same company. In order to coordinate

on the same standard, one of the two groups has to incur considerable learning costs and in most cases also costs for buying the software package related to the other standard.

The situation is conveniently modeled as an n-person coordination game or in a simplified way as a 2-person coordination game as depicted in Figure 15.1. The n-person form requires the payoffs $\Pi_i(n_i)$ of the strategies s_i (with $i = 1, 2$) to be stated explicitly as a function of the size of the group that already chose s_i, n_i:

$$\Pi_i(n_i) = 3n_i$$

It follows that s_i is preferable to the other strategy s_{-i} if $n_i > n_{-i}$. Even if there are different parts of the population that would—not considering the network externality—prefer s_1 and s_2, there is a point from which on the network utility exceeds the utility from the "intrinsic" preferences. Generalized URN scheme models and an agent-based model of this developed by Arthur (1989) and Arthur et al. (1983) and discussed in detail in Section 13.6 show very clear results.

Note that potential commercial vendors of the two standards will have a strong incentive, to capture a large user base as fast as possible, to be—if in any way possible—*first mover*, or to engage in a *price war* if this fails. Once one of the vendors is able to establish herself in a dominant position, her competitors are virtually without any chances to compete with her (two exceptions are discussed in Section 15.2.4). The implications of this in conjunction with the considerations from Section 15.2.1 are clear. Commercial vendors undergo a high risk by

		Player B	
		s_1 Standard 1	s_2 Standard 2
Player A	s_1 Standard 1	3 3	0 0
	s_2 Standard 2	0 0	3 3

FIGURE 15.1 Coordination game.

entering a contested software sector. In order to be competitive, they have to incur considerable development costs—whether they will be able to recover them later will depend if they are able to establish a significant user base before any potential competitors do. It is clear that large, well-established firms have considerable advantages since they can afford to undergo more such risks and to fail more often without going bankrupt. As is widely acknowledged, they are, however, less likely to come up with radically new products and radical innovations in general (Nooteboom, 1994). Established firms tend to try to circumvent this by acquiring small startups and their products along with them; this also allows the large firm to selectively only invest in successful ideas that have already taken off.

Further, once a competitor is established in a software industry, i.e., once she has driven out all her competitors, she will be able to set the prices according to her pleasing. She will also be in control of the technical standards and have the ability to change them without handing the specifications to other parties, thereby further deterring potential competitors. The price for all this—in terms of opportunity costs—is borne by the society as a whole.

15.2.3 The Resulting Social Dilemma

Since the firms themselves also benefit from the development of human capital in a society, they would collectively be better off if they only could agree on a cooperative culture that would allow the broadest possible access to all goods with zero marginal cost that contribute to the development of skills and human capital in the society. As the benefits of each such contribution are, however, collectively enjoyed by all firms (and by society as a whole) while the costs are borne privately only by the contributing firm, we face an n-person social dilemma situation.

For a formal representation of the problem consider the following simplified example: in a society with $n = 1000$ equal-sized firms each firm develops a product with zero marginal cost. The development costs for each of the goods are 100 (of a certain monetary unit, say million dollars). If the firm releases the good into the public domain, it will have to bear the development costs in full but each of the 1000 firms (including the one developing the good) will obtain an additional payoff of 1 million dollars generated by the enhanced human capital levels. Let the strategies be denoted s_{PD} (for public domain) and s_{PR} (for proprietary) and the numbers of firms following both strategies n_{PD} and $n_{PR} = 1000 - n_{PD}$. In turn, the respective payoff functions are

$$\Pi_{PD}(n_{PD}) = -100 + n_{PD}$$

$$\Pi_{PR}(n_{PD}) = n_{PD}$$

s_{PR} is always strictly dominant but since the number of firms is larger than 100, the Pareto optima are those strategy combinations where none or at most 100 firms play s_{PR}.[11]

---

[11]To see this, consider the payoffs for the cases (A) $n_{PD} = n$, (B) $n_{PD} = n - x$ with $0 < x < 100$, (C) $n_{PD} = n - 100$, and (D) $n_{PD} = n - x$ with $x > 100$. In case (A), $\Pi_{PD} = n - 100$, Π_{PR} does not exist, because no one plays s_{PR}. In case (B), there are $n - x$ agents obtaining payoff $\Pi_{PD} = n - 100 - x$ as well as x firms getting $\Pi_{PR} = n - x$. In case (C), firms get at most $\Pi_{PR} = n - 100$, but there are $n - 100$ firms getting even less, $\Pi_{PD} = n - 200$. The strategy configurations (C) are therefore Pareto dominated by (A). Since in all cases (D) the maximal payoffs are even lower than in case (C), only outcomes (A) and (B) are Pareto optima. Note that none of the outcomes (B) for any $\tilde{x}$ can be Pareto dominated because for lower $x < \tilde{x}$ the maximum payoffs (the payoffs of s_{PR}) are lower than for $\tilde{x}$ while for higher $x > \tilde{x}$ the number of agents obtaining the high payoff Π_{PR} is lower than for $\tilde{x}$. Further note that for each x in cases (B) there are permutations and thus $n!/x!$ different and distinguishable outcomes, all of which are Pareto optima.

Therefore for $n > 100$ we always obtain a dilemma structure.

Now, the above case is simplified in that it does not allow mixed strategies,[12] in that it does not consider repetitions (in this case, cooperative strategies with credible threats, i.e., n-person equivalents to TFT would introduce another, cooperative, equilibrium), and in that it assumes the firm size to be homogeneous.

Consider another simplified model which does not require the latter assumption. Let a population of firms be composed of two sub-populations, PD and PR. Let the population shares (measured in output) be denoted p_{PD} and $p_{PR} = 1 - p_{PD}$ and the respective output sizes of the populations y_{PD} and y_{PR}, such that

$$p_{PD} = \frac{y_{PD}}{y_{PD} + y_{PR}}$$

Assume that the future size of an arbitrary firm i be determined by

$$y_{i,t+1} = (1 - \alpha_i)y_i + CG = (1 - \alpha_i)y_{i,t}$$
$$+ 1.2 \frac{1}{y_{PD,t} + y_{PR,t}} \sum_j \alpha_j y_{j,t}$$

where $0 \le \alpha_i \le 1$ is firm i's share of output it contributes to a collective good CG, the remainder $(1 - \alpha_i)$ is reinvested privately. While the private investments are directly transformed into future output, the future output is enhanced by the collective good, which generates for each firm an additional output of 120% of the average contribution to the collective good. Assume that PR firms do not contribute to the collective good ($\alpha_{PR} = 0$) while PD firms contribute their entire output ($\alpha_{PD} = 1$). It follows that the respective sizes of the population shares develop according to

$$y_{PD,t+1} = 0 + 1.2 \frac{1}{y_{PD,t} + y_{PR,t}} \sum_{j \in PD} y_{j,t}$$

$$y_{PR,t+1} = y_{PR,t} + 1.2 \frac{1}{y_{PD,t} + y_{PR,t}} \sum_{j \in PD} y_{j,t}$$

from which the future population shares

$$p_{PD,t+1} = \frac{y_{PD,t+1}}{y_{PD,t+1} + y_{PR,t+1}}$$

$$p_{PR,t+1} = \frac{y_{PR,t+1}}{y_{PD,t+1} + y_{PR,t+1}}$$

can be computed. Since the relation between the future shares is preserved if the computation uses the current shares instead of the current absolute size,

$$\tilde{y}_{PD,t+1} = 0 + 1.2 \frac{1}{p_{PD,t} + p_{PR,t}} p_{PD,t} = 1.2 p_{PD,t}$$

$$\tilde{y}_{PR,t+1} = p_{PR,t} + 1.2 \frac{1}{p_{PD,t} + p_{PR,t}} p_{PD,t}$$

$$= (1 - p_{PD,t}) + 1.2 p_{PD,t}$$

i.e.,

$$\frac{y_{PD,t+1}}{y_{PD,t+1} + y_{PR,t+1}} = \frac{\tilde{y}_{PD,t+1}}{\tilde{y}_{PD,t+1} + \tilde{y}_{PR,t+1}}$$

the system is conveniently and completely described by the recurrence equation

$$p_{PD,t+1} = \frac{\tilde{y}_{PD,t+1}}{\tilde{y}_{PD,t+1} + \tilde{y}_{PR,t+1}}$$
$$= \frac{1.2 p_{PD,t}}{1 - p_{PD,t} + 1.2 p_{PD,t} + 1.2 p_{PD,t}}$$
$$= \frac{1.2 p_{PD,t}}{1 + 1.4 p_{PD,t}}.$$

with p_{PR} following as $p_{PR} = 1 - p_{PD}$ for each time period.

The equilibrium condition for dynamic systems in difference equations (as covered in

---

[12]However, the game does not have a mixed strategy equilibrium.

more detail in Chapters 10 and 11), $p_{PD,t+1} = p_{PD,t}$ yields two equilibria,

$$p_{PD,1}^* = 0$$
$$p_{PD,2}^* = 1/7$$

which are conveniently interpreted as a population with no cooperation at all ($p_{PD,1}^*$) and a divided population ($p_{PD,2}^*$) with a cooperating minority (that contributes to the public domain). A stability analysis using the method introduced in Chapters 10 and 11 shows that $p_{PD,2}^*$ is stable while $p_{PD,1}^*$ is not (see also Exercise 2).

In this case, the model suggests that a population with a small minority of firms that support the public domain with their goods will emerge. This is due to the fact that they themselves also benefit from their own contribution. Since the private investments of noncontributing firms do not generate growth effects, their growth will exceed the growth their contribution induces in the already larger noncontributing share of the population. If private investments also generate growth effects or if the growth effects produced by the public good are smaller, the divided population equilibrium would be much closer or equal to $p_{PD,1}^*$ with the share of contributing firms also lower. This equilibrium and with it the stable cooperating (contributing) minority does, however, exist as long as the property of a socially beneficial collective good is preserved in the model (i.e., as long as growth from contributions to the collective good exceeds growth from private investment). The equilibrium is also preserved if more than two strategies are allowed or even if the firms may freely choose the extent of their contribution to the public good. This setting, in turn, is much more realistic and may be applied to real economic systems inferring that contributions to public goods are self-supporting to a certain extent though this extent is probably much smaller than socially desirable. It is obvious that different kinds of government intervention can encourage or ensure much larger contributions to the public domain and thus a much more rapid development.

15.2.4 The Strategy Space in Industries with Network Externalities

Size Effects and Price Wars

As mentioned above, when network externalities are present firms are faced with very different decision problems than in sectors that are not subject to network externalities or where network externalities do not play a dominant role (see also Chapters 3 and 4 and Section 13.6). To be successful, an installed base is crucial; it increases the utility of other potential users and convinces them to join the network and purchase the good. This is true to the extent that depending on different sizes of the expected user base, different cost levels may be feasible for the vendor such that production is still profitable. The cost may obviously include gifts to the initial user base, i.e., paying the first cohort of users for adopting the standard. For more detailed analyses of the industrial economics of network externalities, see Shy (2001) or Heinrich (2013).

Consider the following model: an industry with network externalities is contested by two producers, A and B. Customers may only use one of the two goods provided by A and B, in turn choosing strategy s_A or s_B. Let p_A and p_B denote the population share of customers using the two goods, this equals the market shares of A and B. Further assume that customers reconsider their choices leading to dynamic process following the replicator equation known from Chapters 8 and 11:

$$\frac{dp_i(t)}{dt} = p_i(t)\left(\Pi_i(t) - \sum_{j\in\{A,B\}} p_j(t)\Pi_j(t)\right) \quad i = A, B$$

		Player 2	
		s_A Standard A	s_B Standard B
Player 1	s_A Standard A	$1 + \alpha$ / $1 + \alpha$	1 / 1
	s_B Standard B	1 / 1	$1 + \beta$ / $1 + \beta$

FIGURE 15.2 Price war coordination game.

where Π_i are the expected payoffs of choosing the respective strategy; note that the sum is simply the average payoff. Assume that the expected payoffs arise from the underlying game as depicted in Figure 15.2. Parameter $\alpha > 0$ is controlled by the first producer while the second producer controls parameter $\beta > 0$, both thereby being able to manipulate the game and the game's dynamics (its fixed points and their stability) in order to obtain a larger market share.

The expected payoffs are as follows:

$$\Pi_A(t) = 1 + \alpha p_A(t)$$
$$\Pi_B(t) = 1 + \beta(1 - p_A(t))$$

Substituting this into the replicator equation yields (writing the $p_i(t)$ simply as p_i for convenience):

$$\frac{dp_A}{dt} = p_A(1 - p_A)((\alpha + \beta)p_A - \beta) \quad (15.1)$$

with the dynamic of the other population share $p_B(t)$ of course following as $p_B = 1 - p_A$. The stability determining eigenvalue is the linearization of the function

$$\lambda(p_A) = \frac{\partial dp_A(t)/dt}{\partial p_A(t)} = -3(\alpha + \beta)p_A^2$$
$$+ 2(\alpha + 2\beta)p_A - \beta$$

There are three equilibria:

$$p_{A,1}^* = 0, \quad p_{A,2}^* = 1, \quad p_{A,3}^* = \frac{\beta}{\alpha + \beta}$$

$p_{A,1}^*$ and $p_{A,2}^*$ are stable and $p_{A,3}^*$ is always unstable.[13] In turn, and unsurprisingly for a coordination game, the two equilibria standing for complete monopolization for either of the competitors are stable with an unstable market sharing equilibrium in between. The significance of the latter unstable equilibrium lies in the fact that it separates the basins of attraction of the two stable equilibria. For $p_A < p_{A,3}^*$, the dynamic goes toward $p_{A,1}^*$, for $p_A > p_{A,3}^*$, it goes toward $p_{A,2}^*$. Each competitor would therefore work to have $p_{A,3}^*$ shifted as close as possible to the respective other one's monopolization equilibrium; A would try to increase α in order to shift $(\beta/\alpha + \beta)$ close to 0; B would try to increase β so that $(\beta/\alpha + \beta)$ will be close to 1. α and β may be seen as gifts by the respective company to potential users to convince them to switch to their standard, not to the other one. If increasing these parameters induces costs for the two companies, the companies face a trade-off. Increasing their parameter makes them more likely to win the price war and to be able to appropriate monopoly benefits later on, but it also increases the overall sunk cost which they cannot recover in case they lose the battle.

The IT economy offers plenty of examples for such standard wars:

- between *PC operating systems*, especially in the late 1980s and early 1990s, the major contenders being Microsoft's DOS/Windows product line, Apples Mac OS's, Be Inc.'s BeOS. It was only later that with GNU/Linux an open-source alternative entered the stage;
- between *web browsers* in the 1990s with major contenders Microsoft Internet Explorer and Netscape Navigator;

[13]For $\alpha = 0$, the first and the third fixed point would be marginally stable (but α is by definition required to be strictly positive); for $\beta = 0$, the second and the third fixed point would be marginally stable (but β is by definition required to be strictly positive).

- again between web browsers in more recent years with major contenders Internet Explorer and the open-source browser Mozilla Firefox, as well as Google's Chrome and Apple's Safari;
- between *social media systems* (Google+ and Facebook);
- between *web search engines* in the late 1990s (Google, Lycos, Yahoo, Bing) and again more recently (Google, Yandex, and others);
- between *microprocessor architectures* in the 1980s (Intel, Motorola, Sequent, National Semiconductor, IBM) and again in the 2000 (Intel, AMD, IBM (PowerPC));
- between *data storage systems*, VHS and Betamax in the 1980s, blue-ray and HD DVD discs in the 2000s, and perhaps also between floppy discs, optical discs (CD, DVD, HD DVD, blue-ray), and USB flash storage devices over a longer period of time since the 1990s, though these product lineages may be perceived to serve slightly different purposes.

Compatibility (Interoperability) and Incompatibility

Vendors of standard setting products are generally able to control and fine-tune the degrees of compatibility of their products. When faced with a competitor who offers a product which is compatible to their own, thereby trying to break into their industry segment, they can redefine the standard to add obstacles or to remove the compatibility altogether. Often, compatibility can be controlled to such an extent that an asymmetric compatibility structure results. For instance, one product is able to actively communicate with the other while the other can only accept incoming messages from this product. Or—this being often the case with word processing software—one product can open the other product's native file format but not vice versa.

Consider the following simple model: assume—similar to the model in the previous section—a setting with two competitors and a large number of users choosing one of the two producers' products. It shall again be modeled with the same replicator equation and shall again be driven by the users' expected outcome from the two options resulting from a normal form game with two parameters α and β controlled by competitors A and B, respectively. However, this time, the producers do not offer transfers to their consumers; they reduce the compatibility of their competitor's product to their own. A increases α to diminish an s_B player's return against s_A players; an increase in β reduces s_A players benefits from communicating with s_B users.

Computing the expected payoffs and substituting into the replicator equation result in a dynamic system (consisting of only one differential equation) identical to Eq. (15.1). Consequently, the equilibria and their stability properties are also identical (see also Exercise 3). The monopolization equilibria are stable, and unstable population division equilibrium exists. Both competitors strive to increase their respective parameter α or β in order to shift the population sharing equilibrium such that the size of their basin of attraction is maximized.

Note that this example, suggesting that rational competitors will always try to be as incompatible as possible to other standards, is simplified. In more complex models, this is not necessarily the case, particularly if only compatibility offers the firm in question an option to take over the other firm's market share. Another example would be one with large positive benefits from compatibility from which also the two standard vendors benefit and the effects of which outweigh what they hope to gain with the compatibility battle.

Controlling a Sector, Planned Obsolescence, and Refusal to Innovate

Once a commercial vendor gains absolute control of a sector, especially one with zero marginal cost, she can not only set the prices in this sector to whatever she pleases, she can also decide about the direction and pace of innovation (if any) without having to defend her position in the market and she can change the standard and require the users to pay for new versions as often as she likes.[14]

Users may react by refusing to update. However, by simply changing specifications, the producer may remove backwards compatibility thereby reducing the users utility from working with older versions and eventually forcing them to update. Indeed, there are recurring fights between Microsoft and other software firms that produce applications for Microsoft's operating system Windows. Microsoft places no particular value on backward compatibility (or is intentionally removing backward compatibility); users and application producers on the other hand were not always willing to switch to the newest Windows versions resulting in the complete failure of Windows ME and later Windows Vista.

Further, while firms in a dominating position in their sector are not forced to innovate, the IT industry is highly interconnected and develops quick enough to ensure that their entire sector would quickly become obsolete if they do not keep up with other parts of the IT industry. However, a similar effect may be observable and indeed pretty well known. Microsoft Windows, which enjoyed a dominating position in the operating system sector with no serious competitors at least between 1995 and 2010, is frequently ridiculed for being unreliable, badly designed, and generally flawed—yet it is still the most widely used PC operating system. The company has been alleged to have a policy of "ship(ping) it on Tuesday and get it right by version 3" (Anderson, 2001).

Tied Standards

At the same time, other firms followed different strategies. Apple, for instance, while trailing badly behind Microsoft in the PC operating systems sector in the late 1990s managed to stabilize its position and to return with a powerful assault on several established and emerging hardware and software sectors in the 2000s. This included not only smartphones, MP3 players, tablet computers but also the established markets of PC operating systems and web browsers.[15]

Apple's great advantage over many years was not only the sale of an integrated system starting with the hardware but also including operating system, application software, peripheral devices, and services. That all these sectors generate network externalities of their own is obvious. Further, they are not independent of each other. It is therefore possible to use network externalities in one of them strategically to improve one's position in another one. This has probably also played a part in Microsoft's final success in the browser war of the 1990s (see above). It was discussed as a side issue in Microsoft's antitrust lawsuit in the late 1990s and early 2000s, Microsoft tied its web browser Internet Explorer to the Windows operating system (and vice versa: it was demonstrated that the operating system did not function properly without the web browser). The phenomenon is known as standard tying in the literature with an early game theory analysis by Choi (2004) and more recently an evolutionary analysis with replicator models by Heinrich (2014).

Two-Sided Networks

Some standards or technologies with network externalities have two or multiple distinct and separable groups of users. To gain a

---

[14]For more detail on the related issue of planned obsolescence, see Choi (1994).

[15]Note that since recently Apple produces a Windows version of its native web browser Safari, possibly indicating preparations for an assault on Microsoft's core business.

dominating position for one standard it is in such cases often sufficient to acquire a large user base in one of these groups. Since both groups generate network externalities for the other group as well, this will increase the incentives of users from the other group to adopt this standard. A common example is PC operating system: an operating system as a successful technology needs both users and vendors of complementary application programs. Losing the support of one of the two groups would render it unattractive to the other group. This effect is related to the effect of tied standards as detailed above; the strategic options for monopolists in control of the standard or technology are equivalent.

Profitable Piracy

Product piracy is generally only feasible if there are considerable profit margins since the pirate would otherwise not be able to produce cheaper than the rightful owner of the brand or patent and would be unable to cover her additional costs incurred by avoiding detection and prosecution. If profit margins are high, product piracy is feasible and widespread. For goods with zero marginal costs, the profit margin for the pirate—who did not have to cover the development costs—is equal to the price she charges. However, there is no significant product piracy in the traditional sense of the word (a second, illegal, producer who pretends to be the rightful owner of the brand). This is because with zero production costs, everyone is able to copy a software package or database and redistribute it for free. Over the recent years and with the emergence of better and better communication technologies, software piracy has developed into a major grievance of the commercial software industry and—even more so—of the music and entertainment industry.[16]

In essence, not every hacker has been as idealistic as Robert Stallman. Many do not care about how software or information is licensed and pragmatically focus on sharing what they have. While this, as explained above, reduces the vendor's profits and puts her attempts to recover her development costs in jeopardy, it does also—given that the product already exists—help to make efficient use of it. It opens it to a larger group of people who can benefit from it and who in turn can put their skill and creativity to use in other areas thereby benefiting the society as a whole instead of keeping the product to the small club whose well-informed members are willing and able to pay for it. Software piracy adds openness to the information economy. It may have played an important part in the great success of the IT economy, as important perhaps as the technological advances.

Many of the firms that deal with goods which are prone to software piracy are—understandably—furious. Software piracy is illegal but large parts of the population nevertheless engage in it on a gigantic scale. Nevertheless, it should be noted that it is largely illegal only because copyright law and intellectual property rights have been further restricted since the 1970s in many countries to make it illegal; it would have been rather difficult to prosecute someone for copying information without commercial intentions on the basis of the laws as they were 1970. While, like in other sectors, some firms go bankrupt, the industry as a whole does not seem to be in danger. In fact, there is also another aspect to software piracy. In order to establish themselves in a sector, vendors need, as discussed above, to create an installed base. Thus, they benefit greatly if they can extract revenues from those customers willing to pay and give the software as a gift to those who are not,

---

[16]For an empirical evaluation whether the music industry actually suffered any losses due to piracy, see Oberholzer-Gee and Strumpf (2007).

i.e., if they can exercise price discrimination. Piracy offers several ways to do that: illegal copies are most likely made more often by users who cannot afford the software, they are made more often by users with better skills, and they are employed more often for private, noncommercial use. There is at least anecdotal evidence that companies actively employ such strategies, for instance Jeff Raikes, the former head of the Microsoft business group, quoted: "If they are going to 'pirate' somebody, we want it to be us rather than somebody else." (Darmon et al., 2009). The phenomenon is commonly referred to as profitable piracy; for detailed analyses, see Shy (2001), Peitz and Waelbroeck (2006), Darmon et al. (2009), or Le Texier and Gordah (2011).

Niche Construction

Finally, the deliberate creation of incompatibility as discussed above can be driven to the extreme of trying to split off a part of a sector so that the incompatible products are no longer substitutes and that re-introducing compatibility would no longer make sense. This can be done for software by adding new features or by tying it to other standards or software products (thereby also involving standard tying as mentioned above).

Being successful at splitting niches off established sectors with a dominant product or standard is not easy, especially not when attempted using a top-down approach, i.e., the company designs the product and the users have to like it. There are more successful examples with bottom-up approaches: a company funds an open-source community that develops an alternative software in a contested sector. If the open-source software is successful, the company enters the newly created niche with a commercial product. Sun Microsystems has reportedly used such niche construction techniques with Openoffice (which was open source, the proprietary equivalent being Staroffice) and in a different way with Java

(by making it freely available thereby building a large community) (Luksha, 2008). Other examples may include Google's various new software products.

Open Source as a Business Strategy

Commercially funded open-source communities may be useful for the creation of new niches before the commercial vendor enters the niche, but there are many other ways to strategically make use of open-source communities.

At the core of many such strategies is the insight that the open distribution of the source code of a program invites a wide range of improvement suggestions and contributions to bug fixing from the user community. This makes development cheaper and speedier, adds to information security as well as to the users trust in the reliability of the software, and allows a greater focus on the users' needs. On the other hand, gaining an installed base is important in order to be successful in the long run.

Many open-source business models then focus on covering their costs from either selling complementary products to the open-source software (such as hardware or data or other software) or—more often—offering support services for the software including installation and maintenance. For software for commercial purposes, the support is most likely the bigger source of revenue anyway. Further, with a rapidly developing IT industry, some have come to understand software more as a service (including support) than a product. We will return to these considerations in the following section.

Examples include Sun Microsystems (supporting the text editor Openoffice, see above), Red Hat and IBM (supporting and profiting from Linux in various ways), as well as Google (which relies on and works with many open-source communities).

15.3 THE ECONOMICS OF OPEN SOURCE

15.3.1 Open Source in Practice

In the first few decades of electronic information and communication technology, before the emergence of widely available global digital communication networks (starting with the ARPANET in the 1970s and transforming into today's internet in the late 1980s and early 1990s), software in general, and licensing in particular, was not a big issue. Code was to a larger extent than today adjusted to the hardware and was freely shared among programmers—the world that Richard Stallman fought to preserve in the 1980s. With the emergence of proprietary closed source licensing in the 1980s, this all changed. The specific change came down to the refusal of software vendors to make the source code of the programs available to the users; the programs were now distributed in a compiled form, in binary code, unreadable to humans, and therefore impossible to modify—alongside with a license that fitted this practice. It is practically impossible to recreate the source code from binary (while compiling source code into binary is easy).

With the growth of the software industry—also in terms of revenue and financial potential—came the emergence of software licensing practically as a branch of law. Licenses grew increasingly detailed and included more and more provisions about what the user was and was not allowed to do. At some point, the open-source communities, specifically Stallman's FSF, started writing their own open-source licenses called GPL. The later versions of the GPL (GPLv3) are special in the way that they require all software licensed with this license and furthermore every software that includes code which has ever been so licensed to be open source forever. It has therefore been called a "viral license" because it spreads to every software package it touches. Of course, this restrictive[17] form of open-source licensing is not in the interest of every open-source programmer— particularly if the open-source project is somehow tied to or shares code with a commercial project. For this and for other reasons[18] earlier versions of the GPL are still in use and a number of less restrictive licenses exist, including the LGPL (Lesser General Public License), the BSD Licenses (Berkley Software Distribution Licenses, named after a UNIX-like operating system, BSD), and others.

Open source started with Stallman's proclamation that software should be free. In the early times of open-source software, it was not specified what exactly this means. That there are, in fact, two different meanings, "free as in *'free beer'* and free as in *'free speech'*" surfaced only later. Open source requires the latter but not the former, that is, it is possible to charge money for open-source software which is nevertheless open source and still allows the user to change the software; it is also possible for closed source software to be gratis (freeware) without making the source available to the user. It should be noted that nonfree open-source software is rather an exception because it would be hard to prevent people from compiling and using the openly available source without paying (even though they may violate the license in the process).

Open-source software is usually organized around a project leader with—depending on the size of the project—no, one, or several inner and outer circles of developers, with or without special groups developing particular modules of the software and with or without

---

[17]More restrictive open-source licenses do not allow to redistribute open-source code commercially, even in modified or improved versions; more permissive ones, however, do.

[18]For example, some programmers find GPLv3 just too restrictive.

particular task forces. The projects may also and do generally involve the users to some extent, usually at least for making improvement suggestions and for debugging (submitting bug reports). The internal governance also differs widely. Raymond (2000) of the OSI popularized the metaphor of the *cathedral and the bazaar*: some projects are developed by a closed group, are not open to the participation of random volunteers and also tend to be less open to suggestions from others (cathedral style). Others specifically welcome participation of previously uninvolved people (bazaar style); they may be more democratic, they may include complex voting systems and other decision mechanisms, but may also be prone to some forms of bureaucratization. While bazaar style organization forms are specific to open-source projects, cathedral style organization is, in effect, similar to the organization of commercial software producers. While some find that open-source software generally tends to be more *modular* (Bonaccorsi and Rossi, 2003) in order to allow many groups of programmers to interact productively in a self-organized and efficient way, this feature also plays an increasingly important role in commercial and closed source softwares. Open-source software does, however, probably have a pioneering role with regard to this and to many other aspects.

15.3.2 Open Source in Theory

When open source as a phenomenon became an important part of the software industry in the 1990s, when the open-source communities grew beyond small groups of idealists like Stallman, when open-source software packages became technological leaders in some of the software sectors, the phenomenon began to puzzle economists and other rational choice theorists alike.

Why would someone work for free? Why would they make the results of their work available to everyone to continue, to use, even to sell? Why would they not instead sell their products as there obviously are users that would be willing to pay? They are generally highly qualified. Why would they not at least work for a commercial software producer to be paid for their work?

The open-source communities' answers are simple (Stallman, 1985, Raymond, 2000). (i) They required the program anyway and see no reason why it should not be used by others as well; (ii) they just enjoy fixing problems; and (iii) they, like Stallman, dislike the commercial closed source software industry and the culture of obscurity, obfuscation, and distrust it produces and set out to initiate a more cooperative programming culture either in their spare time, as a side effect of commercial projects, or, if they enjoy other funding, as their regular occupation.

Rational choice theorists naturally find it hard to believe that just this is enough to sustain a larger open-source community. Though few deny that it plays a part, a number of other approaches have been put forward; they are summarized in, for instance, Lerner and Tirole (2002), Lakhani and von Hippel (2003), and Bitzer and Geishecker (2010). Programming good open-source software may (i) help building reputation in order to gain well-paying employment opportunities in the future. It may (ii) even serve as a signaling strategy as only very skilled programmers can develop and maintain a project that is successful on a global scale; this in turn may deter competitors from even trying. (iii) Expectation of reciprocity and (iv) avoidance of punishment by the community for not contributing may also pose a motivation to contribute. (v) In some cases, the software firms make strategic decisions to support open-source projects and direct their programmers to contribute as part of their jobs. Finally (vi), a newer approach is to explain contributions to open-source software by recognition and social approval in the open-source community (Greiff and Paetzel, 2012). Many of these explanations are generic approaches to solve social dilemma games, not specific to the open-source phenomenon. While a social dilemma structure is involved here, open-source programmers and firms do not necessarily perceive it this way as the relation to other sectors, network externalities, and the embeddedness into social and political issues on a larger scale may overlay the dilemma structure.

If open-source software is commercially funded or supported, similar questions could be asked: Why would anyone fund an open-source project if the open-source community would develop the program in question anyway and the benefactor will only enjoy the same rights as everyone else even if the project was only completed because of her generous donations? In this case, the situation in question is not a dilemma game. If the benefactor is in need of exactly such a program, it is perfectly rational for her to fund its development. This is even more true if she offers goods complementary to that program (such as technical support) or if network externalities generated by the program benefit the benefactor's products.

One of the interpretations of open-source principle is that it is, in fact, a concept for a *gift exchange economy* (Raymond, 2000; Berdou, 2011). That is, it affects a mode of production that is not based on scarceness of resources, not on trade, and not on the allocation of resource in a "free market" but rather on free sharing of abundant goods. Since there is no theoretical limit to the economic production of goods with zero network externalities, they are theoretically always abundant and any scarcity is artificially introduced. For such goods, economic principles based on gift exchange concepts rather than scarcity concepts would be both desirable and efficient. Since inefficiency is the main argument against gift exchange economies, the existence of open-source communities in reality is a key aspect for this discussion.

15.3.3 Open Source in Reality

Since the 1990s and especially since the later 2000s, open-source software enjoys increasing popularity with open-source software packages playing dominating roles in a number of software sectors (as mentioned in Section 15.1). This may be due to the fact that open source is better suited than closed source software for a number of important features a software package should be able to accomplish. This includes bug fixing (the correction of errors), user-led innovation, quick release- and update cycles, and building user trust in the security and safety to use the software. Some of these are immediate consequences of public availability of the source code so that everyone can read and analyze it and is free to search for and uncover potential security holes. Others result from the existence of a community of active users around the developer community and a vivid communication between the two.

This does not only acknowledge the specific properties of goods with zero marginal cost, it also makes use of them—the specifics being essentially unlimited capacities to reproduce the software, significant network externalities, and the likelihood of the emergence of software piracy if the software is not distributed for free anyway. Parts of the benefits bestowed by positive network externalities may be reintegrated into the production process, for example, widely used open-source software is much less likely to still contain severe errors and produce program crashes. Also, computer systems and software packages assume more and more the characteristics of services instead of products. For instance, in more complex packages it is important to continuously install updates in order to not only fix newly detected security holes but also ensure that the software remains compatible with other software packages, that new features are included, etc. To maintain the benefits of positive network externalities it is also important that users go along with these update cycles and, if possible, to understand the nature of the software's continuing development—something that users of commercial closed source software are unlikely to do since already the form in which they mostly obtain the software (purchasing it on a storage medium, usually a DVD) suggests otherwise.

As detailed above, this makes several business models with open-source software feasible, the most common ones being to sell complementary products or support for the open-source software. The latter is the business model of Red Hat that maintains a GNU/Linux distribution,[19] offers support for this system mainly to commercial users and is also the largest contributor to the funding for the Linux kernel development. Another example is Google's development of open-source operating systems (Android OS, Chrome OS) and other software (e.g., the Chromium browser) that allows to get a foothold in the PC and smartphone software sector.

Many of the larger open-source software packages that are not directly developed by commercial software vendors such as Google are today funded by foundations and employ a number of developers as permanent employees. The foundations, in turn, are funded by various sources with large contributions coming from large commercial players in the software industry which use the network externalities generated by the open-source software in many of the above discussed strategic ways.

15.3.4 Open Source Everywhere

For sometime now, different initiatives have attempted to transfer the concept of open source from the IT industry to various other economic sectors including automobile manufacturing (open-source cars), biotech and medicine (Rohde et al., 2011), computer hardware, laboratory equipment manufacturing (Pearce, 2012), etc. It should be noted that in this case only the designs are free while the materials may still be quite expensive and potentially very hard to obtain. This does, of course, undermine one of the central characteristics of open-source software: marginal production cost is negligible for software but not in hardware industries such as these. Still, other characteristics, that may prove important, are similar. The development costs for engine design or for biotechnological products are much larger than the immediate production costs; modular product designs render the development and innovation process much more flexible, and open standards may help allowing a swift introduction of promising new technologies.

While some open-source projects in non-IT-related industries enjoyed some success, they generally failed to copy the success of open-source software or even to gain wider attention. Also, their success was largely limited to fields that share some characteristics with the IT industry, namely huge development costs. The costs of copying the design specifics are, of course negligible, as is always the case for information and data.

Open-source hardware products are not widely available not least because they—until now—failed to attract the critical mass of developers and labor required to make the product feasible for a broader audience beyond small highly trained and highly specialized groups. Open source may, however,

---

[19]A distribution is a compilation of the operating system and large numbers of peripheral applications—in the case of GNU/Linux—most of them open source. The user may download and install the compiled packages from the online resource of the distribution; the distribution then cares for maintaining compatibility between the different packages, keeping them up to date, and relieves the user of the time-consuming process of compiling each one of the software packages.

yet play a significant role in the innovation of new technologies in different hardware and manufacturing sectors, as well as in genetics, medicine, and biotech. Rohde et al. (2011), for instance, discuss an example in which large numbers of researchers collaborated to quickly analyze the genome of a then virulent pathogen. Since it has become possible to apply for patents on organisms, open source may also offer a way to keep organisms in public domain in order not to lose the entire agricultural sector to a handful of patent holders.[20] Similar considerations may apply to the pharmaceutical industry.

15.4 POLICY IN THE WEIGHTLESS ECONOMY: INTELLECTUAL PROPERTY RIGHTS, OPEN STANDARDS, AND OTHER ISSUES

15.4.1 Intellectual Property Rights

The consequences of modern intellectual property rights law in agriculture and also in computing betray a disturbing lack of foresight on the part of the law makers. Today's world is faced with the patenting of life forms and the absolute dominance of very few patent holders on the one hand and the copyrighting of trivialities[21] and legal battles with nonpracticing patent holding companies (or patent trolls) on the other hand. The economic role of intellectual property rights and patents has changed over the past decades; in the process the crime of software piracy was invented and huge barriers to innovation and development

have arguably been erected; barriers that have partly been torn down again by both software piracy (illegally) and open-source software (legally). Patents on the other hand fulfill today not only the traditional function of protecting innovations but also strategic functions such as protecting dominant market positions and obstructing innovation by competitors then.

While a mechanism to protect and encourage innovation is necessary the current law of patents and intellectual property rights arguably overshoots that goal and should be reconsidered.

Openness

The emergence of a wide field of goods with zero marginal cost (the software industry) made new products and technologies available to larger groups of the population at an unanticipated scale. This also led to major transformations in many other sectors and of social life as a whole; it made information, skills, education much more widely accessible and arguably led to additional economic growth over the past decades (in spite of the various crashes and crises). All this results from the openness of the technologies, the potential of innovations to quickly spread throughout the population. The importance of this particular aspect has until now only been acknowledged insufficiently. The concept of open source is particularly well suited to ensure openness.

Network Externalities

Information and communication technology is subject to large network externalities; this

---

[20]Over the recent decades plant variety used in agriculture has globally decreased largely due to the emergence of a few—partly genetically engineered—more efficient crop varieties and to increasing regulation and requirements for standardization. This happening at the same time with the inception of a radically new understanding of intellectual property law helped to create a very asymmetric ownership structure of the major food crop's genomes (Blakeney, 2011).

[21]The most striking examples might be the "progress bar" (patented for Sony in 2007) and "one-click buying" (patented for Amazon in 1999).

leads to vast possibilities and also quickly to lock-in situations. If it is intended to influence the development of the industry (for instance by propagating an *open standard*), this must be done within a narrow critical time window after which the industry is locked in to a point where no public or private entity could alter the trajectory in any way significantly. It may also be beneficial to the economy to avoid long standard wars that delay innovation in other industries until one of the standards has emerged victorious. Public institutions can exercise influence easily by developing a standard themselves, requiring it to be open, or even simply by endorsing a private standard; something the US Department of Defense has frequently and successfully done in the process of the emergence of the internet (earlier ARPANET) and other computer science standards.

Size Is Power

Large competitors have for various reasons advantages over small players in the IT industry and similar fields. These crucially include not only network externalities but also patenting law and other aspects. This has resulted in the emergence of heavily *asymmetric industry structures* (monopolies and oligopolies) in various software sectors, including price wars before one firm was able to achieve a monopoly status and possibly loss in product quality afterwards. It may, in certain cases, be necessary for public policy to avoid such outcomes. To accomplish this an antitrust case with the goal of splitting a firm up (as has been attempted with Microsoft in the 1990s and early 2000s) is probably neither sufficient nor even helpful. Instead, it should be avoided that the monopolist can use specific strategic means to deter market entry—such as obscure standards, incompatibility-generating changes to the standard (or generally control of standards), and patenting of broad concepts. Requiring important standards to be open and,

if possible, governed by a neutral party would most likely be more successful than employing antitrust law.

Path Dependence

The development of industries with network externalities is path dependent and nonergodic, and there is no reason to expect such sectors to approach long-term equilibria when even the underlying characteristics of the products defy—as shown above—equilibrium analyses (compare Chapters 4, 7, 10, and 11). This does, however, not mean that the development path is at every point particularly sensitive to, say, regulatory taxes or other fiscal policy measures. Instead, there are occasional opportunities to put the development path onto another trajectory, particularly in times of the emergence of new standards and also when other, related sectors undergo major changes.

15.5 CONCLUSION

Aaron Swartz has always been interested in programming and computer technology. He involved with several standard setting working groups as a teenager and won a price for creating useful, noncommercial, educational online resources at age 13. As an adult, he fought for the freedom of information (not just software), founded NGO initiatives, and wrote his "Open Access Guerrilla Manifesto" in 2008. Also in 2008, he uploaded US federal court documents, which are technically public, to the public internet. He later did the same with other, not openly and freely accessible digital repositories (this time scientific papers). After having already been investigated for the incident in 2008, he was arrested and charged with, among other counts, computer fraud. After being prosecuted for charges that could have earned him several decades in prison and a million dollar in fines, he committed suicide in early 2013. He was 26 years old. Representatives from both major parties in the United States (Republicans and Democrats) have since worked to change intellectual property law to avoid cases like Swartz's where individuals are threatened with draconic punishment for minor copyright infringements.

This chapter not only gave an introduction to the information economy and economic aspects of open source but also tried to convey the spirit of the idea of open source, an idea that was central to the work and also targeted in the prosecution of Aaron Swartz.

The chapter showed that the great success of both the IT economy and open-source communities was driven by the negligible marginal costs and the network externalities of the goods in question. With methods introduced in earlier chapters (Chapters 2, 8, and 11) it analyzed the properties of IT and open source, also detailing on what motivates open-source programmers and summarizing with a selection of policy recommendations. The chapter argued that openness of information, data, and software is the central moment in the development of the IT economy—an openness that is a main concern of future socioeconomic development.

Chapter References

Anderson, R., 2001. Why information security is hard—an economic perspective. In: Proceedings of the 17th Annual Computer Security Applications Conference, 2001, doi:10.1109/ACSAC.2001.991552.

Arthur, W.B., 1989. Competing technologies, increasing returns, and lock-in by historical events. Econ. J. 99 (394), 116–131.

Arthur, W.B., Ermoliev, Y.M., Kaniovskii, Y.M., 1983. A generalized URN problem and its applications. Cybernetics. 19, 61–71.

Berdou, E., 2011. Organization in Open Source Communities: At the Crossroads of the Gift and Market Economies. Routledge, New York, NY/London.

Bitzer, J., Geishecker, I., 2010. Who contributes voluntarily to OSS? an investigation among German IT employees. Res. Policy. 39 (1), 165–172.

Blakeney, M., 2011. Recent developments in intellectual property and power in the private sector related to food and agriculture. Food Policy. 36 (S1), S109–S113.

Bonaccorsi, A., Rossi, C., 2003. Why open source software can succeed. Res. Policy. 32 (7), 1243–1258.

Choi, J.P., 1994. Network externality, compatibility choice, and planned obsolescence. J. Ind. Econ. 42 (2), 167–182.

Choi, J.P., 2004. Tying and innovation: a dynamic analysis of tying arrangements. Econ. J. 114 (492), 83–101.

Darmon, E., Rufini, A., Torre, D., 2009. Back to software "Profitable Piracy": the role of information diffusion. Econ. Bull. 29 (2), 453–553.

Greiff, M., Paetzel, F., 2012. Reaching for the stars: an experimental study of the consumption value of social approval. MAGKS Discussion Paper 08-2012, available on SSRN, doi:10.2139/ssrn.2127067.

Heinrich, T., 2013. Technological Change and Network Effects in Growth Regimes: Exploring the Microfoundations of Economic Growth. Routledge, Oxon, UK/New York, NY.

Heinrich, T., 2014. Standard wars, tied standards, and network externality induced path dependence in the ICT sector. Technol. Forecast. Soc. Change. 81, 309–320.

Lakhani, K.R., von Hippel, E., 2003. How open source software works: "Free" user-to-user assistance. Res. Policy. 32 (6), 923–943.

Lerner, J., Tirole, J., 2002. Some simple economics of open source. J. Ind. Econ. 50 (2), 197–234.

Le Texier, T., Gordah, M., 2011. Peer-to-peer networks and complementary goods: the impact of openness and innovation on profitable piracy. Econ. Anal. 44 (1–2), 15–37.

Luksha, P., 2008. Niche construction: the process of opportunity creation in the environment. Strategic Entrepreneurship J. 2 (4), 269–283.

Nooteboom, B., 1994. Innovation and diffusion in small firms: theory and evidence. Small Bus. Econ. 6 (5), 327–347.

Oberholzer-Gee, F., Strumpf, K., 2007. The effect of file sharing on record sales: an empirical analysis. J. Polit. Econ. 115 (1), 1–42.

Pearce, J.M., 2012. Building research equipment with free, open-source hardware. Science. 337 (6100), 1303–1304.

Peitz, M., Waelbroeck, P., 2006. Why the music industry may gain from free downloading—the role of sampling. Int. J. Ind. Organ. 24 (5), 907–913.

Raymond, E.S., 2000 (1998). The Cathedral and the Bazaar, <http://catb.org/~esr/writings/cathedral-bazaar/cathedral-bazaar> (accessed October 2013).

Rohde, H., Qin, J., Cui, Y., et al., 2011. Open-source genomic analysis of shiga-toxin-producing E. coli O104:H4. N. Engl. J. Med. 365 (8), 718–724.

Shy, O., 2001. The Economics of Network Industries. Cambridge University Press, New York, NY.

Stallman, R.M., 1983. GNU Project Initial Announcement. <http://www.gnu.org/gnu/initial-announcement. html> (Full text of Richard M. Stallman's posting in the Usenet newsgroup in 1983; accessed October 2013).

Stallman, R.M., 1985. The GNU Manifesto, <http://www.gnu.org/gnu/gnu.html> (accessed October 2013).

Williams, S., 2002. Free as in Freedom—Richard Stallman's Crusade for Free Software. O'Reilly, <http://oreilly.com/openbook/freedom> (accessed October 2013).

Further Reading

Chesbrough, H., Vanderhaverbeke, W., West, J. (Eds.), 2006. Open Innovation: Researching a New Paradigm. Oxford University Press, Oxford, UK.

Colombatto, E. (Ed.), 2004. The Elgar Companion to the Economics of Property Rights. Edward Elgar, Cheltenham, UK/Northampton, MA.

Lessig, L., 2002. The Future of Ideas: The Fate of the Commons in a Connected World. Random House Digital, New York, NY/Toronto, Canada.

Wu, T., 2010. The Master Switch: The Rise and Fall of Information Empires. Alfred A. Knopf, New York, NY.

Further Reading—Online

For further reading, see the textbook website at http://booksite.elsevier.com/9780124115859

EXERCISES

1. Section 15.2.1 describes an n-person game between a producer of a good with zero variable cost and a number of consumers, their respective strategies being to allow (other) consumers to access the good for free.

   a. Write the game as a simplified 2-person game between one producer and one consumer. Do Nash equilibria and Pareto optima coincide? Are there Nash equilibria in mixed strategies?

   b. Write the game as an n-person game. Is the structure (Nash equilibria, Pareto optima, and coincidence between these) retained?

	Player 2	s_A Standard A	s_B Standard B
Player 1	s_A Standard A	1 1	1 − α 1 − β
	s_B Standard B	1 − β 1 − α	1 1

FIGURE 15.3 Compatibility war coordination game.

2. Consider the replicator dynamic model given in Section 15.2.3.

   a. Show that $p^*_{PD,2}$ is stable and $p^*_{PD,1}$ is not.

   b. Could the model also be analyzed using an agent-based simulation? If so, how? Would this yield the same result?

3. Consider the replicator dynamic model in Section 15.2.4 in the part on compatibility and incompatibility (on the basis of the game matrix in Figure 15.3).

   a. Show that it leads to the same dynamic system as given in the first part of the section in Eq. 15.1.

   b. Show that it yields the three equilibria and their respective stability properties as stated in Section 15.2.4.

   c. How does the system change if the parameters are constrained to $0 < \alpha < 1$ and $0 < \beta < 1$? Is the equilibrium structure retained?

4. Concept of open source

   a. What is open-source software? How does it differ from freeware?

   b. Open-source programmers do not receive a monetary revenue from selling their products. Why do they engage in open-source programming nevertheless? Give nine possible approaches to explain this.

   c. Why did open-source communities first emerge in the software industry and not, say, in the manufacturing sector?

Networks and Innovation—The Networked Firm, Innovation Systems, and Varieties of Capitalism

"Despite the considerable amount of research devoted to economic growth and development, economists have not yet discovered how to make poor countries rich. As a result, poverty remains the common experience of billions." **Costas Azariadis and John Stachurski**[1]

"Capitalism, then, is by nature a form or method of economic change and not only never is but never can be stationary. ...The fundamental impulse that sets and keeps the capitalist engine in motion comes from the new consumers, goods, the new methods of production or transportation, the new markets, the new forms of industrial organization that capitalist enterprise creates. ...This process of Creative Destruction is the essential fact about capitalism. It is what capitalism consists in and what every capitalist concern has got to live in." **Joseph A. Schumpeter**[2]

[1]"Poverty Traps," in: Philippe Aghion and Steven N. Durlauf (eds.), *Handbook of Economic Growth*, Volume 1, Part A, San Diego: Elsevier, 2005, p. 295.

[2]*Capitalism, Socialism and Democracy*, New York: Harper, 1975/1942, p. 82.

The Microeconomics of Complex Economies.
DOI: http://dx.doi.org/10.1016/B978-0-12-411585-9.00016-6

16.1 OVERVIEW

The focus of this chapter is on how to understand and possibly strengthen the innovation capacity of economic systems. An *innovation is an invention*, or more generally, novelty, brought to or applied *in the economic sphere*. By definition, innovation is thus resulting in *changes* in production, or industrial or sectoral economic *structures*. It is, as is any emergent structure, the outcome of decisions and activities of individual agents and their interactions.

The more complex production processes become, the more problematic the reduction of sources of economic progress to the results of the efforts of a few "extraordinary" members of society (as for instance reflected in Schumpeter's early conception of the entrepreneur, see Chapter 12) becomes. In fact, as far as radical (as opposed to incremental) innovations are concerned, by far the largest contributors of underlying inventions have been

government research facilities. Companies tend to focus on changes in existing products and structures, or on variations of existing products (Lazonick, 2009). For the advancement of technologies and introduction of new types of goods *coordinated and cooperative* efforts of some kind are generally required, in research groups, amongst companies, and in all kinds of (informal) partnerships of different actors. This becomes increasingly necessary as production processes and value chains are disintegrated, in coordinated value-added chains, clusters, networks, or hierarchies (see Chapter 4). Issues of *standard setting, coordination*, via hierarchy or among equals, and *consent* about the direction of changes move to the center of attention when we turn to the implementation of innovations within existing production structures. Changes have to stay compatible to other, and others', components, or entail concerted complementary changes by others. The institutional framework that structures interactions plays an important part in how these surrounding processes develop and actions are undertaken.

The functional borders of companies are difficult to define in these circumstances while their legal borders are clear ("blurring boundaries"; see also Chapter 4 and the examples of the Third Italy and Silicon Valley referred to there). Additionally, as pointed out in Chapter 13 in the discussion of Nelson and Winter's evolutionary institutional theory of the firm, routines are what keeps a large organization functional. The changes introduced by innovations may easily clash with existing routines, leading to resistance on the part of the actors who are to implement them, and problems during the restructuring of the routines due to frictions when old routines and new necessities do not coincide well. Changes in single processes and organization structures may turn out not to be compatible with the rest. A critical issue to a company's success becomes *how to organize production processes in networks and maintain innovation capacities.*

Consequently, a number of conditions that help or hinder the process of successfully innovating are difficult, in many cases impossible, to grasp within the structures of any equilibrium economics. *Innovation itself,* captured by Schumpeter's five categories, as new products, new markets, new organization, new inputs, new sources of raw material, or in the distinction between product and process innovation (or radical and incremental innovation), is by nature *disequilibrating.* It is the result of learning processes and subsequent changes of and/or improvements in products. That means *uncertainty* is a constitutive element of innovation processes. A reduction of this uncertainty to risk and a clearly defined innovation production function will hinder the clear view on a number of crucial aspects in the process, and as a consequence will only be of limited usefulness when it comes to answering questions

about the advantageous structures for fostering innovation capacities.

The institutional framework that agents face has a significant influence on the overall innovation performance observed, as *institutions structure agents' interactions* (see Chapters 1 and 3). They can, of course, not reduce the fundamental uncertainty related to the innovation itself, but they can set up a system in which other areas pose less of a threat to individual agents, allowing them to increase their control over their environment to some degree, at least. They likewise influence how well the communication between agents, for transmitting new knowledge, can work. For an understanding of observed performance, an understanding of the institutional framework is consequently a core aspect. In the following, we will introduce *conditions that can help support innovation processes* and improve a system's innovation performance.

One major aspect that unites the concepts that will be presented in more detail here is their recognition that agents find themselves in *strategic interactions.* The institutional framework that structures these interactions can broaden agents' abilities to respond to strategic challenges in their environment and can increase their capacities for interaction and the exchange of knowledge (see Chapters 1, 12, and 13). The last point also takes at least implicit notice of the fact that innovation is the result of a path-dependent and cumulative process, where *changes and advances in technology build on existing technology.* The creation of novelty (innovation) and its spread (imitation) jointly lay the basis for future further advances (new combinations; innovation as well as their imitation by others are thus necessary for permitting a continuing process of change). Thus, systems, as complex interaction structures, may show different performances, and given path dependency in this may differ persistently. Supporting agents' efforts for achieving technological advances and the understanding of the different direction that innovation and specialization processes have taken are the objectives of all concepts introduced here.

In the second section of this chapter, we briefly explain the neoclassical understanding of innovation in order to contrast it with the understanding embodied in the approaches presented subsequently in this chapter. In the third section, we present a conceptualization that allows a more detailed comparison of production networks with regard to their ability to maintain their innovative capacity. We go *beyond the neoclassical market-hierarchy dichotomy* by integrating the institutional content of a network (as all firms are members of some kind of network) into the conceptualization. The fourth section takes up the concept of *Innovation Systems*, meaning the joint (coordinated and cooperative) innovative capacity of various production chains or networks. The concept is originally formulated on the national level but can also be adapted to apply to smaller entities. In the fifth section, we introduce a regional development concept that was developed in parallel to the innovation systems concept, namely, the *Theory of Endogenous Development*. This concept is formulated specifically with a view on offering a framework for supporting regional policy makers in their efforts of furthering development in their respective regions. Finally, in the sixth section we present the *Varieties of Capitalism* concept. Derived from an analysis of developed economies, this concept offers a framework for capturing persistent differences between these economies, arriving at some ideal types that show distinct features in their institutional structures and derived from that in the functioning of their economic sectors in general and their respective innovation focuses and performances more specifically. Finally, a brief restatement of the commonalities and complementarities among the concepts introduced in this chapter will be offered.

16.2 TOWARDS A COMPLEXITY-BASED UNDERSTANDING OF INNOVATION

The concepts presented in this chapter are united by a number of characteristics that not only relate them to one another but at the same time distinguish them from approaches to innovation derived from neoclassical theory (for different integrations of innovation into formal approaches, see Antonelli and de Liso, 1997). There are different approaches for integrating technological change, as the outcome of innovation processes, into models in the neoclassical approach, depending on the question focused on in the respective analysis. This is, of course, in itself not problematic—depending on the focus you pursue, aspects of the framework can be treated more superficially and simplified, or have to be integrated in a more detailed fashion. However, we can state that the treatment of innovation processes that we find in neoclassical formulations leave some aspects outside the scope of the respective treatments that have been found to be integrative aspects of the whole process.

When the focus is on the results of successful outcomes that are reflected in *long-term growth* dynamics, *innovation* is basically *taken as given*—either directly time dependent or automatically mirrored in productivity increases following investment decisions. Its integration into the model then conforms to standard assumptions and axioms regarding individual behavior and capacities. In this case, all uncertainty surrounding the process is removed. Either, all possible technologies are known, and some are momentarily barred from utilization by prohibitive costs, or the technology space is known, and agents face certain probabilities for finding improvements, so that investment decisions can be based on their expected values. In this second case, we will require complete knowledge of changes in the price vector and demand patterns following successful innovations, permitting the cost–benefit analysis on which the actual investment decision is based. We also continue to find perfect information within the system as a whole, economic motivations as the sole source of individual motivations, perfect transferability of any information available, opportunistic behavior, and an independence from overall structures and nonprice influences (for neoclassical growth models, see Acemoglu, 2008, and especially chapter 15 for the treatment of technological change).

For innovation proper, there are two neoclassical, so-called *linear* models of innovation—one emphasizing effects and incentives on the supply side and the other on the demand side (Himmelweit et al., 2002, chapter 15). The supply-side approach is called *technology push*—basic research is publicly funded and disseminated. The process itself is assumed to advance linearly from *basic research* to *applied research and development* and from there to the introduction of the *new product or process*. The outcomes of R&D efforts are available to all concerned agents as knowledge can be perfectly codified and transferred without incurring costs or problems. In the case of public sector R&D, the availability is free, research and scientific advances are characterized as public goods. Advances that are achieved in private companies are incorporated in their products and brought to the market that way, where they can be copied effortlessly or, in case of patent protection, utilized after payments of appropriate licensing fees. Applied research still aims at expanding knowledge, but commercial use plays an important part in directing resources already, development then centers on commercializing results. When this process has borne fruit, demand leads to finding which output combination (point on an isoquant) is actually realized. The demand side is therefore inconsequential in the process of introducing possibilities for new products, and only influencing eventual prices and quantities based on exogenously given preferences of the consumers. The role of policies here is to ensure a continued flow of new knowledge. This can, for instance, be achieved through public provision or incentive schemes for stimulating private sector activities, through subsidies aimed at overcoming "market failures" that arise here due to the inappropriability of outcomes by the innovator, or through the granting of patents to ensure exclusive rights of use at least for a time.

A *demand-pull* view centers on the direction of creative efforts undertaken with a view on satisfying existing wants. A linear view—technology to demand or demand to technology—neglects a number of factors that have come to be understood as important contributors to processes of innovation and change. Even focusing only on technology and demand, an integration of feedback processes between these can enhance our understanding for actually observable change (for an overview, Himmelweit et al., 2002, chapter 15).

The concepts presented here, in contrast, all incorporate a notion of *innovation processes* as shaped by *feedback loops* among the different stages they go through. Additionally, they contain an understanding of the importance of *tacit knowledge* (resulting from experience) in technological capacities, which can consequently not be codified perfectly and, for that matter, communicated without friction and loss. Furthermore, a broader *accumulation of capacities and knowledge* (development of absorptive capacity) is a necessary condition for private agents in order to effectively utilize and then develop technologies further. Such accumulation is the foundation for further advances in the future. The *social embeddedness* of the entire process plays an important role for the understanding of innovation capacities. Finally, the *uncertainty* related to matters of novelty and resulting potential problems to be taken care of by agents are included as well.

Acquiring technological knowledge is a long *process, cumulatively building* on earlier knowledge and already existing capabilities. This process needs supportive structures in a number of fields, from the quality of the workforce that is present through financial means for financing research and implementation, and continued access to information. Furthermore, it is acknowledged that *innovation* is (increasingly) the *outcome of cooperative efforts*, laying an additional emphasis on institutional provisions for the strengthening of coordination and cooperation between agents in situations characterized by strategic interdependence. The coordination of agents is therein often reached on the basis of nonprice signals. The recognition of the tacit knowledge component likewise means that *interactive learning* and *knowledge sharing* in production processes is an important source of improvement (learning by doing, learning by using, etc.) that is more easily shared the better the basis for cooperation and trust among the involved agents, and their movement between different involved entities. Not only is R&D hence increasingly in need of cooperation, but also the innovation capacities likewise increase, the closer the contact between agents.

The policy focus is accordingly on the institutional framework and provisions therein to strengthen the relations among the agents as well as supporting them through, broadly understood, infrastructural measures (including service provisions, etc.). As we see, the focus of the systems approaches to innovation is rather different than in the linear approaches, developed from an understanding of innovation and the innovation process that is more closely oriented on real-world processes. In fact, the concepts introduced here have been formulated based on empirical observations and regularities found therein, then abstracting from these in order to formulate a general framework for addressing questions of interest. In contrast, the way forward chosen in much of mainstream economics starts from a given set of axioms and assumptions formulated to enable the construction of mathematical equilibrium models that are then adapted to the single case under investigation (see Table 16.1 for a brief overview over the distinct conception behind innovation presented here). A general problem that has been found with the latter is that even though it is perfectly possible to set up one model to match one case, the transferability of results to similar cases and samples quite

TABLE 16.1   Different Understandings of Critical Aspects Concerning Innovation

Neoclassical Innovation Characteristics	Innovation Characteristics in Network and Systems Approaches
Linear view	Feedback loops
Frictionless knowledge transfer	Tacit knowledge
No problems adopting others' innovations	Absorptive capacities have to be developed
Innovation space known—risk	Innovation space unknown—uncertainty
Expected value and cost–benefit analysis in investment	Open-ended process, unforeseeable results
Economic incentives (price and profit) sole drivers of the process	Curiosity, experimentation, marketing of the outcomes of process (creation of demand)
Policies focused on "market mechanism" where possible, subsidies where public good character dominant	Policies focused on infrastructure for capacity building, communication and knowledge dissemination, interaction, and cooperation

often fails. They may offer what appears to be the foundation for a good statistical fit, and hence description of a sample, without providing actual explanations of processes (see Chapters 5 and 6; also, for instance, Berg and Gigerenzer, 2010).

16.3 FIRMS IN CLUSTERS AND NETWORKS—AN ORGANIZATIONAL TRIANGLE

Production processes are generally organized in some form of *network*. In joint production processes, companies specialize in individual steps of the overall process, the combination of these specific contributions resulting in the final product. In order to be able to combine the contributions at different stages of the production process, the efforts of individual contributors have to be coordinated (see Chapter 4). That does not only mean the characteristics and specifics of the distinct parts that are added in the creation of the final product have to be clear but also includes aspects such as the timing of the delivery of certain parts from one firm to another (a broadly understood coordination on technological and behavioral standards). The more complex the production process gets, the more pronounced the need for a coordination of the individual efforts becomes, and the more specialized activities get, the more important *nonprice based forms of coordination* become as the usual assumptions regarding markets' coordinating powers become less and less applicable (see also Chapters 3 and 4). This is related to the information requirements during the process as well as more general aspects that concern the fact that the presumed market mechanism, coordination through prices, may work in an environment characterized by numerous agents, whereas once their number is reduced, aspects of power and negotiation move to center stage.

16.3.1 Transaction Costs and Market Versus Hierarchy Optimization

In conceptualizing organization, economics mostly focuses on one aspect, namely the choice of "optimal" size and structure by the agents involved based on the minimization of costs resulting from the operations they carry out. This goes back to R. Coase who raised the question what the place of firms was in economies given that in the neoclassical world of perfect information and zero transaction costs there was no reason to rely on hierarchies instead of markets for the organization and execution of production activities (or, more generally speaking, the coordination of agents). He concluded that in the real world, transactions do cause costs and that for some transactions, costs could be reduced if they were not taken to the market place but executed within hierarchical structures (Coase, 1937). It would then prove advantageous to have certain steps of a production process not be mediated through market exchanges but in the controlled environment of a firm with its hierarchical structure.

In the conceptualization of organizational forms developed from this insight it is assumed that all influence factors can be expressed in terms of the *cost they signify for a transaction*. Extensions in some of the contributions to the new institutional economics, or new organizational economics (as for instance in Williamson 1975, 1985, 2005), acknowledge a number of influence factors but continue to fold them into the transaction cost dimension. Thus, the transaction cost conceptualization limits the relevant organizational categories to a *one-dimensional extension* between the atomistic *market* on the one hand and a complete *hierarchy* on the other. All mixed forms, meaning production processes in which more than one firm are involved (firms signifying hierarchy), are thought of as lying between those two poles (effectively erasing any additional insights and information that might have been gained from the additional influences acknowledged). Transactions that are not adequate for market exchanges due to their inherent costs (risk premium, insurance premium, information costs, and so on; in general, costs related to guarding against other agents' opportunistic behavior, which these will by assumption show) are carried out within a hierarchy; those for which market processes are adequate (offering cost advantages), are left to market exchanges. How long the value-added chain within one firm is, is assumed to be the result of a calculation setting costs related to market transactions against costs for the same transaction within a hierarchical order, with the boundaries of the firm determined by the point where the cost of a transaction is the same in a market as in a hierarchy. As with many approaches, the presumptive ceteribus paribus comparison of different situations introduces a number of problems once it is attempted to take this view to informing observers about real-world structures. Synergies among agents who do not interact based on price signals alone, market power of the larger hierarchies inflecting observable prices and changing conditions, or friction within large hierarchies leading to losses of efficiency are difficult to integrate. Once large hierarchies exist, it is difficult to find the reference point against which their cost is to be evaluated. Exchanges of information and the maintenance of innovation capacity is likewise outside the scope of this dimension to address, leading to limited applicability in a number of questions involving real-world relevant questions such as the longer term viability of specific structures. These factors do, however, have an influence in real-world situations where the simple counterfactual of taking prices and (difficult to impossible to calculate) internal costs for single items or services as given and comparing them, cannot be met.

16.3.2 The Networked Firm

In reality, production networks take on a *variety of shapes* and their institutional structure exerts a significant influence on its production and innovation capacities. Information regarding these alternative shapes and structures hence contains the key to insights for a number of relevant questions regarding (market) structures and innovation processes that cannot be gained from the perspective of a market-hierarchy dichotomy alone. Reducing the explanation of firm size and structure to be able to accommodate all sources of influence in the transaction cost dimension reduces the information available for attempts of increasing the innovation capacity of production networks. As far as the question of the innovation capacity of a network is concerned such additional information may well prove crucial to arriving at distinct and empirically relevant conclusions. Hence, the conceptualization we present here includes direct interdependence and hence an institutional dimension for approaching the organization of activities in networks of production. Incorporating this interdependence and institutional dimension to capture problem-solving capacities of the actors in networks, we take a step beyond the neoclassical dichotomy of market and hierarchy.

The construct of a market without any institutional support is unfeasible (which, in the form of property rights and contract enforcement is not denied by anybody, even though "abstracted" from in many analyses then). In fact, what Coase has pointed out is that in his view, the main point that the recognition of the importance of transaction costs entails, is the fact that the formal legal framework will have a noticeable influence on economic activities (Coase, 1992). However, there are a number of influences that result from the relations of the agents in a value-added chain as well. To take an example, relationships between suppliers and customers, as well as relationships amongst producers, develop over time. Such a relationship may evolve in a number of ways and directions depending on how the agents choose to structure their interactions. If over time, then, purely price-based reasons for maintaining a relationship become relatively less relevant in exchange for an increased importance of nonprice relations between agents, this can have a number of consequences. Amongst other things, transaction costs (that do of course play a role, however, subject to more complex influences than the one-dimensional dichotomy referred to above would suggest and permit) may in such a case be reduced in ways that pure market or hierarchy could not achieve. Also, investment behavior can be expected to differ, as relations that are not maintained purely on the base of prices allow the formulation of longer term plans and thus the implementation of longer term projects more easily when the risk of a breakup of relations is reduced (beyond the point where relations can be defined in formal contracts). As a result, the innovation performance in the overall production process can be expected to show a different character depending on how the agents perceive their relationships.

So, different network forms could certainly be subsumed under a transaction cost heading. But some fundamental information about the network would inadvertently be lost in that process. One aspect to which this relates is the kind and direction as well as the overall incidence of innovation. Questions of innovation in and innovation capacity of the agents involved in production processes then cover a field where this information is crucial to understanding the dynamics involved. And innovation is the crucial ingredient to many questions of economic relevance, especially in terms of long-term dynamics and processes. Understanding the conditions that are supportive of innovation success at the level of companies and networks allows structuring the institutional framework so as to better support their efforts, and analyses incorporating this dimension can reveal potentially valuable information and aspects to economic agents and policy makers alike.

16.3.3 The Organizational Triangle

As the institutions governing the relations among the members of a production network become less instrumental, the ceremonial aspect of their character increases. *Ceremonial* aspects are understood as those that exhibit a past-binding character, inhibitive of change. In their pure form, they are without problem-solving capacity. The *instrumental* aspects manifest in a forward-looking character, permitting the search for and introduction of new combinations, thus fostering potential for technological progress and continuous change and improvement in problem-solving capacity (remember the Veblenian institutional dichotomy, as introduced in Chapter 1 and explained in more detail in Chapters 12 and 13). We introduce an *Organizational Triangle* to capture this *institutional dimension of organizational forms* (for a more detailed analysis of different network structures, see Elsner et al., 2010). As shown in Figure 16.1, we depict the conceptualization of organizational forms along a market-hierarchy dichotomy in the horizontal and the additional institutional dimension, the ceremonial–instrumental dichotomy, in the vertical.

In the lower left corner of the triangle, we place a *market with atomistic agents*. All exchanges within the production process are coordinated through price alone; the agents cannot exert influence on each other. The lower right corner represents the point where a whole production process is undertaken within *one vertically*

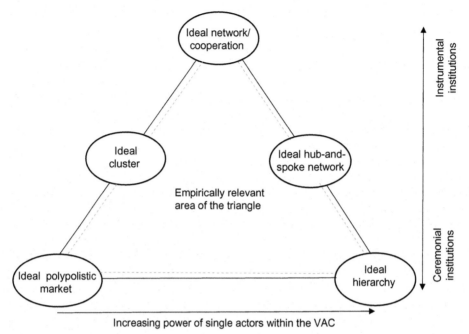

FIGURE 16.1   The organizational triangle.

integrated company in which the relations between the units involved in the process are all governed in *hierarchical structures*. In between these two forms of production, mixtures are placed in which hierarchical and price-based coordination mechanisms jointly play a role. With more steps of a production process executed within a hierarchy, we move to the right in this dimension. Implicitly included is also a notion of increasing power of some agents as we move to the right. This means for instance that when production is organized between two firms, we move further to the right, the more pronounced the power difference between these.

This baseline is empirically void (as are the other edges). Prices are the only relevant variable and transactions are organized in markets or hierarchically depending on where they can be executed relatively more cheaply. There are no institutions incorporated in this dimension. As you can, however, not conceptualize a market or hierarchy without institutions, the

baseline as such cannot take us very far in analyzing production processes. For a market, you need rules that govern the exchange relations between agents and delineate the rights of the agents involved in transactions. And how can you understand a hierarchy without institutions that in fact structure the hierarchy and give shape to the relative positions of the agents involved therein? Even if we admit to very limited institutions at this stage, such as prices and an understanding of positions of power in a hierarchy, the next logical step would be to ask about the determination of prices and decisions about the structure of the hierarchy, necessitating additional rules to be introduced, and so on.

Therefore, the *additional dimension* reflecting the interdependence and the *institutional* aspects of the relation between the agents promises additional and relevant information about the organization of production processes in real-world interdependent settings. This way, we can extend the analytical capacity of a conceptualization of organizational forms to represent real-world network structures, allowing for a more detailed comparative empirical analysis of such forms. The additional dimension contains information regarding the nature of the institutions involved ranging between the problem solving, instrumental on the one hand (that increases as you move upward) and the ceremonial on the other hand (which is higher the closer you get to the baseline, see below). Thereby we can formulate three more theoretical ideal types to complement those on the baseline dimension.

The top corner we label the ideal *institutionalized cooperation* or ideal *informal network*. On the edges, between ideal market and ideal network, and ideal hierarchy and ideal network, we find two hybrid forms again, namely, the ideal *local cluster* between ideal market and ideal network, and the ideal *hub-and-spoke network* between the ideal hierarchy and the ideal network. We define clusters as informal coordination forms, reflected in repeated and lasting vertical and horizontal relations of their respective products. We define networks as more formal (possibly project-based) collaborations based on deliberately contracted cooperation. These relations include a strategic component. Hub-and-spoke networks share characteristics of hierarchies (as we find a hub and the spokes) and we therefore place the ideal type halfway between pure hierarchy and the ideal informal network. Relations in both clusters and networks are governed by both prices and nonprice motives and mechanisms (also see Chapter 4).

16.3.4 The Instrumental and Ceremonial Aspects of the Institutionalized Network Dimension

With the ideal *informally emerged network* on one corner of the triangle, we include an ideal form that is characterized by the *instrumentality*

of its institutional structure. In networks different agents combine their inputs in the production of a final product. These agents interact in production processes, meaning the value-added chain along which they are placed links their efforts. Depending on the internal structure of the network, for instance the ability of the most powerful agent in the network to influence others' decisions or an ability to exchange interaction partners frequently or on short notice, the interaction leaves more or less scope for the development and maintenance of structures that are given to advantageous problem-solving capacities. (Remember that a ceremonially dominated institutional framework still supports agents in coordinating their activities and thus does include some measure of problem-solving capacity, but that the status-driven rationalization of its maintenance reduces this relative to frameworks that are motivated differently; see Chapters 3 and 13.12.) A similar reasoning applies to clusters.

Note that both clusters and networks include *horizontal relations* among firms. The *knowledge transfer* between firms is an important aspect of overall innovation capacity. The more freely knowledge can flow between firms, usually on a basis of institutionalized trust and cooperation, the easier improvements in some part of the cluster or network, can be incorporated by others. At the same time, as all technological advances are the result of new combinations of previously existing technologies, a freer flow of technologies (knowledge) increases the base available for possible new combinations.

The *empirically relevant* space for analyzing organizational forms is the *inside of the triangle*. Analyses of hierarchical, individualistic, and cooperative, as well as instrumental and ceremonial aspects in the relations between the agents involved lay the foundation for this. Instead of ideal types of markets, hierarchies, and networks, we find real-world markets, hierarchies, and networks that have to be considered as sets of institutions. The ceremonial–instrumental dichotomy in the conceptualization of institutions strengthens the analytical capacity of this approach insofar as it relates real-world forms to the basic fact of direct interdependence and their degree of solving related complex decision structures, and thus allows the more precise identification of potential weaknesses (especially in the dynamic, as opposed to static, capacity) of production systems.

The argument for a more ceremonial content in the institutions structuring relationships along value-added chains at the bottom of the triangle can be developed as follows (distinguishing between ceremonial market-based and ceremonial hierarchy-based relations). Remember that the question to be addressed with the help of the triangle centers on the suitability of the organization of production structures. This includes static considerations of effectiveness and efficiency, as well as notions of dynamic effectiveness and innovation capacity.

In an *atomistic market*, where transaction decisions are taken based on prices alone, every single step in a production process has to be executed by a different agent. We have to think of numerous single-entrepreneur firms in this setting. For production processes involving numerous steps, someone with a plan in mind of where to move to and how to get there will buy every single production and service step along the way and then sell the final product. This leaves some open questions (why would one agent be in a position to have a production plan in mind in this setting and what keeps others from copying it, what consequences for the production organization and costs in such potentially monopsonistic markets may there be, and how can this be reconciled with a "perfect competition" assumption, etc.). What can furthermore not be properly integrated are innovation and innovation processes, as— barring a perfect information transmission to

let newly arising requirements or production possibilities immediately lead to adaptations and changes by all relevant single producers—a single agent has no incentives for introducing novelties into a value-added chain. Mechanisms for finding such novelty— absent recurrence to government-financed research facilities, or the simple postulation of their existence—are likewise absent (see above).

Power does not play a role at this point in this dimension. If it existed, it is in turn difficult to see how the different positions of agents in innovation processes were to be justified, as there is no grounds for a logical derivation of such positions. If the way out chosen, on the other hand, involves a "lets imagine change has happened"–"thought experiment," it is not too apparent what questions remained that could adequately be addressed in such an analytical framework.

Another consequence of a dominant price-based motive in interactions is that agents do not invest in their relationships; or, if you think of "perfect" polypolistic spot-market relations, never get to develop them because they cannot count on meeting on a repeated basis (costs and benefits of relations change with changes in the kind of relations; see Chapter 14 as well). There is thus no reason for agents to invest in relationship-specific assets that could not be (or only with difficulty be) recovered should the relationship end. Those specific assets (in the broadest sense, including for instance organizational structures) are the most likely carriers of process innovations—a reduction of investment in such assets should consequently reduce the incidence of such innovations in a production system. Product innovations might still be observed, though, insofar as outside actors with individual new ideas try to enter a market.

When we get to the *purely hierarchical* structures, these rely on noninstrumental rules only, and we see a hierarchy for hierarchy's sake. The problem-solving aspect of the rules has disappeared, only their status-based justification remains. All a pure hierarchy serves for is the establishment of stratification based on rank and the maintenance of that structure—as in the case of the perfect market, there is no room here for a problem-solving technological content. In relations that are structured along such lines, flexibility to react to problems and room to introduce new solutions to problems are by definition absent. That means innovation capacity is absent. Additionally, if an increased control is executed from the top of the hierarchy, the relation to other members of a network need not be based on cooperation and the development of long-term common goals. It is easy to replace members, as others will be able to fill a ceremonial hierarchical position just as well as anybody. The investment in relationship-specific assets is thus a decision that does not make sense in these circumstances as well.

Obviously, these arguments refer to the baseline dimension and not the combinations we find in the empirically relevant inside of the triangle. But of course, as such they do show us the trends we can expect in differently organized value-added chains, depending on the relative weight of the respective aspects in the overall structure. As innovation is a dynamic and aggregative process, a weakening of structures supportive of specific aspects of the innovation process weakens the longer term perspectives of the respective production process. Overall, a less instrumentally organized network, either focusing on short-term prices as the determinant of the network's membership, with relations motivated by attempts at individualistic exploitation and invidious distinction, or on hierarchy and status-relations alone, is going to be less innovative than a more instrumental one with cooperative members.

16.4 NATIONAL INNOVATION SYSTEMS

Studying innovation and innovation performance, it has become obvious that *conventional indicators* (such as R&D spending on the input side and patents on the output side) do not offer a concise overview over or convincing explanations of the dynamic potential of economies (see below). *Growth and innovation trends*, reflecting knowledge embodied in investment as the central contributor to development, *cannot be captured* adequately by these measures. R&D spending is subject to uncertainty, or focused on incremental improvements that are not felt that strongly on a higher level of aggregation, and existing patents only give a very limited perspective on future changes and development potential.

The transmission of information, and for that a foundation for agents on which to acquire and communicate knowledge, is needed for innovation processes to function, as is the recognition of innovation as the outcome of interactive processes. Structures in place that influence how communication and interaction are structured play a key role for innovation success. The concept of national innovation systems (NIS) addresses this issue by strengthening the focus on the linkages of the agents involved in the creation and diffusion of knowledge in an economy. This reflects *innovation processes as interdependent and aggregative*, pursued in complex relationships among agents. There are numerous slightly different definitions of what an NIS is exactly, the original contributions are usually attributed to Freeman (1987), Lundvall (1992), and Nelson (1993) (Box 16.1). The motivation for formulating this approach was the dissatisfaction with national economic policies and their foundation limiting attention to relative wage costs as the only determinants of economies' competitiveness (Lundvall, 2007).

BOX 16.1

SOME DEFINITIONS OF NIS

In the original formulations, NIS has been defined as

> ... the network of institutions in the public and private sectors whose activities and interactions initiate, import, modify and diffuse new technologies (Freeman, 1987);
> ... the elements and relationships which interact in the production, diffusion and use of new, and economically useful, knowledge...

and are either located within or rooted inside the borders of a nation state (Lundvall, 1992);

> ... a set of institutions whose interactions determine the innovative performance... of national firms (Nelson, 1993).

The societal structures enabling innovation and a systemic perspective are hence at the center of the concept.

16.4.1 Understanding Economies and Their Potential as a Function of Their Institutional Framework

For today's economies and their development potential, the recognition of *innovation dynamics* is highly relevant because innovation has more than ever become the result of increasingly *complex and interwoven activities*. The strengthening of innovation systems has to be based on strengthening and improving structures that allow agents to interact and exchange knowledge. As agents' interactions shape the system, *each system may show its own dynamics* and have developed its own specific requirements which have to be addressed.

The dynamic potential of an economy relies not only on the *creation* of knowledge but also crucially on its *accessibility* by economic agents and *dissemination* in the economic sphere. Furthermore, this knowledge is not only the codified type that you can learn independently of contacts to specific people, but includes the tacit kind as well, that is difficult to communicate and hence spread without personal contacts and learning by doing (or using, or copying, etc.). Beyond research collaborations and the improvement of possibilities

of technology flows (and complementary policies to enhance the capacities of firms to find and absorb knowledge), an innovation system with longer term potential thus additionally has to encourage the movement of personnel.

Empirical approaches to measuring the quality of innovation systems thus center on these issues, quantifying knowledge flows between firms, but also relations between firms, and public and private research centers (including universities), the mobility of people between firms, and generally, the speed of the diffusion of new knowledge between firms. An important formal tool is network analyses, based on graph theory, in order to gain a deeper understanding of networks and the relations of agents within these networks (see Section 13.11).

16.4.2 Innovation Processes in Complex Environments

Development dynamics underline the increasing importance of a conception of innovation systems that recognizes the nature of innovation (as interdependent and cumulative) and that reflects the principal components that a strengthening of a production system has to involve. These are the recognition of the importance of knowledge and innovation for an economy's dynamic potential and the growing number of agents that are involved in the creation of knowledge, as well as their increasingly strategic relations during the process of knowledge creation and innovation diffusion and the necessity of increasingly collective efforts during these processes.

The recognition of the complexity (due to the agents involved and their relations as well as the nature of knowledge and innovation itself) of processes creating and disseminating new knowledge as well as the system character of development and technological advances are likewise becoming more central. This also recognizes that there are *numerous potential sources of innovations* along the whole value-added chain, the process not simply being a mechanical matter of (government-financed) science providing and firms utilizing.

Technology and the level of technology that can be employed depend on two complementary components, the knowledge embodied in the machine on the one hand, hence the physical capital available, and the skill of the people operating these machines, the human capital they have acquired. Technological change builds on existing knowledge in a cumulative fashion (Ayres, 1996/1944). For technologies to be transferable between companies, matching general skills has to be distributed more broadly in the population (in an area).

16.4.3 Perspectives on Policy

When it comes to policies, the understanding of innovation processes and the innovation system at hand is of course indispensable for the design of conscious attempts for improvements of the functioning of the NIS. Path dependency in economic development patterns underlines the need for understanding

the specific innovation system of a country or region when attempts are made to strengthen the respective dynamic potential. An influence on links between agents in production and innovation processes can be exerted through numerous instruments at the disposal of policy makers, in the form of the structure of the taxation system, access to financing, and also policies regulating competition in markets, or the shape and direction of the intellectual property protection versus information diffusion system, as well as formal and informal means for encouraging longer term relations among agents, for instance. An aspect to bear in mind, though, is that a too narrow focus on identifiable existing potential (comparative advantages) may result in the specialization on low-value-added activities without a chance to move out of these. As the development experiences of all developed economies have shown, a shift in focus to areas where competences had not existed before has proven the crucial impulse for long-term increases in per capita income (Amsden, 2001; Chang, 2002, 2008; Gerschenkron, 1962; and many others).

Understanding the innovation process as in the NIS framework allows for new approaches to understanding the potential and capacity of, even the need for, public policy formulations. Traditionally, or, if you prefer, derived from neoclassical formulations, the focus and justification of policies has been on the correction of "market failures," in this case underinvestment in the development of new technologies due to an only partial ability to capture the resulting benefits (partial appropriability). Therefore, R&D spending and support for private efforts (tax breaks, patents, etc.) have long dominated the agenda of policy makers. A better understanding of the much more intricate nature of the diffusion of knowledge in innovation processes leads to a recognition of systemic aspects of the process, where systemic failures are the problems that are faced. This changes not only the basis for but also the focus of policies. Enhancing the possibilities for inter-actions among the agents increases in impor-tance, focusing on encouraging joint research activities and other cooperative relations, especially also in informal relations and the resulting channels for knowledge flows (see Chapter 17 for a more general explanation of possibilities of policy makers based on the general principles of interactive processes that you have been introduced to throughout this book). The ability to absorb new technologies and knowledge is crucial to the individual firms' success, and their connections to others increase the chance that they will find or develop capacities for achieving this.

16.5 ENDOGENOUS DEVELOPMENT THEORY

A challenge that firms and policy makers face in an era of increasingly global competition and production networks lies at the heart of the endogenous development theory as well—that in an era of an increasing importance of global relations in the economic sector, the importance of *regional production systems* increases at the same time. The response to this increased com-petition fosters the drive towards new modes of organization in cities and in regional production systems as strategic responses are sought to the growing challenges confronted (for an in-depth formulation of the concept, see Vázquez Barquero, 2002). After focusing on the national level in the preceding section where the overall framework for policies is set, thus, we focus on the possibilities for *regional agents* here to foster development dynamics on the level they can influence, in a bottom-up perspective.

16.5.1 Foundations of the Concept

The understanding behind the endogenous development approach is that the creation and diffusion of innovation in the production system,

flexibility in the organization of production, agglomeration and diversity economies that emerge in cities, and the development of the institutional framework are the key components to and drivers of the competitiveness of local and regional production systems. When condi-tions can be advantageously influenced there, economies (external as well as internal) result, reducing production costs, and relations between agents are strengthened, reducing transaction costs, and furthering cooperation, thus laying the basis for the possibility of a self-sustained devel-opment of the region in question. We also find a reference to the fact that capital accumulation is in the final analysis an accumulation of tech-nology and of knowledge, complemented by the abilities of the people working in production processes. The same concept of technology, and hence of technological progress as a cumulative process under true uncertainty, characterized by path dependence, as that introduced before is reflected here.

During these processes, firms are of course always *embedded* in the *wider regional context* and system of relations between enterprises. Every decision they take is conditioned by the milieu they find themselves in and the development of the strategic relationships that form their environment. Their decisions have repercus-sions for the other firms and the innovation capacity of the system as a whole because the stock of knowledge in a given region has benefi-cial external effects and the more pronounced so, the higher the level of connectedness of the agents in territories. Firms are the principal focus for this concept, as their strategic decisions in oligopolistic markets are the carriers of inno-vations (for example, see Chapter 4).

16.5.2 Four Main Focuses—Firms, Flexibility, Cities, and Institutions

Firm networking is the crucial ingredient through which growth and structural change are achieved, while the size of the firms joined in such a network is not a matter of great importance (meaning you want to deepen relations among agents, and strengthen structures, for nonprice-based coordination as well as transfers of tacit knowledge). Where local firms are engaged in networking activities, multiple internal markets are generated as well as less specific meeting areas which in turn facilitate the exchanges of products, services, and especially knowledge. Exchanges of products and the transmission of messages and information in turn strengthen paths for the diffusion of innovation. Specialization in production is hence the predominant objective here (many of the original case studies analyzed industrial districts in Europe, and especially in the Mediterranean; see Chapter 4).

Advances in the *flexibility* of the organization of production processes have contributed to increasing local competitiveness where networks of more autonomous subsidiary plants are integrated into a territory. Considerable organizational advances also include the increase of strategic alliances and agreements among firms. The results can be conceived of as scale economies in production systems as well as in research and development where alliances are focusing on innovation. Obviously, firm systems and strategic alliances among them have a positive impact on transaction costs as well.

The preferential space for these developments is *cities*, the places of production activities. They are uniquely suitable for the creation and development of new industrial and service spaces because of their development potential and capacity to generate externalities. The important aspect is not their size, but the functions they perform. These center on the potential for agglomeration economies that play an important role for the advantages economic agents can gain in cities. Providing the infrastructure and supporting agents in behavior that lead to the realization of potential economies is a central

focus of policies (see section 16.5.3). General competitive pressures can trigger local strategic responses that, if successful, help bring about endogenous development processes. The development potential and externalities are captured as *Marshallian* specialization and *Jacobian* diversification *externalities*. Marshallian externalities describe effects that result from specialization. If companies in a territory are active in a particular (sub-)sector or industry, knowledge is generated in this specific field. If knowledge exchanges between producers can be stimulated (exchanges of information, personnel, etc.) innovativeness and competitiveness can be increased. An additional advantage (of such *industrial districts*) is seen to lie in an available pool of suitably qualified labor on which companies can draw to meet short-term changes in requirements. The diversification view puts a heavier emphasis on knowledge spillovers between sectors and industries (for a study of these externalities, see van der Panne, 2004).

Of course, development processes have profound *institutional and cultural roots*. The agents in a society shape its economic development and the unique features of each society shape the capacity to support and strengthen development processes, or hinder them, as agents act within the specific institutional structure of a territory. Those cities and regions with institutional structures that are flexible enough to interact and integrate external actors have an advantage. The encouragement of the production of public goods and a framework within which actors are more willing to cooperate in learning and the creation of innovation enhances that advantage. Territories with highly developed institutional structures allow companies to better profit from existing training and research facilities. The institutional structure also fosters the formation of strategic relationships, especially where it encourages repeated interactions and stimulates the building of trust between agents, reinforcing cooperation amongst them. Maintaining the instrumentality of institutional structures becomes a critical factor for continued improvements to be realized (see Chapters 4 and 14).

16.5.3 Policy Focus and Implications

Then, local and regional actors play a rather pronounced role and can actively influence their territories' potential by introducing organizational, technological, productive, and commercial changes. In the most successful cases, development strategies are designed by *interacting local groups* of involved agents. One of the main axes of local development policy is the diffusion of innovation and knowledge. Intermediate organizations and local initiatives can be set up for fostering improved conditions for firms and for supporting the formation of networks of actors, in strategic partnerships and cooperation.

We can hence distinguish a move from regional and industrial policies to territorial development policies. Traditional regional growth policy was developed from a focus on concentrated growth models (growth poles) and hence promoted regional distribution of income and employment by attracting external resources to the target area. Local development policy aims at overcoming imbalances by fostering development *from within a territory*. The urban/industrial concentration–diffusion model considered economic development in functional terms; the mobility of production factors would produce redistribution and restore equilibrium between richer and poorer regions. Recently proposed local development strategy is based on a territorial approach to regional development and assumes that local institutions, development paths, and local resources condition economic growth processes. For this reason, the mobilization of local endogenous factors plays a crucial role in the formulation of policies (see Chapter 14).

The change/development model is based on the diffusion of innovation and knowledge

in firms and society, increased flexibility in production processes, an improvement of the urban environment where people live and produce, and an institutional system that is favorable to the creation and development of firms. Involvement in the processes is likewise distinct; not the provision of funds is the mainstay of policies, but rather a *decentralized management through intermediate organizations and agencies* (technological institutes, business innovation centers, training centers). Diffusion of innovation and knowledge, flexible organization of production, urban and institutional development together generate increased efficiency in the performance of the production system. Territories are most successful when all of these converge to reinforce their effects—in fact, due to the strategic interaction among agents, local development policies are a significant factor as they act as catalysts to the process through the local initiatives they design and help to implement (see Chapters 4 and 17).

16.6 VARIETIES OF CAPITALISM

In 2001, Hall and Soskice (2001) introduced their notion of sustained Varieties of Capitalism (VoC). Their understanding regarding the function and effects of institutions in political economies has led them to a conceptualization that allows a broad classification of developed economies with reference to two ideal types as liberal market economies (LMEs) and coordinated market economies (CMEs) (and Mediterranean economies as a, potentially instable, hybrid form).

16.6.1 Beyond the Predominant Understandings of Institutions at the Time

The ways in which the influence of the institutional structure on agents' behavior was mainly understood at the time of their writing can, according to them, be captured in three broad categories:

- *One* is seeing institutions as socializing agencies that are external to the agents and that create a set of norms for and attitudes in the actors who operate where they are valid.
- The *second* focuses on the effects institutions can have, understanding them primarily in terms of the power that an institutional structure grants to some agents due to the hierarchy and resource control it establishes.
- *Finally*, institutions are seen as a combination of sanctions and rewards in the face of which agents adjust their behavior so that behavioral patterns can be predicted relatively easily when the institutional structure is known. (Note that the concept of institutions that finds expression here is different from that introduced in Chapters 1, 12, and 13.)

Even though pointing to important influence factors, *each of these conceptualizations leaves out*, according to Hall and Soskice, the whole field of *strategic interactions* that are so important for actors' behavior in reality. In fact, given that these interactions are so central to the outcomes eventually achieved, the institutions that matter most will accordingly be those that provide the frame for these interactions. The focus of their analysis is hence on those institutions that have a particular influence on the structure of strategic interactions.

16.6.2 Institutional Influence and Strategic Interactions

More specifically, it is the institutions that shape the strategic interactions of firms (that stand at the center of the analysis) and here

institutions with particular influence in five broad fields:

- The *first* field is industrial relations, especially the institutions shaping wage bargaining and the bargaining regarding working conditions.
- The *second* refers to the field of vocational training and education, taking up both sides that are involved there. The problem of firms to secure a suitably qualified workforce is taken into account just as the decision of workers regarding how much to invest in the development of their skills, as well as the decision, what kind of skills to invest in (in general terms, whether to focus on general skills or on skills that are more industry- or even company-specific).
- *Also included* is the field of corporate governance, because of its influence on accessing means of finance.
- The *fourth* field is that of inter-firm relations, where problematic decisions arise in questions regarding the sharing of proprietary information, for instance given the risk of exploitation in joint ventures.
- And, *finally*, the institutions that influence the relations of companies to their employees matter. On the one hand there are those regarding the guarantee of suitable competencies on the side of the employees, but there are also influences on the collaboration among employees for the furthering of the objectives of the firm.

These institutions are interpreted as not standing alone; on the contrary, Hall and Soskice assume that a single institution's contribution to companies' problem solving cannot be understood in isolation. Rather, they postulate an *interaction and interdependence between institutions*, leading to a dependence of the returns of institutions on their combination with others that may support similar behavior patterns and decisions. From the complementarities of institutions emerge the ideal types of market economies they propose.

16.6.3 LMEs and CMEs

For them, two ideal types of economies emerge from the comparison of economies in these fields, the mentioned LMEs and the CMEs. In LMEs, coordination is achieved mainly via hierarchies and competitive market arrangements. The outcomes that are observed accordingly tend to be understood in terms of supply and demand. In CMEs, we find a much more pronounced reliance on nonmarket relationships for the coordination of agents (among others, more extensive relational or incomplete contracts, network monitoring based on the exchange of private information, and more reliance on collaboration instead of a focus on competitive relationships).

That means that companies located in economies organized in a coordinated manner operate with a *broader set of institutions and structures of cooperation* than those in LMEs. The role of business associations, trade unions, networks of cross-shareholdings, and legal or regulatory systems shaped in a way that makes the sharing of information and collaboration easier is much more pronounced here supporting the strategic interactions that matter for firms' success. All of these have come to fulfill, among others, one central function, which is the reduction of uncertainty for the involved actors through a stabilization of the environment in which they operate. Additionally, they enhance the agents' capacity of, or encourage their willingness of, sharing information, and also monitoring others' behavior and, if need be, sanctioning those that do not act according to agreed courses of action. A primary function of these *institutions* is to allow the agents to *coordinate on strategies that offer them a higher return* in situations that can in principle be understood as multiple equilibrium games. As coordination (on an equilibrium)

is often based on informal institutions, the concept acknowledges their importance in non-cooperative environments, and thus allows the integration of history and culture into the concept as actors are usually socialized to follow certain rules and norms and learn these in the interaction with other members of the group over time.

An important aspect to this is furthermore what Hall and Soskice call *deliberative institutions*, those that make it easier for actors to discuss matters (multilaterally) and outline a common course of action. The possibility to deliberate questions and problems likewise makes the coordination in situations allowing for multiple equilibria easier at the same time that it also strengthens the information base, the common knowledge of the actors. Overall, such institutions offer a set of strategic options and capacities that agents would not have at their disposal without them.

16.6.4 Beyond the Market-Hierarchy Dichotomy

We can appreciate better now, how the concept differs from those proposed in the transaction cost economics (market-hierarchy dichotomy) in two fundamental ways. *First* of all, aspects of organization and coordination that go beyond market and hierarchy are fundamental parts of the concept, giving recognition to the necessity and importance of these forms for agents in settings of strategic uncertainty. The enhanced ability to *signal credible commitments* is an especially important effect of these. And in fact, differences in these institutional sets are crucial for the distinction between the different types of developed economies.

The *second* fundamental difference derives from the perspective on the relationship between firms and institutional structure. In the "new institutional (transaction cost) economics," it is assumed that the relevant institutional structures are created by the agents (firms) in order to allow the efficient execution of their undertakings. That means that "(institutional) structure follows (firm) strategy." The idea of an institutional structure emerging from the directed actions of individual agents is, however, one that is doubtful in its implications, and especially in matters of institutions that ease coordinated actions by the economic agents. It is much more plausible to assume that firms are faced with an institutional structure that is not (completely) controlled by them. And then it is only plausible to assume that firms will adopt behavioral patterns that make use of the opportunities they face. Then, firms will *employ modes of coordination that find relatively stronger support from the institutions in place* (hence, strategy follows structure and we arrive in a path-dependent setting). This opens the door to introducing a concept of a "comparative institutional advantage" (to which we will return a little further on in this section). We have to caution here against a unidirectional interpretation of influences again, but still can follow the assumption that in a given institutional structure a drastic overhaul is less likely than the adoption

of new rules, or the adaptation of existing ones, that are largely compatible with the existing ones.

For illustrating the last point, we can use a simple graphical representation, such as that given in Figure 16.2.

What Figure 16.2 illustrates is the notion that different kinds of coordinating measures may be drawn on, and, depending on the overall framework, may lead to comparable economic outcomes. However, note that a number of criticisms have been formulated with a view on the conceptualization proposed (see below), and that these may impact the evaluation of outcomes, or, indeed, the classifications of the systems, and their outputs. The pure cases of the conceptualization will not be encountered. In real-world economic systems, coordination through price mechanism and in arms-length relations is still embedded into a regulatory framework guaranteeing overall stability, and public sector providing infrastructure, research, and substantial demand and risk reduction for innovation sectors (such as seen in the example of the military-industrial complex in the USA

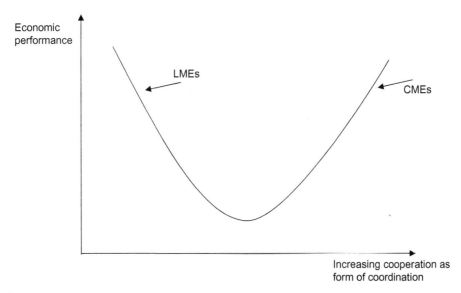

FIGURE 16.2 Type of coordination and economic performance.

after World War II, for instance). Also note that narrow indicators are more prone to offering a potentially distorted view, as effects in other parts of the overall system (such as the shift of cost to nature, for instance) can be more easily ignored. Such additional effects may become noticeable, once the timeframe for an evaluation changes, for instance.

16.6.5 Consequences for Production Structures in Different Economies

The *different general patterns of coordination* find their reflection in a number of characteristics of the specific economies. As examples, we can refer to investment behavior and innovation performance; more specifically, the direction and kind of innovation more likely to be pursued. As companies in *CMEs* are more likely to be engaging in *longer lasting relationships*, time horizons under which specific investments can amortize are longer. We can expect relatively *more relationship-specific assets* to be included in the investment portfolio of companies as they should be more willing to make the commitments embodied in these investments. Production in CMEs requires a higher level of industry- or company-specific skills from the workforce (decisions for the acquisition of which are easier given the justifiable expectations of longer employment durations in one company). In *LMEs*, on the other hand, investments can be expected to be more focused on assets that are *not relationship-specific*, but can be switched to other uses, or be used in other business relationships. Skills are likewise of a more general, more easily transferable kind.

That means that companies in CMEs have advantages in the production of products where quality counts primarily, as a result of deeper specialization and focus in production as a possibility in these environments. Companies in LMEs have advantages where prices matter more, as reduced protection of

labor and the available set of general skills tend to favor less skilled and lower price production processes. As far as the innovation performance is concerned, we also find a reflection of these aspects there. Finally, according to Hall and Soskice, the incremental innovations that help maintain competitiveness in the production of capital goods are more likely to occur in CMEs, whereas the radical innovations that are required in fast-moving technology sectors may be more likely in LMEs (note the critique below, however).

16.6.6 Challenges and Focuses for Policy Makers

Challenges for economic policy makers likewise differ under the VoC perspective compared to the neoclassical approach. Derived from the neoclassical approach the problem was conceived of as defining the actions that firms were to take in order to achieve long-term objectives set out for the economy. Then, incentives were to be designed to get agents to do what was desired of them—in a way, one could say the problem was understood as getting private agents to cooperate with the government agents (for instance, setting incentives to induce behavior by private agents that can overcome market failures). The focus on strategic interaction among private agents and the results derived from this allows a quite different formulation of the problem set for economic policy makers. When companies can only achieve their objectives through collaboration, how to get private agents to cooperate has to be the objective, and the support for and formulation of an institutional structure that helps make this easier has to be the objective of economic policy. (A similar strand of argumentation will be taken up in Chapter 17.)

How this can be done differs depending on the overall framework (Figure 16.2). In this reading, sometimes national economic performance can be improved when the functioning of market mechanisms is improved (through regulation reducing complexity and uncertainty, for instance). However, in other instances improved capacities for coordinating with other agents in situations of strategic interaction are the key to an improved performance. An "incentive compatibility" has to be maintained as enhancing coordination in strategic interactions is a difficult task, which includes the fostering of information sharing among agents and improvements in private agents' ability to make credible commitments, and the shaping of expectations regarding others' behavior that allows for a cooperative strategy to be chosen (see also *recognized interdependence and futurity*, presented in Chapters 3, 14, and 17). These things cannot be mandated but depend on the willingness of private agents to play their part.

16.6.7 VoC and (the Challenges of) Globalization

As an additional point, we can address the consequences for the understanding of how to face the challenges from increasingly globalized economic activities. The usual understanding of globalization that we are confronted with rests on three pillars, based on which challenges and dangers for economies are identified and subsequent policy recommendations formulated:

- *One* basic assumption in the general view on globalization is that firms are essentially identical everywhere.
- The *second* is that competitiveness tends to be reduced to unit labor costs.
- The *third* that a specific political dynamic would result from these aspects, namely an enhanced negotiating power of businesses being able to force governments to implement changes in the domestic institutional frameworks firms face

(lowering labor costs, reducing tax rates, withdrawing from regulatory tasks).

Each of these pillars can be called into question once the VoC perspective is adopted, resulting in a whole different evaluation of the situation and potential problems that may arise as a consequence.

As we have seen, following the VoC approach, *firms develop distinct strategies* depending on where they are located, and hence are not identical. They may in fact split their operations to benefit from specific conditions that support specific parts of their operations; and they can use aspects of the different institutional structure to their own advantage, whether they split their operations or concentrate everything in one specific location. The institutional environment exerts a significant influence in any case, as said, because strategies and structures follow the institutions that are in place for coordinating their activities, at least to some degree. Given these specific strategies and structures, *firms will not automatically move* their operations to where labor is cheapest. As can be appreciated from the above, a number of additional factors influence the overall effectiveness of operations as competitive advantages also result from the institutional structures within which specific activities are undertaken (not denying that, of course, qualified labor available at a lower price is attractive). As a result, there is *no reason to suspect a uniform direction of policy making to be the only reasonable way*. If competitive advantages derive from strategies designed to benefit from specific institutional provisions, and if different institutional provisions favor different kinds of coordination and as a consequence different kinds of activities, then nations may actually prosper by getting more diverse, creating institutional niches for companies to locate in. The arguments and negotiating positions of the agents then change as it becomes clear that their relation can be seen as one of mutual dependency in which cooperation can improve everyone's long-term position, instead of continued (distributional) conflict in a de facto zero-sum relation.

16.6.8 Some Extensions and Basic Critique of the VoC Concept

As (should be the case) in every scientific discussion, the proposals forwarded by Hall and Soskice have been met with criticism as well. For an overview, see Kesting and Nielsen (2008). Main points on which the criticism centers are the game-theoretic analogies employed by Hall and Soskice, the close orientation on rational choice approaches to institutions and institutional change going hand in hand with this perspective, as well as the likewise related lack of including the political dimension that a study of political economies would demand. *Cultural, historical, and social elements* influencing development paths and current shapes of analyzed economies *are lost* in this way. Furthermore, the *ideal types* they derive are seen as *too limited*. Additionally, the attempt to closely link two limited ideal types and real-world examples that are shaped by cultural and historical experiences limits the insights that can be gained from the exercise. It is, as Kesting and Nielsen show, variously pointed out that ideal types would serve much better as the basis for case studies, if it was not attempted to fit one country with one ideal type, but rather to try and identify which aspects of an institutional structure conform to which type. Thereby, an enhanced *understanding of institutional dynamics and possible development paths* to be followed would become possible.

Some criticism has also been put forward by Lazonick (2009), one aspect of which refers to the *assumption of the innovation ability of the different ideal types*. As we have pointed out above, government financing of research has been an important factor, and has in fact increased in importance over the last decades,

for the steady flow of new technologies into the economic sphere of societies. This covers knock-offs from military and space programs, general military research, but basic research in pharmacy and biotechnology as well, for instance. This publicly mandated and financed research has nothing to do with the organization of the relation of agents in the economic sphere. We can in fact distinguish differences in the direction of government-financed research, between orientations leaning more towards the military and more towards civilian undertakings (Niosi et al., 1993), but resulting inventions are, again, not influenced by the organization of the economic sphere. The ease with which inventions may be turned into innovations may, on the other hand, well be have a connection to that organizational structure, as the LME-prototype economy may be more prone to introducing radical innovations due to reduced possibilities for resistance from existing interests.

Another aspect Lazonick refers to is the continuing change of especially the Anglo-Saxon economies, along a direction that lead to structures with an influence on companies' innovation capabilities again. The point here is the *financialization* of the economic sphere—the movement to (short-term) financial indicators such as stock prices for measuring companies' success. This has increasingly induced companies to adopt a short-term time horizon in their operations and a focus of actions on influencing these indicators. A prime example is buybacks that serve the manipulation of stock prices. As Lazonick shows, over the last decade, this has grown by exceptional degrees, leading some of the largest companies in the US economy to spend substantial parts, more than 100% in some cases, of their net profits on such operations. These means, then, are not available any longer for financing longer term operations and R&D operations internally. This dynamic signifies a noticeable change in direction compared to the earlier postwar decades (see Chapters 4 and 7). Coinciding calls for increased government presence in research and education in general by company representatives complete the picture of an increasing shift of private companies' risk and costs to the general public.

16.7 CHAPTER CONCLUSION: MAIN ASPECTS OF THE ABOVE CONCEPTS

The concepts introduced in this chapter largely share the view of *innovation* as an interactive and cumulative process. The level on which the respective authors have focused differs, though, ranging from *firm networks* to the *regional systems* (which may overlap with the cluster and network views, however) to the *national level of innovation systems*. This has been complemented by a concept centering on the differences within *large-scale national institutional frameworks* and the development directions most likely to be observable in these. Given the common view on innovation, it is not surprising that they share *general policy recommendations* for strengthening the innovation capacity of systems.

The novelty character of the innovation is stressed, which goes hand in hand with uncertainty during invention and innovation processes. Innovation is disequilibrating and a potential threat to existing structures and interests, within companies as well as beyond companies. Uncertainty characterizes the process of introducing an innovation, a new product, for instance, just as previous invention processes. Even though companies can influence and create demand (see Chapter 7), they are not guaranteed success. Innovation manifests in changing economic structures; on a sectoral level, in the companies present in that sector, as well as on a higher aggregate level, concerning the overall composition of economic activity in an economy, for instance. The complex and complicated advanced technologies that have come to be utilized in large parts of modern economies rely on substantial coordinated and even cooperative effort in their application. This is likewise true for the interactions in innovation processes behind changes in them. How to foster structures that support agents in those processes is a core aspect of successful innovation policies. One stress is the necessity for *establishing structures* that enable and incentivize agents to make effective use of existing capacities and endowments; or, in a prior step, to develop the absorptive capacities required for effectively operating and changing advanced technology. Crucially, given the cumulative nature of technological changes, this includes the ability to diffuse novelty through the production fabric of the system under investigation. As existing production structures are to be supported in their functioning and innovation capabilities, we can assume that incremental innovations are the natural first focus for agents then. However, to the degree that potential capacities are to be realized in a territory the establishment of new structures in a territory is not neglected either.

From assessing existing networks for their innovation capability, we have moved to analyzing the national framework influencing the innovation ability of the companies located within the respective borders. Within this *national system* it has turned out to be advantageous to delegate responsibilities to *local* or *regional* actors who have a better understanding of the territory in question than agents at higher administrative levels can have, and help to establish a regional framework and regional structures for supporting the activities of agents in that territory. Finally, we have turned to the potential constraints that advantageous changes in institutional structures may be subject to as single institutions complement one another and the targeted change of one or some of them without reference to the overall institutional system may then easily produce undesired results (for a systemic policy approach, see Chapter 17).

In terms of the topics that have resurfaced throughout this textbook, we can identify the strengthening of structure that fosters *strategic cooperation* of directly interdependent agents as a crucial component to maintaining the ability for long-term, instrumental, change. A balance between the capacity for self-organization in the system, hierarchy for direction and standard setting, stabilization and turbulence because of novelty, as well as the continued maintenance of instrumentality in structures, among others, may demand *trade-offs between different objectives* therein and at times, however. Which ways are open for achieving continuously advantageous results, without short-term disadvantageous disruptions and adverse consequence will in part depend on the structures in place (see Chapter 17).

Chapter References

Acemoglu, D., 2008. Introduction to Modern Economic Growth. Princeton University Press, Princeton, NJ.

Amsden, A., 2001. The Rise of the Rest—Challenges to the West from Late-Industrializing Economies. Oxford University Press, Oxford.

Antonelli, G., de Liso, N., 1997. Introduction: an appraisal of the economic analysis of technological change. In: Antonelli, G., de Liso, N. (Eds.), Economics of Structural and Technological Change. Routledge, London, New York, pp. 1–47.

Ayres, C.E., 1996. The Theory of Economic Progress (internet edition). <http://cas.umkc.edu/econ/Institutional/ Readings/Ayres/tep/TEP.html>.

Berg, N., Gigerenzer, G., 2010. As-if behavioral economics: neoclassical economics in disguise? Hist. Econ. Ideas. 18 (1), 133–166.

Chang, Ha-Joon, 2002. Kicking Away the Ladder: Development Strategy in Historical Perspective. Anthem, London.

Chang, Ha-Joon, 2008. Bad Samaritans: The Myth of Free Trade and the Secret History of Capitalism. Bloomsbury Press, New York, NY.

Coase, R.H., 1937. The nature of the firm. Economica. 4, 386–405.

Coase, R.H., 1992. The institutional structure of production. Am. Econ. Rev. 82 (4), 713–719.

Elsner, W., Hocker, G., Schwardt, H., 2010. Simplistic vs. complex organization: markets, hierarchies, and networks in an organizational triangle—a simple heuristic to analyze real-world organizational forms. J. Econ. Issues. 44 (1), 1–29.

Freeman, C., 1987. Technology and Economic Performance: Lessons from Japan. Pinter, London.

Gerschenkron, A., 1962. Economic Backwardness in Historic Perspective, A Book of Essays. The Belknap Press of Harvard University Press, Cambridge, MA.

Hall, P.A., Soskice, D., 2001. Varieties of Capitalism: The Institutional Foundation of Comparative Advantage. Oxford University Press, Oxford.

Himmelweit, S., Simonetti, R., Trigg, A., 2002. Neoclassical and Institutionalist perspectives on Economics Behavior—Microeconomics. Thomson, London.

Kesting, S., Nielsen, K. (Eds.), 2008. Varieties of Capitalism and New Institutional Deals: Regulation, Welfare and the New Economy. Edward Elgar, Cheltenham, Northampton.

Lazonick, W., 2009. Sustainable Prosperity in the New Economy. W.E. Upjohn Institute for Employment Research, Kalamazoo, MI.

Lundvall, B.-A. (Ed.), 1992. National Innovation Systems: Towards a Theory of Innovation and Interactive Learning. Pinter, London.

Lundvall, B.-A., 2007. National innovation systems— analytical concept and development tool. Ind. Innov. 14 (1), 95–119.

Nelson, R.R. (Ed.), 1993. National Innovation Systems: A Comparative Analysis. Oxford University Press, New York, Oxford.

Niosi, J., Saviotti, P., Bellon, B., Crow, M., 1993. National systems of innovation: in search of a workable concept. Technol. Soc. 15 (2), 207–227.

Van der Panne, G., 2004. Agglomeration externalities: Marshallian versus Jacobian. J. Evol. Econ. 14 (5), 593–604.

Vázquez Barquero, A., 2002. Endogenous Development, Networking, Innovation, Institutions and Cities. Routledge, London.

Williamson, O.E., 1975. Markets and Hierarchies: Analysis and Anti-Trust Implications—A Study in the Economics of Internal Organization. Free Press, New York, NY.

Williamson, O.E., 1985. The Economic Institutions of Capitalism: Firms, Markets, Relational Contracting. Free Press, New York, NY.

Williamson, O.E., 2005. Transaction cost economics. In: Ménard, C., Shirley, M.M. (Eds.), Handbook of New Institutional Economics. Springer, Berlin, pp. 41–68.

Further Reading—Online

For further reading, see the textbook website at http:// booksite.elsevier.com/9780124115859

17

Policy Implications: New Policy Perspectives for Private Agents, Networks, Network Consultants, and Public Policy Agencies*

"The philosophers have only interpreted the world in various ways; the point is to change it." Karl Marx[1]

OUTLINE

*Claudius Gräbner has contributed some sections to this chapter.

[1]"Theses on Feuerbach," in: Friedrich Engels, *Ludwig Feuerbach & the Outcome of Classical German Philosophy*, New York: International Publishers, 1996/1886, p. 84.

The Microeconomics of Complex Economies.
DOI: http://dx.doi.org/10.1016/B978-0-12-411585-9.00017-8

In Chapters 4, 6, 7, 15, and 16, we have explained how the real world is a complex system and why neoclassical mainstream economics does not reflect this properly. In Chapters 8—11, we have provided the analytical approaches and tools of modeling complex economic systems more appropriately. Chapters 12—14 provided the history of complex economic theorizing and a number of current core models and approaches to complexity economics. Finally, Chapters 15 and 16 again, showed important areas of application, where complexity economics can be illustrated to provide appropriate analysis, i.e., information economics on the one hand and innovation, firm networks, and economic development on the other. The present chapter explains policy implications of complexity microeconomics and therefore draws on the issues explained there.

17.1 POLICY IMPLICATIONS OF COMPLEXITY (MICRO-) ECONOMICS

17.1.1 The Flawed Neoclassical Mainstream Benchmark: "Second Best" or "Worst," and a New Basic Policy Perspective

It was shown in a number of examples that, as soon as we only slightly alter assumptions of the neoclassical core model, in this way starting to consider that the economic system is complex indeed, the alleged neoclassical "benchmark" of a perfect market economy simply dissolves and there is *no longer an obvious, predetermined benchmark for policy orientations*. In this case we have to acknowledge that reality is not even a rough approximation of that ideal model; that model just turned out to be too artificial, designed after other criteria than explaining (and improving) reality. As it has hardly anything to do with reality, we cannot even say that or how real policy measures would be close to, or galaxies away from, whether they would approach or stride away from that ideal.

For instance, the *Theory of the Second Best* (see Section 5.7.1) demonstrated this in close logical and theoretical connection to the neoclassical core model. If the "perfect state" is not available—for instance, because one of the many required strict assumptions, e.g., perfect information, or convex indifference curves, is violated—the then available next best result most probably will require a violation of most other optimality conditions as well. This means that a gradual move from any system state toward a first-best solution is usually not possible. As a result, when changing the slightest assumption, reflecting real-world complexity, we cannot say how and how far we will end up deviating from the abstract ideal and where we will find ourselves in the *universe of possible system states* (see Chapter 10 on this)—perhaps in one of the worst in terms of the "perfect" ideal.

Policy would then have to adopt a *systemic perspective* rather, considering all conditions of the system simultaneously—which, in turn requires a considerable *complexity of the policy system in control of the economic system* (see on "Ashby's Law" described in the next section).

For a *pragmatic, real-world-oriented policy*, the real situation then has to be carefully analyzed in order to be able to find out how a "relatively good" result may be reached. In effect, the simple policy-kit, the usual "market-oriented" "there-is-no-alternative" policy prescriptions that the partial and general equilibrium approaches postulate and require ("more ideal market!") is not adequate, and it gets unfruitful, as said, as soon as the slightest deviations from the perfect set of assumptions of the first best have to be acknowledged.

Given that the usual policy proposals in today's real world are, if only implicitly, rooted in one or the other way in the neoclassical core model, this will help increase our awareness of how an argument for or against certain policy positions may be structured and on which grounds it is defended.

Direct interdependencies among agents, particularly among firms in a fragmented value-added chain (VAC) or in an oligopolistic market structure, have been real-world instances above, as well as imperfect and asymmetric information, collective goods, network technologies with network externalities, or the existence of power, among others (again, see Chapters 4–7).

17.1.2 The Complexity of Economic Systems, and a Systemic Approach to Policy

We have explained in Chapters 6, 10, and 11 that complex systems may display unpredictable motions, i.e., bifurcations, or phase transitions and "chaos," rather than unique stable equilibria. Complexity has to do with the *variety* in the network of its interdependent elements, e.g., the *heterogeneity* of its agents in the case of a socioeconomic system.

A Minimum Complexity of a Controlling Policy System

If a (socioeconomic) system in a dynamic (often unpredictable) motion is to be stabilized in order to have its dependent variables remain in (or enter into) some aimed-at value areas, even after the independent variables or the functions have changed, a controlling system, a policy system in our case, must have a neutralizing influence on the independent variables or the system functions. Variety, in *information theory* and *cybernetics*, is considered to denote, e.g., the total *number of possible states of a system*. As the famous *Ashby's Law*, developed by W. Ross Ashby (Ashby, 1956), already stated, the number of possible states of the controlling system must be at least equal to the number of possible states of the system to be controlled. As has been formulated in the same vein, *only "variety can absorb variety"* (Beer, 1979). In other words, the complexity of a policy system to control the complex socioeconomic system must be at least as large as the complexity of the latter.

This explains a lot, when we consider the battles over the different economic policy paradigms in the transitions of the 1970s from an earlier interventionist paradigm to a "neoliberal" (de-)regulation regime of "letting the markets do by themselves." As argued in more detail in Chapter 4, one of the public arguments of "neoliberal" think tanks, corporation leaders, mainstream economists, and leading politicians was that selective policy interventions into the "market system" in the era of welfare-state interventionism—falsely and crudely alleged to be Keynesian—had led to some "over-complexity" (particularly, as perceived then, of the policy system). It had also been argued that, besides (but perhaps just because of) "over-complexity," this had triggered all kinds of *evasions of the economic system and its agents*, so that an increasing number of *interventions would*

be neutralized, if not worsened, by the system, requiring ever more interventions, which, overall, would worsen problems rather than reduce them. The idea usually cited here is Hayek's "road to serfdom"—a crude and simplistic, fearful metaphor (for a revived and ongoing debate on Hayek's "road to serfdom," see, e.g., Farrant and McPhail, 2010).

The true core of this argument is that in capitalist "market" societies, with their increasing oligopolistic corporate power, governments never dared to *intervene with a consistent, systemic, and long-run approach*. With isolated, halfhearted, and inconsistent interventions in the given policy regime, which is, in contrast to money-capital, kept divided in national units, the "system" and its leading agents could *avoid* any public objective to be realized and *evade* any intervention measure. Examples become public on a daily basis nowadays, be it *tax evasion* of an estimated 40% of the global money-capital, hoarded in tax havens, or be it the obvious support even from governments of leading industrial countries (individual states of the USA, or Ireland, the UK or Germany) for global industrial and financial corporations that virtually have been freed from paying taxes in many places of the USA or in the EU (see, e.g., the Apple and Amazon cases, which are registered in Ireland in order to avoid tax paying for their EU branches). Phenomena like these have been evidence for some global race to the bottom among national social and tax standards.

The policy problem, of course, is even more complicated as appears at first sight. Under complexity and path-dependent process, small causes, which may easily be overlooked, may have large effects later on, as we have explained throughout this textbook. Therefore, it has been argued by information theorists, monitoring the factors relevant for the variety and complexity of the system and making *ongoing experience, learning,* and *policy adaptations* is always critically required.

Collective Rationality: Social-Choice Versus Procedural, Discourse, and Substantial Conceptions of Democracy

Note that the *controlling policy system* itself needs to have, and to further, some qualification. Its collective rationality might stem from a whole set of interaction and verbal communication procedures and mechanisms, including different *interaction, discourse,* and *voting* mechanisms at different levels. Some collective rationality may be gained in these ways—while we should be aware of all kinds of static voting problems potentially involved here, such as the so-called *Arrow Paradox* of static preference aggregation by voting, that have been an issue in Social-Choice, or Public-Choice theory for long.

Kenneth Arrow's (1950) paradox, or impossibility theorem, stated that, when voters have at least three alternatives to vote on and each has a particular ranked preference order among them, no *ordinal* (or rank-order) voting system can convert these preferences of the individuals into a complete and transitive social welfare ranking, if they have to meet also a specific set of apparently very general criteria. These criteria are an *unrestricted domain, nondictatorship, Pareto efficiency,* and *independence of irrelevant alternatives* (compare the *rationality criteria* for utility functions as explained in Chapter 5). These simple "fairness" criteria, for instance, say: (i) If every voter prefers alternative X over alternative Y, then the group must prefer X over Y. (ii) If every voter's preference between X and Y remains unchanged, then the group's preference between X and Y shall also remain unchanged, independent on how they vote on them (even if voters' preferences between other pairs like X and Z, Y and Z, or Z and W change). (iii) There is no "dictator," i.e., no single voter possesses the power to always determine the group's preference.

The theorem is usually cited in discussions on elections and voting, in order to stress the impossibility of a *superior collective* or *common*

rationality. Note, however, that, e.g., voting that uses cardinal utility is not covered by the theorem. The theorem also depends on the notion of strict independence of individual preferences, i.e., it is a strictly *static logical issue* with no consideration of democratic discourse with the opportunity of some *endogenous change* or convergence *of individual preferences.* Contemporary "Social-Choice" theory nevertheless uses this theorem when dealing with issues of democracy, although it is just a logical exercise (which nevertheless was innovative, surprising, and enlightening in the beginning). Thus, this theorem has been much criticized on the basis of its restrictive and flawed assumptions, such as ordinal utility with its reduced utility information, or the inadequateness of applying the Pareto criterion to issues of democratic voting, i.e., the neglect of interindividual utility comparability, further, its lack of evaluation of basic needs, the dynamics of individual capabilities, etc. (for the most comprehensive critique, see Sen, 1970/1984, 2008).

A Systemic, Experience- and Learning-Based, Nonmyopic Policy Approach

Some collective rationality, if gained in a discourse process with "endogenous preferences," will, at any rate, have to be complemented through procedures of further *collective learning from policy experience.* We will address the issue again in some more detail in Section 17.2.

In all, a first *policy conclusion* may be the following:

- Complexity microeconomics is reflected in a basic *complexity-policy* approach that must be *systemic,* in the sense that it always needs to be prepared for evading reactions and to further *intervene at a multitude of different systemic points,* often *simultaneously,* or in an *anticipated sequence.* While in the 1970s the "neoliberal" paradigmatic turnaround was prepared—by the way, also in a very systemic, consequential, and very long-run approach—by public campaigns suggesting upcoming "chaos" from Keynesian welfare-state interventionism (which sanctified even the bloody "neoliberal" putsch in Chile in 1973, legitimized that way by F.A. Hayek and M. Friedman)—a systemic complexity-policy approach would have to enlighten the public that a collectively rational systemic intervention will have to be an ongoing process, and a sequence of action, experience, and learning on the side of the policy-makers and the public itself, which has to be kept involved.

17.1.3 Further "Complexity Hints for Economic Policy"

As we have explained and exemplified in Chapters 6, 10, 11, and 13, complex systems are dynamic, evolutionary, path-dependent, emergent, and open-ended, with properties also often called *autopoietic/morphogenetic* (self-creating), often also considered *homeostatic/hysteretic/equifinal* (path preserving), but also have multiple equilibria, often complicated orbits, show idiosyncratic sudden changes, are, thus, chaotic, i.e., nonpredictable—and no longer analytically or probabilistically solvable. Against that background, for instance, Salzano and Colander (2007) have considered particular "complexity hints for economic policy" (see also, e.g., Ivarola et al., 2013; for further implications of complexity economics for epistemological "meta"-theorizing, see Chapter 18).

In general, they argue, those more real-world systems "can be discovered by a combination of analytics and computer simulations" (Salzano and Colander, 2007, p. XI; see also Chapters 9–11), and, thus, complexity economists' policy recommendations would generally be *less certain, less clear-cut, less apodictic*, and postulating than the usual mainstream normative policy prescriptions ("more market!") based on the specific, ideal "market model."

As complex systems usually have a *huge number of possible states* (a large number of degrees of freedom), among them a large number of *states resulting from evasive moves of agents* against policy regulations, they may particularly remain homeostatic and equifinal, returning to their previous path after some external shock, or after some discretionary policy intervention in our case. Thus, there exists some basic *undecidability of policy* (Salzano and Colander, 2007, p. XVII). This, obviously, requires a basic *"change in the worldview that is currently dominant in policy circles"* (Velupillai, 2007, in Salzano and Colander, 2007, p. 275; italics added). Velupillai (2007) also argues, for instance, that a reorientation of policy has to focus on proper *institutional design* (Velupillai, 2007, p. 276), which we will further develop in the remainder of this chapter.

In all, a second *policy conclusion* may be as follows:

- Policy will, among others, have to be *more inductive*, i.e., prepared to *act on the temporal dimension*, pursue measures that are valid and appropriate only for *certain contexts and time windows* and are set up to permanently collect new knowledge and experience. With some undecidability, uncomputability, and other indeterminate problems (Velupillai, 2007, pp. 280ff.), policy issues can only be solved pro tempore (p. 278).

Velupillai (2007) formally shows that appropriate and stabilizing institutional design measures will be impossible to be determined just on the basis of calculating the system to be controlled. A "non-algorithmic step must be taken" (p. 285) rather, for the system to be controlled in order to (faster) *move it into a basin of attraction*, which has self-organizing, equilibrating, or stabilizing properties. As there is no general algorithm for an endogenous motion, or a political moving, of the system in this direction, Velupillai considers "nonalgorithmic" political measures, in order to try moving the system toward a generally satisfying equilibrium. (For policy examples, see Section 17.2.)

A third *policy conclusion* might follow:

- *Stabilizing potentially volatile complex systems* through *reducing the complexity of individual decision situations* would also involve *institutional solutions* that include a *collective commitment* and *self-binding* for some appropriate *time period* to decisions taken earlier (in terms of investment in capital, effort, brain, etc. made before, thus reducing volatility and turbulence) (see also Velupillai, 2007, p. 289). Politics then would basically be the art of determining the *proper point in time for a new change* or a new phase of letting systemic volatility increase.

Also, Gallegati et al. (2007), in the edited book of Salzano and Colander mentioned above, have elaborated on policy implications of complexity. They focus on the *size distribution* (of firms) in (economic) systems (particularly in the national networks of firms), i.e., a *high degree of centrality of large hub firms* in that case, and demonstrate the high levels of *systemic volatility* connected with a large number of such heterogeneity of (large and small) agents, with aggregate fluctuations resulting from such *"idiosyncratic volatility"* (p. 300) (for a discussion of such *"scale-free"* network structures with a power-law distribution of firm size, see Section 13.11 above).

Thus, another *policy conclusion* may be concluded from complexity economics:

- In order to stabilize turbulent economic systems, policy should also *control for volatility*. As an example for such a policy, Gallegati, Kirman, and Palestrini recommend a policy to *reduce the legal protection of intellectual property rights* (IPR), to reduce discretionary and arbitrary use of them, and to smooth and live up the *overall innovation* and growth rates (op. cit.) (on that, see also Chapter 15 and Section 17.4 below). Second, and connected with that, the overall *concentration of firms has to be reduced*, in order to *reduce aggregate*

fluctuations. Technically, the overall *network centrality degree*, or, in statistical terms, the power-law size distribution, i.e., a high power concentration in the economy, should be *reduced* and agents' size distribution *made more even* (again, see Section 13.11 for such network structures). The latter would also apply to the volatility of the financial sector, as the authors argue.

In the following, we make a step further, from such general principles and orientations to a more specific policy model that designs and shapes specific conditions of effective agents' interactions to promote the institutional emergence of cooperation. We will specifically refer in this context to basic game theory (GT) models as explained in Chapters 3, 13, and 14.

17.2 INTERACTIVE AND INSTITUTIONAL ECONOMIC POLICY: A LEAN POLICY APPROACH FOR A COMPLEX, INTERACTIVE, AND EVOLUTIONARY ECONOMY, BASED ON THE GAME-THEORETIC PERSPECTIVE

17.2.1 "Self-Organization" of Systems— And a Role for Social Evaluation, "Meritorization," and Policy

A Solution Possible ...

Let us consider typical contemporary "market"-based (macro-)economic problems, such as, e.g., mass unemployment, increasing precarious labor, increasing income vulnerability for an increasing number of people, increasingly uneven income and wealth distribution, limitless work such as overtime work, Sunday work, etc., increasing precariousness of health and old-age insurance, underinnovation and underinvestment, business cycle volatility, inflation/deflation, uncontrollable financial speculation and financial crises, food and resource speculation, nature climate deterioration, etc. Such phenomena we may explain (and, in fact, have explained in specific ways in this textbook, as in Chapters 4 and 7) as ultimately rooted in uni-, bi-, or multilateral defective behaviors among individualistic agents in fragmented structures and typically dilemma-prone social decision situations and processes. Note, however, that there, of course, is no simple, direct, or static and stable causal relation between complex and intricate microeconomic decision structures and highly aggregative macro situations and processes.

We have referred, for such problems, to the approaches of *Axelrod, Schotter, Lindgren*, and many others in this textbook (see Chapter 13 for the relevant selected approaches). A large variety of approaches, models, and simulations have demonstrated that in an evolutionary process, institutions of cooperation may emerge from dilemma-prone structures if specific conditions can emerge (see, e.g., Liebrand and Messick, 1996; Lindgren, 1997; Offerman and Sonnemans, 1998; Oltra and Schenk, 1998; Eckert et al., 2005; Demange and Wooders, 2005; Traulsen and Nowak, 2006; Jun and Sethi, 2009; among innumerable others).

... But Uncertain and Fragile

The process of the evolutionary and self-sustaining solution of such problems through *emerging proper instrumental institutions of cooperation*, which we have illustrated to be basically feasible in a self-organizing process (see Chapters 3, 10, 11, 13, and 14), however, turns out to be in fact

1. *highly uncertain* to take off at all,
2. often very *time-consuming* while taking off and during the process of sufficient stabilization, and
3. lastingly *fragile* and prone to backslides (after it has taken off).

And there is no guarantee that conditions are existent so that proper self-organization

will come about with sufficient *certainty, stability*, and *speed*. Technically, we have argued, this is reflected in the existence of at least two potential Nash equilibria (NE) in the Prisoners' Dilemma supergame (PD-SG), a superior and an inferior one. Building on this, the fundamental problem that always remains is the basic social dilemma structure. An individualistic culture then implies that the process may be highly time-consuming and unstable, if taking off at all. The more individualistic the culture is the greater generally is the incentive to defect and even to deviate from an already-established institution of cooperation. Model simulations of evolutionary processes have lent additional credibility to this surmise (see, e.g., Lindgren, 1997 and his approach in Chapter 13).

A Social Evaluation, and "Meritorization" Criteria

Therefore, basically, a specific type of public policy intervention, ideally representing a different, broader, more collective and more long-run rationality attained in different processes as indicated above, is called for to initiate, stabilize, and accelerate the learning, coordination, and cooperation process of the private agents.

The process of learning coordination and cooperation has been considered a *social production process*, i.e., the common and collective generation of a Pareto-improving behavior, or Pareto-superior economic situation, with a collective good always involved (see, e.g., Chapters 1, 3, and 14 on the ubiquity of the PD).

The support of a process of proper common/collective problem-solving through the intervention by an *external agency* with a different, more long-term and broader rationality and common/collective action capability then presupposes a certain *social valuation*, or what often has been called a *meritorization*, of the good or situation previously produced in the spontaneous, decentralized individualistic system, often considered to be a "market" (for the theory of instrumental social evaluation in the *institutionalist* tradition of John R.

Commons, see both the conceptions of a *negotiated economy*—Nielsen, 1992; Nielsen and Pedersen, 1988—and the *instrumental value principle*—Tool, 1979, 1994; further Myrdal, 1958; for *meritorization* in the theory of fiscal policy, see the classic Musgrave, 1959, 1987). This social valuation will have to consider either a complete blockage of superior action, i.e., a still dominant mutual defection, or the large time requirement of the process of producing the superior result of common cooperation, or the fragility of such a cooperative outcome.

Note that a *merit good* is defined as a good that basically can be produced in the spontaneous decentralized individualistic system ("market"), the production of which, however, appears inferior from a collective or social point of view (Musgrave), traditionally in terms of price and quantity, but, in our case, mainly in terms of uncertainty of production, time consumed for production, and fragility of production (possibility of a backslide). Thus, the *public policy agent evaluates the "market" outcome* and takes action to improve the outcome in these good-dimensions.

In terms of goods, this process then transforms

1. what originally was a *public good,*
2. but then potentially emerged, under certain conditions, in an evolutionary interaction and learning process in a spontaneous, decentralized, individualistic, *private system* through institutionalized cooperation, as a kind of private good, as generated by the collectivity of private agents (with a continuing non-exclusion and non-rivalry),
3. which, because of the uncertainties, failures, and deficiencies of that very process, as mentioned, will be publicly valuated as insufficiently produced and will thus be transformed through public action into what then will be a *merit good.*

Through that social/public valuation, or meritorization, the public policy agent will *embed* the private decentralized interaction mechanism and process in the private interaction system into a broader sociopolitical mechanism and *instrumental value system*. Economic policy intervention then will be specified as the *public promotion* of proper and self-sustaining emergence *of institutionalized cooperation* among private agents.

17.2.2 The Typical Economic Problem, and a New Private—Public Interrelation

Typical (Macro-) Economic Problems as Individualistic Cooperation Failure (Market Failure) in Complex Economies

Most economic problems in "market economies" with individualist cultures can be explained as cooperation failure. There is no such thing as an ideal "market (economy)," and *real-world markets fail* to generate the coordination/cooperation required for problem-solving in complex environments—and the more so the more deregulated they are. This may come about, as you may have learned in this textbook, on the basis of the *mixed* (i.e., partly convergent, partly antagonistic) *interests*, as they are modeled in social dilemmas or stag-hunt type coordination problems, and the result reflected through some *ceremonial dominance* (see Section 13.12), which in turn corresponds to a culture of dominating individualistic defection. This may include any kind of economic problem which exists due to the lack of the ability of the "market" to properly adjust to the basic conditions of complexity through gaining an effective collective action capability. The comment on the complex micro—macro causal chains made above in Section 17.2.1 applies.

In real-world terms, we may think of macro-problems of macroeconomic business cycles, labor market depression, financial market speculations and related meltdowns, etc., and also of "meso"-level problems and processes of decline of whole regions, sectoral problems, etc., as mentioned before (see, e.g., Cooper and John, 1988, presented in Chapter 13).

And again, many coordination (namely all stag-hunt or technology-choice type) problems imply that most of the individualistic private agents involved would be willing to act in a problem-solving, Pareto-improving manner, but cannot do so because they do not know, whether the others will do the same. The same applies, under certain conditions (as reflected, for instance, by the simple PD-SG single-shot solution), to social dilemma problems (which then are transformed into a stag-hunt type coordination problem; see Chapter 3). And problem-solving in these cases indeed requires coordinated or cooperative action.

As mentioned before, we may consider coordination or cooperation failure as a *deficient social production process*.

As an example, we may consider an economy that faces a *strong and fast structural change* in production technology and/or demand in a cluster of industries. But without a proper behavioral adaptation process, GDP and employment may come under pressure. Individual companies, industries, and clusters, and the economy as a whole might be able to better maintain and increase their sales, their industry-wide returns, their industrial-regional products, and, finally, the national income and the rate of employment by quickly adjusting the industrial production structure. The industrial production structure, in turn, may be better and faster adjusted, particularly with less *social costs*, less layoffs and unemployment, less breakdowns of firms, less regional downturns, etc., if firms could be preserved and become capable of handling the adaptation required in an ongoing concern, through coordinated active investment strategies. However, in contrast to that, they usually individualistically abstain from moving forward and investing, just downsize their firms, and mutually wait for the others' expansive actions. As any *business cycle*, boom or bust,

this, be it at macro or sectoral levels, is a *collective-good problem* (again, e.g., Cooper and John, 1988; for the financial sector and the global *financial crisis* as a social dilemma, see, e.g., Batrancea, 2009; Hilbe et al., 2013; for the classic application to development as a stag-hunt/assurance game, see Sen, 1967). *Coordinated restructuring and expansive company behavior*, in production, R&D, or marketing projects, to develop new products and sales opportunities, together with commonly used new (soft) infrastructures, would appear to be critical here to help stabilize and improve the industrial and/or regional structures, and macro-performance, and to keep social costs within limits—*coordinated and cooperative smooth structural change*, while firm organizations keep performing rather than downsizing or going bankrupt (for more details and case studies at the "meso-"sized level, see, e.g., Elsner, 2000a,b, 2001; Englmaier and Reisinger, 2008).

A New Private–Public Interrelation Defined

Economic problems, such as a decreasing or insufficiently growing GNP, the sudden vulnerability of a relevant number of skilled jobs, the vulnerability and collapse of public finance, or any other crisis or shock impact, as we are experiencing particularly in the financial-crisis world, normally provokes a policy response at the macro-level under the postulate to "Increase the GDP!" or "Maintain and create jobs!". Pursuing this objective usually requires that certain common/collective conditions of production and innovation are maintained or improved; examples of such conditions are *"location factors"* in a wide sense, such as the improvement of some regional/industrial structure, innovation quantity and qualities, etc. The latter "good" or "process outcome" will indeed, at some level, be subject to a stag-hunt or dilemma problem in the interactions among the private agents.

In mainstream economics, the *collective-good problem* has been regarded as implying a purely public task. But in the era of "neoliberal" policy conceptions, this public task has been dealt with by deregulating "the market," i.e., basically solving complex problems with an inadequate, individualized, noncooperative structure (see, e.g., Chapter 4 for more details). This, in fact, tends to worsen the problem by making the basic cooperation-failure problem ubiquitous. But the conventional collective-good perspective as such already unduly directed responsibility away from the private agents; these indeed have—in pursuing their individual economic interests—considerable interests to contribute to solving these common or collective problems. The problems then can indeed be better solved through *a new kind of public and private interaction* supportive of improving the common or collective conditions of production and innovation among the *private* agents.

However, coordination/cooperation failure and lock-in, as mentioned, usually result among private agents engaging in some kind of complex interaction as has been explained, e.g., in Chapter 4, and the present policy approach exactly starts form *initiating/unlocking, accelerating*, and *stabilizing* this process among private agents through a new and clearly specified kind of public intervention (for this basic idea of policy-making, see also, e.g., Axelrod, 1984/2006; Benz, 1995; Block, 2000; Cohen, 2001, 163ff.; Deroian, 2001; Doran, 2001; Crouch, 2005; Ahdieh, 2009; Dolfsma and Leydesdorff, 2009; among countless others).

Note again that we assume that the potential *outcome of the private interaction* process can be *related to an economic policy objective* in such a way that it can be subject to social valuation or *meritorization*. We basically assume that the private agents can indeed produce a *good* that has a potential *public value* in addition to its *private values*.

The new policy perspective in the following explains a relation between the interaction process among privates and the potentially emergent institution of cooperation on the one hand and specific economic *policy instruments* supporting specific *favoring factors of that very interaction* system on the other, thus promoting the particular emergence of that institution.

Making Use of the Interests of the Private Agents in the Collective Good

The public policy agent, in promoting cooperation, can *utilize the individual interests of the private agents in that (merit) good* in order to sway *private agents to contribute* to its production. In contrast to policy conceptions based upon the conventional neoclassical collective-good argument, the public policy agent, thus, does *not have to fully produce the collective good in lieu of the private agents* but may incite the private agents to produce it themselves as a merit good. Therefore, this, basically, also allows for a *leaner policy* approach, which is structural and does not have to shift big amounts of money as subsidies in the usual well-known ways, even practiced under the "neoliberal" regime.

The argument here will not simply be that public authorities can sway private individuals to contribute to commonly valued goals through a set of subsidies or similar incentives. The closer analysis of the interactive process among private agents, as explained and applied in this textbook, allows for a better *specification of the policy approach and its instruments*. Among them will be the awareness of the importance of the common future for the private agents, i.e., recognized interdependence and futurity, as explained in Chapters 3, 13, and 14 and already explained by Axelrod (1984/2006). Conventional instruments, such as *subsidies* or *infrastructural projects*, the latter indirectly supporting the activities and benefits of private agents, or monetary measures, are given new significance in this context. They may support the Pareto-superior outcome; but, as said, traditional fiscal and monetary policy instruments (fiscal subsidies to industrial companies, abundant money supply and interest-rate subsidies to fiscal-sector corporations) will have a significantly smaller role to play (compared to nonpecuniary instruments) in inducing the intended effects, i.e., they need to be much smaller than is usually practiced, as we will explain below.

Starting Points of a New Policy Perspective

We have extended simple Single-Shot solution as introduced in Chapter 3 with regard to several aspects (see, e.g., Chapters 3, 8, 13, 14) to show how an institution of cooperation may emerge in a process of interaction among agents, assumed at the outset to be conventional, individualistic, short-term maximizers. This implied showing how individuals may change their behaviors.

We have also argued that individualistic behavior and its ceremonial motivation (warrant) (see Section 13.12), as represented in a PD and its individualistic outcome (NE), can indeed be taken as a *worst case view of a reality*, in which the social rules and institutions of coordination and cooperation have in fact been weakened under the "neoliberal" regime. In this sense, it has been argued

> that neoclassical rationality [...] is simply a case in which the parental bent is severely repressed. It could arise only in a cultural setting in which there is a trained incapacity to consider the impact of one's behavior on the well-being of others (Bush, 1999a, p. 146).

It thus appears necessary to introduce a supra-individualistic rationality and mechanism into the interaction process of the individualistic private, i.e., an additional public policy intervention, following a collective rationality, to initiate, accelerate, and stabilize the institutionalization of coordination through cooperation, which cannot be brought forth with sufficient certainty, speed, and stability by the spontaneous, individualistic, and decentralized system (the "market" economy) alone.

17.2.3 "Meritorics" for a Negotiated Economy and for an Instrumental Institutional Emergence

The conception of the *merit good*, as developed by R.A. Musgrave in the framework of the economics of public finance, as mentioned, has been revived since the 1980s, and its basis has been further developed, even by Musgrave himself (see, e.g., Brennan and Lomasky, 1983; Musgrave, 1987; Ver Eecke, 1998, 2008), from one of simply "wrong individual preferences" to one that substantiates meritorization (the positive social valuation) on the basis of "community preferences," which have evolved from *historical processes of interaction beyond the "market"* (see Musgrave, 1987, p. 452). So it also stresses a *social evaluation* of the outcomes of the "market" through some social decision-making broader than, relatively independent of, and superior to the "market."

For our purpose, we will therefore define a merit good as a good basically resulting from the decentralized, spontaneous, individualistic structure, and related process, which is evaluated through a *social decision-making* process on the grounds of its deficient quantity, quality, relative price, and—as new dimensions discovered in deficient decentralized, spontaneous, individualistic processes—the time span needed for its production as well as the certainty or stability of acquiring it through that "market" process (see also again Ver Eecke, 1998).

Against this background, the problem of neoclassical mainstream economics is that it has not developed a conception of social decision-making that can be regarded as an allocation mechanism independent of and with priority over the "market," on the basis of which the problematic results of the "market" could be evaluated and (de-)meritorized. Neoclassical public-choice theory, restricted to areas that the "market" leaves aside, however, basically faces the same individualistic problems of coordination/cooperation that are faced in individualistic dilemmas within the "market" (refer to Arrow's impossibility theorem discussed earlier).

Evolutionary-institutional economics, in the philosophical tradition of *pragmatism*, has claimed that democratic and *participative sociopolitical decision-making* should be independent of the "market" and should have priority over it. The conceptions of a *negotiated economy* and of the *instrumental value principle* of a truly *discretionary economy* were elaborated to reflect the view that the "market" has to be deliberately embedded in a wider sociopolitical process (see, e.g., Commons, 1934/1990, 612ff., 649ff.; Tool, 1979; Nielsen and Pedersen, 1988; Hargreaves Heap, 1989; Ramstad, 1991; Nielsen, 1992; Hayden, 1994, 2006).

We will not go into this philosophical and political-science discussion any deeper here (but see Chapter 18 on some of these issues of "science and politics"), but will simply assume an economic policy agent who is legitimized through a process of participatory democratic decision-making. In this very process, *public policy objectives* should be developed and operationalized, which then will provide the criteria for the concrete meritorizations required. This is in the traditions of pragmatistic understanding of democracy as process rather than static voting (again, refer to the Arrow Paradox above); the issues are not primarily in some abstract static "majority rule" but about the substantial "process by which majorities [...] are formed" (Bush, 1987, p. 1109), and such process would be heavily interconnected "with the process of inquiry upon which instrumental valuing depends" (ibid.). In this way, substantial, participative, and *discursive democracy* might support, embedded in institutionalization processes dealt with in this textbook, *collective long-run rationality* and "nonalgorithmic" (Velupillai), "discretionary" (Tool) *action capacity* (beyond static public-choice paradoxes), and with this an increasing dominance of instrumental values and instrumentally warranted patterns of

behavior. Modeling such democratic, participatory, and discursive process may be, and, in fact, has been, done in the realm of *cooperative GT* (see, e.g., McCain, 2009).

On this background, the economic policy agent may employ *instruments* related to the interactive process of the private agents to *change critical conditions of the private interactions*, aiming at

1. *deblocking* (*unlocking*, *breaking-out*, or *initiating*),
2. *accelerating*, and
3. *stabilizing* (*perpetuating*)

the provision of the (then) merit good through promoting *common*, i.e., parallel, coordinated action of trust generation (in coordination problems of the stag-hunt type) and/or *collective*, i.e., directly cooperative action (in social dilemma problems).

Figure 17.1 illustrates the logical sequence of this conception of a *new meritorics*, i.e., of the specified interactions between the public policy agent and the interaction system of the private agents.

Start reading the figure from the bottom and follow the numbers in the boxes. It then illustrates, at a glance, the argument already developed in Chapters 3, 13 (Section 13.12), and 14 and applied to policy in Section 17.2 so far. The collective social dilemma problem, a cooperation issue, with the usual one-shot Pareto-inferior NE outcome (1), then will be played recurrently in a sequential process, perhaps transforming the problem structure into a stag-hunt type coordination problem (2). This may have three types of outcome: a quick, successful, and stable institutionalization of cooperation or rule-based coordination (3a), a very time-consuming and fragile emergence of the Pareto-superior coordination/cooperation, where public meritorization may justify to accelerate and stabilize the process (3b), and a complete blockage of Pareto-improving action and superior outcome through individualistic behavior with a persistent short-run future perspective, where public meritorization will provide reason for public agency to deblock, unlock, or initiate the whole process of institutionalization of coordination/cooperation (3c). The first case will then lead to corresponding outcomes (4) that will be approved by, and pass, the meritorization process (5)/(6)/(7) and lead to a self-policing, self-stabilizing circuit (3a)–(4)–(7). In the other two cases, meritorization (5)/(6)/(7) will cause policy actions, as explained.

Note again that we assumed a somewhat *staged social* (collective, or socioeconomic) *production process* in the sense of an interaction among private agents in some specified (perhaps, e.g., local/regional) arena on a specified and limited issue (e.g., a common local location factor favoring all local firms), which in turn contributes to a major good, which is relevant for the "big," "macro" policy objective (contributing to maintaining or creating jobs, to increasing GDP(-growth), etc.)—thus a

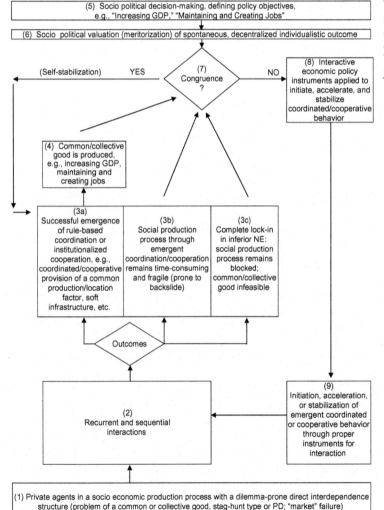

FIGURE 17.1 A sequence of the interactive social production process of a collective (merit) good with interactive economic policy intervention. Read from bottom, following the numbers. *Adapted from Elsner (2001).*

connection between the private interaction process and the public meritorization of its outcome, and the, then possible, cooperation-supporting policy intervention addressed to that very interaction process among the private agents (for a detailed real-world example, see again Elsner, 2000a,b, 2001; for the specific instruments, see below, Section 17.2.5).

Before we turn to the specifics of *how* this interactive economic policy approach may proceed, namely, which kind of *instruments* and measures are appropriate in this process, we will discuss two general implications of the approach as developed so far.

17.2.4 General Implications

A Paradigm Change Toward a Leaner Policy

One of the obvious insights is that the *private* agents receive a specific *benefit* from, and thus have a specific *interest* in, the production of the good (which is originally collective, later possibly private, and finally has to become merit), regardless of the fact that it generally cannot be adequately produced by them (because of coordination and cooperation failures inherent in their spontaneous individualistic interactions). Thus, the public policy agent, when making the good better feasible through meritorization and a corresponding improvement of specific conditions of coordination and cooperation, can also *call the private agents in to contribute* to its generation. In contrast to the conventional neoclassical collective goods analysis, we, in this way, come to recognize that the state is by no means solely responsible for producing (and financing) a collective solution. As said, basically, this allows for a *leaner, less expensive policy* approach. This is the case in a specific and better-defined way, different from the more general argument of "neoliberal" economists and politicians that their "market-conform" structural reforms, or "market order" policies

are generally cheaper and more complexity-reducing than any "interventionism." Our approach defines a new public–private relationship based on the insights of real-world complex economic systems.

A related insight from the PD-SG analysis was that the solution of the collective-good problem, or dilemma structure, is a *gradual* problem in an evolutionary process. This implies that a complete abolishment of the dilemma structure is by no means necessary for the public policy agent in order for the private agents to be able to better solve the cooperation problem. For instance, if the public policy agent subsidized cooperative behavior to such an extent that a cooperative strategy would strictly dominate defection for all agents in a PD, this might well be a very costly solution in terms of public subsidies. (Besides this, it would also be a trivial one in a theoretical sense.) Social problem-solving, indeed, can already effectively be promoted gradually by simply *weakening the dilemma structure* and/or *improving its relation to the expectations* according to the single-shot solution—in this way gradually promoting a *more cooperative culture*. As you may have seen in Chapter 3 (and its exercises) already, small additional rewards for common cooperation may already be effective. With proper *gradual changes in the incentive structure* relative to expectations, the probability of cooperative solutions will already increase, i.e., institutionalized cooperation may come into existence with increased certainty, speed, and stability (persistence).

Generally speaking, a leaner policy becomes feasible because the approach allows for a *clearer definition of the relative interests*, or *benefits*, as well as the *relative responsibilities*, or *costs*, of the private and public policy agents with respect to the cooperative social solution—as opposed to often fuzzy "public–private partnerships" so much en vogue recently (and which of course are not always flawed and ineffective, but usually depend on the power relation between the public and private agents involved).

Meso-Economics and Structural (Regional and Industrial) Policies as New Focuses

A second implication refers to the issue of social learning in evolutionary processes, as explained earlier in, e.g., Chapters 3, 8, 13, and 14. As we have seen in Chapters 13 and 14, learning social problem-solving by way of the formation of institutions of cooperation is critically dependent upon some social characteristics, such as *group, arena* and/or *platform size, neighborhood/proximity, interaction density*, and reduced *mobility* (for the latter factor, see, e.g., Glaeser et al., 2002), and certain *network structures*, be these given at the beginning of the process or emergent properties (for the issues of local interaction, neighborhood structures, and selective matching, see also, e.g., Stanley et al., 1994; Kirman, 1998; Oltra and Schenk, 1998; Sandler, 2004; Traulsen and Novak, 2006; Spiekermann, 2009, and, of course, the literature given in Chapters 13 and 14).

The problem-solving capacity emerging in evolutionary interaction processes thus largely depends on *meso-sized network structures* such as small-world networks, both as received and adapting through the process. These include social or professional groups of various kinds and other meso-economic arenas and platforms like *communities, regions, industries* or *local clusters* of industry branches, agent *networks*, etc. (see again Chapters 4, 13, and 14). In all, meso- (cluster and network) economics may become one of the focal points of the evolutionary theory of social learning and institution building, and consequently also a new focal point in an interactive, or institutional, economic policy approach related to such evolutionary process.

Insofar as emerged meso-economic entities provide the platforms for more effective cooperative solutions to complex economic problems,

they also provide a prime level or focus for the promotion of cooperation and for an interactive/institutional economic policy that is oriented toward the critical factors and favorable conditions of such institution building. Against this background, economic policy would have to focus more on meso-economic or structural-policy approaches different from conventional micropolicies, which is conventional "competition" (and antitrust) policy and pecuniary individual-firm subsidization programs, and conventional macro-policies (monetary and fiscal policies). In contrast, it should be committed to the *conditions of institution building* in local, regional, industrial, and other medium-sized social units, i.e., to the *deep structure* of the economy (see, e.g., Dopfer et al., 2004; for such *microeconomic policy* overviews as intended here, see, e.g., Cohen, 2001; Tisdell and Hartley, 2008; for the *institutional design* perspective, see, e.g., Hurwicz, 1987; Calvert, 1995; Croskery, 1995).

This policy perspective has indeed been applied to manifold areas of industrial and regional issues, cluster and network, and innovation and information issues (see, e.g., Elsner, 2000a,b, 2001; Cossentino et al., 1996; Pratt, 1997; Deakin et al., 1997; Cellini and Lambertini, 2006; Borrás and Tsagdis, 2008; among many others).

17.2.5 The Axelrodian Policy Model: A Basic PD-Informed Interactive/Institutional Economic Policy and a Related Instrumentation

A General View Based on the Single-Shot Inequality

Since such institutional emergence, as explained in the foregoing, will normally not automatically and easily occur—particularly not in times of crises and turbulence, when conditions of widespread strong uncertainty, fears, and distrust may lead to reinforced ceremonial behavior, i.e., mutual blockage of cooperation or even a breakdown of institutions that once had emerged—it remains an issue of proper policy action.

Recall the basic dilemma game ($b > a > c > d$), and the possibility for a change of the problem structure in a supergame:

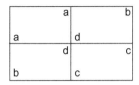

Conditional cooperation can become a NE in the repeated game if the discount factor for future payoffs δ is large enough to fulfill the single-shot condition $(\delta > (b - a)/(b - c))$ (see Chapter 3). A basic GT-informed policy conclusion, based on the simple single-shot approach, may be the following: It is, in general, obviously favorable for cooperation if b and c were relatively low and a and δ were relatively high. The algebraic logic of a *related policy action* resulting from this is also rather obvious. From that inequality, the following functional equation results:

$$\delta_{min} = ! \ (b - a)/(b - c) = 1 - [(a - c)/(b - c)]$$

with the following policy-relevant marginal conditions:

$$\frac{\partial \delta_{min}}{\partial (b - a)} = \frac{1}{(b - c)} > 0 \qquad (17.1)$$

$$\frac{\partial \delta_{min}}{\partial (b - c)} = -\frac{(b - a)}{(b-c)^2} < 0 \qquad (17.2)$$

$$\frac{\partial \delta_{min}}{\partial a} = -\frac{1}{(b - c)} < 0 \qquad (17.3)$$

$$\frac{\partial \delta_{min}}{\partial b} = \frac{(a - c)}{(b-c)^2} > 0 \qquad (17.4)$$

$$\frac{\partial \delta_{min}}{\partial c} = \frac{(b - a)}{(b-c)^2} > 0. \qquad (17.5)$$

First, note that δ always needs to be equal or larger than δ_{min} for the emergence of a second NE through the repetition in the supergame. Second, the partial derivatives above show that

1. the relative change of δ_{min} against a relative change of $(b - a)$ is positive,
2. the relative change of δ_{min} against a relative change of $(b - c)$ is negative,
3. the relative change of δ_{min} against a relative change of a is negative,
4. the relative change of δ_{min} against a relative change of b is positive, and
5. the relative change of δ_{min} against a relative change of c is positive.

The policy recommendations, thus, as further explained and illustrated below, are

1. to reduce $(b - a)$, in order to increase the probability that the single-shot inequality condition of the solution of a social dilemma over time will be solved, as common cooperation becomes relatively more attractive in terms of payoffs, in this way the requirement for its solution in terms of future expectations, δ, relaxed; thus, reduce the incentive to defect, b, while increasing the incentive to cooperate, a;
2. to increase $(b - c)$, in order to increase the probability that the social dilemma will be solved (as in (1)); thus, reduce the payoff for common defection, c, even more than reducing the incentive to defect, b;
3. to increase the incentive to cooperate, a, in order to support the solution of the social dilemma, as above; i.e., increase a so that the requirement of δ_{min} might even decrease, i.e., be relaxed, if everything else remains equal, as above;
4. to reduce the incentive to defect, b, so that the requirement of δ_{min} may be relaxed and the probability of solution increased, as above;
5. to reduce the payoff for common defection, c, so that the requirement of δ_{min} is relaxed and the solution supported, as above.

Note again that the PD payoff structure in the underlying game need not be dissolved as such by policy action, which would probably imply a politically expensive solution and a theoretically trivial one. So the problem that remains, and cannot be solved by hyperrational individuals coined for an ideal "market," is the very social dilemma structure, i.e., a dominant incentive to defect, an incentive in favor of an *individualistic culture*. And the more individualistic the culture is, the *heavier the weight of the dilemma structure in relation to the future expectation of commitment* will be in terms of the relations of *a*, *b*, *c*, and (*a* then relatively small) δ.

Not only does the public policy agent have to publicly identify and evaluate the specific characteristics of the good she wants the private agents to cooperatively produce (mirroring the Pareto-superior economic situation), she must also involve the private agents into behaviors, measures, and projects to be pursued in coordinated and cooperative ways, thus helping to

1. *increase their awareness of their complex and dilemma-prone interdependence* (*recognized interdependence*, see Bush, 1999b),
2. *increase their expectations of always having a common future* to meet again (δ), and
3. *enable them in specific ways to learn to cooperate.*

The resulting instruments then are obvious.

Instruments I: Rewarding Cooperation

The first specific complex of instruments of such interactive/institutional economic policy is very obvious, according to the recommendations (1)–(5) in the previous section. The single-shot inequality above also shows that the more successful the public policy agent is in integrating the private agents into a future-bound process, i.e., the higher the discount parameter δ, the less the increase of the relative rewards for cooperation need to be.

However, this tradeoff between the rewards for cooperation (*a*) and the "shadow of the common future" (Axelrod), δ, does not necessarily imply a contrast between *quantitative* (namely, pecuniary) and *qualitative* instruments, i.e., offering *pecuniary* subsidies as opposed to promoting more favorable *expectations* (of meeting again, future commitment). As has often been shown from practical experience, the extra incentives from the public policy agent, which reward cooperation, may also consist of *nonpecuniary* benefits (for instance, of *early* and/or *selective information* about public planning for those involved, see, e.g., Calvert, 1995; Elsner, 2001; also, e.g., Klein, 1990; for intrafirm policies, e.g., Cabrera and Cabrera, 2002).

Instruments II: Enlarging the "Shadow of the Future"

The second complex of instruments of interactive/institutional economic policy is not that obvious, in practical terms. It refers to the *probability of meeting again* (in a future interaction). Cooperation could be promoted if the discount parameter could be increased, i.e., if future interactions became more probable or *future awareness* of the agents increased.

However, this can also be subject to policy control. As Axelrod (1984/2006) already mentioned, the public policy agent can indeed increase the importance of future interactions by organizing cooperation in the form of *frequent project-based meetings*, or make it permanent, e.g., by dividing projects into several subinteractions, *connecting different projects* so that the agents will meet again in different arenas/platforms, connecting projects *over time*, etc.

Obviously, in all, there is ample opportunity for the public policy agent to deliberately *design the conditions of interaction* to promote cooperation in a variety of subject areas that private agents are jointly interested in.

A Policy Approach for Different Types of Policy Agents

This is *institutional policy* since it specifically refers to the processes of institutional emergence, and it is *double interactive* as it refers in an interactive way to the conditions and intermediate results of the interaction processes of the private agents.

Finally, it has been shown to be applicable by enlightened interdependent and interacting *agents themselves*, as their own policy strategy, e.g., in their cluster, their value-added chain, their innovation network, etc., or by an "enlightened" neutral private *cluster* or *network advisor/consultant/counselor* hired by the parties involved. As far as this has its inherent limits, the *public policy agent's* state activity, exerted, to be sure, through a *new type of "enlightened" public policy agents* or personal representatives, is required (see again, e.g., Calvert, 1995; Elsner, 2001; Dixit, 2001).

17.2.6 Further Game-Theoretically Informed Policy Issues

Other GT normal-form structures and evolutionary insights, beyond the single-shot solution and the Axelrodian policy suggestions, have further policy implications that altogether seem to contribute to and to complete that new policy perspective. Beyond the two policy suggestions in the previous section ("Instruments I" and "Instruments II"),

1. *improving the payoff structure in favor of coordination/cooperation* (weakening dilemmas and making their interdependence structure less intricate) and
2. *increasing the awareness of the agents for their common future,*
   these will be briefly considered here, noting that there are manifold overlaps among these issues and that they have to be further operationalized in a future comprehensive complexity-policy approach:
3. *Promote recognition of interdependence*: Private agents involved in directly interdependent and interactive settings may, in the real world, not be (fully) aware

of the setting or system they are involved in, as they are considered boundedly rational, i.e., with limited calculation capacity, anyway. Particularly, they may not be aware of the character of the incentive structure or not even know all payoffs (namely, in individualistic cultures, they may not know those payoffs yet that can be gained through superior coordination or mutual cooperation, as they may have never experienced them). *Recognized interdependence*, thus, has been a long-standing issue in the pragmatist/instrumental policy conception of original evolutionary-institutional economists (see again Bush, 1999b; see also again, e.g., Doran, 2001; Cabrera and Cabrera, 2002). This may include qualifying knowledge about the specific character of the interdependence structure (see, e.g., Ahdieh, 2009) or fostering *frequent repetition* (e.g., Calvert, 1995).

After the financial crisis 2007ff. and the Great Recession 2008ff., for instance, much literature has appeared with critical reflections of the legal frameworks of the "markets," where it has been argued that the current legal frameworks would not prevent social dilemmas, greed, and aspired exploitation. Thus, there would be a role for countervailing institutions to foster a *more enlightened self-interest* (e.g., Clements, 2013).

4. *Favor equality*: One of the basic, although often only implicit, conditions of GT-solutions is equity/equality/symmetry of payoffs among agents. It is a factor of transparency, less volatility, and better controllability of the resulting process. GT has come from different angles and analyses to conclude that not only "state activism cannot be avoided" but also we have "to favour policies of equality" (Hargreaves Heap, 1989, p. 224). Most intricate, thus, may be socially asymmetric structures like Battle-of-the-Sexes games

and—even more so—anti-coordination games of the Chicken type, or other structures with interpersonally extreme asymmetric incentives.

The practical win-win character and superior macro (socioeconomic) performance of more equal societies has indeed been widely supported in international empirical investigations (see, e.g., Wilkinson and Pickett, 2009).

We have to be aware, of course, that symmetric payoffs are only loosely indicating social equality.

5. Increase *transparency and awareness through support of memorizing, monitoring, and reputation*: Above recognized interdependence and recognized futurity, particularly in structured populations with permanent partner change and many one-shot encounters, state action needs to focus on transparency through some organized common/collective memory (transparency over time), improved monitoring capabilities, and reputation building and utilization of reputation chains (which, in fact, has become a major issue in the *internet economy* nowadays). All these mechanisms facilitate solutions by improving opportunities of positive or negative sanctioning (see, e.g., Doran, 2001; see also Chapters 14 and 15).

6. *Support general trust and assurance*: In more intricate coordination problems, i.e., stag-hunt type structures, less general trust in populations will be equivalent with greater risk aversion and thus will tend to favor inferior solutions, as we have explained both in terms of modeling and comparative international empirical evidence (see Chapters 3 and 14). This also refers to one of the earlier policy-relevant applications of GT, Sen's Assurance Game mentioned before (Sen, 1967; see also, e.g., Englmaier and

Reisinger, 2008 on public information policies).

7. *Reduce volatility, increase stability, to facilitate and improve social learning, broadest investment, minimum certainty, trust, experimentation/innovation, and social-capital building*: We have explained in different theoretical, model-based, and empirical contexts (see, e.g., model and case study in Chapter 14; also, e.g., Glaeser et al., 2002 on the empirical tradeoff between *mobility* and *social-capital* building in the USA) that in large anonymous populations with initially frequent random partner change, cooperative solutions depend on the strength of the capability of partner selection and of building *stable and long-run relations*.

This, in fact, is what the global corporate economy does by way of *local clusters* and *networks* in reaction to increasing turbulences of globalization (see Chapter 4).

8. *Support experimentation/behavioral innovation to generate minimum critical masses of cooperators*: In the population approach (Chapter 3) and in more particular models (Chapters 13 and 14), you may have seen that invadability of defective/individualistic cultures by a cooperative culture typically requires a minimum critical mass of experimenters/innovators (which, in turn, then may grow up to some maximum critical mass or maximum portion of the population). Promoting such minimum critical mass also may relate to a policy strategy of *unlocking* of mutual blockages (see also point (12)).

9. *Care for size and human scope: promote inner meso-structures, mid-sized platforms, neighborhoods, and communities, and small worlds*: An important insight of applied GT-based evolutionary modeling was that cooperative solutions largely depend on "mid-sized" arenas, clusters, or neighborhoods so that meso-economic

carrier groups and networks of institutionalized cooperation may emerge better, easier, faster, and more stably in evolutionary processes (again, see Chapters 13 and 14).

International empirical evidence on greater trust and superior macro-performance seems to support this policy perspective and includes higher levels of industrial spatial *clustering* and industrial *networking* (see Chapter 4, and also, e.g., Klein, 1990). Note that such decentralization needs to be interrelated with proper *long-distance interconnections* among clusters (see point (10)) and centralization of the societal meritorization process (see, e.g., Doran, 2001).

10. *Besides local clustering, care for some long-distance interaction, small worlds*: We have also explained that the overall effectiveness of populations, or systems, also require their organization in *network structures* that not only display a relatively *strong clustering*, but also some *long-distance relations*, so that the *average path length* among any two nodes (agents) in the whole system nevertheless remains relatively short and, thus, we may expect information, innovation, favorable expectations, and cooperative behaviors to *diffuse quickly through the whole system* (defecting behavior, of course, might diffuse quickly as well in this structure, though). We have explained this approach to *network analysis* in Sections 13.10 and 13.11 with the Watts–Strogatz model of network analysis. As explained, such a small-world network as described, with intense clustering but also a short average path length through the whole system, is a type of graph, in which most nodes can be reached from every other node through a small number of steps (nodes in between).

Note that, for instance, also the human brain is organized like an ideal small world, with clusters of neural nodes but also long-distance connections (axons). Small-world networks tend to contain subnetworks, which have connections between almost any two nodes within them, a high clustering coefficient. But also, many pairs of nodes will be connected by short paths, a small mean shortest-path length of the network.

Regrettably, in reality, often efficiency is reduced through *large hub agents* (or "gatekeepers") that dispose the long-run relations among clusters, i.e., a higher centrality degree (see Section 13.11 also on the Barabási–Albert model of scale-free networks).

This all implies that policies will have to *support clustering and networking* to favor quick information diffusion in dense interaction systems, but also, at the same time, *support long-distance relations* that care for the in- and outflows of potentially new kinds of information, knowledge, and behaviors into other meso-sized groups, clusters, subnetworks, or regions, *without letting hubs become too powerful.*

11. *Create "focuses" for socially most preferred equilibria out of multiple equilibria.* Schelling put forward the idea of the existence, in interdependent decision-making, of an exogenous "focus," which people apply in favor of one (in the best case: the Pareto-optimal) equilibrium out of several or many possible equilibria in a coordination problem, where otherwise a Pareto-superior equilibrium would not be selected automatically through the interaction process.

Out of the myriad of possible equilibria of solving the problem of two people "to meet each other in New York on a certain day at noon," without having been able to talk on the location (a dating game)—one of Schelling's examples—such an exogenous or a priori focus of many people would be to select the option "at Grand Central Station at noon" for their decision.

This may become part of a policy strategy, if agents do not have a common exogenous a priori focus or standard or *social rule to select* the superior equilibrium. Policy then can *shape such selection in favor of a socially preferred equilibrium* (or attractor) by *creating such a focus/standard/social rule* through public instruction or statement of public intent, particular operating procedures, and the like (see, e.g., Calvert, 1995, pp. 68–70).

12. *Promote breakout in critical time windows*: Lock-in, as explained, is an indispensable kind of coordination or cooperation with given network technologies. Coordination then may be based on an inferior technology; or an earlier superior technology may have become an inferior one through technological change. Particularly, institutionalized cooperative arrangements, or (informally) institutionalized networks, are subject to *life cycles* with *degeneration* and *institutional lock-in*, in which their character may change through *ceremonial encapsulation*, and in this way their problem-solving capacity will be reduced, as explained (see Chapter 1 and Section 13.12).

Good *network governance*, thus, is a continuous task also of any interactive, institutional policy to prevent degeneration, ceremonial encapsulation, regressive institutional change, and lock-in—and to care for *unlocking* and progressive institutional change, *without endangering productive coordination* and generating too much instability and turbulence (for the issue of *breakout*, be it in the sense of just technological lock-in based on increasing returns or network externalities (W.B. Arthur) or on the institutional degeneration mentioned

(P.A. David), see, e.g., Deroian, 2001; Dolfsma and Leydesdorff, 2009).

Particularly for technological lock-in in technology choice under network externalities, we have a more detailed focus in the following in the framework of applied information and innovation economics. Breakout here will be connected to the principle of *standard- and information openness*. Specifically, a breakout needs to be related to the provision of a *new lock-in superior to the previous one*. For this, there will be typically only critical time windows open. Outside of these time windows, the change required might be considerably more difficult and expensive (see Chapter 15 and Section 17.3.1).

Note that we cannot treat models and relatively abstract theory as immediate and full one-to-one mappings of reality. The above, therefore, have been called issues that follow from GT modeling and theoretical and analytical insights, but are not considered strict policy requirements or prescriptions, which would follow directly from theory and analytical results. We have compared above mainstream political prescriptions with the different character of the policy perspective resulting from a complexity (micro-) economics. We will finally reflect on such methodological issues of how to use one's knowledge, gained from complexity microeconomics, in reality in Chapter 18.

17.3 POLICY IMPLICATIONS FOR INFORMATION AND INNOVATION IN FIRMS, NETWORKS, AND OPEN-SOURCE COMMUNITIES

Particularly in Chapters 15 and 16, we have *applied* our general analyses and tools to the complex issues of

1. *information economics*, effective information diffusion, and shared knowledge, under

conditions of network effects, cumulative tendencies toward one standard out of competing ones, and, thus, under given conditions of oligopolistic and power-based structures, tendencies toward monopolization;

2. *innovation and network economics*, with the *theory of the firm* as factually embedded in networks in manifold ways, effective and less effective ones, the fact of the *organization of innovation in systems*, local and national, and the broader theory of *development* as innovation processes, broadly understood, in a factual *variety of (national) economic systems*, existing simultaneously and persistently, and often even diverging rather than converging.

The policy implications as developed and considered there were quite considerable and entail a number of policy discussions.

17.3.1 Policies to Realize the Potentials of Existing Knowledge: Moderating "Property Rights" and Developing Openness as a General Principle

Intellectual Property Rights and Openness

Under the influence of most powerful oligopolistic players, governments, since the 1990s, have raised legal fences of protection for what those players call their IPRs. Any short line of programming—as a famous US court case on the little program for "click&buy" in the early 2000s showed—can now be protected against competition, even if it is, as in most cases, pretty general knowledge, based on a truly *societal process of knowledge generation and sharing*. The myth of a causal chain behind that, however, alleged that otherwise agents would have no incentives to, and no longer would, invest in producing new knowledge, inventions, and innovations.

Thus, the world today is faced with the patenting even of life forms, typically reaped from the open nature (in other countries than those, where the big players then patent their booties), the dominance of few patent holders, often buying and holding patents in their portfolios just to improve their shareholder value, the copyrighting of trivialities, and legal battles with those *nonpracticing patent holding companies* (or *patent trolls*). Patents do not only have the traditional function of protecting innovation but also the strategic function of *protecting dominant positions* and *obstructing innovation* by competitors. The role of IPRs and patents, thus, has changed over the past decades and the crime of software *piracy* was virtually invented through that process in the last couple of decades. In fact, barriers to innovation and development have been erected, which, in turn, have been questioned by both software piracy (illegally) and *open-source communities* (legally).

One *policy implication* resulting is the following:

• For more effective *societal problem-solving*, the protection and encouragement of knowledge flow, diffusion, and innovation on the *broadest basis of agents* seems to be required and the current law of patents and IPR overshoots should be reconsidered and reversed. The big players' profit might be somewhat reduced through such increased competition through many upcoming smaller agents and a *diversity of business models*, and they would have to prove their superiority under conditions of more competition with servicing customers—the *open-source business model* of Red Hat, IBM, and the like. The upside of it will be the unleashing, mobilization, and utilization of a considerable societal creative potential on a more even socioeconomic basis.

The emergence of a wide field of goods with zero marginal cost made new products and technologies available to larger groups of the population at an unanticipated scale. It made information, skills, and education more widely accessible. The openness of technologies, the potential of innovations to quickly spread throughout the population, has until now only insufficiently been acknowledged. The concept of open source is particularly well suited to ensure openness.

A Critical Political Time Window for Technological-Openness and Antimonopoly Strategies

Information and communication technology is subject to network externalities, as said, which entails opportunities but also may easily and quickly lead to lock-in situations. Some policy conclusions are the following:

- Influencing the development of the industry (for instance by propagating an open standard) must be done within a narrow critical time window, after which the industry is locked-in to a degree, where the public policy agent may no longer be able to alter the trajectory without considerable costs. It may also be beneficial to the economy to *avoid long standard wars that delay innovation*. Public policy agencies can exercise influence easily by developing a *public standard* themselves, requiring it to be open, or even by endorsing a private standard—something the US Department of Defense has frequently and successfully done in the process of the emergence of the *Internet* and other computer science standards. We have already explained in Section 17.2.6 how lock-ins are usually necessary under given technological and organizational conditions and not always disadvantageous, and thus a breakout is not desirable any time.
- It may also be necessary for public policy to avoid asymmetric power-based, oligopolistic and monopolistic industry structures and long standard/price wars. To accomplish this, an *antitrust case* with the goal of *splitting a firm up* (as has been attempted with *Microsoft* in the 1990s and early 2000s)

does no longer appear to be applicable and effective, let alone sufficient. It must also be avoided that the oligopolists can use the means to *deter entry*—such as obscure standards, incompatibility-generating changes to the standard (or, generally, control of standards), patenting of too broad concepts, etc. Requiring important *standards to be open*, possibly *governed by a neutral party*, would most likely be successful.

17.3.2 Perspectives on Innovation and Development Policies

Innovation Policies

An understanding of the innovation system is of course required for the design of innovation policies. In particular, the path dependence of an innovation system of a nation or region is necessary, when attempts are made to strengthen the dynamic potential. From analyses of innovation systems as referred to in Chapter 16, we may conclude some policy recommendations:

- *Links among agents* in production and innovation can be shaped through numerous instruments at the disposal of policy-makers: the structure of the taxation incentives, access to subsidized finance and credit, the regulation of competition and antitrust, the structures of IPR protection versus *information-diffusion systems*, or formal and informal means for encouraging longer term relations among agents (for this, see Section 17.2).

On the background of traditional neoclassical policy postulates, the focus and justification of policies has been on the correction of "market failures," in this case *underinvestment* in the development of new technologies, but also of innovative organizational solutions for extended collective action capabilities, due to an often only partial ability to capture the resulting benefits (partial appropriability). Therefore, R&D spending and support for private efforts (tax breaks, patents, etc.) have long dominated the innovation-policy agenda.

A better understanding of the much more intricate nature of the *diffusion of knowledge* in innovation processes, however, leads to recognition of *systemic* aspects of the process and systemic failures are the problems that are faced. This changes the focus of policies, and a policy conclusion can be formulated as following:

- *Enhancing the opportunities for interactions* among agents, focusing, e.g., on encouraging *joint research activities* and other coordinated and cooperative relations, especially informal relations and the channels of knowledge flows, has to be a new policy focus. The *capacity to absorb new knowledge* (absorption capacity) is crucial to the individual firms' success, and their network relations to others increase the chance that they will find or develop capacities for achieving this (on networks, see Sections 13.10 and 13.11).

Endogenous Development Policies, Local and National

Local and regional agents, coordinated and embedded by supra-regional entities and agencies, play a rather pronounced role in development strategies. One of the main axes of local development policy is, again, the *diffusion of knowledge and innovation*. Intermediate organizations and local initiatives can be set up to improve conditions for supporting networks.

We can identify indeed a move from generalist policies to territorial cluster- and network-oriented development policies. While traditional regional growth policy was developed from a focus on concentrated growth in growth poles and promoted attracting external resources to the target area, local development policy aims at

development from within a territory. The traditional model considered economic development in functional terms, for instance, the mobility of production factors restoring equilibrium between richer and poorer regions. More recently proposed local development strategies, in contrast, assume that local institutions, development paths, and local resources condition growth processes, so the mobilization of *endogenous* local factors plays a more central role.

The development and change model is based on the *diffusion processes* of innovation and knowledge among firms, clusters, networks, and society, an improvement of the urban environment where people live and produce, and an institutional system that is favorable to the creation and development of firms, clusters, and networks. Not the provision of funds is the mainstay of such policies, but rather a properly embedded decentralized management through intermediate organizations and agencies (technological institutes, business innovation centers, training centers, knowledge transfer agencies, open-source, standardization, and coordination agencies, etc.).

Local and regional entities, however, must be coordinated and *embedded in larger, usually national, frameworks*, in order to prevent their being exploited and played off against each other by more powerful global commercial players, but also to prevent too large *Myrdalian backwash effects* and promote Myrdalian *spread* effects across the boundaries of local centers and regional agglomerations.

Economic policies likewise differ under the *Varieties of Capitalism* perspective as compared to neoclassical postulates of just compensating for "market failures." The focus on strategic interaction, clustering, and networking among private agents and the results derived from this suggest a different formulation of the problem set for economic policy. When companies can achieve their objectives through cooperation only, how to get private agents to cooperate has to be the critical issue, and the support for and formulation of an institutional structure that helps make this easier has to be the objective of economic development policy.

How this can be done differs, depending on the overall framework. Sometimes national economic performance can be improved through market regulation, thus reducing complexity and uncertainty, for instance. In other instances, improved capacities for coordination and cooperation with other agents are the key to an improved performance. It includes fostering information-sharing among agents or improvements in private agents' abilities to make credible commitments, or the shaping of expectations regarding others' behavior that allows for a cooperative strategy to be chosen (again, see Chapter 16 for more details).

17.4 FINAL CONCLUSIONS

In all, complexity economics, including evolutionary-institutional GT reasoning, has been of considerable use in the development and specification of new *systemic*, *interactive*, and *institutional policy* perspectives. These basically define *new relations* among *interacting private agents* and between these and the *public policy agent*, which turned out to be considerably different from those, often too ambiguous, flawed, and opaque, public–private partnerships, which have been so fashionable in theory and policy in recent decades, but often ended in dubious alliances, but also different from any pragmatic, predominantly subsidizing policies—with their financial aids, grants, subsidized credits, tax breaks, informal subsidies from public infrastructure use, including particularly public R&D provision from universities, and many other overt or hidden subsidies—and mostly expensive for the tax payer in the end.

The new perspectives are in line with an understanding of economic policy to solve problems by unlocking, initiating, accelerating, and stabilizing coordination and cooperation and, in this way, the emergence of institutions of cooperation with superior economic performance. Private agents have to make their recurrent contributions here according to the payoffs they can yield from the common and collective solutions.

The policy perspective of shaping interaction conditions for interacting private agents in a long-termed, consistent, and systemic approach requires a deliberate, qualified, and powerful public policy agency, which is virtually no longer existent after four decades of "neoliberal" shrinking of the state and of public action capability for the long-run future.

The approach makes further use of the older political-economic conception of *merit goods*, which mirrors the relation between the system of private agents and the public policy agent in the system of goods. However, obviously, not every private cooperative action may aim at a potential merit good (for potential oligopolistic *collusion* against third parties and the general public, for instance, see Chapter 7). An institutional arrangement carefully designed through a *strong role for the public policy agent* in relation to individual private agents, i.e., by a "strong state," will make the difference between cooperation at the expense of third parties and cooperation to solve common problems in a "progressive," i.e., less powerful or ceremonial way, not at the expense of third parties (see Section 13.12 for the definition of such "progressive" institutional change).

The public policy agent and the general public always need to be aware of existing private power structures. In order to *reliably* and *sustainably* define public objectives and corresponding "merit goods," to *credibly* set incentives vis-à-vis powerful corporate agents and to ensure a reasonable *distribution of the win-win benefits among both the private agents and between private agents and the general public*, the public policy agent needs to have considerable *independent power*. And it accordingly has to act in a *qualified* and *consistent* manner (see, e. g., Klein, 1990; Elsner, 2001), which, in turn, requires some *participative*, continuous, and *transparent decision-making process* (e.g., Nielsen, 1992). Obviously, the current public-opinion building and decision-making systems are still far away from that.

A public policy agent pursuing a conception of interactive/institutional economic policy may basically be able to initiate, accelerate, and stabilize the formation of a *strong culture of cooperation* so that, in an evolutionary process, an extremely individualistic culture may fade away behind the "veil of history." It appears that increasing the effectiveness of real problem-solving justifies the effort of further elaborating such an interactive/institutional economic policy paradigm.

The approach has been applied to issues of *network structures*, *firm size distribution*, related *systemic volatility*, and to information, knowledge, innovation, and development economics, with a number of specific complexes of policy measures, all focused in perspective to *information diffusion*, *shared knowledge*, *reducing volatility and complexity*, promoting *recognized interdependence* and interaction, *futurity*, coordination, and cooperation, *clustering* and *networking*, and, with this, *innovation* in a broad sense, improving socioeconomic *performance* and human *well-being*. The idea that the economy exists and works to improve human well-being in this way may become a tangible human experience again.

Chapter References

Ahdieh, R. B., 2009. The visible hand: coordination functions of the regulatory state. Available at: <http://ssrn.com/abstract=15222127> (accessed 23.10.13.).

Arrow, K.J., 1950. A difficulty in the concept of social welfare. J. Polit. Econ. 58 (4), 328–346.

Ashby, W.R., 1956. An Introduction to Cybernetics. Chapman & Hall, London.

Axelrod, R., 1984. The Evolution of Cooperation. Basic Books, New York, NY, 2nd 2006.

Batrancea, L.-M., 2009. A game theoretic approach to the 2008 world financial meltdown. Int. J. Bus. Res. 9 (2), <http://www.freepatentsonline.com/article/International-Journal-Business-Research/208535089.html> (accessed 06.12.13.).

Beer, S., 1979. The Heart of Enterprise. John Wiley, London, New York.

Benz, A., 1995. Beyond the public—private divide: institutional reform and cooperative policy making. A New German Public Sector? Reform, Adaptation and Stability. Dartmouth, Aldershot, Brookfield (pp. 165–187).

Block, F., 2000. Disorderly coordination: the limited capacities of states and markets. In: Burlamaqui, L., Castro, A.C., Chang, H.-J. (Eds.), Institutions and the Role of the State. Edward Elgar, Cheltenham, Northampton, pp. 53–71.

Borrás, S., Tsagdis, D., 2008. Cluster Policies in Europe. Firms, Institutions, and Governance. Edward Elgar, Cheltenham, Northampton.

Brennan, G., Lomasky, L., 1983. Institutional aspects of "merit goods" analysis. Finanzarchiv, N.F. 41, 183–206.

Bush, P.D., 1987. The theory of institutional change. J. Econ. Issues. XXI, 1075–1116.

Bush, P.D., 1999a. Veblen's "Olympian detachment" reconsidered. Hist. Econ. Ideas. 7 (3), 127–151.

Bush, P.D., 1999b. Recognized interdependence. In: O'Hara, P.A. (Ed.), Encyclopedia of Political Economy, Vol. 2. Routledge, London, New York, pp. 963–964.

Cabrera, À., Cabrera, E.F., 2002. Knowledge-sharing dilemmas. Organ. Stud. 23 (5), 687–710.

Calvert, R.L., 1995. The rational choice theory of institutions: implications for design. In: Weimer, D.L. (Ed.), Institutional Design. Kluwer, Boston, Dordrecht, London, pp. 63–94.

Cellini, R., Lambertini, L., 2006. Differential game-theoretical analysis and industrial policy. In: Bianchi, P., Labory, S. (Eds.), International Handbook on Industrial Policy. Edward Elgar, Cheltenham, Northampton, pp. 415–431.

Clements, M.T., 2013. Self-interest vs. greed and the limitations of the invisible hand. Am. J. Econ. Sociol. 72, 949–965.

Cohen, S.I., 2001. Microeconomic Policy. Routledge, London, New York (Chapter 9).

Commons, J.R., 1934. Institutional Economics. Its Place in Political Economy. Macmillan, New York, NY (repr. New Brunswick: Transaction Publishers, 1990).

Cooper, R., John, A., 1988. Coordinating coordination failures in Keynesian models. Q. J. Econ. 103, 441–463.

Cossentino, F., Pyke, F., Sengenberger, W. (Eds.), 1996. Local and Regional Response to Global Pressure: The Case of Italy and its Industrial Districts. ILO, Geneva.

Croskery, P., 1995. Conventions and norms in institutional design. In: Weimer, D.L. (Ed.), Institutional Design. Kluwer, Boston, Dordrecht, London, pp. 95–112.

Crouch, C., 2005. Capitalist Diversity and Change. Recombinant Governance and Institutional Entrepreneurs. Oxford University Press, Oxford, New York.

Deakin, S., Goodwin, T., Hughes, A., 1997. Co-operation and trust in inter-firm relations: beyond competition policy. In: Deakin, S., Michie, J. (Eds.), Contracts, Co-operation, and Competition. Oxford University Press, Oxford, pp. 339–369.

Demange, G., Wooders, M., 2005. Group Formation in Economics. Networks, Clubs, and Coalitions. Cambridge University Press, Cambridge, New York.

Deroian, F., 2001. Lock-out in social networks. In: Kirman, A., Zimmermann, J.B. (Eds.), Economics with Heterogeneous Interacting Agents. Springer, Berlin, Heidelberg, pp. 57–72.

Dixit, A., 2001. On modes of economic governance. CESifo Working Paper Series 589.

Dolfsma, W., Leydesdorff, L., 2009. Lock-in & break-out from technological trajectories: modeling and policy implications. Technol. Forecast. Soc. Change. 76, 932–941.

Dopfer, K., Foster, J., Potts, J., 2004. Micro-meso-macro. J. Evol. Econ. 14, 263–279.

Doran, J., 2001. Intervening to achieve co-operative ecosystem management: towards an agent based model. J Artif. Soc. Social Simul. 4 (2).

Eckert, D., Koch, S.t., Mitloehner, J., 2005. Using the iterated Prisoner's Dilemma for explaining the evolution of cooperation in open source communities. In: Scotto, M., Succi, G. (Eds.), Proceedings of the First International Conference on Open Source Systems, Genoa.

Englmaier, F., Reisinger, M., 2008. Information, coordination and the industrialization of countries. CESifo Econ. Stud. 54 (3), 534–550.

Elsner, W., 2000a. A simple theory of cooperative industrial policy. model building and practical experience. In: Elsner, W., Groenewegen, J. (Eds.), Industrial Policies After 2000. Kluwer Academic Publishers, Boston, Dordrecht, London, pp. 113–143.

Elsner, W., 2000b. An industrial policy agenda 2000 and beyond. In: Elsner, W., Groenewegen, J. (Eds.), Industrial Policies After 2000. Kluwer Academic Publishers, Boston, Dordrecht, London, pp. 411–486.

Elsner, W., 2001. Interactive economic policy: toward a cooperative policy approach for a negotiated economy. J. Econ. Issues. XXXV (1), 61–83.

Farrant, A., McPhail, E., 2010. Does F.A. Hayek's "road to serfdom" deserve to make a comeback? Challenge. 53 (4), 96–120.

Gallegati, M., Kirman, A., Palestrini, A., 2007. Implications of scaling laws for policy-makers. In: Salzano, M., Colander, D. (Eds.), Complexity Hints for Economic Policy. Springer, Milan, Berlin, Heidelberg, New York, pp. 291–302.

Glaeser, E.L., Laibson, D.I., Sacerdote, B., 2002. An economic approach to social capital. Econ. J. 112, 437–458.

Hargreaves Heap, S.P., 1989. Rationality in Economics. Basil Blackwell, Oxford, New York.

Hayden, F.G., 1994. Institutional theory of economic policy. In: Hodgson, G.M., Samuels, W.J., Tool, M.R. (Eds.), The Elgar Companion to Institutional and Evolutionary Economics, vol. 1. Edward Elgar, Aldershot, Brookfield, pp. 392–397.

Hayden, F.G., 2006. Policymaking for a Good Society. The Social Fabric Matrix Approach to Policy Analysis and Program Evaluation. Springer, New York, NY.

Hilbe, C., Chakra, M.A., Traulsen, A., 2013. The evolution of strategic timing in collective-risk dilemmas. PLoS One. 8 (6), e66490, <http://www.ncbi.nlm.nih.gov/pmc/articles/PMC3682992/> (accessed (06.12.13.).

Hurwicz, L., 1987. Inventing new institutions: the design perspective. Am. J. Agric. Econ. 69 (2), 395–419.

Ivarola, L., Marqués, G., Weisman, D., 2013. Expectation-based processes—an interventionist account of economic practice: putting the direct practice of economics on the agenda of philosophy of economics. Economic Thought—Hist. Philos. Method. 2 (2), 20–32.

Jun, T, Sethi, R., 2009. Reciprocity in evolving social networks. J. Evol. Econ. 19, 379–396.

Kirman, A.P., 1998. Economies with interacting agents. In: Cohendet, P., et al., (Eds.), The Economics of Networks. Springer, Berlin, Heidelberg, New York, pp. 17–51.

Klein, D.B., 1990. The microfoundations of rules vs. discretion. Constit. Polit. Econ. 1 (3), 1–19.

Liebrand, W.B.G., Messick, D.M. (Eds.), 1996. Frontiers in Social Dilemmas Research. Springer, Berlin.

Lindgren, K., 1997. Evolutionary dynamics in game-theoretic models. In: Arthur, W.B., Durlauf, S.N., Lane, D.A. (Eds.), The Economy as an Evolving Complex System II. Addison-Wesley, Reading, MA, pp. 337–367.

McCain, R., 2009. Game Theory and Public Policy. Edward Elgar, Cheltenham, Northampton.

Musgrave, R.A., 1959. The Theory of Public Finance: A Study in Public Economy. McGraw-Hill, New York, NY.

Musgrave, R.A., 1987. Merit goods. The New Palgrave. A Dictionary of Economics. Macmillan, London, Basingstoke (pp. 452–453).

Myrdal, G., with a contribution of Paul Streeten, 1958. Value in Social Theory: A Selection of Essays on Methodology. Harper, New York, NY.

Nielsen, K., 1992. The mixed economy, the neoliberal challenge, and the negotiated economy. J. Soc. Econ. 21, 325–351.

Nielsen, K., Pedersen, O.K., 1988. The negotiated economy: ideal and history. Scand. Polit. Stud. 2, 79–101.

Offerman, T., Sonnemans, J., 1998. Learning by experience and learning by imitating successful others. J. Econ. Behav. Organ. 34, 559–575.

Oltra, V., Schenk, E., 1998. Evolution of cooperation with local interactions and imitation. In: Cohendet, P., et al., (Eds.), The Economics of Networks. Springer, Berlin, Heidelberg, New York, pp. 205–222.

Pratt, A., 1997. The emerging shape and form of innovation networks and institutions. In: Simmie, J.M. (Ed.), Innovation, Networks and Learning Regions? Jessica Kingsley Publishers, London, Bristol, pp. 124–136.

Ramstad, Y., 1991. From desideratum to historical achievement: John R. Commons's reasonable value and the "negotiated economy" of Denmark. J. Econ. Issues. XXV, 431–439.

Salzano, M., Colander, D., 2007. Complexity Hints for Economic Policy. Springer, Milan, Berlin, Heidelberg, New York.

Sandler, T., 2004. Global Collective Action. Cambridge University Press, Cambridge, New York.

Sen, A.K., 1967. Isolation, assurance and the social rate of discount. Q. J. Econ. 81 (1), 112–124.

Sen, A.K., 1970/1984. Collective Choice and Social Welfare. Holden-Day, San Francisco, CA (repr. 1970, Elsevier).

Sen, A.K., 2008. Social choice. In: Durlauf, S.N., Blume, L.E. (Eds.), The New Palgrave Dictionary of Economics, second ed. Palgrave Macmillan, London, Basingstoke.

Spiekermann, K.P., 2009. Sort out your neighbourhood. Public good games on dynamic networks. Synthese. 168, 273–294.

Stanley, E.A., Ashlock, D., Tesfatsion, L., 1994. Iterated Prisoner's Dilemma with choice and refusal of partners, Santa Fe Institute Studies in the *Science of Complexity*. In: Langton, C.G. (Ed.), Artificial Life III, proc. vol. XVII. Addison-Wesley.

Tisdell, C., Hartley, K., 2008. Microeconomic Policy. A New Perspective. Edward Elgar, Cheltenham, Northampton.

Tool, M.R., 1979. The Discretionary Economy: A Normative Theory of Political Economy. Goodyear Publishing, Santa Monica, CA.

Tool, M.R., 1994. Instrumental value theory. In: Hodgson, G.M., Samuels, W.J., Tool, M.R. (Eds.), The Elgar Companion to Institutional and Evolutionary Economics, vol. 1. Edward Elgar, Aldershot, Brookfield, pp. 406–412.

Traulsen, A., Nowak, M.A., 2006. Evolution of cooperation by multilevel selection. PNAS. 103 (29), 10952–10955.

Velupillai, K. V., 2007. The impossibility of an effective theory of policy in a complex economy. In: Salzano, M., Colander, D. (Eds.), Complexity Hints for Economic Policy. Springer, Milan, Berlin, Heidelberg, New York, pp. 273–290.

Ver Eecke, W., 1998. The concept of a "merit good". The ethical dimension in economic theory and the history of economic thought or the transformation of economics into socio-economics. J. Soc. Econ. 27, 133–153.

Ver Eecke, W., 2008. The concept of "merit good" and the history of economic thought. Ethical Dimensions of the Economy. Making Use of Hegel and the Concepts of Public and Merit Goods. Springer, Berlin, Heidelberg (pp. 91–112).

Wilkinson, R., Pickett, K., 2009. The Spirit Level. Why More Equal Societies Almost Always Do Better. Allen Lane/Penguin, London, New York.

Further Reading—Online

For further readings on the chapter issues, see the textbook website: http://booksite.elsevier.com/9780124115859

How to Deal with Knowledge of Complexity Microeconomics: Theories, Empirics, Applications, and Actions*

"The degree to which economics is isolated from the ordinary business of life is extraordinary and unfortunate. [...] This separation of economics from the working economy has severely damaged both the business community and the academic discipline. [...] Today, a modern market economy [...] requires an intricate web of social institutions to coordinate the working of markets and firms across various boundaries. At a time when the modern economy is becoming increasingly institutions-intensive, the reduction of economics to price theory is troubling enough. It is suicidal for the field to slide into a hard science of choice, ignoring the influences of society, history, culture, and politics on the working of the economy." **Ronald Coase**[1]

"The proof of the pudding is in the eating." **Spanish-English medieval proverb.**

"...and the proof of knowledge is in its application in inter-actions, its adaptation and enhancement in practice — rather than its consumption and wastage." **(Wolfram Elsner, Torsten Heinrich, Henning Schwardt)**

*This chapter was coauthored by Claudius Gräbner.

[1]Nobel Laureate in Economics, "Saving Economics from the Economists," *Harvard Business Review*, December 2012.

The Microeconomics of Complex Economies.
DOI: http://dx.doi.org/10.1016/B978-0-12-411585-9.00018-X

18.1 WHAT IS SCIENTIFIC KNOWLEDGE?

When we study the behavior of scientists in a scientific community, or the way of how theories are (or should be) built, or if we ask questions about how the "truth" can, if existent, be revealed, and what the relation between scientists, "reality," action, and policy is, we are in the realm of the *philosophy* (and, in fact, also *sociology*) *of science* (or *epistemology*), of which *methodology* is a part, and we are working with "meta-theories," i.e., theories about theories and science.

18.1.1 Scientific Systems: *Models, Theories, Approaches*

Mathematical Models

We have explained, throughout this textbook, a number of formal *systems of mathematical equations* that usually are called *models* (e.g., in Chapters 3, 5–7, 13, and 14). Such formal models are usually quite well specified in their assumptions, variables, parameters, hypotheses, proofs, and results. However, even the most formal system of equations cannot tell us much without some qualitative, verbal *storytelling*, in which it is *embedded* and which *interprets* its hypotheses, proofs, and results. Some mathematical economists called for a strict separation of theory and interpretation in the process of modeling. "An axiomatized theory has a mathematical form that is completely separated from its economic content. [...] The divorce of form and content immediately yields a new theory whenever a novel interpretation of a primitive concept is discovered" (Debreu, 1986, p. 1265). But even Debreu acknowledged that the purely formal model requires some *interpretation* in order to serve as guidance for behavior or policy.

The story embedding such a system of equations may be either somewhat broader in its potential scope of applications than the algebraic part of the model or, in some parts, it may be narrower. The verbal qualification may be more or less specified, while the formal part of the model may be in parts more specific, with a narrow scope of applications, while in other parts more general. So all depends on how the different components of the overall model *relate to reality*.

One might be surprised that a discussion about the relation to reality was led even in the field of *mathematics*. On the one hand, the *"formalist school" of mathematics*, most famously represented by the German David Hilbert and the French "Bourbaki" group (a collective pseudonym for a cooperation of mathematicians between the mid-1930s and the early 1980s), was seeking a clear distinction between mathematical objects and their interpretation. It saw mathematics as the formal study of symbols and structures without any reference to what these structures represent in the real world. The *"intuitive school" of mathematics*, on the other hand, argued that a meaningful analysis of symbols always entails an idea of what the symbols stand for. Therefore, Bertrand Russell, tending toward the latter, compared a formalist mathematician with a watchmaker "who is so absorbed in making his watches look pretty that he has forgotten their purpose

of telling the time, and has therefore omitted to insert any works" (Russell, 2009/1903, p. xxxii).

Theories and Approaches

Also, we have presented other *systems of thought* as "models," i.e., those that were less mathematical but *more verbal*, more storytelling, perhaps combined with a rough scheme of variables and relations (see, e.g., Chapters 1 and 12 and Section 13.12). We are used to term such more *conceptual* systems that usually *apply to very large areas* of reality, such as "the economy," theories. Note that the *scope of applications* typically is broader than with a mathematical model and its story, but mostly the relation to reality is simply less specified in such a more general theory. But more *specific propositions* or *hypotheses* can perhaps be derived from general theories.

Further, we have provided, throughout this book, whole sets of *analytical tools* and "approaches" to formally model and logically analyze *propositions about economic relations among economic entities* (like agents, goods, social behaviors/rules/institutions, payoffs, quantities, prices, ...), such as *game theory* to model and analyze *direct interaction*, or *replicators* and phase diagrams to model and analyze *evolutionary process* (see Chapters 2 and 8–11).

18.1.2 *Pattern Modeling* and Case Studies as Method

We have also provided more *applied theoretical systems*, with a "mid-range" generality, specified and applied to more specified and, thus, narrower fields, such as the modern global corporate economy, the information, innovation, and IT-economies, and policy systems (see Chapters 4 and 15–17).

Finally, we have provided *case studies*, which represent a very specific analysis. They serve to explain a real-world phenomenon exhaustively and in great detail, but it is more difficult to generalize their results as they are very time and space dependent.

In all, as you see, we have dealt with a *wide range of thought systems*, more or less specified, more or less general, and more or less formal.

Beyond all differences among them, most of the models of complexity microeconomics we have introduced in this textbook should be interpreted in the epistemological tradition of *pattern modeling*, i.e., to be *holistic, systemic, evolutionary*, but applied and not too abstract, i.e., in a *mid-range level of abstraction* (Wilber and Harrison, 1978). Holistic means that the *relations* among parts and between them and the whole receive particular attention (for an exemplary approach, see Section 18.7). This is in contrast to neoclassical models with their atomistic view according to which everything has to be explained in terms of the behavior of isolated individuals (see Chapter 5). Pattern models are systemic in the sense that they expect the different parts of a system to be interrelated and that they seek to understand the nature of these relations. As a consequence of the holistic and systemic view, neither the single agent nor the aggregate of all agents can be understood if studied in isolation (note the relation to the concept of *reconstitutive downward effects* described in Sections 3.2.4 and 14.4). In other words, because the economy is complex, i.e., it consists of many directly interdependent and interactive agents, the whole is considered to be "more than the sum of its parts," as repeatedly explained throughout this textbook. One consequence is that simple aggregation as assumed in neoclassical theory is impossible, as has been argued earlier in relation to the concept of *emergence* (see Chapters 1, 3, 6, 8–11, and 14). Finally, pattern models are evolutionary in the sense that the cumulative changes in the nature of the

relations among agents and social structures in their environment are seen as a fundamental aspect of social reality.

18.1.3 Scientific Systems and *Reality*: Is Strict *Testing* Possible?

With all of these scientific *systems of statements*, we need to determine and qualify their scientific status, or real-world *relevance*, *informational content*, area of *applicability* and degree of *generality*, degree of correctness or *truth*, empirical *verifiability* and *falsifiability*, i.e., their overall "fruitfulness." We would have to analyze their implied specific statements, *propositions* and *forecasts*, their (more general) *axioms* and (more specific) *assumptions*, explicitly made or tacitly presumed, and their *"auxiliary" statements* about the specific conditions of their application to reality or empirical data. Ideally, every scientific system should be able to be cast in the form of *variables*, independent and dependent ones, *parameters*, *value areas* of application, strict formal *relations*, and exactly forecasted *results*. A sufficiently specified proposition should ideally then assume the form of an *"if-then"* hypothesis.

One will immediately realize that such an ideal scientific system would be an extremely complicated thing. In fact, the whole bandwidth of scientific systems mentioned earlier and provided in this textbook consists of more or less complicated systems. Even if we could objectively *"measure,"* i.e., exactly and objectively relate "reality" to exact theoretically derived variables, parameters, and relations (more on that discussed later), it would be extremely difficult to strictly *"verify"* or even only *"falsify"* something through the instance of "reality"—as the usual *textbook methodology and epistemology* require and suggest. The modern classic for the standard textbook methodology/epistemology is *Karl W. Popper* (e.g., Popper, 1959/1934) and his "critical rationalist" approach.

18.2 POSITIVISM AND CRITICAL RATIONALISM

The particular philosophy of science, which is based on the view that information derived from measuring logical and mathematical variables and relations through some *objective sensory experience* or *test* is not only possible but the exclusive source of authoritative knowledge, has been called positivism since the early nineteenth century. According to this view, there is valid knowledge ("truth") only in scientific knowledge attained that way, i.e., through strict and *objective empirical evidence*. In this tradition, it has always been assumed that *science* is indeed able to provide its theories in a form that can be strictly, if not verified, at least *straightforwardly* and *objectively falsified*, once and for all, against reality. The strength of a scientific theory, it is claimed, lies in the very fact that it is or can be made open to such falsification. This means that if a theory cannot, in principle, be falsified, it does not constitute a scientific system. For that purpose, a scientific system must *demarcate the areas of application* of its propositions, i.e., the *specific implications* of its more abstract theories, in order *not to be immune* against such empirical refutation.

Popper further developed this epistemology and coined the term "critical rationalism" to characterize it. Logically, he argued, no number of confirming outcomes at the level of experimental testing can finally confirm a scientific theory, as there may occur any contradicting instance in future testing; but a single counterexample would prove the theory, from which the specific implication was derived, to be false. In this view, theories are only tentative, for the time being, propositions thus just are *hypotheses* or "conjectures." While classical nineteenth century positivist rationalism held that it is the theory most likely to be true that one should prefer, Popper's critical rationalism held that it is the least likely, or most easily falsifiable, the simplest and at the same time most general, theory that explains known facts and that one should prefer and put to test in order to generate scientific progress through falsification and subsequent theory improvement. In this view, it is more important to make falsification as easily as possible, than to reveal truth via induction, let alone to *immunize* theory against such testing and potential falsification.

18.3 MODEL PLATONISM: THE IMMUNIZING EPISTEMOLOGICAL PRACTICE OF MAINSTREAM ECONOMICS UNDER SCRUTINY

18.3.1 The *Axiomatic Method* and the Original Criticism

In the framework of such *critical rationalist* logic of testing and of falsifiability of propositions, with their surrounding system of axioms, assumptions, auxiliary hypotheses on the conditions of application, etc., a classic critique of the *deviating practice* of neoclassical mainstream economics from the critical rationalist practice was developed under the characterization of Model Platonism by philosopher and economist *Hans Albert* already in the 1950s and 1960s (see, e.g., Albert, 1971/1963). Model Platonism is characterized by a number of *strategies to immunize the neoclassical economic model against reality*, i.e., against empirical test and falsifiability. These include, according to Albert, strategies to work excessively with sets of *axioms* (the so-called axiomatic method), which by definition are inaccessible to reality, and with assumptions that leave unexplained and *unspecified the areas of application* of the neoclassical propositions, in order to attain a mathematical model with a predetermined unique and "optimal" equilibrium (see Chapters 5 and 6).

Note, however, that the original motivation to advocate and develop the axiomatic method, which is most famously related to the work of GET theorist *Gerard Debreu* (who was trained as a mathematician), was to discipline scientific scrutiny. Debreu expected the axiomatic method to require the researchers to constantly aspire greater rigor, weaker assumptions, greater simplicity, stronger conclusions, and greater generality of their results (see, e.g., Debreu, 1991, p. 4).

However, as Albert argued, neoclassical economic practice alleges *general laws of behavior* in combination with an excessive use of *ceteris paribus clauses*, which in turn claim unrestricted, general validity, and leave the areas of their application deliberately largely unspecified. Thus, for instance, the neoclassical allegation of a "rational" behavior, where individuals always *maximize their utility*, and firms always maximize their profit, *cannot be put to the empirical test*, and thus not be falsified, as it is constructed by neoclassical economics in a way so that it appears *always true*, if axioms and assumptions (including catch-all ceteris paribus clauses), particularly about "rationality," apply. So the area of application is left unspecified, so that *any behavior can be claimed to be utility maximizing* anytime (see also as a famous critic, Sen, 1977, p. 323). This, e.g., entails the problem explained in Chapters 5 and 6 that there is more than one preference relation being able to "explain" an observed choice.

Note again that, according to the "critical rationalist" ideal, propositions should have been put forward in the form of *"if-then" hypotheses*, stating the *"ifs"* in a strict and empirically accessible way-and the *"thens"* as well. According to the critical Model Platonism analysis, this

has never been the praxis of neoclassical mainstream economics.

18.3.2 Econometric Testing and Meta-Regressions . . .

Note that even econometric testing cannot serve as the strict and objective testing tool that the neoclassical mainstream claims it to be, as *econometric data usually fit with different functional forms* and usually many functional forms can be adapted to a certain data set through parametrical fine-tuning (on *measurement issues* in general, see Sections 10.4 and 10.6). Similarly, researchers can influence the outcome of their study by varying the set of control variables in their econometric model. The bias resulting from this kind of manipulation is called *specification bias*. The discussion on the validity and reliability of econometric testing in economics has indeed been fundamental and ongoing for decades (see, e.g., McCloskey and Ziliak, 1996; Nell and Errouaki, 2011).

An important tool to measure specification biases is meta-regression. Meta-regressions are the statistical analysis of econometric literature. It uses regression analysis to explain the variation among reported regression estimates (see, e.g., Stanley, 2013, p. 207).

18.3.3 . . . and Publication Biases

Meta-regressions helped to identify not only specification biases as mentioned earlier but also publication biases, i.e., the bias arising because reviewers tend to accept papers consistent with the dominating theoretical and methodological (econometric) view more frequently, researchers expect results to be consistent with the dominant theoretical view and because having statistically highly significant results increases the probability that a paper gets published (see, e.g., Stanley, 2013, p. 211; Card and Krueger, 1995a).

One of the most prominent meta-analyses was that of Card and Krueger (1995a,b), which showed that there is no empirical evidence for a policy-relevant adverse-employment effect of a minimum wage. This finding was confirmed by, e.g., Doucouliagos and Stanley (2009), who also showed a significant publication bias in that context.

18.3.4 Replicability of Results and Data Transparency—Toward a New Academic Ethics

Another possibility to enhance the significance of econometric studies than the use of meta-regressions would be a more frequent replication of existing work.

As a prominent recent example, in 2010, *C. Reinhart and K. Rogoff* published a paper, in which they showed that economic growth will decline if the debt of a nation exceeds 90% of its GDP (Reinhart and Rogoff, 2010). This finding had a significant impact on policy measures in the frame of a "neoliberal" austerity policy era in most countries during the global fiscal crisis, and in particular in the European currency union in the Euro crisis, as it was taken as evidence for the necessity of strict austerity measures. Later, after a graduate student had problems in replicating the study for his seminar paper, the finding was shown to be false (Herndon et al., 2013). The cause was an accidental omission of some rows in the Excel spreadsheet by the authors.

Independently of what particular mistake occurred in that case it is an instance of the requirement of data transparency and replicability as a precondition for econometric testing.

It is of course not sufficient to resolve the other measurement problems identified above.

As a reaction to many similar incidences and long-standing and continuing debates on *flawed publication practices* and theoretical—methodological biases of mainstream journals, the *American Economic Association* (AEA) decided, after long discussions, to publish papers in its journals, mainly the *American Economic Review*, only "if the data used in the analysis are clearly and precisely documented and are readily available to any researcher for purposes of replication" (AEA, 2013). According to general *AEA standards* on *conflicts of interest and data transparency*, adopted already in 2012:

1. [e]very submitted article should state the sources of financial support for the particular research it describes. If none, that fact should be stated.
2. Each author of a submitted article should identify each interested party from whom he or she has received significant financial support, summing to at least $10,000 in the past three years, in the form of consultant fees, retainers, grants and the like. The disclosure requirement also includes in-kind support, such as providing access to data. If the support in question comes with a non-disclosure obligation, that fact should be stated, along with as much information as the obligation permits. If there are no such sources of funds, that fact should be stated explicitly. An 'interested' party is any individual, group, or organization that has a financial, ideological, or political stake related to the article.
3. Each author should disclose any paid or unpaid positions as officer, director, or board member of relevant non-profit advocacy organizations or profit-making entities. A 'relevant' organization is one whose policy positions, goals, or financial interests relate to the article.
4. The disclosures required above apply to any close relative or partner of any author.
5. Each author must disclose if another party had the right to review the paper prior to its circulation.
6. For published Articles, information on relevant potential conflicts of interest will be made available to the public.

This indicates that the *conventional methods* of the mainstream "normal science" of *modeling and testing* have come under scrutiny recently and will have to give way to a *new ethics of economic research and publication* and new epistemological considerations.

18.3.5 The Model Platonism Critique Then and Now

Albert, in contrast to the practice he criticized, postulated a *real-world approach* to economics to investigate *real motives, values, instincts, traits, habits, social rules,* and *predispositions* of agents. With this, he appeared way ahead of his time in the 1950s and 1960s, anticipating nowadays' evolutionary, institutional, and complexity economics, as well as behavioral and experimental lab economics.

This critique of the practice of the dominant theory, approach, and perspective in economics has been taken up recently and further developed, applying it to the more recent developments of the economic mainstream. *J. Kapeller* recently has overhauled that epistemological critique (see Kapeller, 2012, 2013) and modernized the analysis of the axiomatic-propositional logic of neoclassical economics, which, in fact, has further developed over the last decades to better immunize it against new conflicting empirical evidence. He applies it to recent developments such as *behavioral finance* and the *mainstream parts of experimental economics* and confirms its widespread *thought-experimental* style and *apriorism*.

According to Kapellar, the neoclassical epistemology was modernized by its adherence by presenting their models as just devices for *storytelling and metaphors*, while, however, *maintaining the normative "superior insights"*: utility maximization, profit maximization, and market equilibrium. Then any specific research results, how critical ever, are interpreted and presented in a way that they fit these a priori superior insights. He describes the neoclassical

research praxis of performing most interesting research on, e.g., asymmetric information and uncertainty, social dilemmas and the commons, oligopolistic games, or network externalities, where they *no longer stick to any one of their conventional core propositions*, but then give the results an interpretation consistent with the narrow frame of a *perfect, optimizing,* and *equilibrating market economy*. This again indicates the danger of sticking to vague concepts such as utility maximization, which may be, as said, consistent with almost any empirical phenomenon.

The praxis of interpreting results, which are at odds with the assumptions of a model but which can be generated as the outcome of the model by calibrating it in a favorable manner as evidence for the given theory, is closely related to the epistemology of *methodological instrumentalism*, nowadays dominant in economics, as we will explain in Section 18.4.

In this way, a schizophrenic economics, a scientific discipline in the state of *cognitive dissonance* emerged, where any new knowledge from critical and cutting-edge research must be interpreted according to an *apriority*, the "perfect-market economy," which then appears as a more or less *ideological must*. No critical cutting-edge research result, then, will be able to change the dominant policy rhetoric or their *textbooks*. It results in a scientific discipline somehow *apart from reality* in its *mass teaching, media rhetoric,* and *policy advice*. On the "rhetoric of economics," see particularly Section 18.5.

18.4 FROM "IF" TO "AS IF": MILTON FRIEDMAN AND METHODOLOGICAL INSTRUMENTALISM

18.4.1 Friedman: *Logical Positivism, Eternal Laws,* and "Good Predictions"

Popper, as said, required scientific statements to be formulated in a clear "if-then" structure with clearly defined areas of application of the "if" component. And Albert demonstrated that the neoclassical practice fundamentally differs from that. The dominant view in economics indeed is different from the postulates of critical rationalism. The key contribution to the methodology of neoclassical economics is an essay of Milton Friedman on "positive economics" (1953), in which he refuted the view that the quality of a scientific theory could be judged by the realism of its assumption and claimed that the only way to evaluate a theory is to judge its *ability to generate good predictions* for the system under investigation. He even argued that "the more significant the theory, the more unrealistic the assumptions" have to be. So he proposed to replace the "if" in Poppers rationalism by an "as if," i.e., the requirement to make good predictions *"as if" real-world agents behaved like, e.g., rational agents* in the neoclassical sense.

Some clarifications are needed before scrutinizing this apparently odd statement in more detail. Friedman stands in the tradition of *logical positivism*. According to logical positivism, it is the task for the scientific community to reveal eternal or *general laws*, i.e., laws that are time- and space-invariant. One such law could be the utility maximizing behavior of economic agents. The researcher creates a hypothesis by applying general laws $L_1, L_2, ..., L_n$ on some initial conditions $C_1, C_2, ..., C_m$ he observes in reality. Using the rules of logical *deduction*, he then derives the hypothesis H, which should be tested against reality. If it coincides with reality, the model cannot be refuted. Note that as the general laws are expected to be time- and space-invariant, in this framework explanation (for past and present) and prediction (for the future) are logically equivalent. If the deduction is conducted before the situation described by the hypotheses has taken place, the model *predicts* state H. If H lies in the past, the model *explains* H. So there is no logical difference between explanation and prediction.

Viewed against this background, one is able to understand Friedman's claim that a theory should be judged on its ability to produce good predictions alone. As assumptions (for him) are abstractions from reality, they are necessarily false and there is "no criterion by which to judge whether a particular departure from realism is or is not acceptable," i.e., to judge which degree of "nonrealism" is still acceptable (Friedman, 1953, p. 32). His allegation that "the more significant the theory, the more unrealistic the assumptions" must be understood as the contention that more realistic assumptions draw explanatory power away from the general laws and thus limit the power of the general law to contribute to the theoretical explanation (of the hypothesis). A good general law simply would not require the information entailed in a realistic assumption to predict (viz. explain) a situation.

18.4.2 Critiques: Assumptions, Predictions, and Strict Testing

The view of Friedman received extensive critique from inside economics and other disciplines such as philosophy of science, but although even renowned mainstream economists such as *Paul Samuelson* (see, e.g., Samuelson in Archibald et al., 1963) refuted Friedman's approach, it is still used to defend the standard unrealistic *assumptions* as deployed in neoclassical theory, with no specification of its areas of application. Friedman's methodological instrumentalism can therefore be considered just one of the obvious *immunization strategies* in the sense of Albert and Kapeller (see Section 10.3.5).

Specifically, the approach is deficient in its crude use of the concept of "assumptions." For example, according to *Musgrave* (1981), there are three different kinds of assumptions.

Some assumptions entail the supposition that a factor has an effect on the subject under investigation, but that this effect is not relevant for the phenomenon to be explained. Galileo, e.g., assumed that air resistance had no effect on heavy objects falling down a short distance. Although this was false in the strict sense, heavy objects falling down a short distance behave "as if" there is no air resistance as the effect of air resistance in this context is indeed negligible. Such assumptions have therefore been called *negligibility assumptions* (Musgrave, 1981, p. 378). The appropriateness of such assumptions has indeed to be evaluated by testing the predictive power of the corresponding theory (a negligibility assumption is not justified if the subject under investigation was a feather as the effect of air resistance was not negligible in this case).

Another type of assumptions is called *domain assumptions* and specifies the domain of applicability of the corresponding theory. If the researcher figures out that his theory applies only if a certain effect is not present, then he might restrict his theory to situations, in which this effect is absent by stating its absence as a domain assumption (Musgrave, 1981, p. 379). There is nothing wrong about this as long as it is done in a transparent manner.

The third kind of assumptions are assumptions, of which the researcher knows that they are false and merely introduces them as an intermediate step in developing a more sophisticated theory or as an intermediate step in explaining his theory to an audience. One might assume that the solar system consists only of the sun and one planet, prove some results, and then show that the results also hold if there is more than one planet. The assumption that there was only one planet in the solar system is then called a *heuristic assumption* (Musgrave, 1981, p. 383).

Although Friedman's argument has some merit for negligibility assumptions, it is not true for domain assumptions. In fact, "the more unrealistic domain assumptions are, the less testable and hence less significant is the theory.

Contrariwise, the more significant the theory, the more widely applicable it will be" (Musgrave, 1981, p. 382). Neither is it applicable to heuristic assumptions. In the end, Musgrave showed that Friedman's methodological instrumentalism is flawed already because it lacks an adequate taxonomy of assumptions.

Another one of the fundamental problems of Friedman's approach is that it still relies heavily on the *strict (econometric) testing of scientific hypotheses*, which is impossible, as we explain in Musgrave, 1981. It will therefore not be possible, even if the hypotheses were formulated in a way that allows potential falsification, to evaluate the quality of its predictions.

Finally, throughout this textbook, examples of complex modeling and system simulations have demonstrated that *general laws* are very rare in economics (if existent at all). The logical positivist research program, on which Friedman's methodological instrumentalism is built, however, rests on the idea of time- and space-invariant laws. If there were no such laws, the logical equivalence between prediction and explanation could not be established.

18.5 EMULATING WRONG IDEALS: THE McCLOSKEY CRITIQUE OF THE *RHETORIC OF ECONOMICS*

As in any science, economists seek to persuade others of their arguments. With reference to the ancient Greeks, the scrutiny of writings with this (or any other) intention is called "rhetoric" (McCloskey, 1998/1985, p. 4). Deidre McCloskey, however, stated that rhetoric is of particular importance for economists because today two different forms of methodology in economics exist, the official and the unofficial. Economics is done according to the latter although it is claimed officially that it is done according to the former.

The official methodology is that of *"modernism."* It is deeply rooted in logical positivism, behaviorism, and operationalism and represented by Friedman (Friedman, 1953), and *Gary Becker* and *George Stigler* (Stigler and Becker, 1977). This approach was already reviewed in Section 18.4.

The way economics is actually done by researchers, McCloskey argues, does not follow this methodology. This fact is appreciated by her as she criticizes the modernist approach. In fact, she argues, modernism, as it is an outdated perspective on how science should work, is not accepted in other scientific disciplines including mathematics and physics. Instead, an unofficial methodology is applied and it is according to the standards of this unofficial methodology that the quality of economic arguments is assessed. The big problem is that economists are unconscious about this underlying methodology. The reason is that most economists only are educated to use implicit and naïve rhetoric: the *rhetoric of mathematics and statistics*, which relies on the scrutiny of mathematical formulas and statistical tests of significance.

However, what is needed according to McCloskey is an explicit and learned rhetoric. It would allow the reader to read scientific texts in alternative ways than it was intended by the writer and thus to understand the persuasive element in his arguments and to identify the underlying, usually implicit methodological considerations. Only if these elements are recognized, the scientific message can be understood and then supported or debunked (McCloskey, 1998/1985, p. 19).

This entails considering the extensive use of *literal figures* by economists in their writings. She argues that the fact that even the mathematical or statistical articles are full of literary is not a problem as such but that the unconsciousness of the scientific community about it is problematic. Examples of literary figures are *analogies* ("If the law of demand for ice cream holds, so it must for gasoline."), *individual introspection* ("What would I do if the price of gasoline doubled?"), *thought experiments* ("What would my friends do if the price gasoline doubled?"), and *metaphors* ("game theory," "the market is represented by supply and demand," "children are durable goods," "elasticity," "depression," "equilibrium"). McCloskey (1983, 1998/1985) particularly criticizes the use of the term *"statistical significance"* in econometrics, as while it leaves open the most important questions (quality and construction of the sample, economic significance of the repressor, standards to which the repressor is to compared, etc.), it is usually a sufficient argument for the acceptance or rejection of the economic hypothesis.

All these ways of convincing others of one's own argument are not just crude tools — although they are unscientific according to the official methodology of economics. Still, they are accepted, and what McCloskey is criticizing *inter alia* is that economists never reflect their normative basis, according to which it is judged whether an argument is accepted or not. This yields a *scientific praxis* that is full of *implicit assumptions* and obscure arguments, and in which only a small fraction of evidence is brought to discussions.

Consider, e.g., the work of Esther Duflo and Abhijit Banerjee (Duflo and Banerjee, 2011), who introduced randomized controlled field experiments into development economics. Although it is argued that this technique constitutes hard evidence in contrast to "wishy-washy evidence" of cross-country growth regressions and case studies (see Banerjee, 2007), in their book, Duflo and Banerjee make extensive use of *storytelling, thought experiments*, and *metaphors*, in order to make their arguments more persuasive for other scientists and policy makers (Labrousse, 2010). Again, this is not a bad thing as such. According to McCloskey, any serious argument in economics will use *metaphors* and *stories* not just as an ornament but for the sake of the argument (see, e.g., McCloskey, 1983, p. 503; McCloskey,

1985, p. 19). But mainstream economists, she says, are not able to reflect on these literal figures and ask themselves why they are necessary, as according to the official methodology they were useless. So what is really needed in economics is a *transparent and reflected scientific praxis* that takes methodological considerations seriously.

18.6 CRITICAL RATIONALISM VERSUS *PARADIGMS*

18.6.1 Modern Measurement Theory and the *Duhem–Quine Thesis*

After all, the practice of the economic mainstream basically never followed the critical-rationalist ideal of empirical testing and falsification. But when a scientific discipline never has practiced critical rationalism, the question emerges, whether critical rationalism is in fact an adequate description of doable scientific practice. Most criticisms of Popper's philosophy of science, in fact, refer to the falsification element.

The latter was intended as a method ensuring that "science" is stronger than nonscience, as "science" would have survived this particularly rigorous selection method. But, in fact, *modern measurement theory* has shown, even for the "exact" natural sciences, that there is *no objectively correct* or *true way of measuring*.

Already the famous physicist *W. Heisenberg* argued that measuring more than one property of a physical particle simultaneously with perfect precision is naturally impossible. This is known as the *uncertainty principle* of quantum mechanics or as the *Heisenberg principle*.

Further, when we look at some "real" object, we do it with a particular *perspective*, according to the prejudices of our specific *world view*, and to the *presetting and allowances of our scientific theory*. Accordingly, the measuring and *testing equipment* itself usually is

constructed in a biased way to show us things the way we have conceptualized them before. We usually see, what we expected to see, and even new detections will usually remain within the larger frame of our prevalent and preexisting *habits of thought*. For instance, even Albert Einstein claimed that he was working within the Newtonian frame, just generalizing it.

The famous Durhem–Quine thesis (according to Pierre Duhem, 1861–1916, and Willard Van Orman Quine, 1908–2000) argues exactly that way, stating, in particular, that it is *impossible to test a single hypothesis* on its own, since each one comes as *part of an environment of axioms, assumptions, models, theories, auxiliary hypotheses, core examples,* and *empirical prototypes*. Thus, in case of a "falsification," we could only say that that whole package would have been falsified, but could not conclusively say, which element of the whole system would have to be replaced (note the analogy to the theory of the second best in Chapters 5 and 17). This is just a reflection of the fact that also *scientific thought systems are complex* systems.

So it has been argued by many philosophers of science that strict falsificationism would have killed, for instance, the theories of Darwin and Einstein from their very beginnings. When they were first advanced, each of them still was at odds with some then available evidence, and only later more evidence — often only attained *within* the theoretical perspective they had newly provided — became available, which gave them the critical support needed.

So even if we could expose a single hypothesis to some empirical test against measurement data, the theory carried by the current scientific community would not be easily given up.

The discovery of the planet Neptune may serve as an example: the existence of the planet was mathematically predicted before it could be directly observed. The then relevant scientific community knew about the irregularities of the orbit of the planet Uranus before, but did not abandon the Newtonian laws of gravitation for that empirical nonfit. Rather, astronomers searched for a disturbing mass, and thus concluded that there had to exist another undiscovered planet in relation to Uranus. That was Neptune. It was a strong confirmation of the Newtonian gravitational theory.

Above that, "*reality*," in the form of empirical *data*, usually is not that clear and selective to allow for a clear decision on whether some evidence contradicts a hypothesis or just is a sign of flaws in the hypothesis, or in the evidence. See already our comment on *econometric testing* above. Thus, "evidence" is not at all the strict instance of judging a theory as falsificationism seemed to assume.

Finally, falsificationism has also been questioned on purely logical grounds, as a *logical impossibility* similarly applies to verification and *falsification*. For instance, it is not clear how falsificationism would deal with a statement like "For every metal, there is a temperature at which it will melt." The hypothesis cannot be falsified by any possible observation, for there is always a higher temperature possible than the tested one, at which the metal may in fact melt. Nevertheless, this proposition is with no doubt acknowledged as a scientific hypothesis.

18.6.2 Scientific Systems as *Paradigms*, and *Scientific Revolutions*

Thomas Kuhn (Kuhn, 1970/1962) and *Imre Lakatos* (Lakatos, 1970) have, against these changes revolution of our perception of scientific cognition and measurement, reformulated epistemology in the sense of a systemic or holistic view of science. According to Kuhn's most influential book "The Structure of Scientific Revolutions," scientists work within a "paradigm" rather than a "theory," and a

falsificationist methodology either is impossible or, if strictly applied, would make science virtually impossible.

No scientific or theoretical system ever solves all the empirical "*puzzles*," with which a scientific discipline is confronted at a given time. But that very imperfection of the data-theory fit exactly defines the further search activity of the normal course of a scientific discipline, the *normal science*, which takes place *within* a given environment of axioms, assumptions, theories, core models, and historical reference examples—called a *paradigm*. If every failure to fit measurement data would lead to theory rejection, all theories would have to be rejected at all times. Rather, the test of a single hypothesis will be done by referring to that environment as an evaluative instance, and that evaluative theoretical system cannot itself be legitimated.

But how then can a scientific system (a theory, and, in fact, a paradigm) be refuted at all? Kuhn's answer is, it will not be dropped unless the "*anomalies*" it has to face become ever more, and ever more severe, *and* unless *another paradigm is offered*, which has been developed already so far that it can solve the most pressing puzzles and anomalies of the discipline better than the old one. Note that the new one need not solve *all* puzzles and anomalies itself, but it solves the most relevant, actually the most pressing ones better. Thus, "refuting a theory" assumes the form of a *scientific revolution between whole sequential paradigms*.

The classical example was the so-called *Copernican Shift*, when the geocentric paradigm (the earth as a disk and center of the universe) contradicted ever more observations gained through ever better telescope technology. The old world view was not given up until a new holistic explanation was present—and even then it was, as is well known, perilous for the representatives of the new paradigm to contend it.

Note that this is also a *sociological and a social-psychological, evolutionary*, and *cumulative process* of a *complex system and its scientific community*, which so far carried the older paradigm. And again, only when the existing paradigm comes into a severe crisis because it can no longer solve an increasing number of ever more pressing puzzles *and* if there is offered a new paradigm, *scientific development* ("progress") will occur. However, this will occur *not as a piecemeal, marginal falsificationist improvement*, but as a paradigmatic revolution, a systems (ex-)change. Normal science in the old paradigm will only then be abandoned by that scientific community.

Lakatos elaborated on and operationalized that paradigmatic epistemology by defining paradigms as so-called *research programs*. A research program contains a *hard core* of axioms and assumptions, often with a core model and historical core reference that cannot be abandoned or altered without abandoning the paradigm altogether. More *specific theoretical systems*, specific models, or single propositions are formulated in order to explain evidence that may threaten the hard core. These are termed *auxiliary hypotheses* and considered *life-belts* around the core. They may be altered or abandoned, as empirical discoveries require, in order to protect the core.

Such ad hoc amendments may be *progressive*, when they enhance the program's explanatory or predictive power, e.g., make it more generally applicable. Such normal science is permissible until it generates ever more misfit with observations (anomalies) and some better system will be devised and the old research program replaced. The difference between a progressive and a *degenerative* research program lies in whether changes to its auxiliary hypotheses have achieved a greater explanatory/predictive power or whether they have been made simply out of the necessity of offering some response in the face of new and troublesome evidence. Doing mainly the latter

has been a major accusation of philosophers of science and critical economists against the practice of neoclassical mainstream economics.

Note again that, in all, *scientific development* ("progress"), not only of economics, is also an *interactive and evolutionary social process of a scientific community*, interrelated with, of course, other influential *economic and political forces* involved (and sometimes also with some societal groups as "stakeholders" of more general common goods), and as such it also can only be a matter of an *emergent collective evaluation*.

18.7 CRITICAL REALISM

Against the background of socioeconomic systems as *complex* systems and the *paradigmatic perspective* on (economic) science and scientific development, a social science epistemology was developed under the label of critical realism (rather than critical rationalism explained earlier). Its founding father was the British philosopher *Roy Bhaskar* who elaborated, for the social sciences, on the fundamental (*ontological*) distinction between *individuals* and *society*, and, accordingly, *agency* and *structure*. Although any social structure is inconceivable without individual agents, it usually has, as an *emergent complex system*, very different properties than its constitutive elements, the individual agents (e.g., Bhaskar, 1998/ 1979, 34ff.). Note that this epistemological approach conforms to our analyses of complex and evolutionary economic systems as dealt with throughout this textbook (see, e.g., Chapters 6, 9, 11, or 14 for greater detail). The epistemological approach here is the same as with all complex systems, including the complex socioeconomic systems that we have dealt with throughout this textbook.

A related fundamental aspect of critical realism is, thus, the rejection of both *methodological individualism* (see Chapter 5) and *methodological collectivism*, the latter regarding socioeconomic phenomena exclusively at the macro-level of the social structure.

Methodological individualism, the standard view of most mainstream economics, seeks to explain social phenomena entirely through the actions of individuals. Neoclassical economics exhibits this ontology, when all motions in their models are generated by the behavior of some utility-maximizing agent (see Chapter 6 for a critique of the neoclassical ontology). Aggregation then takes place through the representation of the agents via one single representative agent. It therefore has been considered *methodological reductionism*.

Methodological collectivism was first expressed by French sociologist Emile Durkheim, whose objects of investigation were solely social facts. These would influence the behavior and thinking of individuals and act as effective constraints on them (Durkheim, 1982/1895, 52). In this way, social *structure* is the only source for explaining individual *agency*, while structure itself would exist entirely independent of the behavior of the individuals (loc. cit., 59).

Critical realism holds that social *structure* and *individuals* (and their *agency*) are *interdependent*. As stated by *Tony Lawson*, one of the leading representatives of critical realism (Lawson, 1994, 520): "Structure and human agency, in sum, each presuppose, although neither can be reduced to, or explained completely in terms of, the other." Critical realist theory, thus, considers individuals and society as two different ontological layers and the *interplay* between them is an important

research object for critical realism. For instance, while individuals are acting according to their own reasoning, this reasoning is influenced by social circumstances, but, in turn, also contributes (generally as an *unintended consequence*) to the transformation of social structure (Lawson, 1994, 521).

Reality, which is considered independent of the single researcher, then consists of three different "domains" (Lawson, 1994, 513): the *experience* of the state of affairs (i.e., the *empirical* domain), the *objects* causing the experience (the *actual* domain), and a domain including the *underlying structures*, *mechanisms*, *powers*, and *tendencies* (the *nonfactual* domain). The most important task for economics is to explain the latter, because it allows explaining human activities and social structures by revealing the underlying mechanisms, which are not simply observable. By not reflecting on this distinction, neoclassical economics, unconsciously, would be concerned with the empirical domain alone and therefore be incapable of producing real insights into the functioning of the economy.

And as *social structures* (because of the constant process of mutual transformation with individual behavior) are *space and time dependent*, critical realists give priority to the *explanation* of behavior and structures over prediction as in the dominating mainstream methodological approach (see Section 18.4 on Friedman).[2] Specifically, as social structures can be transformed by individuals, and individuals are considered reasoning subjects, agents may *change their behavior*, after socioeconomics provided them with reasonable new explanations

---

[2]Note that there are many examples of theories incapable of providing adequate predictions but still entailing an enormous explanatory content even in the natural sciences. Consider the biological theory of Darwinian evolution. It explains numerous natural phenomena in a satisfactory manner; still it is not able to yield adequate prediction, simply because of the complexity of the biological systems. But this does not disqualify it as a good scientific theory. For many physical systems, the non-predictability has been rigorously proven by applying the tools of dynamical systems and chaos theory. The impossibility to make predictions for (well-understood) systems with sensible dependence on initial conditions is exemplified by the literal figure of Laplace's demon (Laplace, 2007 [1901], p. 4).

for socioeconomic phenomena, and thus *transform social structures* (Lawson, 2003). This *additional feedback mechanism* makes social systems and socioeconomic analysis, and in particular forecasting, *even more complex*. Some of the related phenomena are known under the labels *self-fulfilling* or *self-destroying prophecy* of new scientific knowledge.

Note, however, that the *financial crisis and Great Recession 2007ff.* has indeed been *forecasted* by complexity economists (in contrast to mainstream economists), such as Steve Keen, Mark Buchanan, or Ping Chen, who were running *complex models of the economy*.

Finally, critical realism elaborates on the *other-orienting* character of human practice. People do things because of their *relation* to other people, their own position in relation to the position of the other person. The employee, for instance, deals in a certain way with the employer because of the relative social positions the two are in in a certain socioeconomic system or structure (Lawson, 1997, 159). The other-orientation exactly exists because of learned *social rules and institutions*, which reflects, at the epistemological level, the substantial analyses of the socioeconomic system and its processes in this textbook.

18.8 REALITY, "REALISM," AND CONSTRUCTIVISM

What we may generally learn from the foregoing is that *socioeconomic reality is usually not simply what it appears to be at the surface of the immediate phenomena* but that there is a particular microeconomic *deep structure* behind that. Therefore, *realism* is not "realistic," not real world, if not "critical"—this seems to be the message of the critical realist research program. One must always look behind that veil of immediate impressions and everyday consciousness and perceptions; and this exactly is why we have received an academic education.

So always think twice, and try to apply theories, models, and analytical tools that you have learned in this textbook, to reality.

Particularly, the *"market"* or *"market economy"*—as you may have learned in this textbook in different contexts and from different angles—is not what we are usually told it is, and what powerful opinion leaders claim them to be. "Markets" can be everything and nothing. Being just decentralized, spontaneous forms and mechanisms, in which prices play some role, they basically are *underdetermined* and *undetermined* in their processes and results unless "embedded" in some specific set of formal or informal social rules and institutions. Particularly, deregulated markets often generate some over-complexity and thus *over-turbulence* for the individual decision-maker, which then often leads to races for the short-run maximum, for one-shot extra gains, intentions of exploitation, in a word to *defective behavior and inferior results*. Therefore, "markets" may become useful, functioning tools of coordination (among other useful tools) only if *properly embedded* in sets of what are *their counter-principles and -mechanisms*, such as complexity-reducing sets of rules and institutions, or of specifically acting, "enlightened" government (see Chapter 17 for more details). Rules and institutions may assume the form of networks of cooperation, and networks of networks, i.e., *networks of institutions*, or whole *institutional arrangements*.

Another epistemology (or meta-theory) encouraging a more critical view on the subjects under investigation is what can broadly be put under the label of "constructivism." Constructivists differ from critical realists in that they neglect any reality independent from the scientist and explain the effects of social structures on individuals only by the interpretation these structures are given by the individuals. Constructivists claim that "facts" are constructed by scientists rather than being objectively true. Therefore, constructivist research relies on different tools than those presented throughout this textbook, especially on *discourse analysis* (see, e.g., Keller, 2012; McCloskey, 1983, 1998/1985), *deconstruction* (Derrida, 1997), and *genealogy* (Foucault, 1977). Note, however, that constructivism is a relatively new and less settled, and a very broad and diverse area of epistemological research, which still is evolving (for more details, see, e.g., Berger and Luckmann, 2011; Searl, 2010). Also note that the idea that our *perception of reality* is critical, which is connected to all kinds of *relativistic* and *subjectivist* views in the history of philosophy, beginning in ancient times, and which found a prominent expression in modern epistemology in the *Duhem−Quine thesis* above, nowadays has been elaborated in a theory of *framing*, which refers to concepts of how individuals, groups, and societies perceive and communicate about reality. This particular set of theories and meta-theories are relevant in media studies, sociology, psychology, linguistics, and political science. And famous "heterodox" economists, such as *Kenneth E. Boulding* and *Albert O. Hirschman*, have been pioneering this epistemological conception building, particularly perception and discourse theories, as well (e.g., Boulding, 1956; Hirschman, 1970).

18.9 EPISTEMOLOGICAL PLURALISM

It should have become obvious throughout this textbook, and through this chapter in particular, that it is hard, if not impossible, to imagine an effective scientific discipline with only one "monist" scientific paradigm. This is hard to comprehend even beyond the social sciences (in the natural sciences), but particularly hard in the social sciences and in economics. Despite the nowadays dominating position of neoclassical economics, the intellectual landscape of economics is in fact *diverse*, with continuously *competing paradigms*,

indeed a *contested area*. See already Chapters 5, 6, 10, 12, and 13 for the rich and diverse arrays of economic thought, conceptualizing, and modeling.

On top of that, frontiers of economics with other disciplines are fluid, and, again, this is the case beyond just neoclassical *"economic imperialism,"* which alleges to be able to explain any social phenomenon with the preconception of *individualistic rationality* and conventional *marginal analysis*. Productive interaction with other disciplines may be based on *agent-based complexity economics*, with multiple and heterogeneous agents, genuine *"socioeconomics,"* and *true interdisciplinarity* on an equal footing of the disciplines as *potential mechanism* and *asset of scientific progress*.

So why is *economics a multi-paradigmatic science*? And is this a good thing or not?

In the philosophy of science, the view that important phenomena can be fully explained only by the presence and combined use of several perspectives, approaches, and paradigms is called pluralism or *epistemological pluralism*, a *methodology for scientific progress*. In fact, most sciences are organized in a pluralistic way. Complex phenomena can be better analyzed, it is assumed, if analyzed from *different paradigmatic perspectives*.

Even the subject matter of *mathematics* seems to require a pluralistic scientific community with the classical and constructivist school of mathematics, to name only two out of many (Hellmann and Bell, 2006, p. 69).

But why should a pluralism of paradigms, including theories and methodologies, be important? Critical realists deployed the figure of closed versus *open systems* in order to clarify this issue. If one studies a closed system, then knowledge is always held with certainty and a superior methodology can be identified. But the prerequisites for a system to be a closed system are very specific:

- All the relevant variables must be identifiable and clearly classifiable as exogenous or endogenous. And only the latter proven to affect the system and do so in a unique, nonambiguous, predetermined way.

- The relations between the different variables must be entirely random or completely known.
- The components of the system must be separable (i.e., atomistic and independent) and of a constant nature. Their relationships among each other are known.

If these criteria are not fulfilled (and it is clear that for the real-world economic system they are not), knowledge is only held with *uncertainty*, such that one unique monist "school of truth" cannot be identified. Therefore, pluralism is necessary for advancing scientific knowledge.

The insight that pluralism, particularly in economics, is necessary is not new. Already in 1992 the *American Economic Review* (Vol. 82, p. xxv) published a *"Plea for a Pluralistic and Rigorous Economics."* Among others, it said: "[...] we call for a new spirit of pluralism in economics, involving critical conversation and tolerant communication between different approaches." It had been initiated by Geoffrey Hodgson, Uskali Mäki, and Donald McCloskey and was signed by many leading researchers such as W. Brian Arthur, Kenneth E. Boulding, Richard M. Cyert, Paul A. Davidson, Richard Day, Christopher Freeman, Bruno Frey, Eirik Furubotn, John K. Galbraith, Nicolas Georgescu-Roegen, Richard Goodwin, Clive W.J. Granger, Geoffrey Harcourt, Robert Heilbroner, Albert O. Hirschman, Charles Kindleberger, Janos Kornai, David Laidler, Harvey Leibenstein, Hyman Minsky, Franco Modigliani, Richard Nelson, Mancur Olson, Luigi Pasinetti, Mark Perlman, Paul A. Samuelson, Martin Shubik, Herbert A. Simon, Jan Tinbergen, Douglas Vickers, and E. Roy Weintraub, among others, with four Nobel Laureates among them. The subscribers themselves represented a broad array of perspectives and approaches in economics.

Against this background, it appears even more regrettable that the situation has not fundamentally changed since. When Elinor Ostrom received the Nobel Prize in economics in 2009, it turned out that a whole generation of Ph.D. students of leading US universities did not even know her name, as documented on certain Ph.D. discussion websites. Note, however, that most of the names above will be familiar to you after having worked through the present textbook.

Although indispensable for scientific progress, pluralism of course implies some difficulty for the scientific praxis of individual scientists. Economists belonging to different paradigms have difficulties interacting with each other. They often do not share the same languages, ontological, epistemological, and methodological ideas, perspectives, axioms and assumptions, core models and core examples, and therefore often have difficulties to understand the arguments offered by others. In economics, the problem appears to be particularly severe, as economists usually are not trained to be particularly sensitive to differences in methodology and perspective, and many methodological arguments are used only implicitly (see Section 18.5). However, these issues have to be addressed explicitly in order to allow an open discourse, which is necessary in order to identify the strengths and weaknesses of certain approaches and to decide *which approach is best-suited to address certain questions* (Dow, 1997, p. 89). As Kuhn (1970/1962, p. 202) put it, "what the participants in a communication breakdown can do is recognize each other as members of different language communities and then become translators." Note that an individual economist for logical reasons cannot be a "pluralist economist."

Currently, still most undergraduate and graduate programs in economics prescribe primarily and exclusively a simplistic and reduced version of neoclassical economics. Economic methodologies, history of economic thought, or *training in the capability of paradigm switching* (being able to view an economic issue from different perspectives) are rarely addressed in greater detail. The conventional approach has always presupposed, as Paul Samuelson once put it, "a scientific consensus about 'good economics', a core of foundational concepts, which are accepted by all but a few right and left wing writers" (Samuelson, 1967, pp. 197f.). But although this is not the case, mainstream economists take their methodological approach as given and methodological reflections are hardly considered necessary (Dow, 2009, p. 55). As GET theorist Frank Hahn (1992) puts it: "Economists are not equipped for discussing methodology and it does not matter." Lawson (1992) argued that this statement in itself represents a methodological position, and, in fact, it summarizes the current situation and provides evidence for D. McCloskey's argument that most neoclassical economists only deploy naïve rhetoric.

As the economy is a complex and open system, pluralism indeed is necessary. In order to make pluralism work, however, different schools would have to spend effort on *training their discourse and paradigm-switching capabilities*.

The different "heterodoxies" have indeed led a *discourse on such proactive epistemological pluralism* over the last two or three decades, and many economists have concentrated on elaborating a new *ethics of pluralism in economics* (S. Dow, J.B. Davis, E. Fullbrook, J.E. Reardon, and others). The have founded an international umbrella association named *International Confederation of Associations for Pluralism in Economics* (ICAPE) or the *Association for Integrity and Responsible Leadership in Economics and Associated Professions* (AIRLEAP). Ph.D. students in many countries have launched declarations, associations, groups, and networks at local and national levels under the labels of *"post-autistic"* or "pluralistic" movements. Books and journals on the subject have been edited or launched, such as the *International Journal of Pluralism and Economics Education* (IJPEE). The discussion has led to a whole series of book publications, handbooks, and special issues of journals since the 1990s,

and has reached even into mainstream outlets (see, e.g., Arnsperger, 2010; Garnett et al., 2009; Fullbrook, 2009; Reardon, 2009; Groenewegen, 2007; Salanti and Screpanti, 1997; Denis, 2009).

However, the threat to a proactive epistemological pluralism "beyond just plurality" is more severe than ever and stems from something that many just consider a technicality and objective, neutral procedure just to safeguard quality in the discipline, i.e., the *ranking of journals*, and based on that, of individual economists, departments, schools, universities, publishers, etc. The problem here is that the discipline is confronted here with most severe *methodological and statistical flaws* and more *fundamental misconceptions* as many alternative rankings and calculations have demonstrated. The results have not proven to be stably replicable in any other attempt (see Section 18.3.4 for this criterion). The official *citation-based impact factors* represent an extremely *self-referential and circular cumulative system*, which in effect *reduces the remaining diversity and plurality* of the discipline with increasing speed currently (see, e.g., Lee and Elsner, 2011).

The foundations for improvement, however, to, e.g., increase the diversity and thus resilience of the complex scientific system of economics or to *avoid "advising" the world economy into another big crash* like the ones of 1929ff. and 2007ff. lie in a more pluralistic education. We do hope to contribute to such a future of economics through the present textbook.

18.10 FURTHER "APPLYING" YOUR KNOWLEDGE ON COMPLEX ECONOMIES: *ACTION AND EXPERIENCE*, ENLARGING RATHER THAN CONSUMING KNOWLEDGE THROUGH ITS USE

18.10.1 Policies in a Broad Understanding

We have discussed above an important dimension of "applying" the theoretical and analytical knowledge learned, i.e., confronting it with *reality* by *measuring* in different ways. But the proof of the pudding is not only in measuring it but in the "eating." "Eating" here means some *"doing,"* or *practice*, or *action*. However, rather than being "consumed," knowledge will be enlarged in such repeated "proof." We have explained in Chapter 17 that "applying" our complexity economics knowledge implies *"policies" in a broad understanding*, challenging us as "politicians" at *different (spatial and social) levels* and in *different roles*.

This begins in the smallest of our interactions, bilateral, *two-person interactions*, where we can apply our knowledge to analyze and determine the game structure at hand, and develop, suggest, or try to contribute to, *sustainable solutions*.

In *larger networks*, where we may be involved as *party*, we are likewise challenged to suggest, after proper analysis, *network and interaction structures*, rules and institutions for better structure, *governance*, process, and outcome. Even being party in a network, we are not like a pinball, determined to just react or behave in our short-run individualistic interest, which in the mid-term may turn out, as we have learned, not to yield the best payoff at all. Here as well, sustainable common or collective solutions might be the true challenge.

Finally, of course, we all are mostly better in advising others than in helping ourselves. So even if you will not be trained, after having graduated, as a *management consultant*, there will be ample opportunity in a professional life to assume the role of providing advice—after a proper analysis of a multi-agent interaction structure, its complexity features, ongoing processes, and outcomes so far—for a better network structure in terms of agents and relations, better incentive structures, and rules and institutions to be established—again, for a better governance, process, and outcome, for instance for an R&D firm network.

So there will be ample opportunity to apply your knowledge learned here as a future "politician" in a broad array of levels, areas, problems, processes, outcomes, and roles.

18.10.2 Knowledge, Expanding, and Transforming

Information and knowledge, as you will experience then, is the only "production factor" or "raw material" or "input" that will not wear out or be consumed by application and use, but on the contrary, will *expand through such application and experience*. As we do *not* have, and will never have, perfect knowledge and foresight, there is no way other than attaining experience.

The chance we will have then, though, is that our knowledge not just gets more and more, but gets better and better, settled, condensed, *assuming higher qualities*. You may learn that you may start in some case with dealing with just masses of *data*; you may then condense, structure, and transform data to usable *information*. You may further settle this information into a broader personal potential that can be retrieved in different situations, i.e., *knowledge*. Knowledge is something that often (if *"tacit"*) is not easily imitable by others, although much of it must be *shared* with others in order to be useful for yourself at all, as you may have learned in this book in many contexts. After some years of practice of learning, knowledge accumulation, applying, and experiencing, you may find that another, final, dimension of "knowing" opens up, perhaps the highest form of knowing, i.e., *"wisdom."* Wisdom will sometimes tell you that you should not follow the immediate impulse or dominant incentive, nor do what the data, or information, or your knowledge would tell you to—and with that, you may find, you will often fare better in the long run.

This is what *Adam Smith*, already in the TMS in the year 1759, the very beginning of modern economics, called *prudence* (see Chapter 12). Prudent behavior opens doors, including economic opportunities, that otherwise would remain closed. It enables processes that otherwise would remain blocked or quickly get locked-in in petrified inferior situations. For Adam Smith already, it was a reflection of the human agency capacity of *empathy*, entailing, as we have coined it here, *recognized interdependence* and *futurity* (see, e.g., also Chapters 1 and 3 and Section 13.12), the way to productive interactive process, *coordination*, and *cooperation* combined with appropriate *openness*, *innovation*, and *change* (for that see Chapters 15–17)—in a word, *"welfare"* or "well-being," not to speak of the more fashionable conception of *"happiness."*

Note how we can build bridges in this epistemological perspective, in the end, from the very beginning of modern economics (1759) to cutting-edge innovation economics and open-source worlds in modern IT, and from Chapter 1 through Chapters 15–17. Nothing less than building these bridges will be required from you in the course of a good and successful professional lifetime.

18.11 A FINAL "APPLICATION": GOVERNANCE FOR THE *RES PUBLICA*, AND POLICY

Last but not least, it should have become clear throughout this textbook that the analysis of complex structures, and of dynamic, evolutionary, and complex process, and their *institutional*, complexity-reducing *equilibria* or *attractors* (solutions), their *self-organizing*, morphogenetic, or autopoietic capacities, can *under no circumstances justify a blind trust or blind hope for a general "good"* (*let alone "optimal"*), and self-sustainable *self-organization* (a "self-administering," "self-policing," etc. "natural order") of any

spontaneous decentralized system, at least not with due certainty or within due course of time (see Chapters 10, 11, or 17 for more details)—thus, in general, there is *no "spontaneous order"* that would not have to become *subject to some social evaluation, meritorization,* and action.

Thus, in the end, we are reminded that we also are, and for some reason have evolved, biologically as well as culturally, into *"political animals."* As such we may hope to be able one day to *generate appropriate governance structures*—themselves always subject to some evolution—for some self-policing system, or network, or network of networks, for the whole *res publica*. In that sense, we all are required to act as *"politicians"* in the core areas of *public* policies (beyond the roles mentioned in Section 18.7), i.e., take part in a future participative and proactive democratic process.

After we have applied our knowledge in generating proper governance structures on smaller spatial levels, as network members involved, or as neutral advisors of such networks, as mentioned, the remainder of required "application," or action, is *politics and policies*. These should become politics and policies, which are better informed than those we have nowadays, in order also to *set some formal rules and institutions* for, to *structure* and *embed, restrict* and *empower* "markets," and any spontaneous decentralized systems, for a better socioeconomy, better "welfare," "well-being," or maybe even "happiness" of the greatest number.

Chapter References

Albert, H., 1971/1963. Modell-Platonismus—Der neoklassische Stil des ökonomischen Denkens in kritischer Beleuchtung. In: Topitzsch, E. (Ed.), Logik der Sozialwissenschaften. Kiepenheuer & Witsch, Berlin, pp. 406–434.

American Economic Association, 2013. American Economic Review: Data Availability Policy. <http://www.aeaweb.org/aer/data.php> (accessed 27.11.13.).

Archibald, G.C., Simon, H.A., Samuelson, P.A., 1963. Discussion. Am. Econ. Rev., P&P. 53 (2), 227–236.

Arnsperger, C., 2010. Critical Political Economy: Complexity, Rationality, and the Logic of Post-Orthodox Pluralism. Routledge, London, New York.

Banerjee, A.V., 2007. Making Aid Work. MIT Press, Cambridge, MA.

Berger, P.L., Luckmann, T., 2011. The Social Construction of Reality: A Treatise in the Sociology of Knowledge. Open Road Media, New York, NY.

Bhaskar, R., 1998/1979. The Possibility of Naturalism. A Philosophical Critique of the Contemporary Human Sciences. third ed. Routledge, London, New York.

Boulding, K.E., 1956. The Image: Knowledge in Life and Society. Michigan University Press, Chicago, IL.

Card, D.E., Krueger, A.B., 1995a. Time-series minimum wage studies: a meta-analysis. Am. Econ. Rev., P&P. 85 (2), 238–243.

Card, D.E., Krueger, A.B., 1995b. Myth and Measurement: The New Economics of the Minimum Wage. Princeton University Press, Princeton, New York.

Debreu, G., 1986. Theoretical models: mathematical forms and economic content. Econometrica. 54 (6), 1259–1270.

Debreu, G., 1991. The mathematization of economic theory. Am. Econ. Rev. 81 (1), 1–7.

Denis, A., 2009. Pluralism in economics education. Int. Rev. Econ. Educ. 8 (2), (special issue).

Derrida, J., 1997. Of Grammatology. Johns Hopkins University Press, Baltimore.

Doucouliagos, H., Stanley, T.D., 2009. Publication selection bias in minimum-wage research? A meta-regression analysis. Br. J. Ind. Relat. 47 (2), 406–428.

Dow, S., 1997. Mainstream economic methodology. Cambridge. J. Econ. 21 (1), 73–93.

Dow, S., 2009. History of thought and methodology in pluralist economics education. Int. Rev. Pluralism Econ. Educ. 8 (2), 41–57.

Duflo, E., Banerjee, A., 2011. Poor Economics. A Radical Rethinking of the Way to Fight Global Poverty. Public Affairs, New York, NY.

Durkheim, E., 1982/1895. The Rules of Sociological Method. Macmillan, London (W.D. Halls, Trans.).

Garnett, R., Olsen, E., Starr, M. (Eds.), 2009. Economic Pluralism. Routledge, London, New York.

Foucault, M., 1977. Discipline & Punish. Random House, New York, NY.

Friedman, M., 1953. The methodology of positive economics. Essays in Positive Economics. University of Chicago Press, Chicago, IL (repr. 1953; pp. 3–16, 30–43).

Fullbrook, E. (Ed.), 2009. Pluralist Economics. Zed Books, London.

Groenewegen, J. (Ed.), 2007. Teaching Pluralism in Economics. Edward Elgar, Cheltenham, Northampton.

Hahn, F.H., 1992. Reflections, royal economic society. Newsletter. 77, 5.

Hellmann, G., Bell, J.L., 2006. Pluralism and the foundations of mathematics. In: Kellert, S.H., Longino, H.E., Kenneth Waters, C. (Eds.), Scientific Pluralism. University of Minnesota Press, Minneapolis, London, pp. 64–79.

Herndon, T., Ash, M., Pollin, R., 2013. Does high public debt consistently stifle economic growth? A critique of Reinhart and Rogoff. Working Paper No. 322, Political Economy Research Institute, University of Massachusetts, Amherst.

Hirschman, A.O., 1970. Exit, Voice, and Loyalty: Responses to Decline in Firms, Organizations, and States. Harvard University Press, Cambridge, MA.

Kapeller, J., 2012. In: Elsner, W. (Ed.), Modell-Platonismus in der Oekonomie. Zur Aktualität einer klassischen epistemologischen Kritik, Series Institutionelle und Sozial-Ökonomie, vol. 20. P. Lang, Frankfurt/M.

Kapeller, J., 2013. "Model Platonism" in economics: on a classical epistemological critique. J. Inst. Econ. 9 (2), 199–221.

Keller, R., 2012. Doing Discourse Research. An Introduction for Social Scientists. Sage, London.

Kuhn, T.S., 1970/1962. The Structure of Scientific Revolutions. University of Chicago Press, Chicago, IL.

Labrousse, A., 2010. Nouvelle économie du développement et essais cliniques randomisés: une mise en perspective d'un outil de preuve et de gouvernement. Revue de la régulation. 7 (1), <http://regulation.revues.org/7818> (accessed 27.11.13.).

Lakatos, I., 1970. Falsification and the methodology of scientific research programmes. In: Lakatos, I., Musgrave, A. (Eds.), Criticism and the Growth of Knowledge. Cambridge University Press, Cambridge, pp. 91–195.

Laplace, P.S.M., 2007/1901. A Philosophical Essay on Probabilities. Cosimo Inc, New York, NY.

Lawson, T., 1992. Methodology: non-optional and consequential, letter to editor. R.E.S. Newsletter (October), 2–3.

Lawson, T., 1994. The nature of post Keynesianism and its links to other traditions: a realist perspective. J. Post Keynesian Econ. 16 (4), 503–538.

Lawson, T., 1997. Economics and Reality. Routledge, London, New York.

Lawson, T., 2003. Reorienting Economics. Routledge, London, New York.

Lee, F.S., Elsner, W., 2011. Evaluating economic research in a contested discipline: rankings, pluralism, and the future of heterodox economics. Am. J. Econ. Sociol. 69 (5), (special issue).

McCloskey, D.N., 1983. The rhetoric of economics. J. Econ. Lit. 22 (2), 481–517.

McCloskey, D.N., 1985. The loss function has been mislaid: the rhetoric of significance tests. Am. Econ. Rev., P&P. 75 (2), 201–205.

McCloskey, D.N., 1998/1985. The Rhetoric of Economics. second ed. University of Wisconsin Press, Chicago, IL.

McCloskey, D.N., Ziliak, S.T., 1996. The standard error of regressions. J. Econ. Lit. 34 (1), 97–114.

Musgrave, A., 1981. Unreal assumptions in economic theory: the F-twist untwisted. Kyklos. 34 (3), 377–387.

Nell, E.J., Errouaki, K., 2011. Rational Econometric Man: Transforming Structural Econometrics. Edward Elgar, Cheltenham, Northampton.

Popper, K.R., 1959/1934. The Logic of Scientific Discovery. Basic Books, New York, NY (1934 in German).

Reardon, J. (Ed.), 2009. Handbook of Pluralist Economics Education. Routledge, London, New York.

Reinhart, C.M., Rogoff, K.S., 2010. Growth in a time of debt. Am. Econ. Rev., P&P. 100 (2), 573–578.

Russell, B., 2009/1903. Principles of Mathematics. Routledge, New York, NY.

Salanti, A., Screpanti, E. (Eds.), 1997. Pluralism in Economics: New Perspectives in History and Methodology. E. Elgar, Cheltenham, Northampton.

Samuelson, P., 1967. Economics. seventh ed. McGraw-Hill, New York, NY.

Searl, J.R., 2010. The Construction of Social Reality. Simon and Schuster, New York, NY.

Sen, A.K., 1977. Rational fools. A critique of the behavioral foundations of economic theory. Philos. Public Aff. 6 (4), 317–344.

Stanley, T.D., 2013. Does economics add up? An introduction to meta-regression analysis. Eur. J. Econ. Econ. Policies: Intervention. 10 (2), 207–220.

Stigler, G.J., Becker, G.S., 1977. De Gustibus Non Est Disputandum. Am. Econ. Rev. 67 (2), 76–90.

Wilber, C.K., Harrison, R.S., 1978. The methodological basis of institutional economics: pattern model, storytelling, and holism. J. Econ. Issues. 12 (1), 61–89.

Further Reading—Online

For further reading, see the textbook website at http://booksite.elsevier.com/9780124115859

Index

Printed in the United States
By Bookmasters